CONSTRUCTION PLANNING, EQUIPMENT, AND METHODS

CONSTRUCTION PLANNING, EQUIPMENT, AND METHODS

Third Edition

R. L. Peurifoy

Consulting Engineer
Bryan, Texas

McGraw-Hill Book Company

New York   St. Louis   San Francisco   Auckland   Bogotá   Düsseldorf
Johannesburg   London   Madrid   Mexico   Montreal   New Delhi
Panama   Paris   São Paulo   Singapore   Sydney   Tokyo   Toronto

CONSTRUCTION PLANNING, EQUIPMENT, AND METHODS

Copyright © 1979, 1970, 1956 by McGraw-Hill, Inc. All rights reserved. Printed in the United States of America. No part of this publication may be reproduced, stored in a retrieval system, or transmitted, in any form or by any means, electronic, mechanical, photocopying, recording, or otherwise, without the prior written permission of the publisher.

234567890 DODO 79

This book was set in Times Roman by Science Typographers, Inc.
The editors were Julienne V. Brown and Frances A. Neal;
the cover was designed by Albert M. Cetta;
the production supervisor was Charles Hess.
New drawings were done by J & R Services, Inc.
The printer and binder was R. R. Donnelley & Sons Company.

Library of Congress Cataloging in Publication Data

Peurifoy, Robert Leroy,   date
  Construction planning, equipment, and methods.

  Bibliography: p.
  Includes index.
  1. Building. I. Title.
TH145.P45   1979   624   78-16761
ISBN 0-07-049760-5

CONTENTS

Preface   xiii
List of Abbreviations and Symbols   xv

1 Introduction   1

The engineer and construction / The construction industry / Types of
construction contracts / Construction economy and the
engineer / Construction economy and the contractor / Value
engineering / Making a value engineering study / Objections to value
engineering studies / Examples of value engineering studies / The time
value of money

2 Job Planning and Management   15

Construction activities / The critical path method / Definitions
of terms and symbols / Steps in critical path scheduling / Developing a
critical path schedule / Determining total float / Determining
free float / Applying the critical path method to overlapping
activities / Updating an arrow diagram / The time-grid diagram
method / Advantages of the time-grid diagram / Conducting a crash
program / Determining the minimum total cost of a project / Manual
versus computer analyses of critical path methods / Preparing a
construction schedule for a highway project / Clearing the right of
way / Drainage structures / Earthwork / Concrete pavement /
Scheduling resources / Delivering materials / Scheduling
laborers / Financing the project / Job layout / Project control during
construction / Keeping equipment records / Project
supervision / Construction-cost control / Cost-control records

**3 Factors Affecting the Selection of Construction
Equipment**   61

Standard types of equipment / Special equipment / The cost of
owning and operating construction equipment / Depreciation
costs / Straight-line depreciation / Declining-balance

                                                       v

method / Sum-of-the-years-digits method / Investment
costs / Operating costs / Economic life of construction
equipment / Costs of depreciation and replacement / Costs of
investments / Maintenance and repair costs / Downtime
costs / Obsolescence costs / Economic life of equipment that serves
other equipment / Sources of construction equipment

4 Engineering Fundamentals   89

Rolling resistance / The effect of grade on the required
tractive effort / The effect of grade in locating a borrow pit / The
effect of altitude on the performance of internal-combustion
engines / The combined effect of pressure and temperature on the
performance of internal-combustion engines / Drawbar
pull / Rimpull / Acceleration

5 Soil Stabilization and Compaction   105

Glossary of terms / Properties of soils / Swell and shrinkage /
Types of soils / Soil tests / Laboratory tests / Field tests /
Nuclear determination of moisture density of soils / Soil
stabilization / Stabilizing soils with hydrated lime / Asphalt-soil
stabilization / Cement-soil stabilization / Specifications for compacting
soils / Tamping rollers / Smooth-wheel rollers / Pneumatic-tired
rollers / Pressure bulb theory of load distribution / Pneumatic-tired
rollers with variable inflation pressures / Vibrating compactors /
Densification of soils by explosive vibrations / Installation
of the explosives / Deep densification of soils using a terra-probe
vibrator / Production rates using the terra-probe vibrator / Limitations
on the classifications of soils that may be compacted by the terra-probe
vibrator / Cost considerations / Conclusions regarding the method of
deep-sand vibratory compaction

6 Tractors and Related Equipment   144

Tractors / Crawler tractors with direct drive / Crawler tractors
with torque converter and power-shift transmissions / Wheel
tractors / Performance data for wheel tractors /
Gradability / Bulldozers / Crawler-mounted versus
wheel-mounted bulldozers / Moving earth with bulldozers / The output
of bulldozers / Clearing land / Types of equipment
used / Tractor-mounted bulldozers / Tractor-mounted special
blades / Tractor-mounted rakes / Tractor-pulled chains / Tractor-pulled
root plows / Tree crusher / Disposal of brush / Production rates / Cost
of clearing land / Ripping rock / Determining the rippability of
rock / Determining the speed of sound waves in rock / Types of
rippers / Economy of ripping rock / Front-end loaders / Production
rates for crawler-tractor-loaders / Production rates for
wheel-tractor-loaders

7 Scrapers 188

Types and sizes of scrapers / Performance charts / Cycle time for a
scraper / Operating efficiency and production / Increasing the
production rates of scrapers / Applying the load-growth curve to scraper
loading / The effect of rolling resistance on the production of
scrapers / Analyzing the performance of a wheel-type scraper

8 Excavating Equipment 206

Useful lives of power shovels and backhoes, draglines and clamshells,
and cranes / Power shovels / Selecting the type and size power
shovel / Shovel dimensions and clearances / The output of power
shovels / The effect of the depth of cut on the output of a
power shovel / The effect of the angle of swing on the output of a power
shovel / The effect of job conditions on the output of a power
shovel / The effect of management conditions on the output of a
power shovel / Draglines / Types of draglines / The size of a dragline /
The output of a dragline / The effect of the depth of cut and the
angle of swing on the output of a dragline / The effect of the size of
the bucket and the length of the boom on the output of a
dragline / The effect of the class of material on the cost of excavating
earth / Cranes / Safe lifting capacities of cranes / Specifications for
cranes / Working ranges of cranes / Rated loads for hydraulic
cranes / Clamshells / Hoes / Trenching machines / Wheel-type
trenching machines / Ladder-type trenching machines / Production rates
for trenching machines / Earth-and-rock saws / Wheel
excavators / Trap-loading materials

9 Trucks and Wagons 262

Rear-dump trucks / Bottom-dump wagons / Capacities of trucks and
wagons / Performance capabilities of trucks and wagons / Balancing
the capacities of hauling units with the size of excavator / The effect of
the size of trucks on the cost of hauling earth / The effect of the size of
the excavator on the cost of excavating and hauling earth / The effect
of grade on the cost of hauling earth with trucks / The effect of rolling
resistance on the cost of hauling earth / The effect of altitude on the
performance of hauling equipment

10 Operation Analyses 286

Motion and time studies / Duration of a time study / Statistical methods
of determining the number of observations needed / Time-lapse moving
pictures / Motion and time study for a concrete paver / Example of job
planning in constructing roof trusses / Applying motion and time studies
to building houses / Applying the theory of queues to determine the most
economical number of hauling units

11 Belt-Conveyor Systems 309

Representative belt-conveyor systems / Conveyor belts / Idlers / Idler friction / Power required to drive a belt conveyor / Power required to move an empty belt / Power required to move a load horizontally / Power required to move a load up an inclined belt conveyor / Driving equipment / Conveyor-belt take-ups / Holdbacks / Trippers / Examples illustrating the use of belt-conveyor systems

12 Compressed Air 334

Definitions of gas-law terms / Boyle's and Charles' laws / Energy required to compress air / Effect of altitude on the power required to compress air / Air-compressor definitions and terms / Stationary compressors / Portable compressors / Compressor capacity / Effect of altitude on capacity of compressors / Intercoolers / Aftercoolers / Receivers / Loss of air pressure in pipe due to friction / Loss of air pressure through screw-pipe fittings / Loss of air pressure in hose / Recommended sizes of pipe for transmitting compressed air / Recommended sizes of hose for transmitting compressed air / Diversity or capacity factor / Air required by pneumatic equipment and tools / Effect of altitude on the consumption of air by rock drills / The cost of compressed air / The cost of air leaks / The cost of using low air pressure

13 Drilling Rock and Earth 364

Definitions of terms / Bits / Jackhammers / Drifters / Wagon drills / Track-mounted drills / Rotary-percussion drills / Piston drills / Blasthole drills / Shot drills / Diamond drills / Manufacturers' report on drilling equipment and techniques / Selecting the drilling method and equipment / Selecting the drilling pattern / Rates of drilling rock / The effect of air pressure on the rate of drilling rock / Determining the optimum air pressure for drilling rock / Determining the increase in production resulting from an increase in air pressure / The effect of increased air pressure on the costs of maintenance and repairs of drills / Conducting a study to determine the economy of increasing air pressure / Test to determine the effect of air pressure on the rate of penetration of a drill / Drilling earth / Sizes and depths of holes drilled into earth / Removal of cuttings / Earth-boring machines

14 Blasting Rock 406

Definition of terms / Dynamite / Ammonium nitrate explosives / Slurries / Stemming / Firing charges / Safety fuse / Electric blasting caps / Delay blasting caps / Primacord / Primadet delay blasting caps / Handling misfires / Presplitting rock / Increasing efficiency of explosives with holes drilled at an angle / Proper spacing of blastholes / Monitoring the seismic effect of blasting / Care in the use of detonating cord / Transporting and handling explosives / Storing explosives

15 Tunneling   426

Scope of this subject / Types of earth excavated for tunnels / Types of rocks / Physical defects of rocks / Preliminary explorations / Number of entrances / Sequence of operations for drill and blast construction / Driving tunnels in rock / Drilling rock / Drill mountings for small tunnels / Drill jumbos / Drilling patterns / Loading and shooting holes / Driving tunnels with tunnel-boring machines / The essential parts of a mole / The operation of a mole / Methods of transporting muck / Sizes of moles / Limits on the types of earth or rock that can be excavated by moles / Rates of driving tunnels with moles / Production experiences with moles / Mangla dam tunnels / Mersey river tunnels / New developments in tunneling / San Francisco bay area rapid transit system / Japan tunnel mole / Tunnel in alluvial soil makes fast advance at low cost / Multihead tunneling machine / Use of laser beams to guide moles / Accuracy of laser beams / Advantages of using moles / Disadvantages of using moles / Ventilating tunnels / Volume of air required for ventilation / Size and capacity of vent pipe / Dust control / Mucking / Locomotives / Ground support / Using rock mechanics studies to design tunnel supports and linings / Rock bolting / Controlling groundwater / The cross sections of tunnels / Thickness of concrete linings / Sequence of lining a tunnel / Reinforcing steel / Forms for concrete linings / Tunnel lining by the pumping method / Placing the concrete lining / Tunnel lining with pneumatic placers / The use of precast concrete segments to line tunnels

16 Foundation Grouting   491

Need for grouting / Exploring to determine the need for grouting / Material used for grout / Drilling patterns / Drilling injection holes / Preparations for grouting / Washing the seams / Grouting pressures / Equipment for cement grouting / Injecting cement grout / Pressure grouting with asphalt / Clay grouting / Chemical grouting / Examples describing grouting operations / Determining the effectiveness of grouting

17 Piles and Pile-driving Equipment   506

Types of piles / Timber piles / Precast concrete piles / Cast-in-place concrete piles / Raymond step-taper concrete piles / Monotube piles / Advantages and disadvantages of cast-in-place concrete piles / Steel-pipe piles / Steel piles / The resistance of piles to

penetration / Pile hammers / Drop hammers / Single-acting steam
hammers / Double-acting steam hammers / Differential-acting steam
hammers / Hydraulic hammers / Diesel hammers / Vibratory pile
drivers / Performance factors for vibratory drivers / The Foster vibro
driver-extractor / Jetting piles / Driving piles below water / Pile-driving
formulas / Loss in energy due to impact / Energy losses due to causes
other than impact / Analysis of pile-driving problems / Michigan
pile-driving tests / Selecting a pile-driving hammer / Drilled and
underreamed foundations

18 Pumping Equipment   550

Classification of pumps / Reciprocating pumps / Diaphragm
pumps / Centrifugal pumps / Air-operated centrifugal-type sump
pumps / Performance of centrifugal pumps / Loss of head due to
friction in pipe / Loss of head due to friction in rubber hose / Selecting
a pump / Wellpoint systems / Capacity of a wellpoint system

19 Cofferdams   574

Forces acting on a cofferdam / Seepage of water under
cofferdams / Types of cofferdams / Earth-fill cofferdams / Rock-fill
cofferdams / Ohio-River-type cofferdams / Crib-type
cofferdams / Single-wall steel-sheet-piling cofferdams / Diaphragm-type
cellular cofferdams / Circular-type cellular cofferdams / Designing
circular-type cellular cofferdams / Economy of cofferdam
height / Freezing a cofferdam / Freezing soil for temporary ground
support / Cost of freezing ground / The effect of the properties of the
ground on the shape of the frozen zone / Electroosmosis

20 The Production of Crushed-Stone Aggregate   602

Types of crushers / Jaw crushers / Gyratory crushers / Cone
crushers / Hammer mills / Roll crushers / Rod and ball mills / Sizes
of stone produced by jaw and roll crushers / Log washers / Sand
preparation and classification machines / Selecting crushing
equipment / Scalping crushed stone / Feeders / Surge piles / Screening
aggregate / Revolving screens / Vibrating screens / Efficiency
factors / Deck factors / Aggregate-size factors / Determining the size
screen required / Portable crushing and screening plants / Flow
diagrams of aggregate-processing plants / Example of crushed-stone
aggregate plant / Handling crushed-stone aggregate

21 Forms for Concrete Structures   644

Form requirements / The cost of forms / Designing a project for form
economy / The constructor and form economy / Materials for
forms / The size of form sections / Properties of lumber / Pressure

produced by concrete / Fundamentals of form design / Stresses due to bending / Shearing stresses / Compression stresses / Deflection of forms / Wall forms / Column forms / Allowable loads on wood shores / Forms for beam-and-slab-type floor construction / Maximum spans for wood joists and wood stringers / Forms for beams

22 Concrete   670

Design of concrete mixtures / Handling and batching materials / Batching the aggregate / Concrete mixers / Outputs of construction mixers / Central mixing plants / Paving mixers / Transit-mixer and agitator trucks / Handling and transporting concrete / Hand buggies / Power-driven buggies / Buckets / Hoisting concrete with a crane versus a material tower / Chutes / Belt conveyors / Placing concrete with pumps / Placing concrete using the shotcrete method / Placing concrete / Curing concrete / Placing concrete in cold weather / Placing concrete in hot weather / Placing concrete in water

Appendix A   Cost of Owning and Operating Construction Equipment   699

Appendix B   Definitions of Certain SI Units   709

Appendix C   Alphabetical List of Units with Their SI Names and Conversion Factors   710

Appendix D   Factors for Converting Certain U.S. Customary (English) Units to Metric Units   711

Appendix E   U.S. Customary (English) Unit Equivalents   712

Appendix F   Metric Unit Equivalents   713

Index   715

PREFACE

Since publication of the second edition of this book many improvements in methods and equipment have proved beneficial to the construction industry. The author hopes that coverage of these improvements in this, the third edition, will increase the value of the book to the reader.

New material includes: expanded coverage of value engineering, soil stabilization and compaction, deep soil densification, clearing land, power shovels, draglines, cranes, and backhoes; operation analyses, air compressors, rock drills and methods; new methods of driving tunnels with moles; guidance of moles with laser beams; mucking; the use of precast concrete lining segments for tunnels; improved pumps and methods for placing concrete linings in tunnels; pressure grouting with chemicals; newer types of pile-driving equipment and methods; current information on pumping equipment and on freezing cofferdams; new methods of producing aggregate; revised dimensions of lumber for use as formwork for concrete structures; and more coverage of the use of conveyor belts, pumps, and shotcrete for placing concrete.

The book contains many new photographs of construction equipment and methods.

Many of the tables show values in both U.S. Customary (also called English) and metric (SI) units. Appendixes are included to assist the reader in converting values from U.S. Customary to metric units. Also, other tables listing conversion factors of interest to the reader are included.

The number of publications and sources of information listed under References has been increased substantially. Names and addresses of the manufacturers of construction equipment illustrated and described in the book are given as an aid to persons who may wish to contact the manufacturers.

The use of generic masculine pronouns has been retained in text references to individuals whose gender is not otherwise established. It should be emphasized that this has been done solely for succinctness of expression and such references are intended to apply equally to men and women.

The author is deeply grateful to the many persons who have given generous assistance in obtaining much of the information appearing in the book.

Comments from readers will be welcomed.

R. L. Peurifoy

LIST OF ABBREVIATIONS
AND SYMBOLS

AGC	Associated General Contractors of America, Inc.
bbl	barrel
bhp	brake horsepower
bm	bank measure, volume of earth prior to loosening
°C	Celsius temperature
cfm	cubic feet per minute
const.	construction
cpm	cycles per minute
cps	cycles per second (hertz)
cu ft	cubic foot
cu m	cubic meter
cu yd	cubic yard
cwt	100 pounds
deg	degree
est	estimated
°F	Fahrenheit temperature
f.o.b.	free on board
fmp	feet per minute
fps	feet per second
ft	foot
ft-lb	foot-pound
gal	gallon
gpm	gallons per minute
hp	horsepower
hr	hour
in.	inch
kW	kilowatts
lb	pound
lin ft	linear foot
M	1,000

m	meter
m^3	cubic meter
max	maximum
M fbm	1,000 feet board measure of lumber
min	minute, minimum
mm	millimeter
mph	miles per hour
op	operation
plf	pounds per linear foot
psf	pounds per square foot
psi	pounds per square inch
rpm	revolutions per minute
$S4S$	smooth on 4 sides for lumber
sec	second
sq ft	square foot
sq in.	square inch
square	100 square feet of area
sq yd	square yard
std	standard
tph	tons per hour
wk	week
yd	yard
yr	year

INTRODUCTION

THE PURPOSE OF THIS BOOK

The efforts of an engineer, who designs a project, and the constructor, who builds the project, are directed toward the same goal, namely, the creation of something which will serve the purpose for which it is built in a satisfactory manner. Construction is the ultimate objective of a design. It is hoped that this book will assist the reader in more fully understanding the construction industry. It is hoped that the material presented in the book will illustrate how the application of engineering fundamentals and analyses to construction activities may reveal methods of improving the quality, while at the same time reducing the costs, of construction.

THE ENGINEER AND CONSTRUCTION

When the prospective owner of a project under consideration recognizes a need for the project, he usually employs an engineer to make a study to determine whether the project is justified. If the study indicates that it is justified, an engineer will be engaged to prepare the plans and specifications and usually to supervise the construction of the project. It is the duty of the engineer to design that project which will most nearly satisfy the needs of the owner at the lowest practical cost. The engineer should study every major item to determine if it is possible to reduce the cost without unduly reducing the service which the project will furnish. It may be possible to change the design, modify the requirements for construction, or revise portions of the specifications in such a manner that the cost of the project will be reduced without sacrificing its essential value. An engineer who practices this philosophy is rendering a real service to his client. Thus, it seems evident that an engineer should be reasonably familiar with construction methods and costs if he is to design a project that is to be constructed at the lowest practical cost.

THE CONSTRUCTION INDUSTRY

Construction is essentially a service industry, whose responsibility is to convert the plans and specifications prepared by an engineer or an architect into a finished project.

The construction of projects involves thousands of details and complex interrelationships among owners, architects, engineers, general contractors, specialty contractors, manufacturers, material dealers, equipment distributors, governmental bodies and agencies, labor, and others.

The contractor assumes the responsibility for the delivery of the completed facility at a specified time and cost. In so doing, he accepts legal, financial, and managerial obligations.

Construction accounts for 15 out of every 100 jobs and consumes more basic and finished materials than any other industry.

Under the stimulus of increasing demand for its services, the construction industry has expanded and is expanding in geographical scope and technological dimension.

TYPES OF CONSTRUCTION CONTRACTS

Although there are many types of construction contracts, the three types that are of primary interest are lump-sum, unit-price, and cost-plus-a-fixed-fee contracts. Each of these is described briefly below.

Lump-sum contract The terms of this contract provide that the owner will pay to the contractor a specified sum of money for the completion of a project conforming to the plans and specifications furnished by an engineer or an architect. It is common practice for the owner to pay to the contractor a portion of this money at specified intervals, such as monthly, with the amount of each payment depending on the value of the work completed during the prior period of time, or according to some other schedule. Under the terms of this contract, a contractor may earn a profit or he may sustain a loss, depending on the total amount of the contract and the total cost of constructing the project.

Unit-price contract The terms of this contract provide that the owner will pay to the contractor a specified amount of money for each unit of work completed in a project. The units of work may be any items whose quantities can be determined, such as cubic yards of earth, linear feet of concrete pipe, square yards of concrete pavement, tons of asphalt pavement, etc. Payments are usually made by the owner to the contractor at specified intervals during the period of construction, with the amount of each payment depending on the value of the work completed during the prior period of time. Under the terms of this contract a contractor may earn a profit or he may sustain a loss, depending on the amount that he receives and the total cost of constructing the project.

Cost-plus-fee contract Under the terms of this contract the owner agrees to reimburse the contractor for specified costs, usually on-site costs, incurred by the contractor in constructing a project, plus an additional fee, which is essentially a management fee, to reimburse the contractor for the costs incurred at his head office resulting from the construction of the project. Items of expense covered by the fee include, but are not limited to, salaries, rent, taxes, insurance, interest on money borrowed to finance the project, the cost of trips made by persons to the project, expediting the delivery of materials to the project, etc. Under the terms of this contract, a contractor may realize a profit, or he may sustain a loss.

Contractors frequently are required to furnish a performance bond for each project. The bond, which is issued by an approved surety, protects the owner by guaranteeing that the project will be completed satisfactorily for the contract price. In the event the original contractor fails to complete the project, it then becomes the responsibility of the surety to obtain satisfactory completion by engaging another contractor or by using some other method which is acceptable to the owner. The cost of the performance bond, amounting to approximately 1 percent of the cost of the project, is paid for by the contractor.

Contractors tend to specialize in the types of work which they construct. Although there are no clear lines separating the fields of construction, they may be roughly divided into building, highway, heavy, railroad, pipeline, municipal, marine, steel erection, etc. Several of these can be subdivided into smaller fields. The reasons for specializing are primarily a matter of business discretion. Few contractors, if any, can afford to own all the different types of equipment required for construction in all engineering fields. A contractor who attempts to own and operate such a large quantity of equipment might find himself "equipment-poor." As it costs money to own equipment, even though it is not working, idle equipment represents a continuing loss to the owner. The cost of owning equipment is discussed in Chap. 3.

CONSTRUCTION ECONOMY AND THE ENGINEER

The cost of a project is influenced by the requirements of the design and the specifications. Prior to completing the final design the engineer should give careful consideration to the methods and equipment which may be used to construct the project. Requirements which increase the cost without producing commensurate benefits should be eliminated. The ultimate decisions of the engineer should be based on a reasonable knowledge of construction methods and costs.

The cost of a project may be divided into five or more items: materials, labor, equipment, overhead and supervision, and profit. The last item is beyond the control of the engineer, but he does have some control over the cost of the first four items.

If the engineer specifies materials which must be transported great distances, the costs may be unnecessarily high. Requirements for tests and inspections of materials may be too rigid for the purpose for which the materials will be used. Frequently substitute materials are available which are essentially as satisfactory as materials whose costs are considerably higher.

The specified quality of workmanship and methods of construction have considerable influence on the amount and class of labor required and the cost of labor. Complicated concrete structures are relatively easy to design and to reduce to drawings, but they may be exceedingly difficult to build. A high-grade concrete finish may be justified for exposed surfaces in a fine building, but the same quality of workmanship is not justified for a warehouse. The quality of workmanship should be in keeping with the type of project.

Engineers should keep informed on the developments of new construction equipment, as such information will enable them to modify the design or construction methods to permit the use of economical equipment. The use of a dual-drum concrete-paving mixer, instead of a single-drum mixer, will increase the production of concrete materially and for most projects will reduce the cost of the pavement. The use of the high-capacity earth loader and large trucks may necessitate a change in the location, size, and shape of a borrow pit, but the resulting savings may easily justify the change. The use of wellpoint systems for controlling ground water has eliminated the need of cofferdams for many projects. The development of underreamed footings has changed the foundation designs for many structures from load-bearing piles to less expensive types of supports.

The following list indicates methods which an engineer may use to reduce the costs of construction:

1. Design concrete structures with as many duplicate members as practical in order to permit the reuse of forms without rebuilding.
2. Simplify the design of the structure where possible.
3. Design for the use of cost-saving equipment and methods.
4. Eliminate unnecessary special construction requirements.
5. Design to reduce the required labor to a minimum.
6. Specify a quality of workmanship that is consistent with the quality of the project.
7. Furnish adequate foundation information where possible.
8. Refrain from requiring the contractor to assume the responsibility for information that should be furnished by the engineer or for adequacy of design.
9. Use local materials when they are satisfactory.
10. Write simple, straightforward specifications which clearly state what is expected. Define the results expected, but within reason permit the contractor to select the methods of accomplishing the results.

11. When possible, use standardized specifications, ones with which the contractors are familiar.
12. Hold prebidding conferences with contractors in order to eliminate uncertainties and to reduce change orders to a minimum.
13. Use inspectors who have sufficient judgment and experience to understand the project and have authority to make decisions.

Other examples, illustrating methods of effecting economy in construction, will be found in succeeding chapters of this book.

CONSTRUCTION ECONOMY AND THE CONTRACTOR

One desirable characteristic of a successful contractor is a degree of dissatisfaction over the plans and methods under consideration for constructing a project. Complacency in members of the construction industry will not contribute toward developing new equipment, new methods, or new construction planning, all of which are desirable for continuing improvements in the products of the industry at lower costs. A contractor who does not keep informed on new equipment and methods will soon discover that his competitors are underbidding him. It is hoped that the analyses and examples presented in this book will impress on the reader the value of carefully studying each project in order to select the methods and equipment that will produce the greatest construction economy.

Suggestions for possible reductions in construction costs by the contractor include, but are not limited to, the following:

1. Prebidding studies of the project and the site to determine the effect of:
    a. Topography
    b. Geology
    c. Climate
    d. Sources of material
    e. Access to the project
    f. Housing facilities if required
    g. Storage facilities if required
    h. Labor supply
    i. Local services
2. The use of alternate construction equipment, having higher capacities, higher efficiencies, higher speeds, more maneuverability, and lower operating costs.
3. The payment of a bonus to the key personnel for production in excess of a specified rate.
4. The use of radios as a means of communication between the headquarters office and key personnel on projects covering large areas.
5. The practice of holding periodic conferences with key personnel to discuss plans, procedures, and results. Such conferences should produce better

morale among the staff members and should result in better coordination among the various operations.

6. The adoption of realistic safety practices on a project as a means of reducing accidents.
7. Considering the desirability of subcontracting specialized operations to other contractors who can do the work more economically than the general contractor.
8. Considering the desirability of improving shop and serving facilities for better maintenance of construction equipment.

VALUE ENGINEERING

This is a formalized application of a specialized branch of engineering whose objective is to effect economy in the cost of constructing a project. A government agency, a corporation, or a private owner of a project to be designed and constructed usually uses its architect and/or engineer to make the necessary preliminary predesign studies and then design the project most suitable to serve the purposes for which the project will be constructed, presumably at the lowest costs consistent with the overall objectives of the project. Following the completion of the plans and specifications, a contract is awarded to the successful bidder; it may also be a negotiated contract. The terms of the contract provide that the contractor may use his own staff or engage one or more value engineers to make a study of the design, specifications, materials, and methods of construction to determine if any of these items can be modified to permit the construction of the project at a cost less than the amount of the contract without reducing the quality or usefulness of the project.

Value engineering may be applied to a project in one or two stages. The first stage is during or immediately after the completion of the plans and specifications, and prior to their release to contractors. The purpose of this study is to determine if modifications can be made in the design, or if substitutions can be made in the specified materials, to reduce the cost of the project without sacrificing the quality. If economies can be effected, the net savings will accrue to the owner of the project. The net savings, if any, will be the total reduction in cost less the cost of the value engineering study.

The second stage for a value engineering study is after a contract is awarded for the construction of the project. This study is made by the contractor, under the direction of his own value engineer, or under the direction of a professional value engineer engaged by the contractor. If such a study indicates that reductions in cost can be effected, the contractor is invited to submit to the owner detailed statements describing the modifications, with estimates showing the anticipated reductions in costs. If the owner, usually after consultation with his architect and/or engineer, approves the modifications, with reductions in cost, the resulting net savings are shared by the contractor and the owner on a preagreed basis, frequently in equal amounts.

MAKING A VALUE ENGINEERING STUDY

A value engineering study should be made by one or more persons who are thoroughly versed in methods of construction and the materials to be used in a project. As a means of implementing the study, certain questions, such as the following, should be asked regarding the project:

1. What is it?
2. What is its purpose?
3. What does it cost?
4. What modifications are possible?
5. What will such modifications cost?
6. What effect, if any, will the modifications have on the time required to complete the project?

An application of each of these questions to each phase of the project may reveal that certain reductions in costs are possible without sacrificing the quality or function of the project. With the approval of the owner, these modifications can then be adopted.

Because of the greater possibility for reduction in cost, a value study should be concentrated on those items that represent the larger costs in the project and those that are repetitive. Items whose potential savings will not equal or exceed the costs of studies should be disregarded.

In a report to the Congress of the United States of America in February 1975, the Environmental Protection Agency estimated that at least 107 billion dollars was required to control pollution from municipal sources. The figure implies the necessity of implementing cost controls to ensure that Federal funds are being used effectively. Recent studies by the EPA indicate that value engineering applied during the design phase of waste treatment facilities can potentially minimize the cost, not only for the construction phase but over the life cycles of the facilities as well [1].

OBJECTIONS TO VALUE ENGINEERING STUDIES

Although numerous studies have demonstrated that reductions in costs are possible, there may be some objections by contractors to such studies and any recommended modification. Possible objections include the following:

1. How would it affect the project with regard to cost?
2. How would it affect the project with regard to time?
3. How would it affect the owner-contractor relationship?
4. How would it affect the architect-contractor or engineer-contractor relationship?
5. What is the probability of the modification's being approved?

The answers to questions 1 and 2 mean that any modification resulting in a reduction in cost should be evaluated in terms of the cost of any delay in completing the project.

If the owner of a project has invited the contractor to recommend modifications, the owner-contractor relationship should not be affected adversely.

Most contractors are hesitant to recommend modifications that seem to reflect adversely on the ability or integrity of the architect or engineer who designed the project, for understandable reasons. Contractors do not wish to jeopardize their relationships with the architect or engineer who designed the project by appearing to criticize the design.

If a contractor recommends one or more modifications that are not approved by the owner, or are approved after what seems to be undue delay, the contractor may be reluctant to make additional recommendations. Prompt action by the owner should eliminate this possible objection.

In many instances contractors may modify their methods of construction within the scope of the specifications which specify end results instead of methods, to take advantage of improved equipment and methods, without prior approval of the owner. If such modifications result in a reduction in the cost of constructing a project, the reduction will accrue to the contractor.

EXAMPLES OF VALUE ENGINEERING STUDIES

The examples presented below illustrate how value studies reduced (or might have reduced) the costs of the projects to which they apply. The examples are included to illustrate the possible or realized advantages of value studies. Their inclusion is not intended to imply that each recommendation had merit.

Example The design of a building required the installation of a number of sliding doors to be fabricated from an expensive panelling material available in one stock size, namely, 4 ft 0 in. wide by 8 ft 0 in. long. The specified sizes of the doors were 2 ft 7 in. wide by 4 ft 1 in. high, equal to an area of 11 sq ft, to be cut from a panel whose area was 32 sq ft. The excess material, amounting to 21 sq ft for each panel, would be wasted because it could not be used elsewhere in the project. Prior to awarding a contract for the construction of the building, the owner, who was familiar with construction practices, directed that the sizes of the doors be modified to 4 ft 0 in. by 4 ft 0 in. In addition to reducing the cost, the modification improved the function of the doors.

Example A contractor was awarded a contract to construct a concrete taxiway, 75 ft wide by approximately 1,500 ft long, for an existing airport. The specifications required that the taxiway be constructed in five strips, each 15 ft wide, with dowels of 2-in.-diameter steel pipe installed at 18-in. spacings in the joint between adjacent strips. Prior to starting construction the contractor offered to reduce the amount of the contract by $25,000 if he were permitted to lay three strips, each 25 ft wide. The decision in analyzing this alternate method should be based on determining if the purpose of the runway would be better served by five strips 15 ft wide or three strips 25 ft wide.

Example It was estimated that a radio facility designed for the U.S. Department of Defense, Bureau of Yards and Docks, would cost $16,845,620 as originally designed. When the design was subjected to a value engineering analysis by a consultant, it was determined that certain modifications could be made without affecting the operating function of the facility, which reduced the cost to $14,999,521. The fee paid for the investigation was $600. Thus the net saving was $1,840,099 [2].

Example Following the completion of a combination flood control and hydroelectric dam, whose cost was approximately $76,000,000, the contractor released an article listing six modifications, which, if they had been adopted, would have reduced the cost of the project by an estimated $7,200,000 [3].

The suggested modifications in methods and materials, together with the estimated savings, are listed and briefly described below.

Care and diversion of the river If a cofferdam lower than the one specified had been permitted (with the contractor to assume the risk of any costs resulting from the overtopping of the dam) and combined with a provision for flood waters to be diverted through a portion of the dam, the cost of this item could have been reduced by an estimated $500,000.

Height differential limited to 20 ft This limitation on height differential reportedly forced a shutdown of concreting operations for 3 months during the second-stage conversion and retarded concreting progress for 4 months thereafter. This requirement reportedly delayed the completion of the project at least 6 months, resulting in an increase in costs of at least $500,000.

Concrete lifts limited to 30 in. This limitation, which was applied to a portion of the concrete placed in the dam, increased the cost of cleanup and curing, with a resulting increase of at least $300,000 in the cost of the project.

Refrigeration The requirement that concrete be cooled before, during, and after placement resulted in an additional estimated cost of $1,400,000.

Five-day limit between successive lifts This requirement was estimated to have delayed the completion of the project by 3 months, at an additional cost of at least $250,000.

Aggregate The requirement that the aggregate for the project be produced from a quarry 7 miles from the dam, instead of permitting the use of natural sand and aggregate from a nearby quarry, as originally contemplated, increased the cost of the project by at least $4,250,000.

Example A reinforced concrete bridge to be constructed in Hawaii was designed to be built on falsework. Because the superstructure was 150 ft (45.7 m) above the ground, the contractor chose to build it by cantilevering out from the piers, thus eliminating the need for falsework. The savings resulting from this change in construction plans, amounting to about $400,000, were shared equally by the contractor and the owner [4].

Persons interested in pursuing this subject further may wish to obtain one or more of the publications listed in the bibliography at the end of this chapter.

THE TIME VALUE OF MONEY

The time value of money is a relationship between the value of money today and its value at some future date, considering the interest charged or paid for the use of money. For example, if $100 is borrowed today for a period of 1 year at an interest rate of 8 percent per year, it will be necessary to repay the $100 plus an additional $8 to cover the cost of interest, for a total of $108. Thus, for the stated condition, $100 today is equal to $108 1 year hence. If $100 is borrowed today at a rate of interest of 8 percent per year, with $50 plus accrued interest to be paid at the end of 6 months, and the balance to be paid at the end of 1 year, the payments will be

1. $T = \$50 + \$100 \times 0.04 = \$ \ 54$
2. $T = \$50 + \$50 \times 0.04 = \quad 52$
   Total repaid $\qquad = \$\overline{106}$

For this condition $100 today is equal to $54 to be paid in 6 months plus $52 to be paid in 12 months

When an asset is purchased with the provision that the cost of the asset will be liquidated over several pay periods, at a specified rate of interest, it is necessary to know in advance the amount of each payment to be made. Because of the interest charge the sum of the delayed payments will exceed the amount that would be paid for a cash purchase.

Formulas will be developed for use in determining the time value of money.

Space in this book does not permit an exhaustive discussion of this subject, but a number of excellent books devoted entirely to this subject are available.

Formulas Prior to developing the time-value formulas it is necessary to list and define the symbols that will be used.

$P =$ a present amount of money
$T =$ a future amount of money n periods from today that is equivalent to P with interest rate i
$R =$ uniform end of period payment in a series of payments continuing for a duration of n periods
$i =$ rate of interest per interest period
$n =$ number of interest periods

In the formulas which will be developed the rate of interest should conform to the interest period. For example, if the repayment of a loan is to be made every 3 months in four installments at 8 percent interest per year, there will be four interest periods, and the interest rate will be 2 percent per period.

Formulas for single payments If P dollars are borrowed or invested at an interest rate i per period for several periods, with the earned interest to be retained and compounded at the end of each period, the future amounts at the end of the periods will be

End of first period: $\quad T = P + Pi$
End of second period: $T = P + Pi + (P + Pi)i = P(1 + i)^2$
End of nth period: $\quad T = P(1+i)^n$

This is the future amount for a single payment P, with the interest rate i compounded at the end of each interest period.

$$T = P(1 + i)^n \qquad (1\text{-}1)$$

The formula may be revised to determine the amount that must be invested today to provide T dollars at the end of n periods.

$$P = \frac{T}{(1 + i)^n} = T\frac{1}{(1 + i)^n} \tag{1-2}$$

Formulas for uniform end-of-period payments The debt created by the purchase of an asset is frequently liquidated by making uniform end-of-period payments for the necessary number of periods. A formula for determining the amount of payment R can be developed.

If a uniform amount R is invested at the end of each period for n periods at compound interest i per period, the total amount at the end of n periods will be

$$T = R\left[(1 + i)^{n-1} + (1 + i)^{n-2} + \cdots + (1 + i) + 1\right] \tag{a}$$

Multiply both sides of formula by $(1 + i)$.

$$T(1 + i) = R\left[(1 + i)^n + (1 + i)^{n-1} + \cdots + (1 + i)\right] \tag{b}$$

Subtract (a) from (b) to give

$$Ti = R(1 + i)^n - 1$$

Then

$$R = T\frac{i}{(1 + i)^n - 1} \tag{1-3}$$

This is referred to as a sinking fund formula because it determines the uniform end-of-period investment R that must be made in order to provide the amount T at the end of n periods.

In order to determine the uniform end-of-period payment R required to liquidate a current debt P in n periods substitute for T in formula (1-3) its value from formula (1-1).

$$R = P(1 + i)^n \frac{i}{(1 + i)^n - 1} = P\frac{i(1 + i)^n}{(1 + i)^n - 1} \tag{1-4}$$

This may be referred to as a liquidating or capital recovery formula.

The expression

$$\frac{i(1 + i)^n}{(1 + i)^n - 1}$$

is called the liquidating factor. Tables appearing in appropriate books on mathematics give the values for this factor and the factors in formulas (1-1) to (1-3) for values of i and n. Table 1-1 gives the values of these factors for interest rates of 6, 8, and 10 percent for values of n from 1 through 10 interest periods. Tables in books on mathematics and engineering economy cover a much broader range of values.

Table 1-1 Compound amount factors

Single payment			Uniform period payments		
			6% compound interest		
(1)	(2)	(3)	(4)	(5)	(6)
n	$(1 + i)^n$	$\dfrac{1}{(1 + i)^n}$	$\dfrac{i}{(1 + i)^n - 1}$	$\dfrac{i(1 + i)^n}{(1 + i)^n - 1}$	$\dfrac{(1 + i)^n - 1}{i}$
1	1.060	0.9434	1.0000	1.0600	1.000
2	1.124	0.8900	0.4854	0.5454	2.060
3	1.191	0.8396	0.3141	0.3741	3.184
4	1.262	0.7921	0.2286	0.2886	4.375
5	1.338	0.7473	0.1774	0.2374	5.637
6	1.419	0.7050	0.1434	0.2034	6.975
7	1.504	0.6651	0.1191	0.1791	8.394
8	1.594	0.6274	0.1010	0.1610	9.897
9	1.689	0.5919	0.0870	0.1470	11.491
10	1.791	0.5584	0.0759	0.1359	13.181
			8% compound interest		
1	1.080	0.9259	1.0000	1.0800	1.000
2	1.166	0.8573	0.4808	0.5608	2.080
3	1.260	0.7938	0.3080	0.3880	3.246
4	1.360	0.7350	0.2219	0.3019	4.506
5	1.469	0.6806	0.1705	0.2505	5.867
6	1.587	0.6302	0.1363	0.2163	7.336
7	1.714	0.5835	0.1121	0.1921	8.923
8	1.851	0.5403	0.0940	0.1740	10.637
9	1.999	0.5002	0.0801	0.1601	12.488
10	2.159	0.4632	0.0690	0.1490	14.487
			10% compound interest		
1	1.100	0.9091	1.0000	1.1000	1.000
2	1.210	0.8264	0.4762	0.5762	2.100
3	1.331	0.7513	0.3021	0.4021	3.310
4	1.464	0.6830	0.2155	0.3155	4.641
5	1.611	0.6209	0.1638	0.2638	6.105
6	1.772	0.5645	0.1296	0.2296	7.716
7	1.949	0.5132	0.1054	0.2054	9.487
8	2.144	0.4665	0.0874	0.1874	11.436
9	2.358	0.4241	0.0736	0.1736	13.579
10	2.594	0.3855	0.0628	0.1628	15.937

Examples The following examples will illustrate the use of these formulas.

Example What will be the value 8 years hence of an investment of $1,000 made today at an interest rate of 8 percent compounded annually? Use formula (1-1) and column 2 of Table 1-1.

$$T = 1,000 \times 1.851 = \$1,851$$

Example What single investment made today at 8 percent compound interest will provide $4,000 at the end of 8 years? Use formula (1-2) and column 3 of Table 1-1.

$$P = 4,000 \times 0.5403 = \$2,161.20$$

Example What uniform payment must be made at the end of each year for 5 years, at an interest rate of 8 percent, to liquidate a current debt of $20,000? Use formula (1-4) and column 5 of Table 1-1.

$$R = 20,000 \times 0.2505 = \$5,010$$

If this debt is to be liquidated by making uniform payments at the end of each month for 5 years and at an interest rate of 8 percent per year, the interest rate per monthly period will be $\frac{8}{12} = \frac{2}{3}$ percent and the number of periods will be $5 \times 12 = 60$. For this condition

$$R = 20,000 \times 0.02028 = \$405.60$$

It will be noted that the total amount of payments under the latter plan are less than under the former plan because interest is applied only to the unliquidated portion of the debt.

Example A common practice used in determining the amount of the uniform monthly payments required to liquidate a debt created by the purchase of construction equipment at a specified rate of interest is to calculate the charge for interest for the debt for the entire period of repayment, and then add this amount to the initial debt. The total debt plus interest charge is then divided by the number of months over which the debt is to be paid to determine the amount of the monthly payments.

For example, assume that a unit of equipment is purchased with a balance of $20,000 to be paid in 12 equal monthly installments, at a quoted 10 percent interest rate. The total debt including interest will be

Balance due	$= \$20,000$
Interest charge, $0.10 \times \$20,000 =$	$2,000$
Total amount	$= \$22,000$

Amount of monthly payments: $22,000 \div 12 = \$1,833.33$

What is the true annual rate of interest? The interest rate is determined by using formula (1-4) and solving for i.

Given $P = \$20,000$, $R = \$1,833.33$, and $n = 12$, find i.

SOLUTION The solution is as follows:

$$\frac{R}{P} = \frac{1,833.33}{20,000.00} = 0.09167$$

Rewriting formula (1-4), we have

$$\frac{R}{P} = \frac{i(1 + i)^n}{(1 + i)^n - 1} = 0.09167$$

In order to determine the true rate of interest per period, 1 month, it is necessary to enter a table of compound amount factors, such as Table 1-1, column 5, and for $n = 12$ seek a factor value equal to 0.09167. An examination of mathematical tables gives the following results:

For $i = 1\frac{1}{2}\%$, $\quad \frac{R}{P} = 0.09167$

Thus the rate of interest is 1.50 percent per month, or approximately 18 percent per year. When the value carried into the table does not appear in the table, it is necessary to interpolate to find the correct rate of interest.

PROBLEMS

1-1 Solve the following problems with the rate of interest equal to 10 percent compounded annually:

(a) If $10,000 is invested today, what will its value be after 10 years?

(b) What single amount must be invested today to produce $20,000 at the end of 4 years?

(c) If $1,000 is invested today, and an equal amount is invested at the end of each year for 10 years, what will be the value at the end of 10 years?

(d) If $1,000 is invested today, and an equal amount is invested at the end of each year for 5 years with no further investment made, what will be the value at the end of 10 years?

1-2 Solve the following problems with the rate of interest equal to 8 percent compounded annually:

(a) If a debt of $20,000 is created today, what uniform end-of-year payments must be made to amortize the debt at the end of 10 years?

(b) What uniform end-of-year payment must be made to create a sinking fund whose value will be $40,000 at the end of 10 years?

(c) If $1,000 is invested today and an equal amount is invested at the end of each 2 years for 10 years, what will be the value at the end of 10 years?

1-3 Solve the following problems with the rate of interest equal to 10 percent compounded annually:

(a) If $10,000 is borrowed today to be repaid in 10 years with equal end-of-year payments, what will be the value of the unpaid principal at the end of 5 years?

(b) If $1,000 is invested today and an equal amount is invested at the end of each year for 8 years, with no further investments made, what will the value be at the end of 12 years?

(c) Assume that $20,000 is borrowed today to be repaid in 10 equal year-end payments. If, after making the sixth payment, no further year-end payments are made, what payment will be required to liquidate the debt at the end of 15 years?

REFERENCES

1. Tufty, Harold G.: EPA Makes Value Engineering (VE) Mandatory on Projects over $10 Million, *Civil Engineering*, vol. 46, pp. 101–103, September 1976.
2. Value Engineering Hits Contracting, *Engineering News-Record*, vol. 172, pp. 23–25, May 14, 1964.
3. White, Ross: A Contractor Assays the Specifications for Bull Shoals Dam, *Civil Engineering*, vol. 21, pp. 32–33, November 1951.
4. Contractor-Designer Interaction, *Civil Engineering*, vol. 46, p. 62, December 1976.
5. VE Saves, Pays on Some Jobs, *Engineering News-Record*, vol. 173, pp. 17–18, November 5, 1964.
6. Dell'Isola, A. J.: Everybody Benefits from Value Engineering, *Constructor*, vol. 47, pp. 40–42, December 1965.
7. Cox, Allen E.: Why Value Engineering in the Construction Industry? *Constructor* vol. 47, pp. 40–44, August 1965.
8. Cox, Allen E.: Why Engineering in Construction? *Constructor*, vol. 47, pp. 42–44, September 1965.
9. Dell'Isola, A. J.: Value Engineering in Construction, *Civil Engineering*, vol. 36, pp. 58–61, September 1966.
10. Miles, Lawrence D.: "Techniques of Value Analysis and Engineering," 2nd ed., McGraw-Hill Book Company, New York, 1972.

CHAPTER TWO

JOB PLANNING AND MANAGEMENT

GENERAL INFORMATION

This chapter deals with the planning that is necessary prior to starting actual construction on a project. Such planning should facilitate the construction by establishing:

1. The time for delivering materials
2. The types, quantities, and duration of equipment needs
3. The classification and numbers of laborers needed and the periods during which they will be needed
4. The extent to which financial aid, if any, will be needed
5. The time required to complete the project

A contractor should do some of this planning prior to bidding a project, since such planning frequently will reveal factors which will affect the cost of the project, and thus will influence the amounts shown in a bid.

CONSTRUCTION ACTIVITIES

Most projects are divided into construction activities to facilitate job planning. A construction activity is a portion of a project which may be performed by a classification of laborers or perhaps a single type of equipment. For example, in constructing a reinforced-concrete retaining wall the project might be divided into the following activities:

1. Excavate earth, machine.
2. Excavate earth, hand.
3. Build forms.
4. Place reinforcing steel.
5. Place concrete.
6. Cure concrete.
7. Remove forms.
8. Finish concrete surface.
9. Backfill with earth.

In planning the construction of a highway requiring a new location the project might be divided into the following activities:

1. Move to the project and set up the plant.
2. Clear and grub the right of way.
3. Perform the earthwork, cut and fill.
4. Excavate for drainage pipe.
5. Install drainage pipe.
6. Backfill around drainage pipe.
7. Place the base material.
8. Place the pavement.
9. Shape the shoulders.
10. Clean up and remove the plant.

In order to estimate the progress in constructing the project, the job planner should determine the quantity of work to be constructed for each activity expressed in an appropriate unit. Then he should estimate the probable rate at which the work will be performed, allowing for estimated loss in time owing to bad weather or any other cause. From this information it will be possible to estimate the total time required to complete each activity. The estimated starting date and completion date for each activity should be determined. In scheduling the activities the job planner should consider the desirable sequential relationships between the activities. For example, in constructing a concrete foundation unit it will be necessary to complete the excavation before concrete can be placed.

THE CRITICAL PATH METHOD

The critical path method of planning, analyzing, and controlling a construction project has become a useful tool for engineers, architects, contractors, and others who are associated with construction. Many government and private

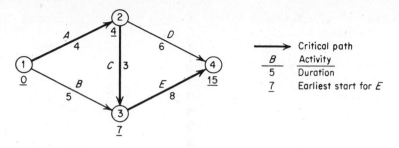

Figure 2-1 Arrow diagram.

agencies require the preparation and use of this method when planning the construction of a project.

In order to analyze a project by using the critical path method it is necessary to divide the project into activities. The number of units of work required to complete each activity should be determined. Then the time required to complete each activity, considering available equipment and labor, should be estimated in appropriate units, such as days, weeks, or months. Also, it is necessary to determine the time sequence in which the activities should be constructed. For example, concrete for a beam can not be placed until the forms have been erected and the reinforcing steel has been placed.

Table 2-1 List of activities, durations, and precedences

Activity	Duration	Activities which immediately precede	follow
A	3	None	B, C, D
B	5	A	E
C	4	A	F, G
D	6	A	G, H
E	4	B	I
F	5	C	J
G	3	C, D	K
H	6	D	L
I	5	E	N
J	7	F	O
K	4	G	P
L	5	H	M, Q
M	3	L	P
N	4	I	S
O	5	J	S, T
P	6	K, M	T
Q	4	L	R
R	4	Q	T
S	5	N, O	U
T	4	O, P, R	U
U	3	S, T	None

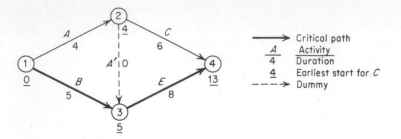

Figure 2-2 Arrow diagram.

Each activity should be identified by a symbol or an appropriate description or both, and then listed in column form, with the duration of the activity, together with the activities which immediately precede and follow it, given. (This procedure is illustrated in Table 2-1.) Then the interrelationship of the activities can be indicated by a network or arrow diagram, in which each arrow represents an activity. Figure 2-1 illustrates an arrow diagram for a simple project involving five activities, designated by the letters, A, B, C, D, and E, for which the durations are estimated to be 4, 5, 3, 6, and 8 days, respectively.

Activities A and B can be started at the same time. Activities C and D cannot be started until A is completed. Activity E cannot be started until B and C are completed. An examination of Fig. 2-1 reveals that the minimum total time required to complete the project is the sum of the durations of activities A, C, and E, which is equal to 15 days. This is the critical path for the network.

If the project illustrated in Fig. 2-1 is modified by eliminating activity C, with the condition that activity E cannot be started until activities A and B are completed, a method must be used to indicate this requirement in the network. Since activity C does not appear in the network, it must be replaced with a dummy arrow, as illustrated in Fig. 2-2. A dummy is not a true activity, and it requires no time for completion. The critical path now lies along activities B and E.

DEFINITIONS OF TERMS AND SYMBOLS

Because terms and symbols are used in analyzing a project and constructing the arrow diagram, it is necessary to define these items.

Activity An activity is the performance of a specific task, such as placing reinforcing steel. It requires time to perform an activity.

Event An event represents the completion of an activity. It requires no time in itself. It is usually indicated on the arrow diagram by a number enclosed in a circle.

Arrow An arrow is drawn to represent each activity included in the network for a project, joining two events. An arrow is designated by two numbers, one at the tail and one at the head, with the number at the head always larger than the number at the tail. The length of the arrow has no relation to the duration of the activity which it represents.

Network This is an arrow diagram drawn to represent the relations of the activities and events. It is common practice to start time and the first arrow or arrows at the left end of the network and to proceed to the right.

Dummy A dummy is an artificial activity, represented on the arrow diagram by a dotted line, which indicates that an activity following the dummy cannot be started until the activity or activities preceding the dummy are completed. A dummy activity does not require any time.

Duration This is the estimated time, expressed in any desired unit, required to perform an activity.

Earliest start: ES This is the earliest time that an activity can be started.

Earliest finish: EF This is the earliest time that an activity can be finished. It is the earliest starting time plus the duration of an activity: $EF = ES + D$.

Latest start: LS This is the latest time that an activity may be started without delaying the completion of a project: $LS = LF - D$.

Latest finish: LF This is the latest time that an activity can be finished without delaying the completion of a project: $LF = LS + D$.

Total float: TF This is the amount of time that the start or finish of an activity can be delayed without delaying the completion of a project: $TF = LF - EF = LS - ES$. In Fig. 2-1 the earliest time for event 3 is the sum of the durations for activities A and $C = 4 + 3 = 7$ days. Because activity B has a duration of only 5 days, it can be completed 2 days prior to event 3. Thus its total float is $7 - 5 = 2$ days. If the start or finish of activity B is delayed 2 days, it will not delay the completion of the project.

Free float: FF This is the amount of time that the finish of an activity can be delayed without delaying the earliest starting time for a following activity. $FF = ES$ (following activity) $- EF$ (of this activity).

Critical path The critical path is the series of interconnected activities through the network for which each activity has zero float time. The critical path determines the minimum time required to complete a project.

The uses of these terms and symbols are illustrated more fully in the examples which appear below.

Persons who wish more comprehensive information on this subject may obtain such information from books devoted to the treatment of the critical path method.

STEPS IN CRITICAL PATH SCHEDULING

For persons who wish to apply the critical path method of scheduling the construction of a project it is suggested that the following steps be used.

1. Prepare a list of activities for the project.
2. Estimate the duration of each activity.
3. Determine which activity or activities immediately precede each activity.
4. Determine which activity or activities immediately follow each activity.
5. Draw a network with the activities and events properly interconnected.
6. Assign numbers to the events, being sure that the number at the head of each arrow is larger than the number at the tail of the arrow.
7. Prepare a chart with vertical columns and horizontal lines on which to list each activity with an appropriate designation: duration, earliest start, earliest finish, latest start, latest finish, and total float. A column for free float may be included, if this information is desired.
8. Determine which activities lie on the critical path.

DEVELOPING A CRITICAL PATH SCHEDULE

The following example illustrates a method of scheduling a project by the critical path method. Table 2-1 illustrates a form that can be used to tabulate the activities, together with the estimated durations, and the activities that immediately precede and follow each activity. Although the activities are designated by letters in this example, it is desirable in actual practice to designate

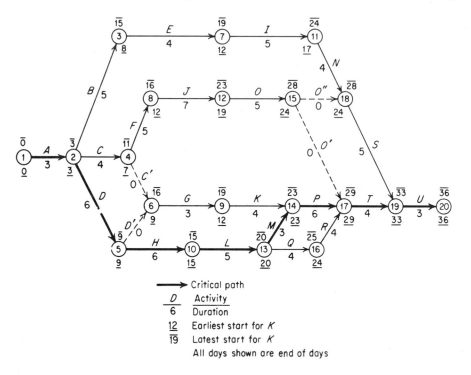

Figure 2-3 Arrow diagram.

each activity by appropriate descriptive words. Thus this example is intended to demonstrate how an arrow diagram and the related information are developed. This table provides the information specified in steps 1 through 4 of the preceding section.

Steps 5 and 6 are illustrated by Fig. 2-3. In this figure it will be noted that there are four dummies. The dummies C' and D' indicate that activities C and D, respectively, must be completed before activity G can be started. If activity G is drawn directly from event 4, without dummy C', it will be necessary to draw dummy D' from event 5 to event 4. This then will indicate that activity F cannot be started until activity D is completed, which is not true. Thus the two dummies O' and O'' are required for the same reasons.

In the figure the heavy lines representing activities A, D, H, L, M, P, T, and U lie on the critical path. The estimated time required to complete the project is 36 working days.

Table 2-2 lists the activities, events, durations, starts, finishes, total floats, and free floats. Numbers appearing in the events columns should be taken from the arrow diagram after it is completed and the events numbered thereon.

Table 2-2 List of activities and related information

Activity	Events		D	ES	EF	LS	LF	TF	FF
A*	1	2	3	0	3	0	3	0	0
D	2	3	5	3	8	10	15	7	0
C	2	4	4	3	7	7	11	4	0
C'	4	6	0	7	7	16	16	9	2
D*	2	5	6	3	9	3	9	0	0
D'	5	6	0	9	9	16	16	7	0
E	3	7	4	8	12	15	19	7	0
F	4	8	5	7	12	11	16	4	0
G	6	9	3	9	12	16	19	7	0
H*	5	10	6	9	15	9	15	0	0
I	7	11	5	12	17	19	24	7	0
J	8	12	7	12	19	16	23	4	0
K	9	14	4	12	16	19	23	7	7
L*	10	13	5	15	20	15	20	0	0
M*	13	14	3	20	23	20	23	0	0
N	11	18	4	17	21	24	28	7	3
O	12	15	5	19	24	23	28	4	0
O'	15	17	0	24	24	29	29	5	0
O''	15	18	0	24	24	28	28	4	0
P*	14	17	6	23	29	23	29	0	0
Q	13	16	4	20	24	21	25	1	0
R	16	17	4	24	28	25	29	1	1
S	18	19	5	24	29	28	33	4	4
T*	17	19	4	29	33	29	33	0	0
U*	19	20	3	33	36	33	36	0	0

* These activities are on the critical path.

Note: All days shown are the ends of days.

Perhaps the easiest method of completing this table is to determine and record the earliest start time and finish time for each activity, including the dummies. The earliest start time for an activity is the controlling earliest finish time for the one or more immediately preceding activities. If two preceding activities have earliest finish times of 12 and 16 days, respectively, the 16 days will determine the earliest start time for the following activity.

After the minimum time required to construct the project is determined, 36 days for this project, the latest finish times for each activity can be determined by working backward from the 36 days. For example, the latest finish times for activities S and T are determined by subtracting the duration of activity U, namely 3 days, from 36 to give 33 days. The latest start time for activity S is its latest finish time minus the duration of S, namely 5 days, to give a value of 28 days. This procedure is applied along each path of activities.

The symbol *19* appearing under event 12 in Fig. 2-3 indicates that 19 days is the earliest finish time for activity J and the earliest start time for activity O. The symbol *23* appearing above event 12 indicates that 23 days is the latest finish time for activity J and the latest start time for activity O.

DETERMINING TOTAL FLOAT

The total float of an activity is the number of days or other appropriate units of time that the start or finish of an activity may be delayed without delaying the completion time for the overall project. Referring to Fig. 2-3 it will be noted that the earliest finish date for activity B is the end of the eighth day, while the latest finish time is the end of the fifteenth day. Thus there is a leeway of $15 - 8 = 7$ days for completing activity B. This is the total float designated in Table 2-2. The total float of 7 days may be allocated to any one of the activities along the path B, E, I, N, or it may be allocated in parts to more than one activity, provided the total delays do not exceed 7 days.

DETERMINING FREE FLOAT

This is the number of days that the finish of an activity may be delayed without delaying the earliest start for a following activity. Referring to Fig. 2-3 and Table 2-2, it will be noted that activity B can be finished at the end of the eighth day and that activity E, which follows, can be started as early as the end of the same day, which is the beginning of the ninth day. Thus activity B has no free float. Activity O is followed by activities S and T, whose earliest start dates are the end of the twenty-fourth and the end of the twenty-ninth days, respectively. Because the earliest of the early starts of the following activities determines the free float, which in this instance is activity S, activity O has zero free float.

Activity K may be completed as early as the end of the sixteenth day, but the following activity cannot be started until the end of the twenty-third day. Thus activity K has a free float of $23 - 16 = 7$ days.

APPLYING THE CRITICAL PATH METHOD TO OVERLAPPING ACTIVITIES

Sometimes it is necessary to apply the critical path method to overlapping activities, which may seem to present a difficult problem to the planner. For example, assume that a bridge requires six intermediate piers consisting of concrete caps supported by steel piles. All piles will be driven before any caps are started.

The construction of the caps might be divided into three activities: the erecting of forms, the placing of reinforcing steel, and the placing of concrete. If this plan is used in preparing the arrow diagram, it will be necessary to show all forms completed with one activity arrow, before placing any reinforcing steel, and likewise all reinforcing for all caps must be placed before any concrete is placed. However, the adopted schedule for constructing the caps provides that after the forms for two caps are erected, the reinforcing will be placed in the forms. Then after the reinforcing is placed, the concrete for these two caps will be placed. In the meantime the forms for other caps will be erected, in units of 2, using the side forms from the caps previously constructed, followed by placing reinforcing and concrete. A diagram containing only three arrows cannot represent these activities correctly. It is necessary to divide the three previously listed activities into three activities each, for a total of nine activities, with each activity represented by an arrow in the diagram.

The sequential information appears in Table 2-3, and the arrow diagram for

Table 2-3 Sequential information for pier caps

| Activity | Activities which immediately | |
	precede	follow
J—drive piles		K
K—erect forms for caps 1 and 2	J	L, N
L—place reinforcing for caps 1 and 2	K	M, O
M—place concrete for caps 1 and 2	L	P
N—erect forms for caps 3 and 4	J	O, Q
O—place reinforcing for caps 3 and 4	L, N	P, R
P—place concrete for caps 3 and 4	M, O	S
Q—erect forms for caps 5 and 6	N	R
R—place reinforcing for caps 5 and 6	O, Q	S
S—place concrete for caps 5 and 6	P, R	

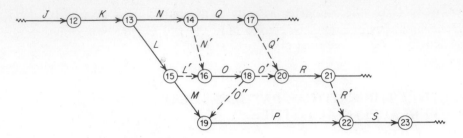

Figure 2-4 Arrow diagram for pier caps.

this portion of the project is illustrated by Fig. 2-4. An appropriate duration must be assigned to each of the nine activities.

UPDATING AN ARROW DIAGRAM

During the construction of a project it may become evident that the project is behind schedule. Under such conditions it may be desirable to determine the current status of the project and also the probable revised completion date. One method of updating an arrow diagram is to prepare a table showing the number

Table 2-4 Updating a critical path analysis

Activity	D	ES	EF	LS	LF	TF
A	0					
B	0					
C	0					
D*	3	10	13	10	13	0
E	4	10	14	19	23	9
F	3	10	13	17	20	7
G	4	13	17	18	22	5
H*	6	13	19	13	19	0
I	5	14	19	23	28	9
J	8	13	21	20	28	7
K	6	17	23	22	28	5
L*	6	19	25	19	25	0
M*	3	25	28	25	28	0
N	5	19	24	28	33	9
O	5	21	26	28	33	7
P*	6	28	34	28	34	0
Q*	5	25	30	25	30	0
R*	4	30	34	30	34	0
S	6	26	32	33	39	7
T*	5	34	39	34	39	0
U*	3	39	42	39	42	0

* These activities are on the two critical paths.

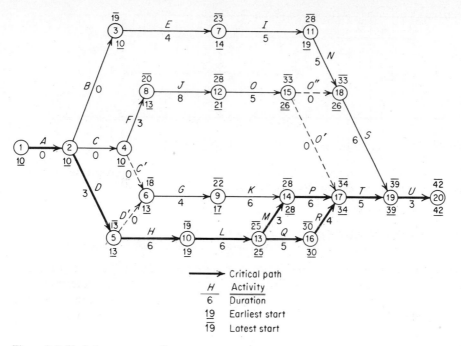

Figure 2-5 Updating an arrow diagram.

of days required to complete each uncompleted activity, effective on the date of the reexamination. Table 2-4 lists this information for the end of the tenth working day for the project analyzed in Table 2-2. Each duration listed in Table 2-4 is the estimate for the remaining number of days required to complete each activity. It will be noted that some estimated durations have been revised.

The arrow diagram can be redrawn with the remaining number of days shown for each activity. For activities already completed, the durations are shown as zero days. As illustrated in Fig. 2-5, the initial time for the starting of the first activity is shown to be the same day as the day of the reexamination, namely, day 10. Thereafter the diagram is completed as if it were an original diagram. It will be noted that there are now two critical paths.

THE TIME—GRID DIAGRAM METHOD

Whereas the lengths of arrows in Fig. 2-3 do not indicate the durations of the activities, the lengths of the arrows in the time-grid diagram of this method are drawn to indicate the durations of the activities which they represent, as illustrated in Fig. 2-6. In preparing a time-grid diagram all arrows representing activities and float are drawn horizontally, with each arrow tail starting at the

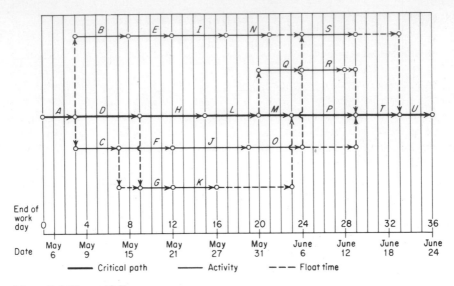

Figure 2-6 Time-grid diagram.

head of the arrow for the immediately preceding activity and then continuing to the right through a path of interrelated activities.

In the diagram vertical lines do not indicate any elapsed time. They simply indicate the precedence of the activities. For example, the broken vertical line from the head of activity A to the tail of activity B indicates that activity A must be completed before activity B can be started.

Because the float times are represented by broken horizontal lines, whose lengths indicate time, it is relatively easy to determine the float time for any activity by an inspection of the diagram. An examination of the diagram might indicate that activities C, F, J, and O have float time of 5 days. However, because activity S cannot be started until activity O is completed, O has the same float time as activity S, namely 4 days.

Because the arrows are drawn to a time scale it is possible to show the calender dates for the activities, which an arrow diagram does not show. Space in the time schedule is provided for working days only. Saturdays, Sundays, and holidays should be excluded unless work will be performed on these days.

Prior to drawing the time-grid diagram, steps 1, 2, 3, 4, and 7 appearing on page 20 should be completed. Step 7 will provide a table which indicates those activities lying on the critical path, that is, those with zero float time. Then, when drawing the diagram, the critical path can be drawn through or near the middle of the diagram, which is usually desirable.

If the name of each activity is written along its arrow and the dates are shown along the bottom of the diagram, the diagram can be a very useful reference during the period of construction.

The diagram in Fig. 2-6 is based on the information listed in Tables 2-1 and 2-2.

ADVANTAGES OF THE TIME–GRID DIAGRAM

Because this diagram shows a time relationship between the activities it is possible by a visual inspection to determine the desirability of shifting the construction schedules for some activities to obtain a better distribution of materials, labor, or equipment, or for other reasons. For example, if activities *J* and *K*, which are shown in Fig. 2–6 to be operated simultaneously, both require carpenters, it will be necessary to provide two crews for a short duration. However, an examination of the diagram reveals that the start of activity *K* can be delayed for 7 days, until activity *J* is finished, without delaying activity *P*. Then the carpenters from activity *J* can be assigned to activity *K*. This is referred to as labor leveling because it permits the use of fewer men for greater periods of time without delaying the completion of the project.

In a similar manner it is possible that altering the schedules for activities, within the periods permitted by float time, may eliminate the need for providing additional equipment on a project for short periods of time only.

UPDATING A TIME–GRID DIAGRAM

The original schedule for a project is shown in Fig. 2-6. If, after a given period of time, it is observed that the project is off schedule, a revised diagram can be prepared, as illustrated in Fig. 2-7. For this figure the information appearing in Table 2-2 is modified as shown in Table 2-4 to reflect the status of the project at the end of the tenth working day, as indicated by the heavy vertical line, and also to adjust for reestimates of the durations of future activities.

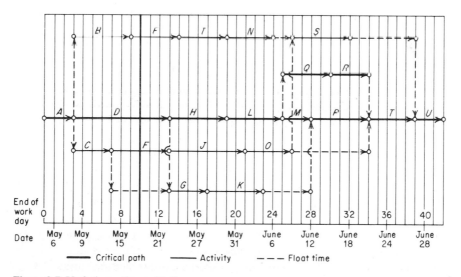

Figure 2-7 Updating a time-grid diagram.

It will be observed that activity *D*, on the critical path, is 4 days behind schedule. Unless this delay can be offset by reductions in the durations of future activities on the critical path, the completion of the project will be delayed 4 days.

CONDUCTING A CRASH PROGRAM

When planning the construction of a project by using the critical path method, it is usual practice to select for each activity a rate of progress that will produce the lowest practical cost. This progress is based on the delivery of materials, if required, the number of laborers available or the number who can work efficiently, and the number and types of equipment that are available, at a minimum cost, for each activity. After the arrow or the time-grid diagram is drawn it is determined that the minimum time required to complete a project is the sum of the durations of those activities lying on the critical path. When a project is constructed under these conditions, it is referred to as a normal program.

However, for some reason it may be desirable to reduce the total time required to complete or construct a project. When the normal time is reduced, the project, or a portion of it, is constructed under a crash program. If a project is constructed under a crash program, it will be necessary to do some or all of the following:

1. Increase the rates of providing materials
2. Increase the number of laborers, which may reduce the productivity per laborer
3. Assign the laborers to overtime work, at premium wage rates
4. Increase the number of units of equipment assigned to critical activities, which may require the rental of equipment not presently owned, or which may reduce the productivity per unit of equipment

If some or all of these steps are adopted, it usually will result in an increase in the cost of those activities that are constructed under a crash program. In order to keep the total increase in cost to a minimum, it is necessary to select for crash operations those activities that will permit the desired reductions in construction time at the least total increase in cost. Because the duration of a project is determined by the activities lying on the critical path, the desired reduction in time should be attained by reducing the durations of one or more activities lying on the critical path. Also, because the cost of a unit reduction in time usually will not be the same for each activity, it is necessary to estimate or determine the increase in the cost per unit of time reduction for each of the critical activities. This increase in cost, which is defined as the cost slope, may be expressed as dollars per hour, dollars per day, or in other suitable units.

Table 2-5 Determining the cost slope for activities under a crash program

	Normal		Crash		Possible reduction, days	Cost slope, dollars per day
Activity	Duration days	Total cost	Duration, days	Total cost		
A	3	$ 876	2	$ 1,164	1	$288
D	6	16,454	4	16,686	2	116
H	6	14,231	4	14,443	2	106
L	5	8,592	4	8,744	1	152
M	3	6,490	3	6,490	0	0
P	6	18,670	4	18,860	2	95
T	4	12,836	3	13,264	1	428
U	3	944	2	1,168	1	224
Q	4	3,848	1	3,986	1	138
R	4	7,614	1	7,814	1	200

Consider the project whose time-grid diagram is illustrated in Fig. 2-6. Assume that it is desired to reduce the total duration of this project from 36 to 32 working days with a minimum increase in cost. Table 2-5 shows the duration and total cost for each critical activity under normal and crash programs, the possible reduction in duration, and the cost slope in dollars per day for reducing the duration of each activity. Because all other activities except Q and R have adequate float, they may be disregarded and constructed under normal conditions.

An examination of Table 2-5 reveals that reductions in the following activities should be considered.

Activity	Possible reduction, days	Cost slope, dollars per day
D	2	$116
H	2	106
P	2	95
Q	1	138

It appears that the desired reduction can be obtained from activities H and P at the least increase in total cost. However, an examination of Fig. 2-5 reveals that activity Q has only 1 day of float. If the duration of P is reduced only one day, the effect on Q may be disregarded. However, if the duration of P is reduced 2 days, it will be necessary to reduce the duration of Q by 1 day, at an extra cost of $138.00, for a total cost for P and Q equal to $95.00 + $138.00 =

$233.00. Thus the reductions in durations for a minimum increase in total cost should be as follows:

Activity	Reduction, days	Cost slope, dollars per day	Total cost
D	1	$116	$116
H	2	106	212
P	1	95	95
Total	4		$423

Because activities C, F, J, O, and S have a float of 4 days the reduction of 4 days in the total duration of the project will cause these activities to lie on a critical path also. Thus there may be more than one critical path for a project.

DETERMINING THE MINIMUM TOTAL COST OF A PROJECT

The total cost of a project includes the following items:

1. Direct costs of materials, labor, and equipment
2. Overhead, job and general
3. Bonus, if any, for early completion, and penalty for late completion
4. Other costs as applicable

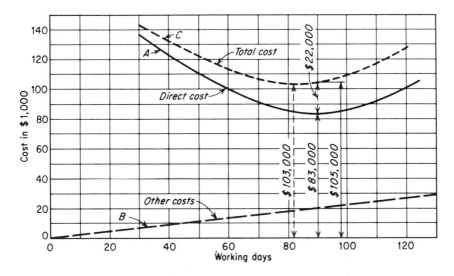

Figure 2-8 Determining minimum total cost of a project.

When scheduling the construction of a project, consideration should be given to selecting the total duration that will result in the lowest total cost. If direct costs only are considered, there will be a duration that produces the lowest costs. However, the costs of overhead, potential penalty, and other items will be increased as the period of construction is extended. This information is illustrated in Fig. 2-8. Curve A gives the estimated direct cost for the indicated numbers of working days. Curve B gives the estimated sum of all costs other than the direct cost. Curve C is the sum of the costs given by curves A and B. The figure indicates a minimum direct cost of $83,000 if the project is constructed in 90 working days. For this duration the other costs will amount to $22,000, to give a total cost of $105,000. If the project is completed in 82 working days, the total cost will be $103,000, which is the minimum possible total cost.

MANUAL VERSUS COMPUTER ANALYSES
OF CRITICAL PATH METHODS

It appears that some users, or potential users, of the critical path method hold the opinion that electronic computers are required to perform the calculations and analyses involved. As demonstrated by Fondahl [1] and others, this is not necessarily correct.

The primary advantages gained from the use of computers are the speed of computations and the elimination of computational errors. It is true that for a project involving a great many activities the speed of computation may justify the cost of using a computer, especially when it is desirable to make studies of resource availabilities involving materials, labor, and equipment. Also, if one wishes to make an exhaustive study of the duration cost relationship for each activity and for the entire project for the purpose of selecting the schedule that will produce the lowest total project cost, the use of a computer may be justified.

The computer is simply a sophisticated calculator. It can produce results which are used in making decisions, but it cannot make the decisions.

When the information required for a critical path study is assembled by a project planner and the calculations are performed manually, the planner will gain a more comprehensive understanding of all aspects of the project, which should enable him to make more intelligent decisions between possible alternates.

PREPARING A CONSTRUCTION SCHEDULE
FOR A HIGHWAY PROJECT

The project described and analyzed below is intended to illustrate the types of information that can be developed for a project. This information will enable the project planner to determine the duration of the overall project; to schedule materials, equipment, and labor; and to schedule the amount and duration of the financing required for the project.

Description of the project The project includes the following quantities and activities, some of which are divided into parts to permit the preparation of an arrow or a time-grid diagram:

Length, 7.20 miles
Width of right of way, 100 ft
Clearing and grubbing, 46 acres
Drainage structures, 12 multibox concrete culverts, two openings, average length 36 ft
Earthwork, 172,400 cu yd bank measure
Concrete pavement, width 24 ft, average thickness 9 in., total area 101,376 sq yd

Clearing the right of way This activity consists of removing all trees and roots to a depth of 12 in. below the surface of the ground and stacking the material in piles along the right of way, where it will be burned. The activity will be performed with a crawler-type tractor equipped with a front-end-mounted combination dozer-rooter blade.

As illustrated in Table 2-6 and Figs. 2-9 and 2-10, this activity is divided into two subactivities, *B* and *C*, to permit the starting of construction on the drainage structures after 3 weeks of clearing have been completed. The balance of the clearing will be completed while the first units of the drainage structures are constructed.

Drainage structures Earth for the drainage structures will be excavated with a backhoe mounted on the rear of a wheel-type tractor, equipped with a dozer blade on the front end.

Project No. _164_
Project _SH1764_
Owner _State Highway Department of Texas_
Location _Brazos County_
Date of project _1975_

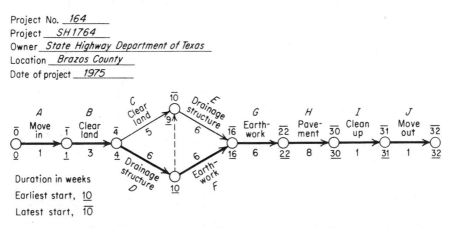

Duration in weeks
Earliest start, 10
Latest start, 10

Figure 2-9 Arrow diagram for a highway project.

Table 2-6 Activity relationships for project number 164

Activity	Duration, weeks*	Activity which immediately precedes	follows
A—move in	1	O	B
B—clear land, part 1	3	A	C, D
C—clear land, part 2	5	B	E
D—drainage structures, part 1	6	B	E, F
E—drainage structures, part 2	6	C, D	G
F—earthwork, part 1	6	D	G
G—earthwork, part 2	6	E, F	H
H—concrete pavement	8	G	I
I—clean up	1	H	J
J—move out	1	I	O

* A week includes 5 working days, ending on Friday. Each duration includes an allowance of approximately 20 percent for estimated time lost because of weather.

After the forms for the structures are erected and the reinforcing is placed, the concrete will be supplied under contract from a local source, using transit-mix trucks.

This activity is divided into two subactivities to permit the starting of earthwork before all culverts are finished.

Earthwork The earthwork, with a balanced cut and fill, will be handled by three wheel-type scrapers and assisted by a crawler tractor during loading operations. As the earth fill is placed, it will be mixed by a tractor-pulled disc harrow,

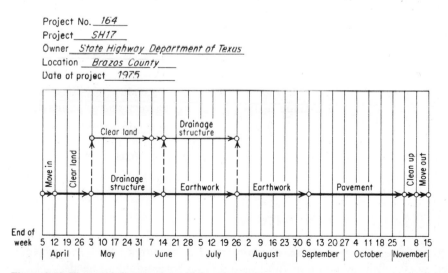

Project No. _164_
Project _SH17_
Owner _State Highway Department of Texas_
Location _Brazos County_
Date of project _1975_

Figure 2-10 Time grid diagram for a highway project.

moistened by a water truck, compacted by two tractor-pulled sheep's-foot rollers, and shaped by two motor graders.

As indicated in Table 2-6, this activity is divided into two subactivities to permit the work to be started at one end of the project as soon as the culverts are constructed for that part of the project.

Concrete pavement The concrete for the pavement will be mixed in a 34 E dual-drum paver and then distributed between side forms, set 24 ft apart. The aggregate will be batched at a central plant and hauled to the paver in triple-batch dump trucks.

The aggregate will be delivered to stock piles adjacent to the batching plant, under contract with a commercial supplier. The aggregate bin will be charged with a clamshell.

The batching plant will be moved to the project during the week prior to the starting of pavement.

SCHEDULING RESOURCES

If construction on a project is to proceed efficiently and at the scheduled rates, it is necessary to know accurately the types and quantities of resources that will be needed and the dates on which they will be needed. Resources include materials, equipment, and labor, by classification and quantities. An analysis of the information obtained from the critical path study will enable the project planner to know in advance what resources will be needed and to arrange for them to be available when they are needed. Also, the dates on which they may be released for use on other projects will be known in advance. Such information should permit the maximum use of all resources.

DELIVERING MATERIALS

The arrow diagram illustrated in Fig. 2-9 or the time-grid diagram illustrated in Fig. 2-10 may be used as a guide in specifying the delivery dates for materials. Materials should be delivered to a project before they are needed. However, excessively early delivery is not desirable because of the possibility that the materials might deteriorate or might congest working areas in which storage space is limited.

SCHEDULING EQUIPMENT USE

Figure 2-11 is an equipment use schedule, which is prepared before the project is started to establish the types, quantities, and dates for equipment needs.

EQUIPMENT USE SCHEDULE
For week ending

Project No. 164
Project SH17
Owner State Highway Department of Texas
Location Brazos County
Date of project 1975

Equipment	Apr 12	Apr 19	Apr 26	May 3	May 10	May 17	May 24	May 31	Jun 7	Jun 14	Jun 21	Jun 28	Jul 5	Jul 12	Jul 19	Jul 26	Aug 2	Aug 9	Aug 16	Aug 23	Aug 30	Sep 6	Sep 13	Sep 20	Sep 27	Oct 4	Oct 11	Oct 18	Oct 25	Nov 1	Nov 8	Nov 15
Truck trailers	1																															2
Crane, crawler		1																			2	2										2
Bulldozers	1	1	1	1	1	1	1	1	1	1	4	4	4	4	4	4	4	4	4	4	4	4										
Bulldozer-hoe		1	1	1	1	1	1	1	1	1	1	1	1	1	1	1																
Trucks, utility		2	2	2	2	2	2	2	2	2	2	2	2	2	2	2	2	2	2	2	2	2	2	2	2	2	2	2	2	2	2	2
Trucks, pickup		2	2	2	2	2	2	2	2	2	2	2	2	2	2	2	2	2	2	2	2	2	2	2	2	2	2	2	2	2	2	2
Trucks, aggregate																						6	6	6	6	6	6	6				
Truck, sprinkler											1	1	1	1	1	1	1	1	1	1	1	1										
Truck, water												1	1	1	1	1	1	1	1	1	1	1	1	1	1	1	1	1	1	1		
Motor graders											2	2	2	2	2	2	2	2	2	2	2	2	1	1	1	1	1	1	1	1	1	1
Sheep's foot roller											1	1	1	1	1	1	1	1	1	1	1	1										
Disk harrow											1	1	1	1	1	1	1	1	1	1	1	1										
Aggregate bin																						1	1	1	1	1	1	1	1	1	1	1
Cement silo																						1	1	1	1	1	1	1	1	1	1	1
Subgrader																							1	1	1	1	1	1	1	1	1	1
Concrete paver																							1	1	1	1	1	1	1	1	1	1
Concrete spreader																							1	1	1	1	1	1	1	1	1	1
Concrete finisher																								1	1	1	1	1	1	1	1	1
Pavement forms																								1	1	1	1	1	1	1	1	1

Figure 2-11 Equipment use schedule.

EMPLOYMENT SCHEDULE

For week ending

Project No. _164_
Project _SH17_
Owner _State Highway Department of Texas_
Location _Brazos County_
Date of project _1975_

Classification	April			May					June				July				August					September				October				November		
	12	19	26	3	10	17	24	31	7	14	21	28	5	12	19	26	2	9	16	23	30	6	13	20	27	4	11	18	25	1	8	15
Foremen	1	1	1	2	2	2	2	2	2	2	2	2	2	2	2	2	1	1	1	1	1	1	1	1	1	1	1	1	1	1	1	1
Mechanic	1	1	1	1	1	1	1	1	1	1	1	1	1	1	1	1	1	1	1	1	1	1	1	1	1	1	1	1	1	1	1	1
Mechanic helper	1	1	1	1	1	1	1	1	1	1	1	1	1	1	1	1	1	1	1	1	1	1	1	1	1	1	1	1	1	1	1	1
Crane operator	1																				1	1	1	1	1	1	1	1	1	1	1	1
Crane oiler	1																				1	1	1	1	1	1	1	1	1	1	1	1
Carpenters				4	4	4	4	4	4	4	4	4	4	4	4	4																
Steel setters				2	2	2	2	2	2	2	2	2	2	2	2	2																
Truck drivers			2	1	1	1	1	1	1	1	2	2	2	2	2	2	2	2	2	2	2	2	1	1	1	1	1	1	1	1	1	2
Tractor operators			1	1	8	8	8	8	8	8	8	8	8	8	8	8	7	7	7	7	7											
Cement batcher																					7	1	1	1	1	1	1	1	1	1		
Aggregate batcher																						1	1	1	1	1	1	1	1	1		
Subgrader operator																						1	1	1	1	1	1	1	1	1		
Paver operator																						1	1	1	1	1	1	1	1	1		
Spreader operator																						1	1	1	1	1	1	1	1	1		
Finisher operator																						1	1	1	1	1	1	1	1	1		
Concrete finishers																						2	2	2	2	2	2	2	2			
Grader operators											2	2	2	2	2	2	2	2	2	2	2	2	2	2	1	1	1	1	1	1	1	1
Laborers	4	2	2	2	8	8	8	8	8	6	8	8	8	8	8	8	8	8	8	8	7	10	8	8	8	8	8	8	8	8	3	3

Figure 2-12 Employment schedule.

Table 2-7 Labor needs by activities

Activity	Classification	Number of workers
Moving in	Foreman	1
	Mechanic	1
	Truck drivers	2
	Crane operator	1
	Crane oiler	1
	Laborers	4
Clear land	Foreman	1
	Tractor operator	1
	Laborers	2
Drainage structures	Foreman	1
	Carpenters	4
	Steel setters	2
	Tractor operator	1
	Truck driver	1
	Laborers	6
Earthwork	Foreman	1
	Tractor operators	7
	Grader operators	2
	Truck driver, water	1
	Mechanic	1
	Laborers	2
Pavement	Foreman	1
	Cement batcher	1
	Aggregate batcher	1
	Clamshell operator	1
	Clamshell oiler	1
	Truck drivers, aggregate	6
	Truck driver, water	1
	Truck driver, forms	1
	Subgrader operator	1
	Paver operator	1
	Spreader operator	1
	Finisher operator	1
	Concrete finishers	2
	Laborers	8
Cleanup	Foreman	1
	Grader operator	1
	Truck driver	1
	Laborers	3
Move out	Foreman	1
	Truck drivers	2
	Crane operator	1
	Crane oiler	1
	Laborers	3

SCHEDULING LABORERS

Table 2-7 illustrates a form which may be used in determining the classification and numbers of laborers required for a project. Reference to Fig. 2-10 will indicate the dates during which these laborers will be needed; the information may also be listed as illustrated in Fig. 2-12. This information is obtained by consolidating by classification the laborers designated for each activity in Table 2-7.

FINANCING THE PROJECT

A construction schedule may be used to estimate the amount of funds that a contractor must provide in financing a project during construction. Most construction contracts specify that the owner will pay to the contractor a stated percent of the value of work completed during each month. The payment for work completed during a month is usually made by the tenth of the following month. Upon completion of the project, the retained funds, usually 10 percent of the contract value of the work, is paid to the contractor. An analysis of the construction schedule will indicate the approximate expenditures and receipts through any desired dates. The excess of expenditures over receipts indicates the amount of financing which the contractor must provide from sources other than the owner.

The estimated expenditures are determined as illustrated in Table 2-8. The amounts shown are the costs of materials, equipment, labor, and general overhead. Although a contractor does not pay an outside party for the use of the equipment, unless it is rented, he must make monthly payments, or other periodic payments, on the equipment until its cost is liquidated. Thus it is proper to include the cost of owning and operating equipment as an expenditure.

Table 2-9 illustrates a form that may be used to estimate the receipts from the owner of the project. The prices received during construction are 90 percent of the contract prices for the respective items. The receipts for a given month are payable to the contractor by the tenth of the following month.

Table 2-10 illustrates a form that may be used to determine the estimated expenditures and receipts for the end of each month during construction. At the end of July the estimated cumulative expenditures amount to $124,860. At this time the cumulative receipts, shown for the end of June and payable by the tenth of July, amount to $59,568. Thus there is a difference of $124,860 − $59,568 = $65,292 which the contractor may have to provide from another source for 10 days.

Information contained in this table should assist a contractor when he discusses with his bank a schedule of financial assistance that he may need from the bank.

Table 2-8 Form for estimating expenditures during construction

Weeks after starting	Activities under construction	Expenditure per week	Cumulative expenditures
1	A	$ 5,680	$ 5,680
2	B	1,540	7,220
3	B	1,540	8,760
4	C, D	1,540	10,300
5	C, D	4,780	15,080
6	C, D	4,780	19,860
7	C, D	4,780	24,640
8	C, D	4,780	29,420
9	C, D	4,780	34,200
10	D	3,240	37,440
11	E, F	13,540	50,980
12	E, F	13,540	64,520
13	E, F	13,540	78,060
14	F, F	13,540	91,600
15	E, F	13,540	105,140
16	E, F	13,540	118,680
17	G	10,300	128,980
18	G	10,300	139,280
19	G	10,300	149,580
20	G	10,300	159,880
21	G	10,300	170,180
22	G	10,300	180,480
23	H	55,500	235,980
24	H	55,500	291,480
25	H	55,500	346,980
26	H	55,500	402,480
27	H	55,500	457,980
28	H	55,500	513,480
29	H	55,500	568,980
30	H	55,500	624,480
31	I	1,200	625,680
32	J	1,860	627,540

JOB LAYOUT

One of the first duties of a superintendent when he assumes the responsibility of starting construction is to prepare a job layout for the project. On this layout he will draw to scale the area available for offices, warehouses, storage of materials, equipment, and earth, and constructing forms and fabricating reinforcing steel. In preparing the job layout, the superintendent should endeavor to arrange all areas to reduce the time consumed in carrying materials from storage areas to

Table 2-9 Estimated receipts during construction

Month	Activities under construction	Weeks under construction	Units completed per week	Unit price received during construction	End-of-period receipts	Total period receipts	Cumulative receipts
April	A	1.0	1	$ 0	$ 0	0	
	B	2.4	6	270.00	3,888	$ 3,888	$ 3,888
May	B, C	4.6	6	270.00	7,452		
	D	4.0	1	3,240.00	12,960	20,412	24,300
June	C	1.0	6	270.00	1,620		
	D	2.0	1	3,240.00	6,480		
	E	2.0	1	3,240.00	6,480		
	F	2.0	14,367	0.72	20,688	35,268	59,568
July	E	4.0	1	3,240.00	12,960		
	F	4.0	14,367	0.72	41,377		
	G	0.6	14,367	0.72	6,207	60,544	120,112
August	G	4.4	14,367	0.72	45,515	45,515	165,627
September	G	1.0	14,367	0.72	10,344		
	H	3.2	12,674	4.41	178,854	189,198	354,825
October	H	4.6	12,674	4.41	257,105	257,105	611,930
November	H	0.2	12,674	4.41	11,179		
	I	1.0	1	0.00	0		
	J	1.0	1	0.00	0	11,179	623,109
Amount retained							69,234
Total amount of contract							$692,343

* Amount payable by the tenth of the following month.

the project. Materials that are similar in use should be stored close together, where possible. The general office and warehouse should be located near the main entrance in order that persons visiting the project for business purposes will not have to travel around the construction areas to reach the office. This should reduce the danger of injuries to visitors and the confusion that frequently is associated with the presence of strangers around a project. If the general warehouse is near the entrance, it will facilitate the delivery of material to be stored in the warehouse and it will also permit closer supervision of materials removed from the warehouse. However, if a warehouse is needed to store heavy materials, such as machines that will be incorporated into the project, it may be desirable to consider using additional warehouses, located nearer the project.

Table 2-10 Estimated expenditures and receipts during construction

Month	Activities under construction	Weeks under construction	Expenditures per week	Expenditures for month	Cumulative expenditures	Total receipts for month	Cumulative receipts*
April	A	1.0	$ 5,680	$ 5,680			
	B	2.4	1,540	3,696	$ 9,376	$ 3,888	$ 3,888
May	B, C	4.6	1,540	7,084			
	D	4.0	3,240	17,960	29,420	20,412	24,300
June	C	1.0	1,540	1,540			
	D, E	4.0	3,240	12,960			
	F	2.0	10,300	20,600	64,520	35,268	59,568
July	E	4.0	3,240	12,960			
	F, G	4.6	10,300	47,380	124,860	60,544	120,112
August	G	4.4	10,300	45,320	170,180	45,515	165,627
September	G	1.0	10,300	10,300			
	H	3.2	55,500	177,600	358,080	189,198	354,825
October	H	4.6	55,500	255,300	613,380	257,105	611,930
November	H	0.2	55,500	11,100			
	I	1.0	1,200	1,200			
	J	1.0	1,860	1,860	627,540	11,179	623,109
Amount retained							69,234
Total amount of contract							$692,343

* Amount payable by the tenth of the month.

Figure 2-13 illustrates a job layout for a multistoried reinforced-concrete frame building. The contractor is fortunate in having adequate area for easy storage of all materials at the job site. This is not commonly the case for buildings erected in congested cities, where storage areas at the job site are limited or nonexistent. If area is not available at the job site, the contractor must obtain storage area as near the site as possible.

PROJECT CONTROL DURING CONSTRUCTION

At specified intervals, usually weekly or monthly, reports should be submitted by the project superintendent to the headquarters office showing the actual progress on each activity during the appropriate time interval or through the

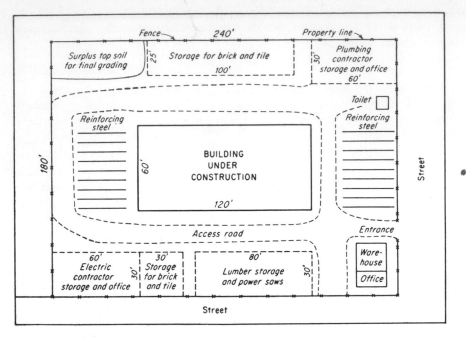

Figure 2-13 Job layout.

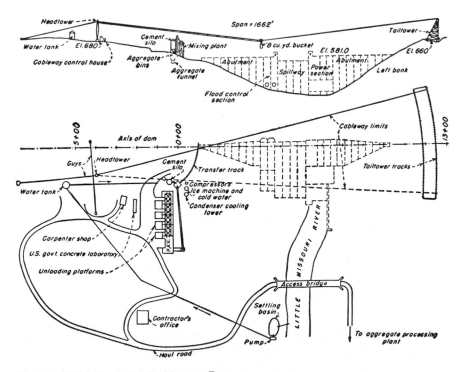

Figure 2-14 Job layout for the Narrows Dam.

effective date of the report. If the progress on one or more activities or on the entire project is behind schedule, such information will be known early enough to take corrective steps.

KEEPING EQUIPMENT RECORDS

When a unit of construction equipment is purchased, it should be assigned a suitable identification, such as a number, to be used throughout its life. An owner of equipment should have a definite plan for keeping a record of the cost of each major unit of equipment. The record may be kept on suitable equipment cards or in ledgers. The information obtained from such records will enable the owner to determine the complete financial history of any unit of equipment. Comparisons may be made between the cost of owning and operating comparable units furnished by different manufacturers as a guide in selecting future units. The information will assist in determining the economic life of equipment. The record should show the original cost, delivered to the owner, the schedule of depreciation, the time it has been used, and the cost of repairs and maintenance. It may be desirable to keep a record of the amount of fuel and lubricating oil consumed.

Figure 2-15 illustrates a form for reporting the use of equipment assigned to a project. The forms are sent to general headquarters weekly in order that the

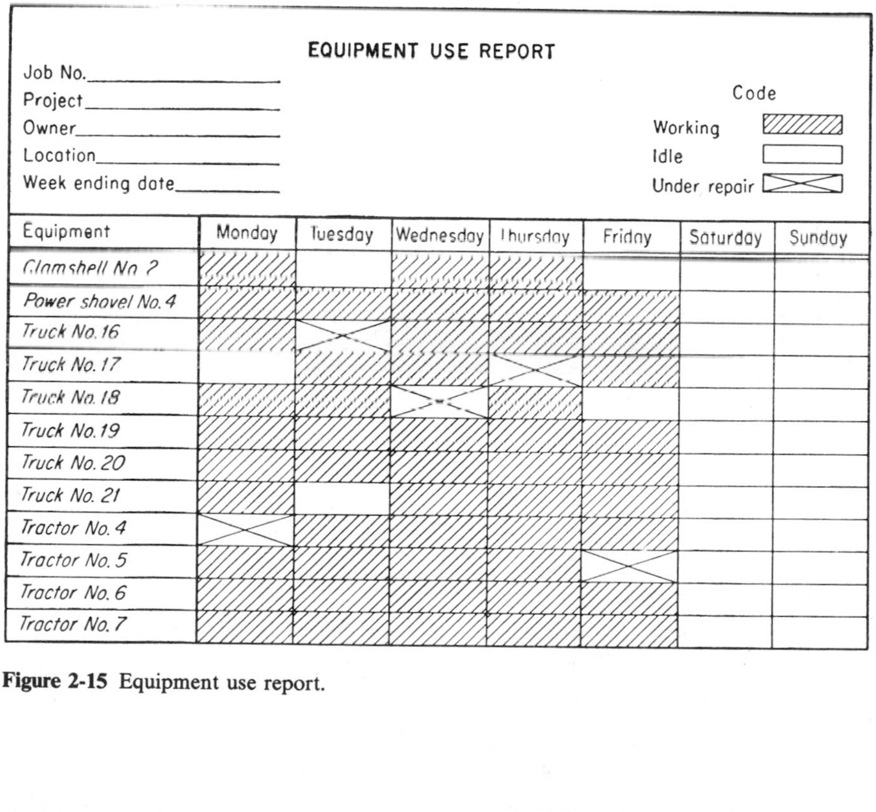

Figure 2-15 Equipment use report.

ENGINE NO. _____ EQUIPMENT NO. __14-82__

DESCRIPTION:
D7 Caterpillar diesel tractor
Arrangement 7B 9435, 7B1713 heavy-duty track roller guards, 4F1867 lighting
system, 3F9549 starting system, 7B7343 crankcase guard, 7B4464 front pull hook,
MD7 Trackson pipelayer with 3500 lb counterweight, serial MD7-681

Purchase Record   **Invoice Record**

Date acquired	New used	Vendor	P.O. No.	V.O. date	V.O. No.	Purchase price	Freight	Tax	Total cost
7/1/75	N	A.T. Fisher Co.	BE108D	8/2/75	JV11 - 8	68,496 80	488 60	3424 84	72,410 04

License Record   **Sales Record**

Year	State	Number	Cost	Title No.		Date sold	To
						Sales price $	
						Book value $	
						Gain or loss $	
						Remarks	

Item	Serial No.	Equipment No.
D7 Caterpillar tractor with pipelayer	3T 6612	14 - 82

Figure 2-16 Equipment ownership cost.

DEPRECIATION RECORD

DESCRIPTION _D7 Caterpillar tractor with pipelayer_ EQUIPMENT NO. _14-82_

Date	Depreciation Rate per mo.	Depreciation Amount	Depreciation To date	Book value	Total cost	Date	Depreciation Rate per mo.	Depreciation Amount	Depreciation To date	Book value	Total cost
7/ 1/75	1,508 54			72,410 04	72,410 04						
7/31/75		1,508 54	1,508 54	70,901 50							
8/31/75		1,508 54	3,017 08	69,392 96							
9/30/75		1,508 54	4,525 62	67,884 42							
10/31/75		1,508 54	6,034 16	66,375 88							
11/30/75		1,508 54	7,542 70	64,867 34							
12/31/75		1,508 54	9,051 24	63,358 80							
1/31/76		1,508 54	10,559 78	61,850 26							
2/29/76		1,508 54	12,068 32	60,341 72							
3/31/76		1,508 54	13,576 86	58,833 18							

Depreciation rate _25_ percent per year

Figure 2-17 Equipment depreciation record.

RENTAL RECORD

DESCRIPTION D4 Caterpillar tractor with pipelayer

EQUIPMENT NO. 14-62

| Date | Rate per month | Rentals | | Date | | Date | Rate per month | Rentals | | Date | |
		Month	To date	In	Out			Month	To date	In	Out
11/75	1,850 00	1,850 00	1,850 00	11/1	11/30						
12/75		1,850 00	3,700 00	12/1	12/31						
1/76	18 days	1,386 00	5,086 00	1/3	1/24						
2/76	16 days	1,206 00	6,292 00	2/5	2/23						
3/76		1,850 00	8,142 00	3/1							
4/76		1,850 00	9,992 00								
5/76	14 days	1,050 00	11,042 00		5/17						
6/76											
7/76	15 days	1,142 00	12,184 00	7/2	7/20						

Figure 2-18 Equipment rental record.

REPAIRS AND OPERATING EXPENSE

DESCRIPTION D4 Caterpillar tractor with pipelayer

EQUIPMENT NO. 14-62

Date	Ref	Description	Repairs	Maintenance	Insurance	License and taxes	Total	Total to date
9/4/75	B 480	Misc. labor & material	38 96					38 96
10/9/75	B 524	Inst. rockguards & labor.	86 45					125 41
11/12/75	A 624	Tune & adjust engine	6 25					131 66
1/8/76	A 648	Labor repairing sideboom	16 80					148 46
4/16/76	A 716	Labor repairing tracks	24 40					172 86
4/24/76	C 562	Insurance – 1 yr.			92 50			265 46
4/26/76	D 236	License & taxes – 1 yr.				128 60		394 06

Figure 2-19 Equipment repair and operating expense record.

information may be transferred to the permanent record for each unit of equipment.

Figure 2-16 illustrates a form which is suitable for recording the cost and a description of a complete unit of equipment.

Figure 2-17 illustrates a form which is suitable for keeping a record of the depreciation of a unit of equipment.

Figure 2-18 illustrates a form which is suitable for keeping a record of the use or rental of a unit of equipment. The contractor who owned this equipment rented it to his job at established monthly rates. The form may be revised to show rental periods in days or weeks, if desirable, or rental periods less than a month may be shown on the form, as illustrated.

Figure 2-19 illustrates a form which is suitable for keeping a record of the cost of repairs and other operating expenses for a unit of equipment.

PROJECT SUPERVISION

The extent and type of supervision required during construction vary considerably with the project. For a small, compact project the supervision may be relatively simple, while a large project, which is spread out over considerable area, such as a dam or a major pipeline, may introduce many supervisory problems. The relationship between all personnel from the contracting company down through the superintendent, foremen, and working crews must be understood clearly. On a project where many men are working side by side with each other there are opportunities for misunderstandings and friction to develop.

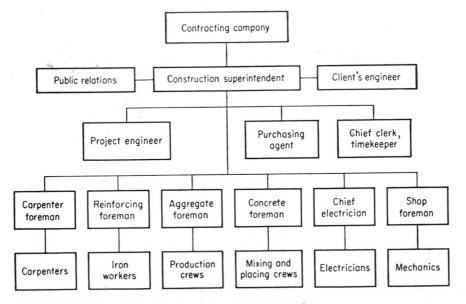

Figure 2-20 Typical organization chart for a construction project.

Jurisdictional arguments may arise regarding responsibility and authority. The foreman should recognize these problems at their inception and should take immediate steps to correct them. If problems arise between the foremen, the superintendent should be prepared to correct them before they reach a serious stage. One practice which has proved successful is to hold regular staff conferences to promote harmony and understanding between key personnel by permitting each one to understand better the problems of the others.

Figure 2-20 illustrates an organization chart which shows the relationship between all major departments of a construction gang. The actual organization of a chart will vary with the particular project.

THE USE OF TWO-WAY RADIO IN SUPERVISING A PROJECT

It is becoming increasingly common practice to use two-way radios, transmitters, and receivers in supervising construction projects. The use of such equipment is especially desirable for a project that is spread out over a large area, where one operation is dependent on another. Among the advantages are the following:

1. Permits quick contacts with the home office, field office, and key personnel on the job.
2. Reduces the time spent by key personnel, such as the superintendent, in rushing from one operation to another.
3. Saves time and cost by increasing the efficiency on a project.
4. Permits equipment to be shifted quickly from one operation to another, thereby reducing delays due to equipment failures, or reduces the amount of equipment required on a project because of the increased efficiency of use.
5. Permits quick contact with the shop in the event that emergency repairs are required for equipment.
6. Expedites the distribution of materials to the different operations.
7. Gives excellent control between concrete-mixing plant and placing operations. In the event of a failure at either location the other can be notified immediately.
8. Permits quick calls for first aid or ambulance in the event of injuries to personnel.

Three types of two-way radio sets are available:

1. Portable
2. Mobile
3. Base station

Portable sets Portable sets may be divided into two types—handset radiophones and packsets.

Handset radiophones weigh 10 to 20 lb and are equipped with wet or dry batteries having a net operating life of about 8 hr. The reception is good for a range of 1 or 2 miles, depending on the terrain and topography.

Packsets are larger than handsets and have longer-life batteries. Some have loudspeakers to permit an entire crew to listen to instructions. The range is about the same as for the handset.

Mobile units Mobile units are installed in trucks, automobiles, scrapers, loaders, at mixer plants, etc. They are operated by the vehicle battery. The power usually ranges from 10 to 60 watts. They have a greater range than the portable set.

Base stations Base-station transmitters and receivers are installed at headquarters for the duration of the project. If a 50- to 60-ft antenna is used, it is possible to send and receive messages up to 60 miles or more. The power may be as high as 250 watts with frequency modulation (FM). Such stations are classified as industrial applications and come under the supervision of the Federal Communications Commission (FCC). The assigned frequencies are so high that the waves travel essentially in a straight line.

In order to obtain a permit to install and operate a base station, it is necessary to submit to the FCC a request for approval, citing the need for a unit. It will be necessary to provide a second-class licensed radio operator at the main station to maintain the radios. Other persons who use the main station or mobile units must be issued licenses as third-class radio operators. The FCC requires weekly frequency checks and periodic reports on the station. Specific call letters and numbers are assigned and must be used at the beginning and end of each conversation.

CONSTRUCTION–COST CONTROL

Few businesses can survive without a knowledge of costs and without an intelligent control of costs. Certainly this is true in the construction industry. A contractor may be an excellent builder, but unless he knows his construction costs, he will never survive the vigorous competition in the industry. If a manufacturer finds that he has lost money on certain items, he may be able to raise the prices enough to assure a profit. However, a contractor who discovers after a project is finished that he has lost money may not have an opportunity to raise the price on the next project, especially if his losses were so great that he cannot finance another project. He may lose money because of one or more reasons, such as

1. Low bid
2. Insufficient knowledge of job conditions
3. Increase in the costs of materials and labor
4. Adverse weather conditions

5. Improper selection of construction equipment
6. Inefficient management and supervision

While it may not be possible to correct the first four difficulties after the project is started, there may be some opportunity to improve item 5, and certainly an alert businessman should correct item 6, or better still he should not let it occur. Cost engineering or cost control will assist in correcting losses resulting from inefficient management and supervision. Cost control is more than mere bookkeeping. Bookkeeping will enable a contractor to determine whether he made a profit after a project is finished. Cost control during the period of construction will enable a contractor to analyze intelligently the performance of labor and equipment. It will show costs and production for labor and equipment. If the costs are higher than were estimated, either the estimate was too low or the costs are too high. If the latter condition is found to exist, it may be corrected while the project is still in operation, thereby providing a profit instead of a loss.

The owner of equipment should use an equipment ledger to provide information concerning each type of major equipment, showing an assigned number, with a description giving the size or capacity and any auxiliary equipment, date of purchase, name of seller, original total cost, estimated total life, and a depreciation schedule (see Figs. 2-16 and 2-17). He should use an equipment-operating ledger to keep a complete record of the cost of each type of equipment (see Fig. 2-19).

Prior to starting construction on a project a contractor should set up a classification of construction accounts in which specific item numbers are assigned to each construction operation. The item numbers that were used in estimating the cost of the project should be used in preparing the classification of construction accounts. This procedure will facilitate the comparison of costs with the original estimates. In setting up the items for which costs are to be estimated and reported during construction, it is well to consider the desirability of dividing an operation into subitems. For example, the costs of concrete in a structure might be subdivided into the costs of producing aggregate, hauling aggregate, mixing and placing concrete, and finishing and curing concrete. If a concrete structure includes various sizes and shapes whose costs vary considerably, it may be desirable to divide the project into subitems for cost purposes.

Cost accounts should provide for the showing of the costs of materials, labor, and equipment separately for each operation if they are to serve the purpose for which they are used. Some contractors follow the practice of grouping the cost of all equipment into one item. This practice is not good, as it does not permit a determination of the true complete cost of a given operation on which the equipment is used. This is especially true of engineering construction for which the cost of equipment may represent a major portion of the total cost. If the cost of equipment includes rental or depreciation, maintenance and repairs, fuel, supplies, etc., a record of the time that the equipment is used on each operation will permit the total cost to be prorated correctly between the several operations. It is not correct to charge to an operation the cost of major repairs because the equipment was assigned to that operation when the repairs were made.

Cost-accounting methods should be realistic, simple, and understandable. They are not an end product, but a means of managing a project. If the men who are supposed to use the information understand it, they will use it. If the information is too complicated, it will be disregarded or used incorrectly.

COST–CONTROL RECORDS

Experience gained on construction projects indicates that it is desirable to use simplified records for obtaining cost information. The forms illustrated in Figs. 2-21 to 2-26 are intended to show how cost information may be recorded and used in a simplified manner.

If the forms are made on the same-size ledger sheets, such as $8\frac{1}{2}$ by 11 in., with two holes punched on the $8\frac{1}{2}$-in. side, all the records from a project may be assembled in one ledger binder when the project is completed. Such information will be of considerable value to estimators in preparing estimates for future projects.

Figure 2-21 is a form for keeping a record of the costs of materials purchased. As the net costs shown in the last column are cumulative through the last entry, it is possible to determine at a glance what the total cost of materials is for a given item.

Figure 2-22 is a form for keeping a record of the man-hours of labor used weekly and to date, the cost of labor per week and to date, the quantity of work completed per week and to date, the unit cost of work completed to date, and the estimated total cost based on the quantity and the indicated unit cost. The indicated saving or overrun is obtained by subtracting from the estimated total cost the product of the budget quantity times the unit cost to date for any desired date. It will be noted that the form is designed to show the item for which the costs apply, such as making forms for footings, piers, walls, and grade beams.

Figure 2-23 illustrates a daily timekeeper's field sheet which is designed to record the number of hours worked during a day by any number of men up to 50. If there are more than 50 men on a project, additional sheets may be prepared with numbers from 51 to 100, 101 to 150, etc. The numbers used on the sheets should coincide with the numbers assigned to the workers. The hours for each worker are shown under the proper classification of work performed, as indicated by the operation symbol near the top of the sheet. Near the bottom of the sheet the total number of man-hours for each operation and the corresponding cost are shown. The sheet provides a space for showing the wage rate per hour and the daily wage earned for each worker. The number of hours worked at regular wage rates and at overtime rates may be shown. The total man-hours shown across the bottom of the sheet should agree with the total hours

MATERIAL COST RECORD

Item
Floor plank and nailers

Job No. _531_

Estimated ___ Budget quantity _136M_ Unit cost _246_ Total cost _33,460_

Date	Bought from	Description	Number					Cost billed	Credits	Net cost to date
			Car	Inv	Check	Statement				
3/3	Brown Lumber Co.	3506 fbm, No. 1 pine, 3 x 8		215	142	9	845.23		845.23
3/4	Brown Lumber Co.	2628 fbm, No. 1 pine, 3 x 8		216	142	9	633.56		1,478.79
3/11	Brown Lumber Co.	2612 fbm, No. 1 pine, 3 x 6		269	171	10	629.70		2,108.49

Figure 2-21 Material cost record.

LABOR COST RECORD

Job No. 531

Symbol FIM

Item
Forms, footings, piers, walls,
and grade beams; Make

Estimated Budget quantity 630 sq Unit cost 22.00 Total cost 13,860.00

Notes	Week ending	Manhours		Labor cost		Quantity		Unit cost to date	Budget quantity x unit cost to date	Indicated	
		For week	To date	For week	To date	For week	To date			Saving	Overrun
	4/12	121	121	968.00	968.00	36	36	26.89	16,941		3,081
	4/19	118	239	944.00	1912.00	64	100	19.12	12,046	1,814	
	4/26	117	356	936.00	2848.00	68	168	16.97	10,691	3,169	
Rain on 4/30	5/3	91	447	728.00	3576.00	32	200	17.88	11,264	2,596	

Figure 2-22 Labor cost record. (*Courtesy of Irving H. Winslow.*)

TIMEKEEPER'S FIELD RECORD

Sheet No. 3

Date 4/26/75

Job No. 531

Man's No.	F1M	F1E	F1S	F2M	F2E	F3M	Rate	Amount	Hours Reg	Hours O.T.	No.
1	8						8.00	64.00	8		1
2		8					8.00	64.00	8		2
3		8					8.00	64.00	8		3
4	4			4			6.00	48.00	8		4
5					8		8.00	64.00	8		5
6				4		4	8.00	64.00	8		6
38						8	6.00	48.00	8		38
39			8				6.00	48.00	8		39
40			8			2	6.00	66.00	8	2	40
Total manhours	32	40	35	44	48	38		1,700.00	224	14	Total
Amount	132.00	296.00	216.00	324.00	344.00	288.00					

Figure 2-23 Timekeeper's field sheet. *(Courtesy of Irving H. Winslow.)*

shown in the vertical column as a check on the accuracy of entries and computations. In a similar manner the total of the amounts shown near the bottom of the sheet should agree with the total amount shown in the vertical column.

In using these forms, it is suggested that a suitable system of symbols be adopted to indicate the various operations. In order to eliminate confusion, the system of symbols should be used uniformly throughout a contractor's operations on all projects. Thus, F1 might indicate forms for foundations, piers, and grade beams; F2, forms for floor beams and girders; F3, forms for floor and roof slab. If a further breakdown is desired, the symbols may be modified to F1M, making forms, F1E, erecting forms, and F1S, stripping forms. These symbols are used on the timekeeper's field sheet.

Figure 2-24 illustrates a payroll record on which the information from the timekeeper's sheet may be permanently recorded. Note that the extreme left and right columns are numbered in groups of 50 to correspond with the numbers used on the timekeeper's sheet. If the spacings of the numbers on the two sheets are made exactly the same, it will be possible to superimpose one sheet partially on the other to simplify the transfer of information from the timekeeper's sheet to the payroll record. In transferring overtime hours from the timekeeper's sheet the hours are shown in the vertical column headed "O.T." for the particular day. When the overtime hours are shown in the payroll-record column headed "Hours," they should be placed in the column headed "$1\frac{1}{2}$" or "2," depending on which overtime rate applies. When overtime hours are extended to the column headed "Pay hr." they are multiplied by the appropriate factor, either $1\frac{1}{2}$ or 2, before they are added to the hours at regular rates. This permits all pay hours to be multiplied by the regular wage rate, thereby eliminating the need of showing more than one wage rate for each worker. Under the column headed "Deductions," the amounts deducted for old-age benefits and for withholding taxes are shown.

The days shown at the head of the several columns may be revised, as desired, to permit any given day to indicate the end of a week, or the names of the days may be replaced by numbers such as 3/15, 3/16, 3/17, etc.

Figure 2-25 illustrates a weekly labor-cost statement on which there are recorded the number of units of work completed, the estimated and actual unit cost to date, and the probable final cost of each operation. The probable final cost is obtained by multiplying the estimated total quantity by the actual unit cost to date. From the probable final cost of a given operation it is possible to estimate the saving or overrun, based on the original estimated cost of the operation. This information may be of considerable value to a contractor in determining the cost status of a project at any time during the period of construction. It will be useful to the estimating department in preparing estimates for future projects.

Figure 2-26 illustrates a material-cost statement which may be prepared weekly or monthly. It assists a contractor by enabling him to determine the status of his material costs through any desired date during construction.

WEEKLY PAYROLL RECORD

Job No. 531
Payroll No. 10

Sheet No. 2
For period from 4/11 to 4/17

No.	Thu R	Thu OT	Fri R	Fri OT	Sat R	Sat OT	Sun R	Sun OT	Mon R	Mon OT	Tu R	Tu OT	Wed R	Wed OT	Hours R	Hours 1½	Hours 2	Pay hr	Rate	Gross amount	OAB	WT	Net amount	Name	WT class	Trade	Check No.	Date paid off	No.
1	8		8		8				8		8		8		40	8		52	8.00	416.00	10.40	12.80	392.80	J.T. Brown	5	Carpenter	521	4/19	1
2	8		8		8		4		8		8		8		40	8	4	60	8.00	480.00	12.00	15.20	452.80	D. Jones	5	Carpenter	522	4/19	2
3	8		8				4		8		8		8		40		4	48	8.00	384.00	9.60	11.60	362.80	C.L. Smith	3	Carpenter	523	4/19	3
4	8		8		8				8		8		8		40	8		52	6.00	312.00	7.80	8.20	296.00	B.L. Avery	1	C. Helper	524	4/19	4
5																													
6																													
7																													
35																													
36																													
37																													
38																													
39																													
40																													

R, hours worked at regular rates
OT, hours worked at overtime rates
OAB, old age benefits
WT, withholding tax

Figure 2-24 Weekly-payroll record (*Courtesy of Irving H. Winslow.*)

LABOR STATEMENT

Job No. 531

Sheet No. 2

Statement No. 11 through 4/17

Symbol	Description	Week's cost	Quantity			Unit cost		Cost			Estimated	
			Unit of measure	Estimated total	Actual to date	Estimated	Actual to date	Estimated total	Actual to date	Probable final	Saving	Overrun
	Forms (Make, erect, strip)											
F1M	Footings		Sq	63	63	16.00	11.88	1,008	748	748	260	
F1E	Piers, walls		Sq	173	173	60.00	54.00	10,380	9,342	9,342	1,038	
F1S	Grade beams	72.00	Sq	173	124	12.00	12.98	2,076	1,610	2,246		170
F2M	Slabs, beams	321.98	Sq	60	32	20.00	20.64	1,200	660	1,238		38
F2E	Girders	421.36	Sq	93	17	54.00	56.18	5,022	956	5,224		202
F2S	Slabs, beams, girders		Sq	93		20.00		1,860		1,860		

Figure 2-25 Weekly labor cost statement. (*Courtesy of Irving H. Winslow.*)

MATERIAL STATEMENT

Sheet No. 2

Job No. 531

Statement No. 1 through 4/19

Description	Unit of measure	Estimated			Actual to date			Probable final cost	Indicated	
		Quantity	Unit cost	Total cost	Quantity	Unit cost	Total cost		Saving	Overrun
Steel and iron										
Steel reinforcement and sundry	*Ton*	*27*	*220.00*	*5,940*	*26*	*200.00*	*5,224*	*5,400*	*540*	
Steel sash	*Sq ft*	*5,580*	*1.50*	*8,360*	*5,580*	*1.38*	*7,732*	*7,732*	*628*	
Miscellaneous iron				*3,200*			*232*	*3,200*		
Total				*17,500*			*13,188*	*16,332*	*1,168*	
Concrete and masonry										
Ready-mixed concrete	*Cu yd*	*449*	*25.40*	*11,400*	*275*	*24.20*	*6,664*	*10,866*	*534*	
Brick – common red	*M*	*134*	*55.20*	*10,720*				*10,720*		

Figure 2-26 Material cost statement. *(Courtesy of Irving H. Winslow.)*

PROBLEMS

2-1 Prepare an arrow diagram and a list of starts, finishes, and total floats for a project involving the listed activities:

Activity	Duration	Activities which immediately	
		precede	follow
A	3	None	B, C
B	5	A	D, E
C	4	A	F, I
D	7	B	G
E	6	B	H
F	11	C	H
G	6	D	J
H	4	E, F	K
I	3	C	K, L
J	6	G	M
K	5	H, I	N
L	7	I	O
M	5	J	P
N	3	K	P
O	2	L	P
P	4	M, N, O	None

2-2 Prepare an arrow diagram and a list of starts, finishes, and total floats for a project involving the listed activities:

Activity	Duration	Activities which immediately	
		precede	follow
A	3	None	C
B	5	None	D, E
C	4	A	F, G
D	8	B	F, G
E	9	B	H, I
F	6	C, D	J, K, L, M
G	8	C, D	K, L, M
H	6	E	K, L, M
I	5	E	P
J	4	F	N
K	7	F, G, H	O
L	6	F, G, H	Q
M	7	F, G, H	P
N	4	J	R
O	8	K	R
P	4	I, M	R
Q	5	L	R
R	3	N, O, P, Q	None

2-3 Prepare a time-grid diagram for the project of Prob. 2-2, for which the durations are expressed in days. Assume a week of 5 days, with work to start on the first Monday in May of the current year. Show the calendar days for the starting and finishing of each activity, with no lost time due to weather or other causes.

CHAPTER THREE

FACTORS AFFECTING THE SELECTION OF CONSTRUCTION EQUIPMENT

GENERAL INFORMATION

A problem which frequently confronts a contractor as he plans to construct a project is the selection of the most suitable equipment. He should consider the money spent for equipment as an investment which he can expect to recover, with a profit, during the useful life of the equipment. A contractor does not pay for construction equipment; the equipment must pay for itself by earning for the contractor more money than it cost. Unless it can be established in advance that a unit of equipment will earn more than the cost, it should not be purchased.

A contractor can never afford to own all types or sizes of equipment that might be used for the kind of work he does. It may be possible to determine what kind and size of equipment seem most suitable for a given project, but this information alone will not necessarily justify the purchase of the equipment. Perhaps the project under consideration is not large enough to justify the purchase, because the cost cannot be recovered before the completion of the project, and it may not be possible to dispose of the equipment at the completion of the project at a reasonable price. A contractor may own a type of equipment, which is presently idle, that is less desirable than the proposed equipment, but, considering the probable heavy depreciation for the proposed equipment and the uncertainty that it can be used on future projects, the apparently ideal equipment may prove to be more expensive than equipment now owned by the contractor.

Any time a unit of equipment will pay for itself on work that is certain to be done it is good business to purchase it. For example, if a unit of equipment costing $25,000 will save $50,000 on a project, a contractor is justified in purchasing it, regardless of the prospects of using it on additional projects or the prospects of selling it at a favorable price when the project is finished.

STANDARD TYPES OF EQUIPMENT

There is no clear definition of standard equipment. Equipment that is standard for one contractor may be special equipment for another contractor. It depends on the extent to which a contractor will use it in his construction operations. Another method which is sometimes used to distinguish between standard and special equipment is the extent to which it is commonly manufactured and available to prospective purchasers. Thus, a 1-cu-yd diesel-powered crawler-mounted power shovel is standard equipment, whereas a 30-cu-yd shovel is classified as special equipment. The larger shovel is manufactured for a specific purchaser.

Contractors should confine their purchases to standard equipment unless a project definitely justifies the purchase of special equipment. Delivery of standard equipment may be obtained more quickly. Standard equipment can be used economically on more than one project. Repair parts for standard equipment may be obtained more quickly and economically than for special equipment. If a contractor no longer needs a unit of standard equipment, he can usually dispose of it more easily and at a more favorable price.

SPECIAL EQUIPMENT

One definition of special equipment is equipment that is manufactured for use on a single project or for a special type of operation. Such equipment may not be suitable or economical for use on another project. An example of special equipment is a 40-cu-yd power shovel used to remove the overburden in strip

Figure 3-1 Canal trimmer.

mining coal. Another example is the hydraulic dredge which was constructed primarily for use in building the Ft. Randall Dam. Another special type of equipment is the canal trimmer illustrated in Fig. 3-1. This equipment is used for the final trimming of the bottom and sides of an earthen canal, prior to placing the watertight membrane, such as concrete or asphalt surfacing. However, as this type of equipment is becoming more common in canal construction, it might be considered as standard. Although belt-conveyor systems are sometimes used to transport aggregates several miles in constructing dams, such installations probably should be considered as special equipment.

The examples which follow illustrate methods that may be used to select equipment for given projects.

Example The project is a concrete dam requiring 1,200,000 tons of crushed-stone aggregate. If the aggregate is hauled from the quarry to the project, by trucks, it will be necessary to build a haul road with several drainage structures at an estimated cost of $280,000. It is doubtful that any salvage value can be realized from the structures after the project is completed. It is estimated that the cost of hauling the aggregate with trucks, including the cost of maintaining the haul road, will be $0.20 per ton.

If the aggregate is transported by a belt-conveyor system, it is estimated that the cost of the system will be $640,000. It is estimated that the conveyor system will have a salvage value of $60,000 following the completion of this project. The difference between the initial cost of this system and the net salvage value is defined as depreciation. The operating costs, including investment, as explained on pages 68 and 71, maintenance, repairs, electrical energy, and labor are estimated to be $0.12 per ton. The total estimated cost and the cost per ton will be as follows.

Using trucks:
Haul road	=$280,000	
Hauling, 1,200,000 tons @ $0.20 per ton	= 240,000	
Total cost	=$520,000	
Cost per ton, $520,000 ÷ 1,200,000 tons	=	0.433

Using a belt conveyor:
Belt-conveyor system	=$640,000	
Less salvage value	= 60,000	
Depreciation	=$580,000	
Transporting, 1,200,000 tons @ $0.12 per ton	= 144,000	
Total cost	=$624,000	
Cost per ton, $624,000 ÷ 1,200,000 tons	=	0.520

The analysis indicates that the use of a belt-conveyor system is not justified.

Example A study was made to determine the economy of using special equipment for trimming the earthen surface of a canal before placing the concrete lining. The soil was sandy clay. The canal had a 14-ft wide bottom and had 1:1 side slopes. On similar projects the cost of trimming the bottom and slopes using draglines, bulldozers, graders, and hand labor had varied from $0.60 to $0.80 per sq yd. A specially constructed self-propelled trimmer, similar to the one illustrated in Fig. 3-1, was estimated to cost $186,000. It was estimated that the trimmer could be used an average of 1,600 hr per year for a total of 4 years. The equipment should trim an average of 50 lin ft of canal per hour.

The estimated cost of trimming per square yard was determined as follows:

Width of canal, including slopes and bottom, 52 ft
Speed, 50 lin ft per hr
Area trimmed, 50 × 52 ÷ 9 = 289 sq yd per hr
Total cost of equipment, $186,000

The cost of owning and operating construction equipment is determined by methods illustrated on pages 65 to 72 of this book.

The cost per hour will be:

Equipment	= $ 78.60
Labor, including supervision	= 48.00
Total cost	= $126.60
Cost per sq yd, $126.60 ÷ 289 =	0.432

From this analysis it is evident that purchase of the special trimmer is justified, provided the stated conditions apply. Sometimes a decision to purchase or not to purchase equipment is dependent on the volume of work that it must perform in order to justify the purchase cost. How many miles of canal must be trimmed by this unit to justify its purchase? For the equipment described in the previous example, the determination could be made as follows:

Estimated cost of trimming without using the special trimmer, $0.70 per sq yd
Cost of special trimmer, $186,000
Estimated life, 4 yr
Estimated hr used per yr, 1,600
Annual costs:

Depreciation, $186,000 ÷ 4	=	$46,500
Maintenance and repairs @ 100% of depreciation	=	46,500
Investment, 15% of average value, 0.625* × 186,000 × 0.15	=	17,437
Fuel, lubrication, and other expenses, 1,600 hr @ $14.00 per hr	=	22,400
Total annual cost	=	$132,837
Cost per hr, $132,837 ÷ 1,600 hr =		83.02

Annual cost, excluding depreciation:

Maintenance and repairs	=	$46,500
Investment	=	17,437
Fuel, lubricating oil, and other expenses	=	22,400
Total cost	=	$86,337
Cost per hr, $86,337 ÷ 1,600	=	53.96

Based on a cost of $53.96 per hr for equipment, excluding the cost of depreciation, the cost of trimming the canal will be:

Equipment cost	=	$ 53.96
Labor cost	=	48.00
Total cost per hr	=	$101.96
Area trimmed per hr, 50 × 52 ÷ 9 = 289 sq yd		
Cost per sq yd, $101.96 ÷ 289	=	$0.35
Cost per sq yd without trimmer	=	0.70
Saving in cost per sq yd using trimmer	=	$0.35

The saving in cost per mile of canal resulting from use of the trimmer could be determined as follows:

No. sq yd per ft of canal, 52 ÷ 9	=	5.78
No. sq yd per mile, 5,280 × 5.78	=	305,184
Saving in cost per mile, 305,184 × $0.35 = $10,681		

* See Table 3-3.

In order to justify purchase and use of this machine, during its useful life it must produce a saving in the cost of trimming canals equal to or greater than the cost of the machine. The number of miles of canal that it must trim in order to produce this saving will be

$$\frac{\text{Total cost}}{\text{Saving per mile}} = \frac{186,000}{10,681} = 17.41 \text{ miles}$$

Thus, for the stated conditions, it will be necessary for the machine to trim at least 17.41 miles of canal during its useful life just to recover the initial cost. Any production in excess of 17.41 miles will result in a profit from the purchase and operation of the machine.

REPLACEMENT OF PARTS

A factor which may be overlooked by a prospective purchaser of equipment is the ease and speed with which replacement parts may be obtained. All equipment parts are subject to failure, regardless of the care which they receive. A truck with a broken axle is useless until the axle is replaced. A broken part in a power shovel may delay an entire project for weeks, while waiting for the part to be manufactured and shipped. Prior to purchasing equipment, the buyer should determine where spare parts are obtainable. If parts are not obtainable quickly, it may be wise to purchase other equipment, for which parts are quickly available, even though the latter seems less desirable. This is an argument for standard equipment.

THE COST OF OWNING AND OPERATING CONSTRUCTION EQUIPMENT

There are several methods of determining the probable cost of owning and operating construction equipment. No known method will give exact costs under all operating conditions. At best the estimate is only a close approximation of the cost. Carefully kept records for equipment previously used should give information which may be used as a guide for the particular equipment. But there is no assurance that similar equipment will involve similar costs, especially if the equipment is used under different conditions. Factors which affect the cost of owning and operating equipment include the cost of the equipment delivered to the owner, the severity of the conditions under which it is used, the number of hours it is used per year, the number of years it is used, the care with which the owner maintains and repairs it, and the demand for used equipment when it is sold, which will affect the salvage value.

When it is necessary to estimate the cost of owning and operating equipment prior to purchasing it, cost records, based on past performance, will not be available. The costs which should be considered include depreciation, maintenance, repairs, investment, lubrication, and fuel, if fuel is required to operate it.

DEPRECIATION COSTS

Depreciation is the loss in value of equipment resulting from use or age. The owner of equipment must recover the loss in the value of equipment during its useful life, or he will sustain an equipment loss on those projects where the equipment is used. The total cost of a unit of equipment should include the purchase price, the cost of transporting it to the purchaser, and the cost of unloading and assembling it at its destination.

While any reasonable method may be used for determining the cost of depreciation, the following three are most commonly used:

1. Straight-line method
2. Declining-balance method
3. Sum-of-the-years-digits method

Each of these methods is approved by the U.S. Internal Revenue Service for income tax purposes.

If a unit of equipment is continued in use after it is completely depreciated, no additional depreciation charge may be made against it when determining profit or loss from its use for income tax purposes.

Straight-line depreciation When the cost of depreciation is determined by this method, it is assumed that a unit of equipment will decrease in value from its original total cost at a uniform rate. The depreciation rate may be expressed as a cost per unit of time, or it may be expressed as a cost per unit of work produced. The depreciation cost per unit of time is obtained by dividing the original cost, · less the estimated salvage value to be realized at the time it will be disposed of, by the estimated useful life, expressed in the desired units of time, which may be years, months, weeks, days, or hours. For example, a given unit of equipment, whose original cost is $12,000, may have a useful life of 2,000 hr per year for 5 years and a salvage of $2,000. The cost of depreciation is determined as follows:

Total depreciation, $12,000 − $2,000   = $10,000
Annual cost of depreciation, $10,000 ÷ 5   = $2,000
Hourly cost of depreciation, $2,000 ÷ 2,000 = $1.00

Another method of estimating the straight-line cost of depreciation is to divide the original cost, less the estimated salvage value, by the probable number of units of work which it will produce during its useful life. This method is satisfactory for equipment whose life is determined by the rate at which it is used instead of by time. Examples of such equipment include the pump and discharge pipe on a hydraulic dredge, rock crushers, rock-drilling equipment, rubber tires, and conveyor belts.

Declining-balance method Under this method of determining the cost of depreciation, the estimated life of the equipment in years will give the average percent of depreciation per year. This percent is doubled for the 200 percent declining-balance method. The value of the depreciation during any given year is determined by multiplying the resulting percent by the value of the equipment at the beginning of that year. While the estimated salvage value is not considered when determining depreciation, the depreciated value is not permitted to drop below a reasonable salvage value.

When the cumulative sum of all costs of depreciation is deducted from the original total cost, the remaining value is designated as the book value. Thus, if a unit of equipment whose original cost was $10,000 has been depreciated a total of $6,000, the book value will be $4,000.

Example This example illustrates how the declining-balance method of determining the cost of depreciation may be applied to a unit of equipment.

Total cost, $10,000
Estimated salvage value, $1,000
Estimated life, 5 years
Average rate of depreciation, 20% per year
Double this rate of depreciation, 2 × 20 = 40%
Cost of depreciation, first year, 0.40 × $10,000 = $4,000.00
Book value at the start of the second year   = 6,000.00
Cost of depreciation, second year, 0.40 × $6,000 = 2,400.00

Table 3-1 gives the schedule of depreciation costs for this equipment.

The method outlined in the example may be used for any reasonable useful life. The depreciation per year may be continued until the book value of the equipment is reduced to a reasonable salvage value.

Sum-of-the-years-digits method Under this method of determining the cost of depreciation, all the digits representing each year of the estimated life of the equipment are totaled. For an estimated life of 5 years, the sum of the digits will be 1 + 2 + 3 + 4 + 5 = 15. Deduct the estimated salvage value from the total

Table 3-1 Annual cost of depreciation using the declining-balance method

End of year	Percent depreciation	Depreciation for the year	Book value
0	0	$ 0	$10,000.00
1	40	4,000.00	6,000.00
2	40	2,400.00	3,600.00
3	40	1,440.00	2,160.00
4	40	864.00	1,296.00
5	40	518.40	777.60
5*	. . .	296.00	1,000.00

* The value of the equipment may not be depreciated below a reasonable minimum salvage value. If this value is $1,000, the lower figures will apply; otherwise the upper figures will apply.

Table 3-2 Annual cost of depreciation using the sum-of-the-years-digits method

End of year	Depreciation ratio	Total depreciation	Depreciation for the year	Book value
0	0	$9,000	$ 0	$10,000
1	5/15	9,000	3,000	7,000
2	4/15	9,000	2,400	4,600
3	3/15	9,000	1,800	2,800
4	2/15	9,000	1,200	1,600
5	1/15	9,000	600	1,000

Total cost = $10,000
Estimated salvage value = 1,000
Total cost of depreciation = $ 9,000
Estimated useful life, 5 years
Sum of the years digits, 15

cost of the equipment. During the first year, the cost of depreciation will be $\frac{5}{15}$ of the cost less salvage value. During the second year, the cost of depreciation will be $\frac{4}{15}$ of the cost less the salvage value. Continue this process for each year through the fifth year. Table 3-2 gives the schedule of depreciation costs for a unit of equipment under the stated conditions.

MAINTENANCE AND REPAIRS

The cost of maintenance and repairs will vary considerably with the type of equipment, the service to which it is assigned, and the care which it receives. If a bearing is greased and adjusted at frequent intervals, its life will be much longer than if it is neglected.

The annual cost of maintenance and repairs may be expressed as a percent of the annual cost of depreciation or it may be expressed independently of depreciation. In any event, it should be sufficient to cover the cost of keeping the equipment operating. The annual cost of maintenance and repairs for a power shovel may vary from 80 to 120 percent of the annual cost of depreciation, with 100 percent a fair average value. The annual cost for certain types of rock-crushing equipment may be much higher, while for an electric motor it will be lower. Experience records serve as a guide in estimating these costs. Appendix A gives representative estimates of the costs of maintenance and repairs for construction equipment.

INVESTMENT COSTS

It costs money to own equipment, regardless of the extent to which it is used. These costs, which are frequently classified as investment costs, include interest on the money invested, taxes of all types which are assessed against the equipment, insurance, and storage. The rates for these items will vary somewhat among different owners, with location, and for other reasons.

There are several methods of determining the cost of interest paid on the money invested in equipment. Even though the owner pays cash for the equipment, he should charge interest on the investment, as the money spent for the equipment could be invested in some other asset which would return interest to the owner. The possibility of earning interest on money is lost to the equipment owner when he spends the money for equipment.

Some equipment owners charge a fixed rate of interest against the full purchase cost of the equipment each year it is owned. This method gives an annual interest cost which is higher than it should be. Each year that equipment is used the owner should deduct from its earnings an amount equal to the annual cost of depreciation. Since this money is retained by the owner, it reduces his net investment in the equipment. After the equipment has been used for the estimated depreciation period, expressed in years or units of production, the owner will have recovered its original cost through the reserve for depreciation. In any event, the interest charged should be based on a realistic value for the equipment, instead of its original cost.

The average annual cost of interest should be based on the average value of the equipment during its useful life. This value may be obtained by establishing a schedule of values for the beginning of each year that the equipment will be used. The calculations given below illustrate a method of determining the average value of equipment:

Original cost of equipment, $25,000
Estimated useful life, 5 yr
Average annual cost of depreciation, $25,000 ÷ 5 = $5,000

(1) Beginning of year	(2) Cumulative depreciation	(3) Value of equipment
1	0	$25,000
2	$ 5,000	20,000
3	10,000	15,000
4	15,000	10,000
5	20,000	5,000
6	25,000	0

Total of values in column 3   = $75,000
Average value, $75,000 ÷ 5   = $15,000
Average value as % of original cost, $\dfrac{\$15,000 \times 100}{\$25,000} = 60$

Thus, the average value of equipment having an estimated life of 5 years is 60 percent of the original cost.

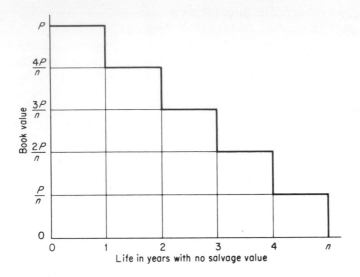

Figure 3-2 Value of equipment by year.

An alternate method of determining the average value of equipment having no salvage value, based on straight-line depreciation, is to develop an equation for this purpose. Figure 3-2 indicates the value of a unit of equipment whose initial cost is represented by P at the beginning of each year during its estimated life of n years.

$$\bar{P} = \frac{P + P/n}{2} = \frac{Pn + P}{2n}$$

$$= \frac{P(n + 1)}{2n} \tag{3-1}$$

where P = total initial cost
$\bar{P}$ = average value
n = life in years

Example Consider a unit of equipment costing $25,000, with a life of 5 years and no salvage value. Using Eq. (3-1), we have

$$\bar{P} = \frac{25,000(5 + 1)}{2 \times 5} = \$15,000$$

Table 3-3 gives the average value of equipment, with no salvage value, for various years of life, expressed as a percent of the initial cost.

If the equipment will have a salvage value at the time it is disposed of, after n years of use, its average value is determined by referring to Fig. 3-3. The average value is the sum of the values at the beginning of the first year and the beginning of the last year divided by 2.

$$\bar{P} = \frac{P + (P - S)/n + S}{2} = \frac{Pn + P - S + Sn}{2n}$$

$$= \frac{P(n + 1) + S(n - 1)}{2n} \tag{3-2}$$

Table 3-3 Average value of equipment with no salvage value

Estimated life, yr	Average value as % of original cost
2	75.00
3	66.67
4	62.50
5	60.00
6	58.33
7	57.14
8	56.25
9	55.55
10	55.00
11	54.54
12	54.17

Example Consider a unit of equipment costing \$25,000, with an estimated salvage value of \$5,000 after 5 years. Using Eq. (3-2), we get

$$\bar{P} = \frac{25,000(5 + 1) + 5,000(5 - 1)}{2 \times 5}$$

$$= \frac{150,000 + 20,000}{10} = \$17,000$$

Because insurance and taxes are usually paid on the depreciated value of equipment, it is proper to use the average value of equipment in determining the average annual cost of insurance and taxes.

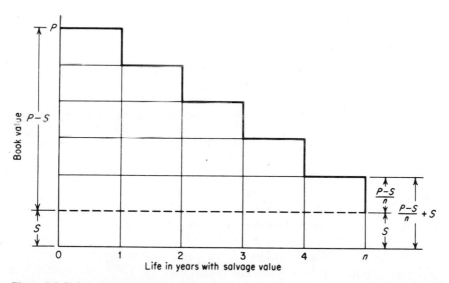

Figure 3-3 Value of equipment by year.

It is common practice to combine the cost of interest, insurance, taxes, and storage and to estimate them as a fixed percent of the average value of the equipment. The present national average rate is about 15 percent, which includes interest at 10 percent and insurance, taxes, and storage at 5 percent per year.

OPERATING COST

Construction equipment which is driven by internal-combustion engines requires fuel and lubricating oil, which should be considered as an operating cost. While the amounts consumed and the unit cost of each will vary with the type of equipment, the conditions under which it is used, and location, it is possible to estimate the cost reasonably accurately for a given project.

The person who is responsible for selecting the equipment should estimate the conditions under which the equipment will operate. There are at least two conditions which will apply to most projects, the extent to which the engine will operate at full power all the time, and the actual time that the unit will operate in an hour or a day.

While the power unit in a piece of equipment may be capable of developing a given horsepower when operating at maximum output, it is well known that maximum output usually will not be required at all times. For example, the full power of an engine may be required while a power shovel is loading the dipper, but during the balance of the cycle the demands on the engine are reduced considerably. The full power of a tractor will be required while it is loading a scraper with earth, and possibly while it is climbing an embankment, but for the rest of the round-trip cycle it is possible that less than the maximum power will be required. Consider the gasoline-engine-driven air compressor that is heard so frequently. For a short time the engine will operate at full power, then it will idle for a while, these conditions alternating as the air is used.

HORSEPOWER RATINGS

Because the horsepower ratings specified in the literature of various manufacturers are not determined under the same operating conditions, it is not possible to compare the work capability of different engines with a high degree of accuracy. The power may be specified for standard conditions, namely at a barometric pressure of 29.9 in. of mercury and at a temperature of 60°F, or it may be specified for normal operating conditions, with altitudes up to 2000 ft above sea level and at temperatures up to 85°F. The specified power may be the maximum that the bare engine can develop or it may be the flywheel power with all accessories attached to the engine. The accessories will vary with engines, but usually include a fan, generator, fuel pump, water pump, air cleaner, and lubricating oil pump. Each of these accessories requires power, for a combined demand that may equal 20 or 25 percent or more of the rated flywheel power of the engine. Thus an engine rated at 200 fwhp may develop 250 hp when rated as a bare engine.

FUEL CONSUMED

When operating under standard conditions a gasoline engine will consume approximately 0.06 gal of fuel per flywheel horsepower hour, while a diesel engine will consume approximately 0.04 gal per flywheel horsepower hour. A horsepower hour is a measure of the work performed by an engine.

In order to determine the work performed by an engine it is necessary to know the average power generated by the engine and the duration of this performance. Engines used in the construction industry seldom operate at a constant output or at the rated output, except for short periods of time. A tractor engine may operate at maximum power when it is loading a scraper or negotiating an adverse slope. During the balance of its cycle the demand on the engine will be reduced substantially, resulting in a decreased consumption of fuel. Also, construction equipment is seldom operated the entire 60 minutes in an hour.

Consider a power shovel with a diesel engine rated at 160 fwhp. When used to load trucks the engine may operate at maximum power while filling the dipper, requiring 5 sec out of a cycle time of 20 sec. During the other 15 sec the engine may operate at not more than one half of its rated power. Also the shovel may be idle for 10 to 15 min, or more, during an hour, with the engine providing only that power required for internal operation.

Assume that this shovel operates 50 min per hr, to give an operating factor = $(50/60) \times 100 = 83.3$ percent. The approximate amount of fuel consumed in an hour can be determined as follows:

> Rated output at flywheel = 160 hp
> Engine factor:
> $\quad$ Filling the dipper, $\frac{5}{20} \times 1$ $\qquad\qquad$ = 0.250
> $\quad$ Rest of cycle, $\frac{15}{20} \times 0.5 \times 1$ $\qquad$ = 0.375
> $\qquad$ Total factor $\qquad\qquad\qquad\qquad$ = 0.625
> Time factor $\frac{50}{60}$ = 0.833
> Operating factor = $0.625 \times 0.833 = 0.520$
> Fuel consumed per hr = $0.520 \times 160 \times 0.04 = 3.33$ gal

For other operating factors the quantity of fuel consumed should be estimated in a similar manner.

LUBRICATING OIL

The quantity of lubricating oil used by an engine will vary with the size of the engine, the capacity of the crankcase, the condition of the piston rings, and the number of hours between oil changes. For extremely dusty operations it may be desirable to change oil every 50 hr, but this is an unusual condition. It is common practice to change oil every 100 to 200 hr. The quantity of oil consumed by an engine per change will include the amount added during the change plus the make-up oil between changes.

A formula which may be used to estimate the quantity of oil required

$$q = \frac{\text{hp} \times f \times 0.006 \text{ lb per hp - hr}}{7.4 \text{ lb per gal}} + \frac{c}{t} \tag{3-3}$$

where q= quantity consumed, gph
  hp= rated horsepower of engine
  c= capacity of crankcase, gal
  f= operating factor
  t= number of hours between changes

The above formula is based on an operating factor of 60 percent. It assumes that the quantity of oil consumed per rated horsepower hour, between changes, will be 0.006 lb. Using the formula, for a 100-hp engine with a crankcase capacity of 4 gal, requiring a change every 100 hr, the quantity consumed per hour will be

$$q = \frac{100 \times 0.6 \times 0.006}{7.4} + \frac{4}{100} = 0.049 + 0.04 = 0.089 \text{ gal per hr}$$

EXAMPLES ILLUSTRATING THE COST OF OWNING AND OPERATING CONSTRUCTION EQUIPMENT

Example Determine the probable cost per hour for owning and operating a 3/4-cu-yd diesel-engine-powered crawler-type power shovel. The following information will apply:

Engine, 160 hp
Crankcase capacity, 6 gal
Hours between oil changes, 100
Operating factor, 0.60
Fuel consumed per hr, $160 \times 0.6 \times 0.04 = 3.9$ gal
Lubricating oil consumed per hr,

$$\frac{160 \times 0.6 \times 0.006}{7.4} + \frac{6}{100} = 0.138 \text{ gal}$$

Useful life, 5 yr, with no salvage value
Hours operated per yr, 2,000
Shipping weight, 56,000 lb

Cost to owner:

List price, f.o.b factory, including bucket	= $119,350
Freight cost, 56,000 lb @ $2.40 per cwt	= 1,344
Taxes, $119,350 @ 5%	= 5,967
Unloading and assembling at destination	= 359
Total cost to owner	= $127,010
Average investment, 0.60 × $127,010	76,207

Annual cost:

Depreciation, $127,010 ÷ 5 yr	= $25,402
Maintenance and repairs, 100% of depreciation	= 25,402
Investment, 0.15 × $76,207	= 11,431
Total annual fixed cost	= $ 62,235

Hourly cost:

Fixed cost, $62,235 ÷ 2,000 hr	= $31.12
Fuel, 3.9 gal @ $0.50	= 1.95
Lubricating oil, 0.138 gal @ $1.60	= 0.22
Grease, 0.5 lb @ $0.30	= 0.15
Total cost per hr, excluding labor	= $33.44

Example Determine the probable cost per hour for owning and operating a 25-cu-yd heaped capacity bottom-dump wagon with six rubber tires. Because the tires will have a different life than the wagon, they should be treated separately. The following information will apply:

Engine, 250 hp diesel
Crankcase capacity, 14 gal
Time between oil changes, 80 hr
Operating factor, 0.60
Fuel consumed per hr, $250 \times 0.6 \times 0.04 = 6.0$ gal
Lubricating oil consumed per hr,

$$\frac{250 \times 0.6 \times 0.006}{7.4} + \frac{14}{80} = 0.30 \text{ gal}$$

Other lubricants used per hr, 0.50 lb
Useful life, 5 yr, with no salvage value
Life of tires, 5,000 hr
Repairs to tires, 15% of cost of depreciation of tires

Cost to owner:

Cost delivered, including freight and taxes	= $92,623
Less cost of tires	= 12,113
Net cost less tires	= $80,510
Average investment, 0.6 × 92,623	= $55,744

Annual cost:

Depreciation, $80,510 ÷ 5 yr	= $16,102
Maintenance and repairs, 50% of depreciation	= 8,051
Investment, 0.15 × $55,744	= 8,362
Total annual fixed costs	= $32,515

Hourly cost:

Fixed cost, $32,515 ÷ 2,000 hr	= $16.26
Tire depreciation, $12,113 ÷ 5,000 hr	= 2.42
Tire repairs, 0.15 × $2.42	= 0.36
Fuel, 6.0 gal @ $0.50	= 3.00
Lubricating oil, 0.30 gal @ $1.60	= 0.48
Grease, 0.50 lb @ $0.30	= 0.15
Total cost per hr, excluding labor	= $22.67

As noted, the costs determined in the previous examples do not include any allowances for the salvage value of the equipment, if any, at the end of its useful life. If it is anticipated that there will be a realizable salvage value at the end of the indicated useful life, the cost of depreciation and the value for the average investment should be modified, using the methods illustrated on pages 70 and 71 respectively.

The hourly cost of owning and operating construction equipment, as illustrated in the previous examples, will vary with the conditions under which the equipment is operated, and the job planner should analyze each job to determine the probable conditions.

If a power shovel is used to excavate a soft material, the life of the dipper teeth, wire rope, and other parts which are affected by the wear and strain will be relatively long. Repair costs will be relatively low. However, if the shovel is used to excavate rock or other hard materials, the dipper teeth, wire rope, clutch linings, and certain gear parts will be subjected to greater strains and the life of each will be reduced. Repair costs will be correspondingly increased. Likewise, the consumption of fuel will be affected by digging conditions.

If trucks are operated over straight, reasonably level, smooth roads, the cost of repairs will be lower than when the same trucks are operated over poorly maintained roads, with steep hills, ruts, or deep sand. A study of statistical information showing the cost per mile for operating automotive equipment over roads having different types of surfaces will reveal surprisingly large variations in the costs. These variations will apply to trucks used for hauling materials.

ECONOMIC LIFE OF CONSTRUCTION EQUIPMENT

The owner of construction equipment should be interested in obtaining the lowest possible cost per unit of production. In order to accomplish this objective he must follow an informed program of equipment replacement. When should equipment be replaced? If the owner replaces it too soon, he will experience an unnecessary capital loss, whereas, if he waits too long, the equipment will have passed its period of economic operation.

In order to determine the most economical time to replace equipment, accurate records of maintenance and repair costs and downtime must be kept for each machine. The owner must consider all costs related to the ownership and operation of the equipment, and the effect which continued use will have on these costs.

The costs to be considered are as follows:

1. Depreciation and replacement
2. Investment
3. Maintenance and repairs
4. Downtime
5. Obsolescence

Table 3-4 Depreciation and replacement costs

End of year	Replacement cost	Salvage value	Loss on replacement	Cumulative hours of use	Cumulative cost per hr
0	$20,000	$20,000	0	0	0
1	21,000	15,000	$ 6,000	2,000	$3.00
2	22,000	12,000	10,000	4,000	2.50
3	23,000	10,000	13,000	6,000	2.17
4	24,000	8,500	15,500	8,000	1.94
5	25,000	7,000	18,000	10,000	1.80
6	26,000	6,000	20,000	12,000	1.67
7	27,000	5,200	21,800	14,000	1.56
8	28,000	4,500	23,500	16,000	1.47

An analysis of the effect which hours of usage will have on each of these costs will establish the time at which a machine should be replaced. The following example will illustrate a method of conducting an analysis to determine each of these costs.

Initial cost of equipment, $20,000
No. of hours used per yr, 2,000
Cost per hr to own and operate equipment, $6.00

Costs of depreciation and replacement When considering the replacement of equipment it is necessary to know the salvage value of the machine and the replacement cost of an equal machine. Because the average cost of construction equipment has been increasing at a rate of approximately 5 percent per year during the past 10 years, and it appears that this rate of increase will continue, it is necessary to reflect this increase in a depreciation and replacement analysis. The salvage value should be the actual amount that can be realized on a trade in for a replacement machine.

Table 3-4 includes the necessary information for this analysis. Note that the replacement cost is increased 5 percent per year to provide for increases in the cost of equipment.

Costs of investment Table 3-5 gives the cumulative costs per hour for this equipment. The investment is assumed to be 15 percent per year on the value of the equipment at the beginning of the year. The owner of equipment should use an interest rate which is appropriate to his operations.

Maintenance and repair costs Table 3-6 lists the costs of maintenance and repairs for the equipment and the calculated cost per cumulative hour. Because of the large variation in the cost of maintenance and repairs, depending on the conditions under which equipment is used, it is important to keep accurate records of these costs.

Table 3-5 Investment costs

Year	Investment, start of year	Depreciation	Investment, end of year	Investment cost	Cumulative investment cost	Cumulative use, hr	Cumulative cost per hr
1	$20,000	$5,000	$15,000	$3,000	$3,000	2,000	$1.50
2	15,000	3,000	12,000	2,250	5,250	4,000	1.32
3	12,000	2,000	10,000	1,800	7,050	6,000	1.18
4	10,000	1,500	8,500	1,500	8,550	8,000	1.07
5	8,500	1,500	7,000	1,275	9,825	10,000	0.98
6	7,000	1,000	6,000	1,050	10,875	12,000	0.91
7	6,000	800	5,200	900	11,775	14,000	0.84
8	5,200	700	4,500	780	12,555	16,000	0.79

Downtime costs Downtime is the time that a machine is not working because it is undergoing repairs or adjustments. Downtime tends to increase with usage. Availability is a term that indicates the portion of the time that a machine is in actual production or is available for production, expressed as a percent. For example, if a machine is down 5 percent of the time, its availability is 95 percent.

If a machine whose operating cost is $6.00 per hour has an average downtime of 5 percent, the cost per hour for this downtime will be 0.05 × $6.00 = $0.30. If the machine is used 2,000 hr per year, the annual cost will be 2,000 × $0.30 = $600. Table 3-7 shows the downtime and the cumulative cost per hour for this time.

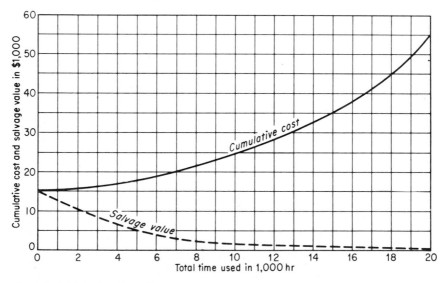

Figure 3-4 Cost of equipment.

Table 3-6 Maintenance and repair costs

Year	Annual cost	Cumulative cost	Cumulative use, hr	Cumulative cost per hr
1	$ 880	$ 800	2,000	$0.44
2	1,620	2,500	4,000	0.63
3	2,250	4,750	6,000	0.79
4	2,740	7,490	8,000	0.94
5	3,360	10,850	10,000	1.09
6	3,870	14,720	12,000	1.23
7	4,740	19,460	14,000	1.39
8	5,480	24,940	16,000	1.56

Productivity is a measure of the ability of equipment to produce at its original rate. If the productivity of a machine decreases with usage, the effect of this decrease is to increase the cost of production, which is equivalent to an increase in the cost per hour for continuing to use the equipment. For example, if the cumulative cost per hour in the seventh column of Table 3-7 is $0.68 and the productivity factor is 0.90, this decrease in productivity has the effect of increasing the cumulative cost per hour to $0.68 ÷ 0.90 = $0.76 per hour. The costs shown in the last column should be used for equipment whose productivity decreases with usage.

Obsolescence costs It has been the history of construction equipment that continuing improvements in the productive capacities have resulted in lower production costs. These improvements, whose advantages can be gained only by the replacement of older equipment with newer equipment, decrease the desirability of continuing to use the older equipment. For example, if a new machine will reduce production costs by 10 percent, when compared with production

Table 3-7 Downtime costs

Year	Down-time, %	Cost per hr	Down-time cost, yr	Cumulative down-time cost	Cumulative hours	Cumulative cost per hr	Productivity factor	Cumulative cost per hr
1	3	$0.18	$ 360	$ 360	2,000	$0.18	1.00	$0.18
2	6	0.36	720	1,080	4,000	0.27	0.99	0.27
3	8	0.48	960	2,040	6,000	0.34	0.98	0.35
4	10	0.60	1,200	3,240	8,000	0.41	0.96	0.42
5	12	0.72	1,440	4,680	10,000	0.47	0.96	0.49
6	14	0.84	1,680	6,360	12,000	0.53	0.94	0.56
7	17	1.02	2,040	8,400	14,000	0.60	0.92	0.65
8	20	1.20	2,400	10,800	16,000	0.68	0.90	0.76

Table 3-8 Obsolescence costs per hour for the life of the equipment

Year	Obso- lescence factor	Equipment cost per hr	Obsolescence cost per hr	Obsolescence cost per yr	Cumulative cost	Cumulative use, hr	Cumulative cost per hr
1	0	$6.00	$ 0	$ 0	$ 0	2,000	$0.00
2	0.05	6.00	0.30	600	600	4,000	0.15
3	0.10	6.00	0.60	1,200	1,800	6,000	0.30
4	0.15	6.00	0.90	1,800	3,600	8,000	0.45
5	0.20	6.00	1.20	2,400	6,000	10,000	0.60
6	0.25	6.00	1.50	3,000	9,000	12,000	0.75
7	0.30	6.00	1.80	3,600	12,600	14,000	0.90
8	0.35	6.00	2.10	4,200	16,800	16,000	1.15

costs for an existing machine, the existing machine will suffer a loss in value equal to 10 percent. This is defined as an obsolescence loss. Failure to take advantage of this potential reduction in production cost through the acquisition of new equipment will result in a higher than necessary production cost for the owner of old equipment.

During the past years productive improvements of construction equipment have averaged about 5 percent per year, and it appears that future improvements may continue at the same rate.

Table 3-8 illustrates the effect of obsolescence costs resulting from the continued use of equipment that might be replaced with newer equipment which is capable of producing at a lower cost.

Summary of costs Table 3-9 lists the five separate costs that should be considered in determining the desirability of replacing the machine.

Table 3-9 Summary of cumulative costs per hour

Item	Year							
	1	2	3	4	5	6	7	8
Depreciation and replacement	$3.00	$2.50	$2.17	$1.94	$1.80	$1.67	$1.56	$1.47
Investment	1.50	1.32	1.18	1.07	0.98	0.91	0.84	0.79
Maintenance and repairs	0.44	0.63	0.79	0.94	1.09	1.23	1.39	1.56
Downtime	0.18	0.27	0.35	0.42	0.49	0.56	0.65	0.76
Subtotal	5.12	4.72	4.49	4.37	4.36	4.37	4.44	4.58
Obsolescence	0.00	0.15	0.30	0.45	0.60	0.75	0.90	1.15
Total	5.12	4.87	4.79	4.82	4.96	5.12	5.34	5.73

Table 3-10 Losses resulting from improper equipment replacement
Excluding obsolescence losses

Replaced at end of year	Cumulative hours	Cumulative cost per hr	Minimum cost per hr	Extra cost per hr	Total loss
1	2,000	$5.12	$4.36	$0.76	$1,520
2	4,000	4.72	4.36	0.36	1,440
3	6,000	4.49	4.36	0.13	780
4	8,000	4.37	4.36	0.01	80
5	10,000	4.36	4.36	0.00	0
6	12,000	4.37	4.36	0.01	120
7	14,000	4.44	4.36	0.08	1,120
8	16,000	4.58	4.36	0.22	3,520

Because some, but not all, types of equipment experience obsolescence losses resulting from improvements in production, the table gives the summarized results in two sets of values. If obsolescence is not a factor in the descision to replace a machine, the most economic life is 4 years. However, if the replacement is delayed to the end of the fifth year, the additional cost is not significant.

If the machine is subject to a 5 percent obsolescence loss per year, it should be replaced at the end of the third year.

Table 3-10 lists the annual and cumulative losses resulting from replacing the equipment too early or too late with obsolescence losses excluded. Table 3-11 shows the same results with obsolescence losses included.

The extra cost per hour appearing in column 5 of Tables 3-10 and 3-11 is obtained by subtracting the cost in column 4 from the cost in column 3 for the given year, which latter costs are obtained from Table 3-9.

Table 3-11 Losses resulting from improper equipment replacement
Including obsolescence losses

Replaced at end of year	Cumulative hours	Cumulative cost per hr	Minimum cost per hr	Extra cost per hr	Total loss
1	2,000	$5.12	$4.79	$0.33	$ 660
2	4,000	4.87	4.79	0.08	320
3	6,000	4.79	4.79	0	0
4	8,000	4.82	4.79	0.03	240
5	10,000	4.96	4.79	0.17	1,700
6	12,000	5.12	4.79	0.33	3,960
7	14,000	5.34	4.79	0.55	7,700
8	16,000	5.73	4.79	0.94	15,040

Table 3-12 Downtime costs considering the cost of time lost by serviced equipment

Based on working 2,000 hr per yr

Year	Downtime, percent	Cost per hr	Downtime cost per yr	Cumulative Downtime cost	Cumulative Hours	Cumulative Cost per hr
1	3	$ 1.68	$ 3,360	$ 3,360	2,000	$1.68
2	6	3.36	6,720	10,080	4,000	2.52
3	8	4.48	8,960	19,040	6,000	3.17
4	10	5.60	11,200	30,240	8,000	3.78
5	12	6.72	13,440	43,680	10,000	4.37
6	14	7.84	15,680	59,360	12,000	4.93
7	17	9.52	19,040	78,400	14,000	5.60
8	20	11.20	22,400	100,800	16,000	6.30

Economic life of equipment that serves other equipment If a machine works alone, the method of determining its economic life illustrated in Tables 3-4 through 3-11 will apply. An example of this condition is a dragline excavating a drainage ditch, wasting the excavated earth in a spoil bank adjacent to the ditch. However, if this dragline is used to load trucks, a delay in production will idle the trucks, perhaps with the cost of the trucks and drivers continuing during the delay. For this condition the total cost of the delay is chargeable to the dragline. The effect of considering this cost is to increase the unit cost of production, and to reduce the economic life of the dragline when it is used as a service unit.

One method of alleviating this increasing cost per unit of production is to replace the older machine with one having a higher availability factor, and to assign the older machine to operations where it can work alone.

Another method of alleviating the increased costs is to maintain a high availability factor for the machine by adopting a good maintenance program and replacing worn parts prior to failure at the end of a shift or over a weekend, when the machine is not in use.

If a tractor-mounted front-end-loader, whose cost is $16.00 per hr, including the operator, is used to load four trucks, whose costs are $10.00 per hr each, including the drivers, the information appearing in Table 3-7 should be modified to reflect the higher total cost, namely $16.00 + (4 × $10.00) = $56.00 per hour. Table 3-12 shows the effect of combining the cost of the loader and the cost of the nonproductive time of the trucks resulting from the downtime of the loader. This is the proper method of determining the cost to a project when a primary unit of equipment, which serves other equipment, experiences a breakdown.

SOURCES OF CONSTRUCTION EQUIPMENT

Contractors and other users of construction equipment frequently are concerned with a decision as to whether to purchase or rent equipment. Under certain conditions it is financially advantageous to purchase, whereas under other conditions it is more economical and satisfactory to rent it. It is the purpose of this article to assist a user in determining which method is the more economical.

There are at least three methods under which a contractor may secure the use of construction equipment. He may

1. Purchase it
2. Rent it
3. Rent it with an option to purchase it at a later date

The method selected should be the one that will provide the use of the equipment at the lowest total cost, consistent with the use that the contractor will make of the equipment. Each method has both advantages and disadvantages which should be considered prior to making a decision. If cost is the only factor to be considered, an analysis of the cost under each method should give the answer. If other factors should be considered, they should be evaluated and applied to the cost as a basis on which to reach a decision. The correct decision for one contractor will not necessarily apply for another contractor. For example, a given contractor may engage in work that requires the use of wellpoint systems for most of his projects, while another may require the use of such a system only once every two or three years. It is probable that the former should purchase the equipment, while the latter should rent it. Thus, a contractor probably should purchase equipment that he will use frequently, and he should rent equipment that he will use only rarely.

The purchase of equipment, as compared with renting it, has several advantages, including the following:

1. It is more economical if the equipment is used sufficiently.
2. It is more likely to be available for use when needed.
3. Because ownership should assure better maintenance and care, purchased equipment should be kept in better mechanical condition.

Among the disadvantages of owning equipment are the following:

1. It may be more expensive than renting.
2. The purchase of equipment may require a substantial investment of money or credit that may be needed for other purposes.
3. The ownership of equipment may influence a contractor to continue using obsolete equipment after superior equipment has been introduced.
4. The ownership of equipment designed primarily for a given type of work may induce a contractor to continue doing that type of work, whereas other work requiring different types of equipment might be available at a higher profit.
5. The ownership of equipment might influence a contractor to continue using the equipment beyond its economical life, thereby increasing the cost of production unnecessarily.

Consider a crawler tractor equipped with a bulldozer blade, whose delivered cost is $30,500. It is assumed to have a useful life of 5 years, it will be used an estimated 2,000 hr per year, and it will have an estimated salvage value of $3,000. Using methods previously developed, the estimated hourly cost of owning and operating this tractor, excluding wages paid to the operator, are determined to be $7.92.

While there are no uniformly established rental rates for construction equipment, the Associated Equipment Distributors (P.O. Box 97724, Chicago, Illinois 60690,) publishes annually a booklet entitled *Nationally-Averaged Rental Rates for Construction Equipment*, which gives representative rates found to be in effect in the United States. For the specified bulldozer the rental rate would be $2,651 per month of 175 hr, or $15.15 per hour. Adding the estimated cost of minor maintenance and repairs, fuel, and lubrication, the total cost per hour, excluding the operator, would be $17.47.

If the bulldozer is used 2,000 hr per year, it is much cheaper to purchase than to rent it. However, if the equipment is used less than 2,000 hr per year, the hourly cost of owning it will vary inversely with the number of hours that it is used per year. While certain costs, such as maintenance and repairs, fuel, lubrication, and greasing, are related to the use of the equipment, other costs, including depreciation and investment, are pretty well independent of use.

An equation which should give the approximate number of hours of use per year, for which the cost of owning or renting the equipment will be the same, may be developed. Because of necessary assumptions and variations in operating conditions, this equation should not be expected to give results that are accurate to the hour, but it may be used as a guide. Let

P = the delivered cost of the new equipment

S = the estimated salvage value at the end of its useful life

N = number of years of useful life

p = ratio of the annual cost of maintenance and repairs divided by the annual cost of depreciation, based on using the equipment 2,000 hr per year

q = a factor equal to p when the equipment is used 2,000 hr per year, but less than p if the equipment is used less than 2,000 hr per year

i = sum of the annual cost of interest, insurance, taxes, and storage, expressed as a fraction of the average value of the equipment. It is assumed to be 13 percent = 0.13

Q = a factor to be multiplied by the original cost of equipment in order to determine its average value during its useful life, expressed as a fraction. Table 3-3 lists the values of this factor, which must be converted to fractions.

C = cost per month for renting equipment, excluding the costs of fuel, lubricating, greasing, and wages

$p/3$ = average cost per hour for maintenance and repairs for rented equipment, which must be paid by the renter

n = number of hours used per year for which the cost per hour for owning or renting the equipment will be the same

Use these terms and symbols to determine the annual cost of owning and operating equipment.

$$\text{Depreciation} = \frac{P - S}{N}$$

$$\text{Maintenance and repairs} = q\frac{P - S}{N}$$

$$\text{Investment} = iQP$$

The cost per hour will be

$$\text{Cost} = \frac{P - S}{Nn} + q\frac{P - S}{Nn} + \frac{iQP}{n} \tag{a}$$

The cost per hour for renting the equipment will be

$$\text{Rental only} = \frac{C}{175}$$

$$\text{Repairs} = \frac{1}{3}p\frac{P - S}{Nn}$$

The cost per hour will be

$$\text{Cost} = \frac{C}{175} + \frac{1}{3}p\frac{P - S}{Nn} \tag{b}$$

Equating Eqs. (*a*) and (*b*), we have

$$\frac{P - S}{Nn} + q\frac{P - S}{Nn} + \frac{iQP}{n} = \frac{C}{175} + \frac{1}{3}p\frac{P - S}{Nn}$$

Solving for *n* gives

$$n = \frac{525\left[P - S + q(P - S) + NiQP\right] - 175p(P - S)}{3NC} \tag{3-4}$$

For the bulldozer previously considered the following values will apply:

$$P - \$30,500$$
$$S = \$3,000$$
$$P - S = \$27,500$$
$$N = 5$$
$$p = 0.9$$
$$q = 0.2 - 0.000035n$$
$$i = 0.13$$
$$Q = 0.60$$
$$C = \$2,651$$

Substituting these values in Eq. (3-4) and solving for *n* we get

$$n = 600 \text{ hr}$$

Thus, for the given equipment and conditions, it will be more economical to rent equipment that will be used less than 600 hr per year and to purchase equipment that will be used more than 600 hr per year.

RENTING EQUIPMENT WITH AN OPTION TO PURCHASE

Under this plan one may rent equipment at the prevailing rate with a provision that he may purchase it at a later date if he wishes to do so. In the event he decides to purchase it, a specified portion of the rent that he has paid may be applied to the original purchase price of the equipment. The agreement may specify that 90 percent of the rent paid may be applied to the purchase.

The effect of this plan, neglecting interest, is to increase the purchase cost of the equipment by 10 percent of the amount that will have been paid in rent. However, because it is not necessary for the renter to pay interest, taxes, and insurance on the equipment that he is renting, the resulting savings in these costs will reduce the increase in the purchase cost.

Apply this plan to the bulldozer previously specified. If, after renting it for 8 months, the renter wishes to purchase it, the amounts involved will be as follows:

$$
\begin{aligned}
\text{Original cost} &= \$30,500 \\
\text{Rent paid, 8 months at \$2,651} &= \$21,208 \\
\text{Amount applied to the purchase, } 0.9 \times \$21,208 &= \underline{19,087} \\
\text{Balance due} &= \$11,413
\end{aligned}
$$

Thus, the renter can purchase the bulldozer, with 4 years and 4 months of useful life remaining, for less than one-half of its original cost. If he will need the unit, it should be purchased. Also, any salvage value that he may realize from the disposal of the unit will reduce his cost of buying and using it.

The cost per hour for buying and using it for 4 years and 4 months can be determined as follows:

$$
\begin{aligned}
\text{Additional cost} &= \$11,413 \\
\text{Estimated salvage value} &= \underline{3,000} \\
\text{Net depreciation} &= \$8,413
\end{aligned}
$$

Average value during useful life, from equation (3-2)

$$\overline{P} = \frac{P(n+1) + S(n-1)}{2n}$$

$$\overline{P} = \frac{\$11,413(4.33 + 1) + \$3,000(4.33 - 1)}{2n} = \$8,178$$

Annual cost:

$$
\begin{aligned}
\text{Depreciation, } \$8,413 \div 4.33 \text{ yr} &= \$1,945 \\
\text{Maintenance and repairs, same as calculated for new equip-} & \\
\text{ment, } 90\% \times \frac{\$30,500 - \$3,000}{5 \text{ yr}} &= 4,950 \\
\text{Investment, } 15\% \times \$8,178 &= \underline{1,227} \\
\text{Total annual or fixed cost} &= \$8,122
\end{aligned}
$$

Cost per hour:

Fixed cost, $8,122 ÷ 2,000 hr	=$ 4.06
Fuel, 5 gal @ $0.50	= 2.50
Lubricating oil and grease	= 1.25
Total cost per hour	=$ 7.81

Thus, a contractor who has paid rent on this unit for 8 months can now purchase it under conditions that will enable him to own and operate it during the balance of its useful life at a very favorable cost.

PROBLEMS

Note: Assume an investment cost equal to 15% per year for the average value of the equipment.

3-1 Using the straight-line method of depreciating equipment, determine the annual cost of depreciation for a tractor whose total initial cost is $46,580 if the assumed life is 5 years, with an estimated salvage value of $6,000.

3-2 Using the double-declining-balance method, determine the cost of depreciation each year for 5 years for the tractor of Prob. 3-1.

3-3 Using the sum-of-the-years-digits method, determine the cost of depreciation each year for 5 years for the tractor of Prob. 3-1. What is the book value of the tractor at the end of three years?

3-4 A power shovel whose total initial cost was $66,340 was assumed to have a useful life of 5 years, with a salvage value of $6,000. It has been depreciated by the double-declining-balance method for 4 years. What is its book value?

3-5 A power shovel whose total initial cost is $72,390 has an estimated useful life of 6 years, with an estimated salvage value of $6,000. Prepare a table listing the annual costs of depreciation and the book value at the end of each of the 6 years based on the straight-line, double-declining-balance, and sum-of-the-years-digits methods of computing the annual cost of depreciation.

3-6 Prepare a graph with curves showing the book values of the power shovel of Prob. 3-5 during the 6 years of its life.

3-7 Determine the average value of a unit of equipment whose total initial cost is $36,000, with an estimated salvage value of $4,000 after 6 years.

3-8 Determine the probable cost per hour for owning and operating a power shovel for the following conditions:

Engine, 180-hp diesel
Crankcase capacity, 5 gal
Time between oil changes, 100 hr
Operating factor, 0.50
Useful life, 5 yr
Hours used per yr, 2,000
Total initial cost, $92,480
Estimated salvage value after 5 yr, $8,000
Annual cost of maintenance and repairs equals 80% of annual depreciation
Cost of fuel, $0.50 per gal
Cost of lubricating oil, $1.60 per gal
Cost of other oils and grease, $0.20 per hr

3-9 Determine the probable cost per hour for owning and operating a wheel-type tractor-pulled scraper for the following conditions:

Engine, 240-hp diesel
Crankcase capacity, 6 gal
Time between oil changes, 80 hr
Operating factor, 0.60
Useful life, 5 yr
Hours used per year 2,000
Annual cost of maintenance and repairs, 75% of annual depreciation
Life of tires, 5,000 hr
Repairs to tires, 15% of the depreciation of tires
Total initial cost, $76,620
Cost of tires, $18,240
Estimated salvage value, $8,000
Cost of fuel, $0.50 per gal
Cost of lubricating oil, $1.60 per gal
Cost of other oils and grease, $0.25 per hr

3-10 Determine the probable cost per hour for owning and operating the tractor-pulled scraper of Prob. 3-9 if it will be used only 1,600 hr per year, with all other conditions remaining the same.

CHAPTER FOUR

ENGINEERING FUNDAMENTALS

GENERAL INFORMATION

In this chapter many problems related to excavating, hauling, and placing earth will be discussed. With the constantly growing volume of earthwork for dams, levees, highways, airports, and other projects the need for selecting the most suitable construction equipment is becoming increasingly important. Persons in the construction industry, including contractors and engineers, should understand the effects which the selection of equipment and methods has on the cost of handling earth. It is hoped that the analyses of problems related to earthwork will assist in demonstrating how effective the application of engineering can be in determining the cost of earthwork.

ROLLING RESISTANCE

Rolling resistance is a resistance which is encountered by a vehicle in moving over a road or surface. This resistance varies considerably with the type and condition of the surface over which a vehicle moves. Soft earth offers a higher resistance than hard-surfaced roads such as concrete pavement. For vehicles which move on rubber tires the rolling resistance varies with the size, pressure, and the tread design of the tires. For equipment which moves on crawler tracks, such as tractors, the resistance varies primarily with the type and condition of the road surface. If a truck is driven off a hard-surfaced highway into a field of soft earth, the resistance to moving is increased materially, as all drivers know. If a loaded wheelbarrow has a well-inflated pneumatic tire, it is much more easily pushed along a concrete sidewalk than when the tire is semideflated or soft. The difference is due to changes in the rolling resistance. A narrow-tread high-pressure tire gives lower rolling resistance than a broad-tread low-pressure tire on a hard-surfaced road. This is the result of the smaller area of contact between the tire and the road surface. However, if the road surface is soft and the tire tends to sink into the earth, a broad-tread low-pressure tire will offer a lower rolling resistance than a narrow-tread high-pressure tire. The reason for this condition is that the narrow tire sinks into the earth more deeply than the broad tire and thus is always having to climb out of a deeper hole, which is equivalent to climbing a steeper grade. As explained later in this book, the type and size tires selected for earth-hauling equipment should be determined after the condition of the haul road is known.

The rolling resistance of an earth-haul road probably will not remain constant under varying climatic conditions or for varying types of soil which exist along the road. If the earth is stable, highly compacted, and well maintained with a grader, and if the moisture content is kept near the optimum, it is possible to provide a surface with a rolling resistance about as low as for concrete and asphalt. It is possible to add moisture, but following an extended period of rain it may be difficult to remove the excess moisture, and the haul road will become muddy, with an increase in rolling resistance. Providing good surface drainage will speed the removal of the water and should permit the road to be reconditioned more quickly. For a major earth project it is good economy to provide a patrol grader, sprinkler trucks, and probably rollers to keep the haul

Table 4-1 Representative rolling resistances for various types of wheels and surfaces

In pounds per 2,000 lb-ton or kilograms per metric ton of gross load

Type of surface	Steel tires, plain bearings	Crawler-type track and wheel	Rubber tires, anti-friction bearings	
			High pressure	Low pressure
Smooth concrete	40	55	35	45
	(20)	(27)	(18)	(23)
Good asphalt	50–70	60–70	40–65	50–60
	(25–35)	(30–35)	(20–33)	(25–30)
Earth, compacted and maintained	60–100	60–80	40–70	50–70
	(30–50)	(30–40)	(20–35)	(25–35)
Earth, poorly maintained	100–150	80–110	100–140	70–100
	(50–75)	(40–55)	(50–70)	(35–50)
Earth, rutted, muddy, no	200–250	140–180	180–220	150–200
	(100–125)	(70–90)	(90–110)	(75–100)
maintenance	280–320	160–200	260–290	220–260
Loose sand and gravel	(140–160)	(80–100)	(130–145)	(110–130)
Earth, very muddy, rutted, soft	350–400	200–240	300–400	280–340
	(175–200)	(100–120)	(150–200)	(140–170)

road in good condition. As illustrated under the subject of trucks, the maintenance of low rolling resistance is one of the best financial investments an
earth-moving contractor can make.

Although it is impossible to give completely accurate values for the rolling
resistances for all types of haul roads and wheels, the values given in Table 4-1
are reasonably accurate and may be used for estimating purposes. Rolling
resistance is expressed in pounds of tractive pull required to move each gross ton
over a level surface of the specified type or condition. For example, if a loaded
truck having a gross weight equal to 20 tons is moving over a level road whose
rolling resistance is 100 lb per ton, the tractive effort required to keep the truck
moving at a uniform speed will be

20 tons × 100 lb per ton = 2,000 lb

If it is desirable to determine the rolling resistance of a haul road, this can
be done by towing a truck or other vehicle whose gross weight is known along a
level section of the haul road at a uniform speed. The tow cable should be
equipped with a dynamometer or some other device which will permit the
average tension in the cable to be determined. This tension is the total rolling
resistance of the gross weight of the truck. The rolling resistance in pounds per
gross ton will be

$$R = \frac{P}{W} \tag{4-1}$$

where R = rolling resistance, lb per ton
$\quad\;\; P$ = total tension in tow cable, lb
$\quad\;\; W$ = gross weight of truck, tons

If it is necessary to tow the loaded truck up or down a sloping haul road, an
appropriate correction for the effect of the slope may be applied to the tension
in the tow cable, as explained in the following article. In order to apply a
correction it is necessary to know the grade of the haul road over which the test
is being conducted.

THE EFFECT OF GRADE ON REQUIRED TRACTIVE EFFORT

When a vehicle moves up a sloping road, the total tractive effort required to
keep the vehicle moving is increased approximately in proportion to the slope of
the road. If a vehicle moves down a sloping road, the total tractive effort
required to keep the vehicle moving is reduced in proportion to the slope of the
road. The most common method of expressing a slope is by percent. A 1 percent
slope is one where the surface rises or drops 1 ft vertically in a horizontal
distance of 100 ft. If the slope is 5 percent, the surface rises or drops 5 ft per 100
ft of horizontal distance. If the surface rises, the slope is defined as plus, while if
it drops, the slope is defined as minus. All automobile drivers know that a plus
slope retards, while a minus slope aids, an automobile traveling along a highway.
The same forces apply to construction equipment moving over a road. This is a

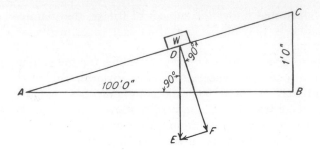

Figure 4-1 The effect of grade on the performance of a tractor or truck.

physical property which is not affected by the type of equipment or the condition or type of the road.

The effect of grade is to increase, for a plus slope, or decrease, for a minus slope, the required tractive effort by 20 lb per gross ton of weight for each 1 percent of grade. While this amount is not strictly correct for all slopes, it is sufficiently accurate for most construction projects.

Figure 4-1 illustrates the method of determining the effect of grade on tractive effort. The line AB is horizontal. The slope of AC is 1 percent. DE is perpendicular to AB. DF is perpendicular to AC. EF is parallel to AC. Triangle DEF is similar to triangle ABC. For practical purposes the length of AC is 100 ft. W is a 1-ton weight, represented by the vector DE. P is the component of W parallel to AC.

From the similarity of triangles,

$$\frac{EF}{ED} = \frac{P}{W} = \frac{BC}{AC} \qquad \text{or} \qquad P = W\frac{BC}{AC} = 2{,}000 \text{ lb} \times \frac{1}{100} = 20 \text{ lb}$$

If BC is increased to 2 ft,

$$P = 2{,}000 \text{ lb} \times 2/100 = 40 \text{ lb}$$

For any given slope the approximate value of P in pounds per ton is

$$P = 2{,}000 \text{ lb} \times \frac{\% \text{ slope}}{100} = 20 \text{ lb} \times \% \text{ slope}$$

Example Consider the effect of grade on the total tractive effort of a truck whose gross weight is 20 tons. The truck will be driven up a road whose slope is 5 percent. The additional tractive effort resulting from the slope is

$$P = 20 \text{ tons} \times 20 \text{ lb per ton} \times 5\% = 2{,}000 \text{ lb}$$

Thus, the truck engine must continually deliver to the driving wheels 2,000 lb of rimpull to overcome the effect of the slope. If the truck is moving down the same slope, the effect of the grade will be to help the engine and truck, which is equivalent to adding 2,000 lb to the rimpull of the truck.

If a tractor is towing a load, the combined gross weights of the tractor and its towed load should be used in determining the effect of the gráde.

Table 4-2 The effect of grade on the tractive effort of vehicles
In pounds per ton or kilograms per metric ton of gross weight

Slope, %	Lb per ton	Kg per m ton	Slope, %	Lb per ton	Kg per m ton
1	20.0	10.0	12	238.4	119.2
2	40.0	20.0	13	257.8	128.9
3	60.0	30.0	14	277.4	138.7
4	80.0	40.0	15	296.6	148.3
5	100.0	50.0	20	392.3	196.1
6	119.8	59.9	25	485.2	242.6
7	139.8	69.9	30	574.7	287.3
8	159.2	79.6	35	660.6	330.3
9	179.2	89.6	40	742.8	371.4
10	199.0	99.5	45	820.8	410.4
11	218.0	109.0	50	894.4	447.2

Table 4-2 gives values for the effect of slope, expressed in pounds per gross ton or kilograms per metric ton of weight of the vehicle.

THE EFFECT OF GRADE IN LOCATING A BORROW PIT

Sometimes engineers and contractors do not give sufficient consideration to the grade or slope of the haul road in locating borrow pits. It is desirable, when possible, to locate a borrow pit at a higher elevation than the fill, in order that the slope down the haul road may help the loaded trucks or other hauling equipment by permitting them to carry larger loads or to travel at higher speeds. Since the vehicles will be empty when returning up the haul road from the fill to the borrow pit, the effect of the grade will be considerably less. This item is discussed in detail in Chap. 9, on trucks and wagons (see pages 274 to 277).

COEFFICIENT OF TRACTION

The total energy of an engine in any unit of equipment designed primarily for pulling a load can be converted into tractive effort only if sufficient traction can be developed between the driving wheels or tracks and the haul surface. If there is not sufficient traction, the full power of the engine cannot be used. The wheels or tracks will slip on the surface. Thus, the coefficient of traction between rubber tires or crawler tracks and different haul surfaces is of importance to the operators of hauling units.

The coefficient of traction may be defined as the factor by which the total load on a driving tire or track should be multiplied in order to determine the maximum possible tractive force between the tire or track and the surface just before slipping will occur. For example, the driving tires of a truck rest on a

Table 4-3 Coefficients of traction for various road surfaces

Surface	Rubber tires	Crawler tracks
Dry, rough concrete	0.80–1.00	0.45
Dry clay loam	0.50–0.70	0.90
Wet clay loam	0.40–0.50	0.70
Wet sand and gravel	0.30–0.40	0.35
Loose, dry sand	0.20–0.30	0.30
Dry snow	0.20	0.15–0.35
Ice	0.10	0.10–0.25

level haul road of dry clay. The total pressure between the tires and the road surface is 8,000 lb. In testing the tires for slippage by applying a driving force to the wheels, it is found that slippage will occur when the tractive force between the tires and the surface is 4,800 lb. The coefficient of traction is 4,800 ÷ 8,000 = 0.60.

The coefficient of traction between rubber tires and road surfaces will vary with the type of tread on the tires and with the road surface. For crawler tracks it will vary with the design of the grouser and the road surface. These variations are such that exact values cannot be given. Table 4-3 gives approximate values for the coefficient of traction between rubber tires or crawler tracks and road surfaces which are sufficiently accurate for most estimating purposes.

> **Example** Assume that a rubber-tired tractor has a total weight of 18,000 lb on the two driving tires. The maximum rimpull in low gear is 9,000 lb. If the tractor is operating in wet sand, with a coefficient of traction of 0.30, the maximum possible rimpull prior to slippage of the tires will be 0.30 × 18,000 lb = 5,400 lb. Regardless of the power of the engine, not more than 5,400 lb of tractive effort may be used because of the slippage of the wheels. If the same tractor is operating on dry clay, with a coefficient of traction of 0.60, the maximum possible rimpull prior to slippage of the tires will be 0.60 × 18,000 lb = 10,800 lb. For this surface the engine will not be able to cause the tires to slip. Thus, the full power of the engine may be used.

THE EFFECT OF ALTITUDE ON THE PERFORMANCE OF INTERNAL–COMBUSTION ENGINES

An internal-combustion engine operates by combining oxygen from the air with the fuel and then burning the mixture to convert latent energy into mechanical energy. The power of an engine is a measure of the rate at which it can produce energy from fuel. For each charge of fuel and air into a cylinder there must be a correct ratio between the quantity of fuel and air if the maximum efficiency and power are to be obtained from the engine. The ratio between the quantities should be that which will provide just enough oxygen to supply the requirements of the fuel for complete combustion. If the density of the air is reduced because of altitude, the quantity of oxygen in a given volume of air will be less than for the same volume of air at sea level. As each cylinder of an engine draws in a given volume of air prior to the firing stroke, there will be less oxygen in the cylinder if the density of the air is reduced. Since the ratio of the oxygen and fuel should remain constant, it will be necessary to reduce the quantity of fuel supplied to an engine at high altitudes. This is usually done by adjusting the carburetor. The effect on the engine is to reduce the power. A human being experiences the same effect when he engages in physical work at a high altitude. Although he breathes the same volume of air, he may not get enough oxygen to supply his requirements.

If the density of the air decreased uniformly with the altitude, it would be possible to express the loss in power of an engine due to altitude by means of a simple formula with a high degree of accuracy. Actually this is not true.

For most practical purposes it is sufficiently accurate to assume that for four-cycle gasoline and diesel engines the loss in power due to altitude will be equal to approximately 3 percent of the sea-level horsepower for each 1,000 ft above the first 1,000 ft. Thus, for a four-cycle engine with 100 belt hp at sea level, the power at 10,000 ft above sea level would be determined as follows:

$$\text{Sea-level power} = 100 \text{ hp}$$

$$\text{Loss due to altitude,} \quad \frac{0.03 \times 100 \times (10{,}000 - 1{,}000)}{1{,}000} = 27 \text{ hp}$$

$$\text{Effective power} = 73 \text{ hp}$$

For the two-cycle engine, which is becoming increasingly more popular in the diesel field, the loss in power due to altitude is approximately 1 percent of the sea-level horsepower for each 1,000 ft above the first 1,000 ft. This type engine has its air supplied, under a slight pressure, by a blower, whereas the four-cycle engine depends on the suction of the pistons for the supply of air. If the engine described in the previous paragraph is a two-cycle, the power at 10,000 ft above sea level would be determined as follows:

$$\text{Sea-level power} = 100 \text{ hp}$$

$$\text{Loss due to altitude,} \quad \frac{0.01 \times 100 \times (10{,}000 - 1{,}000)}{1{,}000} = 9 \text{ hp}$$

$$\text{Effective power} = 91 \text{ hp}$$

The two previous problems indicate that, other factors being equal, at high altitude a two-cycle engine will give better performance than a four-cycle engine.

The effect of the loss in power due to altitude may be eliminated by the installation of a supercharger. This is a mechanical unit which will increase the pressure of the air supplied to the engine, thus permitting sea-level performance at any altitude. If equipment is to be used at high altitudes for long periods of time, the increased performance probably will more than pay for the installed cost of a supercharger.

A contractor who has established production rates for his equipment at or near sea level will make a serious mistake if he uses those production rates in bidding a job to be constructed at a high altitude. He must install superchargers or apply a correction factor, as more fully explained hereafter under the subjects of trucks and tractors.

THE EFFECT OF TEMPERATURE ON THE PERFORMANCE OF INTERNAL–COMBUSTION ENGINES

Many persons who have driven an automobile through a desert during a hot afternoon have noticed that the performance of the automobile seems sluggish. If driving was continued into the night after the temperature had decreased appreciably, the performance of the engine seemed to improve noticeably. This experience was not imaginary. An internal-combustion engine will develop a higher horsepower at a low air temperature than at a high temperature. The effect of temperature on the performance of an internal-combustion engine has been determined from laboratory tests. The next section discusses the combined effect of pressure and temperature on the performance of internal-combustion engines.

THE COMBINED EFFECT OF PRESSURE AND TEMPERATURE ON THE PERFORMANCE OF INTERNAL–COMBUSTION ENGINES

When an internal-combustion engine is tested to determine its power, it is necessary to conduct the tests under standard conditions in order that the results may be significant. Standard conditions mean a temperature of 60°F and average sea-level barometric pressure, equivalent to 29.92 in. of mercury (in Hg). As the power of the engine usually is determined with a brake or a dynamometer, the result is expressed as the brake horsepower (bhp) of the engine or as flywheel horsepower (fwhp).

If a test must be conducted under other than standard conditions, the horsepower may be determined by using the formula

$$H_c = H_o \frac{P_s}{P_o} \sqrt{\frac{T_o}{T_s}} \tag{4-2}$$

where H_c = corrected bhp for standard conditions
H_o = observed bhp, as determined from tests
P_s = standard barometric pressure, 29.92 in. Hg
P_o = observed barometric pressure, in. Hg, at time of test
T_o = absolute temperature, °F, equal to 460 + observed temperature
T_s = absolute temperature for standard conditions, equal to 460 + 60 = 520°F

**Table 4-4 Average barometric pressures
for various altitudes above sea level,**
In inches of mercury

Altitude above sea level, ft	Barometric pressure in. Hg
0	29.92
1,000	28.86
2,000	27.82
3,000	26.80
4,000	25.82
5,000	24.87
6,000	23.95
7,000	23.07
8,000	22.21
9,000	21.36
10,000	20.55

Example A gasoline engine was tested under the given conditions and was found to develop the indicated horsepower. It is desired to convert the results to bhp for standard conditions.

Observed hp, 86.43
Observed pressure, 29.52 in. Hg
Observed temperature, 42°F

Substituting these values in formula (4-2), we get

$$H_c = 86.43 \times \frac{29.92}{29.52} \sqrt{\frac{460 + 42}{520}} = 86.07 \text{ hp}$$

Thus, this engine should develop 86.07 bhp if tested under standard conditions.

Formula (4-2) may be used to determine the probable effective horsepower of a four-cycle engine at any temperature and altitude. From Table 4-4 determine the probable barometric pressure for the given altitude. Estimate the probable temperature. Apply this information to formula (4-2), and solve for the effective horsepower.

Example A tractor is operated by a four-cycle diesel engine. When tested under standard conditions, the engine developed 130 fwhp. What is the probable horsepower at an altitude of 3,660 ft, where the average daily temperature is 72°F?
    The information for use in formula (4-2) will be as follows:

$H_c = 130$
$P_s = 29.92$ in.
$P_o = 26.14$ in. (from Table 4-4)
$T_s = 520°F$
$T_o = 460 + 72 = 532°F$

Table 4-5 Correction factors for determining the effective horsepower of four-cycle engines
For various altitudes and temperatures

Altitude above sea level, ft	Temperatures, °F								
	110	90	70	60	50	40	20	0	−20
0	0.954	0.971	0.991	1.000	1.008	1.018	1.039	1.062	1.085
1,000	0.920	0.937	0.955	0.964	0.974	0.984	1.003	1.025	1.048
2,000	0.887	0.904	0.921	0.930	0.938	0.948	0.968	0.988	1.010
3,000	0.855	0.872	0.888	0.896	0.905	0.914	0.933	0.952	0.974
4,000	0.825	0.840	0.856	0.865	0.873	0.882	0.899	0.918	0.938
5,000	0.795	0.809	0.825	0.833	0.842	0.849	0.867	0.885	0.904
6,000	0.767	0.781	0.795	0.803	0.811	0.820	0.836	0.853	0.872
7,000	0.738	0.752	0.767	0.775	0.782	0.790	0.806	0.823	0.840
8,000	0.712	0.725	0.739	0.746	0.754	0.762	0.776	0.793	0.811
9,000	0.686	0.699	0.713	0.720	0.727	0.734	0.748	0.764	0.782
10,000	0.682	0.675	0.687	0.693	0.707	0.707	0.722	0.737	0.753

Find H_o.

Rewriting formula (4-2) and substituting the given information, we get

$$H_o = H_c \frac{P_o}{P_s} \sqrt{\frac{T_s}{T_o}}$$

$$= 130 \times \frac{26.14}{29.92} \sqrt{\frac{520}{532}} = 112.7 \text{ hp}$$

Thus the probable horsepower of the engine will be reduced to 112.7 as a result of the increased altitude and temperature.

Table 4-5 gives factors by which the horsepower of a four-cycle engine, as determined under standard conditions, may be multiplied to obtain the probable horsepower for various altitudes and temperatures. Owing to variations in the barometric pressure at any altitude as the result of changes in climatic conditions, the factors may vary slightly with climatic conditions.

The two-cycle diesel engine operates under different conditions from those which apply to a four-cycle engine. Therefore, the correction factors given in Table 4-5 will not apply to two-cycle engines. If similar information is desired, it should be requested from the manufacturer.

DRAWBAR PULL

The available pull which a crawler tractor can exert on a load that is being towed is referred to as the drawbar pull of the tractor. The pull is expressed in pounds. From the total pulling effort of an engine there must be deducted the pull required to move the tractor over a level haul road before the drawbar pull can be determined. If a crawler tractor tows a load up a slope, its drawbar pull will be reduced by 20 lb for each ton of weight of the tractor for each 1 percent slope.

The performance of crawler tractors, as reported in the specifications supplied by the manufacturer, is usually based on the Nebraska tests. In testing a tractor to determine its maximum drawbar pull at each of the available speeds, the haul road is calculated to have a rolling resistance of 110 lb per ton. If a tractor is used on a haul road whose rolling resistance is higher or lower than 110 lb per ton, the drawbar pull will be reduced or increased, respectively, by an amount equal to the weight of the tractor in tons multiplied by the variation of the haul road from 110 lb per ton.

Example A tractor whose weight is 15 tons has a drawbar pull of 5,684 lb in sixth gear when operated on a level road having a rolling resistance of 110 lb per ton. If the tractor is operated on a level road having a rolling resistance of 180 lb per ton, the drawbar pull will be reduced by 15 tons $\times$ (180 − 110) = 1,050 lb. Thus, the effective drawbar pull will be 5,684 − 1,050 = 4,634 lb.

The drawbar pull of a crawler tractor will vary indirectly with the speed of each gear. It is highest in the first gear and lowest in the top gear. The specifications supplied by the manufacturer should give the maximum speed and drawbar pull for each of the several gears. The following is an example:

Gear	Speed, mph	Drawbar pull, lb
1st	1.72	28,019
2d	2.18	22,699
3d	2.76	17,265
4th	3.50	13,769
5th	4.36	10,074
6th	7.00	5,579

RIMPULL

Rimpull is a term which is used to designate the tractive force between the rubber tires of driving wheels and the surface on which they travel. If the coefficient of traction is high enough to eliminate tire slippage, the maximum rimpull is a function of the power of the engine and the gear ratios between the engine and the driving wheels. If the driving wheels slip on the haul surface, the maximum effective rimpull will be equal to the total pressure between the tires and the surface multiplied by the coefficient of traction. Rimpull is expressed in pounds.

If the rimpull of a vehicle is not known, it may be determined from the formula

$$\text{Rimpull} = \frac{375 \times \text{hp} \times \text{efficiency}}{\text{speed, mph}} \quad \text{lb} \tag{4-3}$$

The efficiency of most tractors and trucks will range from 80 to 85 percent. For a rubber-tired tractor with a 140-hp engine and a maximum speed of 3.25 mph in first gear, the rimpull will be

$$\text{Rimpull} = \frac{375 \times 140 \times 0.85}{3.25} = 13,730 \text{ lb}$$

The maximum rimpull in all gear ranges for this tractor will be as follows:

Gear	Speed, mph	Rimpull, lb
1st	3.25	13,730
2d	7.10	6,285
3d	12.48	3,576
4th	21.54	2,072
5th	33.86	1,319

In computing the pull which a tractor can exert on a towed load, it is necessary to deduct from the rimpull of the tractor the tractive force required to overcome the rolling resistance plus any grade resistance for the tractor. It will be noted that the rubber-tired tractor differs from the crawler tractor in this respect. For example, if a tractor whose maximum rimpull in the first gear is 13,730 lb weighs 12.4 tons and is operated up a haul road with a slope of 2 percent and a rolling resistance of 100 lb per ton, the pull available for towing a load will be determined as follows:

Max rimpull $\qquad\qquad\qquad\qquad\qquad$ = 13,730 lb
Pull required to overcome grade,

$\qquad$ 12.4 × 20 × 2 = 496 lb
Pull required to overcome rolling resistance,

$\qquad$ 12.4 × 100 = 1,240 lb
Total pull to be deducted $\qquad\qquad$ = $\underline{\text{1,736 lb}}$
Pull available for towing a load $\qquad$ = 11,994 lb

ACCELERATION

Acceleration is the increasing of the speed of a moving vehicle by the application of surplus power from the engine, that is, power which is not required to keep the vehicle moving at a uniform speed. The rate of acceleration depends on the weight of the vehicle and the surplus rimpull that is available for accelerat-

Table 4-6 Approximate rate of accelerating a 1-ton weight

Accelerating rimpull, lb	Acceleration, mph per min
5	3.3
10	6.6
20	13.2
30	19.8
50	33.0
100	66.0
200	132.0
300	198.0

ing. Unless surplus rimpull is available, the speed of the vehicle cannot be increased.

Although it is impossible to analyze a hauling unit to determine the exact rates of acceleration for given conditions, it is possible to obtain results which are sufficiently accurate for most estimating purposes. Such an analysis is based on Newton's second law of motion. The basic law is expressed by the formula

$$F = \frac{W}{g} a \tag{4-4}$$

where $F =$ an accelerating force, lb
   $W =$ weight to be accelerated, lb
   $g =$ acceleration of gravity, 32.2 ft per sec per sec
   $a =$ acceleration of weight W, ft per sec per sec

Assume that a force of 10 lb is available to accelerate a weight of 1 ton, 2,000 lb. If this information is inserted in formula (4-4) and the formula is rewritten, we get

$$a = \frac{Fg}{W} = \frac{10 \times 32.2}{2,000} = 0.161 \text{ ft per sec per sec}$$

Expressed in words this means that for each second of elapsed time that the 10-lb force is applied the weight will undergo an increase in velocity of 0.161 fps. This is equivalent to an increase in speed of 0.11 mph per sec. In 1 min the speed will be increased by $60 \times 0.11 = 6.6$ mph. If the force is increased from 10 to 20 lb, the rate of acceleration will be increased to 13.2 mph per min.

Table 4-6 gives approximate rates of accelerating a 1-ton weight, in mph per minute, for various accelerating rimpulls. In the table the accelerating rimpull is expressed in pounds, and the weight remains constant at 1 ton.

Example A practical application may be made to a loaded truck. Assume that the truck and its load weigh 40,850 lb and that the truck has a 125-hp engine. The maximum speed in first gear is 3.0 mph. For this speed the rimpull is obtained from formula (4-3), using an assumed efficiency of 81 percent.

$$\text{Rimpull} = \frac{375 \times 125 \times 0.81}{3.0} = 12,620 \text{ lb}$$

The maximum speeds and rimpulls for various gears are as follows:

Gear	Maximum speed, mph	Rimpull, lb
1st	3.0	12,620
2d	5.2	7,275
3d	9.2	4,120
4th	16.8	2,250
5th	27.7	1,365

The haul road is level, with a rolling resistance of 60 lb per ton.

It is desired to determine the approximate total time required to bring the truck from a stationary position to the top speed in fifth gear. It is assumed that the rimpull in excess of that required to overcome rolling resistance will be available to accelerate the truck. Wind resistance will be neglected, which may be a factor in some cases. The weight of the loaded truck is $40,850/2,000 = 20.425$ tons. The rimpull required to overcome rolling resistance is $20.425 \times 60 = 1,225$ lb. This rimpull must be deducted from the maximum rimpull of the truck in each gear in order to obtain the rimpull available for accelerating the truck.

The maximum rimpulls available for accelerating the truck are approximately those given below. In actual operation the available rimpulls will probably be less than the amounts given when a truck goes into any gear because of the reduction in power of an engine at a reduced speed. If the truck is equipped with a torque converter instead of just gears and a clutch, it is more probable that the rimpulls will be available throughout the accelerating ranges.

Gear	Maximum accelerating rimpull, lb
1st	11,395
2d	6,050
3d	2,895
4th	1,025
5th	140

In actual operation of the truck the maximum accelerating rimpulls will probably not be available, especially in the lower gears, because of the reluctance of the driver to apply the full power of the engine, and also because of higher mechanical losses in the lower gears. Therefore, the first three values should be modified downward, and perhaps the other two should be reduced somewhat, according to the judgment and experience of the job planner.

The time required to bring the speed of the truck up to 3.0 mph in first gear would be determined as follows:

$$\text{Maximum accelerating rimpull per ton} = \frac{11,395}{20.425} = 557 \text{ lb}$$

If this rimpull is reduced to an effective value of 300 lb per ton, it will produce an acceleration of 198 mph in 1 min. The time required to produce an acceleration to 3.0 mph will be $3.0/198 = 0.015$ min. When the shift is made to second gear, the speed should be 3.0 mph. It is to be increased to 5.2 mph, for a gain of 2.2 mph. The time required to increase the speed from 3.0 to 5.2 mph would be determined as follows:

$$\text{Maximum accelerating rimpull per ton} = \frac{6,050}{20.425} = 296 \text{ lb}$$

Table 4-7 Approximate time required to accelerate a truck

Gear	Top speed, mph	Required accelera- tion, mph	Accelerating rimpull, lb per ton		Accelera- tion, mph per min	Time to accelerate to top speed, min
			Maximum	Effective		
1st	3.0	3.0	557	300	198	0.015
2d	5.2	2.2	296	200	132	0.017
3d	9.2	4.0	141	100	66	0.061
4th	16.8	7.6	50	40	26.4	0.288
5th	27.7	10.9	7	6	4.0	2.725

Total time, no allowance for shifting gears. 3.106
Add for five gear shifts @ 4 sec each 0.333
Total elapsed time. 3.439

If this rimpull is reduced to an effective value of 200 lb per ton, it will produce an acceleration of 132 mph in 1 min. The time required to produce an acceleration of 2.2 mph will be

$$\frac{2.2}{132} = 0.017 \text{ min}$$

In a similar manner the time required to accelerate to top speed in each of the other three gears can be determined. The results are given in Table 4-7. The total time given in Table 4-7 must be increased by the total time required to shift gears. If time is started when the shift is made into first gear, there will be five shifts. It should be possible to make a shift in 4 sec without undue rushing.

The time given in Table 4-7 may be used as a guide, but it should be modified by the judgment of the job planner. For example, if the rolling resistance of the haul road is reduced to 50 lb per ton, the maximum accelerating rimpull in fifth gear will be increased to 16.8 lb per ton. If the effective rimpull is assumed to be 14 lb per ton, the acceleration will be increased to 9.25 mph in 1 min. The time required to increase the speed from 16.8 to 27.7 mph will be reduced from 2.725 min to

$$\frac{10.9}{9.25} = 1.18 \text{ min}$$

If the rolling resistance of the haul road is increased to 70 lb per ton, the truck will not be able to attain top speed in fifth gear. From this example, it may be seen that the rolling resistance of a haul road is especially effective on the performance of a loaded vehicle in its top gear.

PROBLEMS

4-1 A four-wheel tractor whose operating weight is 42,469 lb is pulled up a road whose slope is +3 percent at a uniform speed. If the average tension in the towing cable is 3,680 lb, what is the rolling resistance of the road?

4-2 Consider a wheel-type tractor-pulled scraper whose gross weight is 116,270 lb, including the tractor, scraper, and its load. What is the equivalent gain in horsepower resulting from hauling this vehicle down a 4 percent slope instead of up the same slope at a speed of 15 mph? (Note: 1 hp equals 33,000 ft-lb of work per minute.)

4-3 A wheel-type tractor-pulled scraper having a combined loaded weight of 146,000 lb is push loaded down an 8 percent slope by a crawler tractor whose weight is 58,460 lb. What is the equivalent gain in loading force for the scraper and the tractor resulting from loading the scraper downslope?

4-4 A tractor has a 300 hp engine under standard conditions. What is the power of the engine when it is operating at an altitude of 9,000 ft above sea level and at a temperature of 80°F?

4-5 A four-cycle gasoline engine was tested under the given conditions and was found to develop the indicated horsepower. Determine the horsepower for standard conditions.

      Observed hp, 98.64
      Observed temperature, 70°F
      Observed atmospheric pressure, 23.52 in. Hg

4-6 A wheel-type tractor with a 180-hp engine has a maximum speed of 4.35 mph in first gear. Determine the maximum rimpull of this tractor in each of the indicated gears if the efficiency is 80 percent.

Gear	Speed, mph
1st	4.35
2d	7.60
3d	12.40
4th	18.30
5th	28.55

4-7 If the tractor of Prob. 4-6 weighs 18.2 tons and is operated over a haul road whose slope is +3 percent with a rolling resistance of 70 lb per ton, determine the maximum external pull of the tractor in each of the five gears.

4-8 If the tractor of Prob. 4-6 and 4-7 is operated down a 3 percent slope whose rolling resistance is 70 lb per ton, determine the maximum external pull of the tractor in each of the five gears.

CHAPTER FIVE

SOIL STABILIZATION AND COMPACTION

INTRODUCTION

Soils are used extensively in and with many types of construction; they are used to support structures, to support pavements for highways and airports, and as dams and levees to resist the passage of water. Some soils may be suitable for use in their natural state, while others must be excavated, processed, and compacted in order to serve their purposes.

A knowledge of the properties, characteristics, and behavior of soils is highly important to those persons who are associated with the design or construction of projects involving the use of soils. A great deal of useful knowledge related to the properties and characteristics of soils has been developed by Mr. R. R. Proctor since he initiated a scientific study to determine the density-moisture relationship of soils in 1933. His original methods or modifications thereof are now used in specifying the methods of processing soils used for construction purposes.

GLOSSARY OF TERMS

The following glossary is used to define the terms that are used with soils.

AASHTO   American Association of State Highway and Transportation Officials.

Aggregate, coarse   Crushed rock or gravel.

Aggregate, fine   Sand or fine crushed stone used for filling voids in coarse aggregate.

Backfill Material used in refilling a cut or other excavation.

Bank A mass of soil rising above an average level, or any soil which is dug from its original position.

Bank measure A measure of the volume of earth in its natural position before it is excavated.

Base The layer of material in a roadway or airport runway section on which the pavement is placed.

Binder Fine aggregate or other materials which fill voids and hold coarse aggregate together.

Borrow pit An excavation from which fill material is excavated.

Clay A soil composed of particles less than $\frac{1}{256}$ mm in size.

Cohesion The quality of some soil particles to be attracted to like particles, manifested in a tendency to stick together, as in clay.

Cohesive materials A soil having properties of cohesion.

Compacted volume A measurement of the volume of a soil after it has been subjected to compaction.

Core The impervious portion of an embankment, such as a dam.

Density The ratio of the weight of a material to its volume.

Embankment A fill whose top is higher than the adjoining natural ground.

Fines Soil or crushed stone whose particles are small size.

Grain-size curve A graph of the analysis of a soil showing the percentage of sizes by weight.

Granular material A soil, such as sand, whose particle sizes are such that they do not stick together.

Impervious A material that resists the flow of water through it.

In situ Soil in its original or undisturbed position.

Lift A layer of soil placed on top of soil previously placed in an embankment.

Liquid limit The water content, expressed as a percent of the weight of water to the dry weight of the soil, at which the soil passes from a plastic to a liquid state.

Optimum moisture content The percent of moisture, by weight, at which the greatest density of a soil can be obtained by compaction.

Pass A working trip or passage of an excavating, grading or compaction machine.

Plasticity index The numerical difference between a soil's liquid limit and its plastic limit.

Plastic limit The lowest water content, expressed as a percent of the ratio of the weight of moisture to the dry weight of soil, at which the soil remains in a plastic state.

Proctor, or proctor test A method developed by R. R. Proctor for determining the moisture-density relationship in soils subjected to compaction.

Proctor, modified A moisture-density test of more rigid specifications than the Proctor test.

Silt A soil composed of particles between $\frac{1}{16}$ mm and $\frac{1}{256}$ mm in size.

Soil The loose surface material of the earth's crust.

Stabilize To make soil firm and to prevent it from moving.

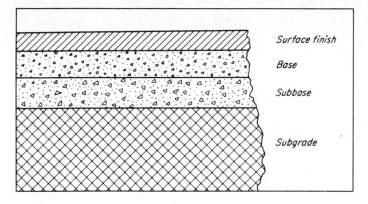

Figure 5-1 Methods of constructing a high-quality pavement.

Subbase   The layer of selected material placed to furnish strength to the base of a road. In areas where the construction goes through marshy, swampy, unstable land it is often necessary to excavate the natural materials in the area of the roadway and replace them with more stable materials. The material used to replace the unstable natural soils is generally called subbase material, and when compacted it is known as the subbase.

Subgrade   The surface produced by grading native earth, or cheap imported materials which serve as a base for a more expensive paving.

PROPERTIES OF SOILS

Prior to discussing earth handling or analyzing problems involving earthwork it is desirable to become more familiar with some of the physical properties of earth. These properties have a direct effect on the ease or difficulty of handling earth, the selection of equipment, and the production rates of the equipment.

Swell and shrinkage It is well known that the volume and density of earth undergo considerable changes when the earth is excavated, hauled, placed, and compacted. Because of these changes it is necessary to specify whether the volume is measured in its original position, in the loose condition, or in the fill after compaction.

The bank-measure volume is the volume of the earth measured in the borrow pit, trench, canal, or cut prior to loosening. This is the volume on which payment usually is based.

The loose-measure volume is the volume of the earth after it has been removed from its natural position and deposited in trucks, scrapers, or spoil piles.

The compacted volume, or fill volume, is the volume of the earth after it has been placed in a fill, such as a dam, and compacted. For projects requiring compacted earth fill the volume in the fill may be used as the basis of payment.

The volume of earth should be expressed in cubic yards, regardless of whether it is bank measure, loose, or compacted.

When the volume of earth increases because of loosening, this increase is defined as swell. It is expressed as a percent of the original undisturbed volume. Thus, if the earth removed from a hole having a volume of 1 cu yd is found to have a loose volume of 1.25 cu yd, the gain in volume is 0.25 cu yd, or 25 percent. This particular earth is then said to have a swell of 25 percent. The values of swell vary considerably for different classes of earth, as indicated in Table 5-1.

When earth is placed in a fill and compacted under modern construction methods, it will usually have a smaller volume than in its original condition. This reduction in volume is the result of an increase in the density and is illustrated by the difficulty frequently encountered in driving wood stakes into a fill after the earth has been thoroughly compacted by sheep's-foot tamping rollers, pneumatic tires, or other compacting equipment. This reduction in volume from

Table 5-1 Representative properties of earth and rock*

| Material | Weight, lb per cu yd (kg per m³) | | Percent swell | Swell factor* |
	Bank	Loose		
Clay, dry	2,700	2,000	35	0.74
	(1,600)	(1,185)	35	0.74
Clay, wet	3,000	2,200	35	0.74
	(1,780)	(1,305)	35	0.74
Earth, dry	2,800	2,240	25	0.80
	(1,660)	(1,325)	25	0.80
Earth, wet	3,200	2,580	25	0.80
	(1,895)	(1,528)	25	0.80
Earth and gravel	3,200	2,600	20	0.83
	(1,895)	(1,575)	20	0.83
Gravel, dry	2,800	2,490	12	0.89
	(1,660)	(1,475)	12	0.89
Gravel, wet	3,400	2,980	14	0.88
	(2,020)	(1,765)	14	0.88
Limestone	4,400	2,750	60	0.63
	(2,610)	(1,630)	60	0.63
Rock, well blasted	4,200	2,640	60	0.63
	(2,490)	(1,565)	60	0.63
Sand, dry	2,600	2,260	15	0.87
	(1,542)	(1,340)	15	0.87
Sand, wet	2,700	2,360	15	0.87
	(1,600)	(1,400)	15	0.87
Shale	3,500	2,480	40	0.71
	(2,075)	(1,470)	40	0.71

* The swell factor is equal to the loose weight divided by the bank weight per unit of volume.

the bank-measure volume is defined as shrinkage. It is expressed as a percent of the original undisturbed volume. Thus if the earth removed from a hole having a volume of 1 cu yd is found to have a compacted volume of 0.9 cu yd, the loss in volume is 0.1 cu yd, or 10 percent. For this condition the earth is said to have a shrinkage of 10 percent. For any given class of earth the percent of shrinkage will vary with the extent and degree of compaction and the amount of moisture present during compaction.

Table 5-1 gives representative values for swell for different classes of earth. These values will vary with the extent of loosening and compaction. If more accurate values are desired for a specific project, tests should be made on several samples of the earth taken from different depths or from different locations within the proposed cut. The test may be made by weighing a given volume of undisturbed, loose, and compacted earth. A container having the same volume should be used in determining the weight for each of the three conditions.

The percent swell and shrinkage may be determined from Eqs. (5-1) and (5-2), respectively.

$$S_w = \left(\frac{B}{L} - 1 \right) \times 100 \tag{5-1}$$

$$S_h = \left(1 - \frac{B}{C} \right) \times 100 \tag{5-2}$$

where S_w = % swell
  S_h = % shrinkage
  B = weight of undisturbed earth
  L = weight of loose earth
  C = weight of compacted earth

The weights of earth usually are expressed in pounds per cubic foot.

Example Determine the percent swell and shrinkage for earth whose weights are as follows:

Undisturbed, 92 lb per cu ft
Loose, 76 lb per cu ft
Compacted, 108 lb per cu ft

The percent swell will be

$$S_w = \left(\tfrac{92}{76} - 1 \right) \times 100$$

$$= (1.21 - 1) \times 100 = 21\%$$

The percent shrinkage will be

$$S_h = \left(1 - \tfrac{92}{108} \right) \times 100$$

$$= (1 - 0.85) \times 100 = 15\%$$

Similar results may be obtained by using a calibrated container to measure the volume of a given quantity of earth in the undisturbed, loose, and compacted states.

To illustrate the use of Table 5-1, 10 cu yd of earth in a borrow pit may occupy 12.5 cu yd in a truck and 9 cu yd in a compacted fill.

Types of soils Soils may be classified according to the sizes of the particles of which they are composed, by their physical properties, or by their behavior when the moisture content varies.

A contractor is concerned primarily with five types of soils: gravel, sand, silt, clay, organic matter, and combinations of these types.

Gravel is a rocklike material whose particles are larger than $\frac{1}{4}$ in. Sizes larger than 10 in. are usually called boulders.

Sand is a disintegrated rock whose particles vary in sizes from those of gravel down to 0.002 in. It may be classified as coarse or fine sand, depending on the sizes of the grains. Sand is a granular, or noncohesive, material whose strength is not affected by its moisture content.

Silt is a very fine sand, and is thus a granular material whose particles are smaller than 0.002 in. It is a noncohesive material, and it has little or no strength. It compacts very poorly.

Clay is a cohesive material whose particles are microscopic in size. The cohesion between the particles gives clays a high strength when dry. Clays are subject to considerable changes in volume with variations in moisture content. When clays are combined with granular soils, the strengths of such soils are increased greatly.

Organic matter is a partly decomposed vegetable matter. If it is present in soil that is used for construction purposes, it should be removed and replaced with a more suitable soil.

Soils existing under natural conditions may not contain the several types in the desired ratios to produce the necessary properties for construction purposes. For this reason it may be necessary to obtain soils from several sources and then blend them as they are placed in a fill.

If the material in a borrow pit consists of layers of different types of soils, the specifications for the project may require the use of excavating equipment that will dig through the several layers in order to mix the soil.

Soil tests Prior to preparing the specifications for a project representative samples of soil are collected and tested in laboratories to determine their properties, including the dry unit weight and the percent of moisture required for maximum compacted density. The optimum moisture content is the ratio of the weight of water to the dry weight of soil, expressed as a percent, that will permit the soil to be compacted to the maximum density with the least effort.

Figure 5-2 shows moisture-density curves which illustrate the effect of varying amounts of moisture on the density of a soil subjected to equal compactive efforts, for the standard and modified Proctor tests. It will be noted that the modified Proctor gives a higher density at a lower moisture content than the standard Proctor at a higher moisture content. The optimum moisture for the standard Proctor is 17 percent versus 14 percent for the modified Proctor.

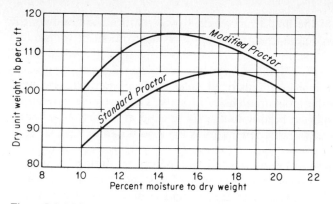

Figure 5-2 Moisture-density curves for fixed compaction.

The modified Proctor test may be used because it is more reflective of the heavier equipment used today in compacting soils.

Laboratory tests The laboratory test that is accepted by highway departments and other agencies is the Proctor test. For this test a sample of soil consisting of $\frac{1}{4}$ in. and finer material is used. The sample is divided into three equal parts, and moisture is added. Each part is placed separately in a cylindrical steel mold whose inside diameter is 4.0 in. and whose height is 4.59 in., and then compacted by dropping a 5.5-lb rammer, with a circular base, 25 times from a height of 12 in. above the specimen. The specimen is removed from the mold and weighed immediately; then it is dried to a constant weight to remove all moisture and weighed again to determine the moisture content. The test is repeated, using varying amounts of water in the samples, until the moisture content that produces the maximum density is determined. This test is designated as AASHTO T 99-70.

The modified Proctor test, designated as AASHTO T 180-70, is performed in a similar manner, except that a rammer whose weight is 10 lb is dropped 18 in.

Field test The specifications for a project may require a contractor to compact the soil to a 90 percent relative density, based on the standard Proctor test. If the laboratory density of the soil is determined to be 120 lb per cu ft, the contractor must compact the soil to a density of 0.9×120 lb $= 108$ lb per cu ft.

Field tests are conducted by removing samples of compacted soil from the fill at random locations, and then determining the damp and dry weights of each sample. The volume of the hole can be determined by several methods. The most common method is to fill the hole with dry sand from a container of known weight. The difference in the weight of the container, before and after the hole is filled, will determine the weight of sand used, from which the volume of the hole can be determined. If the wet weight and the dry weight of the sample and the volume of the hole from which it was removed are known, the dry-weight density can be determined. Also, the moisture content of the sample can be determined.

Nuclear determination of moisture density of soils Nuclear methods are used extensively to determine the moisture-density of soils. The instrument required for this test can be transported readily to the fill, placed at a location where a test is to be conducted, and within a few minutes the results can be read directly from the indicators.

The device utilizes the Compton effect of gamma-ray scattering for density determinations and hydrogenous thermalization of fast neutrons for moisture determinations. The emitted rays enter the ground, where they are partially absorbed and partially reflected. Reflected rays pass through Geiger-Müller tubes in the surface gauge. Counts per minute are read directly on a reflected-ray counter gauge and are related to moisture and density calibration curves.

Advantages of the nuclear method when compared with the Proctor method include the following:

1. Decreases the time required for a test from as much as a day to a few minutes, thereby eliminating potentially excessive delays for the contractor, e.g., waiting for the results from Proctor tests.

Figure 5-3 Density-moisture gauge and scaler. *(Troxler Electronic Laboratories, Inc.)*

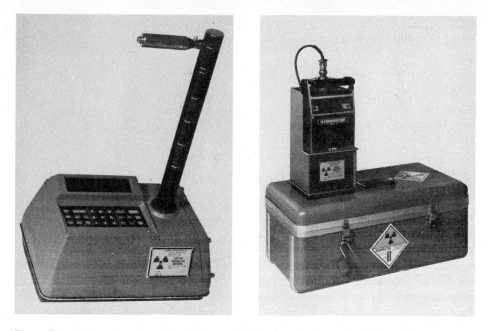

Figure 5-4 (*a*) Percent test nuclear soil gauge; (*b*) depth moisture gauge. (*Campbell Pacific Nuclear Corporation.*)

2. Does not require the removal of soil samples from the site of the tests.
3. Provides a means of performing density tests on soils containing large-sized aggregates and on frozen materials.
4. Reduces or eliminates the effect of the personal element, and possible errors, that may occur in performing Proctor tests.

Instruments are available that will measure moisture and density of soils at depths up to 200 ft or more below the surface of the ground. The measurements are performed by drilling holes in the soil to the desired depths, installing aluminum tubing in the holes temporarily, then lowering nuclear sensing probes down the tubing and making the tests at the desired depths. Figure 5-6 illustrates an instrument that can be used to conduct deep tests.

Because nuclear tests are conducted with instruments that present a potential source of radiation, an operator should exercise reasonable care to assure that no harm can result from the use of the instruments. However, by following the instructions furnished with the instruments and exercising proper care, exposure can be maintained well below the limits set by the Nuclear Regulating Commission (NRC), formerly the Atomic Energy Commission. In the United States a license is required to own, possess, or use nuclear-type density- and moisture-measuring instruments. A license may be obtained from the Nuclear Regulating Commission, and where required from state and/or local government agencies.

Figure 5-5 (*a*) Nuclear moisture-density meter; (*b*) soil moisture-temperature meter and cells. *(Soiltest, Inc.)*

114

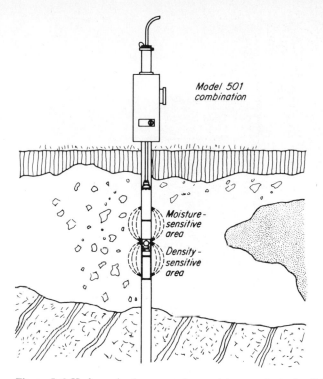

Model 501
combination

Moisture-
sensitive
area

Density-
sensitive
area

Figure 5-6 Hydroprobe for measuring moisture content of soil below the surface of the ground. *(Campbell Pacific Nuclear Corporation.)*

SOIL STABILIZATION

Many soils are subject to differential expansion and shrinkage when they undergo changes in moisture content. If pavements are to be constructed on such soils, it is highly desirable to stabilize them to prevent or reduce the changes in volume in order to protect the pavements from excessive damages.

Stabilization may be applied to a soil in its natural position or as it is placed in a fill. Also, stabilization may be applied to the subgrade, subbase, or base material.

Methods of stabilizing soils include, but are not limited to, the following operations:

1. Blending and mixing heterogeneous soils to produce more homogeneous soils.
2. Incorporating hydrated lime into soils that are high in clay content.
3. Blending asphalt with the soil.
4. Mixing portland cement with the soil.
5. Incorporating various types of salts into the soils.
6. Incorporating certain chemicals into the soils.
7. Compacting the soils thoroughly after they are processed.

Figure 5-7 Disk harrow used to blend soil. *(Rome Industries.)*

Blending and mixing soils If the soils that are to be used in a fill are heterogeneous in their original states, such as in a borrow pit, they may be mixed during excavation by using equipment such as a power shovel or a deep-cutting belt loader to excavate through several layers in one operation. When such material is placed on a fill, it may be subjected to further blending by several passes with a disk harrow, as illustrated in Fig. 5-7.

Figure 5-8 Using stabilizer to blend soils. *(Seaman Corporation.)*

Figure 5-9 Self-propelled soil stabilizer. *(RayGo, Inc.)*

Stabilizing soils with hydrated lime The plasticity index of soils with high clay content can be reduced substantially by incorporating hydrated lime into the soil using a disk harrow or other stabilizing equipment, such as the pulverizer illustrated in Fig. 5-8.

When the subgrade of a highway constructed in Kansas damaged the pavement substantially as a result of differential changes in volume as the moisture content varied, the state specified that for an extension of the highway the upper 6 in. of the subgrade should be stabilized with 5 percent by weight of hydrated lime. The decision was based on the results of laboratory tests performed on untreated and treated samples of the subgrade, as listed in Table 5-2 [1]. The explanation for this soil improvement lies in a base exchange reaction occurring between the lime and clay particles, which causes the clay to agglomerate and become more granular and porous. After compaction, a cementing reaction occurs between the lime and free silica and alumina in the clay, resulting in a substantial improvement in the strength and stability of the soil.

The stabilizing procedure for this project involved spreading the lime, preliminary mixing, followed by a 48-hr curing period, remixing, and compacting, followed by a 7-day damp curing period.

Asphalt-soil stabilization When asphalts, such as MC-3 or RC-3, are mixed with granular soils, usually in amounts of 5 to 7 percent of the volume of the soil, this treatment will produce a much more stable soil. Some soils have been stabilized

Table 5-2 Laboratory test data for raw soil and lime-soil mixture

Sample number	Liquid limit, percent lime				Plasticity index, percent lime				Percent swell at optimum moisture	
	0	3	5	7	0	3	5	7	0% lime	5% lime
501	56	55	54	53	29	24	19	17	8.6	0.2
502	49	45	43	43	27	14	9	6	4.4	0.1
503	37	43	44	44	14	13	14	13	3.7	0.4
504	29	38	38	38	7	9	7	6	. . .	. . .
505	45	44	40	40	24	16	7	4	. . .	. . .
506	44	49	40	40	23	10	6	5	3.5	0.0
507	49	45	43	37	27	13	9	1	4.5	. . .
508	46	43	42	42	25	9	7	7	4.9	0.1
511	39	46	43	44	18	19	9	9	5.2	. . .
512	44	37	36	36	24	10	0	4	. . .	. . .

by adding 10 to 15 percent of minus 200-mesh fines to fill the interstices in the soils and then mixing this blend with asphalt.

The moisture content of the soil must be low at the time the asphalt is added. Also, it is necessary to allow the volatile oils to evaporate from the bitumen before finishing and rolling the material.

Soils treated in this manner may be used as finished surfaces for low traffic density secondary roads, or they may serve as base courses for high-type pavements.

Cement-soil stabilization Soil-cement is one of the most generally used types of mixed-in-place paving. It is particularly economical and convenient in areas where the soil is clay or silt and native deposits of gravel or rock are scarce. The ratio of cement to soil is usually from 5 to 7 percent by weight.

The construction methods involve spreading the portland cement uniformly over the surface of the soil, then mixing it into the soil, preferably with a pulverizer-type machine, to the specified depth, followed by fine grading and compaction. If the moisture content of the soil is low, it will be necessary to sprinkle the surface with water during the processing operation. The material should be compacted within 30 min after it is mixed, using tamping- or pneumatic-tired rollers, followed by final rolling with smooth-wheel rollers. It may be necessary to apply a seal of asphalt or other acceptable material to the surface to retain the moisture in the mix.

SPECIFICATIONS FOR COMPACTING SOILS

Today the compaction of soil placed in an embankment for construction purposes is considered to be a necessity. There may be differences of opinion regarding the degree of compaction justified and regarding the methods of attaining the required compaction. The owner desires the most dense and stable embankment possible at the lowest cost. The contractor desires to satisfy the requirements of the specifications at the lowest construction cost.

Specifications governing compaction may be one of the following types:

1. Method only
2. Method and end result
3. Suggested method and end result
4. End results only

Method only specifications If the specifications for a project direct the contractor to place the soil in lifts of a specified depth, with the soil having a specified moisture content, with the provision that a specified type of roller having a specified weight is to be used to compact the soil by making a specified number of passes over each lift, the contractor will have no choice except to comply with the requirements of the specifications. If the owner prescribes this type of specifications, he will be obligated to accept the responsibility for the results.

Method and end result specifications For most projects this is not a satisfactory specification. Unless extensive predesign tests have been performed on soil samples, which eliminate the possibility of the soil behaving differently than is expected, it is probable that a specified method of compacting the soil will result in excessive costs because compacting operations will be continued after adequate compaction is attained, or compaction operations may be discontinued before adequate density is attained. In any event, the contractor should not be held responsible for the end results.

A further objection to the use of this type of specification is that it may not permit a contractor to make use of methods which he has found to be economical and effective. Thus, the use of this type of specification may result in an unnecessarily high cost for the project.

Suggested method and result specifications This type of specification seems to be more desirable than the two types previously described. It leaves a contractor free to select any reasonable method and equipment which he may have learned from vast experience will provide the required density. Experienced contractors are quite ingenious, and if given an opportunity to use this experience, they frequently can attain the specified results at a significant reduction in costs.

At the same time this type of specification can serve as a guide to a less-experienced contractor.

End result only specifications Several states and agencies are moving toward a policy of using this type of specification. The argument for the use of this policy is that the owner is interested primarily or solely in the end result. For example, the specifications dictate that the soil shall be compacted to 95 percent relative density, based on the modified Proctor test. Unless there are justified reasons for prescribing the methods to be used, the contractor should be permitted to select his own methods, which may be substantially less expensive than other prescribed methods.

TYPES OF COMPACTING EQUIPMENT

Compaction is attained by applying energy to a soil by one or more of the following methods:

1. Kneading action
2. Static weight
3. Vibration
4. Impact
5. Explosives

Many types of compacting equipment are available, including the following:

1. Tamping rollers
2. Smooth-wheel rollers
3. Pneumatic-tired rollers
4. Vibrating rollers, including tamping, smooth-wheel, and pneumatic
5. Self-propelled vibrating plates and/or shoes
6. Manually propelled vibrating plates
7. Manually propelled compactors
8. Vibratory compactors for deep sand

On some projects it may be desirable to use more than one type of equipment to attain the desired results and to effect the greatest economy.

Tamping rollers Tamping rollers are of the sheep's-foot type or modifications thereof. This roller, which may be towed by a tractor or self-propelled, consists of a hollow steel drum on whose outer surface there are welded a number of projecting steel feet, which on different pieces may be of varying lengths and cross sections. A unit may consist of one or several drums mounted on one or more horizontal axles. The weight of a drum may be varied by adding water or sand to produce unit pressures under the feet up to 750 psi or more.

As a tamping roller moves over the surface, the feet penetrate the soil to produce a kneading action and a pressure to mix and compact the soil from the bottom to the top of the layer. With repeated passages of the roller over the surface, the penetration of the feet decreases until the roller is said to walk out of the fill.

The specifications may prescribe one of the following as a means of attaining the desired compaction:

1. The number of passes of a roller, producing a specified unit pressure under the feet, over each layer of soil.
2. Repeated passes of a roller, producing a specified unit pressure under the feet, over each layer of soil until the penetration of the feet does not exceed a stated depth.
3. Repeated passes of a roller over each layer until the soil is compacted to a specified density.

Sheep's-foot rollers are quite effective in compacting clays and mixtures of sand and clay. However, they cannot compact granular soils such as sand and gravel. Also, the depth of a layer of soil to be compacted is limited to approximately the length of the feet.

Figure 5-10 illustrates tractor-pulled sheep's-foot rollers on a project, and Fig. 5-11 illustrates a self-propelled tamping roller and dozer.

Modified tamping rollers Figure 5-12 illustrates a modification of a tamping roller for which the feet are replaced by segments or pads. Some types are designed to permit the addition of ballast to increase the pressure under the pads.

Figure 5-10 Tractor-pulled sheep's-foot rollers.

Figure 5-11 Self-propelled tamping roller and dozer. *(RayGo, Inc.)*

Figure 5-12 Self-propelled segmented roller. *(Marathon-LeTourneau Company.)*

122

Figure 5-13 Tractor-pulled ballasted grid roller. *(Hyster Company.)*

Another modification of the tamping roller, designated as a grid roller, is illustrated in Fig. 5-13. When this roller is ballasted with concrete blocks, it is capable of producing very high soil pressures, and when it is used to compact soil containing rocks, the high concentration of pressure on rocks projecting above the surface of the soil is effective in shattering the rocks and forcing the broken pieces into the soil to produce a relatively smooth surface.

Figure 5-14 Articulated drum-type compactor. *(RayGo, Inc.)*

Figure 5-15 Three-wheel two-axle roller *(Shovel Supply Company)*.

Smooth-wheel rollers These rollers may be classified by type or by weight.

A three-wheel two-axle roller is illustrated in Fig. 5-15a. The front wheel is used for steering, while the two rear wheels are used for driving the unit. A two-wheel tandem roller of varying size is available. A three-wheel tandem roller differs from the two-wheel tandem unit in that it has three drums and three axles. This unit can be more effective than the two-wheel tandem or the three-wheel two-axle units in eliminating or reducing transverse surface roughness because of the concentration of pressure on the middle wheel when the unit passes over high spots in the surface being compacted.

Smooth-wheel rollers may be classified by weight, which is usually stated in tons. The rolls are steel drums, which may be ballasted with water or sand to increase the weights. If a roller is designated as 14–20 tons, it means that the minimum weight of the machine only is 14 tons and that it can be ballasted to give a maximum weight of 20 tons.

Specifications governing these rollers may be of two types, one type simply designating the weight, and the other type designating the weight per linear inch of roll, such as 300 lb per in. of roller width. Specifying the weight only does not necessarily indicate the compressive pressure under the wheels. Specifying the minimum weight per linear inch of width is a more definitive method, and appears to be superior to the former method.

When compacting cohesive soils these rollers tend to form a crust over the surface, which may prevent adequate compaction in the lower portions of a lift.

Figure 5-16 Pneumatic-tired roller. *(Galion Manufacturing Division, Dresser Industries, Inc.)*

However, these rollers are effective in compacting granular soils, such as sand, gravel, and crushed stone, and they are also effective in smoothing surfaces of soils that have been compacted by tamping rollers.

Pneumatic-tired rollers These are surface rollers which apply the principle of kneading action to effect compaction below the surface. They may be self-propelled or towed. They may be small or large-tired units.

The small-tired units usually have two tandem axles with four to nine tires on each axle. The rear wheels are spaced to travel over the surfaces between the front wheels, which produces a complete coverage of the surface. The wheels may be mounted in a manner that will give them a wobbly-wheel effect to increase the kneading action on the soil. Usually the weight of a unit may be varied by adding ballast to suit the material being compacted.

Large-tired rollers are available in sizes varying from 15 to 200 tons gross weight. They utilize two or more big earth-moving tires on a single axle. The air pressure in the tires may vary from 90 to 150 psi. Because of the heavy loads and high tire pressures they are capable of compacting all types of soils to greater depths. These units are frequently used to proof roll subgrades and bases on airfields and earth-fill dams.

Figure 5-17 Self-propelled 50-ton pneumatic roller. *(Shovel Supply Company.)*

Figure 5-18 Pneumatic-tired roller with variable inflation pressure. *(Bros TT Division, American Hoist International Corporation.)*

Table 5-3 Effect of variations in gross weight and tire inflation pressure on ground contact pressure

Gross weight, lb		7,650		15,300		22,500		25,000	
Tire size	Inflation pressure, psi	Ground contact pressure							
		Psi*	Pli†	Psi	Pli	Psi	Pli	Psi	Pli
7.50 × 15	35	33	125	39	237	44	333	46	369
4 or 6 ply	45	38	127	45	241	50	338	51	374
	55	44	129	50	243	55	341	57	377
	60	46	131	53	245	58	344	61	380
7.50 × 15	50	43	145	50	250	56	342	58	378
10 ply	60	47	152	54	254	60	347	62	382
	70	50	162	58	258	64	350	66	385
	80	54	175	62	264	68	354	70	389
	90	58	183	65	272	71	359	74	392
7.50 × 15	50	43	153	50	250	57	343	59	378
12 ply	60	47	164	55	256	61	347	64	383
	70	51	170	59	264	66	351	68	386
	80	55	184	62	270	70	357	72	392
	90	58	202	66	276	73	364	76	397
	100	62	218	69	289	76	369	79	402
	110	65	224	72	293	79	375	82	406
7.50 × 15	50	47	158	57	253	63	348	65	385
14 ply	60	50	170	59	260	67	353	68	389
	70	52	181	62	268	69	358	72	394
	80	55	192	65	276	73	365	75	399
	90	57	210	68	281	76	370	78	405
	100	61	225	71	290	79	377	82	408
	110	65	230	75	293	83	385	85	417
	120	68	239	79	301	87	391	89	423
	130	71	243	82	318	90	400	93	431

Source: Firestone Tire and Rubber Company.
* Ground contact pressure in psi.
† Ground contact pressure in lbs per in. of tire width.

There are at least four methods of indicating the compacting ability of pneumatic rollers; these are

1. The gross weight of the unit
2. The gross weight per wheel
3. The weight per inch of tire width
4. The air pressure in the tires

Because the area of contact between a tire and the ground surface over which it passes varies with the air pressure in the tire, specifying the total weight or the weight per wheel is not necessarily a satisfactory method of indicating the compacting ability of a roller. A more definitive method of designating the compacting ability is to specify the gross weight, the number and sizes of tires, and the tire inflation pressure.

Table 5-3 illustrates the effect of gross vehicle weight and tire inflation pressure on the ground contact pressure and the load per inch of tire width.

Figure 5-19 illustrates a graphical method of determining the ground contact pressure for a 13.00 × 24 18-ply smooth compactor tire subjected to varying loads and inflated to varying air pressures. Similar information is available from tire manufacturers for other tire sizes and loads.

As indicated by the dashed lines, a wheel load of 8,000 lb and an inflation pressure of 60 psi gives a ground contact pressure of 70 psi. The contact area for the tire will be 8,000 lb ÷ 70 psi = 114.3 sq in.

Pressure bulb theory of load distribution This theory is related to the distribution of a load, and thus to the unit soil pressure, when the load is applied to the soil through a circular object. Because the contact area between a tire and the ground approximates a circle, the theory can be applied to pressures in the soil under tires with slight modifications. Figure 5-21 illustrates the ratios of unit pressures to ground contact pressure at varying depths below the surface of the ground.

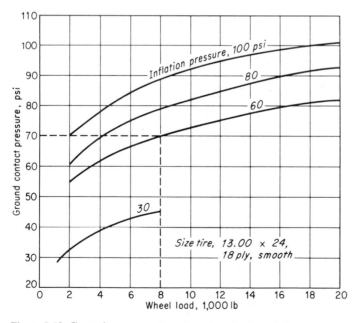

Figure 5-19 Ground pressure at varying wheel loads and air pressures.

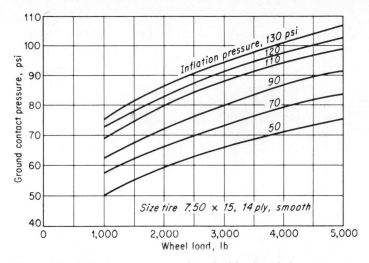

Figure 5-20 Ground pressure at varying wheel loads and air pressures.

Pneumatic-tired rollers with variable inflation pressures When a pneumatic-tired roller is used to compact soil through all stages the first passes over a lift should be made with relatively low tire pressures to increase flotation and ground coverage. However, as the soil is compacted the air pressure in the tires should be increased up to the maximum specified value for the final pass. Prior to the development of a method of varying the air pressure while a roller is in operation it was necessary to (1) vary the pressure in the tires, (2) vary the weight of the ballast on the roller, or (3) keep rollers of different weights and tire

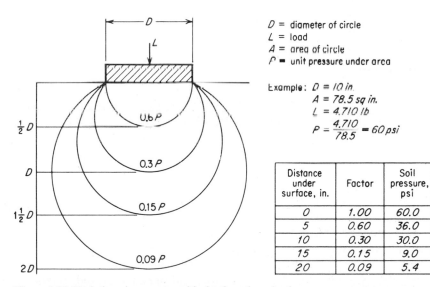

Figure 5-21 Variations in pressure with depth under a load.

Figure 5-22 Towed-type vibrating sheep's-foot roller.

pressures on a project in order to provide units to fit the particular needs of a given compaction condition.

Several manufacturers produce rollers that are equipped to permit the operator to vary the tire pressure without stopping the machine. The first passes are made with relatively low tire pressures. As the soil is compacted, the tire pressure is increased to suit the particular conditions of the soil. The use of this type of roller usually permits adequate compaction with fewer passes than were required by the constant pressure rollers.

Vibrating compactors Certain types of soils such as sand, gravel, and relatively large stones respond quite well to compaction produced by a combination of pressure and vibration. When these materials are vibrated, the particles shift their positions and nestle more closely with adjacent particles to increase the density of the mass.

Several types of compactors have demonstrated their abilities to produce excellent densification of these soils. They include

1. Vibrating sheep's-foot rollers
2. Vibrating steel-drum rollers
3. Vibrating pneumatic-tired rollers
4. Vibrating plates or shoes

Vibrating sheep's-foot, steel-drum, pad-type, and pneumatic-tired rollers are actuated by separate engines mounted on the rollers, or in some cases by

Figure 5-23 Towed-type vibrating drum roller. *(Bros TT Division, American Hoist International Corporation.)*

hydraulic drives which rotate horizontal shafts on which one or more eccentric weights are mounted. Vibrations may vary from 1,000 to 5,000 per min, with the actual number corresponding to the natural resonant frequency of vibrations for the given soil. In addition to compacting the soil, the drum- and pad-type rollers tend to shatter the rock particles near the surface and thus leave a relatively smooth surface.

During the construction of the Cougar dam on the McKenzie River in Oregon the U.S. Army Corps of Engineers conducted tests using 5- and 10-ton vibratory steel-drum rollers to determine the effectiveness of these machines in compacting the rockfill portion of the dam [2]. The larger roller, having a static weight of 10 tons and a dynamic force of 20 tons, demonstrated its ability to consolidate lifts of rock 36 in. thick, with individual rocks varying in sizes up to 24 in. The rollers were towed over the fills at speeds between 1.5 and 2 mph,

Figure 5-24 Self-propelled vibrating drum roller. *(Bros TT Division, American Hoist International Corporation.)*

while vibrating at frequencies of approximately 1,400 vpm. Settlement was measured after two, four, and six passes, with the following results:

Number of passes	Relative % of compaction
2	60
4	83
6	100

In general, better compaction efficiencies and economy are attained by moving vibrating compactors at relatively slow speeds, 1.5 to 2.5 mph. Slow speeds permit a greater flow of vibratory energy into the soil.

Manually operated vibratory plate compactors Figure 5-26 illustrates a self-propelled vibratory-plate compactor used for consolidating soils and asphalt (hot or cold mix) in locations where larger units are not practical. These gasoline- or diesel-powered units are rated by centrifugal force, exciter revolutions per minute, depth of vibration penetration (lift), feet per minute travel, and area of coverage per hour.

Figure 5-25 Vibrating drum-type roller. *(Hyster Company.)*

Figure 5-26 Self-propelled vibro-plate. *(Wacker Corporation.)*

133

Figure 5-27 Self-propelled vibrating compactor. *(RayGo, Inc.)*

Manually operated vibratory tamping compactors Figure 5-27 illustrates a compacting unit of this type which may be used in locations where larger units are not practical.

Manually operated rammer compactors Figure 5-28 illustrates a gasoline-engine-driven rammer used for compacting cohesive or mixed soils in confined areas. These units range in impact from about 300 to 900 or more ft-lb per sec at an impact rate up to 850 per minute, depending on the specific model. Performance criteria include pounds per blow, area covered per hour, and depth of compaction (lift) in inches. Rammers are self-propelled in that each blow moves them ahead slightly to contact new soil.

Densification of soils by explosive vibrations [7, 8] In a loose, saturated, granular soil, a sudden shock or vibration causes localized spontaneous liquefaction and displacement of the soil grains. The weight of the soil is temporarily transferred to the liquid and the soil particles fall into a much denser pattern, aided by the weight of the soil above. In a dry soil, the shock and vibration cause the particles to move to a new denser and more compact pattern. The moment soil particles are freed or loosened from their initial orientation, even small pressures are effective in realigning them in a more compact mass. This process is not reversible, and the new density is permanent.

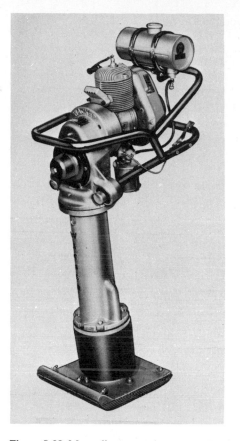

Figure 5-28 Manually operated rammer. *(Wacker Corporation.)*

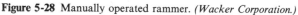

The maximum result is obtained in a soil that is either dry or completely saturated. As the water content of the soil decreases from 100 percent saturation to the retained or absorbed water content around each grain of soil, less densification is obtained because of the increase in capillary tension between the grains. This effect becomes more pronounced as the soil becomes finer. The effect of capillary tension can be overcome by ponding or flooding the area, then allowing adequate time for the water to seep downward to meet the existing water level. Although the quantity of water required to saturate the soil is not great, an increased head will reduce the time required to attain full saturation.

A slight amount of superimposed weight is advantageous in reorienting the soil particles. The upper 2 to 3 ft (0.6 to 0.9 m) of soil usually undergoes only a slight increase in density unless completely saturated to the surface. Even when the soil is saturated, the increase in density is not as pronounced as it is at deeper elevations. If it is necessary to compact this upper layer of soil, vibratory compaction may be attained by using conventional mechanical equipment.

Table 5-4 Types of equipment suited for compacting soils

Type compactor	Soil best suited for	Maximum effect in loose lift, in.	Density gained in lift	Maximum weight, tons
Sheep's foot	Clay, silty clay, gravel with clay binder	7 to 12	Nearly uniform	20
Steel tandem two-axle	Sandy silts, most granular material with some clay binder	4 to 8	Average*	16
Steel tandem three-axle	Same as above	4 to 8	Average*	20
Steel three-wheel	Granular or granular-plastic material	4 to 8	Average* to uniform	20
Pneumatic, small-tire	Sandy silts, sandy clays, gravelly sand and clays with few fines	4 to 8	Average* to uniform	12
Pneumatic large-tire	All types	? to 24	Uniform	50
Vibratory	Sand, silty sands, silty gravels	3 to 6	Uniform	30
Combinations	All	3 to 6	Uniform	20

*The density may decrease with depth.

After the initial shock, other charges exploded in the same area will cause further settling, but each successive charge produces a smaller effect until no appreciable or useful settling can be obtained. The ratio for any series of charges, empirically obtained, shows that the first quarter of a charge causes approximately 60 percent densification, the second quarter causes 25 percent more, the third quarter 10 percent more, and last quarter 5 percent more. This condition is one of the factors affecting the spacing of the holes to assure that a sufficient number of overlapping effects will be applied to each location in any area.

Spacings, depths, and sizes of explosive charges The densification of soils by means of explosives is different from regular blasting in that no craters can be blown in the soil and there is no debris from the explosion of the charges. The energy from an explosion must be contained entirely within the ground.

The approximate sizes and depths of charges can be determined from existing formulas, tempered with experience and checked by trial tests conducted at the site of the operation. The amount of each charge will vary according to the type of soil, depth of strata, desired amount of densification, spacing of holes, present ground-water level, nearness of structures, overlapping effect of charges, and type of explosive used. Experience has indicated that the center of an explosive charge should be below the center of the mass of soil to be densified at approximately the two-thirds point down. It may be necessary to have separate charges in the same hole when cohesionless strata are separated by layers of cohesive soil or when operating near existing buildings or structures. For such conditions, delay electric blasting caps may be used to permit firing at delayed intervals, thereby reducing the energy per firing.

Horizontal spacings of holes may vary from 10 to 25 ft (3.0 to 7.5 m) and are governed by the depth of the strata, the size of the charge, and the overlapping effect of adjacent charges. Spacings closer than 10 ft (3.0 m) in saturated soils should be avoided, unless carefully investigated for safety, because of possible propagation of sensitive explosions of adjacent charges.

The firing pattern should allow a number of charges to act on one particular area. However, the pattern should leave an area on one or two sides to permit excess pore water to escape from a square. Reduction of the voids in a volume of soil results in release or displacement of a large volume of water, the quantity depending on the depth, the original void ratio, and the amount of densification of the soil.

Installation of the explosives. After the spacings, depths, and sizes of charges have been determined and a sequence of shots or firing pattern has been established, the locations of the holes are marked out. One method of producing the holes for the charges is to use one or more nonsparking plastic or aluminum pipes of the desired sizes, which can be self-jetted into the soil to the correct depth. An explosive charge with an electric blasting cap and lead wires is then placed in each hole through the pipe. After the pipe is withdrawn, the hole is filled and tamped with a wooden rod.

After the charges for a given pattern have been installed, the blasting caps are tested individually using a galvanometer. Then the charges are fired according to the schedule of delays previously determined.

Publications are available which furnish dependable information on the transportation, storage, handling, and use of explosives [9, 10]. Most manufacturers of explosives can furnish useful information on this subject. Local regulations, licenses, permits, and prejudices must also be respected when using explosives.

Deep densification of soils using a terra-probe vibrator [11] This method of vibrator compaction is accomplished by the use of a vibratory pile-driving apparatus together with an open-end tubular probe; the probe is driven into and extracted from the soil to be compacted on certain modular spacings [12]. When the driving and extracting phases are accomplished, densification of the soil

Figure 5-29 Vibratory probe in position to densify the soil. *(L. B. Foster Company.)*

occurs both inside and outside the probe, with the concentration of vibratory energy creating extreme densification inside the probe and with densification outside the probe diminishing with distance.

To date, the vibratory pile driving apparatuses used have been in the frequency ranges of 720 to 1,100 cpm (11 to 19 Hz), the normal operating frequency being 900 cycles per min (15 Hz). The vibrator has been able to create amplitudes of 3/8 to 1 in. (9.5 to 25 mm). The vibrator creates vertical energy by counter-rotating eccentric weights, which cancel out the horizontal effects and give vertical vibrations only.

Figure 5-30 Vibrating probe at maximum penetration in densifying soil. *(L. B. Foster Company.)*

The best probe material used has been an open-end 30-in. (760 mm) pipe of 3/8 in. (9.5 mm) wall thickness with 4- to 6-in. (100- to 150-mm) wide and 1/2-in. (13-mm) thick steel bands spaced 5 to 10 ft (1.5 to 3 m) apart on the outside of the pipe, together with wider driving and clamping bands at the bottom and top of the probe. Tests using other diameters have revealed that smaller diameters give less densification inside the pipe, while larger diameters require more vibratory energy and thicker and heavier probe material. The probe is usually 10 to 15 ft (3 to 4.6 m) longer than the maximum penetration depth, to allow for any flexing of the probe, particularly when probes more than 50 to 55 ft long (15 to 17 m) are used. This also allows for any cut-off requirements during application.

The probe is attached to the vibrator by means of a hydraulic clamp; this permits the vertical vibratory energy produced to travel to the probe material undiminished, as the probe, hydraulic clamping head, and vibrating transmission case act as a unit.

A mobile crane of sufficient size and capacity is required to handle the vibrating unit and the probe length during driving and extracting operations.

An overburden of sand is required before beginning the operation to compensate for the settling that will result from the compaction. About a 12 percent shrinkage allowance has been satisfactory for most applications, but a hydraulic fill with a relatively low density may require a 15 percent allowance.

Spacing of the probes. The dimensions of the modular spacings of the probes are dependent on the required relative density of the soil. Test patterns of several different spacings should be run initially to determine the required spacing to give the desired density. Square patterns have been used with spacings varying from 3 to 8 ft (0.9 to 2.4 m). Square spacings seem to offer better results and faster operations than other patterns. Also, if additional probes are needed, they can be placed in the centers of the square patterns. Small lathing stakes are generally used to indicate the location of each probe setting.

Production rates obtained with the terra-probe. Compaction by this method is very expeditious, resulting in an average rate of about 15 probes per hour. For projects requiring shallow probes in loose soils the rate could be higher, while for projects requiring deeper probes in denser soils the rate could be lower.

During earlier applications of this method, tests were conducted by allowing the probes to sink to the lowest desired depths and then continuing the vibrations for several minutes to determine if additional densification was produced. The tests revealed that little, if any, additional densification resulted.

Limitations on the classifications of soils that may be compacted by the terra-probe. The use of this method should be limited to saturated cohesionless soils. Because densification of soils by this method causes the grains to assume new positions that reduce the volume of voids in the mass, it is necessary for the grains to be free at least temporarily and to be submerged in water; only saturated cohesionless soils will respond to the vibrations effectively. If unsaturated sands are to be densified by this method they should be submerged or saturated by adding sufficient water to bring the upper level to near the surface of the ground.

In some test applications, this method was unsuccessful in densifying the soils. These soil conditions were:

1. Saturated sand with sieve analysis indicating 60 percent passing the No. 100 sieve, 52 percent passing the No. 120 sieve, and 5 percent passing the No. 200 sieve.
2. Dry soil with 80 percent passing the No. 100 sieve and 50 percent passing the No. 200 sieve.
3. Dry material for an 11-ft (3.1-m) shallow depth, with the sieve analysis indicating 85 percent passing the No. 40 sieve, 25 percent passing the No. 100 sieve, and 12 percent passing the No. 200 sieve.

In some projects, in which the upper layers of soil consist of mud, muck, and silt, it will be necessary to remove all the undesirable material, because it will not be densified by the vibratory method. The replacement material should be a granular cohesionless soil that will respond to vibratory densification. In some instances it may be necessary to screen the replacement material in order to remove any silt or clay balls.

Cost considerations. In all applications of the numerous techniques and methods available, consideration of costs becomes important. The terra-probe method, because vibratory energy accelerates its applications, has some interesting cost considerations. An over-all cost consideration should include the following items:

1. Cost of soil removal, if required
2. Cost of replacement soil, if required
3. Cost of necessary soil overburden, if required
4. Cost of a testing program
5. Cost of the vibratory compaction method

The first four costs will be directly related to each project site, as each may or may not be applicable.

The cost of the vibratory compaction method can vary depending on the size of the area, the initial soil density, the required density, and the depth to be compacted. Because the mobilization and demobilization costs would be the same for a small or a large project, the unit cost for a small project would be higher. With other conditions remaining the same, the cost per unit volume should be less for projects requiring deep probes. A higher specified density, requiring closer spacing of probes, will result in a higher cost per unit of volume than the wider spacing permitted with lower density requirements.

The depth of compaction is a factor of consideration, but it is less significant than other factors because of the speed provided by the vibratory device used. Overall probing time for a hole 25 ft (7.6 m) deep would not be doubled if the depth were increased to 50 ft (15 m) under the same soil conditions because the time required to move between the probes would be the same for both depths and the time required to penetrate the additional depth would be a matter of a few seconds for most projects.

The costs of the vibratory compaction method have varied for the reasons given heretofore, but a bracketing of the cost range has been established for several projects. The costs have ranged from about $0.70 per cu yd ($0.91 per m³) to about $1.10 per cu yd ($1.40 per m³) of compacted soil. This cost range is inclusive of the varying density requirements and includes a marine-type operation involving more equipment than a land operation. None of these applications was larger than 100,000 cu yd (76,000 m³) in volume. Therefore, it is realistic to assume that projects of 500,000 to 1,000,000 cu yd (380,000 to 760,000 m³) would have a lower unit cost, and that for projects of 5,000,000 cu yd to 10,000,000 cu yd (3,800,000 m³ to 7,600,000 m³) the unit costs might be in the $0.30 per cu yd to $0.40 per cu yd ($0.39 per m³ to $0.52 per m³) range. None of these costs includes the contractor's profit. Also, localized union labor requirements could affect the costs.

Conclusions regarding the method of deep-sand vibratory compaction. This method of vibratory compaction, though simple, represents an advance in the engineering field and in the construction industry. The availability of vibratory pile-driving devices, the employment of their best features learned through job experiences, and their effectiveness in cohesionless soils have led to this method of compacting deep sand.

The employment of this method provides the following advantages:

1. An effective means for compacting a range of saturated sands
2. An expedient method of compaction because of the speed of driving and extracting made available by the vibratory pile-driving device
3. Less expensive compaction than that obtained by other means of compaction because of the high production rates
4. Adjustable modular spacings to adapt to final density requirements and job site conditions
5. An effective method of compacting soil to substantial depths
6. A compaction method where lower initial density can make the method more expedient than higher initial density
7. A means of densification of some soils to reduce the soil liquefaction hazards of earthquakes
8. A method of compaction for use in land reclamation.

In order to increase the effectiveness of this method the following recommendations are made:

1. That an *in situ* test pattern procedure of two or three modular spacings be used to establish a grid pattern for probe holes for each application
2. That a quality control of the highest order be used in dredging out of undesirable material, in cleaning the bottom of the excavation, and in the dredge fill operation to ensure that only good compactable material is used for replacement
3. That this method not be used for compacting soils less than 12 to 13 ft (3.7 to 4.0 m) deep, because other methods of compacting generally are more economical
4. That when this method is used to compact soils 12 to 20 ft (3.7 to 6.1 m) deep, closer spacings of probes be used than for holes more than 20 ft (6.1 m) deep.

PROBLEMS

5-1 A given soil weighs 120 lb per cu ft *in situ*, 96 lb per cu ft loose, and 128 lb per cu ft when compacted in a fill. Determine the percent swell and shrinkage for this soil.

5-2 The capacity of a truck is 16 cu yd of earth. If the earth weighs 110 lb per cu ft *in situ* and 95 lb per cu ft loose, what is the capacity of the truck expressed in cubic yards bank measure?

5-3 If earth is placed in fill at the rate of 180 cu yd per hr, and the dry weight of the earth is 2,890 lb per cu yd, how many gallons of water must be supplied each hour to increase the moisture content of the earth from 4 to 10 percent by weight?

5-4 Earth whose *in situ* weight is 112 lb per cu ft, loose weight is 90 lb per cu ft, and compacted weight is 120 lb per cu ft is placed in a fill at the rate of 240 cu yd per hr, measured as compacted earth, in layers whose compacted thickness is 6 in. Sheep's-foot roller drums, each 5 ft wide, are pulled by a tractor at a speed of 2 mph, with an operating factor of 75 percent. Determine the number of drums required to provide the necessary compaction if eight drum passes are specified for each layer of earth.

5-5 If a multiwheel pneumatic roller whose 7.50 × 15 14-ply tires are inflated to 90 psi, and whose wheel loads are 2,800 lb each, is used to compact a soil, what is the maximum compacted depth of a layer of earth that can be compacted to a unit pressure of not less than 50 psi at the bottom of the layer? Assume that the ground contact area for a tire is a circle whose area in square inches equals the wheel load divided by the ground contact pressure.

REFERENCES

1. Lime Stabilized Subgrade for Kansas "I" Project, *Roads and Streets*, vol. 102, pp. 112–115, February 1959.
2. Bertram, George E.: *Proceedings of the Second Panamanian Conference on Soil Mechanics and Foundations*, Sao Paulo, Brazil, vol. I, pp. 444–452, 1963.
3. Morris, M. D.: Earth Compaction, Construction Methods and Equipment, 1961.
4. Williamson, A. O.: "Compaction and Compaction Techniques," Bros Incorporated, Minneapolis, Minnesota.
5. "Handbook of Compactionology," Bros Incorporated, Minneapolis, Minnesota, 1964.
6. Compaction Answers are Getting Closer, *Roads and Streets*, vol. 111, pp. 110–124, January 1968.
7. Prugh, Byron J.: Densification of Soils by Explosive Vibrations, *Journal of the Construction Division, Proceedings of the American Society of Civil Engineers*, vol. 89, pp. 79–100, March 1963.
8. "Nuclear Methods of Measuring Soil Density and Moisture," STP No. 293, American Society for Testing and Materials, 1916 Race Street, Philadelphia, Pennsylvania 19103, March 1961.
9. "Blasters' Handbook," 12th ed., E. I. Du Pont de Nemours & Company, Inc., Wilmington, Delaware 19898, 1949.
10. "Safety in the Handling and Use of Explosives," Pamphlet No. 17, Institute of Makers of Explosives, 420 Lexington Avenue, New York, New York 10017, 1966.
11. Jones, II. W.: Densification of Sand for Drydock by Terra-Probe, *Journal of the Soils Mechanics and Foundation Division, Proceedings of the American Society of Civil Engineers*, vol. 99, pp. 451–470, June 1973.
12. Anderson, Robert D.: New Method for Deep Sand Vibratory Compaction, *Journal of the Construction Division, Proceedings of the American Society of Civil Engineers*, vol. 100, pp. 79–95, March 1974.

TRACTORS AND RELATED EQUIPMENT

TRACTORS

TRACTOR USES

Tractors have many uses as construction equipment. While their primary purpose may be to pull or push loads, they are also used as mounts for many types of accessories, such as front-end shovels, rippers, bulldozer blades, sidebooms, hoes, trenchers, and others. There are sizes and types to fit almost any job for which they are usable.

TYPES OF TRACTORS

Tractors may be divided into two major types:

1. Crawler
2. Wheel

Wheel tractors are either two-wheel or four-wheel.
In selecting a tractor several factors should be considered; these include, but are not limited to, the following:

1. The size required for a given job
2. The kind of job for which it will be used—bulldozing, pulling a scraper, ripping, clearing land, etc.
3. The type of footing over which it will operate, i.e., high-tractive or low-tractive efficiency
4. The firmness of the haul road
5. The smoothness of the haul road

6. The slope of the haul road
7. The length of haul
8. The type of work it will do after this job is completed

Crawler tractors Crawler tractors are usually rated by size or weight and power. The weight is important on many projects because the maximum tractive effort that a unit can provide is limited to the product of the weight times the coefficient of traction for the unit and the particular road surface, regardless of the power supplied by the engine. Table 4-3 (page 94) gives the coefficients of traction for various surfaces.

Most manufacturers make crawler tractors with some or all models equipped with a choice of direct drive or torque converter and power-shift drives.

Crawler tractors with direct drive Table 6-1 gives pertinent information and performance data for tractors equipped with direct drives. Some manufacturers' specifications list two sets of drawbar pulls—rated and maximum. The rated is the drawbar pull that can be sustained for continuous operation, while the maximum is the drawbar pull that the tractor can exert for a short period while lugging the engine, such as when passing over a soft spot in the ground, which requires a temporary higher tractive effort. Thus, the rated pull should be used for continuous operation. Also, the available drawbar pull is subject to the limitations on traction developed between the tracks and the ground.

Some manufacturers rate their engines under standard conditions, namely at 60°F and sea-level elevation, while others rate their engines under more representative operating conditions, such as 85°F and up to 2,500 ft elevation above sea level. As indicated in Chap. 5, the two methods do not give the same results.

Crawler tractors with torque converter and power-shift transmissions Many crawler tractors are available with torque converter drives and power-shift

Figure 6-1 Crawler tractor pushing a self-loading scraper. *(Caterpillar Tractor Company.)*

Table 6-1 Representative specifications and performance data for crawler tractor equipped with direct drive

Approximate oper- ating weight, lb	18,300	32,000	47,000
Flywheel hp	93	160	235
Drawbar hp	75	128	187
Ratio, lb per hp	197	200	200

Performance data

	Speed, mph	fpm	Drawbar pull, lb	Speed, mph	fpm	Drawbar, pull, lb	Speed, mph	fpm	Drawbar, pull, lb
Gear, forward									
1st	1.7	150	17,240	1.5	132	32,500	1.5	132	44,400
2d	2.7	238	10,470	2.2	193	22,700	1.9	167	34,500
3d	3.7	326	7,090	3.1	272	15,000	2.7	238	24,100
4th	5.2	458	4,670	4.6	405	9,390	3.5	307	17,750
5th	6.8	598	3,190	5.9	518	6,770	4.6	405	13,000
6th							6.3	555	8,450
Gear, reverse									
1st	2.1	185	13,670	1.8	158	28,470	1.5	132	43,700
2d	3.3	290	8,180	2.5	220	18,935	2.0	176	33,900
3d	4.6	405	5,440	3.7	325	12,390	2.7	238	23,700
4th	6.4	563	3,480	5.4	475	7,620	3.6	317	17,400
5th							4.6	405	12,700
6th							6.4	563	8,250

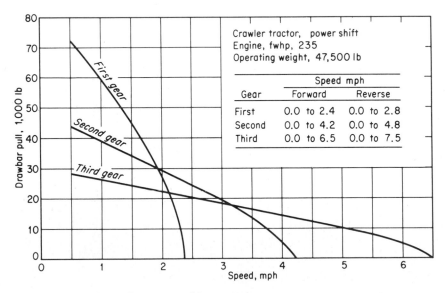

Figure 6-2 Drawbar pull versus speed for a crawler tractor.

transmissions which eliminate shifting gears. These drives provide an efficient flow of power from the engine to the tracks by automatically selecting the speed which is most suitable for the load pulled by the tractor.

Figure 6-2 illustrates the performance curves for a tractor equipped with a torque converter and a three-speed transmission. Assume that the tractor must provide a drawbar pull of 50,000 lb. The figure indicates that the tractor should be operated in first gear and that it will have a maximum speed of 1.33 mph. If the required drawbar pull is 10,000 lb, this pull can be provided by each of the three gears. However, because the tractor can provide the required pull in third gear at a speed of 5 mph, it should be operated in this gear. The gear selected should be the highest one that will provide the required pull in order to operate at the highest possible speed.

The equivalent drawbar pull which a tractor must provide, regardless of whether it is a direct-drive or power-shift type, is the algebraic sum of the pull required by the towed load, the effect of grade on the tractor, and the effect of increased or decreased rolling resistance on the tractor.

Figure 6-3 illustrates a two-wheel tractor-pulled scraper.

Example Consider the tractor whose performance data is illustrated in Fig. 6-2. The tractor must provide a drawbar pull of 12,000 lb to tow an attached load up a 6 percent grade over a haul road having a rolling resistance of 80 lb per ton. Determine the equivalent required drawbar pull and the maximum speed for the tractor.

The weight of the tractor is 23.75 tons.

The equivalent drawbar pull is as follows:

1. Required by towed load   = 12,000 lb
2. Required by grade, $23.75 \times 6 \times 20$ = 2,850 lb
  Subtotal   = 14,850 lb
3. Reduction in rolling resistance, $23.75(110 - 80)$ = 712 lb
  Total   = 14,138 lb

An examination of Fig. 6-2 indicates that the tractor can operate in third gear at a speed of 4 mph.

Figure 6-3 Two-wheel tractor-pulled scraper. *(WABCO Construction and Mining Equipment Group.)*

Wheel tractors One of the primary advantages of a wheel tractor compared with a crawler tractor is the higher speed possible with the former, in excess of 30 mph for some models. However, in order to attain a higher speed a wheel tractor must sacrifice pulling effort. Also, because of the lower coefficient of traction between rubber tires and some soil surfaces, the wheel tractor may slip its wheels before developing its rated pulling effort.

The traction developed by a wheel tractor is expressed in pounds, rimpull. This is a measure of the tractive effort which the engine is capable of delivering to the surface supporting the driving wheels. The net drawbar pull of a wheel tractor is obtained by deducting from the available rimpull the pull required to overcome the rolling resistance of the unit when it is traveling on a level haul surface or by deducting from the product of the coefficient of traction and the gross weight on the pulling wheels the pull required to overcome the rolling resistance, using whichever value is the smaller. As the speed is increased

Table 6-2 Representative specifications for two-wheel tractors

Approximate weight, lb (kg):	32,200 (14,560)		17,740 (8,050)	
Engine hp (kW)	275 (205)		180 (134)	
Ratio, lb per hp (kg/kW)	117 (71)		98 (60)	
Tire sizes, in. (mm)	24.00 × 29 (610 × 738)		21.00 × 25 (534 × 635)	

		Performance data		
Speed Gear	Speed, mph (km/h)*	Rimpull, lb (kg)†	Speed, mph (km/h)*	Rimpull, lb (kg)†
1st	2.16 (3.48)	25,000‡ (11,380)	3.41 (5.50)	15,850 (7,175)
2nd	4.18 (6.73)	17,100 (7,785)	7.25 (11.70)	7,450 (3,380)
3rd	7.15 (11.50)	10,050 (4,560)	12.63 (20.35)	4,280 (1,945)
4th	12.18 (19.60)	5,880 (2,670)	22.28 (35.90)	2,420 (1,100)
5th	20.00 (32.20)	3,580 (1,620)	35.03 (56.35)	1,540 (700)
Reverse	2.79 (4.49)	25,000‡ (11,380)	4.35 (7.00)	12,440 (5,650)

 * To convert mph to km/h, multiply mph by 1.609.
 † To convert lb to kg, multiply lb by 0.454.
 ‡ These rimpulls are limited by the maximum traction resulting from the weights on the tires, when pulling loaded scrapers.

through the selection of higher gears, the rimpull will be decreased in approximately the same proportion. Thus, for a given unit whose engine is operated at a rated power, the product of the speed times the rimpull will remain approximately constant.

Performance data for wheel tractors While most wheel tractors are equipped with torque converters and power-shift transmissions, some are equipped for direct drive. For this reason performance data will be presented for both types.

Table 6-2 illustrates the type of specifications provided for wheel tractors equipped for direct drive.

Figure 6-4 illustrates the type of information that may be provided for a wheel tractor by the manufacturer. The unit consists of a two-wheel tractor and a two-wheel scraper having the following specifications:

Engine fwhp, 250
Scraper capacity
  Struck, 14 cu yd
  Heaped, 18 cu yd

Weight of unit, lb:	Tractor	Scraper	Total
Empty	33,570	14,730	48,300
Loaded	49,670	40,630	90,300
Distribution	55%	45%	100%

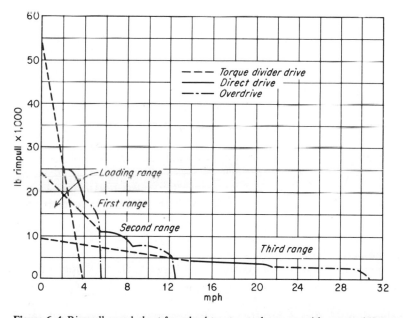

Figure 6-4 Rimpull-speed chart for wheel tractor and scraper with power-shift transmission. Usable rimpull will depend on traction available and total weight of tractor drive wheels. *(Caterpillar Tractor Company.)*

The tractor is equipped to permit torque divider drive, direct drive, or overdrive in each gear range. When an engine is capable of providing the required rimpull, the overdrive should be used in order to make use of the higher speed.

The figure is a performance chart whose purpose is to enable the user of the unit to determine the maximum possible speed for a given load and haul condition, as illustrated by the following example.

Example Determine the maximum speed for the tractor of Fig. 6-4 for the stated conditions.

Gross vehicle weight loaded, 88,000 lb
Grade   = 6%
Rolling resistance, 80 lb per ton =   4%
  Total resistance   = 10%
Required rimpull, 88,000 × 0.10 = 8,800 lb

Figure 6-4 reveals that this rimpull can be provided by any one of the three gear ranges. However, the maximum speed, 8 mph, is obtained in the second range using direct drive.

Another type of performance chart is illustrated in Fig. 6-5. This chart is applicable for a two-wheel tractor and a two-wheel scraper having the following specifications:

Engine fwhp at 2,100 rpm, 398
Scraper capacity
  Struck, 24 cu yd
  Heaped, 32 cu yd

Weight of unit, lb:	Tractor	Scraper	Total
Empty	51,700	27,650	79,350
Loaded	81,270	78,080	159,350
Distribution	51%	49%	100%

The tractor is equipped with a six-speed power-shift transmission with an overdrive in the top five speed ranges. The total resistance in percent of vehicle weight is the algebraic sum of the resistances resulting from grade and rolling resistance. The maximum speed is determined by applying the following steps:

1. Start with the appropriate vehicle weight on the lower left horizontal scale.
2. Read up this weight line to the intersection with the sloping total resistance line.
3. From this intersection read horizontally to the right to the intersection with the speed range performance curve.
4. From this intersection read down to the lower right scale to determine the vehicle speed.

If the application of step 3 results in the intersection of two speed range curves, use the curve which gives the higher speed.

The following example illustrates the method of using Fig. 6-5.

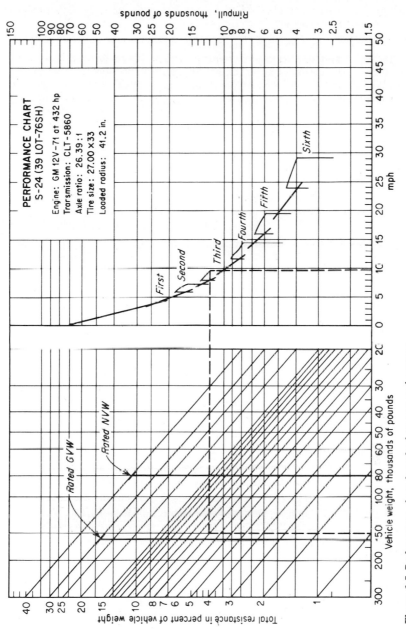

Figure 6-5 Performance chart for wheel tractor and scraper.

Example Determine the maximum speed for the tractor for the stated conditions.

Gross vehicle weight loaded, 150,000 lb
Grade   = 5%
Rolling resistance, 60 lb per ton   = 3%
   Total resistance   = 8%

The two dashed lines, representing steps 1, 2, and 3, indicate that the tractor can operate in the third speed range, using normal or overdrive position. Because the use of overdrive will permit a speed of 9.5 mph, whereas normal will permit a speed of only 8 mph, the former should be used.

GRADABILITY

Gradability is defined as the maximum slope, expressed as a percent, up which a crawler or wheel-type prime mover may move at a uniform speed. The gradability may be determined for an empty or a loaded vehicle. Thus, the gradability of a tractor only will be greater than for a tractor that is pulling a loaded vehicle. Gradability may be specified for any desired gear.

The forward motion of a prime mover is limited by the following factors:

1. The power developed by the engine and available as drawbar pull or rimpull.
2. The rolling resistance of the haul road.
3. The gross weight of the prime mover and its load.
4. The grade to be negotiated. Adverse grade adds to the resistance, while favorable grade subtracts from the resistance.

The gradability of a crawler tractor is determined by subtracting from the available drawbar pull the total pull required to overcome the rolling resistance on the unit and any load that it will pull. The surplus drawbar pull, if it is less than the coefficient of traction multiplied by the weight of the tractor, is then available to negotiate a grade. As the drawbar pull of a crawler tractor, taken from the manufacturer's specifications, is usually based on a rolling resistance of 110 lb per ton, any rolling resistance in excess of this amount should be applied to the weight of the tractor. The entire rolling resistance on the towed load should be used. In order to provide a reasonable factor of safety, not more than 85 percent of the rated drawbar pull of a tractor should be used in determining the gradability of the unit.

Example Determine the gradability of a crawler tractor pulling a high-pressure rubber-tired self-loading scraper and its load. The following information is available:

Tractor horsepower, 180
Weight of tractor, 40,500 lb or 20.25 tons
Drawbar pull in 1st gear, 33,714 lb
Available drawbar pull 0.85 × 33,714 = 28,600 lb
Weight of loaded scraper, 78,960 lb or 39.48 tons
Haul road, rutted, uneven earth
Rolling resistance for tractor, 160 lb per ton

Excess rolling resistance for tractor, 50 lb per ton
Rolling resistance for scraper, 210 lb per ton

The gradability is determined as follows:

Rolling resistance of tractor, 20.25 × 50	=	1,012 lb
Rolling resistance of scraper, 39.48 × 210 =		8,291 lb
Combined rolling resistance	=	9,303 lb

Drawbar pull available to overcome grade:

Maximum available drawbar pull	=	28,600 lb
Required for rolling resistance	=	−9,303 lb
Pull available for grade	=	19,297 lb

Combined weight of tractor and loaded scraper:

Tractor, 20.25 tons
Scraper, 39.48 ton
   Total 59.73 tons

Pull required per ton per 1% grade, 20 lb
Pull required per 1% grade for the total load, 20 × 59.73 = 1,195 lb
Maximum possible grade, $\dfrac{19,297}{1,195}$ = 16%

For the tractor alone the maximum possible grade will be:

Maximum available drawbar pull	=	28,600 lb
Pull required for rolling resistance =		−1,012 lb
Pull available for grade	=	27,588 lb

Pull required per 1% grade, 20 × 20.25 = 405 lb
Maximum possible grade, $\dfrac{27,588}{405}$ = 68%, provided the tracks do not slip

The gradability of a wheel-type tractor or a truck can be determined in the same manner as for a crawler tractor. However, if the manufacturer's specifications furnish sufficient information, the gradability for any gear can be determined from the formula

$$K = \frac{972 \times T \times G}{R \times W} - \frac{N}{20} \qquad (6\text{-}1)$$

where K = gradability, %
 T = rated engine torque, lb-ft
 G = total gear reduction for particular gear selected
 R = rolling radius, the radius of the loaded driving wheels, in., measured from center of axle to surface of ground
 W = gross weight of complete unit, lb
 N = rolling resistance, lb per ton

Example Determine the gradability of a wheel-tractor-pulled wagon and its load, when operating in third gear at sea level. The following information will apply:

Rated torque at 2,100 rpm, 750 lb-ft
Total gear reduction, 41.0
Rolling radius, loaded, 29.38 in.
Gross weight, 138,500 lb
Rolling resistance, 50 lb per ton

$$K = \frac{972 \times 750 \times 41.0}{29.38 \times 138,500} - \frac{50}{20} = 7.3 - 2.5 = 4.8\%$$

The value, 4.8 percent, is obtained by using the full torque of the engine. If only 85 percent of the torque is considered, as a safety precaution, the gradability will be

$$K = 7.3 \times 0.85 - 2.5 = 6.2 - 2.5 = 3.7\%$$

If the rolling resistance of the haul road is permitted to increase to 80 lb per ton, and 85 percent of the torque is considered, the gradability will be

$$K = 6.2 - 80/20 = 6.2 - 4.0 = 2.2\%$$

Table 6-3 gives representative gradability for a wheel-tractor-pulled wagon, both empty and loaded, operating at sea level, based on using the full engine torque. In addition, the following information is applicable:

Engine, 300 belt hp
Rated torque at 2,100 rpm, 750 lb-ft
Rolling radius, 29.38 in.
Empty weight of tractor and wagon, 58,500 lb
Gross weight with load, 138,500 lb
Coefficient of traction, 0.6
Rolling resistance, 40 lb per ton

An appropriate performance chart, such as Fig. 6-5, can also be used to determine the gradability of a tractor, as illustrated by the following example.

Example Determine the gradability of the tractor represented in Fig. 6-5 when it is operating with a gross vehicle weight of 150,000 lb at a uniform speed of 10 mph. The steps are as follows:

1. Read up the 10-mph line to the intersection with the normal drive curve for the fourth speed range.
2. Read horizontally to the left to the intersection with the 150,000-lb vehicle weight line.
3. Read upward to the left, parallel with the sloping total resistance lines, to the value 6.7 percent, which is the combined resistance of the grade and the rolling resistance.
4. Deduct the rolling resistance of the haul road, expressed as a percent, from the 6.7 percent. The remainder is the maximum grade up which this vehicle can operate at a uniform speed. For example, if the rolling resistance is 60 lb per ton, equal to 3 percent, the maximum grade will be $6.7 - 3.0 = 3.7$ percent.

Table 6-3 Representative gradability of a wheel tractor and wagon

Gear	Speed		Gear reduction	Gradability, %	
	mph	(km/h)		Empty	Loaded
1st	3.1	(5.0)	116.9:1	22.0*	18.8
2d	5.2	(8.3)	70.3:1	22.0*	10.5
3d	9.0	(14.5)	41.0:1	15.3	5.3
4th	15.7	(25.2)	23.5:1	7.8	2.2
5th	24.7	(39.7)	14.9:1	4.3	0.6
Reverse	4.1	(6.6)	90.0:1	22.0*	14.0

* These values are limited by the maximum traction between the tires and the haul road.

BULLDOZERS

GENERAL INFORMATION

The term bulldozer may be used in a broad sense to include both a bulldozer and an angledozer. These machines may be further divided, on the basis of their mountings, into crawler-tractor- or wheel-tractor-mounted. Based on the method of raising and lowering the blade a bulldozer may be classified as cable-controlled or as hydraulically controlled. Each type of equipment has a place in the construction industry. For some projects either type will be satisfactory, while for other projects one type will be superior.

Bulldozers are versatile machines on many construction projects, where they may be used from the start to the finish for such operations as:

1. Clearing land of timber and stumps
2. Opening up pilot roads through mountains and rocky terrain
3. Moving earth for haul distances up to approximately 300 ft
4. Helping load tractor-pulled scrapers
5. Spreading earth fill
6. Backfilling trenches
7. Clearing construction sites of debris
8. Maintaining haul roads
9. Clearing the floors of borrow and quarry pits

Bulldozers are mounted with blades perpendicular to the direction of travel, while angledozers are mounted with the blades set at an angle with the direction

Figure 6-6 Hydraulic-controlled bulldozer. *(Caterpillar Tractor Company.)*

of travel. The former push the earth forward, while the latter push it forward and to one side. Some blades may be adjusted to permit their use as bulldozers or angledozers. The size of a bulldozer is indicated by the length and height of the blade. Plates may be installed at the ends of a blade to reduce the spillage when a machine is used for moving earth.

CRAWLER-MOUNTED VERSUS WHEEL-MOUNTED BULLDOZERS

At one time bulldozers were mounted on crawler tractors only. However, with the development of wheel tractors, bulldozers have been mounted on them also. Each type of mounting has advantages under certain conditions. For some jobs the conditions are such that either type may be used satisfactorily.

Among the advantages claimed for the crawler-mounted bulldozer are the following:

1. Ability to deliver greater tractive effort, especially in operating on soft footing, such as loose or muddy soil
2. Ability to travel over muddy surfaces
3. Ability to operate in rocky formations, where rubber tires might be seriously damaged
4. Ability to travel over rough surfaces, which may reduce the cost of maintaining haul roads
5. Greater flotation because of the lower pressures under the tracks
6. Greater use versatility on jobs

Among the advantages claimed for wheel-mounted bulldozers are the following:

1. Higher travel speeds on the job or from one job to another
2. Elimination of hauling equipment to transport the bulldozer to a job
3. Greater output, especially when considerable traveling is necessary
4. Less operator fatigue
5. Ability to travel on paved highways without damaging the surface

If the equipment user has a job which is large enough to justify the purchase of special equipment, he should select the equipment that is most suitable for the particular job. However, since small jobs will seldom justify the purchase of special equipment, it is desirable to select equipment which can be used on other jobs. Under the latter conditions the selection of versatile equipment will usually be a wise choice.

Figure 6-7 illustrates a crawler-mounted bulldozer opening up construction on a precarious mountain road-building job where sharp rocks predominate. For work of this type the crawler-mounted bulldozer is usually superior to the wheel-mounted. Figure 6-8 illustrates a wheel-mounted bulldozer.

Figure 6-7 Crawler-tractor-mounted bulldozer. *(Caterpillar Tractor Company.)*

Figure 6-8 Wheel-tractor-mounted bulldozer. *(Caterpillar Tractor Company.)*

MOVING EARTH WITH BULLDOZERS

Under certain conditions bulldozers are satisfactory machines for moving earth for such jobs as excavating ponds for stock water, trench silos, and highway cuts, stripping the topsoil from land or ore deposits, constructing low levees, backfilling trenches, spreading material on fills, etc. In general, haul distances should be less than 300 ft. Either a crawler-mounted or a wheel-mounted tractor may be used, a crawler-mounted machine having an advantage on short hauls with soft or muddy ground, and a wheel-mounted machine possibly having an advantage on longer hauls and firm ground.

The output of a bulldozer will vary with the conditions under which it operates. During the first passes over a given lane most of the initial earth will spill off the ends of the blade to form a windrow on each side of the lane. After these windrows have been built up to form a trench, further end spillage will be reduced or eliminated, with a substantial increase in output. Steel plates on the ends of a blade will reduce end spillage. On some jobs two bulldozers, working side by side, with adjacent ends of the blades in contact, have been used to increase the output as much as 50 percent over the combined output of two machines working separately. If earth can be pushed downhill, the output of a machine will be increased substantially because of the advantage of the favorable grade and the ability to float larger quantities of earth ahead of the machine. Figure 6-9 illustrates two bulldozers operating under favorable conditions, namely, downhill dozing, slot excavation, side-by-side operation, and floating extra earth ahead of the machine.

THE OUTPUT OF BULLDOZERS

The blade of a bulldozer has a theoretical capacity which varies with the class of earth and the size of the blade. If the capacity of a blade is known, one can determine the approximate output of a machine by estimating the number of passes it will make in an hour.

Example Estimate the approximate output of a bulldozer for the following conditions:

Material, sandy loam topsoil, weight 2,700 lb per cu yd bm
Swell, 25%
Haul distance, 100 ft, over level ground, with bulldozer operating in a slot
Crawler tractor, 72 drawbar hp
Moldboard size, 9 ft 6 in. long, 3 ft 0 in. high
Rated moldboard capacity, 3.6 cu yd loose volume
Net moldboard capacity, 3.6 ÷ 1.25 = 2.9 cu yd bm
Operating factor, 50-min hr
Probable round-trip time

Pushing, 100 ft @ 1.5 mph	= 0.758 min
Returning, 100 ft @ 3.5 mph	= 0.324 min
Fixed time, loading and shifting gears	= 0.320 min
Total time	= 1.402 min

Trip per hr, 50 ÷ 1.402 = 35.7
Output per hr, 35.7 trips @ 2.9 cu yd = 103.4 cu yd bm

Figure 6-9 Operating two bulldozers side by side.

The output given in the example is based on favorable operating conditions which permit a load equal to the maximum capacity of the dozer. For most projects the load will be less than the maximum possible capacity. For example, if the earth is ordinary soil, the load might be reduced to 2.0 cu yd bank measure. With other conditions remaining the same the output per hour will be

35.7 trips @ 2.0 cu yd = 71.4 cu yd bm

The approximate capacity of a bulldozer blade may be determined from the size of the load pushed by the blade. Actual measurements of representative loads will give better results than estimates. For example, if a blade 9 ft 6 in. long by 3 ft 0 in. high is used to push earth in a slot or trench whose height is about equal to that of the blade, it is possible to fill the blade to full length and height. Although the shape of the front slope of the earth will be irregular, assume that it is equivalent to a 2 : 1 slope. The size of the load will be 9 ft 6 in. long, 3 ft 0 in. high, and 6 ft 0 in. wide. The loose volume will be

$$\frac{9.5 \times 3 \times 6}{2 \times 27} = 3.2 \text{ cu yd}$$

For a swell of 25 percent the net volume will be

3.2 ÷ 1.25 = 2.56 cu yd bm

Table 6-4 Representative blade capacities and bulldozer output

In cubic yards bank measure

Blade length	Blade height, in.	Tractor, drawbar hp	Forward speed, fpm	Reverse speed, fpm	Blade capacity, cu yd	Output, cu yd per hr Haul distance, ft			
						100	200	300	400
11 ft 3 in.	$45\frac{1}{2}$	130	150	326	4.8	184	105	74	57
10 ft 3 in.	$45\frac{1}{2}$	80	123	334	4.4	152	86	60	46
9 ft 6 in.	38	65	123	343	2.8	98	55	38	29
8 ft 2 in.	38	65	123	343	2.4	84	47	33	25
7 ft 2 in.	$32\frac{1}{2}$	43	150	167	1.5	47	26	18	14
5 ft 8 in.	$27\frac{1}{2}$	32	150	185	0.9	29	16	11	9
11 ft 2 in.	43	210*	141	712	4.2	178	103	73	56
11 ft 3 in.	36	122*	141	712	3.0	127	74	52	40

* These values are flywheel horsepower for wheel-mounted dozers.

If the dozing is done without slots, the capacity of the blade will be reduced by approximately 25 percent. Also, if the earth is so hard that a full load cannot be moved, the capacity must be reduced accordingly.

Table 6-4 gives approximate blade capacities and outputs in cubic yards bank measure for various sizes of blades and tractors. The information given in the table is based on pushing full loads in slots. It is assumed that the tractors will push the loads forward in first gear, then return for another load in reverse gear. It is assumed that the tractors will operate 50 min per hr. For other job conditions the outputs given in the table must be modified.

CLEARING LAND

LAND CLEARING OPERATIONS

Clearing land may be divided into several operations, depending on the type of vegetation, the condition of the soil and topography, the amount of clearing required, and the purpose for which the clearing is done, as listed below.

1. Complete removal of all trees and stumps, including roots
2. Removing all vegetation above the surface of the ground only, leaving stumps and roots in the ground
3. Disposing of vegetation by stacking and burning it
4. Knocking all vegetation down then chopping or crushing it to or into the surface of the ground, or burning it later

5. Killing or retarding the growth of brush by cutting the roots below the surface of the ground

TYPES OF EQUIPMENT USED

Several types of equipment are used for clearing land, with varying degrees of success. Included are the following:

1. Tractor-mounted bulldozers
2. Tractor-mounted special blades
3. Tractor-mounted rakes
4. Tractor-pulled chains and steel cables
5. Special machines with pusher bars, and drum-type wheels equipped with blades to chop the vegetation as the machine passes over it

Tractor-mounted bulldozers Whereas bulldozers were used extensively during the past to clear land, they are now being replaced by special blades mounted on tractors. There are at least two valid objections to the use of bulldozers. Prior to felling large trees they must excavate earth from around the trees and cut the main roots, which leaves objectionable holes in the ground, and requires much time. Also, when stacking the felled trees and other vegetation they transport considerable earth to the piles, which makes burning more difficult.

Tractor-mounted special blades Two types of special blades are used to fell trees; both are mounted on the front ends of tractors.

One is a single-angle blade with a projecting stinger on the lead side, extending ahead of the blade, so that it may be forced into and through a tree to split and weaken it. Thus, if a tree is too large to be felled in one pass, the trunk may be split and removed in parts. Also, the tractor may make a pass around a tree with the stinger penetrating the ground to cut the main horizontal roots of the tree. Figure 6-10 shows this blade in use. It may be used to remove stumps and to stack material for burning.

Another type of special blade is a V blade, with a protruding stinger at its lead point, as illustrated in Fig. 6-11. The sole effect of the blade permits it to slide along the surface of the ground, thereby cutting vegetation flush with the surface. However, it can be lowered below the surface to remove stumps. Also, the blade may be raised to permit the stinger to pierce a tree above the surface of the ground. Other special blades are shown in Figs. 6-12 and 6-13.

Tractor-mounted rakes Figure 6-14 illustrates a tractor-mounted rake which can be used to grub and pile trees, boulders, and similar materials without transporting excess quantities of soil. Granular material, such as sand and gravel, flows between the teeth readily. Optional tooth spacing is available for use under

Figure 6-10 Land-clearing blade piercing tree with stinger. *(Rome Industries.)*

Figure 6-11 Tractor-mounted V blade for clearing land. *(Fleco Corporation.)*

Figure 6-12 Tractor-mounted V blade splitting a large tree. *(Fleco Corporation.)*

Figure 6-13 Tractor-mounted clearing blade. *(Rome Industries.)*

Figure 6-14 Tractor-mounted land-clearing rake. *(Fleco Corporation.)*

varying soil conditions. However, some plastic material may tend to combine with the vegetation and clog the spaces between the teeth.

This rake can be an effective tool when stacking the cleared material in piles for burning.

Tractor-mounted clamp rakes Figure 6-15 illustrates a tractor-mounted clamp rake which can be used to pick up felled trees and brush and transport them to sites for burning or to other sites for disposal. For some projects this method of handling the material is better than using a tractor-mounted rake to push it over the surface of the ground. Using this type of rake reduces or eliminates the soil transported to the stack. Also, because of its higher reach, the clamp rake can be more effective in reshaping a pile of material to increase the rate of burning.

Tractor-pulled chains Figure 6-16 illustrates a heavy chain pulled by two crawler tractors, which is effective in felling trees and partially eliminating brush when used to clear semiarid land. The effectiveness of the chain may be increased by welding steel sections, such as short lengths of rail, to the links perpendicular to the chain. The extra weight holds the chain closer to the surface of the ground and removes more of the smaller brush and other vegetation.

A second trip over the previously chained area several months after the first pass, with the chain pulled in the opposite direction, will further reduce the quantity of surviving vegetation.

Tractor-pulled root plows Figure 6-17 illustrates a tractor-mounted root plow which has been very effective in killing small trees and brush, especially when it

Figure 6-15 Tractor-mounted clamp rake. *(Fleco Corporation.)*

Figure 6-16 Tractor-pulled chain used to clear land. *(Caterpillar Tractor Company.)*

Figure 6-17 Tractor-pulled root plow.

is used in clearing semiarid land. The plow floats under the surface of the ground at a predetermined depth to slice the roots of the plants below the bud zones, thereby preventing many of them from resprouting.

This method of clearing land is economical and effective when used on a project in which it is not necessary to disturb the surface of the ground, such as clearing the right-of-way for a transmission line, or to increase the grazing capacity of range land.

Tree crusher Figure 6-18 illustrates a machine that has been used effectively in crushing and shredding trees and other vegetation. When the machine moves over land to be cleared, the beam mounted on the front pushes the trees ahead and downward, thereby permitting the grouser-type cutter blades attached to the drum-type wheels to chop or shred the vegetation to small pieces that may be left at the site or disposed of by stockpiling and burning.

Because this method produces only partial clearing of land, its use should be limited to projects which do not require complete clearing, such as right-of-ways for transmission lines, lake beds, etc.

Cutting trees with a shear Figure 6-19 illustrates a tractor-mounted shear which may be used to cut trees above the surface of the ground. This machine is especially useful for felling only selected trees without disturbing others.

Figure 6-18 Tree-shredding machine. *(Marathon-LeTourneau Company.)*

Figure 6-19 Tractor-mounted grapple shear cutting a tree. *(Rome Industries.)*

Figure 6-20 Burning brush with forced draft and fuel oil. *(Fleco Corporation.)*

DISPOSAL OF BRUSH

When brush is to be disposed of by burning, it should be piled in stacks and windrows, with a minimum amount of soil. Shaking a rake while it is moving the brush will reduce the amount of soil present.

If the brush and trees are burned while the moisture content is high, it may be necessary to provide a continuous external source of fuel, such as oil, to maintain satisfactory combustion. The burner illustrated in Fig. 6-20, which consists of a gasoline-engine-driven pump and a propeller, is capable of maintaining a fire even under adverse conditions. The liquid fuel is blown into the pile of material as a stream while the propeller furnishes a supply of air to assure vigorous burning.

PRODUCTION RATES

As previously stated, the rate of clearing land will depend on several variables, including, but not limited to, the following: (1) density of vegetation, (2) sizes and kinds of trees, (3) kind of soil, (4) topography, (5) rainfall, (6) types of equipment used, (7) skill of equipment operators, and (8) requirements of the specifications governing the project.

Formula (6-2) may be used as a guide in estimating the required time to fell trees only, using a shear-type cutting blade illustrated in Fig. 6-10, mounted on a crawler tractor of the size indicated in Table 6-5 [1]. Prior to preparing an estimate, the estimator should visit the project to be cleared in order to obtain information needed to evaluate the variable factors in the formula. With this information reasonably applicable values can be assigned to the factors listed in

Table 6-5 Representative times in minutes for cutting trees with tractor-mounted blades

Size tractor, fwhp	Base time B	Time to cut a tree*				Time per foot for diameters above 6 ft F
		1–2 ft dia. M_1	2–3 ft dia. M_2	3–4 ft dia. M_3	4–6 ft dia. M_4	
93	40	0.8	4.0	8.0	25	. . .
130	28	0.5	2.0	4.0	12	4.0
190	21	0.3	1.5	2.5	7	2.0
320	18	0.3	0.5	1.5	4	1.2

* The times listed are for cutting trees flush with the surface of the ground. If it is necessary to remove the stumps, the times should be increased by 50 percent.

Table 6-5. Thus we have

$$T = B + M_1N_1 + M_2N_2 + M_3N_3 + M_4N_4 + DF \tag{6-2}$$

where T = time per acre, min

B = base time required for a tractor to cover an acre with no trees requiring splitting or individual treatment, min

M = time required per tree in each diameter range, min

N = number of trees per acre in each diameter range obtained from a field survey

D = sum of diameter in feet of all trees per acre, if any, larger than 6 ft in diameter at ground level

F = time required per foot of diameter to fell trees larger than 6 ft in diameter, min

Formula (6-2) may also be used to estimate the time required to stack felled trees into windrows spaced approximately 200 ft apart, by letting M_1, M_2, etc., represent the time required to move a tree into a windrow. Table 6-6 gives representative values for the time required to pile trees.

Table 6-6 Representative times in minutes for stacking trees with tractor-mounted blades

Size tractor, fwhp	Base time B	Time to stack a tree				Time per foot for diameters above 6 ft F
		1–2 ft dia. M_1	2–3 ft dia. M_2	3–4 ft dia. M_3	4–6 ft dia. M_4	
93	35	0.3	0.6	2.5	. . .	. . .
130	28	0.2	0.4	1.5	3.0	. . .
190	24	0.1	0.3	1.0	2.0	0.4
320	20	0.0	0.1	0.7	1.2	0.2

COST OF CLEARING LAND

The cost of clearing land varies considerably with the factors previously listed. Very little information on this subject has been released. However, in 1958 the Agricultural Experiment Station of Auburn University, Auburn, Alabama, conducted tests to determine the cost of clearing land using three sizes of crawler tractors, equipped with bulldozer blades and with shearing blades, such as the one illustrated in Fig. 6-10. The results of the tests have been published in a booklet [2].

For test purposes an area of 24 acres was divided into 12 plots of 2 acres each, with dimensions 198 ft wide by 440 ft long. Each size tractor cleared two plots using a bulldozer blade and two plots using a shearing blade. The net time required to fell, stack, and burn the material from each plot was determined. The trees consisted of pine, oak, hickory, and gum, distributed by species, size, and density as listed in Table 6-7. The diameters of the trees were measured at breast height.

The trees were felled, and then pushed along the surface of the ground and stacked in windrows not more than 198 ft apart, after which they were burned. During the burning operation the timber was pushed into tighter stacks to increase the burning effectiveness, using a tractor-mounted blade.

Table 6-8 shows the average time required by each size crawler tractor and type of blade to fell, stack, and dispose of an acre of timber. The smaller amounts of time required to dispose of trees felled with the shearing blades were the result of the smaller amounts of soil in the roots of trees felled with this type of blade.

Table 6-7 Types of equipment used, species, sizes, and densities of trees

Plot no.	Blade used*	% by species		% by size trees, in.		No. trees per acre
		Hardwood	Pine	To 6	Above 6	
1	B	79	21	87	13	375
2	B	98	2	74	26	285
3	B	97	3	76	24	385
4	B	56	44	87	13	585
5	B	53	47	93	7	680
6	B	78	22	87	13	755
7	S	80	20	86	14	690
8	S	29	71	98	2	1,545
9	S	72	28	82	18	445
10	S	60	40	98	2	710
11	S	89	11	72	28	410
12	S	75	25	76	24	400

* B denotes a bulldozer blade and S denotes a shearing blade.

Table 6-8 Average machine time required, in hours, to clear an acre of land based on size tractor and blade used

| | Time per acre, hr | | | | | |
| | 93 fwhp | | 130 fwhp | | 190 fwhp | |
Operation	B*	S	B	S	B	S
Felling	2.19	1.58	1.71	1.14	0.92	0.71
Stacking	0.52	0.55	0.56	0.60	0.48	0.46
Disposal	1.75	0.84	1.80	0.78	1.93	0.70
Total	4.46	2.97	4.07	2.52	3.33	1.87

* *B* denotes a bulldozer blade and *S* denotes a shearing blade.

RIPPING ROCK

GENERAL INFORMATION

Although rock has been ripped with varying degrees of success for many years, recent developments in methods, equipment, and knowledge have greatly increased the extent of ripping today. Rock that was considered to be unrippable a few years ago is now ripped with relative ease, and at cost reductions, including ripping and hauling with scrapers, amounting to as much as 50 percent when compared with the costs of drilling, blasting, loading with shovels, and hauling with trucks.

The major developments that are responsible for the increase in ripping rock include

1. More powerful tractors
2. Improvements in the sizes and performances of rippers
3. Better instruments for determining the rippability of rocks
4. Improved techniques in using instruments and equipment

DETERMINING THE RIPPABILITY OF ROCK

Prior to selecting the method of excavating and hauling rock it is desirable to determine if the rock can be ripped or if it will be necessary to drill and blast it. Because the rippability of most types of rocks is related to the speed at which sound waves travel through rock it is possible to use seismographic methods to determine with reasonable accuracy if a rock can be ripped.

Rocks which propagate sound waves at low velocities are rippable, whereas rocks which propagate waves at high velocities are not rippable. Rocks having intermediate velocities are classified as marginal. Figure 6-21 indicates the

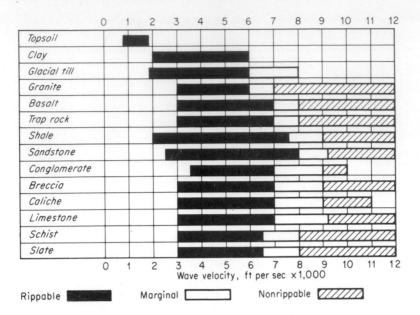

Figure 6-21 Relation between rippability of rock and velocity of sound waves.

velocity ranges for various types of soils and rocks encountered on construction projects. The indication that a rock may be rippable, marginal, or nonrippable is based on using a single-shank hydraulic ripper mounted on a crawler tractor whose engine develops about 385 fwhp. If two such tractors are used in tandem to pull one ripper, the rippability range can be increased somewhat, up to velocities as high as 8,000 to 10,000 fps in some instances. The information appearing in the figure should be used as a guide only. The decision to rip or not to rip rock should be based on the relative costs of excavating, using the methods under consideration, and the equipment available. If smaller tractors are to be used, the upper limits on the velocities of rock to be ripped will be less than those appearing in Fig. 6-21. Field tests may be necessary to determine if a given rock can be ripped economically.

DETERMINING THE SPEED OF SOUND WAVES IN ROCK

Figure 6-22 shows a type of geophysical equipment that is used to determine the velocity of sound waves in soil. Figure 6-23 illustrates the paths followed by sound waves from the wave-generating source through a formation to the detecting instruments. A geophone, which is a sound sensor, is driven into the ground at station 0. Equally spaced points 1, 2, 3, etc., are located along a line, as indicated. A wire is connected from the geophone to the seismic timer, and another wire is connected from the timer to a sledge hammer, or another impact producing tool. A steel plate is placed on the ground at stations 1 through 8, in

Figure 6-22 Geophysical equipment used to determine the velocity of sound waves in soil. *(Soiltest, Inc.)*

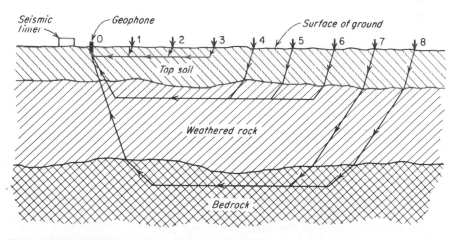

Figure 6-23 Paths of sound waves through formations.

successive order. When the hammer strikes the steel plate, a switch closes instantly to send an electric signal to the timer, which starts the timer. At the same instant the blow from the hammer sends sound waves into the formation, which travel to the geophone. Upon the receipt of the first wave the geophone signals the timer to stop recording elapsed time. With the distance and time known, the velocity of a wave can be determined.

As the distance from the geophone to the wave source, namely the steel plate, is increased, waves from the plate will enter the lower and more dense formation, through which they will travel at a higher speed than through the top soil, and thus will reach the geophone before the waves through the top soil arrive. When the velocity through the denser formation is determined, it will be noted that it has a higher value, which velocity will remain approximately constant as long as the waves travel through a formation of uniform density.

The distance from the geophone to the point along the stations from which the waves reach the geophone first through the lower formation may be determined as illustrated in Fig. 6-24. In this figure the travel times for the waves are plotted against the distances to the impact stations. For each formation the velocity is essentially a straight line. The point of intersection of the velocity lines indicates the critical distance from the geophone.

The depth to the surface separating the two strata depends on the critical distance and the velocities in the two materials. It can be computed from the formula

$$D_1 = \frac{L_1}{2}\sqrt{\frac{V_2 - V_1}{V_2 + V_1}} \tag{6-3}$$

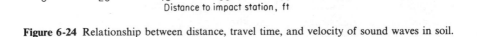

Figure 6-24 Relationship between distance, travel time, and velocity of sound waves in soil.

where D = depth, ft

$\quad L_1$ = critical distance, ft

$\quad V_1$ = velocity of wave in top stratum, fps

$\quad V_2$ = velocity of wave in lower stratum, fps

Solving formula (6-3) for D_1 gives

$$D_1 = \frac{36}{2}\sqrt{\frac{3,000 - 1,000}{3,000 + 1,000}} = 13 \, ft$$

Thus the topsoil has an apparent depth of 13 ft.

Formula (6-4) may be used to determine the apparent depth of the two top strata, namely the topsoil and the weathered rock.

$$D_2 = \frac{C_2}{2}\sqrt{\frac{V_3 - V_2}{V_3 + V_2}}$$

$$+ D_1\left[1 - \frac{V_2\sqrt{V_3^2 - V_1^2} - V_3\sqrt{V_2^2 - V_1^2}}{V_1\sqrt{V_3^2 - V_2^2}}\right] \tag{6-4}$$

where C_2 = 70 ft

$\quad D_1$ = 13 ft

$\quad V_1$ = 1,000 fps

$\quad V_2$ = 3,000 fps

$\quad V_3$ = 6,000 fps

Solving,

$\quad D_2$ = 31 ft

TYPES OF RIPPERS

Figures 6-25 through 6-27 illustrate several types of tractor-mounted hydraulically operated rippers, which are more commonly used than the towed type. The ripper in Fig. 6-25 is using one shank, while the ripper in Fig. 6-26 is using three shanks. The number of shanks used depends on the size of the tractor, the depth of penetration desired, the resistance of the material being ripped, and the degree of breakage of the material desired. If the material is to be excavated by self-loading scrapers, it should be broken into particles that can be loaded into scrapers, usually not more than 24 to 30 in. maximum sizes. Only a field test conducted at the project will demonstrate which method, depth, and degree of breakage is most satisfactory and economical.

Another method of classifying rippers is illustrated in Fig. 6-28. The shank in a is attached to the tractor with a parallel-type linkage, while the shank in b is attached with a hinge- or radial-type linkage.

As the depth of penetration of the parallel-type linkage is varied, the point is kept at a constant angle, which reduces the wear and stabilizes the production.

Figure 6-25 Tractor-mounted hydraulically operated ripper. *(Caterpillar Tractor Company.)*

Figure 6-26 Tractor-mounted hydraulically operated triple-shank ripper. *(Fiat-Allis Construction Machinery, Inc.)*

Figure 6-27 Tractor-mounted parallelogram-type hydraulically operated ripper. *(Soiltest, Inc.)*

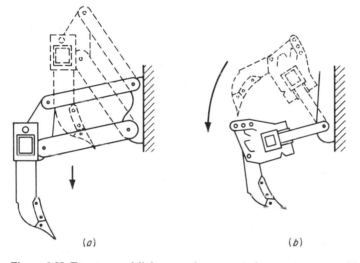

(a)   (b)

Figure 6-28 Two types of linkage used to mount rippers on tractors. (*a*) Parallel: By raising and lowering shank through almost vertical plane, parallel-type linkage keeps points at constant angle at any penetration depth. This holds the tip at its best cutting angle, reduces wear, and smooths output. (*b*) Hinge: The traditional linkage arrangement swings the clevis and shank down through an arc, changing the point angle at various depths. Hinged rippers offer some advantages in boulder-strewn soil.

The angle of the point of the hinge-type linkage will vary as the depth of penetration is varied, which may be a disadvantage with some types of rock. However, hinge-type rippers may offer some advantages when ripping soil containing boulders.

ECONOMY OF RIPPING ROCK

Although the cost of excavating rock by ripping and scraper loading is considerably higher than for earth that requires no ripping, it may be much less expensive than using an alternate method, such as drilling, blasting, shovel loading, and truck hauling. An example of a reduction in cost effected by the use of ripping and scraper hauling is illustrated by the experience of a contractor who constructed a section of Interstate 5 highway in southern Oregon [4]. The rock was sandstone and volcanic agglomerate with some decomposed granite and basalt.

In preparing his estimate the contractor planned to handle most of the material by drilling, blasting, shovel loading, and truck hauling, as indicated in the accompanying table. However, job experience demonstrated that he could handle most of the rock by ripping and scraper loading, with a substantial reduction in the cost, as shown in Table 6-9, which is based on revised estimates made prior to completing the project.

Although the scrapers were strengthened considerably for use on this project, the cost of repairs was approximately double the cost for scrapers used on earth projects. The life of scraper tires was reduced from about 4,000 hr to 1,000 and 1,500 hr, depending on where the scrapers were working. It was necessary to limit the scraper loads to approximately 10 percent below their normal struck capacities. Even under these conditions scrapers maintained an average availability factor of 91.5 percent.

The bibliography at the end of this chapter lists sources containing cost information on ripping rock.

Table 6-9 Ripping rock costs versus alternate methods

	Estimated methods, quantities, and costs			Actual methods and costs	
Method	Cost per cu yd	Volume, cu yd	Total cost	Volume, cu yd	Total cost
Blast, shovel, truck	$0.86	3,100,000	$2,666,000	100,000	$ 86,000
Blast, scraper	0.68	none	none	900,000	612,000
Ripper, scraper	0.46	700,000	322,000	2,800,000	1,288,000
Total		3,800,000	$2,988,000	3,800,000	$1,986,000

FRONT-END-LOADERS

USES

Front-end-loaders are used extensively in construction work to handle and transport bulk material, such as earth and rock, to load trucks, to excavate earth, as bulldozers, etc. They are both satisfactory and economical when used for such purposes.

TYPES AND SIZES

There arc basically two types of front-end-loaders, the crawler-tractor-mounted and the wheel-tractor-mounted, as illustrated in Figs. 6-29 and 6-30, respectively. They may be further classified by the capacities of the buckets or the weights that the buckets can lift. Wheel-mounted units may be steered by the rear wheels, or they may be articulated, to permit steering as indicated in Fig. 6-31, which also gives important dimensional specifications.

Figure 6-29 Crawler-tractor-mounted front-end-loader. *(Caterpillar Tractor Company.)*

Figure 6-30 Wheel-tractor-mounted front-end-loader. *(Caterpillar Tractor Company.)*

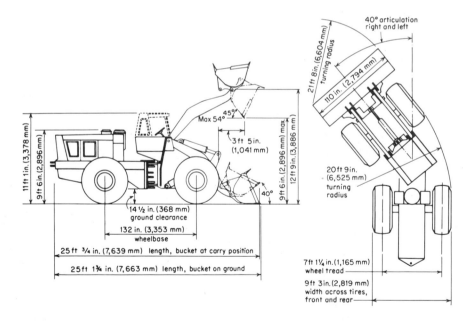

Figure 6-31 Articulated wheel-tractor-mounted loader. *(International Harvester Company.)*

Table 6-10 Bucket selection chart

SAE capacity, cu yd		Weight of material,* lb per cu yd	Weight of material, lb
Struck	Heaped		
4	$4\frac{1}{2}$	1,500	6,750
$2\frac{1}{2}$	3	2,200	6,600
$2\frac{1}{4}$	$2\frac{1}{2}$	2,700	6,750
2	$2\frac{1}{4}$	3,000	6,750
$1\frac{3}{4}$	2	3,300	6,600

* These are loose-measure weights.

OPERATING SPECIFICATIONS

Representative operating specifications for a wheel-tractor loader furnish information such as that listed below.

> Engine flywheel hp @ 2,300 rpm, 119
> Speeds, forward and reverse:
> Low, 0 to 3.9 mph
> Intermediate, 0 to 11.1 mph
> High, 0 to 29.5 mph
> Operating load (SAE)*, 6,800 lb
> Tipping load, straight ahead, 17,400 lb
> Tipping load, full turn, 16,800 lb
> Lifting capacity, 18,600 lb
> Breakout force, maximum, 30,000 lb

The maximum capacity bucket selected for use with this tractor will depend on the weight of the material to be handled, as indicated in the bucket selection chart (Table 6-10). The heaped capacity is based on a slope of 2:1, as approved by the Society of Automotive Engineers (SAE).

PRODUCTION RATES FOR CRAWLER-TRACTOR-LOADERS

The production rate for a tractor loader will depend on the: (1) fixed time required to load the bucket, shift gears, turn, and dump the load, (2) time required to travel from the loading to the dumping position, (3) time required to

---

*The operating load is rated at 50 percent of the tipping load, considering the combined weight of the bucket and the load, measured from the center of gravity of the extended bucket at its maximum reach with standard counterweights and nonballasted tires.

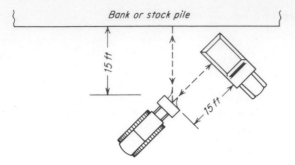

Figure 6-32 Tractor loader loading a truck.

return to the loading position, and (4) the actual volume of material hauled each trip. Figure 6-32 illustrates a typical loading situation, using a crawler-tractor-mounted loader, having the following specifications:

Bucket capacity, heaped, $2\frac{1}{4}$ cu yd

Travel speed by gear:

Forward	mph	fpm
1st	1.9	167
2d	2.9	255
3d	4.0	352
Reverse		
1st	2.3	202
2d	3.6	317
3d	5.0	440

Assume that the tractor will travel at an average of 80 percent of the specified speeds in 2d gear, forward and reverse. The fixed time should be based on time studies for the particular equipment and job.

The cycle time per load will be, in minutes

Fixed time to load, shift, turn, and dump	= 0.40
Haul time, 30 ft ÷ 204 fpm	= 0.15
Return, 30 ÷ 252 fpm	= 0.12
Cycle time	= 0.67 min

Although the rated heaped capacity of the bucket is $2\frac{1}{4}$ cu yd, it is probable that the average volume will be about 90 percent of this capacity for sustained loads. Assume an average capacity of 0.9 × 2.25 = 2.03 cu yd, loose volume.

The production in a 60-min hour will be as follows:

No. cycles, 60/0.67= 90
Volume, 90 × 2.03 = 182.7 cu yd

If the material has a swell of 25 percent, and the tractor has an operating factor of 45 min per hr, the volume per hour in bank measure will be

$$V = \frac{182.7}{1.25} \times \frac{45}{60} = 110 \text{ cu yd}$$

The chart in Fig. 6-33 gives the production rates for crawler-tractor-loaders based on handling earth having a swell of 25 percent and an operating factor of 45 min per hr. The loose weight of the earth is 2,700 lb per cu yd. It is assumed that the actual average volume of earth in a bucket is 90 percent of its rated heaped capacity. The production rates are determined as follows:

Fixed time, 0.40 min
Haul speed, in 2d gear, 0.8 × 255 = 204 fpm
Return speed, in 3d gear, 0.8 × 440 = 352 fpm

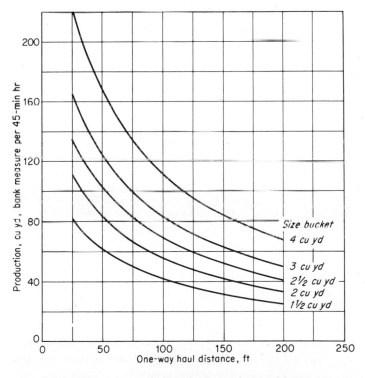

Figure 6-33 Production rates for crawler-tractor-mounted loaders.

Cycle time for one-way distance, ft

Haul distance, ft	25	50	100	150	200
Fixed time	0.40	0.40	0.40	0.40	0.40
Haul time	0.12	0.24	0.49	0.73	0.98
Return time	0.07	0.14	0.28	0.42	0.56
Cycle time, min	0.59	0.78	1.17	1.55	1.94
Trips per hr	76.3	57.8	38.5	29.1	23.2

Volume hauled per hour, in cubic yards bank measure, by sizes of buckets

Size bucket, cu yd		One-way haul distance, ft				
Loose	Bank*	25	50	100	150	200
$1\frac{1}{2}$	1.08	82.3	62.5	41.6	31.5	25.1
2	1.44	110.0	83.5	55.5	42.0	33.5
$2\frac{1}{2}$	1.80	133.0	104.0	69.5	52.5	40.8
3	2.16	164.6	125.0	83.2	63.0	50.2
4	2.88	220.0	167.0	111.0	84.0	67.0

* Based on a swell of 25 percent and an average load equal to 90 percent of the rated capacity.

PRODUCTION RATES FOR WHEEL-TRACTOR-LOADERS

The production rates for wheel-tractor-loaders are determined in the same manner as for crawler-tractor-loaders. However, because they are more maneuverable and can travel faster on smooth haul surfaces, the production rates for wheel units should be higher than for crawler units under favorable conditions.

Consider a wheel unit with a $2\frac{1}{2}$-cu-yd heaped capacity bucket, handling material weighing 2,700 lb per cu yd loose volume, for which the swell is 25 percent. This unit, equipped with a torque converter and a power-shift transmission, has the following speed ranges, forward and reverse:

Low range, 0 to 3.9 mph
Intermediate range, 0 to 11.1 mph
High range, 0 to 29.5 mph

When hauling a loaded bucket, the unit should travel at an average speed of about 80 percent of its maximum speed in the low range. When returning empty, the unit should travel at an average speed of about 60 percent of its maximum speed in the intermediate range for distances less than 100 ft, and at about 80 percent of its maximum speed in the same range for distances of 100 ft and over. The average speeds should be about as follows:

$$\text{Hauling, all distances, } 0.8 \times 3.9 \times 88 \qquad = 274 \text{ fpm}$$
$$\text{Returning, 0 to 100 ft, } 0.6 \times 11.1 \times 88 \qquad = 585 \text{ fpm}$$
$$\text{Returning, 100 ft and over, } 0.8 \times 11.1 \times 88 = 780 \text{ fpm}$$

If the haul surface is not well maintained, or is rough, these speeds should be reduced to realistic values.

Because of the greater maneuverability of the wheel-loader, its fixed time should be slightly less than for a crawler-loader. Assume a fixed time of 0.35 min.

Cycle time

Haul distance, ft	25	50	100	150	200
Fixed time	0.35	0.35	0.35	0.35	0.35
Haul time	0.09	0.18	0.36	0.55	0.73
Return time	0.05	0.09	0.13	0.19	0.26
Cycle time, min	0.49	0.62	0.84	1.09	1.34
Trips per 45-min hr	92.0	72.6	53.7	41.2	33.6

Volume hauled per hour, in cubic yards bank measure, by size of buckets

Size bucket, cu yd		One-way haul distance, ft				
Loose	Bank*	25	50	100	150	200
2	1.44	132.5	104.5	77.2	59.5	40.5
3	2.16	198.0	157.0	116.0	89.0	72.5
4	2.88	264.0	204.5	154.0	118.5	96.6
5	3.60	331.0	261.0	193.0	148.0	122.0
6	4.32	397.0	313.0	231.0	177.0	144.0

* Based on a swell of 25 percent and an average load equal to 90 percent of the rated capacity.

Figure 6-34 illustrates the variations in production rates by sizes of buckets and one-way haul distances.

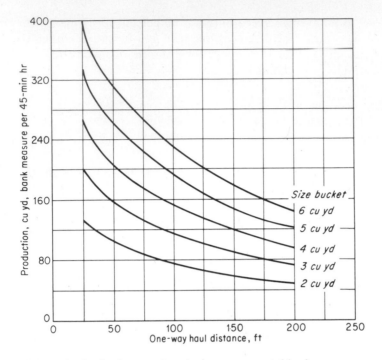

Figure 6-34 Production rates for wheel-tractor-mounted loaders.

PROBLEMS

6-1 If the tractor-pulled scraper for which the rimpull and speed chart of Fig. 6-4 applies hauls a gross vehicle weight of 80,000 lb up a 3 percent slope over a haul road whose rolling resistance is 80 lb per ton, determine the maximum speed range and speed for the vehicle.

6-2 The tractor-pulled scraper for which Fig. 6-4 applies will operate under the following conditions:

Gross vehicle weight, 80,000 lb
Weight on driving wheels, 60 percent of gross weight
Coefficient of traction, 0.5
Rolling resistance of haul road, 90 lb per ton

Determine the maximum grade up which the vehicle can operate in the first speed range in either direct drive or overdrive, considering the available rimpull as limited by the tractor or the coefficient of traction.

6-3 If the tractor-pulled scraper for which Fig. 6-5 applies hauls a gross vehicle weight of 130,000 lb up a 4 percent grade on a haul road whose rolling resistance is 80 lb per ton, determine the maximum speed range and speed for the vehicle.

6-4 Determine the maximum speed of the tractor-pulled scraper for which Fig. 6-5 applies for each of the following conditions:

Gross vehicle weight, 130,000 lb
Weight on driving wheels, 75,000 lb
Coefficient of traction, 0.6
    (*a*) Haul road is level, with a rolling resistance of 80 lb per ton.
    (*b*) Haul road is up a 7 percent grade, with a rolling resistance of 100 lb per ton.
    (*c*) Haul road is down a 5 percent grade, with a rolling resistance of 100 lb per ton.

REFERENCES

1. Latin-American Land Development Seminar, Program and Proceedings, Rome Industries, Cedartown, Georgia 30125.
2. Rome Training Presentations No. 11-A, 11-C, 11-E, 11-F, Rome Industries, Cedartown, Georgia 30125. No dates.
3. Fleco Corporation, P. O. Box 3270, Jacksonville, Florida 32203.
4. "From Brush to Grass," Caterpillar Tractor Company, Form AEO-30060, Peoria, Illinois 61629. No date.
5. Land Improvement Contractors, Caterpillar Tractor Company, Form AEO-30049-01, Peoria, Illinois 61629. No date.
6. "Land Clearing," Caterpillar Tractor Company, Peoria, Illinois, 61629. No date.
7. Marathon-LeTourneau Company, P.O. Box 2307, Longview, Texas 75607.
8. "Cost of Clearing Land," Agricultural Experiment Station of Auburn University, Auburn, Alabama, Circular 133, June 1959.
9. New Developments in Earthmoving-Rippers, *Construction Methods and Equipment*, vol. 47, pp. 149–168, April 1965.
10. How to Rip Economically, *Roads and Streets*, vol. 107, pp. 43–52, December 1964.
11. When to Move Rock with Scrapers, *Roads and Streets*, vol. 108, pp. 44–95, July 1965.
12. Rip Basalt with Big Tractor, *Roads and Streets*, vol. 116, pp. 114–115, October 1973.
13. Alloy Points Rip Hard Sandstone Fast, *Roads and Streets*, vol. 116, p. 114, September 1973.
14. Ripping Increases Production, Saves Trouble, Money, *Roads and Streets*, vol. 115, pp. 78–79, August 1972.
15. Church, Horace K., 433 Seismic Excavation Studies: What They Tell About Rippability, *Roads and Streets*, vol. 115, pp. 86–92, January 1972.
16. Contractor's Own Seismic Study Helps to Set Job Strategy, *Roads and Streets*, vol. 115, pp. 26–28, January 1972.
17. Church, Horace K., Seismic Exploration Yields Data, *Engineering News-Record*, vol. 175, pp. 62–66, August 12, 1965.
18. Crice, Douglas B., The Geophysical Half of Geotechnical Engineering, *Civil Engineering*, vol. 45, pp. 62–65, October 1965.
19. "Handbook of Ripping, A Guide to Greater Profits," 5th ed., Caterpillar Tractor Company, Peoria, Illinois 61629, 1975.

SEVEN

SCRAPERS

GENERAL INFORMATION

Tractor-pulled scrapers have established an important position in the earth-moving field. As they are self-operating to the extent that they can load, haul, and discharge material, they are not dependent on other equipment. If one of them experiences a temporary breakdown, it is not necessary to stop the job, as would be the case for a machine which is used exclusively for loading earth into hauling units, for if the loader breaks down, the entire job must stop until repairs can be made. The self-loading scrapers are available with capacities up to 50 cu yd or more.

These machines are the result of a compromise between the best loading and the best hauling machines, and, as must be expected of any composite machine, they are not superior to other equipment in both loading and hauling Power shovels, draglines, and belt loaders usually will surpass them in loading only, while trucks may surpass them in hauling only, especially when long, well-maintained haul roads are used. However, their ability to load and haul earth gives them a definite advantage on many projects. The development of high-speed wheel-type tractors has increased the economic haul distance for this type equipment up to a mile or more on many projects.

The ability of these machines to deposit their loads in uniformly thick layers will facilitate the succeeding spreading operations. On the return trips to borrow pits the cutting blades of scrapers may be lowered enough to remove high spots, thereby assisting in maintaining the haul roads.

Earth frequently is found in stratified layers, which must be blended by mixing the materials from several layers. The limited depth of cut will not permit scrapers to mix the layers satisfactorily. For this reason shovels and trucks sometimes are used, even though scrapers will handle the earth more economically.

The advantages and disadvantages previously given for crawler compared with wheel tractors will, in most instances, apply to tractor-pulled scrapers.

TYPES AND SIZES OF SCRAPERS

There are two types of scrapers, based on the type of tractor used to pull them—the crawler-tractor-pulled and the wheel-tractor-pulled. The latter type may be further subdivided, as indicated and described.

1. Crawler-tractor-pulled
2. Wheel-tractor-pulled
   a. Single-engine
   b. Twin-engine
   c. Two-bowl tandem
   d. Elevating scraper

These various types are illustrated in Figs. 7-1 through 7-6.

Figure 7-1 Crawler tractor and self-loading scraper.

Figure 7-2 Single-engine wheel-type tractor-pulled scraper. *(International Harvester Company.)*

Figure 7-3 Twin-engine tractor and scraper. *(International Harvester Company.)*

Figure 7-4 Two-bowl tandem scraper unit. *(Euclid, Inc.)*

Figure 7-5 Wheel-type tractor-pulled elevating scraper. *(WABCO Construction and Mining Equipment Group.)*

Figure 7-6 Wheel-type tractor-pulled elevating scraper. *(WABCO Construction and Mining Equipment Group.)*

Crawler-tractor scraper For relatively short haul distances the crawler-type tractor, pulling a rubber-tired self-loading scraper, can move earth economically. The high drawbar pull in loading a scraper, combined with good traction, even on poor haul roads, gives the crawler tractor an advantage for short hauls. However, as the haul distance is increased, the low speed of a crawler tractor is a disadvantage compared with a wheel tractor.

Unless the loading operation is difficult, a crawler tractor can load a scraper without the aid of a bulldozer. However, if there are several scraper units on a job, the increased output resulting from using a bulldozer to help load the scrapers usually will justify the use of a bulldozer.

Wheel-tractor scrapers For longer haul distances the higher speed of a wheel-type tractor-pulled self-loading scraper will permit it to move earth more economically than a crawler-type tractor. Although the wheel-type tractor cannot deliver as great a tractive effort in loading a scraper, the higher travel speed, which may exceed 30 mph for some models, will offset the disadvantage in loading when the haul distance is sufficiently long.

The break-even distance, the haul distance at which the cost of hauling with a crawler or a wheel tractor will be the same, may be determined by making an analysis of a given job. The analysis should consider the class of soil, the condition of the borrow pit, the condition, length, and slope of the haul road, the nature of the fill, and weather.

The size of a scraper The size of a scraper may be specified as the struck, or heaped, capacity of the bowl, expressed in cubic yards. The struck capacity is the volume of the material that a scraper will hold when the top of the material is struck off even with the top of the bowl. In specifying the heaped capacity of a scraper some manufacturers specify the slope of the material above the sides of the bowl with the designation SAE. The SAE (Society of Automotive Engineers) specifies a slope of 2 : 1, measured horizontally and vertically, respectively. Because the slope will vary with the class of material being hauled, the heaped capacity is only an approximate value.

The capacity of a scraper, expressed in cubic yards bank measure, is obtained by multiplying the loose volume in the scraper by an appropriate swell factor, as given in Table 5-1, or more accurately one that is known to apply to the particular soil being handled. Owing to the compacting effect on the earth in a scraper, resulting from the pressure required to force additional earth into the bowl, the swell usually is less than for earth deposited into a truck by a power shovel. Tests indicate that the swell factors given in Table 5-1 should be increased by 10 percent for earth loaded into a conventional scraper. When computing the bank measure volume for an elevating scraper, the swell factors given in Table 5-1 should be used.

If a conventional scraper hauls an average heaped load of 22.5 cu yd of wet earth, for which the adjusted swell factor is $0.80 + 0.08 = 0.88$, the bank-measure volume will be $22.5 \times 0.88 = 19.8$ cu yd.

OPERATING A SCRAPER

A scraper is loaded by lowering the front end of the bowl until the cutting edge, which is attached to and extends across the width of the bowl, enters the ground and, at the same time, raising the front apron to provide an open slot through which the earth may flow into the bowl. As the scraper is pulled forward, a strip of earth is forced into the bowl. This operation is continued until the bowl is filled or until no more earth may be forced in. The cutting edge is raised and the apron is lowered to prevent spillage during the haul trip.

The dumping operation consists of lowering the cutting edge to the desired height above the fill, raising the apron, and forcing the earth out between the blade and the apron by means of a movable ejector mounted at the rear of the bowl.

The elevating scraper illustrated in Fig. 7-6 is equipped with horizontal slats which are operated by two endless chains, to which the ends of the slats are connected. As the scraper moves forward with its cutting edges digging into and loosening the earth, the slats rake the earth upward and into the bowl of the scraper. This action requires less energy than pushing earth upward through material already in the bowl. As a result, this scraper is capable of loading the bowl without assistance from a pusher tractor for some types of soils. Also, the pulverizing action of the slats permits a more complete filling of the bowl, and it permits a more uniform spreading action on the fill.

PERFORMANCE CHARTS

Manufacturers of wheel-type scrapers provide a performance chart for each of their units. This chart contains information that may be used to analyze the performance of a unit under various operating conditions. Figure 7-7 is a performance chart for a scraper whose specifications are as follows:

Engine fwhp at 2,100 rpm, 441
Transmission, torque converter and power-shift, with overdrive and six
   speeds forward
Capacity of scraper:
  Struck, 28 cu yd
  Heaped, 3 : 1 slope, 32 cu yd
  Heaped, 1 : 1 slope, 38 cu yd
Weights (net weight distribution, empty):
  Drive axle, 60.4%   = 55,800 lb
  Scraper axle, 39.6%   = 36,600 lb
    Total   = 92,400 lb
Payload   = 94,000 lb
Total load   = 186,400 lb
Gross weight distribution
  Drive axle, 50%   = 93,200 lb
  Scraper axle, 50%   = 93,200 lb

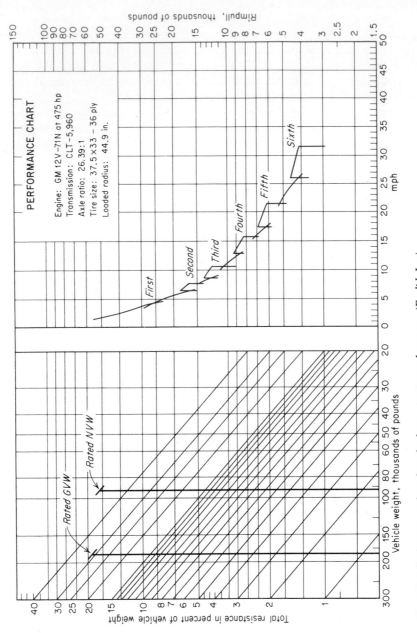

PERFORMANCE CHART

Engine: GM 12V–71N at 475 hp
Transmission: CLT–5,960
Axle ratio: 26.39:1
Tire size: 37.5×33 – 36 ply
Loaded radius: 44.9 in.

Rimpull, thousands of pounds

First
Second
Third
Fourth
Fifth
Sixth

mph

Total resistance in percent of vehicle weight

Rated GVW
Rated NVW

Vehicle weight, thousands of pounds

Figure 7-7 Performance chart for wheel-type tractor and scraper. *(Euclid, Inc.)*

Assume that the scraper is hauling a gross load of 186,400 lb. Use the chart to determine the highest gear and the maximum speed at which it may operate when traveling up a 4 percent grade on a haul road having a rolling resistance of 40 lb per ton, equal to a 2 percent grade. Because the chart is based on zero rolling resistance it will be necessary to add the rolling resistance to the grade resistance to determine the total resistance, which is 6 percent.

The chart is used by applying the following four steps:

1. Find the gross vehicle weight on the lower left horizontal scale, using the weight of 186,400 lb.
2. Read up to slanted total resistance line, namely 6 percent.
3. From the intersection of the two lines read horizontally to the right to the interception with the performance curve. This line intercepts the third speed range overdrive curve.
4. Read down from this interception to the lower scale to determine the maximum vehicle speed, which is 10.6 mph.

The scraper can also operate in the direct drive of the third speed range, but its maximum speed will be slightly less than 9 mph.

The vertical row of figures at the right of the chart indicates the rimpull in 1,000 lb required at 6 percent total resistance to move the unit at a uniform speed slightly larger than 11,000 lb.

If the gradability of this scraper in direct drive third speed range is desired it may be determined from the chart by using the following steps:

1. Read horizontally to the left from the top of the curve for the gear and speed range to the intersection with the vertical line indicating the gross weight of the vehicle.
2. Use this point of intersection to determine the total resistance value from the appropriate slanted resistance line or lines. For the stated conditions the value is about 7.5 percent. Deducting the 2 percent for rolling resistance, the maximum grade is about 5.5 percent.

CYCLE TIME FOR A SCRAPER

The cycle time for a scraper is the time required to load, haul to the fill, dump, and return to the loading position again. The cycle time may be divided into two elements, fixed time and variable time.

The fixed time is the time devoted to other than hauling or returning empty. It includes the time for loading, dumping, turning, accelerating, and decelerating, all of which are reasonably constant under uniform operating conditions. Table 7-1 gives representative time values for each of these fixed-time elements based on favorable, average, and unfavorable conditions. It will be noted that the time indicated for accelerating and decelerating varies with the maximum

Table 7-1 Fixed time elements, in minutes, for wheel scrapers

	Hauling speed ranges, mph (km/h)								
	5 to 8 (8 to 13)			8 to 15 (13 to 24)			15 to 30 (24 to 48)		
Element	(1)*	(2)	(3)	(1)	(2)	(3)	(1)	(2)	(3)
Loading	0.8	1.0	1.4	0.8	1.0	1.4	0.8	1.0	1.4
Dumping-turning	0.4	0.5	0.6	0.4	0.5	0.6	0.4	0.5	0.6
Accelerating-decelerating	0.3	0.4	0.6	0.6	0.8	1.0	1.0	1.5	2.0
Total time	1.5	1.9	2.6	1.8	2.3	3.0	2.2	3.0	4.0

* Columns 1, 2, and 3 indicate the times for favorable, average, and unfavorable conditions, respectively, which will vary with the size and condition of the loading pit and the dumping area.

speed at which a vehicle will travel on the haul road. It takes longer to accelerate to a speed of 20 mph than to a speed of 10 mph, and also it takes longer to decelerate from the higher speed. The times are based on using a pusher tractor of adequate size.

The time required to haul and return depends on the distance traveled and the average speed of the vehicle. Because hauling and returning are usually at different speed ranges, it is necessary to determine the time for each separately.

Example Determine the cycle time for a scraper to haul earth from a pit to a fill 2,000 ft distant under average fixed-time conditions, with an average haul speed of 12 mph and an average return speed of 24 mph.

Because the hauling speed governs the fixed time elements in Table 7-1, the fixed time will be 2.3 min. The individual times are determined as follows:

Fixed time $= 2.3$ min

Haul time, $\dfrac{2,000}{12 \times 88} = 1.9$ min

Return time, $\dfrac{2,000}{24 \times 88} = 1.0$ min

Total time $= 5.2$ min

OPERATING EFFICIENCY AND PRODUCTION

If the scraper cycle time of 5.2 min developed in the previous article could be maintained for a period of 60 min, the unit would make $60/5.2 = 11.5$ trips, and the volume of material hauled would equal the product of the number of trips times the average volume per load. However, scrapers and other types of construction equipment do not operate 60 min per hr. This introduces terms defined as operating efficiency and operating factor. If the scraper operates on the average for a sustained period of time 50 min per hr, its operating efficiency is defined as a 50-min hour, and its efficiency factor is $\frac{50}{60} = 0.83$. The actual operating efficiency of a machine can be determined from a stop-watch study of the machine, conducted for an interval, or intervals, of time that will furnish a representative value for the efficiency. Studies conducted at several different times during a day, and repeated over a period of several days, will give more accurate results than a single study. Many time studies have been made for all or most types of construction equipment, and the results have been very helpful in enabling contractors to increase their operating efficiencies. The studies are more useful if the duration and cause of each delay are recorded for future analysis.

Based on these studies the operating efficiencies of equipment such as scrapers may be classified as follows:

Classification	Operating efficiency, min per hr	Operating factor
Excellent	55	0.92
Average	50	0.83
Fair	45	0.75
Unfavorable	40	0.67

The actual rate of production for any unit of construction equipment should be estimated or determined by applying an appropriate operating factor to its maximum rate of production.

NUMBER OF SCRAPERS SERVED BY A PUSHDOZER

If wheel-type tractor-pulled scrapers are to attain their maximum hauling capacities, they need the assistance of one or more push tractors during the loading operation to reduce the loading and cycle time. Although crawler-type tractor-pulled scrapers are frequently referred to as selfloading units, it may be economically desirable to provide push tractors for them. If using a push tractor will increase the job production enough to more than pay the cost of the tractor, it is good business to use one, regardless of the type of scraper units used.

When using push tractors, it is desirable to match the number of pushers with the number of scrapers. If a pusher or a scraper must wait for the other, it reduces the operating efficiency of the waiting unit and the project and results in an increased production cost.

The pusher cycle time includes the time required to load a scraper plus the time required to move into position to load another scraper. With the cycle time for the scraper and the push tractor determined, formula (7-1) may be used to determine the number of scrapers that a tractor may serve.

$$N = \frac{T_s}{T_p} \qquad (7\text{-}1)$$

where N = number of scrapers served
T_s = cycle time for scraper
T_p = cycle time for pusher tractor

Table 7-2 Representative pusher tractor cycle times

Method of loading	Loading conditions	Cycle time, min
Back track	Favorable	1.7
	Average	2.5
	Unfavorable	3.0
Chain	Favorable	1.2
	Average	1.6
	Unfavorable	2.0
Shuttle	Favorable	1.2
	Average	1.6
	Unfavorable	2.0

The cycle time for a pusher tractor will vary with the conditions in the loading pit, the relative size of the tractor and the scraper unit, and the loading method used by the tractor. Figure 7-8 shows three loading methods that are used, and Table 7-2 lists representative cycle times for each method for favorable, average, and unfavorable conditions.

Favorable loading conditions include loading in a large pit or cut, ripping hard soil prior to loading, loading down grade, maintaining a smooth loading

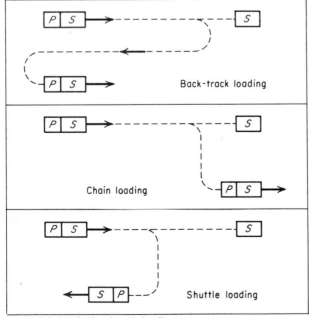

Figure 7-8 Methods of push loading scrapers.

surface, and using a pusher tractor whose power is matched with the size of the scraper. Unfavorable loading conditions are the opposite of those for favorable conditions.

INCREASING THE PRODUCTION RATES OF SCRAPERS

There are at least two methods that a contractor may use to obtain a higher profit on a project involving earthwork. One method is to increase the bid prices on the work. However, competition usually limits the price which he may bid. The alternate method is to organize and operate his equipment in a manner that will assure the maximum production at the lowest cost. The latter method usually offers the best opportunity for attainment. Thus, a contractor should strive to increase the production without increasing his costs. There are several methods whereby he may attain this objective.

Ripping Most types of tight soils will load more easily if they are ripped ahead of the scraper. If the value of the increased production resulting from ripping exceeds the cost of ripping, the soil should be ripped.

When rock is ripped for scraper loading, the depth ripped should always exceed the depth excavated to leave a loose layer of material under the tracks and tires to provide good traction and to reduce the wear on the tracks and tires.

Prewetting the soil Some soils will load more easily if they are reasonably moist. Prewetting can be done in conjunction with ripping, ahead of loading, to permit a uniform penetration of the moisture into the soil.

Also, prewetting soil in the cut can reduce or eliminate the use of water trucks on the fill, thereby reducing the possible congestion of equipment on the fill, and the elimination of excess moisture on the surface of the fill may facilitate the movement of the scrapers on the fill.

Loading down grade [4] When it is practicable to do so, scrapers should be loaded down grade. Each 1 percent of favorable grade is the equivalent of increasing the loading force by 20 lb per ton of gross weight of the push tractor and scraper unit.

Consider a wheel-type scraper unit whose capacity is 30 cu yd, with a net empty weight of 90,000 lb and a gross loaded weight of 170,000 lb. This unit is push loaded by a tractor whose weight is 70,000 lb. The combined empty weight will be 160,000 lb and the gross weight will be 240,000 lb. Assume that loading is done down a 10 percent grade. The increased force available to assist in loading the scraper will be

$$\text{Initial force with the scraper empty} = \frac{160,000}{2,000} \times 10 \times 20 = 16,000 \text{ lb}$$

$$\text{Final force with the scraper loaded} = \frac{240,000}{2,000} \times 10 \times 20 = 24,000 \text{ lb}$$

If the combined drawbar pull and rimpull of the two tractors is 140,000 lb during the loading operation, the effect of down grade loading is to increase the available power by about 11 percent up to 17 percent.

APPLYING THE LOAD-GROWTH CURVE
TO SCRAPER LOADING

Without a critical evaluation of available information it might appear that the lowest cost of moving earth with scrapers is to load every scraper to its maximum capacity before it leaves the cut. However, numerous studies of loading practices have revealed that loading scrapers to their maximum capacities usually will reduce, rather than increase, the rate of production.

When a scraper starts loading, the earth flows into it rapidly and easily, but as the quantity of earth in the bowl increases, the incoming earth encounters greater resistance, and the rate of loading decreases quite rapidly, as illustrated in Fig. 7-9. This figure is a load-growth curve, which shows the relation between the load in a scraper and the loading time. An examination of the curve reveals that during the first 0.5 min the scraper loads about 17 cu yd of earth. During the next 0.5 min it loads an additional 2 cu yd, and, if loading is continued to 1.4 min, the gain in volume during the last 0.4 min is less than 1 cu yd.

The information shown in Fig. 7-9 and Table 7-3 was obtained from a field study of scraper production. The basic information and calculations are given in the following example.

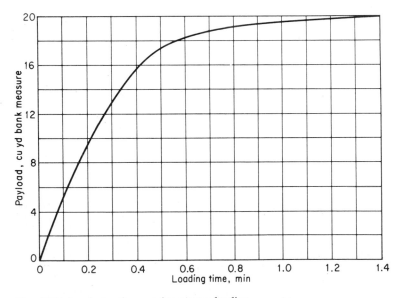

Figure 7-9 Load-growth curve for scraper loading.

Example The equipment used and job conditions were as follows:

Equipment:
  Pusher tractor, 335 fwhp, with power shift
  Scraper tractor, 345 fwhp, two-wheel
  Scraper capacity, struck, 19.5 cu yd, heaped, 27 cu yd
  Net weight of scraper unit, 60,000 lb
Job conditions:
  Earth, sandy clay, swell 33 percent, weight, 3,050 lb per cu yd bm
  Haul distances varied from 500 ft to 10,000 ft
  Haul-road rolling resistance 65 lb per ton; grade, 2 percent adverse for loaded unit
  Combined rolling and grade resistance
    Loaded, $65 + 40 = 105$ lb per ton, or 5.25 percent
    Empty, $65 - 40 = 25$ lb per ton, or 1.25 percent

The calculations and results for a haul distance of 2,500 ft are as follows, based on a 19-cu-yd load, bank measure.

Weight of hauling unit, empty $= 30$ ton

Weight of load, $\dfrac{19 \times 3,050}{2,000} = 29$ ton

Gross vehicle weight $\quad\quad = \overline{59 \text{ ton}}$

Rimpull required, loaded, $59 \times 105 = 6,190$ lb
Maximum speed, 13.8 mph
Actual speed, $0.9 \times 13.8 = 12.4$ mph
Rimpull required, empty, $30 \times 25 = 750$ lb
Actual speed, 22.6 mph
Cycle time, less loading time:

Accelerating and decelerating,	$= 1.0$ min
Turning, dumping, spotting, and boosting	$= 1.1$ min
Hauling, $\dfrac{2,500}{12.4 \times 88}$	$= 2.3$ min
Returning, $\dfrac{2,500}{22.6 \times 88}$	$= 1.3$ min
Total time, excluding loading	$= \overline{5.7 \text{ min}}$

Table 7-3 Variations in the rates of production of scrapers with loading times

Loading time, min	Other time, min	Cycle time, min	Number trips per hr	Payload cu yd	(cu m)	Production, per hr cu yd	(cu m)
0.5	5.7	6.2	8.07	17.4	(13.3)	140	(107)
0.6	5.7	6.3	7.93	18.3	(14.0)	145	(111)
0.7	5.7	6.4	7.81	18.9	(14.5)	147	(112)
0.8	5.7	6.5	7.70	19.2	(14.7)	148*	(113)
0.9	5.7	6.6	7.57	19.5	(14.9)	147	(112)
1.0	5.7	6.7	7.46	19.6	(15.0)	146	(112)
1.1	5.7	6.8	7.35	19.7	(15.1)	145	(111)
1.2	5.7	6.9	7.25	19.8	(15.2)	143	(109)
1.3	5.7	7.0	7.15	19.9	(15.2)	142	(109)
1.4	5.7	7.1	7.05	20.0	(15.3)	141	(108)

* The economical loading time is 0.8 min.

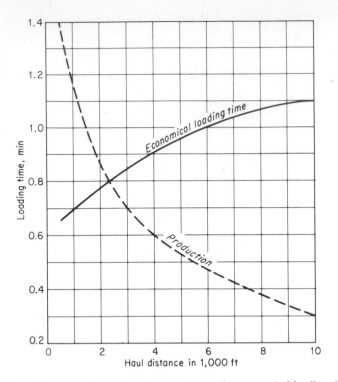

Figure 7-10 The effect of haul distance on the economical loading time of a scraper.

The information appearing in Table 7-3 is based on a 50-min hour.

Figure 7-10 shows that for this equipment and project the economical loading time increases with an increase in the haul distance.

THE EFFECT OF ROLLING RESISTANCE ON THE PRODUCTION OF SCRAPERS

A job condition that is sometimes neglected is the effect of the rolling resistance of the haul road on the production of scrapers, and the cost of hauling earth. A well-maintained road permits faster travel speeds and reduces the costs of maintenance and repairs for the scrapers.

Consider an analysis of the performance of four wheel-type scrapers, hauling earth 1 mile over two level roads whose rolling resistances are 60 lb per ton and 100 lb per ton. The former road receives good maintenance while the latter receives no maintenance. The results of the analysis are given in Table 7-4. The table reflects an increase in the cost of maintenance and repairs for scrapers operating on the poorly maintained road.

Table 7-4. Effect of haul-road maintenance on the production and cost of hauling earth

Item	Haul-road maintenance	
	Good	Poor
Fixed scraper time, min	2.4	2.4
Travel time, min	4.2	6.2
Total cycle time, min	6.6	8.6
Trips per 50-min hr	7.58	5.82
Payload, cu yd bm	16	16
Production, cu yd per hr	121	93
Production, cu yd per hr for 4 scrapers	484	372
Cost per hr for scrapers:		
4 × $31.60	$126.40	
4 × $34.00		$136.00
Cost per hr for pusher loader	33.00	33.00
Cost per hr for motor grader	16.50	none
Total cost per hr	$175.90	$169.00
Cost per cu yd	$0.363	$0.454
Percent increase in cost per cu yd		22

ANALYZING THE PERFORMANCE OF A WHEEL–TYPE SCRAPER

The following example analyzes the performance of a wheel-type scraper for the specified equipment and job conditions.

Example See Fig. 7-7 for performance chart.

Tractor engine, 441 fwhp
Scraper capacity
   Struck, 28 cu yd
   Heaped 3:1 slope 32 cu yd
Net weight of empty unit = 92,400 lb
Maximum payload   = 94,000 lb
Maximum gross weight = 186,400 lb
Weight on drive axle   = 93,200 lb
Weight on scraper axle = 93,200 lb
Total length of haul, 4,000 ft as follows:
   1,200 ft of +4% grade loaded
   1,400 ft of +2% grade loaded
   1,400 ft of −2% grade loaded
Type soil, sandy clay, weight 3,100 lb per cu yd bm, swell 33%
Loose weight of soil, 3,100 × 0.75* = 2,320 lb per cu yd
Rolling resistance, 80 lb per ton = 4%

---

* See Table 5-1 for the value of the swell factor.

Figure 7-10, which probably applies to this scraper with reasonable accuracy, indicates an economical loading time of 0.9 min, and Fig. 7-9 indicates a load equal to 96 percent of the rated capacity, namely $0.96 \times 32 = 30.7$ cu yd, loose measure. The weight of the load will be $30.7 \times 2,320 = 71,200$ lb, which is below the specified maximum weight.

The actual weight will be

Empty   = 92,400 lb
Load   = 71,200 lb
   Gross weight = 163,600 lb

Use Fig. 7-7 to determine the speed for each section of the road, hauling and returning.

Distance, ft	Grade, %	Total resistance, %	Speed, mph	Travel time, min
Hauling				
1,200	4	8	9.5	1.44
1,400	2	6	11.0	1.45
1,400	−2	2	31.5	0.60
Returning				
1,400	2	6	21.5	0.75
1,400	−2	2	31.5	0.60
1,200	−4	0	31.5	0.60
Total travel time				5.44

Table 7-1 indicates a fixed time of 3.0 min for a speed range up to 30 mph and average conditions. The cycle time will be

Fixed time, min   = 3.00
Travel time, min   = 5.44
  Cycle time, min   = 8.44

The speeds shown in the above table can be attained provided there are no obstacles or conditions to cause delays along the haul road. Thus, the cycle time of 8.44 min is the minimum for the specified conditions. If delays are anticipated, the travel speeds and the cycle time should be adjusted to reflect the anticipated conditions. The production per 50-min hour is determined as follows:

Volume per load, 30.7 cu yd loose measure
Payload, $30.7 \times 0.75 = 23.0$ cu yd
Number of trips per hr, $\dfrac{50}{8.44} = 5.93$
Volume hauled per hr, $5.93 \times 23 = 136$ cu yd

PROBLEMS

7-1 The tractor-pulled scraper for which Fig. 6-5 applies weighs 47,460 lb empty. Its average load of earth will be 16 cu yd, loose measure, whose weight will average 2,640 lb per cu yd. The scraper will be loaded with the assistance of a bulldozer under average conditions. When the scraper is loaded, it will travel up a 3 percent haul road whose rolling resistance is 80 lb per ton, to a fill 2,500 ft distant. Determine the probable cycle time for this unit to make a round trip.

If the operating factor for the scraper is 0.75, how many trips should it make in one hour?

If the earth swells 23 percent, what volume of earth should the scraper haul per hour, expressed in cubic yards bank measure?

7-2 If the scraper of Prob. 7-1 is push loaded by a bulldozer of adequate size, how many scrapers can a bulldozer serve under favorable, average, and unfavorable conditions when using the back-track and chain methods of loading?

7-3 If the scraper of Prob. 7-1 hauls earth, as previously specified, under the following job conditions, determine the probable cycle time per trip based on an operating factor of 1.0. The total one-way haul distance will be 3,700 ft and will consist of three sections whose conditions are as follows:

Section	Distance, ft	Slope, %	Rolling resistance, lb per ton
1	1,200	0	80
2	1,800	−3	75
3	700	−2	90

The scraper will return along the same haul road.

Assume average conditions for determining the fixed time.

If the operating factor is 0.83, what is the probable volume of earth hauled per hour by each scraper, expressed in cubic yards bank measure?

7-4 If the scraper for which Table 7-3 applies spends 1.2 min obtaining its load, what is the lost income per hour based on a contract price of $0.56 per cu yd for the earth, when compared with the production possible under the most economical loading time?

7-5 Two contractors use the same types of scrapers, for which Table 7-3 applies, and the same types of bulldozers to help load the scrapers. The loading pits and the haul roads are the same.

Contractor A uses a chain method of push loading his scrapers for 0.8 min. He has a fleet of eight scrapers and as many bulldozers as required to load the scrapers.

Contractor B uses a back-track method of loading his scrapers for 1.3 min. He has a fleet of eight scrapers and as many bulldozers as required to load the scrapers.

The cost per hour for a scraper is $39.50 and that for a bulldozer is $28.50, including the operators. Using the production and cycle times for scrapers given in Table 7-3, determine the cost of loading and hauling a cubic yard of earth for each contractor.

REFERENCES

1. International Harvester Company, 401 North Michigan Avenue, Chicago, Illinois 60611.
2. Euclid, Inc., 22221 St. Clair Avenue, Cleveland, Ohio 44117.
3. WABCO Construction and Mining Equipment Group, 2300 N. E. Adams Street, Peoria, Illinois 61639.
4. Three Scrapers in Tandem Make Fast Work Moving Earth at Building Site, *Construction Methods and Equipment*, vol. 51, pp. 66-69, September 1969.

EIGHT

EXCAVATING EQUIPMENT

INTRODUCTION

This chapter will deal with the listed types of equipment which are used to excavate earth and related materials and to lift items frequently used in construction operations. The equipment includes the following machines:

1. Power shovels
2. Backhoes
3. Draglines
4. Clamshells and cranes
5. Trenching machines
6. Wheel-mounted belt loaders

The first four machines belong to a group which is frequently identified as the Power Crane and Shovel Association family [1]. This association has conducted and supervised studies and tests which have provided considerable information related to the performance, operating conditions, production rates, economic life, and cost of owning and operating equipment in this group. Also, the association has participated in establishing and adopting certain standards that are applicable to this equipment. The results of the studies, conclusions and actions, and the standards have been published in technical bulletins and booklets.

Some of the information published by the Power Crane and Shovel Association is reproduced in this book, with the permission of the association.

USEFUL LIVES OF POWER SHOVELS AND BACKHOES, DRAGLINES AND CLAMSHELLS, AND CRANES

Table 8-1 lists illustrative useful lives of these machines in both years and working hours based on the assumption that they will be used 1,800 hr per year. These values are presented primarily for illustrative purposes, which should not imply that all machines of these types will experience the same usages and useful lives. Therefore it is recommended that each owner of such equipment adopt a realistic expected useful life for the equipment that will be used under conditions that will apply to his operations.

In two-shift operation, a machine might be expected to last about half as many years as indicated in the tables, but it should last about as many working hours as indicated.

POWER SHOVELS

GENERAL INFORMATION

Power shovels are used primarily to excavate earth and load it into trucks or tractor-pulled wagons or onto conveyor belts. They are capable of excavating all classes of earth, except solid rock, without prior loosening. They may be mounted on crawler tracks, in which case they are referred to as crawler-mounted. Such shovels have very low travel speeds, but the wide treads give low soil pressures, which permit them to operate on soft ground. They may be mounted on rubber-tired wheels. Single-engine self-propelled units are powered and operated from the excavator cab. The non-self-propelled units mounted on the rear of trucks, which are referred to as truck-mounted, have separate engines for operating them. Rubber tire-mounted shovels, which have higher travel speeds than the crawler-mounted units, are useful for small jobs where considerable traveling is necessary and where the road surfaces and ground are firm. Figure 8-1 illustrates a crawler-mounted shovel, Fig. 8-2 a wheel-mounted shovel, and Fig. 8-3 a truck-mounted shovel.

THE SIZE OF A POWER SHOVEL

The size of a power shovel is indicated by the size of the dipper, expressed in cubic yards. In measuring the size of the dipper the earth is struck even with the contour of the dipper. This is referred to as the struck volume, as distinguished from the heaped volume which a dipper may pick up in loose soil. Owing to the swelling of a soil when it is loosened, the bank-measure volume of a dipper will

Table 8-1 Illustrative useful life figures for power shovels and backhoes, draglines and clamshells, and cranes*

Shovels and backhoes

| Machine sizes, cu yd | | Useful life | | | |
| | | Crawler-mounted | | Rubber-tire-mounted | |
Over	Through	Years	Working hours*	Years	Working hours*
0	$\frac{5}{8}$	8	14,400	10	18,000
$\frac{5}{8}$	1	10	18,000	11	19,800
1	$1\frac{3}{4}$	11	19,800	13	23,400
$1\frac{3}{4}$	$2\frac{1}{2}$	13	23,400		
$2\frac{1}{2}$	$3\frac{1}{2}$	15	27,000		
$3\frac{1}{2}$	5	16	28,800		

Draglines and clamshells

| Machine sizes, cu yd | | Useful life | | | |
| | | Crawler-mounted | | Rubber-tire-mounted | |
Over	Through	Years	Working hours*	Years	Working hours*
0	$\frac{5}{8}$	10	18,000	10	18,000
$\frac{5}{8}$	1	11	19,800	13	23,400
1	$1\frac{3}{4}$	13	23,400	15	27,000
$1\frac{3}{4}$	$2\frac{1}{2}$	14	25,200	17	30,600
$2\frac{1}{2}$	$3\frac{1}{2}$	16	28,800	18	32,400
$3\frac{1}{2}$	5	17	30,600	19	34,200

Cranes

| Machine sizes, tons | | Useful life | | | |
| | | Crawler-mounted | | Rubber-tire-mounted | |
Over	Through	Years	Working hours*	Years	Working hours*
0	18	12	21,600	13	23,400
18	35	14	25,200	15	27,000
35	60	16	28,800	17	30,600
60	90	18	32,400	18	32,400
90	120	19	34,200	19	34,200
Over 120		20	36,000	20	36,000

* The total working hours are based on 1,800 working hr per year.
Source: Power Crane and Shovel Association [1b]

Figure 8-1 Crawler-mounted power shovel. *(Northwest Engineering Company.)*

be less than the loose volume. It is possible that a dipper may be heaped sufficiently to give a bank-measure volume equal to the rated size of the dipper. However, this condition will not occur except for easy digging soils, under favorable conditions, and the assumption should not be made unless field tests indicate it to be correct. If a 2-cu-yd dipper, excavating a soil whose swell is 25 percent, is able to fill the dipper to its struck volume only, the bank-measure volume will be $2 \div 1.25 = 1.6$ cu yd.

Figure 8-2 Wheel-mounted power shovel.

Figure 8-3 Truck-mounted power shovel.

Power shovels are commonly available in the following sizes: $\frac{3}{8}$, $\frac{1}{2}$, $\frac{3}{4}$, 1, $1\frac{1}{4}$, $1\frac{1}{2}$, 2, and $2\frac{1}{2}$ cu yd, which are classified by the Power Crane and Shovel Association as commercial sizes. Larger sizes may be available, or they can be manufactured on special order.

THE BASIC PARTS AND OPERATION OF A SHOVEL.

The basic parts of a power shovel include the mounting, cab, boom, dipper stick, and dipper. These parts for a cable-controlled shovel are illustrated in Fig. 8-4.

With a shovel in the correct position, near the face of the earth to be excavated, the dipper is lowered to the floor of the pit, with the teeth pointing into the face. A crowding force is applied through the shipper shaft, and at the same time tension is applied to the hoisting line to pull the dipper up the face of the pit. If the depth of the face is just right, considering the type of soil and the size of the dipper, the dipper will be filled as it reaches the top of the face. If the depth of the face, referred to as the depth of cut, is too shallow, it will not be possible to fill the dipper completely without excessive crowding and hoisting tension, and possibly not at all. This subjects the equipment to excessive strains and reduces the output of the unit. If the depth of the face is greater than is required to fill the dipper, when operating under favorable crowd and hoist, it will be necessary to reduce the depth of penetration of the dipper into the face if the full face is to be excavated or to start the excavation above the floor of the

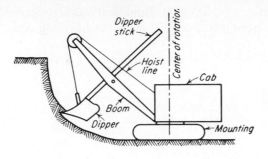

Figure 8-4 Basic parts and operation of a power shovel.

pit. The material left near the floor of the pit will be excavated after the upper portion of the face is removed.

The general operations of a hydraulically controlled shovel differ from those of a cable-controlled shovel primarily in that the operating forces of the former are produced by pistons instead of by cables.

SELECTING THE TYPE AND SIZE POWER SHOVEL

One of the problems which confronts the purchaser of a power shovel is the selection of the type and size. Several factors will affect the selection.

In selecting the type of shovel the prospective purchaser should consider the probable concentration of work to be performed. If there will be numerous small jobs in different locations, the mobility of the rubber-tired-mounted shovel will be a distinct advantage. If the work will be concentrated in large jobs, mobility will be of less importance and the crawler-mounted shovel will be more desirable. A crawler-mounted shovel usually is less expensive than the rubber-tired-mounted unit and can operate on ground surfaces which are not firm enough to support the latter type unit.

In selecting the size of a shovel, the two primary factors which should be considered are the cost per cubic yard of material excavated and the job conditions under which the shovel will operate.

In estimating the cost per cubic yard the following factors should be considered:

1. The size of the job, as a larger job may justify the higher cost of a large shovel.
2. The cost of transporting a large shovel will be higher than for a small one.
3. The depreciation rate for a large shovel may be higher than for a small one, especially if it is to be sold at the end of a job, owing to the probable greater difficulty of selling a large shovel.
4. The cost of downtime for repairs for a large shovel may be considerably greater than for a small one, owing to increased delays in obtaining parts for a large shovel, especially if the parts must be manufactured to order.
5. The combined cost of drilling, blasting, and excavating rock for a large shovel

may be less than for a small shovel, as a large machine will handle bigger rocks than a small one. This may permit a saving in the cost of drilling and blasting.
6. The cost of wages per cubic yard will be less for a large shovel than for a small one.

The following job conditions should be considered in selecting the size of a shovel:

1. High lifts to deposit earth from a basement or trench into trucks at natural ground level will require the long reach of a large shovel.
2. If blasted rock is to be excavated, the large-size dipper will handle bigger rocks.
3. If the material to be excavated is hard and tough, the dipper of the large shovel, which exerts higher digging pressures, will handle the material more easily.
4. If the time allotted for the completion of a project requires a high hourly output, a large shovel must be used.
5. The size of available hauling units should be considered in selecting the size of a shovel. If small hauling units must be used, the size of the shovel should be small, whereas if large hauling units are available, a large shovel should be used.
6. The weight limitations imposed by most states for hauling on highways may restrict the size of a shovel if it is to be hauled over state highways. Also, the clearance of bridges and underpasses may restrict the size.

SHOVEL DIMENSIONS AND CLEARANCES

In considering the size of a power shovel for a project it may be desirable to know the dimensions of the boom and the dipper stick and the maximum cutting height, digging radius, dumping radius, and dumping height. Figure 8-5

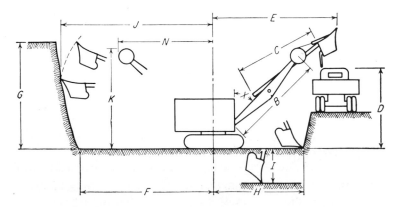

Figure 8-5 Clearance diagram for a power shovel.

Table 8-2 Dimensions and clearances for power shovels for 45° boom angle

Size dipper, cu yd	Length std boom, ft	Length std handle, ft	Max cutting height, ft	Max digging radius, ft	Max dumping height, ft	Max dumping radius, ft
$\frac{3}{8}$	13–15	11–13	17–19	22	13–15	18–20
$\frac{1}{2}$	15–16	12–13	19–24	21–24	14–16	19–20
$\frac{3}{4}$	17–18	13–15	21–27	25–28	15–17	22–24
1	20	16	23–27	31–32	15–18	23–25
$1\frac{1}{4}$	21	16	23–27	31–32	16–19	24–27
$1\frac{1}{2}$	21–23	16–18	24–29	32–33	18–20	28–30
$1\frac{3}{4}$	22–24	16–18	26–30	32–33	18–20	28–30
2	22–25	17–19	26–30	33–36	19–20	30–33
$2\frac{1}{2}$	25–26	18–19	28 35	35 38	19–21	32–34

is a clearance diagram for a shovel. Table 8-2 gives representative dimensions and clearances for power shovels. The clearances are for a boom angle of 45°. For boom angles other than 45° the clearances will be more or less than the values given in Table 8-2. Manufacturers' specifications should be consulted for exact values of the clearances. The maximum dumping height and radius are especially important when a shovel in a pit is loading trucks at natural ground level.

Table 8-3 Approximate shovel digging and loading cycles for various angles of swing*

Size of shovel dipper, cu yd	Easy digging Moist loam, light sandy clay Angle of swing, deg				Medium digging Good common earth Angle of swing, deg				Hard, tough digging Hard tough clay Angle of swing, deg			
	45	90	135	180	45	90	135	180	45	90	135	180
$\frac{3}{8}$	12	16	19	22	15	19	23	26	19	24	29	33
$\frac{1}{2}$	12	16	19	22	15	19	23	26	19	24	29	33
$\frac{3}{4}$	13	17	20	23	16	20	24	27	20	25	30	34
1	14	18	21	25	17	21	25	29	21	26	31	36
$1\frac{1}{4}$	14	18	21	25	17	21	25	29	21	26	31	36
$1\frac{1}{2}$	15	19	23	27	18	23	27	31	22	28	33	38
$1\frac{3}{4}$	16	20	24	28	19	24	28	32	23	29	34	39
2	17	21	25	30	20	25	29	34	24	30	35	41
$2\frac{1}{2}$	18	22	27	32	21	26	31	36	25	31	37	43

* The time is in seconds with no delays when digging in optimum depths of cut and loading trucks on the same grade as the shovel.

Source: Power Crane and Shovel Association [1c].

OPTIMUM DEPTH OF CUT

The optimum depth of cut is that depth which produces the greatest output and at which the dipper comes up with a full load without undue crowding. The depth varies with the class of soil and the size of the dipper. Values of optimum depths for various classes of soils and sizes of dippers are given in Table 8-4.

Table 8-4 Ideal outputs of power shovels in cubic yards (cubic meters) per 60-min hour, bank measure

Class of material	Size of shovel, cu yd (cu m)								
	$\frac{3}{8}$	$\frac{1}{2}$	$\frac{3}{4}$	1	$1\frac{1}{4}$	$1\frac{1}{2}$	$1\frac{3}{4}$	2	$2\frac{1}{2}$
	(0.29)*	(0.38)*	(0.57)*	(0.76)*	(0.95)*	(1.14)*	(1.33)*	(1.53)*	(1.91)*
Moist loam, or light	3.8	4.6	5.3	6.0	6.5	7.0	7.4	7.8	8.4
sandy clay	(1.1)†	(1.4)†	(1.6)†	(1.8)†	(2.0)†	(2.1)†	(2.2)†	(2.4)†	(2.6)†
	85	115	165	205	250	285	320	355	405
	(65)‡	(88)‡	(126)‡	(157)‡	(190)‡	(218)‡	(244)‡	(272)‡	(309)‡
Sand and gravel	3.8	4.6	5.3	6.0	6.5	7.0	7.4	7.8	8.4
	(1.1)	(1.4)	(1.6)	(1.8)	(2.0)	(2.1)	(2.2)	(2.4)	(2.6)
	80	110	155	200	230	270	300	330	390
	(61)	(84)	(118)	(153)	(176)	(206)	(229)	(252)	(298)
Good common earth	4.5	5.7	6.8	7.8	8.5	9.2	9.7	10.2	11.2
	(1.4)	(1.7)	(2.1)	(2.4)	(2.6)	(2.8)	(2.9)	(3.1)	(3.4)
	70	95	135	175	210	240	270	300	350
	(54)	(73)	(103)	(134)	(160)	(183)	(206)	(229)	(268)
Hard, tough clay	6.0	7.0	8.0	9.0	9.8	10.7	11.5	12.2	13.3
	(1.8)	(2.1)	(2.4)	(2.7)	(3.0)	(3.3)	(3.5)	(3.7)	(4.0)
	50	75	110	145	180	210	235	265	310
	(38)	(57)	(84)	(111)	(137)	(156)	(180)	(202)	(236)
Wet, sticky clay	6.0	7.0	8.0	9.0	9.8	10.7	11.5	12.2	13.3
	(1.8)	(2.1)	(2.4)	(2.7)	(3.0)	(3.3)	(3.5)	(3.7)	(4.0)
	25	40	70	95	120	145	165	185	230
	(19)	(30)	(53)	(72)	(91)	(110)	(125)	(141)	(175)
Well-blasted rock	40	60	95	125	155	180	205	230	275
	(30)	(46)	(72)	(95)	(118)	(137)	(156)	(175)	(210)
Poorly blasted rock	15	25	50	75	95	115	140	160	195
	(11)	(19)	(38)	(57)	(73)	(88)	(107)	(122)	(149)

* These values are the sizes of shovels in cubic meters.
† These values are the depths of cut in meters.
‡ These values are the ideal outputs in cubic meters.

THE OUTPUT OF POWER SHOVELS

The output of a power shovel is affected by numerous factors, including the following:

1. Class of material
2. Depth of cut
3. Angle of swing
4. Job conditions
5. Management conditions
6. Size of hauling units
7. Skill of the operator
8. Physical condition of the shovel

The output of a shovel should be expressed in cubic yards per hour based on bank-measure volume. The capacity of a dipper is based on its struck volume. In excavating some classes of materials, it is possible for a dipper to pick up a heaping volume which may exceed the struck volume. In order to obtain the bank-measure volume of a dipper of earth, the average loose volume should be divided by 1 plus the swell, expressed as a fraction. For example, if a 2-cu-yd dipper, excavating material whose swell is 25 percent, will handle an average loose volume of 2.25 cu yd, the bank-measure volume will be 2.25 ÷ 1.25 = 1.8 cu yd. If this shovel can make 2.5 cycles per min, which includes no allowance for lost time, the output will be 2.5 × 1.8 = 4.5 cu yd per min, or 270 cu yd per hr. This is an ideal output, which will seldom, if ever, be experienced on a project. Table 8-4 gives the ideal outputs of power shovels, expressed in cubic yards and cubic meters bank measure, for various classes of materials, based on digging at optimum depth with a 90° swing and no delays. In Table 8-4 the upper figure is the optimum depth in feet, and the lower figure is the ideal output in cubic yards.

THE EFFECT OF THE DEPTH OF CUT ON THE OUTPUT OF A POWER SHOVEL

If the depth of the face from which a shovel is excavating material is too shallow, it will be difficult or impossible to fill the dipper in one pass up the face. The operator will have a choice of making more than one pass to fill the dipper, which will increase the time per cycle, or he may carry a partly filled dipper to the hauling unit each cycle. In either case the effect will be to reduce the output of the shovel.

If the depth of the face is greater than the minimum required to fill the dipper, with favorable crowding and hoisting forces, the operator may do one of three things. He may reduce the depth of penetration of the dipper into the face in order to fill the dipper in one full stroke. This will increase the time for a

Table 8-5 Conversion factors for depth of cut and angle of swing for a power shovel

Percent of optimum depth	Angle of swing, deg						
	45	60	75	90	120	150	180
40	0.93	0.89	0.85	0.80	0.72	0.65	0.59
60	1.10	1.03	0.96	0.91	0.81	0.73	0.66
80	1.22	1.12	1.04	0.98	0.86	0.77	0.69
100	1.26	1.16	1.07	1.00	0.88	0.79	0.71
120	1.20	1.11	1.03	0.97	0.86	0.77	0.70
140	1.12	1.04	0.97	0.91	0.81	0.73	0.66
160	1.03	0.96	0.90	0.85	0.75	0.67	0.62

cycle. He may start digging above the base of the face, and then remove the lower portion of the face later. Or he may run the dipper up the full height of the face and let the excess earth spill down to the bottom of the face, to be picked up later. The choice of any one of the procedures will result in some lost time, based on the time required to fill the dipper when it is digging at optimum depth. As indicated in Table 8-4, the optimum depth varies with the class of material and the size of the dipper.

The effect of the depth of cut on the output of a shovel is illustrated in Table 8-5. In the table the percent of optimum depth of cut is obtained by dividing the actual depth of cut by the optimum depth for the given material and dipper, then multiplying the result by 100. Thus, if the actual depth of cut is 6 ft and the optimum depth is 10 ft, the percent of optimum depth of cut is $\frac{6}{10} \times 100 = 60$.

THE EFFECT OF THE ANGLE OF SWING ON THE OUTPUT OF A POWER SHOVEL

The angle of swing of a power shovel is the horizontal angle, expressed in degrees, between the position of the dipper when it is excavating and the position when it is discharging the load. The total time in a cycle includes digging, swinging to the dumping position, dumping, and returning to the digging position. If the angle of swing is increased, the time for a cycle will be increased, while if the angle of swing is decreased, the time for a cycle will be decreased. The effect of the angle of swing on the output of a shovel is illustrated in Table 8-5. For example, if a shovel which is digging at optimum depth has the angle of swing reduced from 90 to 60°, the output will be increased by 16 percent.

The output of a shovel operating at 90° swing and optimum depth, which is obtained from Table 8-4, should be multiplied by the proper conversion factor from Table 8-5 in order to obtain the probable output for any given depth and angle of swing.

> **Example** The use of the tables is illustrated by considering a 2-cu-yd shovel excavating common earth, with a depth of cut of 12 ft and an angle of swing of 60°. The percent of optimum depth is $12/10.2 \times 100 = 118$.
>
> By interpolating in Table 8-5 the factor is found to be 1.115. However, it is doubtful that values beyond two decimal places are significant. Therefore, 1.11 is sufficiently accurate for practical purposes. The probable output of the shovel will be $300 \times 1.11 = 333$ cu yd per 60-min hour.

Although the information given in Tables 8-4 and 8-5 is based on extensive field studies, the reader is cautioned against using it too literally without adjusting it for conditions which will probably exist on a project. As explained later, additional factors must be applied to whatever extent they are necessary in the judgment of the project planner.

THE EFFECT OF JOB CONDITIONS ON THE OUTPUT OF A POWER SHOVEL

As every owner of a power shovel knows, no two excavating jobs are alike. There are certain conditions at every job over which the owner of the shovel has no control. These conditions must be considered in estimating the probable output of a shovel.

A shovel may operate in a large, open pit, with a firm, well-drained floor, where trucks can be spotted on either side of the shovel to eliminate lost time waiting for hauling units. The terrain of the natural ground may be uniformly level, so that the depth of cut will always be optimum. The haul road is not affected by climatic conditions, such as rains. A job of this type is large enough to justify the selection of balanced hauling units. Such a project might be classified as having excellent job conditions.

Another shovel may be used to excavate material for a highway cut through a hill. The depth of cut may vary from zero to considerably more than the optimum depth. The sides of the cut must be carefully sloped. The cut may be so narrow that a loaded truck must move out before an empty truck can back into loading position. As the truck must be spotted behind the shovel, the angle of swing will approximate 180°. The floor of the cut may be muddy, which will delay the movement of the trucks. Light rains may delay operations for several days. A project of this type might be classified as having poor job conditions.

In excavating a basement, which requires the trucks to travel up an earth ramp, a power shovel may be delayed considerably by ground water or rain, by the difficulty of getting hauling units in and out, and by the difficulty of excavating the corners.

Job conditions may be classified as excellent, good, fair, and poor. There is no uniform standard which may be used as a guide in classifying a job. Each job

Table 8-6 Factors for job and management conditions

	Management conditions			
Job conditions	Excellent	Good	Fair	Poor
Excellent	0.84	0.81	0.76	0.70
Good	0.78	0.75	0.71	0.65
Fair	0.72	0.69	0.65	0.60
Poor	0.63	0.61	0.57	0.52

planner must use his own judgment and experience in deciding which condition best represents his job. Table 8-6 illustrates the effect of job conditions on the output of a power shovel.

THE EFFECT OF MANAGEMENT CONDITIONS ON THE OUTPUT OF A POWER SHOVEL

The attitude of the owner of a shovel in establishing the conditions under which a shovel is operated will affect the output of the shovel. While the owner may not be able to improve job conditions, he may take several steps to improve management conditions, including the following:

1. Greasing and lubricating the shovel frequently
2. Checking the shovel parts that are subject to the greatest wear, and replacing worn parts while the shovel is not being operated, as at the end of a shift
3. Replacing badly worn wire rope between shifts
4. Replacing dull dipper teeth with sharp ones, as required
5. Giving the shovel a major overhaul between jobs, if necessary
6. Keeping at the job extra parts that are subject to the greatest wear
7. Keeping the pit floor clean and smooth to permit better truck spotting and to reduce the angle of swing
8. Providing adequate trucks of the correct size to eliminate lost time in loading and waiting for trucks
9. Paying a bonus to the crew for production in excess of an agreed amount to encourage high production
10. Providing a competent supervisor to keep the job running smoothly

Management conditions may be classified as excellent, good, fair, and poor. Table 8-6 illustrates the effect of management conditions on the output of a power shovel.

EXAMPLES ILLUSTRATING THE EFFECT OF THE VARIOUS FACTORS ON THE OUTPUT OF A POWER SHOVEL

It is doubtful that a job planner will be able to select exactly the correct factors to be used in estimating the output of a shovel. As a result, the actual output of a shovel may vary from the estimated output. Experience and good judgment are essential to the selection of the correct factors. If the output is found to fall below that estimated, it may be possible to increase it by modifying the operating conditions.

Example To illustrate the use of the information in Tables 8-4 to 8-6, consider a 1-cu-yd power shovel for excavating hard clay with a depth of cut of 7.5 ft. An analysis of the project indicates an average angle of swing of 75°, job conditions will be fair, and management will be good. Determine the probable output in cubic yards per hour bank measure.

From Table 8-4 the ideal output will be 145 cu yd per hr. The optimum depth is 9 ft.

Percent of optimum depth is $7.5/9 \times 100 = 83.3$
From Table 8-5 the depth-swing factor is 1.04
From Table 8-6 the job-management factor is 0.69
The probable output per hr, $145 \times 1.04 \times 0.69 = 104$ cu yd
For a 50-min hr the probable output will be $0.83 \times 104 = 86$ cu yd

Example This example illustrates the effect of the various conditions on the output of a shovel. Determine the probable output, in cubic yards per hour bank measure, for a 1-cu-yd shovel for each of the conditions given in the table.

	Class of material				
Factors involved	Moist loam	Common earth	Hard clay	Wet clay	Poorly blasted rock
Depth, ft	6.0	10.0	8.0	12.0	Varies
Angle of swing, deg	60	90	120	180	120
Job conditions	Good	Fair	Fair	Poor	Fair
Management conditions	Good	Good	Fair	Poor	Good
Ideal output, cu yd per hr	200	175	145	95	75
Optimum depth, ft	6.0	7.8	9.0	9.0	
Percent optimum depth	100	128	89	133	
Depth-swing factor	1.16	0.94	0.87	0.67	
Job-management factor	0.75	0.69	0.65	0.52	0.69
Probable output, cu yd per hr	174	114	82	33	52

METHODS OF INCREASING THE OUTPUT OF A POWER SHOVEL

A problem which frequently confronts a consultant on the selection and operation of excavating equipment is to analyze a project which is not being operated satisfactorily in order to recommend corrective steps to increase the output and reduce the cost of handling the material.

Example On one such project, where the cost was exceeding the estimate, an analysis was made to determine methods of reducing the cost of excavating and hauling the earth. The material was common earth. The analysis of the operations revealed the following information:

Size of power shovel, $1\frac{1}{2}$ cu yd
Depth of cut, 12 ft
Angle of swing, 120°
Size of trucks, 6 cu yd bm
Round-trip time for a truck, 19 min
No. trucks, 8

The time spent by the shovel in cleaning up the floor of the pit, moving, and undergoing repairs reduced the actual excavating time to about 30 min per hr.

The floor of the pit was rough, muddy, and heavily rutted because of inadequate drainage, which reduced the efficiency of the hauling units.

The output averaged 108 cu yd per hr.

The direct cost of excavating and hauling the earth was determined as follows:

Shovel, operator, and oiler	=	$ 41.25 per hr
Trucks and drivers, 8 @ $15.80	=	126.40 per hr
Direct overhead and supervision	=	16.30 per hr
Total cost	=	$183.95 per hr
Cost per cu yd, $183.95 ÷ 108	=	1.70

The analysis indicated that the output could be increased by taking the following steps:

1. Use a small bulldozer to keep the floor of the pit clean and well drained.
2. Reduce the depth of cut to the optimum.
3. Reduce the angle of swing to 75° by improving the floor of the pit.
4. Improve the job conditions to good by proper maintenance of the pit and haul roads and by excavating at optimum depth.
5. Improve the management conditions to good by properly servicing the equipment at the end of the shifts and by paying a bonus of $0.04 per cu yd, to be divided among the workers, for all production in excess of 120 cu yd per hr.
6. Reduce the round-trip time of the trucks to 15 min by improving the haul road and the pit floor.
7. Provide additional trucks to haul the increased output of the shovel.

If the recommended steps are taken, the probable output of the shovel will be as follows:

Estimated actual excavating time, 50 min per hr
Ideal output, 240 cu yd per hr
Depth-swing factor, 1.07
Job-management factor, 0.75
Probable output, 240 × 1.07 × 0.75 = 193 cu yd per hr

The number of trucks required to haul the earth will be calculated as follows:

Assume trucks operate 50 min per hr
No. trips per hr per truck, 50/15 = 3.33
Volume hauled per hr per truck, 3.33 × 6 = 20 cu yd
No. trucks needed, 193 ÷ 20 = 9.6
Ten trucks are needed.

The revised direct cost of excavating and hauling the earth will be as follows:

Shovel, operator, and oiler	=	$ 41.25
Trucks and drivers, 10 @ $15.80	=	158.00
Direct overhead and supervision	=	16.30
Cost of bulldozer and operator	=	12.65
Cost of bonus, 73 cu yd @ $0.04	=	2.92
Total cost	=	$231.12
Cost per cu yd, $231.12 ÷ 193	=	1.20
Net saving in cost per cu yd	=	0.50

On a project requiring the handling of 100,000 cu yd of earth the direct cost would be reduced from $170,000 to $120,000, which is a net saving of $50,000. This saving is sufficiently large to demonstrate the financial effect of applying intelligent engineering in the selection of equipment and in analyzing an operation. The failure to apply engineering analysis to the operation of a project is one reason why a contractor may complete a project with a loss, while another will complete a similar project with a profit.

DRAGLINES

GENERAL INFORMATION

Draglines are used to excavate earth and load it into hauling units, such as trucks or tractor-pulled wagons, or to deposit it in levees, dams, and spoil banks near the pits from which it is excavated. In general, a power shovel up to a capacity of $2\frac{1}{2}$ cu yd can be converted into a dragline by replacing the boom of the shovel with a crane boom and substituting a dragline bucket for the shovel dipper.

For some projects either a power shovel or a dragline may be used to excavate materials, but for others the dragline will have a distinct advantage compared with a shovel. A dragline usually does not have to go into a pit or hole in order to excavate. It may operate on natural ground while excavating material from a pit with its bucket. This will be very advantageous when earth is removed from a ditch, canal, or pit containing water. If the earth is hauled with trucks, they do not have to go into the pit and contend with mud. If the earth can be deposited along a canal or ditch or near a pit, it frequently is possible to use a dragline with a boom long enough to dispose of the earth in one operation, eliminating the need for hauling units, which will reduce the cost of handling the earth. Draglines are excellent units for excavating trenches when the sides are permitted to establish their angles of repose, without shoring.

One disadvantage in using a dragline compared with a power shovel is the reduced output of the dragline. A comparison of the ideal output of various sizes of draglines with the output of power shovels shows that a dragline will excavate approximately 75 to 80 percent as much earth as a shovel of the same size.

TYPES OF DRAGLINES

Draglines may be divided into three types, as follows:

1. Crawler-mounted (see Fig. 8-6)
2. Wheel-mounted, self-propelled (see Fig. 8-7)
3. Truck-mounted (see Fig. 8-8)

Crawler-mounted draglines can operate on surfaces which are too soft for wheel- or truck-mounted equipment, but their speeds are so slow, frequently less than 1 mph, that it may be necessary to use auxiliary hauling equipment to transport them from one job to another, especially if the distance is great. Wheel- and truck-mounted units may have travel speeds in excess of 30 mph.

Figure 8-6 Crawler-mounted dragline. *(Northwest Engineering Company.)*

Figure 8-7 Wheel-mounted dragline.

Figure 8-8 Truck-mounted dragline.

THE SIZE OF A DRAGLINE

The size of a dragline is indicated by the size of the bucket, expressed in cubic yards, which, in general, is the same size as the dipper of the power shovel into which it may be converted. However, most draglines may handle more than one size bucket, depending on the length of the boom and the class of material excavated. Because the maximum lifting capacity of a dragline is limited by the force which will tilt the machine over, it is necessary to reduce the size of the bucket when a long boom is used or when the material has a high specific gravity. In practice the combined weight of the bucket and its load should produce a tilting force not greater than 75 percent of the force required to tilt the machine over. A longer boom, with a smaller bucket, should be used when it is necessary to increase the digging reach or the dumping radius.

If the material is difficult to excavate, the use of a smaller bucket, which will reduce the digging resistance, may permit an increase in the output of a dragline.

Table 8-7 Typical working ranges for a cable-controlled dragline with maximum counterweights

J, boom length, 50 ft:						
Capacity, lb*	12,000	12,000	12,000	12,000	12,000	12,000
K, boom angle, deg	20	25	30	35	40	45
A, dumping radius, ft	55	50	50	45	45	40
B, dumping height, ft	10	14	18	22	24	27
C, max digging depth, ft	40	36	32	28	24	20
J, boom length, 60 ft:						
Capacity, lb*	10,500	11,000	11,800	12,000	12,000	12,000
K, boom angle, deg	20	25	30	35	40	45
A, dumping radius, ft	65	60	55	55	52	50
B, dumping height, ft	13	18	22	26	31	35
C, max digging depth, ft	40	36	32	28	24	20
J, boom length, 70 ft:						
Capacity, lb*	8,000	8,500	9,200	10,000	11,000	11,800
K, boom angle, deg	20	25	30	35	40	45
A, dumping radius, ft	75	73	70	65	60	55
B, dumping height, ft	18	23	28	32	37	42
C, max digging depth, ft	40	36	32	28	24	20
J, boom length, 80 ft:						
Capacity, lb*	6,000	6,700	7,200	7,900	8,600	9,800
K, boom angle, deg	20	25	30	35	40	45
A, dumping radius, ft	86	81	79	75	70	65
B, dumping height, ft	22	27	33	39	42	47
C, max digging depth, ft	40	36	32	28	24	20
D, digging reach	Depends on working conditions and operator's skill with bucket					

* Combined weight of bucket and material must not exceed capacity.

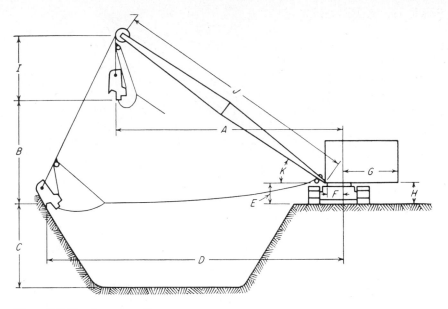

Figure 8-9 Dragline range diagram.

Typical working ranges for a dragline that will handle buckets varying in sizes from $1\frac{1}{4}$ to $2\frac{1}{2}$ cu yd are given in Table 8-7 (see Fig. 8-9 for the dimensions given in the table).

THE BASIC PARTS AND OPERATION OF
A CABLE-CONTROLLED DRAGLINE

The basic parts of a dragline are illustrated in Fig. 8-10.

Excavating is started by swinging the empty bucket to the digging position, at the same time slacking off the drag and the hoist cables. Separate drums on the basic unit are available for each of these cables so that they may be coordinated into a smooth operation. Excavating is accomplished by pulling the bucket toward the machine while regulating the digging depth by means of the tension maintained in the hoist cable. When the bucket is filled, the operator takes in on the hoist line while playing out the drag cable. The bucket is so constructed that it will not dump its contents until it is desired. Hoisting, swinging, and dumping of the loaded bucket follow in that order; then the cycle is repeated. Dumping is accomplished by releasing the drag cable. An experienced operator can cast the excavated material beyond the end of the boom.

Since it is more difficult to control the accuracy in dumping from a dragline as compared with a power shovel, it is desirable to use larger hauling units for dragline loading in order to reduce the spillage. A size ratio equal to at least five to six times the capacity of the bucket is recommended.

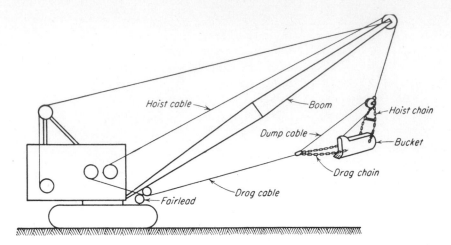

Figure 8-10 Basic parts of a dragline.

Figure 8-11 shows the dragline digging zones. The work should be planned to permit most of the digging to be done in the zones which permit the best digging, with the poor digging zone used as little as possible.

OPTIMUM DEPTH OF CUT

A dragline will produce its greatest output if the job is planned to permit the earth to be excavated at the optimum depth where possible. Table 8-6 gives the

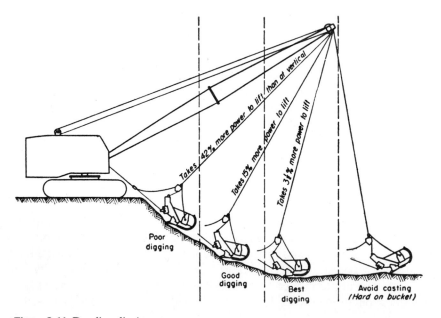

Figure 8-11 Dragline digging zones.

optimum depth of cut for various sizes of buckets and classes of materials, using short-boom draglines.

THE OUTPUT OF THE DRAGLINES

The output of a dragline will vary with the following factors:

1. Class of material
2. Depth of cut
3. Angle of swing
4. Size and type of bucket
5. Length of boom
6. Job conditions
7. Management conditions
8. Method of disposal, casting or loading trucks
9. Size of hauling units, if used
10. Skill of operator
11. Physical condition of the machine

Table 8-8 gives approximate dragline digging and loading cycles for various angles of swing.

The output of a dragline should be expressed in cubic yards per hour bank measure. This quantity may be obtained from field observations, or it may be estimated by multiplying the average loose volume per bucket by the number of

Table 8-8 Approximate dragline digging and loading cycles for various angles of swing*

Size of dragline bucket, cu yd	Easy digging Light moist clay or loam Angle of swing, deg				Sand or gravel Angle of swing, deg				Good common earth Angle of swing, deg			
	45	90	135	180	45	90	135	180	45	90	135	180
$\frac{3}{8}$	16	19	22	25	17	20	24	27	20	24	28	31
$\frac{1}{2}$	16	19	22	25	17	20	24	27	20	24	28	31
$\frac{3}{4}$	17	20	24	27	18	22	26	29	21	26	30	33
1	19	22	26	29	20	24	28	31	23	28	33	36
$1\frac{1}{4}$	19	23	27	30	20	25	29	32	23	28	33	36
$1\frac{1}{2}$	21	25	29	32	22	27	31	34	25	30	35	38
$1\frac{3}{4}$	22	26	30	33	23	28	32	35	26	31	36	39
2	23	27	31	35	24	29	33	37	27	32	37	41
$2\frac{1}{2}$	25	29	34	38	26	31	36	40	29	34	40	44

* The time is in seconds with no delays when digging at optimum depths of cut and loading trucks on the same grade as the shovel.

Source: Power Crane and Shovel Association.

cycles per hour and dividing by 1 plus the swell factor for the earth, expressed as a fraction. For example, if a 2-cu-yd bucket, excavating material whose swell is 25 percent, will handle an average loose volume of 2.4 cu yd, the bank-measure volume will be 2.4 ÷ 1.25 = 1.92 cu yd. If the dragline can make 2 cycles per min, the output will be 2 × 1.92 = 3.84 cu yd per min or 230 cu yd per hr bank measure. This is an ideal output, which will seldom, if ever, be experienced on a project. Table 8-9 gives the ideal outputs of short-boom draglines, expressed in cubic yards bank measure, for various classes of materials, based on digging at optimum depth, with a 90° swing, and no delays. In Table 8-9 the upper figure is the optimum depth in feet, and the lower figure is the ideal output in cubic yards.

Table 8-9 Ideal outputs of short-boom draglines, in cubic yards (cubic meters) per 60-min hour, bank measure

Class of material	Size of bucket, cu yd (cu m)*								
	3.8 (0.29)*	$\frac{1}{2}$ (0.38)*	$\frac{3}{4}$ (0.57)*	1 (0.76)*	$1\frac{1}{4}$ (0.95)*	$1\frac{1}{2}$ (1.14)*	$1\frac{3}{4}$ (1.33)*	2 (1.53)*	$2\frac{1}{2}$ (1.91)*
Moist loam or light sandy clay	5.0 $(1.5)^\dagger$ 70 $(53)^\ddagger$	5.5 $(1.7)^\dagger$ 95 $(72)^\ddagger$	6.0 $(1.8)^\dagger$ 130 $(99)^\ddagger$	6.6 $(2.0)^\dagger$ 160 $(122)^\ddagger$	7.0 $(2.1)^\dagger$ 195 $(149)^\ddagger$	7.4 $(2.2)^\dagger$ 220 $(168)^\ddagger$	7.7 $(2.4)^\dagger$ 245 $(187)^\ddagger$	8.0 $(2.5)^\dagger$ 265 $(202)^\ddagger$	8.5 $(2.6)^\dagger$ 305 $(233)^\ddagger$
Sand and gravel	5.0 (1.5) 65 (49)	5.5 (1.7) 90 (69)	6.0 (1.8) 125 (95)	6.6 (2.0) 155 (118)	7.0 (2.1) 185 (141)	7.4 (2.2) 210 (160)	7.7 (2.4) 235 (180)	8.0 (2.5) 255 (195)	8.5 (2.6) 295 (225)
Good common earth	6.0 (1.8) 55 (42)	6.7 (2.0) 75 (57)	7.4 (2.4) 105 (81)	8.0 (2.5) 135 (104)	8.5 (2.6) 165 (127)	9.0 (2.7) 190 (147)	9.5 (2.8) 210 (162)	9.9 (3.0) 230 (177)	10.5 (3.2) 265 (204)
Hard, tough clay	7.3 (2.2) 35 (27)	8.0 (2.5) 55 (42)	8.7 (2.7) 90 (69)	9.3 (2.8) 110 (85)	10.0 (3.1) 135 (104)	10.7 (3.3) 160 (123)	11.3 (3.5) 180 (139)	11.8 (3.6) 195 (150)	12.3 (3.8) 230 (177)
Wet, sticky clay	7.3 (2.2) 20 (15)	8.0 (2.5) 30 (23)	8.7 (2.7) 55 (42)	9.3 (2.8) 75 (58)	10.0 (3.1) 95 (73)	10.7 (3.3) 110 (85)	11.3 (3.5) 130 (100)	11.8 (3.6) 145 (112)	12.3 (3.8) 175 (135)

* These values are the sizes of the buckets in cubic meters.
† These values are the depths of cut in meters.
‡ These values are the ideal outputs in cubic meters.

**Table 8-10 The effect of the depth of cut and angle of swing on
the output of draglines**

Percent of optimum depth	Angle of swing, deg							
	30	45	60	75	90	120	150	180
20	1.06	0.99	0.94	0.90	0.87	0.81	0.75	0.70
40	1.17	1.08	1.02	0.97	0.93	0.85	0.78	0.72
60	1.24	1.13	1.06	1.01	0.97	0.88	0.80	0.74
80	1.29	1.17	1.09	1.04	0.99	0.90	0.82	0.76
100	1.32	1.19	1.11	1.05	1.00	0.91	0.83	0.77
120	1.29	1.17	1.09	1.03	0.98	0.90	0.82	0.76
140	1.25	1.14	1.06	1.00	0.96	0.88	0.81	0.75
160	1.20	1.10	1.02	0.97	0.93	0.85	0.79	0.73
180	1.15	1.05	0.98	0.94	0.90	0.82	0.76	0.71
200	1.10	1.00	0.94	0.90	0.87	0.79	0.73	0.69

THE EFFECT OF THE DEPTH OF CUT AND THE ANGLE OF SWING ON THE OUTPUT OF A DRAGLINE

The outputs of draglines given in Table 8-9 are based on digging at optimum depths with an angle of swing of 90°. For any other depth or angle of swing the ideal output of the particular unit should be multiplied by an appropriate depth-swing factor. The effect of the depth of cut and the angle of swing on the output of a dragline is given in Table 8-10.

Example A 2-cu-yd short-boom dragline is to be used to excavate hard, tough clay. The depth of cut will be 15.4 ft, and the angle of swing will be 120°. Determine the probable output of the dragline if there are no other factors to affect the output.

The percent of optimum depth, 15.4/11.8 × 100 = 130. From Table 8-10 the correction factor is 0.89. The probable output will be 195 × 0.89 = 173 cu yd per hr. For a 50-min hour the probable output will be

Output = 0.83 × 173 = 143 cu yd

THE EFFECT OF JOB AND MANAGEMENT CONDITIONS ON THE OUTPUT OF A DRAGLINE

The effect of job and management conditions on the output of a dragline will be about the same as for a power shovel. This information is given in Table 8-6.

THE EFFECT OF THE SIZE OF THE BUCKET AND THE LENGTH OF THE BOOM ON THE OUTPUT OF A DRAGLINE

In selecting the size and type bucket, the dragline and bucket should be matched properly in order to obtain the best action and the greatest operating efficiency,

Figure 8-12 Medium-duty dragline bucket.

Figure 8-13 Dragline bucket dumping its load.

which will produce the greatest output of material. Buckets are generally available in three types: light-duty, medium-duty, and heavy-duty. Light-duty buckets are used for excavating materials which are dug easily, such as sandy loam, sandy clay, or sand. Medium-duty buckets are used for general excavating service as digging clay, soft shale, or loose gravel. Heavy-duty buckets are used for mine stripping, handling blasted rock, and excavating hardpan and highly abrasive materials. Buckets are sometimes perforated to permit excess water to drain from the loads. Figure 8-12 shows a medium-duty dragline bucket. Figure 8-13 shows a 1-cu-yd dragline bucket dumping its load on a spoil bank.

Table 8-11 gives representative capacities, weight, and dimensions for dragline buckets.

The normal size of a dragline bucket is based on its struck capacity, which is expressed more accurately in cubic feet. In selecting the most suitable size bucket for use with a given dragline, it is desirable to know the weight of the loosened material to be handled, expressed in pounds per cubic foot. While it is desirable to use the largest size bucket possible in the interest of increasing the output, care should be exercised to see that the combined weight of the load and the bucket does not exceed the safe load recommended for the dragline.

Example The importance of this analysis is illustrated by referring to the information given in Table 8-7. Assume that the material to be handled has a loose weight of 90 lb per cu ft. The use of a 2-cu-yd medium-duty bucket will be considered. If the dragline is to be operated with an 80-ft boom at a 40° angle, the maximum safe load will be 8,600 lb. The approximate weight of

Table 8-11 Representative capacities, weights, and dimensions of dragline buckets

Size, cu yd	Struck capacity, cu ft	Weight of bucket, lb			Dimension, in.		
		Light-duty	Medium-duty	Heavy-duty	Length	Width	Height
3/8	11	760	880		35	28	20
1/2	17	1,275	1,460	2,100	40	36	23
3/4	24	1,640	1,850	2,875	45	41	25
1	32	2,220	2,945	3,700	48	45	27
1 1/4	39	2,410	3,300	4,260	49	45	31
1 1/2	47	3,010	3,750	4,525	53	48	32
1 3/4	53	3,375	4,030	4,800	54	48	36
2	60	3,925	4,825	5,400	54	51	38
2 1/4	67	4,100	5,350	6,250	56	53	39
2 1/2	74	4,310	5,675	6,540	61	53	40
2 3/4	82	4,950	6,225	7,390	63	55	41
3	90	5,560	6,660	7,920	65	55	43

the bucket and its load will be

Bucket, from Table 8-11	= 4,825 lb
Earth, 60 cu ft @ 90 lb per cu ft	= 5,400 lb
Combined weight	= 10,225 lb
Maximum safe load	= 8,600 lb

As this weight will exceed the safe load on the dragline, it will be necessary to use a smaller bucket. Try a $1\frac{1}{2}$-cu-yd bucket, whose combined weight will be

Bucket	= 3,750 lb
Earth, 47 cu ft @ 90 lb per cu ft	= 4,230 lb
Combined weight	= 7,980 lb

If a $1\frac{1}{2}$-cu-yd bucket is used, it may be filled to heaping capacity, without exceeding the safe load of the dragline.

If a 70-ft boom, whose maximum safe load is 11,000 lb, will provide sufficient working range for excavating and disposing of the earth, a 2-cu-yd bucket may be used and filled to heaping capacity. The reduced cycle time, in using the 70-ft boom, will probably offset the increased time required to fill the 2-cu-yd bucket. The ratio of the output resulting from the use of a 70-ft boom and a 2-cu-yd bucket, compared with a $1\frac{1}{2}$-cu-yd bucket, should be approximately as follows:

Output ratio, $\dfrac{60 \text{ cu ft}}{47 \text{ cu ft}} \times 100 = 127\%$

Increase in output $\qquad = 27\%$

The previous example illustrates the importance of analyzing a job prior to selecting the size excavator to be used. The haphazard selection of equipment can result in a substantial increase in the cost of handling of earth.

THE EFFECT OF THE CLASS OF MATERIAL ON THE COST OF EXCAVATING EARTH

Figure 8-14 illustrates the effect which the class of material has on the cost per cu yd bank measure in excavating with draglines. The hourly cost of a machine includes fixed-machine, variable-machine, and labor costs. Each machine is assumed to operate 2,000 hr per year at 75 percent efficiency. Thus, the probable hourly output of any given size machine is obtained by multiplying the ideal output, as given in Table 8-9, by 75 percent. For example, the cost of excavating good common earth using a 1-cu-yd machine is determined as follows:

Operating cost per hr	= $27.60
Ideal output per hr	= 135 cu yd
Probable output, 0.75 × 135	= 101 cu yd
Cost per cu yd, $27.60 ÷ 101	= $0.272

Example This example illustrates a method of analyzing a project to determine the size dragline required. Select a crawler-mounted dragline to excavate 234,000 cu yd bank measure of

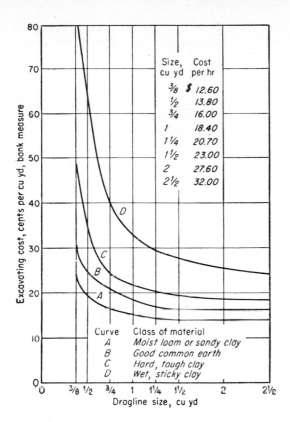

Size,	Cost
cu yd	per hr
3/8	$ 12.60
1/2	13.80
3/4	16.00
1	18.40
1 1/4	20.70
1 1/2	23.00
2	27.60
2 1/2	32.00

Curve	Class of material
A	Moist loam or sandy clay
B	Good common earth
C	Hard, tough clay
D	Wet, sticky clay

Figure 8-14 The effect of the class of material and the size of the bucket on the cost of excavating earth with a dragline.

common earth in digging a canal. The dimensions of the canal will be:

Bottom width, 20 ft
Top width, 44 ft
Depth, 12 ft
Side slopes, 1 : 1

The excavated earth will be cast into a levee along one side of the canal, with a berm of at least 20 ft between the toe of the levee and the nearest edge of the canal. The cross-section area of the canal will be $(20 + 44)/2 \times 12 = 384$ sq ft. If the earth swells 25 percent when it is loosened, the cross-section area of the levee will be $384 \times 1.25 = 480$ sq ft. The dimensions will be

Height, 12 ft
Base width, 64 ft
Crest width, 16 ft
Side slope, 2 : 1

The total width from the outside of the levee to the outside of the canal will be:

Width of levee = 64 ft
Width of berm = 20 ft
Width of canal = 44 ft
Total = 128 ft

It will require a dragline with a boom length of 70 ft to furnish the necessary digging and dumping reaches, which will permit adequate dumping height and digging depth, with a boom angle of 30°.

The project must be completed in 1 year. Assume that weather conditions, holidays, and other major losses in time will reduce the operating time to 44 weeks of 40 hr each, or a total of 1,760 working hours. The required output per working hour will be 133 cu yd. It should be possible to operate with a 150° maximum angle of swing. The management factor should be approximately 0.80.

The required output divided by job-management factor is 133 ÷ 0.80 = 167 cu yd per hr. Assume a depth swing factor of 0.81. The required ideal output is 167 ÷ 0.81 = 206 cu yd per hr.

Reference to Table 8-6 indicates a $1\frac{3}{4}$-cu-yd medium-duty bucket. The combined weight of the bucket and load will be:

Weight of load, 53 cu ft @ 80 lb per cu ft = 4,240 lb
Weight of bucket   = 4,030 lb
   Total weight   = 8,270 lb
   Maximum safe load, from Table 8-5 = 9,200 lb

The equipment selected should be checked to verify whether it will produce the required output

Ideal output, 210 cu yd per hr
Percent of optimum depth, $\dfrac{12.0}{9.5} \times 100 = 126$
Depth-swing factor, 0.82
Job-management factor, 0.80
Probable output, 210 × 0.82 × 0.08 = 138 cu yd per hr

Thus the equipment should produce the required output, with a slight surplus capacity.

CRANES

SAFE LIFTING CAPACITIES OF CRANES

Because cranes are used to hoist and move loads from one location to another, it is necessary to know the lifting capacity and working range of a crane selected to perform a given service. Manufacturers and suppliers furnish this information in literature describing their products.

When a crane lifts a load attached to the hoist line that passes over a sheave located at the boom point of the machine, there is a tendency to tip the machine over. This introduces what is defined as the tipping condition. A machine is considered to be at the point of tipping when a balance is reached between the overturning moment of the load and the stabilizing moment of the machine when the crane is on a firm level supporting surface [2].

During a test to determine the tipping load for a crane, the outriggers, if used, should be lowered to relieve the wheels or crawler tracks of all weight on the supporting surface or ground.

The radius of the load is the horizontal distance from the axis of rotation of the crane to the center of the vertical hoist line or tackle with the load applied.

The tipping load is the load that produces a tipping condition at a specified radius. The load includes the weight of the item being lifted plus the weights of the hooks, hook blocks, slings, and any other items used in hoisting the load but excludes the weight of the hoist rope.

RATED LOADS

The lifting crane rated loads should not exceed the following percentages of tipping loads at specified radii [1(i)].

1. Crawler-mounted machines, 75 percent
2. Rubber-tire-mounted machines, 85 percent
3. Machines on outriggers, 85 percent

The rated loads should be based on the direction of minimum stability from the mounting, unless otherwise specified. No load should be lifted over the front area of the machine except as approved by the crane manufacturer.

CLASSIFICATIONS OF CRANES

Cranes used for lifting shall be classified by a symbol consisting of two numbers based on the rated loads of the crane in the direction of least stability, with the outriggers set if the crane is so equipped.

1. The first number of the group shall be the crane rating radius, expressed in feet, for the maximum rated load, when the crane is equipped with the base boom length.
2. The second number of the group shall be the rated load (expressed in pounds divided by 100 and rounded off to the nearest whole number) when the load is applied at a 40-ft radius, with the use of a 50-ft boom length.

> **Example** To illustrate this method of classifying a crane, assume that a truck-mounted crane is rated at 40 tons at a 12-ft radius when equipped with its base boom length and is rated at 19,600 lb at a 40-ft radius when equipped with a 50-ft-long boom. The classification of this crane would be 40-ton truck-mounted crane, class 12-196.
>
> The number 12 represents the radius in feet for the 40-ton rated load, and the number 196 represents the rated load in pounds divided by 100 at a 40-ft radius.

The literature issued by the manufacturers of cranes, specifying the class of a given unit will generally describe it as a 30-ton truck-mounted crane PCSA Class 12-105, for example. The meanings of the two numerals 12 and 105 are as stated in the foregoing paragraph. The initials represent the Power Crane and Shovel Association.

Manufacturers may furnish literature describing a unit as a 15-ton crawler-mounted crane PCSA Class 10-56. This crane has a rated load of 15 tons at a radius of 10 ft instead of at 12 ft, and a rated load of 5,600 lb at a radius of 40 ft.

SPECIFICATIONS FOR CRANES

Table 8-12 illustrates the kind of information appearing in the specifications issued by the manufacturers of cranes. The crane for which the information

Table 8-12 Lifting capacities in pounds for a 30-ton crane PCSA class 12-105

Specified crane capacities based on 75 percent of tipping load

Length of boom, ft*	Radius, ft	Rated lifting capacity, lb		
		Crane	Clamshell	Dragline
40	12	60,000		
	15	40,000		
	20	27,000		
	25	19,900	10,300	
	30	15,600	10,300	8,800
	35	12,800	10,300	8,800
	40	10,700	9,630	8,800
50	15	40,610		
	20	26,810		
	25	19,710		
	30	15,410	10,300	
	35	12,610	10,300	
	40	10,510	9,460	8,800
	45	8,930	8,035	8,800
	50	7,730	6,955	7,730
60	15	40,420		
	20	26,620		
	25	19,520		
	30	15,220		
	35	12,420	10,300	
	40	10,320	9,290	8,800
60	45	8,740	7,865	8,740
	50	7,540	6,785	7,540
	55	6,600	5,940	5,800
	60	5,800	5,220	5,800

* When used in crane service, this machine can handle a boom whose maximum length is 100 ft.

appearing in Table 8-12 applies is described as a 30-ton crawler-mounted cable-controlled crane PCSA Class 12-105.

WORKING RANGES OF CRANES

Figure 8-15 shows graphically the height of the boom point above the surface supporting the crane and the distance from the center of rotation for the crane for various boom angles for the crane whose lifting capacities are given in Table 8-12.

The maximum boom length for this crane for service with a clamshell, magnet, or dragline is 60 ft. However, if the machine is used for crane service only, the maximum length of the boom may be increased to 100 ft, as illustrated

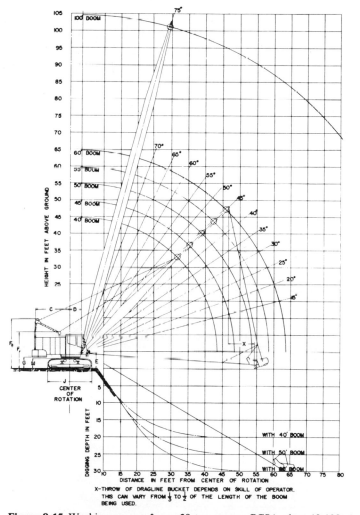

Figure 8-15 Working ranges for a 30-ton crane, PCSA class 12-105, 1- to $1\frac{1}{4}$-cu-yd excavator, nominal rating. *(Northwest Engineering Company.)*

in Fig. 8-15. The length of the boom is increased by adding sections at or near the mid-length of the boom, usually in 5-ft or 10-ft increments.

> **Example** As an example in using the information in Fig. 8-15, determine the minimum boom length that will permit the crane to lift a load 4 ft high to a position 36 ft above the surface on which the crane is operating. The length of the block, hook, and slings that are required to attach the hoist rope to the load is 6 ft. The location of the project will require the crane to pick up the load from a truck at a distance of 25 ft from the center of rotation of the crane. Thus the operating radius will be 25 ft.
>
> In order to lift the load to the specified location, the minimum height of the boom point of the crane must be at least 36 + 4 + 6 = 46 ft above the ground supporting the crane. An examination of the diagram in Fig. 8-15 reveals that for a radius of 25 ft the height of the boom point for a boom 50 ft long is 45 ft, which is not high enough. Thus, the next longer boom, namely 55 ft, must be used. While hoisting the load, the boom angle will be between 65 and 70 deg.

If the block, hook, and slings weigh 1,000 lb, determine the maximum net weight of the load that can be hoisted. It will be necessary to interpolate between the values appearing in Table 8-12 for the answer. For a boom length of 50 ft and a radius of 25 ft the maximum total load is 19,710 lb. For a boom length of 60 ft and a radius of 25 ft the maximum total load is 19,520 lb. By interpolation the load should be $\frac{19,710 + 19,520}{2}$ = 19,635 lb. If the weight of the block, hook, and slings is deducted from the total load, the net weight of the lifted object will be 18,635 lb, which is the maximum safe weight of the object.

Table 8-13 Lifting capacities in pounds for a 25-ton truck-mounted hydraulic crane PCSA class 12-88

Specified crane capacities based on 85 percent of tipping loads

Load radius, ft	Lifting capacity, lb* Boom length, ft						
	31.5	40	48	56	64	72	80
12	50,000	45,000	38,700				
15	41,500	39,000	34,400	30,000			
20	29,500	29,500	27,000	24,800	22,700	21,100	
25	19,600	19,900	20,100	20,100	19,100	17,700	17,100
30		14,500	14,700	14,700	14,800	14,800	14,200
35			11,200	11,300	11,400	11,400	11,400
40			8,800	8,900	9,000	9,000	9,000
45				7,200	7,300	7,300	7,300
50				5,800	5,900	6,000	6,000
55					4,800	4,900	4,900
60					4,000	4,000	4,000
65						3,100	3,300
70							2,700
75							2,200

* The loads appearing above the solid line are limited by the machine stability. The values appearing below the solid line are limited by factors other than machine stability.

RATED LOADS FOR HYDRAULIC CRANES

The rated loads for hydraulic cranes are determined and indicated as for cable-controlled cranes. Table 8-13 lists the rated loads, or maximum safe loads, for a 25-ton truck-mounted crane PCSA class 12-88. The specified loads are limited to 85 percent of the tipping loads over the sides or rear, with the machine supported and leveled on fully extended outriggers, and standing on a firm, uniform supporting surface.

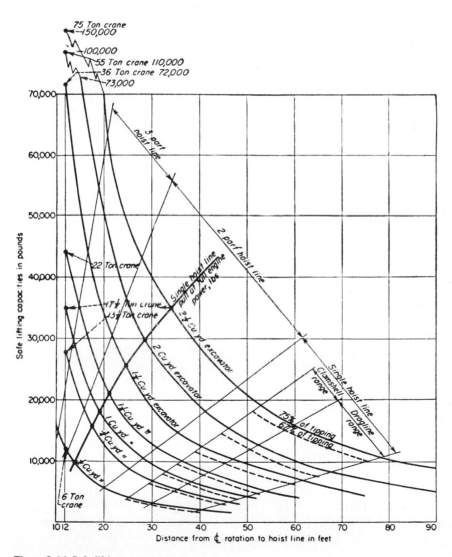

Figure 8-16 Safe lifting capacities of cranes.

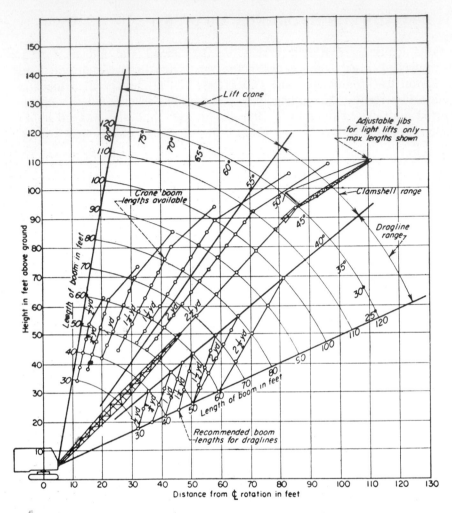

Figure 8-17 Working ranges of cranes.

CLAMSHELLS

GENERAL INFORMATION

Clamshells are used primarily for handling loose materials such as sand, gravel, crushed stone, coal, etc., and for removing materials from cofferdams, pier foundations, sewer manholes, sheet-lined trenches, etc. They are especially suited to vertically lifting materials from one location to another, as in charging

Figure 8-18 Wheel-mounted hydraulic crane with telescoping boom. *(Bucyrus-Erie Company.)*

hoppers and overhead bins. The limits of vertical movement may be relatively large when they are used with long crane booms.

CLAMSHELL BUCKETS

Clamshell buckets are available in various sizes, and in heavy-duty types for digging, medium-weight for general-purpose uses, and lightweight types for rehandling light materials. Manufacturers supply buckets either with teeth that can be removed easily or without teeth. Teeth are used in digging the harder

Figure 8-19 Truck-mounted crane used to drive piles. *(Northwest Engineering Company.)*

types of materials but are not required when a bucket is used for rehandling purposes. Figure 8-20 illustrates a rehandling and a heavy-duty digging bucket.

The capacity of a clamshell bucket is usually given in cubic yards. A more accurate capacity is given as water-level, plate-line, or heaped-measure, generally expressed in cubic feet. The water-level capacity is the capacity of the bucket if it were hung level and filled with water. The plate-line capacity indicates the capacity of the bucket following a line along the tops of the clams. The heaped capacity is the capacity of the bucket when it is filled to the maximum angle of

Figure 8-20 (*a*) Wide rehandling clamshell bucket. (*b*) Heavy-duty clamshell bucket.

repose for the given material. In specifying the heaped capacity the angle of repose usually is assumed to be 45°. The deck area indicates the number of square feet covered by the bucket when it is fully open. Table 8-14 gives representative specifications for medium-weight general-purpose-type buckets furnished by one manufacturer. Figure 8-21 illustrates the use of a clamshell to charge a batching plant.

Table 8-14 Representative specifications for medium-weight general-purpose-type clamshell buckets

	Size, cu yd								
	$\frac{3}{8}$	$\frac{1}{2}$	$\frac{3}{4}$	1	$1\frac{1}{4}$	$1\frac{1}{2}$	$1\frac{3}{4}$	2	$2\frac{1}{2}$
Capacity, cu ft:									
Water-level	8.0	11.8	15.6	23.2	27.6	33.0	38.0	47.0	52.0
Plate-line	11.0	15.6	21.9	32.2	37.6	43.7	51.5	60.0	75.4
Heaped	13.0	18.8	27.7	37.4	45.8	55.0	64.8	74.0	90.2
Weights, lb:									
Bucket only	1,662	2,120	2,920	3,870	4,400	5,310	5,440	6,000	7,775
Counterweights	230	300	400	400	400	500	500	600	600
Teeth	180	180	180	180	180	190	266	300	390
Complete	2,072	2,600	3,500	4,450	4,980	6,000	6,206	6,900	8,765
Dimensions:									
Deck area, sq ft	13.7	16.0	21.8	24.0	29.0	33.4	36.6	40.0	44.6
Width	2′6″	2′6″	3′0″	3′0″	3′5″	3′9″	4′0″	4′3″	4′6″
Length, open	5′5″	6′5″	7′3″	7′10″	8′5″	9′0″	9′2″	9′4″	9′11″
Length, closed	4′9″	5′7″	6′3″	6′9″	7′1″	7′6″	7′11″	8′0″	9′3″
Height, open	7′1″	7′10″	9′1″	9′9″	10′3″	10′9″	10′3″	11′6″	13′0″
Height, closed	5′9″	6′4″	7′4″	7′10″	8′3″	8′9″	8′9″	9′3″	10′4″

Figure 8-21 Feeding a batching plant with a clamshell.

PRODUCTION RATES FOR CLAMSHELLS

Because of the variable factors which affect the operations of a clamshell, it is difficult to give production rates that are dependable. These factors include the difficulty of loading the bucket, the size load obtainable, the height of lift, the angle of swing, the method of disposing of the load, and the experience of the operator. For example, if the material must be discharged into a hopper, the time required to spot the bucket over the hopper and discharge the load will be greater than when the material is discharged onto a large spoil bank. The following example will illustrate a method of estimating the probable output of a clamshell.

> **Example** A $1\frac{1}{2}$-cu-yd rehandling-type bucket, whose empty weight is 4,300 lb, will be used to transfer sand from a stock pile into a hopper, 25 ft above the ground. The angle of swing will average 90°. The average loose capacity of the bucket will be 48 cu ft.
>   The specifications for the crane unit give the following information:

Speed of hoist line, 153 fpm
Swing speed, 4 rpm

Time per cycle (approx.):

Loading bucket	= 6 sec
Lifting and swinging load, 25 ft @ 153 fpm	= 10 sec*
Dumping load	= 6 sec
Swinging back to stock pile	= 4 sec
Lost time, accelerating, etc.	= 4 sec
Total time	= 30 sec

Maximum no. cycles per hr, $\dfrac{60 \times 60}{30} = 120$

Max volume per hr $\dfrac{120 \times 48}{27} = 213$ cu yd

If the unit operates 45 min per hr, the probable output will be $(213 \times 45)/60 = 159$ cu yd per hr loose volume.

If the same equipment is used with a general-purpose bucket to dredge muck and sand from a sheet-piling cofferdam partly filled with water, requiring a total vertical lift of 40 ft, and to discharge it into a barge, the production rate previously determined will not apply. It will be necessary to lift the bucket above the top of the dam prior to starting the swing, which will increase the time cycle. Because of the nature of the material the load will probably be limited to the water-filled capacity of the bucket, which is 33 cu ft. The time per cycle should be about as follows:

Loading bucket	= 8 sec
Lifting load, 40 ft @ 153 fpm	= 16 sec
Swinging, 90° @ 4 rpm	= 4 sec
Dumping load	= 4 sec
Swinging back	= 4 sec
Lowering bucket, 40 ft @ 350 fpm	= 7 sec
Lost time, accelerating, etc	= 10 sec
Total time	= 53 sec

Maximum no. cycles per hr, $\dfrac{60 \times 60}{53} = 68$

Maximum volume per hr, $\dfrac{68 \times 33}{27} = 83$ cu yd

If the unit operates 45 min per hr, the probable output will be $(83 \times 45)/60 = 62$ cu yd per hr loose volume.

HOES

GENERAL INFORMATION

The term hoe applies to an excavating machine of the power-shovel group. It is referred to by several names, such as hoe, backhoe, back shovel, and pull shovel. Figures 8-22 through 8-25 illustrate types of hoes available. As illustrated in Fig.

*A skilled operator should lift and swing simultaneously. If this is not possible, additional time should be allowed for swinging the load.

Figure 8-22 Crawler-mounted cable- and hydraulically operated hoe or pull shovel. *(Northwest Engineering Company.)*

8-26, a power shovel is converted into a hoe by installing a dipper stick and a dipper at the end of the shovel boom. A hoe frequently is equipped with a goose neck boom to increase the digging depth of the machine.

Hoes are used primarily to excavate below the natural surface of the ground on which the machine rests. They are adapted to excavating trenches, pits for basements, and general grading work, which requires precise control of depths.

Figure 8-23 Crawler-mounted hydraulically operated hoe. *(Drott Manufacturing Company.)*

Figure 8-24 Wheel-mounted hydraulically operated hoe. *(Drott Manufacturing Company.)*

Figure 8-25 Crawler-mounted hydraulically operated hoe loading a truck. *(Bucyrus-Erie Company.)*

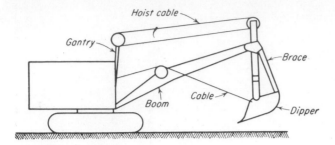

Figure 8-26 Basic parts of a cable-operated hoe.

Because of their rigidity they are superior to draglines in operating on close-range work and dumping into trucks. Because of the direct pull on the dipper, hoes may exert greater tooth pressures than power shovels.

In some respects hoes are superior to wheel- or ladder-type trenching machines, especially in digging utility trenches whose banks are permitted to establish natural slopes and for which trench shoring will not be used. Hoes can remove the earth as it caves in to establish natural slopes, whereas trenching machines cannot do this easily. The reduction in construction costs resulting from the elimination of shoring may be a significant item.

THE BASIC PARTS OF A CABLE-OPERATED HOE

The basic parts of a cable-operated hoe are illustrated in Fig. 8-26. The machine is placed in operation by setting the boom at the desired angle and pulling in on the hoist cable, while releasing the drag cable, to move the dipper out to the desired postition. The free end of the boom is lowered by releasing the tension in the hoist cable until the dipper teeth engage the material to be dug. As the cable is pulled in, the dipper is filled. The dipper is lifted by raising the boom, and then swinging to the dumping position, which may be over a spoil bank or a truck.

WORKING RANGES OF HOES

Figure 8-27 illustrates the terms which are commonly used to identify the dimensions and working ranges of hoes. Table 8-15 gives representative dimensions and clearances for hoes. Dippers are available in various widths to suit the needs of the owner.

Figures 8-28 and 8-29 illustrate a machine which is used to shape ditches, slopes, and other types of earthwork.

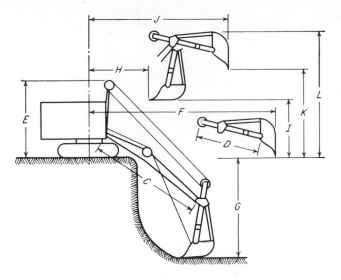

Figure 8-27 Clearance diagram for a cable-operated hoe.

OUTPUT OF HOES

When a hoe is used to dig at moderate depths, the output may approach the output of a power shovel of comparable size digging in the same class of material. However, as the depth is increased, the output of a hoe will decrease considerably. The most effective digging action occurs when the dipper stick is at right angles to the boom. The greatest output will be obtained if digging is

Table 8-15 Representative dimensions and clearances for cable-operated hoes

Size dip-per, cu yd	Length of boom, ft	Length of stick, ft	Max digging radius, ft	Max digging depth, ft	Radius, ft, at beginning of dump	end of dump	Clearance, ft, under dipper at beginning of dump	end of dump
$\frac{3}{8}$	14–15	6–8	23–25	11–12	8–10	17–18	9–10	15–17
$\frac{1}{2}$	16–17	6–8	26–27	15–18	8–10	19–22	9–11	15–18
$\frac{3}{4}$	16–20	7–9	28–33	17–22	8–13	20–27	10–12	16–22
1	18–21	8–10	30–34	20–23	9–11	22–26	12–14	18–21
$1\frac{1}{2}$	22–26	9–11	36–42	25–28	13–15	28–32	14–16	27–30
$1\frac{3}{4}$	24–27	9–12	38–43	26–29	14–16	29–33	15–17	28–31

Figure 8-28 Gradall shaping the side slopes of a ditch. *(The Warner & Swasey Company.)*

Figure 8-29 Gradall cleaning a drainage ditch. *(The Warner & Swasey Company.)*

Figure 8-30 Hoe used to dig a trench.

done near the machine, because of the reduced cycle time, and because the material rolls back into the dipper better when the dipper is pulled upward near the machine. Figure 8-30 illustrates the use of a hoe to excavate a trench.

TRENCHING MACHINES

GENERAL INFORMATION

The term *trenching machine*, as used in this book, applies to the wheel-and ladder-type machines shown in Figs. 8-31 and 8-32, respectively. These machines are satisfactory for digging utility trenches for water, gas, and oil pipelines, telephone cables, drainage ditches, and sewers where the job and soil conditions are such that they may be used. They provide relatively fast digging, with positive controls of depths and widths of trenches, which reduce expensive hand

Figure 8-31 Wheel-type trenching machine. *(The Parsons Company.)*

Figure 8-32 Ladder-type trenching machine. *(The Parsons Company.)*

finishing to a minimum. They are capable of digging any type soil except rock. They are available in various sizes for digging trenches of varying depths and widths. They are usually crawler-mounted to increase their stability and to distribute the weight over a greater area.

WHEEL-TYPE TRENCHING MACHINES

Figure 8-31 illustrates a wheel-type trenching machine. These machines are available with maximum cutting depths exceeding 8 ft, with trench widths varying from 12 in. or less to approximately 60 in. Many of them are available with 25 or more digging speeds to permit the selection of the most suitable speed for any job condition.

The excavating part of the machine consists of a power-driven wheel, on which are mounted a number of removable buckets, equipped with cutter teeth. Buckets are available in varying widths, to which there may be attached side cutters when it is necessary to increase the width of a trench. The machine is operated by lowering the rotating wheel to the desired depth, while the unit moves forward slowly. The earth is picked up by the buckets and deposited onto an endless belt conveyor, which can be adjusted to discharge the earth on either side of the trench.

Table 8-16 gives representative specifications for wheel-type trenching machines. As these specifications do not necessarily include all machines that

Table 8-16 Representative specifications for wheel-type trenching machines

Max trench depth, ft (m)	Trench width, in. (mm)	Engine power, hp (kW)	Wheel speed, fpm (m/sec)	Travel speed, mph (km/hr)	Digging speed, fpm (m/min)
5.5 (1.67)	15–18–21 (380–450–532) 20–23–26 (507–583–660)	55 (41)	36–266 (0.18–1.35)	0.5–2.7 (0.8–4.3)	0.2–10 (0.06–0.30)
6.0 (1.82)	16–18–20 (405–457–517) 20–22–24 (507–559–610) 24–26–28 (610–660–710) 28–30 (710–760)	67 (50)	153–410 (0.78–2.08)	0.16–4.6 (0.26–7.4)	2.8–57.5 (0.08–17.4)
8.5 (2.58)	38–40 (965–1,015) 40–51 (1,015–1,290)	110 (82)	243 (1.23)	1.9 (3.1)	1.3–35.0 (0.42–10.8)

are available, a prospective purchaser should consult the manufacturer's specifications for the particular machine under consideration. The various trench widths for a given machine are obtained by using different bucket widths and installing side cutters.

Wheel-type machines are especially suited to excavating trenches for water, gas, and oil pipelines, buried telephone cables, and pipe drains which are placed in relatively shallow trenches. They also may be used to excavate trenches for sewer pipes up to the maximum digging depths.

LADDER-TYPE TRENCHING MACHINES

Figure 8-32 illustrates a ladder-type trenching machine. By installing extensions to the ladders or booms and by adding more buckets and chain links, it is possible to dig trenches in excess of 30 ft deep with the large machines. Trench widths in excess of 12 ft may be dug. Most of these machines have booms whose lengths may be varied, thereby permitting a single machine to be used on trenches varying considerably in depth. This eliminates the need of owning a different machine for each depth range. A machine may have 30 or more digging speeds to suit the needs of any given job.

The excavating part of the machine consists of two endless chains, which travel along the boom, to which there are attached cutter buckets equipped with teeth. In addition, shaft-mounted side cutters may be installed on each side of the boom to increase the width of a trench. As the buckets travel up the underside of the boom, they bring out earth and deposit it on a belt conveyor, which discharges it along either side of the trench. As a machine moves over uneven ground, it is possible to vary the depth of cut by adjusting the position, but not the length, of the boom.

A modification of the ladder-type machine is one with a vertical boom, illustrated in Fig. 8-33. This machine is available with seven different boom sizes, which permit trench depths varying from 4 ft to 8 ft 3 in. and trench widths varying from 14 to 24 in.

Table 8-17 gives representative specifications for ladder-type trenching machines. The prospective purchaser of a machine should check the manufacturer's specifications for the particular machine under consideration. The various trench widths for a given machine are obtained by using different bucket widths and installing side cutters.

As can be seen from Table 8-17, ladder-type trenching machines have considerable flexibility with regard to trench depths and widths. However, the machines are not suitable for excavating trenches in rock or where large quantities of ground water, combined with unstable soil, prevent the walls of a trench from remaining in place. If the soil, such as loose sand or mud, tends to flow into the trench, it may be desirable to adopt some other method of excavating the trench. Usually, the trench is lined on both sides with sheet piling, lumber or steel, prior to excavating with a clamshell bucket.

Figure 8-33 Vertical-boom trenching machine. *(Barber-Greene Company.)*

SELECTING THE MOST SUITABLE EQUIPMENT FOR EXCAVATING TRENCHES

The choice of equipment to be used in excavating a trench will depend on the job conditions, the depth and width of the trench, the class of soil, the extent to which ground water is present, the width of the right of way for the disposal of excavated earth, and the type of equipment already owned by a contractor.

Table 8-17 Representative specifications for ladder-type trenching machines

Max trench depth, ft (m)	Trench width, in. (mm)	Engine power, hp (kW)	Bucket speed, fpm (m/sec)	Travel speed, mph (km/hr)	Digging speed, fpm (m/min)
4.5 (1.37)	6–8 (152–203)	47 (35)	245–538 (1.24–2.72)	0.7–3.4 (1.1–5.5)	2.2–21.8 (0.67–6.6)
8.5 (2.58)	16–36 (407–920)	55 (41)	96–225 (0.48–1.14)	1.4–3.2 (2.2–5.1)	0.5–13.8 (0.15–4.2)
12.5 (3.81)	16–42 (407–1,070)	74 (55)	135–542 (0.68–2.74)	1.4–3.2 (2.2–5.1)	0.3–9.7 (0.09–2.95)
15.0 (4.57)	18–54 (457–1,370)	90 (67)	103–168 (0.52–0.85)	1.7 (2.7)	0.7–15.5 (0.21–4.75)

If a relatively shallow and narrow trench is to be excavated in firm soil, the wheel-type machine is probably the most suitable. However, if the soil is rock, which requires blasting, the most suitable excavator will be a hoe; a less desirable substitute could be a dragline. If the soil is an unstable, water-saturated material, it may be necessary to use a dragline, hoe, or clamshell and let the walls establish a stable slope. If it is necessary to install solid sheeting to hold the walls in place, neither a hoe nor a dragline will work satisfactorily. A clamshell, which can excavate between the trench braces that hold the sheeting in place, will probably be the best equipment for the job.

Consider the selection of a machine to excavate a trench 24 ft deep and 10 ft wide in soil which is sufficiently firm to require only shoring to hold the walls in place. A trench of this size can be excavated with a ladder-type machine, provided that the length and height of the conveyor belt are adequate to dispose of the earth along one side of the trench. The cross-section area of the trench will be 240 sq ft. If the loose earth has a 30 percent swell, the cross-section area of the spoil pile will be

$$240 \times 1.3 = 312 \text{ sq ft}$$

If the excavated earth will repose with 1 : 1 side slopes, the pile will have a height of 17.6 ft and a base width of 35.2 ft. If a minimum of 4 ft of clearance is required along the side of the trench, the end of the conveyor must have a height clearance of 17.6 ft and a length of approximately 27 ft, measured from the center of the trench. The casting effect on the earth, as it leaves the end of the conveyor belt, may permit the use of a shorter conveyor. Unless the machine under consideration satisfies these clearances, it is probable that difficulties will be experienced in disposing of the earth. A dragline would have no difficulty in disposing of the excavated earth. Also, a dragline can be used to backfill the trench if more suitable equipment is not available.

PRODUCTION RATES OF TRENCHING MACHINES

Many factors will influence the production rates of trenching machines. These include the class of soil, depth and width of the trench, extent of shoring required, topography, climatic conditions, extent of vegetation such as trees, stumps, and roots, physical obstructions such as buried pipes, sidewalks, paved streets, buildings, etc., and the speed with which the pipe can be placed in the trench. Any factors that may affect the progress on a project should be considered in estimating the probable digging speed of a trenching machine.

In laying oil and gas pipes through open, level country, with no physical obstructions to interfere with the progress, it is possible to install in excess of 6,000 ft of pipe in an 8-hr day. This is equivalent to approximately 800 ft per hr, which is not excessive for a wheel-type machine. However, if a trench must be excavated into rock over rough terrain covered with heavy timber, it may not be possible to excavate more than a few hundred feet per day.

If a trench is dug for the installation of sewer pipe, under favorable conditions, it is possible that the machine could dig 300 ft of trench per hour. However, an experienced pipe-laying crew may not be able to lay more than 25 joints of small-diameter pipe, 3 ft long, in an hour. Thus the speed of the machine will be limited to about 75 ft per hr regardless of its ability to dig more trench. In estimating the probable rate of digging a trench, an appropriate operating factor must be applied to the speed at which the machine could dig if there were no interruptions.

Example Estimate the probable average production rate, in feet per hour, in excavating a trench 36 in. wide, with a maximum depth of 12 ft, in hard, tough clay. The trench will be dug for the installation of a 21-in.-diameter sewer pipe, which can be laid at a rate of approximately 30 ft per hr. An examination of the site along the trench reveals that there are obstructions which will reduce the digging speed to approximately 60 percent of the theoretically possible speed. This will require the application of an operating factor of 0.6 to the speed of the machine.

An examination of Table 8-17 indicates a ladder-type machine with a maximum digging depth of 12.5 ft. Considering the class of soil and the depth and width of the trench, the maximum possible digging speed should be about 1 fpm, or 60 ft per hr. The application of the operating factor will reduce the average speed to 36 ft per hr. However, since only 30 ft of pipe can be laid per hour, this will be the controlling speed.

The probable cost per linear foot of trench, for excavating only, should be as follows:

Trenching machines	=	$16.20
Operator	=	7.00
Helpers, 3 men @ $4.00 per hr	=	12.00
Foreman, one-half time charged to excavating	=	4.50
Total cost	=	$39.70
Cost per lin ft, $39.70 ÷ 30 ft per hr	=	1.264

EARTH-AND-ROCK SAWS

As illustrated in Fig. 8-34, this machine consists of a vertical wheel with a horizontal shaft which is supported on an adjustable boom mounted on the rear of a track-type or wheel-type power unit such as a tractor. The machine is used to cut narrow trenches, up to about 6 in. in width and 30 in. or more in depth in frozen earth, caliche, coral, other rocks, and concrete.

The sawing is performed by round carbide-tipped rotating cutters attached to the wheel, with the type selected depending on the properties of the material to be sawed. Their teeth, which are replaceable, rotate freely in their mounting pockets to maintain even tooth wear.

Figure 8-34 Crawler-mounted cutting wheel. *(Vermeer Manufacturing Company.)*

WHEEL EXCAVATORS

Figure 8-35 illustrates a wheel excavator that has been used to produce up to 1,750 cu yd bank measure per hour. The milling action of the wheel permits the excavator to cut almost any material, including weathered and broken rock. The depth of cut, up to 13 ft or more, assures a blending of the materials for the full depth excavated, and the pulverizing action facilitates the placement and compaction of the material on the fill.

As illustrated in the figure, the wheel deposits the excavated material onto a variable-speed conveyor belt which discharges it into either of two hauling units.

TRAP-LOADING MATERIALS

Figure 8-36 illustrates a method of loading materials into hauling units. A machine consisting of a receiving hopper or trap and a belt conveyor is located against a deposit of material to be removed. Bulldozers push the material into a trap, from which a conveyor elevates it and discharges it into hauling units, or onto other belt conveyors.

Figure 8-35 Wheel excavator loading bottom-dump wagons. *(Barber-Greene Company.)*

The best production and economy are attained when the loader is located at the bottom of a hill to permit the bulldozers to push the material downgrade. This method has been used to excavate and transport aggregates and other materials on many projects, such as the Portage Dam in British Columbia, Canada [3].

Figure 8-36 Bulldozers feeding a trap loader. *(Kolman Division, Athey Products Corp.)*

PROBLEMS

8-1 Select the minimum size power shovel that will excavate 110,000 cu yd of ordinary earth in 120 working days of 8 hr each. The average depth of excavation will be 10 ft, and the average angle of swing will be 120°. The job and management factors will be good.

8-2 For each of the stated conditions determine the probable output of a 2-cu-yd power shovel expressed in cu yd per hr, bank measure.

| | Class of earth | | | |
Condition	Moist loam	Moist loam	Common earth	Hard clay
Depth of dig, ft	12	8	11	10
Angle of swing, deg	90	120	60	130
Job conditions	Good	Fair	Excellent	Poor
Management conditions	Excellent	Good	Good	Fair

8-3 A 2-cu-yd power shovel whose cost per hour, including the wages to an operator and an oiler, is $56.00, is assumed to excavate common earth under each of the stated conditions. Determine the cost per cu yd for each condition.

Condition	(1)	(2)	(3)	(4)
Depth of dig, ft	11	13	10	7
Angle of swing, deg	60	90	120	150
Job conditions	Excellent	Good	Fair	Poor
Management conditions	Excellent	Good	Fair	Poor

8-4 Determine the probable production of a 2-cu-yd dragline when excavating tough clay under good job and management conditions. The average depth of cut will be 9 ft and the average angle of swing will be 140°.

8-5 Determine the largest capacity heavy-duty dragline bucket that can be used with a dragline equipped with a 70-ft boom when the boom is operating at an angle of 40°. The earth will weigh 92 lb per cu ft loose measure.

8-6 Select the minimum size crane required to unload concrete pipe weighing 28,000 lb per joint and lower it into a trench when the distance from the center line of rotation of the crane is 30 ft.

8-7 Select the minimum size crane and the minimum length boom required to hoist a load of 36,000 lb from a truck at ground level and place it on a platform 46 ft above the ground. The vertical distance from the boom point of the crane down to the bottom of the load will be 12 ft. The maximum horizontal distance from the center of rotation of the crane to the hoist line of the crane when lifting the load will be 30 ft.

REFERENCES

1. Power Crane and Shovel Association, A Bureau of Construction Industry Manufacturers Association, 111 East Wisconsin Avenue, Milwaukee, Wisconsin 53202.
1a. "Man the Builder, The Functional Design and Job Application of Power Cranes and Excavators," *Technical Bulletin No. 1,* 1971.

1b. "Operating Cost Guide For Estimating Costs of Owning and Operating Power Cranes, Draglines, Clamshells, Backhoes and Shovels, 3/8 thru 5 cu yd-5 thru 125 tons," *Technical Bulletin No.* 2, 1965.
1c. "Proper Sizing of Excavators, Draglines, Clamshells, Backhoes, Shovels and Hauling Equipment," *Technical Bulletin No.* 3, 1966.
1d. "Cable-controlled Power Cranes, Draglines, Hoes, Shovels, Clamshells, Mountings, Attachments, Applications," *Technical Bulletin No.* 4, 1968.
1e. "Power Crane Applications In Industrial Plants," *Technical Bulletin No.* 5, 1954.
1f. "Hydraulic Excavators and Telescoping-boom Cranes," 1974.
1g. "Hydraulic Excavator User's Safety Manual," 1975.
1h. "Operating Cost Guide For Estimating Costs of Owning and Operating Cranes and Excavators," 1976.
1i. "Mobile Power Crane and Excavator Standards," *PCSA Standard No.* 1, 1968.
1j. "Mobile Hydraulic Crane Standards," *PCSA Standard No.* 2, 1968.
1k. "Mobile Hydraulic Excavator Standards," *PCSA Standard No.* 3, 1969.
2. "Crane Load Stability Test Code—SAE J765," SAE Recommended Practice Handbook, Society of Automotive Engineers, Inc., 1967.
3. Low, W. Irvine: Portage Mountain Dam Conveyors System, *Journal of the Construction Division, Proceedings of the American Society of Civil Engineers*, vol. 93, pp. 33-51, September 1967.
4. Construction Industry Manufacturers Association, 111 East Wisconsin Avenue, Milwaukee, Wisconsin 53202.
5. Drott Manufacturing Division of J. I. Case, P. O. Box 1087, Wausau, Wisconsin 54401.
6. Northwest Engineering Company, 201 West Walnut Street, Green Bay, Wisconsin 54305.
7. Vermeer Manufacturing Company, P. O. Box 200, Pella, Iowa 50219.
8. The Warner & Swasey Company, P. O. Box 39127, Solon, Ohio 44139.
9. Barber-Greene Company, 400 North Highland Avenue, Aurora, Illinois 60507.
10. Parsons Company, 200 N. 8th Avenue East, Newton, Iowa 50208.

NINE

TRUCKS AND WAGONS

TRUCKS

In handling earth, aggregate, rock, ore, coal, and other materials, trucks serve one purpose. They are hauling units which, because of their high speeds when operating on suitable roads, have high capacities and provide relatively low hauling costs. They provide a high degree of flexibility, as the number in service may be increased or decreased easily to permit modifications in the total hauling capacity of a fleet. Most trucks may be operated over any haul road for which the surface is sufficiently firm and smooth and on which the grades are not excessively steep. Some units now in use are designated as off-highway trucks because their sizes and total loads are larger than are permitted on highways. These trucks are used for hauling materials on large projects, where the sizes and costs are justified.

Trucks may be classified according to a great many factors, including the following:

1. Size and type of engine—gasoline, diesel, butane, propane
2. Number of gears
3. Kind of drive—two-wheel, four-wheel, six-wheel, etc.
4. Number of wheels and axles and arrangement of driving wheels
5. Method of dumping the load—rear-dump, side-dump
6. Class of material hauled—earth, rock, coal, ore, etc.
7. Capacity, in tons or cubic yards
8. Method of dumping the load for rear dumps, hydraulic or cable

If trucks are to be purchased for general material hauling, the purchaser should select units that are adaptable to the purposes for which they will be used. However, if trucks are to be used on a given project for a given purpose, the purchaser should select trucks that most nearly fit the requirements of the project.

REAR–DUMP TRUCKS

Rear-dump trucks are suitable for use in hauling many types of materials. The shape of the body, such as the extent of sharp angles, corners, and the contour of the rear, through which the materials must flow during dumping, will affect the ease or difficulty of dumping. The bodies of trucks that will be used to haul wet clay and similar materials should be free of sharp angles and corners. Dry sand and gravel will flow easily from almost any shape of body. If quarry rock is to be hauled, bodies should be shallow with sloping sideboards. Figure 9-1 shows a power shovel loading a rear-dump truck.

Figure 9-2 shows a 22-ton single-axle dual-wheel rear-dump truck dumping its load. The body of this truck is approximately 15 ft 3 in. long, 8 ft 4 in. wide, and 3 ft 6 in. deep, inside dimensions. The struck capacity is 14.8 cu yd. It is equipped with 14.00 by 24, 20-ply front tires and 18.00 by 24, 24-ply rear tires.

Figure 9-1 A 100-cu-yd struck capacity rear-dump truck. *(WABCO Construction and Mining Equipment Group.)*

Figure 9-2 Hydraulically operated rear-dump truck. *(WABCO Construction and Mining Equipment Group.)*

BOTTOM–DUMP WAGONS

If units are to be used to haul materials, such as sand, gravel, reasonably dry earth, coal, etc., which flow easily, the use of bottom-dump wagons will reduce the time required to unload the units. Such units are particularly suitable for use

Figure 9-3 Bottom-dump wagon, 150-ton payload, 940-hp diesel engine. *(WABCO Construction and Mining Equipment Group.)*

Figure 9-4 Bottom-dump wagon being loaded by a dragline. *(Euclid, Inc.)*

where the materials are distributed in layers on a fill or are discharged through grizzlies into hoppers. When discharging the loads onto fills, the wagons can dump their loads while moving. When discharging through grizzlies, they will need to stop for only a few seconds. The rapid rate of discharging the load gives these wagons a time advantage over rear-dump trucks.

As the doors through which these units discharge their loads have limited openings, difficulties may be experienced in discharging such materials as wet, sticky clay, especially if they are in large lumps.

Figure 9-5 Bottom-dump wagon approaching the dump. *(Euclid, Inc.)*

These wagons are satisfactory hauling units on projects such as earthen dams, levees, highways, and airports, where large quantities of materials are to be transported and haul roads can be kept in reasonably good condition. They may be loaded by power shovels, draglines, or portable belt loaders.

CAPACITIES OF TRUCKS AND WAGONS

There are at least three methods of expressing the capacities of trucks and wagons: by the load which it will carry, expressed in tons; by its struck volume; and by its heaped volume, the latter two expressed in cubic yards.

The struck capacity of a truck is the volume of material which it will haul when it is filled to the top of the sides, with no material above the sides. The heaped capacity is the volume of material which it will haul when the load is heaped above the sides. The capacity should be expressed in cubic yards. While the struck capacity remains fixed for any given unit, the heaped capacity will vary with the height to which the material may extend above the sides and with the length and width of the body. Wet earth or sandy clay may be hauled with a slope of 1 : 1, while dry sand or gravel may not permit a slope greater than 3 : 1. In order to determine the probable heaped capacity of a unit, it is necessary to know the struck capacity, the length and width of the body, and the slope at which the material will remain stable while the unit is moving. Smooth haul roads will permit a larger heaped capacity than rough haul roads. Because of variations in the heaping capacities of units it may be better to compare them on the basis of their struck capacities. In any event the capacities should be determined or compared in a realistic manner.

The weight capacity may limit the volume of the load when a unit is used to haul heavy material, such as iron ore. However, when the specific gravity of the material is such that the safe load is not exceeded, a unit may be filled to its heaped capacity.

In some instances it is possible to add sideboards to increase the depth of the body of a truck or wagon, thereby permitting it to haul a larger load. This practice probably will increase the hourly cost of operating a unit, because of higher fuel consumption, reduced tire life, more frequent failures of parts, such as axles, gears, brakes, and clutches, and higher maintenance costs. However, if the value of the extra material hauled is greater than the total increase in the cost of operating a vehicle, the overloading is justified. In considering hauling larger volumes of materials, the maximum safe loads on the tires should be checked to prevent excessive overloading, which might result in considerable lost time due to tire failures.

PERFORMANCE CAPABILITIES OF TRUCKS AND WAGONS

The productive capacity of a truck or wagon depends on the size of its load and the number of trips it can make in an hour. The size of the load can be determined from the specifications furnished by the manufacturer. The number of trips per hour will depend on the weight of the vehicle, the horsepower of the engine, the haul distance, and the condition of the haul road.

The productive capacity may be determined as illustrated in the example beginning on page 274, using the rimpulls of the vehicle, if this information is available, the weight of the vehicle, and the condition of the haul road.

Another method of determining the production is to use the performance chart furnished by most manufacturers for their vehicles. Such a chart is illustrated in Fig. 9-6, for a 22-ton rear-dump truck.

Example The specifications for the truck are as follows:

Engine, 225 fwhp
Capacity
   Struck, 14.7 cu yd
   Heaped, 2 : 1, 18.3 cu yd
Net weight empty   = 36,860 lb
Payload   = 44,000 lb
   Gross vehicle weight = 80,860 lb

Determine the maximum speed for the truck when it is hauling a load of 22 tons up a 6 percent grade on a haul road having a rolling resistance of 60 lb per ton, equivalent to a 3 percent adverse grade. Because the chart is based on zero rolling resistance, it is necessary to combine the grade and rolling resistance, which gives an equivalent total resistance equal to $6 + 3 = 9$ percent of the vehicle weight.

The steps in using the chart are as follows:

1. Find the vehicle weight on the lower left horizontal scale.
2. Read up the weight line to the intersection with the slanted total resistance line.
3. From this intersection read horizontally to the right to the intersection with the performance curve.
4. From this intersection read down to find the vehicle speed.

If these four steps are followed, it will be determined that the truck will operate in the second speed range, and that its maximum speed will be 6.5 mph.

The chart should be used to determine the maximum speed for each section of a haul road having a significant difference in grade or rolling resistance.

While a performance chart indicates the maximum speed at which a vehicle can travel, the vehicle will not necessarily travel at this speed. If conditions other than total resistance limit the speed to less than the value given in the chart, the anticipated effective speed should be used.

BALANCING THE CAPACITIES OF HAULING UNITS WITH THE SIZE OF EXCAVATOR

In loading with power shovels, draglines, or belt loaders, it is desirable to use units whose capacities balance the output of the excavator. If this is not done,

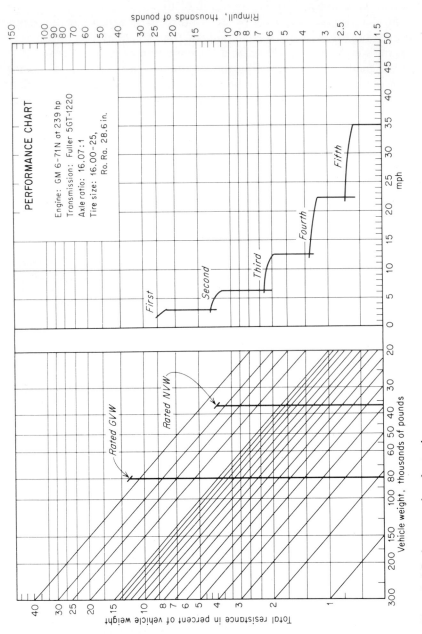

Figure 9-6 Performance chart for truck.

operating difficulties will develop and the combined cost of excavating and hauling material may be higher than when balanced units are used. For example, when an excavator is used to load earth into trucks, the size of the trucks may introduce several factors which will affect the production rate and the cost of handling earth.

1. Advantages of small compared with large trucks:
   a. They are more flexible in maneuvering, which may be an advantage on short hauls.
   b. They may have higher speeds.
   c. There is less loss in production when one truck in a fleet breaks down.
   d. It is easier to balance the number of trucks with the output of the excavator, which will reduce the time lost by the trucks or the excavator.
2. Disadvantages of small compared with large trucks:
   a. It is more difficult for the excavator to load owing to small target for depositing earth.
   b. More total time is lost in spotting the trucks because of the larger number required.
   c. More drivers are required to haul a given output of material.
   d. The greater number of trucks required increases the danger of bunching up at the pit, along the haul road, or at the dump.
   e. The greater number of trucks required may increase the total investment in hauling equipment, with more expensive maintenance and repairs and more parts to stock.
3. Advantages of large compared with small trucks:
   a. Fewer trucks are required, which may reduce the total investment in hauling units and the cost of maintenance and repairs.
   b. Fewer drivers are required.
   c. The smaller number of trucks facilitates synchronizing the equipment and reduces the danger of bunching up by the trucks. This is especially true for long hauls.
   d. They give a larger target for the excavator during loading.
   e. They reduce the frequency of spotting trucks under the excavator.
   f. There are fewer trucks to maintain and repair and fewer parts to stock.
   g. The engines ordinarily use cheaper fuels.
4. Disadvantages of large compared with small trucks:
   a. The cost of truck time at loading is greater, especially with small excavators.
   b. The heavier loads may cause more damage to the haul roads, thus increasing the cost of maintaining haul roads.
   c. It is more difficult to balance the number of trucks with the output of the excavator.
   d. Repair parts may be more difficult to obtain.
   e. The largest sizes may not be permitted to haul on highways.

A rule-of-thumb practice which is frequently used in selecting the size of trucks is to use trucks with a minimum capacity of four to five times the capacity of the excavator bucket or dipper, when loading with a dragline or shovel. The dependability of this practice is discussed in the following analyses.

Example Consider a $\frac{3}{4}$-cu-yd shovel excavating good common earth, with a 90° swing, with no delays waiting for hauling units, and with a 21-sec cycle time. If the dipper and the trucks are operated at their heaped capacities, the swelling effect of the earth should permit each to carry its rated or struck capacity, expressed in cubic yards bank measure. Assume that the number of dippers required to fill a truck will equal the capacity of the truck divided by the size of the dipper, both expressed in cubic yards. The sizes of the trucks considered are based on the struck capacities. Assume that the time for a travel cycle, excluding the time for loading, will be the same for the several sizes of trucks considered. If this is not true, an appropriate travel cycle should be determined for each truck. The time for a travel cycle, which includes traveling to the dump, dumping, and returning to the shovel, will be 6 min.

If 3-cu-yd trucks are used, it will require four dippers to fill a truck. With a shovel cycle of 21 sec it will be necessary to provide a new truck every 84 sec, or 1.4 min. The minimum round-trip cycle for a truck will be 7.4 min. The minimum number of trucks required to keep the shovel busy will be the round-trip time divided by the loading time = 7.4 + 1.4 = 5.3. Thus it will be necessary to use six trucks to keep the shovel busy or else permit the shovel to idle between trucks. Since the time required to load six trucks will be 6 × 1.4 = 8.4 min, the lost time per truck cycle will be 8.4 − 7.4 = 1 min per truck. This will produce an operating factor of

$$\frac{7.4}{8.4} \times 100 = 88 \text{ percent for the trucks}$$

If 6-cu-yd trucks are used, it will require eight dippers to fill a truck. The time required to load a truck will be 168 sec, or 2.8 min. The minimum round-trip cycle for a truck will be 8.8 min. The minimum number of trucks required to keep the shovel busy will be 8.8 + 2.8 = 3.15. For this condition it probably will be cheaper to provide three trucks and let the shovel idle a short time between trucks. The time required to load three trucks will be 3 × 2.8 = 8.4 min. Thus the shovel will lose 8.8 − 8.4 = 0.4 min in loading three trucks. The time lost will be 0.4/8.8 × 100 = 4.5 percent, which is not serious. If four trucks are used, the time required to load them will be 4 × 2.8 = 11.2 min. As this will increase the round-trip cycle of each truck from 8.8 to 11.2 min, the lost time per truck cycle will be 2.4 min per truck. This will result in a loss of

$$\frac{2.4}{11.2} \times 100 = 21.4 \text{ percent of the truck time}$$

which is equivalent to an operating factor of 78.6 percent for the trucks.

If 15-cu-yd trucks are used, it will require 20 dippers to fill a truck. The time required to load a truck will be 420 sec, or 7 min. The minimum round-trip cycle for a truck will be 13 min. The minimum number of trucks required to keep the shovel busy will be 13 + 7 = 1.85. Use two trucks. Since the time required to load two trucks will be 2 × 7 = 14 min, the lost time per truck cycle will be 14 − 13 = 1 min per truck. This will produce an operating factor of $\frac{13}{14} \times 100 = 93$ percent for the trucks.

In the previous example note that the production of the shovel is based on a 60-min hour. This policy should be followed when balancing a servicing unit with the units being served because at times both types of units will operate at maximum capacity if the number of units is properly balanced. However, the average production of a unit, shovel or truck, for a sustained period of time should be based on applying an appropriate efficiency or operating factor to the maximum productive capacity.

THE EFFECT OF THE SIZE OF TRUCKS ON THE COST OF HAULING EARTH

A comparison of the cost of hauling earth with each of several sizes of trucks based on the previous analysis is illustrated in Table 9-1. The information appearing in the table is obtained as illustrated in the following example.

Example Assume that the shovel operates at 80 percent efficiency while it is excavating, with no lost time waiting for trucks.

No. cycles per min, $60 \div 21 = 2.86$
No. cycles per hr, $60 \times 2.86 = 171.6$
Ideal output per hr, $171.6 \times \frac{3}{4} = 128$ cu yd
Output at 80 percent efficiency, $0.8 \times 128 = 102$ cu yd per hr
Travel cycle for each truck, 6 min

If 6-cu-yd trucks are used, the ideal number will be 3.15, as previously determined. If three trucks are used, the output will be $(3.0/3.15) \times 102 = 97$ cu yd per hr.

Cost per hr for a truck and driver		$= \$14.70$
Total cost per hr for trucks, $3 \times \$14.70$		$= \$44.10$
Truck cost while loading,	$\dfrac{2.8 \times \$14.70}{60}$	$= \$ 0.66$
Truck cost per cu yd of earth loaded,	$\dfrac{\$0.66}{6}$	$= \$ 0.110$

The hauling cost per cu yd equals the total truck cost per hour divided by the output per hour, $\$44.10 \div 97 = \$0.456$.

The information given in Table 9-1 indicates that, for the given power shovel and project, the lowest hauling cost will be obtained if three 6-cu-yd trucks are used. For other sizes of power shovels and truck travel cycles the

Table 9-1 Comparison of the cost of hauling common earth with various sizes of trucks, using a $\frac{3}{4}$-cu-yd power shovel for loading

Size truck, cu yd	No. of trucks	Out-put per hr, cu yd	Load-ing time, min	Truck cost per hr		Truck cost at loading		Hauling cost per cu yd
				Per truck	Total	Per truck	Per cu yd	
3	5	96	1.4	$11.20	$56.00	$0.26	$0.086	$0.584
3	6	102	1.4	11.20	67.20	0.26	0.086	0.658
6	3	97	2.8	14.70	44.10	0.66	0.110	0.456
6	4	102	2.8	14.70	58.80	0.66	0.110	0.577
10	2	89	4.6	21.20	42.40	1.62	0.162	0.476
10	3	102	4.6	21.20	63.60	1.62	0.162	0.624
15	2	102	7.0	32.40	64.80	3.78	0.252	0.636
20	2	102	9.3	45.60	91.20	7.06	0.354	0.896

comparative costs given in the table will not necessarily hold true. If the travel cycle for the larger trucks is greater than for the 3-cu-yd trucks, namely, 6 min, the actual time should be used in preparing information similar to that given in the table.

If the size of the excavator is increased, the time lost by the larger trucks at loading will be reduced, which will reduce the hauling cost per cubic yard. One disadvantage in using large trucks, for which costs are paid by the hour, is that the cost of the trucks while they are being loaded will be higher than for smaller trucks. This results from two factors, the longer time required to load and the higher hourly cost of the larger trucks: Since it is desirable to have a truck under the excavator at all times the total hourly truck cost while loading 15-cu-yd trucks will be $32.40, compared with $14.70 for 6-cu-yd trucks, regardless of the size of the excavator. Unless this higher cost for the larger trucks can be recovered by more economical performance during the travel cycle, the use of the larger trucks will not be justified.

THE EFFECT OF THE SIZE OF THE EXCAVATOR ON THE COST OF EXCAVATING AND HAULING EARTH

If the size of the excavator is increased, while the size of trucks remains constant, the resulting increase in the output of the shovel will reduce the time required to load a truck. This will reduce the truck cost per cubic yard during loading. The effect which the size of a power shovel has on the truck cost at loading and the hauling cost is illustrated in Table 9-2. The material will be

Table 9-2 The effect of the size of the power shovel on the cost of hauling earth with 15-cu-yd trucks

| Size shovel, cu yd | Output per hr, cu yd | Truck time | | No. of trucks | Truck cost per hr | Truck cost at loading | | Hauling cost per cu yd |
		Load-ing, min	Round trip, min			Per truck	Per cu yd	
$\frac{1}{2}$	76	11.8	19.8	2	$64.80	$6.38	$0.424	$0.854
$\frac{3}{4}$	108	8.3	16.3	2	64.80	4.48	0.300	0.602
1	125*	6.4	14.4	2	64.80	3.46	0.230	0.520
1	140	6.4	14.4	3	97.20	3.46	0.230	0.694
$1\frac{1}{2}$	191	4.7	12.7	3	97.20	2.54	0.170	0.510
2	231*	3.8	11.8	3	97.20	2.06	0.138	0.420
2	240	3.8	11.8	4	129.60	2.06	0.138	0.540
$2\frac{1}{2}$	280	3.2	11.2	4	129.60	1.72	0.114	0.462
3	312	2.9	10.9	4	129.60	1.58	0.106	0.416

* These values are reduced because the hauling capacities of the trucks limit the outputs.

good common earth, the depth of cut will be optimum, and the angle of swing will be 90°. The operating factor for the shovel will be 80 percent, with no lost time waiting for trucks. Trucks with a heaped capacity of 15 cu yd bank measure will be used to haul the earth. The travel cycle for the trucks will be 8 min. The cost per hour for a truck and driver will be $32.40.

Sample calculations using a 1-cu-yd shovel are as follows:

Ideal output of the shovel, 175 cu yd per hr
Output at 80 percent efficiency, $0.80 \times 175 = 140$ cu yd per hr
Time required to load a truck, $\dfrac{15 \times 60}{140} = 6.4$ min
Round-trip time per truck, with no delays waiting for the shovel,
$\quad 6.4 + 8.0 = 14.4$ min
No. trucks needed, $14.4 \div 6.4 = 2.25$
Output using 2 trucks, $\dfrac{2.0 \times 140}{2.25} = 125$ cu yd per hr
Output using 3 trucks, 140 cu yd per hr

Cost per hr for 2 trucks, $2 \times \$32.40 \quad = \$64.80$
Cost per hr for 3 trucks, $3 \times \$32.40 \quad = \$97.20$
Cost per truck at loading, $\dfrac{6.4}{60} \times \$32.40 = \$ \ 3.46$

Truck costs at loading per cu yd, $\$3.46 \div 15$ cu yd $= \$0.230$
Hauling cost per cu yd, using 2 trucks, $\$64.80 \div 125$ cu yd $- \$0.518$
Hauling cost per cu yd, using 3 trucks, $\$97.20 \div 140$ cu yd $= \$0.694$

Table 9-3 The cost of loading and hauling earth, using various sizes of power shovels and 15-cu-yd trucks

Size shovel, cu yd	Output per hr, cu yd	Shovel cost per hr	No. of trucks	Truck cost per hr	Excavating cost per cu yd	Hauling cost per cu yd	Total cost per cu yd
$\frac{1}{2}$	76	$24.60	2	$64.80	$0.324	$0.854	$1.178
$\frac{3}{4}$	108	27.80	2	64.80	0.258	0.602	0.860
1	125*	28.80	2	64.80	0.230	0.520	0.750
1	140	28.80	3	97.20	0.206	0.694	0.900
$1\frac{1}{2}$	191	42.80	3	97.20	0.224	0.510	0.734
2	231*	59.80	3	97.20	0.260	0.420	0.680
2	240	59.80	4	129.60	0.250	0.540	0.790
$2\frac{1}{2}$	280	67.40	4	129.60	0.242	0.462	0.704
3	312	81.00	4	129.60	0.260	0.516	0.776

* These values are reduced because the hauling capacities of the trucks limit the outputs.

While the information given in Table 9-2 indicates that the cost of hauling earth is reduced as the size of the shovel is increased, the job planner is concerned with the combined cost of excavating and hauling earth. This cost may be obtained by adding the cost of operating the shovel, including labor, to the cost of the trucks. Table 9-3 gives this information. The costs given in the table do not include the cost of moving the equipment to the project and setting it up. The cost of a shovel is based on the cost of owning and operating, with an allowance for the operator and an oiler.

THE EFFECT OF GRADE ON THE COST OF HAULING EARTH WITH TRUCKS

In constructing a fill it frequently is possible to obtain the earth from a borrow pit located either above or below the fill. If the borrow pit is above the fill, the effect of the favorable grade on the loaded truck is to reduce the required rimpull by 20 lb per gross ton for each 1 percent of grade. If the borrow pit is below the fill, the effect of the adverse grade on the loaded truck is to increase the required rimpull by 20 lb per gross ton for each 1 percent of grade. Obviously the grade of the haul road will affect the hauling capacity of a truck, its performance, and the cost of hauling earth. It may be more economical to obtain earth from a borrow pit above, instead of below, the fill, even though the haul distance from the higher pit is greater than from the lower pit. This is an item which should be given consideration in locating borrow pits.

If earth is hauled downhill, it may be possible to add sideboards to the vehicle to increase the hauling capacity, up to the maximum load which the tires can carry. In some instances it will be desirable to use larger tires to permit the trucks to haul greater loads. If the earth is hauled uphill, it may be necessary to reduce the size of the load or the travel speed of the truck, either of which will increase the cost of hauling earth.

> **Example** The following example will illustrate the effect of grade on the cost of hauling earth.
> The project requires 1,000,000 cu yd of earth, bank measure.
> The material will be good common earth, weighing 2,700 lb per cu yd bank measure, with a swell of 25 percent.
> Borrow pit 1 will require an average haul of 0.66 mile up an average grade of 2.2 percent.
> Borrow pit 2 will require an average haul of 0.78 mile down an average slope of 1.4 percent.
> Both borrow pits are easily accessible to the trucks, which will permit spotting on either side of the shovel, whose angle of swing will not exceed 90°. Excavating can be done at optimum depth.
> Job conditions will be excellent, and management conditions will be good. The job-management factor should be not less than 0.80.
> The earth will be excavated with a 3-cu-yd power shovel, with a probable output of $0.80 \times 390 = 312$ cu yd per hr bank measure.
> The average rolling resistance of the haul road is estimated to be 60 lb per ton.
> The coefficient of traction between the truck tires and the haul road will average 0.60.
> The earth will be hauled with bottom-dump wagons, whose estimated heaped capacity will be 15 cu yd bank measure.

The average elevation will be 600 ft above sea level.
The specifications for the trucks are as follows:

Pay-load capacity, 40,000 lb
Engine, diesel, 200 hp
Empty weight, 36,800 lb
Gross weight, loaded, 76,800 lb
Gross weight distribution
      Front axle, 12,000 lb
      Drive axle, 32,400 lb
      Trailer axle, 32,400 lb
Size tires on drive and trailer axles, 24.00 × 25

Gear	Speed, mph	Rimpull, lb
1st	3.2	19,900
2d	6.3	10,100
3d	11.9	5,350
4th	20.8	3,060
5th	32.7	1,945

The maximum usable rimpull of a loaded truck, as limited by the coefficient of traction, will be 32,400 × 0.6 = 19,440 lb. This is sufficiently high to eliminate the danger of tire slippage, except possibly in first gear.

The cost of hauling earth from borrow pit 1 is determined as follows:

The combined effect of rolling resistance and grade on a loaded truck will be

Rolling resistance	=	60 lb per ton
Grade resistance, 2.2 × 20	=	44 lb per ton
Total resistance	=	104 lb per ton

Gross weight of truck, 76,800 ÷ 2,000 = 38.4 tons
Required rimpull, 38.4 × 104 = 3,994 lb
Maximum speed of loaded truck, 11.9 mph

The combined effect of rolling resistance and grade on an empty truck will be

Rolling resistance	=	60 lb per ton
Grade resistance, 2.2 × 20	= −	44 lb per ton
Total resistance	=	16 lb per ton

Weight of empty truck, 36,800 ÷ 2,000 = 18.4 tons
Required rimpull, 18.4 × 16 = 294 lb
Maximum speed of an empty truck, 32.7 mph

The time required for each operation in a round-trip cycle should be about as follows:

Loading, 15 cu yd ÷ 312 cu yd per hr	= 0.0482 hr
Lost time in pit and accelerating, 1.5 min	= 0.0250 hr
Travel to the fill, 0.66 mile ÷ 11.9 mph	= 0.0555 hr
Dumping, turning, and accelerating, 1 min	= 0.0167 hr
Travel to pit, 0.66 mile ÷ 32.7 mph	= 0.0202 hr
Round-trip time	= 0.1656 hr

Assume that the trucks will operate an average of 50 min per hr.

No. trips per hr, $\dfrac{1}{0.1656} \times \dfrac{50}{60} = 5.02$

Volume of earth hauled per truck, $15 \times 5.02 = 75.3$ cu yd per hr

No. trucks required, $312 \div 75.3 = 4.15$

Use four trucks, which will reduce the output of the shovel slightly. If a truck and driver cost \$26.20 per hour, the cost of hauling earth will be

\$26.20 ÷ 75.3 = \$0.348 per cu yd

The cost of hauling earth from borrow pit 2 is determined as follows:

The combined effect of rolling resistance and grade on a loaded truck will be

Rolling resistance   =   60 lb per ton
Grade resistance, 1.4×20 = $-$ 28 lb per ton
  Total resistance   =   32 lb per ton
Gross weight of truck, 38.4 tons
Required rimpull, $38.4 \times 32 = 1{,}229$ lb

The available rimpull in fifth gear is 1,945 lb, which is more than will be required by the truck. Sideboards can be installed to increase the hauling capacity of the truck. The gross load should be limited to a weight that can be pulled by not over 80 percent of the rimpull, with the remaining rimpull reserved to accelerate the truck and to be used on sections of the haul road having higher rolling resistance or less steep grades.

Net available rimpull, $0.8 \times 1{,}945 = $ 1,556 lb
Required rimpull for 15 cu yd   = 1,229 lb
  Surplus rimpull   =   327 lb
Possible additional load, $327 + 32 = 10.2$ tons

Possible additional volume, $\dfrac{10.2 \times 2{,}000}{2{,}700} = 7.55$ cu yd

In order to compensate for the additional weight of the sideboards, the volume of the earth should be increased by not more than 7 cu yd. This will give a total volume of 22 cu yd per load.

The combined effect of rolling resistance and grade on the empty truck will be

Rolling resistance   = 60 lb per ton
Grade resistance, 1.4×20 = 28 lb per ton
  Total resistance   = 88 lb per ton
Weight of empty truck, including sideboards, 19 tons
Required rimpull, $19 \times 88 = 1{,}672$ lb
Maximum speed of an empty truck, 32.7 mph

The time required for each operation in a round-trip cycle should be about as follows:

Loading, 22 cu yd ÷ 312 cu yd per hr   = 0.0707 hr
Lost time in pit and accelerating, 2 min   = 0.0333 hr
Travel to fill, 0.78 mile ÷ 32.7 mph   = 0.0238 hr
Dumping, turning, and accelerating, 1.5 min = 0.0250 hr
Travel to pit, 0.78 mile ÷ 32.7 mph   = 0.0238 hr
  Round-trip time   = 0.1766 hr

Assume that the trucks will operate an average of 50 min per hr.

No. trips per hr, $\dfrac{1}{0.1766} \times \dfrac{50}{60} = 4.72$

Volume of earth hauled per truck, $22 \times 4.72 = 103.8$ cu yd per hr

No. trucks required, $312 \div 103.8 = 3.01$

Use 3 trucks.

If a truck and driver cost $26.20 per hr, the cost of hauling the earth will be

$26.20 \div 103.8 = \$0.252$ per cu yd

A comparison of the cost of hauling the earth from the two pits will reveal the extent of savings that may be effected by using pit 2.

Hauling cost from pit 1	= \$0.348 per cu yd
Hauling cost from pit 2	= 0.252 per cu yd
Reduction in hauling cost	= \$0.096 per cu yd
Reduction in total hauling cost, $1,000,000 \times \$0.096$	= \$96,000

The use of pit 2 instead of pit 1 will result in a saving in hauling cost of

$\dfrac{0.096}{0.348} \times 100 = 27.5$ percent

Another item that is favorable to pit 2 is the reduction in number of trucks from four to three, which will result in a reduction in investment in hauling equipment amounting to approximately $42,000.

THE EFFECT OF ROLLING RESISTANCE ON THE COST OF HAULING EARTH

An important factor which affects the production capacity of a truck or a tractor-pulled wagon is the rolling resistance of the haul road. Rolling resistance is determined primarily by two factors, the physical condition of the road and the tires used on the hauling unit. A great deal can be done to reduce rolling resistance by properly maintaining the road and by selecting proper sizes of tires and then keeping them inflated to the correct pressure. Money spent for these purposes may return dividends, through reduced hauling costs, far in excess of the expenditures. This is one field where the application of engineering knowledge will yield excellent returns.

An earth haul road which is given little or no maintenance will soon become rough, loose, and soft and may develop a rolling resistance of 150 lb per ton or more, depending on the type of soil and weather conditions. If a road is properly maintained with a patrol grader, sprinkled with water, and compacted as required, it may be possible to reduce the rolling resistance to 50 lb per ton or less. Also, sprinkling the road will reduce the damage to hauling equipment by eliminating dust, will reduce the danger of vehicular collision by improving visibility, and will prolong the life of tires because of the cooling effect which the moisture has on the tires.

The selection of proper tire sizes and the practice of maintaining correct air pressure in the tires will reduce that portion of the rolling resistance due to tires. A tire supports its load by deforming where it contacts the road surface until the area in contact with the road will, considering the air pressure in the tires, produce a total force on the road equal to the load on the tire. If the load on a tire is 5,000 lb and the air pressure is 50 psi, the area of contact will be 100 sq in. This neglects any supporting resistance furnished by the side walls of the tire. If, for the same tire, the air pressure is permitted to drop to 40 psi, the area of contact will be increased to 125 sq in. The additional area of contact will be produced by additional deformation of the tire. This will increase the rolling resistance because the tire will be continually climbing a steeper grade as it rotates. The size tire selected and the inflated pressure should be based on the resistance which the surface of the road offers to penetration by the tire. For rigid road surfaces, such as concrete, small-diameter high-pressure tires will give lower rolling resistance, while, for soft road surfaces, large-diameter low-pressure tires will give lower rolling resistance because the larger areas of contact will reduce the depth of penetration by the tires.

Example This example illustrates the effect which rolling resistance has on the cost of hauling earth.

A project requires a contractor to excavate and haul 1,900,000 cu yd of common earth. The contract must be completed within 1 year. By operating three shifts, with 7 hr actual working time per shift, 6 days per week, it is estimated that there will be 5,600 working hours, allowing for lost time due to bad weather. This will require an output of approximately 350 cu yd per hr bank measure, which should be obtained with a 4-cu-yd power shovel.

The job conditions are as follows:

Length of haul, 1 way, 3.5 miles
Slope of haul road, minus 0.5% from borrow pit to the fill
Weight of earth in place, 2,600 lb per cu yd
Swell, 30%
Weight of loose earth, 2,600 ÷ 1.3 = 2,000 lb per cu yd
Elevation, 800 ft above sea level

For hauling the earth the contractor considers using rubber-tire-equipped tractor-pulled bottom-dump wagons, which may be purchased with standard or optional gears. The optional gears will permit the unit to operate at a higher speed. Specifications and performance data are as follows:

	Standard tractor	Optional tractor
Tractor engine	150 bhp	150 bhp
Max speed	19.8 mph	27.4 mph
Mechanical efficiency	82%	82%
Rimpull at max speed	2,330 lb	1,685 lb

Heaped capacity of standard wagon, 32,000 lb or 16 cu yd loose measure, based on 3 : 1 slope
Inside length of wagon, 14 ft 2 in.
Average inside width of wagon, 7 ft 1 in.
Heaped capacity of wagon with sideboard extensions, 2 ft 0 in. high, 46,800 lb, or 23.4 cu yd
    loose measure, based on 3 : 1 slope

	Standard equipment	Optional equipment
Gross weight:		
Tractor and wagon	29,400 lb	29,400 lb
Sideboards	. . . .	1,600 lb
Pay load	32,000 lb	46,800 lb
Total weight	61,400 lb	77,800 lb
Gross weight, tons	30.7	38.9
Delivered cost	$36,200	$36,900
Cost per hr, including driver	$18.30	$19.20*

* The higher cost per hour for the optional equipment is allowed because of the more severe conditions to which it will be subjected.

An analysis of the performance of the standard equipment, operating on a haul road with an estimated rolling resistance of 80 lb per ton, will give the probable hauling cost per cubic yard. This rolling resistance is representative of haul roads which are not carefully maintained.

The combined effect of rolling resistance and grade on a loaded unit will be

Rolling resistance −   80 lb per ton
Grade, 0.5 × 20   = − 10 lb per ton
    Total   =   70 lb per ton
Gross weight of vehicle, 30.7 tons
Required rimpull, $30.7 \times 70 = 2{,}149$ lb
Available rimpull   = 2,330 lb

The tractor can pull the loaded wagon, with a surplus rimpull for acceleration. The rimpull required for the return trip to the shovel will be

14.7 tons × 90 lb per ton = 1,323 lb

which will permit travel at maximum speed.

The time required for each operation in a round-trip cycle should be about as follows:

Volume of earth per load, $16 \div 1.30 = 12.3$ cu yd bm
Loading, 12.3 cu yd ÷ 350 cu yd per hr   = 0.0351 hr
Lost time in pit and accelerating, 1.5 min   = 0.0250 hr
Travel to the fill, 3.5 miles ÷ 19.8 mph   = 0.1770 hr
Dumping, turning, and accelerating, 1.0 min = 0.0167 hr
Travel to pit, 3.5 miles ÷ 19.8 mph   = 0.1770 hr
   Round-trip time   = 0.4308 hr

Assume that the wagons will operate an average of 45 min per hr.

No. trips per hr, $\dfrac{1}{0.4308} \times \dfrac{45}{60} = 1.74$

Volume of earth hauled per wagon, $12.3 \times 1.74 = 21.4$ cu yd per hr
No. wagons required, $350 \div 21.4 = 16.4$

It will be necessary to provide 17 wagons if the specified output is to be maintained. The actual volume of earth hauled per wagon will be $350 \div 17 = 20.6$ cu yd per hr.

Hauling cost per cu yd , $18.30 ÷ 20.6 = $0.889

Let us analyze the performance of the optional equipment to determine whether it will operate at the maximum possible speed while hauling 23.4 cu yd loose measure. It will be necessary to reduce the rolling resistance of the haul road by providing continuous maintenance. While it is possible to reduce the rolling resistance to 40 lb per ton during most of the time the project is in operation, a value of 50 lb per ton will be used in order to provide a margin of safety.

The combined effect of rolling resistance and grade on a loaded unit will be

Rolling resistance=   50 lb per ton
Grade, 0.5 × 20   = − 10 lb per ton
    Total   =   40 lb per ton
Gross weight of vehicle, 38.9 tons
Required rimpull, 38.9 × 40   = 1,556 lb
Available rimpull at 27.4 mph = 1,685 lb

The tractor can pull the load at the maximum speed, with a surplus for acceleration. The rimpull required for the return trip to the shovel will be

15.5 tons × 60 lb per ton = 930 lb

which will permit travel at maximum speed.

The time required for each operation in a round-trip cycle should be about as follows:

Volume of earth per load, 23.4 ÷ 1.30 = 18.0 cu yd bm
Loading, 18 cu yd ÷ 350 cu yd per hr   = 0.0515 hr
Lost time in pit and accelerating, 2 min   = 0.0333 hr
Travel to the fill, 3.5 miles ÷ 27.4 mph   = 0.1277 hr
Dumping, turning, and accelerating, 1.5 min= 0.0250 hr
Travel to pit, 3.5 miles ÷ 27.4 mph   = 0.1277 hr
    Round-trip time   = 0.3652 hr

Assume that the wagons will operate an average of 45 min per hr.

No. trips per hr, $\dfrac{1}{0.3652} \times \dfrac{45}{60} = 2.05$

Volume of earth hauled per wagon, 18 × 2.05 = 36.9 cu yd per hr
No. wagons required, 350 ÷ 36.9 = 9.5

It will be necessary to provide 10 wagons if the specified output is to be maintained. The actual volume of earth hauled per hour per wagon will be 350 ÷ 10 = 35 cu yd.

Hauling cost per cu yd , $19.20 ÷ 35 = $0.549

The reduction in the cost of hauling the earth with the optional equipment will be

Cost using standard equipment   = $0.889 per cu yd
Cost using optional equipment   =   0.549 per cu yd
Reduction in cost   = $0.340 per cu yd
   Total reduction for project, 1,900,000 × $0.340= $646,000

The reduction in the amount of money invested in hauling equipment will be

Using standard equipment, 17 × $36,200= $615,400
Using optional equipment, 10 × $36,900 =   369,000
    Reduction in investment   = $246,400

The reduction in the cost of hauling earth and in the amount of money invested in hauling equipment resulting from the improvement in the rolling resistance of the haul road illustrates the value of analyzing a project. Although the reduction may appear to be unreasonably large, it is possible to produce similar results for many projects involving the hauling of earth. Even the cost of paving the haul road would be justified if this were the only method of reducing the rolling resistance.

Most manufacturers of trucks and tractor-pulled wagons can furnish units with standard or optional gears. For equipment already in service the standard gears may be replaced with optional gears at reasonable costs. Sideboards may be purchased from the equipment manufacturer, or they may be made locally in a machine shop.

Example The effect of rolling resistance on the performance of equipment and the cost of hauling earth is further illustrated in Table 9-4. The information given in the table is based on using the optional tractor-pulled wagons of the previous analysis, an output of 350 cu yd of earth per hour bank measure, a one-way haul distance of 3.5 miles, and a level haul road. If the haul road is not level, similar information may be obtained by combining the effect of rolling resistance and grade.

The speeds and rimpulls of the hauling units are as follows:

Gear	Speed, mph	Rimpull, lb
1st	4.1	11,250
2d	6.5	7,120
3d	10.6	4,360
4th	17.0	2,720
5th	27.4	1,685

The following sample calculations will show how the information given in the table is obtained. Consider a haul road with a rolling resistance of 100 lb per ton.

Table 9-4 The effect of rolling resistance on the cost of hauling earth

Item	Rolling resistance, lb per ton			
	40	60	100	150
Maximum speed loaded, mph	27.4	17.0	10.6	6.5
Maximum speed empty, mph	27.4	27.4	27.4	17.0
Number of trucks required	10	12	15	22
Cost of trucks per hr	$192.00	$230.40	$288.00	$422.40
Volume of earth hauled per hr	350	350	350	350
Hauling cost per cu yd	$0.548	$0.658	$0.824	$1.207
Investment in trucks	$369,000	$442,800	$553,500	$1,141,800

Gross weight of loaded unit, 38.9 tons
Weight of empty unit, 15.5 tons
Required rimpull for loaded unit, $38.9 \times 100 = 3,890$ lb
Maximum speed, 10.6 mph
Required rimpull for empty unit, $15.5 \times 100 = 1,550$ lb
Maximum speed, 27.4 mph

The round-trip time will include fixed time, which should be reasonably constant regardless of the condition of the haul road, plus the travel time to and from the fill.

The fixed time will be

Loading, 18 cu yd ÷ 350 cu yd per hr	= 0.0515 hr
Lost time in pit and accelerating, 2 min	= 0.0333 hr
Dumping, turning, and accelerating, 1.5 min	= 0.0250 hr
Total fixed time	= 0.1098 hr
Travel to the fill, 3.5 miles ÷ 10.6 mph	= 0.3310 hr
Travel to shovel, 3.5 miles ÷ 27.4 mph	= 0.1277 hr
Round-trip time	= 0.5685 hr

Trips per 45-min hr, $\dfrac{1}{0.5685} \times \dfrac{45}{60} = 1.32$

Volume per wagon, $18 \times 1.32 = 23.75$ cu yd per hr
No. wagons required, $350 \div 23.75 = 15$
Actual volume per wagon, $350 \div 15 = 23.3$ cu yd per hr
Hauling cost per cu yd $19.20 \div 23.3 = \$0.824$

THE EFFECT OF ALTITUDE ON THE PERFORMANCE OF HAULING EQUIPMENT

Contractors who have established satisfactory production rates for earth-hauling equipment at one altitude frequently find it desirable to bid on a project located at a different altitude. Unless an adjustment is made for the performance of the equipment at the higher altitude, it is possible that a substantial error may be made in estimating the cost of hauling the earth. As previously discussed, the effect of altitude is to reduce the sea level power of a four-cycle internal-combustion engine by approximately 3 percent for each additional 1,000 ft of altitude above 1,000 ft unless a supercharger is installed on the engine. Power losses of this magnitude are too large to ignore in analyzing a project for bid purposes.

Example This example will illustrate the effect of altitude on the performance of hauling equipment and the cost of hauling earth. The hauling units are commonly used in the construction industry.

The job conditions are as follows:

Weight of earth, 2,700 lb per cu yd bm
Swell, 25%
Weight of loose earth, $2,700 \div 1.25 = 2,160$ lb per cu yd
Haul distance, 1.5 miles, over level road
Rolling resistance, 50 lb per ton

The earth will be excavated with a power shovel, whose output will be 280 cu yd per hr. The specifications for the hauling units are as follows:

Type, tractor-pulled bottom-dump wagons
Tractor engine, 200 bhp
Wagon capacity, 16 cu yd heaped volume
Wagon capacity, 16 ÷ 1.25 = 12.8 cu yd bm
Weight of tractor and wagon   = 36,800 lb
Weight of load, 16 cu yd @ 2,160 lb = 34,560 lb
  Gross loaded weight   = 71,360 lb, or 35.68 tons
Cost per hr, including operator, $21.00

Tractor-performance data at sea level

Gear	Speed, mph	Rimpull, lb
1st	3.0	20,250
2d	5.8	10,450
3d	11.1	5,520
4th	19.4	3,130
5th	30.5	1,990

Compare the performance of a hauling unit at sea level with its performance at 5,000 ft above sea level, all other conditions remaining constant.

Performance at sea level:
  Required rimpull for loaded unit, 35.68 × 50 = 1,784 lb
  Maximum speed loaded, 30.5 mph
  Maximum speed empty, 30.5 mph
The probable round-trip time should be as follows:
  Loading, 12.8 cu yd ÷ 280 cu yd per hr   = 0.0458 hr
  Lost time in pit and accelerating, 1.5 min   = 0.0250 hr
  Travel to the fill, 1.5 miles ÷ 30.5 mph   = 0.0493 hr
  Dumping, turning, and accelerating, 1.5 min = 0.0250 hr
  Travel to pit, 1.5 miles ÷ 30.5 mph   = 0.0493 hr
    Round-trip time   = 0.1944 hr

Assume that units will operate an average of 45 min per hr.

No. trips per hr, $\frac{1}{0.1944} \times \frac{45}{60} = 3.86$
Volume per hr, 12.8 × 3.86 = 49.5 cu yd bm
No. units required, 280 ÷ 49.5 = 5.7
It will be necessary to use six units
Volume hauled per unit, 280 ÷ 6 = 46.7 cu yd per hr
Hauling cost per cu yd, $21.00 ÷ 46.7 = $0.492
Performance at 5,000-ft elevation:
  Loss in available rimpull, $\frac{0.03(5,000 - 1,000)}{1,000} \times 100 = 12\%$
  Correction factor for rimpull at 5,000 ft, 0.88

Available rimpull

Gear	Speed, mph	Rimpull at sea level, lb	Rimpull at 5,000 ft, lb
1st	3.0	20,250	17,820
2d	5.0	10,450	9,196
3d	11.1	5,250	4,620
4th	19.4	3,150	2,772
5th	30.5	1,990	1,751

Required rimpull for loaded unit, 1,784 lb
Maximum speed loaded, 19.4 mph
Required rimpull empty, $15.5 \times 50 = 775$ lb
Maximum speed empty, 30.5 mph
The probable round-trip time should be as follows:

Loading, 12.8 cu yd ÷ 280 cu yd per hr	= 0.0458 hr
Lost time in pit and accelerating, 1.75 min	= 0.0290 hr
Travel to the fill, 1.5 miles ÷ 19.4 mph	= 0.0773 hr
Dumping, turning, and accelerating, 1.75 min	= 0.0290 hr
Travel to pit, 1.5 miles ÷ 30.5 mph	= 0.0493 hr
Round-trip time	= 0.2304 hr

No. trips per hr, $\dfrac{1}{0.2304} \times \dfrac{45}{60} = 3.25$
Volume per hr, $12.8 \times 3.25 = 41.6$ cu yd
No. units required, $280 \div 41.6 = 6.7$
It will be necessary to use 7 units
Volume hauled per unit, $280 \div 7 = 40$ cu yd per hr
Hauling cost per cu yd, $\$21.00 \div 40 = \$0.525$

In the calculations for the 5,000-ft altitude the time lost by a unit in the pit and at the dump was increased by 0.25 min to allow for the effect of the loss in power at this altitude.

PROBLEMS

9-1 A truck for which the information in Fig. 9-6 applies operates over a haul road with a plus 6 percent slope and a rolling resistance of 80 lb per ton. If the gross vehicle weight is 75,000 lb, determine the maximum speed of the truck.

9-2 If the truck of Prob. 9-1 operates on a haul road having a minus 3 percent slope, determine the maximum speed.

9-3 Prepare a table similar to Table 9-1, using a $1\frac{1}{2}$-cu-yd power shovel whose adjusted production will be 170 cu yd per hr.

9-4 A 2-cu-yd power shovel will be used to load common earth into trucks whose capacities are 14.0 cu yd bank measure. Determine the number of trucks required to haul the earth for the following conditions:

For the power shovel:
  Depth of dig, 10 ft
  Angle of swing, 120°
  Job conditions, good
  Management conditions, excellent

For the trucks:
 Weight of earth, 2,900 lb per cu yd bm
 Empty weight of truck, 36,420 lb
 Performance chart of Fig. 9-6 applies
 Assume the time at the dump will be 1.25 min
 Rolling resistance of haul road, 80 lb per ton
 Distance to dump, one mile of minus 2 percent slope and
  0.5 mile of plus 3 percent slope.

Assume that operating conditions limit the average speed of the trucks to 0.75 of the maximum possible speed. Note that the number of trucks should be based on the ideal production rate of the shovel and the no-delay cycle time of the trucks.

REFERENCES

1. WABCO Construction and Mining Equipment Group, 2300 N.E. Adams Street, Peoria, Illinois 61639.
2. Euclid, Inc., 22221 St. Clair Avenue, Cleveland, Ohio 44117.

TEN

OPERATION ANALYSES

GENERAL INFORMATION

In examples appearing earlier in this book methods of determining the probable production rates for various types of equipment are illustrated. One might be justified in questioning the accuracy of the results, especially if they are based on conditions that are assumed to represent those that will occur on a given project. To what extent do actual job conditions conform with the conditions that were assumed when planning a project? It is certain that there will be some variations.

Consider a truck which is loaded by a power shovel. As illustrated in Fig. 10-1, the truck cycle includes at least the following elements:

1. Load
2. Haul
3. Dump
4. Return
5. Spot at the shovel

The minimum cycle time is the sum of the minimum times required for the five elements. The average cycle time is obviously larger than the minimum. Also, there will be cycle times larger than the average time, especially when a number of trucks are used on a job.

Also, the selected rate of production for the shovel is based on an average rate, even though an operating factor of 1.00 is used. Again, there will be rates of production above the average and rates below the average.

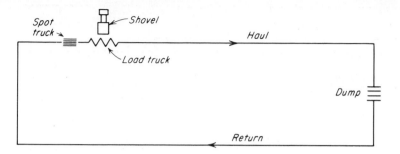

Figure 10-1 Elements in a truck cycle.

Thus, with varying rates of loading trucks and varying truck cycle times, it will not be possible to synchronize the loading and hauling operations for a sustained period of time without experiencing some delays by the shovel waiting for a truck, or by a truck waiting to be loaded.

A contractor should have at least two objectives when he undertakes an analysis of the operations of his personnel or equipment:

1. To determine the average time required for each element and for a cycle
2. To reduce the cycle time by eliminating or decreasing unnecessary delays, and thus to increase production

The next section discusses a type of study which has been used with considerable success in attaining these objectives.

MOTION AND TIME STUDIES

These are studies made by an observer using a stop watch and a clip board, with forms, on which appropriate time elements may be recorded, as they are observed. Consider a truck cycle. The truck is loaded; then it hauls to the dump site, backs into position, dumps its load, and returns to the shovel for another load, where it may have to wait to be served by the shovel, defined here as spotting.

A break point is selected for the beginning and the end of each element. For example, loading time starts when the shovel begins serving the truck, and it ends when the truck begins moving away from the shovel, at which time hauling time starts. Hauling time continues until the truck stops at the dump site, preparatory to backing into dumping position. Dumping time may include turning, backing, and dumping the load. Returning time starts when the truck begins moving away from the dump, and ends when the truck returns to the shovel site. Spotting time is the time required to maneuver into a position for loading. If it is necessary for a truck to wait for position at the dump or at the shovel, additional elements may be included in the cycle, and the time for each

MOTION AND TIME STUDY

Project No. 162	Operation: Power shovel No. 6			Sheet No. 1
Start timing 9:15 am End timing 9:19 am	Operator Jim Brown		Observer J. G. Smith	Date: 6/12/76

Element						Cycles, time in min						Summary	
		1	2	3	4	5	6	7	8	9	10	ΣT	$\bar{T}$
Start		0.00											
Fill dipper	T	0.15	0.12	0.14	0.13	0.14	0.15	0.12	0.17	0.12	0.16	1.40	0.14
	R	0.15	0.59	1.02	1.44	1.91	2.34	2.75	3.22	3.65	4.07		
Swing	T	0.12	0.12	0.10	0.12	0.11	0.10	0.12	0.09	0.09	0.10	1.07	0.11
	R	0.27	0.71	1.12	1.56	2.02	2.44	2.87	3.31	3.74	4.17		
Dump	T	0.09	0.07	0.08	0.09	0.07	0.08	0.08	0.09	0.07	0.08	0.80	0.08
	R	0.36	0.78	1.20	1.65	2.09	2.52	2.95	3.40	3.81	4.25		
Return	T	0.11	0.10	0.11	0.12	0.10	0.11	0.10	0.13	0.10	0.12	1.10	0.11
	R	0.47	0.88	1.31	1.77	2.19	2.63	3.05	3.53	3.91	4.37		
Delay	T												
	R												
Cycle	T	0.47	0.41	0.43	0.46	0.42	0.44	0.42	0.48	0.38	0.46	4.37	0.44

ΣT = sum of element times $\bar{T}$ = average time for element = ΣT/N

Figure 10-2 Time study for a power shovel.

of these additional elements should be recorded. Also, on the form used for recording the time required for each element there should be a space for recording any delays, such as stopping for fuel, water, or tires, and personal delays, etc.

The stop watch should be calibrated to read time in minutes and hundredths of a minute. Once a time study is started the watch should operate continuously, with the observer simply recording the time reading at the beginning of the study and thereafter at the end of each element, which will be the beginning of the following element, until the study is finished. The actual time required for each element can be determined later.

If a study is to be made for a power shovel, the observer can select one location and remain there. However, if a study is to be made for equipment that travels beyond his view, such as a truck or a scraper, the observer should accompany the unit during the full period of study.

Figure 10-2 illustrates a form or observation sheet that can be used to record the time for each element. The entries opposite R are observed on the watch and recorded immediately. The entries opposite T represent the times required for the specified elements, which times are calculated later. This figure is a record of a study made for a power shovel, whose cycle is divided into the elements load, swing, dump, and return, with a further provision for recording any delays.

Dividing the cycle into four elements may or may not be justified. If the average time and the range in times per element are not desired, the study may be limited to determining the cycle times only.

Figure 10-3 illustrates the information obtained from a motion and time study for a wheel-type tractor-pulled scraper. The cycle is divided into five elements, with a further provision for recording any delays. It may be desirable to classify the causes of delays and to indicate them on the sheet, such as

1. Personal
2. Mechanical
3. Service, fuel, oil, water, etc.
4. Other, as applicable

DURATION OF A TIME STUDY

The duration of a time study should permit the observer to record enough cycles to assure results having the desired accuracy. One observation may have some value, but it is highly improbable that it will give the average time of continuing operations. Because of the cost of making the observations and the subsequent calculations, it is desirable to limit the observations to the minimum number required to produce the specified accuracy.

There are time-recording meters that may be attached to construction equipment, which will record the time for each element of a cycle, either automatically or semiautomatically.

MOTION AND TIME STUDY

Project No.	158		Operation:	Scraper No. 4			Sheet No.	1
Start timing	2:14 pm		Operator	Gus Weaver			Date:	6/12/76
End timing	4:10 pm						Observer	J. G. Smith

Element	Load		Haul		Dump		Return		Wait		Cycle	Delay	
Cycle	T	R	T	R	T	R	T	R	T	R	time	T	Type
1	0.86	0.86	3.88	4.74	0.42	5.16	3.16	8.32	0.36	8.68	8.68	0	
2	0.93	9.61	4.24	13.85	0.36	14.21	3.34	17.55	0.24	17.79	9.11		
3	0.78	18.57	4.08	22.65	0.47	23.12	2.86	25.98	0.44	26.42	8.63		
4	0.98	27.40	4.16	31.56	0.34	31.90	2.98	34.88	0.42	35.30	8.88	3.18	6
5	0.82	39.30	4.18	43.48	0.31	43.79	3.04	46.83	0.28	47.11	8.63		
6	0.80	47.91	3.96	51.87	0.38	52.25	2.92	55.17	0.37	55.54	8.43		
7	0.88	56.42	4.22	60.64	0.41	61.05	2.94	63.99	0.46	64.45	8.91		
8	0.96	65.41	4.38	69.79	0.44	70.23	3.18	73.41	0.42	73.83	9.38	2.86	7
9	1.04	77.73	4.14	81.87	0.37	82.24	2.80	85.04	0.52	85.56	8.87		
10	0.92	86.48	4.04	90.52	0.33	90.85	2.84	93.69	0.60	94.29	8.73		
11	0.87	95.16	4.19	99.35	0.34	99.69	2.94	102.63	0.32	102.95	8.66	4.21	6
12	0.92	108.08	4.26	112.34	0.36	112.70	2.86	115.56	0.42	115.98	8.82		
ΣT	10.76		49.73		4.53		35.86		4.85		105.73	10.25	
$\bar{T}$	0.90		4.14		0.38		2.99		0.40		8.81		

ΣT = sum of element times $\bar{T}$ = average time for element

Figure 10-3 Time study for a wheel-type scraper.

When planning a comprehensive time study, consideration should be given to making the observations at intermittent intervals, separated by several hours or days to allow for the effects of varying conditions that may affect the cycle time.

STATISTICAL METHODS OF DETERMINING THE NUMBER OF OBSERVATIONS NEEDED

An observer may use statistical methods to determine the number of observations required to produce results having the specified accuracy, by means of the following procedure.

1. Specify a confidence interval I, which is a time interval, that conforms with the desired accuracy of the study.
2. Specify a confidence coefficient C, which indicates the probability that the results will conform with the desired accuracy.
3. Observe M cycles of the operation being studied.
4. Calculate the sample standard deviation s from the formula

$$s = \sqrt{\frac{\Sigma T^2 - (\Sigma T)^2 / M}{M - 1}} \tag{10-1}$$

Assume that one wishes to obtain an average cycle time with a 90 percent probability that the determined value will be accurate within the specified time interval or tolerance I. Calculate the confidence interval I_m provided by this sample of M observations, using formula (10-2).

$$I_m = 2 t_{0.90}\left(\frac{s}{\sqrt{M}}\right) \tag{10-2}$$

where t is the value of Student's t distribution, as given in Table 10-1 for $C = 0.90$ and $M - 1$ degrees of freedom. For M equal to 10 observations, $t_{0.90} = 1.83$. Substituting these values of M and t into formula (10-2) gives

$$I_M = 2 \times 1.83\left(\frac{s}{\sqrt{10}}\right) = 1.16s \tag{10-3}$$

If I_M, as determined in formula (10-3), is equal to or less than the specified value of I, the number of observations is sufficient. If I_M is greater than the specified value of I, additional observations are required. The total number of observations required N can be determined from formula (10-4).

$$N = \frac{4(t)^2 s^2}{I^2} \tag{10-4}$$

Using the previously selected value of $t = 1.83$, formula (10-4) becomes

$$N = \frac{4(1.83)^2 s^2}{I^2} = \frac{13.4 s^2}{I^2} \tag{10-5}$$

Table 10-1 Values of t for Student's t distribution for $C = 0.90$

M	t	M	t
5	2.13	18	1.75
6	2.02	19	1.74
7	1.94	20	1.73
8	1.90	21	1.73
9	1.86	22	1.72
10	1.83	23	1.72
11	1.81	24	1.71
12	1.80	25	1.71
13	1.78	26	1.71
14	1.77	27	1.71
15	1.76	28	1.70
16	1.76	29	1.70
17	1.75	30	1.70
		Above 30	1.65

The use of formulas (10-1) through (10-5) may be illustrated by applying them to the time study for the power shovel illustrated in Fig. 10-2. Assume that it is desired to be 90 percent certain that the average cycle time obtained from the time study is within ± 0.02 min of the true cycle time. For this condition the confidence interval I will be $2 \times 0.02 = 0.04$ min.

Use formula (10-1) to determine the standard derivation s.

$$\Sigma T^2 = T_1^2 + T_2^2 + T_3^2 + \cdots + T_{10}^2$$

$$= (0.47)^2 + (0.41)^2 + (0.43)^2 + \cdots + (0.46)^2$$

$$= 1.9183$$

$$\Sigma T = 0.47 + 0.41 + 0.43 + \cdots + 0.46 = 4.37$$

$$s = \sqrt{\frac{\Sigma T^2 - (\Sigma T)^2 / M}{M - 1}} = \sqrt{\frac{1.9183 - (4.37)^2 / 10}{10 - 1}} = 0.030$$

Using formula (10-3),

$$I_M = 1.16s = 1.16 \times 0.030 = 0.035$$

Because the value of $I_M = 0.035$ is less than the permissible value of $I = 0.04$, no additional observations are required. Thus the determined average cycle time of 0.44 min is sufficiently accurate for the specified conditions.

If the average cycle time for the scraper study illustrated in Fig. 10-3 is desired for a confidence interval of 0.2 min, the solutions of formulas (10-1) and (10-2) reveal that $N = 22$. Thus it will be necessary to observe at least $22 - 12 = 10$ more cycles to attain the desired accuracy.

The solution of formulas (10-1) through (10-5) at the project are very time consuming. An alternate method of determining the number of observations required uses formula (10-6) to calculate the value of s, which gives reasonable accuracy.

$$s = \frac{R}{d} \qquad (10\text{-}6)$$

where $R =$ the difference between the maximum and the minimum values of the cycle time

$d =$ a conversion factor whose value depends on M, as given in Table 10-2

If the value of s in formula (10-6) is substituted in formula (10-4), the resulting formula will be

$$N = \frac{4t^2R^2}{I^2d^2} \qquad (10\text{-}7)$$

If formulas (10-6) and (10-7) are applied to the cycle times in Fig. 10-2, and the value of d is obtained from Table 10-2 for $M = 10$, the results will be

$$R = 0.48 - 0.38 = 0.10$$

and

$$N = \frac{4 \times (1.83)^2 \times (0.10)^2}{(0.04)^2 \times (3.078)^2} = 8.95 \ or \ 9$$

which confirms the previous findings.

Table 10-2 Values of d factors for time studies using $s = R/d$

M	d	M	d
5	2.326	19	3.689
6	2.534	20	3.735
7	2.704	21	3.778
8	2.847	22	3.818
9	2.970	23	3.856
10	3.078	24	3.891
11	3.173	25	3.925
12	3.258	26	3.956
13	3.336	27	3.985
14	3.407	28	4.012
15	3.472	29	4.038
16	3.532	30	4.053
17	3.588		
18	3.640		

If formula (10-7) is applied to the cycle times for the scraper in Fig. 10-3, under the previously specified conditions,

$$C = 0.90$$
$$I = 0.20$$
$$M = 12$$
$$t = 1.80$$
$$R = 9.38 - 8.43 = 0.95$$
$$d = 3.258$$

$$N = \frac{4(1.80)^2(0.95)^2}{(0.2)^2(3.258)^2} = 27.6 \text{ or } 28$$

An examination of formula (10-7) discloses that, with other factors constant, the number of observations required varies inversely with the square of the confidence interval. For example, the confidence interval for the previous study of the scraper is 0.2 min. This means that there is a 90 percent probability that 28 observations, using the alternate method, or 22 observations, using the more exact method, will give an average cycle time that is within plus or minus 0.1 min of the true value. Because this accuracy might justifiably be considered unrealistic, the interval could be increased to a higher value, such as 0.3 min, for a result within plus or minus 0.15 min of the true value. If I is increased to 0.3, formula (10-7) gives a value of N equal to 12.3. Thus the 12 observations already made are adequate.

TIME–LAPSE MOVING PICTURES

Time-lapse moving pictures have been used recently by a number of contractors to produce permanent photographic records of construction operations [1, 2, 3]. A variable-speed electric-motor-operated camera, usually mounted on a tripod, and a variable-speed projector, at a total cost up to approximately $2,000, are required. The camera may be set to make an exposure at predetermined intervals, such as every 3 sec. While black-and-white film may be used, colored film will enable an observer during projection to identify the different workers and operations better. After the film is processed it may be projected on a screen to enable key personnel to study the operations for the purpose of detecting methods of reducing or eliminating wasted time, or simplifying the operations.

Many types of operations that are confined to limited areas may be photographed, including those involving power shovels, tractor shovels, loading scrapers, building and erecting forms for concrete, placing reinforcing steel and concrete, and others.

If each frame of the film is exposed at a constant time interval, the film may be used for time study purposes. A film may record the actions of several types of equipment or several workers in the area photographed to permit a future study of each. A time study observer is usually limited to a study of one unit of equipment or one man. A film produces a permanent record, which may be rerun for additional studies, whereas a time study made by an observer cannot be rerun.

EQUIPMENT NEEDED FOR TIME–LAPSE MOVING PICTURES

The equipment needed to produce and project pictures will vary somewhat with the extent to which pictures will be made and used, but the following basic items should be considered:

1. A light meter.
2. A camera that will permit manual or automatic tripping of the shutter at the desired frequency. If the camera shutter is to be tripped automatically, it will be necessary to use an electric motor with a variable-speed gear arrangement to trip the shutter at different intervals. A turret-type camera, equipped with a wide-angle, regular and telephoto lens, is desirable; a camera with a zoom lens may also be used.
3. A tripod for the camera.
4. A variable-speed frame-counting projector, either manually or electric-motor operated.
5. A projector screen.
6. A supply of black-and-white or colored film. A standard roll of 16-mm film will produce about 4,000 frames. If a frame is taken every 3 sec continuously, a total of $3\frac{1}{3}$ hr of operations may be recorded on one roll.
7. A supply of cans in which the processed film may be indexed by project and stored.

MOTION AND TIME STUDY FOR A CONCRETE PAVER

A procedure that may be used in conducting a time study is illustrated by the results of a motion and time study for a 34-E dual-drum concrete paver. The procedure may be modified to fit the conditions which apply to other equipment or projects.

   The paver mixed 38.6 cu ft of concrete per batch. The study was conducted for a period of 1 week (48 hr), during which time 2,642 batches or 3,777 cu yd of concrete were produced. During that time there was one rain, which caused a delay of 2.8 hr. For study purposes the delays were divided into major and minor delays. A major delay involved a loss in time of 15 min or more, while a minor delay involved a loss in time of less than 15 min.

   Table 10-3 indicates that under ideal conditions the paver could produce a batch in 0.61 min. This is the no-delay cycle time for the skip.

   Table 10-4 shows the distribution of the total time (48 hr) into losses owing to weather, major delays, and minor delays, and productive time. The last item

**Table 10-3 Ideal paver cycle operation
and time per batch**

Element	Cumulative time, min	
	Batch 1	Batch 2
Skip starts up	0.00	0.61
Water starts in	0.09	0.70
Skip vertical	0.15	0.76
All aggregate in paver	0.22	0.83
Skip down	0.31	0.92
Discharge chute opens	0.34	0.95
Transfer chute opens	0.53	1.14
Transfer chute closes	0.71	1.32
Discharge chute opens	0.94	1.55
Discharge complete	1.14	1.75
Discharge chute closes	1.15	1.76

is the actual time during which the paver was operating, with all delays excluded.

Table 10-5 lists the causes of the delays, excluding weather, the frequencies, and the time losses, and indicates the percent of the net working time lost by each type of delay.

Table 10-6 shows the production of the paver for each of the specified time conditions.

After obtaining the information appearing in Table 10-6, it should be studied to determine to what extent, if any, the delays can be reduced or possibly eliminated. The primary effort should be devoted to those delays which represent the major losses. Will a periodic inspection of the paver enable a mechanic to detect a pending failure of a part in time to permit it to be repaired at the end of a shift?

The cost of labor and equipment on this job can amount to $500 or more per hour. The total time lost in a week, amounting to 19.8 hr, excluding weather, represents a total direct loss of some $9,900 or more. If just half of this loss can

Table 10-4 Distribution of total working time

Time element	Time, hr	% of time
Total time	48.0	100.0
Loss owing to weather	2.8	5.8
Net working time	45.2	94.2
Major delays	6.6	13.8
Minor delays	13.2	27.5
Productive time	25.4	52.9

Table 10-5 Analysis of delays, excluding weather

Cause of delay	No. of delays	Total time, hr	% of net working time
Major delays			
Repair mixer	2	1.2	2.7
Repair cable or bucket	1	0.6	1.3
Repair sheave on boom	1	0.5	1.1
Delay by form crew	4	2.7	6.0
Delay by form grader	2	1.0	2.2
Out of water	2	0.4	0.9
Late start	1	0.2	0.4
Subtotal major delays	13	6.6	14.6
Minor delays			
Batch trucks slow in dumping	1,551	3.9	8.6
Shortage of batch trucks	116	2.4	5.3
Trucks dumped double batch	3	0.3	0.7
Short moves by paver	396	1.8	4.0
Delay due to slow skip	416	0.7	1.5
Bucket slow dumping	1,108	1.4	3.1
Late start	2	0.2	0.4
Repair hoist on skip	1	0.1	0.2
Repair water pump	2	0.4	0.9
Repair concrete bucket	3	0.3	0.7
Out of water	3	0.4	0.9
Delay by form crew	2	0.1	0.2
Delay by finisher	18	1.2	2.7
Subtotal	3,621	13.2	29.2
Total all delays	3,634	19.8	43.8

be saved, it represents a substantial amount, even after paying for the cost of a time study and an analysis of the results of the study.

The largest loss was caused by delays in dumping the batch into the skip, probably the result of slow reaction of the truck drivers or the truck spotter, or both. When human reactions are involved, it is possible to apply certain stimuli to reduce the time required for the reaction. Truck performance demonstrations,

Table 10-6 Production rates for a dual-drum paver

	$\left(\begin{array}{c}\text{Time,}\\\text{hr}\end{array}\right)$	Production rate per hr	
		Batches	Cu yd
Total time	48.0	55.0	78.7
Net working time	45.2	58.5	83.6
Productive time	25.4	104.0	148.5

conducted under a skilled supervisor, using alert drivers, with the other drivers witnessing the demonstration and participating in the discussions, should result in a reduction in these delays.

The loss of 2.4 hr because of a shortage of batch trucks could amount to as much as $1,200 for the week. What would it cost to provide an additional truck?

Classifying the losses by causes should assure a more intelligent and effective program for improving the operating efficiency of this and other projects. Also, time-lapse moving pictures of this operation should provide an excellent opportunity for action studies of both men and equipment, which can pinpoint the causes of delays. Most men who see their mistakes in pictures are inclined to correct them during future work. Pictures are more effective for this purpose than words.

EXAMPLE OF JOB PLANNING IN CONSTRUCTING ROOF TRUSSES

On a multimillion-dollar housing project the contractor chose to use prefabricated lightweight wood roof trusses instead of erecting them in place on each building. Figure 10-4 illustrates the type of truss used. As noted, each truss required seven different sizes and shapes of members, including the $\frac{3}{4}$-in.-thick plywood gusset. Because several hundred identical trusses were required, the fabricating and erecting operations were highly repetitive, thereby permitting economy by job planning.

The contractor selected a site near the center of the project for the storage of stock sizes of lumber, the installation of a bench-type electric-motor-driven radial saw, a 36-in.-high jig-equipped work table, large enough to support a roof truss lying flat, and the spotting of two wheel-mounted flat-bed trailers to receive the finished trusses. Figure 10-5 illustrates the flow diagram for fabricating the trusses.

Stock lumber of appropriate sizes and lengths was stored in a compartmentalized rack at 1. When a given truss member was cut in quantity, a stop was

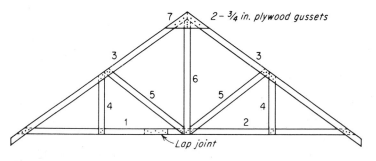

Figure 10-4 Roof truss.

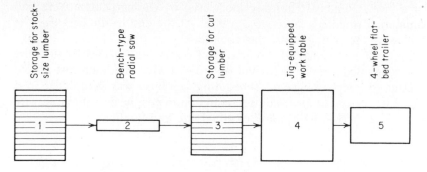

Figure 10-5 Flow diagram for fabricating roof truss.

set on the bench saw to enable the carpenter to saw the members without having to measure them for length or shape. The cut members were stored by size in the rack 3, from which they were transferred to work table 4 as needed. Two carpenters, using only hammers and nails, completed the fabrication of the trusses. Jigs attached to the table permitted the members to be fitted into position quickly and accurately. When a truss was fabricated it was loaded onto a flat-bed trailer. When a trailer was loaded, it was attached to a farm tractor which pulled it to a building, where the trusses were hoisted into position. The tractor was disconnected from the loaded trailer, and attached to an empty trailer for a return trip to the fabricating site.

By preplanning the members to be cut from each length of stock lumber the waste was kept to a minimum.

APPLYING MOTION AND TIME STUDIES TO BUILDING HOUSES

During the early stages of building several hundred homes to only three plans the contractor conducted motion and time studies of all operations as a means of increasing the efficiency of and reducing the cost of construction. The houses were erected on concrete slabs, using wood framing for all walls and the flat roof, metal lath and stucco on the outside walls, sheetrock on the inside walls and ceilings, a composition roof, and steel-sash windows.

He used a central shop to precut all lumber and to preassemble most of the rough-in plumbing. The lumber for a given house was assembled into a single bundle, secured with steel bands, and then delivered to the house site.

When two carpenters and a helper arrived at the slab, they cut the steel bands and proceeded with the erection of the wall frames, assembling panels on the slab, tilting them to vertical positions, plumbing, bracing, and attaching the bottom plates to the concrete slab, using gun-driven studs. Because the lumber was assembled in the bundle in the order that it was used, no time was lost looking for a given member. The only tools used by the carpenters were nail aprons, hammers, carpenter's levels, and a gun. At the end of the first day the framing, including the ceiling joists, was completed.

The delivery of materials and the arrival of craftsmen for each succeeding activity were scheduled to assure efficient operations with minimum lost time.

As a result of preplanning and scheduling, a house was completed in a maximum of 2 weeks and at a substantial reduction in cost when compared with the cost of a single custom-built house of equal size and quality.

APPLYING THE THEORY OF QUEUES TO DETERMINE THE MOST ECONOMICAL NUMBER OF HAULING UNITS

On a given project involving earthwork the most economical number of hauling units is the number that will produce the lowest cost per unit of earth, considering the combined cost of the excavator and the hauling units. If the production rate of the excavator were constant, and if the loads and cycle times of the hauling units were constant, it would be fairly simple to determine the most economical number of hauling units to use on any given project, as illustrated in previous examples appearing in Chap. 9. However, it is well known that truck cycle times are not constant even though the hauling conditions and the number of trucks operating remain constant. There may be times when several trucks are waiting in a queue to be loaded; then later, for no apparent reason, the excavator may have to wait for a truck, resulting in a loss in production. If additional trucks are added to the fleet, to reduce or eliminate the lost production by the excavator, the rate of production will likely be increased, but not enough to compensate for the increased cost of the extra truck or trucks.

The theory of queues can be applied to a situation involving an earth loader and hauling units to analyze statistically the cost of excavating and hauling earth when using varying numbers of hauling units; from this the optimum number of units can be determined. Actual observations and cost determinations made on operating projects have verified the accuracy of this theory [4].

The application of this theory will be illustrated by considering a power shovel used to load trucks, which will haul the earth to a dump site, dump the earth, and then return to the shovel for additional loads, as illustrated in Fig. 10-1. The symbols used in developing and applying the formulas are as follows:

Q = output of shovel in cu yd per hr bank measure
f = operating factor for the shovel, such as a 45-min hr = 0.75
q = capacity of trucks in cu yd bank measure
n = number of trucks in the fleet
P_0 = probability of no trucks in the queue
r = mean arrival rate of truck per hr, excluding loading time, with no delays
$T_a = \dfrac{1}{r}$, cycle time for a truck, excluding loading time, hr

m = number of trucks loaded per hr

$x = \dfrac{m}{r}$, number of trucks needed in the fleet

$T_s = \dfrac{1}{m}$, time to load a truck, hr

C = total cost per hour for shovel and trucks

The production of the shovel in cubic yards per hour will be

$$Q = fmq \tag{10-8}$$

Formula (10-8) gives the ideal rate of production for the shovel. If it must wait for trucks at times, the rate will be reduced, as indicated by formula (10-9):

$$Q = (1 - P_0) fmq \tag{10-9}$$

The total cost per hour for the shovel and trucks will be

$$C = nC_t + C_s \tag{10-10}$$

where C_t = cost per hr per truck

C_s = cost per hr for shovel

The cost per cubic yard will be

$$c = \frac{nC_t + C_s}{Q} \tag{10-11}$$

In order to determine the actual production of the shovel from formula (10-9) it is necessary to determine the values of P_0 when varying numbers of trucks are used. The reader is referred to books on the theory of probability for a complete treatment of this subject. The probability of there being no truck in the queue, resulting in the shovel's having to wait until a truck arrives, is given by the formula

$$P_0(n, x) = \frac{e^{-x}x^n/n!}{\sum\limits_{j=0}^{n}(e^{-x}x^j/j!)} = \frac{p(n, x)}{P(n, x)} \tag{10-12}$$

This is a cumulative Poisson expression, whose values can be determined by using Poisson distribution functions obtained from tables appearing in some handbooks and books treating the theory of probability [5]. Such tables give the values for the numerator and denominator expressions for values n and x [6].

Example Determine the optimum number of trucks, the probable production, and the minimum cost per cubic yard to excavate and haul earth using the following equipment and operating conditions, with volumes in bank measure.

Power shovel, rate of production 300 cu yd per hr when loading
Operating factor, 50-min hr, 0.833
Production per hr, 0.833 × 300 = 250 cu yd
Capacity of trucks, 15 cu yd
Average cycle time for trucks, 0.2040 hr, excluding loading time
Cost per hr for shovel, including operator and oiler, $62.40
Cost per hr for truck and driver, $21.00

From this information the following values are determined:

$Q' = 300$ cu yd per hr
$f = 0.833$
$Q = 0.833 \times 300 = 250$ cu yd per hr
$T_a = 0.2040$ hr
$r = 1 \div 0.2040 = 4.91$
$T_s = 15/300 = 0.050$ hr
$m = \dfrac{1}{0.050} = 20$ trucks loaded per hr
$x = \dfrac{20.0}{4.91} = 4.1$, number of trucks needed

Table 10-7 gives the values of the functions required to evaluate formula (10-12) with x replaced by its value 4.1. The formula may be rewritten as

$$P_0(n, 4.1) = \frac{p(n, 4.1)}{P(n, 4.1)}$$

Most tables give the functions appearing in columns 2 and 3 only. In order to obtain the functions in column 4 it is necessary to subtract from 1 the function appearing in column 3 for the next larger value of n. For example, the function in column 4 for $n = 3$ is obtained by subtracting the function for n equals 4, appearing in column 3. Thus $1 - 0.5858 = 0.4142$.

Applying the values of the functions appearing in Table 10-7 in formula (10-12) gives the values listed for P_0 appearing in Table 10-8. The values of P_0 are the probabilities that there will be no truck in the queue or at the shovel for loading, thus causing a delay for the shovel and a reduction in its rate of production.

Table 10-9 gives the probable production in cubic yards per hour based on using the indicated number of trucks and the probability factors appearing in Table 10-8.

Table 10-10 gives the variations in the cost per cubic yard based on using varying numbers of trucks and formula (10-11). For example, the cost using four trucks is

$$c = \frac{4 \times 21.00 + 62.40}{170} = \$0.81 \text{ per cu yd}$$

Table 10-7 Poisson distribution functions

(1) n	(2) $p(n, 4.1)$	(3) $1 - P(n, 4.1)$	(4) $P(n, 4.1)$
0	0.0166	1.0000	0.0166
1	0.0679	0.9834	0.0845
2	0.1393	0.9155	0.2238
3	0.1904	0.7762	0.4142
4	0.1951	0.5858	0.6093
5	0.1600	0.3907	0.7693
6	0.1093	0.2307	0.8786
7	0.0640	0.1214	0.9427
8	0.0328	0.0573	0.9755
9	0.0150	0.0245	0.9905
10	0.0061	0.0095	0.9966

Table 10-8 Values of P_0

n	$p(n, 4.1) + P(n, 4.1)$	P_0
1	0.0679 + 0.0845	0.804
2	0.1393 + 0.2238	0.622
3	0.1904 + 0.4142	0.460
4	0.1951 + 0.6093	0.320
5	0.1600 + 0.7693	0.208
6	0.1093 + 0.8786	0.124
7	0.0640 + 0.9427	0.068
8	0.0328 + 0.9755	0.034
9	0.0150 + 0.9905	0.015
10	0.0061 + 0.9966	0.006

Table 10-9 Variation in the probable production with the number of trucks used

No. of trucks	$1 - P_0$	Normal production, cu yd per hr	Probable production, cu yd per hr
1	0.196	250	49.0
2	0.378	250	94.5
3	0.540	250	135.0
4	0.680	250	170.0
5	0.792	250	198.0
6	0.876	250	219.5
7	0.932	250	233.4
8	0.966	250	242.0
9	0.985	250	246.5
10	0.994	250	248.5

Table 10-10 Variations in the cost of excavating and hauling earth with the number of trucks used

No. of trucks	Total cost per hr	Production, cu yd per hr	Cost per cu yd
1	$83.40	49.0	$1.71
2	104.40	94.5	1.05
3	125.40	135.0	0.93
4	146.40	170.0	0.81
5	167.40	198.0	0.84
6	188.40	219.5	0.86
7	209.40	233.4	0.89
8	230.40	242.0	0.96
9	251.40	246.5	1.02
10	272.40	248.5	1.10

Example This example presents a graphical solution for the optimization of an excavator-truck earthmoving system by considering it as a cyclic queuing system. Two different situations are analyzed with reference to the variability of the service time of the excavator and the transit time of the trucks. They are: (1) constant service time and constant transit time; (2) constant service time and random transit time. Other conditions may exist and may be analyzed in a similar manner [7].

An earthmoving system composed of one excavator and N trucks may be considered as a queueing system that is described as follows: a truck is loaded, travels to the dump site, dumps, and returns to the back of the queue or, if there is no queue, begins loading immediately. If there is a continuous queue of trucks, the excavator will excavate an average of X cubic yards of earth per hour. If the excavator is idle for a proportion P_0 of the time, the cost per cubic yard of earth moved will be

$$C_N = \frac{K_1 + NK_2}{X(1 - P_0)} = \frac{K_2}{X} F_N\left(\frac{K_1}{K_2} + N\right) \tag{10-13}$$

where K_1 = cost per hr for the excavator, including labor

K_2 = cost per hr for a truck, including labor

$F_N = 1/(1 - P_0)$

The problem is to determine P_0 and hence F_N for any particular N and any particular set of assumptions about the service time and the transit time.

The service time is defined as the time that elapses from the start of loading one truck until the excavator is ready to start loading another truck. The transit time is the time required by a truck between leaving the excavator and arriving at the back of the queue. Both of these times, in general, will be subject to random fluctuations.

If the average service time for a truck is T_s and the average transit time is T_t, R is defined as the ratio T_t/T_s. The standard deviations are $c_s T_s$ and $c_t T_t$. Then c_s and c_t are coefficients of variation.

In the simplest theory, a completely deterministic one, $c_s = c_t = 0$, whereas in the queueing theory approach the probability distributions are negative exponential functions and thus $c_s = c_t = 1$. These two situations may be considered as extremes between which any practical situation will lie.

The following analyses illustrate how this subject may be examined.

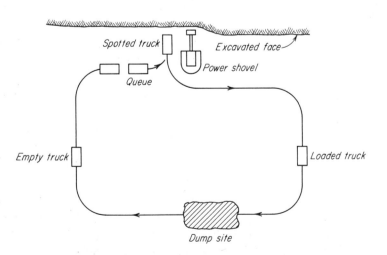

Figure 10-6 Basic elements of an earth-moving operation.

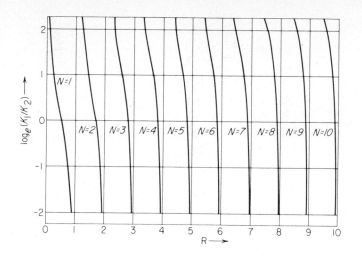

Figure 10-7 Regions of optimal N in the parameter space $\log_e(K_1/K_2) - R$ for the condition $c_s = c_t = 0$.

CONSTANT SERVICE TIME AND CONSTANT TRANSIT TIME When $c_s = c_t = 0$, the optimum value of N in this deterministic analysis is either the integer immediately below $R + 1$ or the integer immediately above. If R_0 is the highest integer that is less than R, the choice lies between $N = (R_0 + 1)$ and $N + 1$.

When $N = R_0 + 1$, the shovel is idle a fraction $(R - R_0)/(R + 1)$ of the time, so that the F_N value is $(R + 1)/(R_0 + 1)$. With $N + 1$ trucks, the shovel is never idle, and therefore $F_{N+1} = 1$.

From Eq. (10-13) it can be seen that the two systems are equally good if $C_N = C_{N+1}$, or

$$\frac{R + 1}{R_0 + 1}\left(\frac{K_1}{K_2} + N\right) = \frac{K_1}{K_2} + N + 1$$

or

$$\frac{K_1}{K_2} = \frac{1 - E}{E}(1 + R_0) \tag{10-14}$$

where $E = R - R_0$

The regions of optimal N are shown in Fig. 10-7 in the parameter space which has axes R and K_1/K_2 at right angles.

RANDOM SERVICE TIME AND RANDOM TRANSIT TIME When service time and transit time are random, the distributions of both times are negative exponential functions, and the system is the cyclic queueing system analyzed by Griffis [6]:

$$P_0 = \frac{1}{\displaystyle\sum_{i=0}^{N} \frac{N!}{(N - i)!}\frac{1}{R^i}} \tag{10-15}$$

In order to avoid numerical calculations using tables of the cumulative Poisson distribution, the values of F_N have been calculated for various values of R. The critical values of K_1/K_2 have been calculated by the procedure of the previous section. Below a critical value of K_1/K_2, N is the optimal number of trucks, whereas immediately above it, $N + 1$ is better. The results of this are shown in Fig. 10-8.

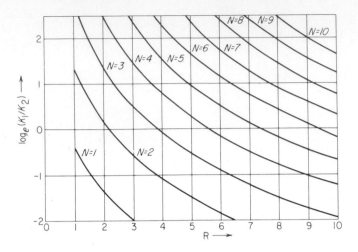

Figure 10-8 Regions of optimal N in the parameter space $\log_e(K_1/K_2) - R$ for the condition $c_s = c_t = 1$.

This representation has the advantage of convenience for an analyst at the site, who does not need to perform any calculations other than those needed to find K_1/K_2 and $R = (T_t/T_s)$. For example, if the ratio of average transit time to average service time is 7 while the ratio of hourly costs is 1.5 (log $K_1/K_2 = 0.405$), the optimum value of N is read from Fig. 10-8 as 6. From Fig. 10-7 in the deterministic analysis, the choice would have been 8 trucks.

Figure 10-9 shows a plot of F_N against R, which reveals that for $R = 7$, $F_6 = 1.50$, whereas for $R = 8$, $F_8 = 1.22$. Because from Eq. (10-13) C is proportional to $F_n(K_1/K_2 + N)$, the difference between C_6 and C_8 (according to the queueing theory calculations) is about 3 percent.

Persons wishing additional information on other conditions related to service time and transit time may refer to the paper presented by Cabrera and Maher [7].

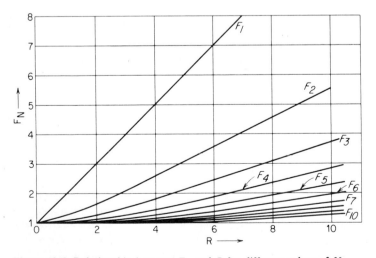

Figure 10-9 Relationship between F_N and R for different values of N_{opt}.

PROBLEMS

10-1 During a motion and time study of the operations of a power shovel, 15 cycle times were observed, with the following results in minutes:

0.52	0.38	0.43	0.46	0.49
0.41	0.36	0.46	0.48	0.43
0.50	0.39	0.41	0.45	0.47

Determine if the average cycle time obtained from these observations is sufficiently accurate for a confidence factor of 0.9 and a confidence interval of 0.03 min.

Use the exact method to determine if sufficient observations have been made. If not, how many additional observations are required?

Use the approximate method to determine the number of observations required.

10-2 Use the observed cycle times listed in Prob. 10-1 and the exact method to determine the number of observations required for each of the following conditions:

$C = 0.9$

$I = 0.02, 0.03, 0.04, 0.05,$ and 0.06 min

10-3 During a motion and time study of trucks hauling earth from a power shovel, the cycle times in minutes for the trucks were as follows:

4.62	4.10	4.96	4.82
4.24	5.12	4.50	4.74
4.68	4.36	4.68	4.88

Use the exact method to determine the number of observations required to obtain an average cycle time for a confidence factor of 0.9 and confidence intervals of 0.15 min, 0.20 min, and 0.30 min.

Make the same determinations using the approximate method.

10-4 Use the theory of queues to determine the optimum number of trucks to use in hauling earth from a power shovel to a fill for the following conditions:

Ideal production for the power shovel, 225 cu yd per hr bm
Operating factor for the power shovel, 0.75
Capacity of trucks, 11 cu yd bm
Average cycle time for trucks, excluding loading time, 0.260 hr
Cost per hr for shovel, including labor, $52.00
Cost per hr for truck and driver, $16.20

Because Table 10-7 gives the values of the Poisson distribution functions for 4.1 trucks only, it will be necessary to use a table of values that apply for the number of trucks needed for this project.

10-5 If the average cycle time for the trucks of Prob. 10-4 is increased to 0.360 hr with no other changes, determine the optimum number of trucks needed.

REFERENCES

1. Fondahl, John W.: Photographic Analysis for Construction Operations, *Proceedings ASCE*, vol. 2483, no. CO2, pp. 9–25, May 1960.
2. Fondahl, John W.: "Construction Methods Improvement by Time-lapse Movie Analysis," Department of Civil Engineering, Stanford University, Stanford, California, January 1962.
3. Oglesby, C. H.: "Techniques for Cost Reduction in Construction," Department of Civil Engineering, Stanford University, Stanford, California, no date.

4. O'Shea, J. B., G. N. Slutkin, and L. R. Shaffer: "An Application of the Theory of Queues to the Forecasting of Shovel-truck Fleet Productions," Department of Civil Engineering, University of Illinois, Urbana, Illinois, February 1964.
5. Burington, R. S., and D. C. May, Jr.: "Handbook of Probability and Statistics with Tables," 1st ed., Handbook Publishers, Inc., Sandusky, Ohio, 1953.
6. Griffis, Fletcher H.: Optimizing Haul Fleet Size Using Queueing Theory, *Proceedings ASCE*, vol. 5753, no. CO1, pp. 75–88, January 1968.
7. Cabrera, J. G., and M. J. Maher: "Optimizing Earthmoving Plant: Solution for the Excavator-Truck System," Highway Research Board No. 454, pp. 7–15, 1973.

ELEVEN

BELT-CONVEYOR SYSTEMS

GENERAL INFORMATION

Belt-conveyor systems are used extensively in the field of construction, where they frequently provide the most satisfactory and economical method of handling and transporting materials, such as earth, sand, gravel, crushed stone, mine ores, cement, concrete, etc. Because of the continuous flow of materials at relatively high speeds, belt conveyors have high capacities.

The essential parts of a belt-conveyor system include a continuous belt, idlers, a driving unit, driving and tail pulleys, take-up equipment, and a supporting structure. Additional accessories, as described later, may be included when desirable or necessary.

A conveyor for transporting materials a short distance may be a portable unit or a fixed installation. Figure 11-1 illustrates a portable conveyor used to stock-pile aggregate which is delivered by trucks. This machine is available in lengths of 33 to 60 ft, with belt widths of 18, 24, and 30 in. It is self-powered with a gasoline-engine drive through a shaft and gearbox to the driving pulley. The operating features include swivel wheels, V-type truck, hydraulic hoist, low-mast height, and antifriction bearings throughout.

When a belt-conveyor system is used to transport materials a considerable distance, up to several miles in some instances, the system should consist of a number of different flights, as there is a limit to the maximum length of a belt. Each flight is a complete conveyor unit which discharges its load onto the tail end of the succeeding unit. Such a system will operate over any terrain provided the slopes do not exceed those for which the given material may be transported.

The limestone rock for the Bull Shoals Dam, whose maximum size was 6 in., was transported 7 miles from the primary crushing plant at the quarry to the

Figure 11-1 Portable belt conveyor.

Figure 11-2 (*a*) Troughing idlers installed. (*b*) Belt transporting aggregate.

dam site. The conveyor system consisted of 21 flights, varying in length from 600 to 2,800 ft, each powered with a 100-hp electric motor. The belts, which were 30 in. wide, were operated at a speed of 525 fpm to deliver 350 cu yd of material per hour. The entire system required 14,000 idlers, which were supported primarily by wood structures. Figure 11-2 illustrates troughing idlers installed on a project and an operating belt transporting aggregate.

THE ECONOMY OF TRANSPORTING MATERIALS WITH A BELT CONVEYOR

One of the first questions that arises in considering the use of a belt conveyor is whether this method of transportation is the most dependable and economical when compared with other methods. The proper way to answer this question is to estimate the cost of transporting the material by each method under consideration. Assume that a belt conveyor is to be compared with trucks for hauling aggregate for a large concrete project.

The net total cost of the conveyor system will include the installed cost of the system, an access road for installing and servicing the system, maintenance, replacements, and repairs, fuel, or electrical energy, and labor, less the net salvage value of the system upon completion of its use. Interest on the investment, plus taxes and insurance, if they apply, should be included. Likewise, any cost of obtaining a right of way for the system should be included. The unit cost of moving the material, per ton or cubic yard, may be obtained by dividing the net total cost of the system by the number of units to be transported.

The cost of transporting the materials by truck will include the cost of constructing and maintaining a haul road, plus the cost of operating the trucks. The unit cost of moving the materials may be obtained by dividing the net total cost by the number of units to be transported.

If either method requires additional handling costs at the source or at the destination, these costs should be included prior to determining the unit cost of moving the materials.

In constructing the Bull Shoals Dam more than 4,500,000 tons of aggregate was transported on belt conveyors at a reported cost of $0.045 per ton-mile. It was estimated that the contractors saved $560,000 on the purchase and installation of the conveyor system compared with a fleet of trucks, plus a haul road and incidentals required for the trucks. In addition, it was estimated that there was a saving of $375,000 on labor operating the system compared with trucks.

REPRESENTATIVE BELT-CONVEYOR SYSTEMS

Figure 11-3 illustrates four belt-conveyor systems based on the location of the drive pulley, the number of drive pulleys, and the take-up method of maintaining the necessary tension in the belt.

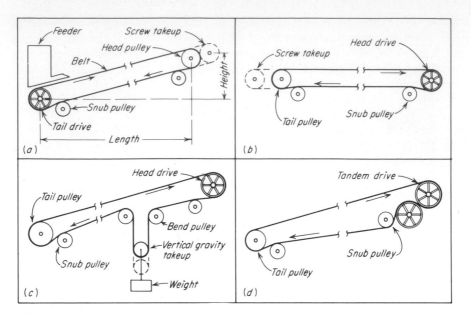

Figure 11-3 Representative belt-conveyor systems.

CONVEYOR BELTS

The belt is the moving and supporting surface on which the material is transported. Many types, sizes, and grades are available, from which the most suitable belt for a given service may be selected.

Belts are manufactured by joining several layers or plies of woven cotton duck into a carcass which provides the necessary strength to resist the tension in the belt. The layers are covered with an adhesive which combines them into a unified structure. Special types of reinforcing, such as rayon, nylon, and steel cables, are employed sometimes to increase the strength of a belt. A measure of the strength of a belt is indicated by the number and weight of the several layers of fabric. The number of layers is expressed as 4-, 6-, 7-, 8-, etc., ply. The weight of each layer of fabric is expressed as 28-, 32-, 36-, 42-, etc., oz, the number indicating the weight of a piece of duck 42 in. wide and 36 in. long. The width of a belt is expressed in inches. Thus, a belt might be specified as a 36-in.-wide 6-ply 42-oz belt.

The top and bottom surfaces of a belt are covered with rubber to protect the carcass from abrasion and injury from the impact at loading. Various thicknesses of covers may be specified. Figure 11-4 illustrates cross sections of belts having different types of construction.

It is necessary to select a belt with sufficient strength to resist the maximum tension to which it will be subjected, as determined by methods which will be developed later.

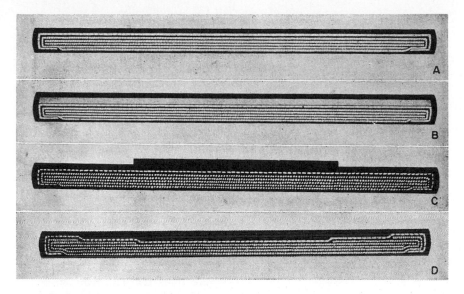

Figure 11-4 Types of conveyor-belt construction. (*a*) Standard. (*b*) Shock pad. (*c*) Stepped pad. (*d*) Stepped ply.

Also, it is necessary to select a belt that is wide enough to transport the material at the required rate. Most belts used on construction projects travel over troughing rollers to increase the carrying capacities. The number of tons that can be transported in an hour will equal the product of the cross-section area of the material in square feet times the belt speed in feet per hour times the weight of the material in pounds per cubic foot divided by 2,000 lb per ton. The area of the cross section will depend on the width of the belt, the depth of troughing, the angle of repose for the material, and the extent to which the belt is loaded to capacity. Figure 11-5 illustrates how the cross-section area may vary with the width of a belt and the angle of repose for the material. In the figure the troughing idlers are set at an angle of 20° above the horizontal. In order to eliminate side spillage, it is assumed that materials will not be placed closer than

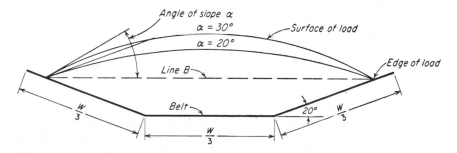

Figure 11-5 Cross-section area of a load on a conveyor belt.

Table 11-1 Areas of cross sections of materials for loaded belts

Width of belt, in.	0.05 W + 1, in.	Area of level load, sq ft	Area of surcharge, sq ft, for angle of repose, deg			Total area, sq ft, for angle of repose, deg		
			10	20	30	10	20	30
16	1.8	0.072	0.029	0.059	0.090	0.101	0.131	0.162
18	1.9	0.096	0.038	0.078	0.118	0.134	0.174	0.214
20	2.0	0.122	0.048	0.098	0.150	0.170	0.220	0.272
24	2.2	0.185	0.072	0.146	0.225	0.257	0.331	0.410
30	2.5	0.303	0.118	0.238	0.365	0.421	0.541	0.668
36	2.8	0.450	0.174	0.351	0.540	0.624	0.801	0.990
42	3.1	0.627	0.241	0.488	0.749	0.868	1.115	1.376
48	3.4	0.833	0.321	0.649	0.992	1.154	1.482	1.825
54	3.7	1.068	0.408	0.826	1.264	1.476	1.894	2.332
60	4.0	1.333	0.510	1.027	1.575	1.843	2.360	2.908

$0.05 W + 1$ in. from the sides of the belt, where W is the width of the belt in inches. It is assumed that the top surface of the material will be an arc of a circle. Table 11-1 gives the cross-section areas for various belt widths and loading conditions. These areas are subject to variation and should not be considered as exact unless the loading conditions are as stated. The area of surcharge is the area above line B of Fig. 11-5.

The carrying capacity of a 42-in. belt, moving 100 fpm, loaded with sand weighing 100 lb per cu ft, with a 20° angle of repose, will be 100 fpm × 100 lb × 1.115 sq ft × 60 min ÷ 2,000 lb per ton = 334.5 tons per hr. The carrying capacity of this belt for other speeds may be obtained by multiplying 334.5 by the ratio of the speed of the two belts.

Table 11-2 gives the approximate carrying capacities of troughed conveyor belts, in tons per hour, for various widths and materials for a speed of 100 fpm. Table 11-3 gives the suggested maximum speeds which are considered good practice for conveyor belts of different widths when handling various kinds of materials. Table 11-4 gives representative allowable working tensions in duck belts for various thicknesses and widths. The pulley diameter is the minimum size that should be used for the indicated service.

IDLERS

Idlers provide the supports for a belt conveyor. For the load-carrying portion of a belt the idlers are designed to provide the necessary troughing, while for the return portion of a belt the idlers provide flat supports. The essential parts of a troughing idler include the rolls, brackets, and base. Antifriction bearings are generally used in idlers, with high-pressure grease fittings to permit periodic lubrication of the bearings. The rolls may be made of steel tubing or cast iron,

Table 11-2 Carrying capacities of troughed conveyor belts, in tons per hour for a speed of 100 fpm*

Width of belt, in.	Max lumps Sized, in.	Max lumps Un-sized, in.	Weight of material, lb per cu ft 30	50	90	100	125	150	160	180	200
14	2	$2\frac{1}{2}$	9	15	28	31	39	46	49	56	62
16	$2\frac{1}{2}$	3	13	21	38	42	52	63	67	75	83
18	3	4	16	27	48	54	67	81	86	97	107
20	$3\frac{1}{2}$	5	20	33	60	67	83	100	107	120	133
24	$4\frac{1}{2}$	8	30	50	90	100	125	150	160	180	200
30	7	14	47	79	142	158	197	236	252	284	315
36	9	18	70	117	210	234	292	351	374	421	467
42	11	20	100	167	300	333	417	500	534	600	667
48	14	24	138	230	414	460	575	690	736	828	920
54	15	28	178	297	534	593	741	890	948	1,070	1,190
60	16	30	222	369	664	738	922	1,110	1,180	1,330	1,480

* Courtesy Hewitt-Robins.

either plain or covered with a composition, such as rubber, where it is necessary to protect a belt against damage due to impact. The diameters of the rolls most commonly used are 4, 5, 6, and 7 in. Large diameter rolls give lower friction and better belt protection, especially when the load includes large lumps of material. Figure 11-6 illustrates troughing and return idlers.

Spacing of idlers Troughing idlers should be spaced close enough to prevent excessive deflection of the loaded belt between the idlers. As indicated in Table

Table 11-3 Maximum speeds of conveyor belts, in fpm*

Kind and condition of material handled	Width of belt, in. 14	16	18	20	24	30	36	42	48	54	60
Unsized coal, gravel, stone, ashes, ore, or similar material	300	300	350	350	400	450	500	550	600	600	600
Sized coal, coke, or other breakable material	250	250	250	300	300	350	350	400	400	400	400
Wet or dry sand	400	400	500	600	600	700	800	800	800	800	800
Crushed coke, crushed slag, or other fine abrasive material	250	250	300	400	400	500	500	500	500	500	500
Large lump ore, rock, slag, or other large abrasive material	. . .	. . .	. . .	. . .	350	350	400	400	400	400	400

* Courtesy Hewitt-Robins.

Table 11-4 Allowable working tension and pulley diameter for conveyor belts*

No. plies	Weight per ply, oz	Width of belt, in.								Diameter of pulley, in.		
		16	18	20	24	30	36	42	48	Head, drive, tripper	Tail, take-up, snub	Bend
3	32	1,440	1,620	.....	.....	.....	......	......	......	16	12	12
3	36	.....	.....	1,800	2,160	.....	......	......	......	20	16	12
3	42	.....	.....	2,200	2,640	3,300	......	......	......	20	16	12
3	48	.....	.....	.....	3,840	.....	......	......	......	24	20	16
4	28	1,600	1,800	2,000	2,400	3,000	......	......	......	20	16	12
4	32	1,920	2,160	2,400	2,880	3,600	4,320	......	......	20	16	12
4	36	.....	.....	2,600	3,120	3,900	4,680	......	......	24	20	16
4	42	.....	.....	.....	.....	4,800	5,760	6,720	......	24	20	20
4	48	.....	.....	.....	.....	6,450	7,750	9,020	......	30	24	20
5	28	2,000	2,250	2,500	3,000	3,750	4,500	......	......	24	20	16
5	32	.....	2,700	3,000	3,480	4,500	5,400	......	......	24	20	16
5	36	.....	.....	3,400	4,080	5,100	6,120	7,140	......	30	24	20
5	42	.....	.....	.....	.....	6,600	7,920	9,240	10,560	30	24	20
5	48	.....	.....	.....	.....	8,700	10,400	12,180	13,920	36	30	24
6	28	.....	.....	3,000	3,600	4,500	5,400	......	......	30	24	20
6	32	.....	.....	.....	4,320	5,400	6,480	7,560	......	30	24	20
6	36	.....	.....	.....	.....	6,300	7,560	8,820	10,080	36	30	24
6	42	.....	.....	.....	.....	.....	9,720	11,340	12,900	36	30	24
6	48	.....	.....	.....	.....	.....	13,000	15,120	17,300	42	36	30
7	28	.....	.....	.....	.....	5,250	6,300	......	......	36	30	24
7	32	.....	.....	.....	.....	6,300	7,560	8,820	10,080	36	30	24
7	36	.....	.....	.....	.....	.....	8,820	10,300	11,780	42	36	30
7	42	.....	.....	.....	.....	.....	......	13,200	15,140	42	36	30
7	48	.....	.....	.....	.....	.....	......	17,640	20,180	48	42	36
8	32	.....	.....	.....	.....	.....	8,640	10,080	11,520	42	30	24
8	36	.....	.....	.....	.....	.....	......	11,760	13,450	48	42	30
8	42	.....	.....	.....	.....	.....	......	......	17,300	48	42	30
8	48	.....	.....	.....	.....	.....	......	......	23,050	54	48	42
9	32	.....	.....	.....	.....	.....	......	11,340	12,900	48	36	30
9	36	.....	.....	.....	.....	.....	......	13,200	15,140	54	48	36

* Courtesy Hewitt-Robins.

11-5, the maximum spacing will vary with the width of the belt and the weight of the load carried. The idler spacing should be reduced at the point where the load is fed onto the belt.

As the sole function of the return idlers is to support the empty belt, the spacing can be increased to approximately 10 ft.

Training idlers Sometimes a conveyor belt is operated under conditions which make it difficult to keep the belt centered on the troughing idlers. If the conditions cannot be corrected sufficiently to keep the belt centered, it may be necessary to install training idlers, spaced 50 to 60 ft apart. Figure 11-7 illustrates a set of training idlers.

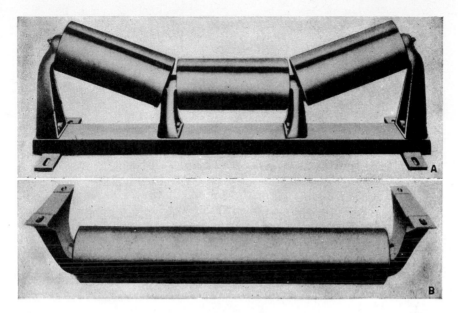

Figure 11-6 Belt idlers. (*a*) Heavy-duty troughing, (*b*) Return.

Idler friction In analyzing a belt conveyor to determine the horsepower required, it is necessary to include the power needed by the idlers. This power will depend on the type and size idler, the kind of bearings, the weight of the revolving parts, the weight of the belt, and the weight of the load. Table 11-6 gives representative friction factors for idlers equipped with antifriction bearings. Manufacturers of idlers will furnish information giving the weights of the revolving parts of their idlers.

Table 11-5 Recommended maximum spacing of troughing idlers*

Width of belt, in.	Weight of material, lb per cu ft		
	30–70	70–120	120–150
14	5 ft 6 in.	5 ft 0 in.	4 ft 9 in.
16	5 ft 6 in.	5 ft 0 in.	4 ft 9 in.
18	5 ft 6 in.	5 ft 0 in.	4 ft 9 in.
20	5 ft 6 in.	5 ft 0 in.	4 ft 9 in.
24	5 ft 6 in.	5 ft 0 in.	4 ft 9 in.
30	5 ft 0 in.	4 ft 6 in.	4 ft 3 in.
36	5 ft 0 in.	4 ft 6 in.	4 ft 3 in.
42	4 ft 6 in.	4 ft 0 in.	3 ft 9 in.
48	4 ft 0 in.	3 ft 3 in.	3 ft 0 in.
24	4 ft 0 in.	2 ft 9 in.	2 ft 6 in.
60	4 ft 0 in.	2 ft 3 in.	2 ft 0 in.

* Courtesy of Hewitt-Robins.

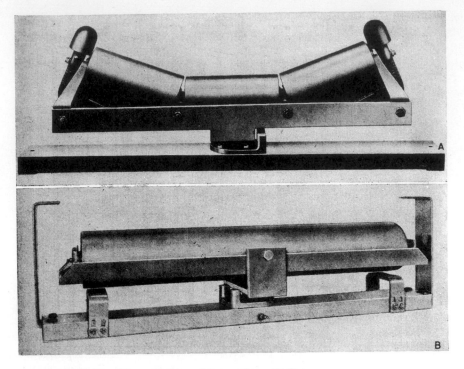

Figure 11-7 Training idlers. (*a*) Reversible troughing. (*b*) Return.

The information in Table 11-6 is used as in the following example.

Example Consider a conveyor 100 ft long, with a 5-ply 32-oz 30-in.-wide belt weighing 6.8 lb per ft. The load will weigh 100 lb per cu ft, or 54 lb per ft of conveyor. The revolving parts will weigh 50 lb for a troughing idler and 31 lb for a return idler. Both idlers are 6 in. in diameter.

From Table 11-6 the idler friction factor is 0.030.

No. troughing idlers required, 100 ÷ 4.5	= 22
Add extra idlers at loading point	= 3
Total no. troughing idlers	= 25
No. of return idlers, 100 ÷ 10	= 10

Total weight of the revolving parts of idlers will be

Troughing, 25 × 50	= 1,250 lb
Return, 10 × 31	= 310 lb
Weight of belt, 200 × 6.8	= 1,360 lb
Weight of load, 100 × 54	= 5,400 lb
Total weight	= 8,320 lb

The force required to overcome idler friction, 8,320 × 0.03 = 249.6 lb.

For a belt speed of 100 fpm the energy required per min will be

100 × 249.6 = 24,960 ft-lb

**Table 11-6 Friction factors
for conveyor-belt idlers
equipped with antifriction
bearings***

Diameter of idler pulley, in.	Friction factor
4	0.0375
5	0.036
6	0.030
7	0.025

* Courtesy Hewitt-Robins.

The horsepower required to overcome idler friction will be

$$P = \frac{24{,}960 \text{ ft-lb per min}}{33{,}000 \text{ ft-lb per min per hp}} = 0.76$$

For other belt speeds the required horsepower will be

$$P = \frac{0.76 \times \text{speed, fpm}}{100}$$

POWER REQUIRED TO DRIVE A BELT CONVEYOR

The total external power required to drive a loaded belt conveyor is the
algebraic sum of the power required by each of the following:

1. To move the empty belt over the idlers
2. To move the load horizontally
3. To lift or lower the load vertically
4. To turn all pulleys
5. To compensate for drive losses
6. To operate a tripper, if one is used

The power required for each of these operations can be determined with
reasonable accuracy for any given conveyor system, as explained later.

POWER REQUIRED TO MOVE AN EMPTY BELT

The power required to move an empty conveyor belt over the idlers will vary
with the type of idler bearings, the diameter and spacing of the idlers, and the
length, weight, and speed of the belt. The energy required to move an empty belt

is given by the equation

$$E = LSCQ \tag{11-1}$$

where E = energy, ft-lb per min
L = length of conveyor, ft
S = belt speed, fpm
C = idler-friction factor, from Table 11-6
Q = weight of moving parts per ft of conveyor

Equation (11-1) may be expressed as horsepower by dividing by 33,000 to give

$$P = \frac{LSCQ}{33,000} \tag{11-2}$$

Representative values of Q are given in Table 11-7. If more accurate values are desired for a given conveyor, they may be determined from the design of the particular conveyor and the weight of the belt used.

Example The use of Eq. (11-2) is illustrated by determining the horsepower required to move a 30-in.-wide belt on a conveyor whose length is 1,800 ft, equipped with 5-in.-diameter idler pulleys, with antifriction bearings. Assume a belt speed of 100 fpm.

From Table 11-6 the value of C will be 0.036.
From Table 11-7 the value of Q will be 26 lb per ft of conveyor length.
The power required to move the empty belt will be

$$P = \frac{1,800 \times 100 \times 0.036 \times 26}{33,000} = 5.10 \text{ hp}$$

Table 11-7 Representative values of Q*

| | Idlers, 5-in.-diameter, steel pulleys | | | | | Weight of conveyor, lb per ft | | | |
| | Troughing | | Return | | Weight of belt, lb per ft | Idlers | | | Q, lb per ft |
Width of belt, in.	Weight of revolving parts, lb	Spacing	Weight of revolving parts, lb	Spacing		Troughing	Return	Belt	
14	18	5'0"	9	10'0"	2.8	3.6	0.9	5.6	10.1
16	20	5'0"	11	10'0"	3.3	4.0	1.1	6.6	11.7
18	22	5'0"	12	10'0"	4.1	4.4	1.2	8.2	13.8
20	24	5'0"	14	10'0"	4.6	4.8	1.4	9.2	15.4
24	26	5'0"	17	10'0"	7.0	5.2	1.7	14.0	20.9
30	31	4'6"	21	10'0"	8.5	6.9	2.1	17.0	26.0
36	36	4'6"	25	10'0"	11.3	8.0	2.5	22.6	33.1
42	40	4'0"	29	10'0"	17.0	10.0	2.9	34.0	46.0
48	45	3'3"	34	10'0"	23.8	13.8	3.4	47.6	64.8
54	74	2'9"	54	10'0"	29.2	26.9	5.4	73.2	105.5
60	80	2'3"	60	10'0"	32.5	35.6	6.0	74.0	115.6

* Courtesy Hewitt-Robins.

Table 11-8 Horsepower required to move empty conveyor belts for a speed of 100 fpm*

Length of con- veyor, ft	Width of belt, in.										
	14	16	18	20	24	30	36	42	48	54	60
50	0.05	0.06	0.07	0.08	0.11	0.14	0.18	0.25	0.35	0.54	0.63
100	0.11	0.13	0.15	0.17	0.23	0.28	0.36	0.51	0.70	1.14	1.25
150	0.16	0.19	0.22	0.25	0.34	0.42	0.53	0.76	1.05	1.71	1.88
200	0.22	0.25	0.30	0.33	0.45	0.56	0.71	1.01	1.40	2.28	2.50
250	0.27	0.32	0.37	0.42	0.56	0.70	0.89	1.27	1.75	2.85	3.13
300	0.33	0.38	0.45	0.50	0.68	0.84	1.07	1.52	2.10	3.42	3.76
400	....	....	0.60	0.66	0.90	1.12	1.43	2.03	2.80	4.56	5.01
500	....	....	....	0.83	1.13	1.40	1.79	2.53	3.50	5.70	6.26
600	....	....	....	1.00	1.35	1.68	2.14	3.04	4.20	6.84	7.51
800	....	....	....	....	1.80	2.25	2.86	4.05	5.60	9.12	10.00
1,000	....	....	....	....	2.26	2.81	3.57	5.07	7.00	11.40	12.50
1,200	....	....	....	....	....	3.37	4.29	6.08	8.40	13.70	15.00
1,400	....	....	....	....	....	3.93	5.00	7.09	9.80	16.00	17.50
1,600	....	....	....	....	....	4.49	5.72	8.10	11.20	18.30	20.10
1,800	....	....	....	....	....	5.05	6.43	9.12	12.60	20.50	22.60
2,000	....	....	....	....	....	5.62	7.15	10.10	14.00	22.80	24.90
2,200	....	....	....	....	....	....	7.86	11.10	15.40	25.10	27.60
2,400	....	....	....	....	....	....	8.58	12.20	16.80	27.40	30.10
2,600	....	....	....	....	....	....	9.29	13.20	18.20	29.60	32.60
2,800	....	....	....	....	....	....	10.00	14.20	19.60	31.90	35.00
3,000	....	....	....	....	....	....	10.70	15.20	21.00	34.20	37.60

* Courtesy Hewitt-Robins.
The power values given in this table are based on the use of 5-in.-diameter idlers. For 4-in.-diameter idlers increase the values by 4 percent. For 6-in.-diameter idlers decrease the values by 17 percent.

Table 11-8 gives representative values for the horsepower required to move empty conveyor belts. The values are based on using 5-in.-diameter idlers with antifriction bearings, and the belt widths given in Table 11-7.

POWER REQUIRED TO MOVE A LOAD HORIZONTALLY

The power required to move a load horizontally may be expressed by Eq. (11-2) if Q is replaced by W, the weight of the load in pounds per foot of belt.

$$P = \frac{LSCW}{33,000} \tag{11-3}$$

This equation may be expressed in terms of the load moved in tons per hour. Let

T = tons material moved per hr

SW = lb material moved per min

$60SW$ = lb material moved per hr

$$T = \frac{60SW}{2,000} = \frac{3SW}{100}$$

Solving,

$$SW = \frac{100T}{3} \tag{11-4}$$

Substituting this value of SW in Eq. (11-3), the horsepower required to move a load horizontally is

$$P = \frac{100LCT}{3 \times 33,000} = \frac{LCT}{990} \tag{11-5}$$

Table 11-9 gives values for the horsepower required to move loads horizontally on conveyor belts. The values are based on using 5-in.-diameter idlers with antifriction bearings. For 6-in.-diameter idlers decrease the values by 17 percent.

Table 11-9 Horsepower required to move loads horizontally on conveyor belts*

Length of con- veyor, ft	Load, tons per hr													
	50	100	150	200	250	300	350	400	500	600	700	800	900	1,000
50	0.09	0.18	0.27	0.36	0.46	0.55	0.64	0.73	0.91	1.1	1.3	1.5	1.6	1.8
100	0.18	0.36	0.55	0.74	0.91	1.1	1.3	1.5	1.8	2.2	2.6	2.9	3.3	3.6
150	0.27	0.55	0.82	1.1	1.4	1.6	1.9	2.2	2.7	3.3	3.8	4.4	4.9	5.5
200	0.36	0.73	1.1	1.5	1.8	2.2	2.6	2.9	3.6	4.4	5.1	5.8	6.6	7.3
250	0.46	0.91	1.4	1.8	2.3	2.7	3.2	3.6	4.6	5.5	6.4	7.3	8.2	9.1
300	0.55	1.1	1.6	2.2	2.7	3.3	3.8	4.4	5.5	6.6	7.7	8.8	9.9	10.9
400	0.73	1.5	2.2	2.9	3.6	4.4	5.1	5.8	7.3	8.7	10.2	11.6	13.1	14.6
500	0.91	1.8	2.7	3.6	4.6	5.5	6.4	7.3	9.1	10.9	12.7	14.5	16.4	18.2
600	1.10	2.1	3.2	4.2	5.3	6.4	7.4	8.5	10.6	12.7	14.8	17.0	19.1	21.0
800	1.40	2.7	4.1	5.5	6.8	8.2	9.5	10.8	13.7	16.4	19.1	22.0	25.0	27.0
1,000	1.70	3.3	5.0	6.7	8.3	10.0	11.7	13.3	16.7	20.0	23.0	27.0	30.0	33.0
1,200	2.0	3.9	5.9	7.9	9.8	11.8	13.8	15.7	19.8	24.0	28.0	32.0	36.0	39.0
1,400	2.3	4.5	6.8	9.1	11.4	13.7	15.9	18.1	23.0	27.0	32.0	36.0	41.0	45.0
1,600	2.6	5.2	7.7	10.3	12.9	15.5	18	21	26	31	36	41	46	52
1,800	2.9	5.8	8.7	11.5	14.4	17.3	20	23	28	35	40	46	52	58
2,000	3.2	6.4	9.6	12.7	15.9	19.1	22	25	32	38	45	51	57	64
2,200	3.5	7.0	10.5	13.9	17.4	21.0	24	28	35	42	49	56	63	70
2,400	3.9	7.6	11.4	15.2	18.9	23.0	27	30	38	46	53	61	68	76
2,600	4.1	8.2	12.3	16.4	20.0	25.0	29	33	41	49	57	65	74	82
2,800	4.4	8.8	13.2	17.6	22.0	26.0	31	35	44	53	62	70	79	88
3,000	4.7	9.4	14.1	18.8	23.0	28.0	33	37	47	56	66	75	85	94

* Courtesy Hewitt-Robins.
    The power values given in this table are based on the use of 5-in.-diameter idlers. For 4-in.-diameter idlers increase the values by 4 percent.

POWER REQUIRED TO MOVE A LOAD UP AN INCLINED BELT CONVEYOR

When a load is moved up an inclined belt conveyor, the power required may be divided into two components: the power required to move the load horizontally and the power required to lift the load through the net change in elevation. The power required to move the load horizontally may be determined from Eq. (11-5). The power required to lift the load through the net change in elevation may be determined as follows: Let

H = net change in elevation, ft

T = tons material per hr

From Eq. (11-4),

$$\frac{100T}{3} = \text{lb material per min}$$

$$\frac{100TH}{3} = \text{energy, ft-lb per min}$$

Dividing by 33,000 gives the horsepower,

$$P = \frac{100TH}{3 \times 33,000} = \frac{TH}{990} \tag{11-6}$$

If the load is moved up an inclined conveyor, the power given in Eq. (11-6) must be supplied from an outside source. If the load is moved down an inclined conveyor, the power will be supplied to the belt by the load.

Table 11-10 Horsepower required to lift a load*

Net lift, ft	Load, tons per hr											
	50	100	150	200	250	300	350	400	500	600	800	1,000
5	0.3	0.5	0.8	1.0	1.3	1.5	1.8	2.0	2.5	3.0	4.0	5.1
10	0.5	1.0	1.5	2.0	2.5	3.0	3.5	4.0	5.1	6.1	8.1	10.0
15	0.8	1.5	2.3	3.0	3.8	4.5	5.3	6.1	7.6	9.1	12.0	15.0
20	1.0	2.0	3.0	4.0	5.1	6.1	7.1	8.1	10.0	12.0	16.0	20.0
25	1.3	2.5	3.8	5.1	6.3	7.6	8.8	10.0	13.0	15.0	20.0	25.0
30	1.5	3.0	4.5	6.1	7.6	9.1	11.0	12.0	15.0	18.0	24.0	30.0
40	2.0	4.0	6.1	8.1	10.0	12.0	14.0	16.0	20.0	24.0	32.0	40.0
50	2.5	5.1	7.6	10.0	13.0	15.0	18.0	20.0	25.0	30.0	40.0	51.0
75	3.8	7.6	11.0	15.0	19.0	23.0	27.0	30.0	38.0	45.0	61.0	76.0
100	5.1	10.0	15.0	20.0	25.0	30.0	35.0	40.0	51.0	61.0	81.0	101
125	6.3	13.0	19.0	25.0	32.0	38.0	44.0	51.0	63.0	76.0	101	126
150	7.6	15.0	23.0	30.0	38.0	45.0	53.0	61.0	76.0	91.0	121	152
200	10.0	20.0	30.0	40.0	51.0	61.0	71.0	81.0	101	121	162	202
300	15.0	30.0	45.0	61.0	76.0	91.0	106	121	152	185	242	303
400	20.0	40.0	61.0	81.0	101	121	141	162	202	242	323	404
500	25.0	51.0	76.0	101	126	151	177	202	252	303	404	505

* Courtesy Hewitt-Robins.

DRIVING EQUIPMENT

A belt conveyor may be driven through the head or tail pulley or through an intermediate pulley. In the event high driving forces are required, it may be necessary to use more than one pulley, with the pulleys arranged in tandem to increase the areas of contact with the belt. Smooth-faced or lagged pulleys may be used, depending on the desired coefficient of friction between the belt and the pulley surface. The pulley may be driven by an electric motor or a gasoline or diesel engine. It is usually necessary to install a suitable speed reducer, such as gears, chain drives, or belt drives, between the power unit and the driving pulley. The power loss in the speed reducer should be included in determining the total power required to drive a belt conveyor. This loss may amount to 5 to 10 percent or more, depending on the type of speed reducer.

The coefficient of friction between a steel shaft and babbitted bearings will be approximately 0.10.

When the power is transmitted from a driving pulley to a belt, the effective driving force, which is transmitted to the belt, is equal to the tension in the tight side less the tension in the slack side of the belt, expressed in pounds.

$$T_e = T_1 - T_2 \tag{11-7}$$

where T_e =effective tension or driving force between pulley and belt
   T_1 =tension in tight side of belt
   T_2 =tension in slack side of belt

The coefficient of friction between a rubber belt and a bare steel or cast-iron pulley is approximately 0.25. If the surface of a pulley is lagged with a rubberized fabric, the coefficient of friction will be increased to approximately 0.35.

When power is transmitted from a pulley to a belt, the tension in the slack side of the belt should not exceed the amount required to prevent slippage between the pulley and the belt. For a driving pulley with a given diameter and speed, the effective tension T_e required to transmit a given horsepower to the belt may be determined from the following equation,

$$P = \frac{\pi D T_e N}{33,000} \tag{11-8}$$

where P =hp transmitted to belt
   D =diameter of pulley, ft
   T_e =effective force between pulley and belt, lb
   N =rpm

The equation may be rewritten as

$$T_e = \frac{33,000P}{\pi DN} \tag{11-9}$$

The ratio T_1/T_e is defined as the pulley tension factor. This factor varies with the type of pulley surface, bare or lagged, and the arc of contact between the belt and the pulley. Values for the factor are given in Table 11-11. The factor

**Table 11-11 Tension factors
for driving pulleys***

Arc of contact, deg	Bare pulley	Lagged pulley
Single-pulley drive		
200	1.72	1.42
210	1.70	1.40
215	1.65	1.38
220	1.62	1.35
240	1.54	1.30
Tandem drive		
360	1.26	1.13
380	1.23	1.11
400	1.21	1.10
450	1.18	1.09
500	1.14	1.06

* Courtesy Hewitt-Robins.

may be expressed as

$$F = \frac{T_1}{T_e} \tag{11-10}$$

If the required effective force T_e between a pulley and a belt whose arc of contact is 210° is 3,000 lb, the minimum tension in the tight side of the belt may be determined from Eq. (11-10) and Table 11-11. From Table 11-11, $F = 1.70$ for a bare pulley.

$T_1 = FT_e$

$= 1.70 \times 3,000 = 5,100$ lb

If the same pulley is lagged, the value of F will be 1.40 and

$T_1 = 1.40 \times 3,000 = 4,200$ lb

For these conditions the minimum values of T_1, T_2, and T_e will be as follows:

	Bare pulley	Lagged pulley
T_1	5,100 lb	4,200 lb
T_e	3,000 lb	3,000 lb
T_2	2,100 lb	1,200 lb

Thus, it is evident that by lagging a drive pulley the tension in a belt may be reduced, possibly enough to permit the use of a lighter and less expensive belt.

Table 11-12 Percent of shaft horsepower required to overcome pulley friction for conveyors with head drive and babbitted bearings*

Length of conveyor, ft	Slope of conveyor, %				
	0	2-10	10-19	19-29	29-36
20	112	93	53	35	28
30	76	63	36	25	19
50	45	38	22	15	13
75	30	25	15	12	9
100	22	19	11	8	7
150	15	14	9	7	6
200	14	11	8	6	5
250	12	10	7	5	5
300	11	8	6	5	4
400	9	6	5	4	4
500	7	6	5	4	3
600	6	5	4	3	3
700	5	4	4	3	3
800	4	4	3	3	3
1,000	4	4	3	3	3
2,000	4	4	3		
3,000	4	3	3		

* Courtesy Hewitt-Robins.
  For antifriction bearings use one-half of the above percentages.

POWER REQUIRED TO TURN PULLEYS

A belt conveyor includes several pulleys, around which the belt is bent. For the shaft of each pulley there is a bearing friction that requires the consumption of power. The power required will vary with the tension in the belt, the weight of the pulley and shaft, and the type of bearing, babbitted or antifriction. For a given conveyor the friction factors for each pulley may be determined reasonably accurately, and from this information the additional power required to compensate for the loss due to pulley friction may be obtained. Table 11-12 gives the percent of the power delivered to a conveyor required to overcome pulley friction for conveyors with head drive and babbitted bearings for all pulley shafts.

CONVEYOR-BELT TAKE-UPS

Because of the tendency of a conveyor belt to elongate after it is put into operation, it is necessary to provide a method of adjusting for the increase in length.

A screw take-up may be used to increase the length of the conveyor by moving the head or tail pulley. This adjustment may be sufficient for a short belt but not for a long belt (see Fig. 11-3).

Another take-up, which is more satisfactory, depends on forcing the returning belt to travel under a weighted pulley, which provides a uniform tension in the belt regardless of the variation in length.

HOLDBACKS

If a belt conveyor is operated on an incline, it is advisable to install a holdback on the driving pulley to prevent the load from causing the belt to run backward in the event of a power failure. A holdback is a mechanical device which permits a driving pulley to rotate in the normal direction but prevents it from rotating in the opposite direction. The operation of a holdback should be automatic. At least three types are available. They are the roller, ratchet, and differential band brake, all of which operate automatically.

A holdback must be strong enough to resist the force produced by the load less the sum of the forces required to move the empty belt, move the load horizontally, turn the pulleys, drive the tripper, and to overcome drive losses.

If a belt conveyor is operated on a decline, the effect of the load is to move the belt forward. If this effect exceeds the total forces of friction, it will be necessary to install a suitable braking unit to regulate the speed of the belt. To overcome this difficulty, an electric motor or generator may be used as the driving unit. In starting an empty belt, the unit will act as a motor, but when the effect of the load is sufficient to overcome all resistances, the unit will act as a generator to regulate the belt speed.

FEEDERS

The purpose of a feeder is to deliver material to a belt at a uniform rate. A feeder may discharge directly onto a belt, or it may discharge the material through a chute in order to reduce the impact of the falling material on the belt. Several types of feeders are available, each of which has advantages and disadvantages when compared with another type. Among the more popular types are the following:

1. Apron
2. Reciprocating
3. Rotary vane
4. Rotary plow

An apron feeder usually receives the material from a gated hopper, which regulates the flow onto the feeder. The feeder consists of a moving, flat, rubber-covered belt or a number of flat steel plates connected to two moving chains. This feeder moves the material from under the hopper and discharges it through a receiving unit onto the conveyor belt. A belt feeder is suitable for handling material consisting of relatively small pieces. If the material contains large pieces of highly abrasive rock or stone, a steel-plate-type feeder will usually prove more satisfactory than a belt type.

A reciprocating feeder consists of steel plate placed under a hopper. The plate is operated through an eccentric drive to produce the reciprocating effect, which moves the material onto the conveyor belt.

A rotary-vane feeder consists of a number of vanes mounted on a horizontal shaft. As the material flows down an inclined plane, the rotating vanes deliver measured amounts to the conveyor. The rate of feeding may be regulated by varying the speed of the rotating vanes.

A rotary-plow feeder consists of a number of plows, or vanes, mounted on a vertical shaft. The plows rotate over a horizontal table onto which the material is allowed to flow. The rate of feeding may be regulated by varying the speed of the plows.

TRIPPERS

When it is necessary to remove material from a belt conveyor before it reaches the end of the belt, a tripper should be installed on the conveyor. A tripper consists of a pair of pulleys which are so located that the loaded belt must pass over one pulley and under the other. As the belt passes over the top pulley, the load will be discharged from the belt into an auxiliary hopper or chute.

A tripper may be stationary or a traveling type. The latter type may be propelled by a hand-operated crank, a separate motor, or the conveyor belt. If a tripper is installed on a conveyor, additional power should be provided to operate it. Figure 11-8 illustrates a belt-propelled automatically controlled tripper.

Example Belt-conveyor design Design a belt conveyor to transport unsized crushed limestone. The essential information is as follows:

Capacity, 300 tons per hr
Horizontal distance, 360 ft
Vertical lift, 40 ft
Maximum size stone, 6 in.
Weight of stone, 100 lb per cu ft
Required belt width, from Table 11-2, 24 in.
Maximum speed, from Table 11-3, 400 fpm
Capacity at 400 fpm, from Table 11-2, 4 × 100 = 400 tons per hr
Required belt speed, $\frac{400 \times 300}{400}$ = 300 fpm

This speed, 300 fpm, will be satisfactory provided the feeder supplies material at a uniform rate. If the rate of feeding is irregular, it may be necessary to increase the speed to assure the specified rate of delivery. The design will be based on a speed of 350 fpm to provide a margin of safety.

Figure 11-8 Belt-propelled automatically controlled tripper.

The power required to operate the loaded conveyor will be as follows:

To drive the empty belt, Table 11-8, $0.81 \times 350/100 =$ 2.84 hp
To move the load horizontally, Table 11-9   = 3.92 hp
To lift the load, Table 11-10   = 12.00 hp
   Subtotal   = 18.76 hp
For pulley friction, Table 11-12, 4% of 18.76   = 0.75 hp
   Subtotal required by belt   = 19.51 hp
For drive losses, 10% of 19.51   = 1.95 hp
   Total power required   = 21.46 hp

Determine the type, size, and number of driving pulleys required to operate the belt. The belt will be driven through a head pulley. When a belt is driven by a pulley, the effective driving force transmitted to the belt is equal to the difference in the belt tensions on the tight side and the slack side, expressed in pounds. This difference is referred to as the effective driving force or tension. Let

T_1 = tight-side tension

T_2 = slack-side tension

T_e = effective tension

$T_e = T_1 - T_2$

The value of T_e can be determined from the horsepower transmitted to the belt and the belt speed in fpm.

$$T_e = \frac{hp \times 33,000}{belt\ speed,\ fpm} = \frac{19.5 \times 33,000}{350} = 1,838\ lb$$

$T_1 - T_2 = 1,838\ lb$

It is desirable to operate the belt at the lowest practical tight-side and slack-side tensions. The necessary tensions are maintained by the take-ups. The maximum slack-side tension will occur as the belt leaves the driving pulley. This tension will equal the tension at the tail pulley plus the weight of the vertical component of the belt. Field observations indicate that the tension in the belt at the loading point should be not less than 20 lb per in. of belt width. This tension will be transmitted to the slack side of the belt at the tail pulley. The minimum possible slack-side tension will be

Tension at tail pulley, 20 × 24   = 480 lb
Weight of belt, 40 ft × 6 lb per ft = 240 lb
　　Total tension　　　　　　 = 720 lb

The values of T_1 and T_2 for each of three driving arrangements will be as follows:

Arc of contact, deg	T_1, lb	T_2, lb
	Single bare drive	
215	1,838 × 1.65 = 3,035	3,035 − 1,838 = 1,197
220	1,838 × 1.62 = 2,980	2,980 − 1,838 = 1,142
	Single lagged drive	
215	1,838 × 1.38 = 2,538	2,538 − 1,838 = 700
220	1,838 × 1.35 = 2,480	2,480 − 1,838 = 642
	Tandem bare drive	
400	1,838 × 1.21 = 2,225	2,225 − 1,838 = 387
450	1,838 × 1.18 = 2,170	2,170 − 1,838 = 332

Regardless of the type of drive selected, the minimum slack-side tension in the belt just as it leaves the head pulley will be 720 lb. Adding the effective tension T_e gives a minimum tight-side tension of 720 + 1,838 = 2,558 lb. If, for a single lagged drive, with an arc of contact of 215°, T_2 is increased to 720 lb, T_1 will be 2,558 lb, which satisfies the tension requirements. Thus, a single lagged pulley will be used to drive the belt.

Reference to Table 11-4 indicates that a 3-ply 42-oz belt has a safe working stress of 2,640 lb, which is satisfactory. The thickness of this belt will permit it to trough satisfactorily. Reference to Table 11-4 indicates that the minimum pulley diameters should be head, 20 in.; tail, take-up, and snub, 16 in.; bend, 12 in.

The troughing idlers should be 5 in. in diameter, spaced 5 ft 0 in. apart, with a maximum spacing of 1 ft 6 in. at the loading point. The return idlers should be 5 in. in diameter, spaced 10 ft 0 in. apart.

Examples illustrating the use of belt-conveyor systems

The following two examples demonstrate some of the advantages of using belt-conveyors on construction projects.

Example 1 When the Los Angeles County Flood Control District prepared an estimate covering the cost of removing 7,300,000 tons of silt, sand, and gravel from the lake bed above the San Gabriel Dam in California, the estimate was based on use of conventional equipment for excavating and hauling the material to a dump site some 800 ft above the lake. It was estimated that the project would cost $7,977,000 and that it would require 857 days to complete the job. The project was awarded to a contractor at a cost of $4,593,000. He completed the project in some 200 days less than the allotted time.

The contractor installed a belt-conveyor system consisting of 165 flights of belts, each 105 ft long and 48 in. wide, to transport the material from the lake to the disposal area. The electric motor selected to power each flight varied from 40 to 100 hp, depending on the slope of the flight. In order to ensure the same rate of flow of the material on each flight all belts operated at the same speed.

A feature of the system was continuous weighing of the material as it moved along on the belt, giving a metered readout of the total tonnage measured from the start of a shift, with another meter showing the cumulative total from the beginning of the week. Still another meter indicated continuously the percent of maximum capacity the belt was carrying at any given time.

The conveyor was loaded at two separate portable stations by tractor-mounted front-end loaders. The method permitted one station to be moved to another location as necessary, while loading was continued at the other station. Grizzlies were installed at the loader stations to remove any boulders that were too large for the conveyor to handle [1].

Example 2 When the earth-filled Portage Dam on the Peace River in British Columbia, Canada, was constructed, it was necessary to transport 57,500,000 cu yd of earth over a distance of approximately 3 miles. The earth was excavated from moraine deposits by bulldozers, which fed the material downhill to trap loaders similar to the ones illustrated in Fig. 8-36. The trap loaders fed portable shuttle conveyors, which transferred the soil to two fixed gathering conveyors. The gathering conveyors then transferred the soil to the permanently installed plant-feed conveyor.

When material in a given location became depleted or an excessively long dozer haul was required, the trap loaders and the shuttle conveyors were moved to new locations nearer the available material.

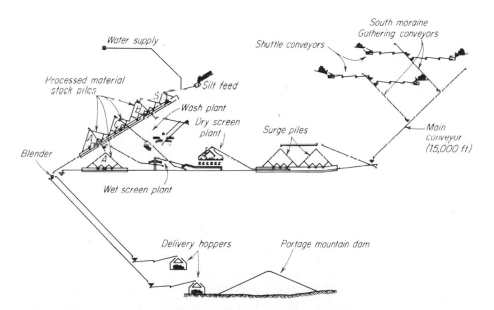

Figure 11-9 Portage Mountain Dam conveying and processing system.

Table 11-13. Details of Belt-Conveyor Equipment for the Portage Mountain Dam

Item	Elevation difference, ft	Belt width, in.	Length of belt, ft	Capacity, tons per hr	Speed, ft per min	Motor horsepower	Location
Belt loaders	------	60	25	3,500	450	1 × 100	Moraine
Shuttle conveyors	Variable	48	100	3,500	600	1 × 100	Moraine
Gathering conveyor	146F*	60	2,000	6,000	800	2 × 500	Moraine
Gathering conveyor	180F	60	1,000	6,000	800	2 × 500	Moraine
Plant feed conveyor	350F	66	15,000	12,000	1,150	4 × 850	Moraine to plant
Conveyor No. 1	98R*	72	655	12,000	900	3 × 500	Surge pile to feed
Conveyor No. 2	75F	72	2,136	12,000	900	2 × 125	Plant feed to blender
Conveyor No. 3	75R	60	540	6,300	700	1 × 500 1 × 200	Surge pile to dry screen
Conveyor No. 4	25R	48	241	2,100	400	1 × 125	$-\frac{3}{8}$-in. material dry screen to stockpile
Conveyor No. 5	14R	48	199	2,100	400	1 × 75	$-\frac{3}{8}$-in. material dry screen to stockpile
Conveyor No. 6	62R	48	364	2,700	600	1 × 200 1 × 100	$-\frac{3}{8}$-in. material dry screen to wet screen
Conveyor No. 7	97R	48	466	3,000	600	2 × 200	Wet screen to stockpile
Conveyor No. 7A	0	48	123	3,000	600	1 × 30	Wet screen to stockpile
Conveyor No. 8	100R	48	502	4,200	700	1 × 500 1 × 200	$-\frac{3}{8}$-in. material to stockpile to wash plant
Conveyor No. 9	16R	48	211	1,800	500	1 × 75	Wash plant to stockpile
Conveyor No. 9A	60R	48	220	1,800	550	2 × 75	Wash plant to stockpile
Conveyor No. 9B	17R	48	94	1,800	550	1 × 75	Wash pile to stockpile
Conveyor No. 10	7F	60	778	6,000	600	1 × 200	Reclaim from stockpile
Conveyor No. A	312F	60	1,907	6,000	800	3 × 500	Blender to dam
Conveyor No. B	303F	60	1,874	6,000	800	3 × 500	Blender to dam
Conveyor A₁ and A₂	Variable	60	122	6,000	800	1 × 200 1 × 75	Blender to dam
Conveyor B₁ and B₂	Variable	60	122	6,000	800	1 × 200 1 × 75	Blender to dam

F designates a fall; R designates a rise.

Because the specifications required a stated grading for the soil, it was necessary to blend different classes of soil before placing it in the dam. Part of the blending was accomplished by the bulldozers before the loads were deposited on the trap loaders. Final blending was performed at the blender, as illustrated in Fig. 11-9.

The soil was hauled by trucks from the delivery hoppers to the dam.

Table 11-13 lists pertinent information concerning the details of the conveyor equipment for the project [2].

PROBLEMS

11-1 Determine the minimum belt width and the minimum belt speed, in fpm, required to transport 400 tph of unsized crushed stone weighing 100 lb per cu ft. The maximum size of the stone is 5 in.

11-2 What is the capacity of a 30-in.-wide belt, in tph, when the belt is transporting gravel weighing 100 lb per cu ft and is moving at the maximum recommended speed?

11-3 A conveyor 400 ft long with a 30-in.-wide 5-ply 36-oz belt is used to transport material weighing 125 lb per cu ft. The angle of repose for the material is 20°. The revolving parts will weigh 36 lb for each troughing idler and 25 lb for each return idler. Both idlers are 5 in. in diameter and are equipped with antifriction bearings. Determine the horsepower required to move this belt at a speed of 300 fpm.

11-4 Using the information given in Table 11-7, determine the horsepower required to move an empty conveyor belt 30 in. wide on a 1,200-ft-long conveyor equipped with 5-in.-diameter idlers with antifriction bearings when the belt is moving at a speed of 300 fpm.

11-5 If the belt of Prob. 11-4 transports 350 tph up a 4 percent slope, determine the power required when the belt is moving at the minimum speed necessary to transport the material. The material weighs 100 lb per cu ft.

11-6 A 4-ply 36-in.-wide belt on a conveyor 600 ft long will be used to transport its maximum capacity of unsized gravel weighing 125 lb per cu ft up a 6 percent slope, using 5-in. antifriction idlers. Determine the power required to operate the belt when it is traveling at its maximum recommended speed.

11-7 Design a conveyor belt system to transport 300 tph of crushed stone under the following conditions:

Weight of stone, 125 lb per cu ft
Horizontal distance, 500 ft
Vertical lift, 70 ft
Use 5-in.-diameter idlers with antifriction bearings.

The design should furnish the following information:

The required width of the belt
The number of plies required for the belt
The required belt speed
The number of 5-in. diameter troughing and return idlers required
The spacing of the idlers
The minimum diameters of the head, tail, take-up, snub, and bend pulleys

REFERENCES

1. Belt-conveyor System Wins Cleanout Job, *Construction Methods and Equipment*, vol. 51, pp. 154-157, March 1969.
2. Low, W. Irvine, Portage Mountain Dam Conveyor System, *Journal of the Construction Division, American Society of Civil Engineers*, vol. 93, pp. 33-51, September 1967.

TWELVE

COMPRESSED AIR

GENERAL INFORMATION

Compressed air is used extensively on construction projects for drilling rock or other hard formations, loosening earth, operating air motors, hand tools, pile drivers, pumps, mucking equipment, cleaning, etc. In many instances the energy supplied by compressed air is the most convenient method of operating equipment and tools.

When air is compressed, it receives energy from the compressor. This energy is transmitted through a pipe or hose to the operating equipment, where a portion of the energy is converted into mechanical work. The operations of compressing, transmitting, and using air will always result in a loss of energy, which will give an overall efficiency less than 100 percent, sometimes considerably less.

FUNDAMENTAL GAS LAWS

As air is a gas, it obeys, within reason, the fundamental laws which apply to gases. The laws with which we are concerned are related to the pressure, volume, temperature, and transmission of air.

DEFINITIONS OF GAS-LAW TERMS

In order to understand the laws which relate to compressed air, it is necessary to define certain terms which are used in developing and applying these laws. The essential definitions are as follows:

> *Gauge pressure*   This is the pressure exerted by the air in excess of atmospheric pressure. It is usually expressed in psi or inches of mercury and is measured by a pressure gauge or a mercury manometer.

Absolute pressure   This is the total pressure measured from absolute zero. It is equal to the sum of the gauge and the atmospheric pressure, corresponding to the barometric reading. The absolute pressure should be used in dealing with the laws of gases.

Psi is the abbreviation for pounds per square inch of pressure.

Psf is the abbreviation for pounds per square foot of pressure.

Vacuum   This is a measure of the extent to which pressure is less than atmospheric pressure. For example, a vacuum of 5 psi is equivalent to an absolute pressure of $14.7 - 5 = 9.7$ psi.

Standard conditions   Because of the variations in the volume of air with pressure and temperature it is necessary to express the volume at standard conditions if it is to have a definite meaning. Standard conditions are an absolute pressure of 14.7 psi and a temperature of 60°F.

Temperature   Temperature is a measure of the amount of heat contained by a unit quantity of gas. It is measured with a thermometer or some other suitable temperature-indicating device.

Fahrenheit temperature   This is the temperature indicated by a thermometer calibrated according to the Fahrenheit scale. For this thermometer pure water freezes at 32°F and boils at 212°F, at a pressure of 14.7 psi. Thus, the number of degrees between freezing and boiling water is 180.

Celsius temperature   This is the temperature indicated by a thermometer calibrated according to the Celsius scale. For this thermometer pure water freezes at 0°C and boils at 100°C, at a pressure of 14.7 psi.

Relation between Fahrenheit and Celsius temperatures   As 180° on the Fahrenheit scale equals 100° on the Celsius scale, 1°C equals 1.8°F. A Fahrenheit thermometer will read 32° when a Celsius thermometer reads 0°.

Let T_F = Fahrenheit temperature and T_C = Celsius temperature. For any given temperature the thermometer readings are expressed by the following equation:

$$T_F = 32 + 1.8 T_C \tag{12-1}$$

Absolute temperature   This is the temperature of a **gas** measured above absolute zero. It equals degrees Fahrenheit plus 459.6 or, as more commonly used, 460.

ISOTHERMAL COMPRESSION

When a gas undergoes a change in volume without any change in temperature, this is referred to as isothermal expansion or compression.

ADIABATIC COMPRESSION

When a gas undergoes a change in volume without gaining or losing heat, this is referred to as adiabatic expansion or compression.

Boyle's law states that when a gas is subjected to a change in volume due to a change in pressure, at a constant temperature, the product of the pressure times the volume will remain constant. This relation is expressed by the equation

$$P_1 V_1 = P_2 V_2 = K \tag{12-2}$$

where P_1 = initial absolute pressure
$\quad\quad V_1$ = initial volume
$\quad\quad P_2$ = final absolute pressure
$\quad\quad V_2$ = final volume
$\quad\quad K$ = a constant

Example Determine the final volume of 1,000 cu ft of air when the gauge pressure is increased from 20 to 120 psi, with no change in temperature. The barometer indicates an atmospheric pressure of 14.7 psi.

$P_1 = 20 + 14.7 = 34.7$ psi

$P_2 = 120 + 14.7 = 134.7$ psi

$V_1 = 1,000$ cu ft

From Eq. (12-2)

$$V_2 = \frac{P_1 V_1}{P_2} = \frac{34.7 \times 1,000}{134.7} = 257.8 \text{ cu ft}$$

BOYLE'S AND CHARLES' LAWS

When a gas undergoes a change in volume or pressure with a change in temperature, Boyle's law will not apply. Charles' law introduces the effect of absolute temperature on the volume of a gas when the pressure is maintained constant. It states that the volume of a given weight of gas at constant pressure varies in direct proportion to its absolute temperature. It may be expressed mathematically by the equation

$$\frac{V_1}{T_1} = \frac{V_2}{T_2} = C \tag{12-3}$$

where V_1 = initial volume
$\quad\quad T_1$ = initial absolute temperature
$\quad\quad V_2$ = final volume
$\quad\quad T_2$ = final absolute temperature
$\quad\quad C$ = a constant

The laws of Boyle and Charles may be combined to give the equation

$$\frac{P_1 V_1}{T_1} = \frac{P_2 V_2}{T_2} = \text{a constant} \tag{12-4}$$

Equation (12-4) may be used to express the relations between pressure, volume, and temperature for any given gas, such as air. It is illustrated by the following example.

Example One thousand cubic feet of air, at an initial gauge pressure of 40 psi and temperature of 50°F, is compressed to a volume of 200 cu ft at a final temperature of 110°F. Determine the final gauge pressure. The atmospheric pressure is 14.46 psi.

$P_1 = 40 + 14.46 = 54.46$ psi

$V_1 = 1,000$ cu ft

$T_1 = 460 + 50 = 510°F$

$V_2 = 200$ cu ft

$T_2 = 460 + 110 = 570°F$

Rewriting Eq. (12-4) and substituting these values, we get

$$P_2 = \frac{P_1 V_1}{T_1} \frac{T_2}{V_2} = \frac{54.46 \times 1,000}{510} \frac{570}{200} = 304 \text{ psi}$$

Final gauge pressure $= 304 - 14.46 = 289.54$ psi.

ENERGY REQUIRED TO COMPRESS AIR

Equation (12-2) may be expressed as $PV = K$, where K is a constant so long as the temperature remains constant. However, in actual practice the temperature usually will not remain constant, and the equation must be modified to provide for the effect of changes in temperature. The effect of temperature may be provided for by introducing an exponent n to V. Thus, Eq. (12-2) may be rewritten as

$$P_1 V_1^n = P_2 V_2^n = K \tag{12-5}$$

For air the values of n will vary from 1.0 for isothermal compression to 1.4 for adiabatic compression. The actual value for any compression condition may be determined experimentally from an indicator card obtained from a given compressor.

When the pressure of a given volume of air is increased by an air compressor, it is necessary to furnish energy to the air. Consider a single compression cycle for an air compressor, as indicated in Fig. 12-1. Air is drawn into the cylinder at pressure P_1 and is discharged at pressure P_2. P_1 does not need to be atmospheric pressure. The initial volume is V_1. As the piston compresses the air, the pressure-volume will follow the curve CD. At D, when the pressure is P_2, the discharge valve will open and the pressure will remain constant while the volume decreases to V_2, as indicated by line DE. Point E represents the end of the piston stroke. At point E the discharge valve will close, and as the piston begins its return stroke, the pressure will decrease along line EB to a value of P_1, when the intake valve will open and allow additional air to enter the cylinder. This will establish line BC.

The work done along the line CD may be obtained by integrating the equation $dW = V\, dP$.

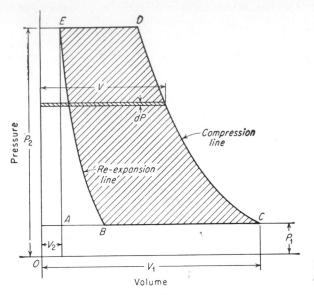

Figure 12-1 Cycle for isothermal compression of air.

From Eq. (12-5), $V^n = K/P$. If both sides of the equation are raised to the $1/n$ power, the equation will be

$$V = \left(\frac{K}{P}\right)^{1/n}$$

Substituting this value of V gives

$$dW = \left(\frac{K}{P}\right)^{1/n} dP$$

Integrating gives

$$W = K^{1/n} \int_1^2 \frac{dP}{P^{1/n}} \tag{12-6}$$

For isothermal compression $n = 1$. Substituting this value in Eq. (12-6) gives

$$W = K \int_1^2 \frac{dP}{P} = -K \log_e \frac{P_2}{P_1} + C$$

When $P_2 = P_1$ and no work is done, the constant of integration is equal to zero. The minus sign may be disregarded. Thus, for isothermal compression of air, the equation may be written as

$$W = K \log_e \frac{P_2}{P_1} \tag{12-7}$$

If it is desired to convert from natural to common logarithms, $\log_e (P_2/P_1)$ may be replaced by 2.302 log (P_2/P_1). For the given compression conditions

$n = 1$, and $K = P_1V_1$. If the compression is started on air at standard conditions, P_1 will be 14.7 psi at 60°F. Since work is commonly expressed in foot-pounds, it is necessary to express P_1 in psf. This is done by multiplying P_1 by 144. When these substitutions are made, equation (12-7) may be written as

$$W = 14.7 \times 144 V_1 \times 2.302 \log \frac{P_2}{P_1}$$

$$= 4{,}883 V_1 \log \frac{P_2}{P_1} \tag{12-8}$$

The value of W is in foot-pounds per cycle. One horsepower is equivalent to 33,000 ft-lb per min. If V_1 in Eq. (12-8) is replaced by V, the volume of free air per minute at standard conditions, the horsepower required to compress V cu ft of air from an absolute pressure of P_1 to P_2 psi will be

$$\text{hp} = \frac{4{,}833 V \log(P_2/P_1)}{33{,}000}$$

$$\text{hp} = 0.1479 V \log \frac{P_2}{P_1} \tag{12-9}$$

Example Determine the theoretical horsepower required to compress 100 cu ft of free air per minute, measured at standard conditions, from atmospheric pressure to 100 psi gauge pressure. Substituting in Eq. (12-9), we get

$$\text{hp} = 0.1479 \times 100 \times \log \frac{114.7}{14.7}$$

$$= 14.79 \times \log 7.8$$

$$= 14.79 \times 0.892$$

$$= 13.2$$

If air is compressed under other than isothermal conditions, the equation for the required horsepower may be derived in a similar manner. However, since n will not equal 1, it must appear as an exponent in the equation. Equation (12-10) gives the horsepower for nonisothermal conditions.

$$\text{hp} = \frac{n}{n-1} 0.0643 V \left[\left(\frac{P_2}{P_1} \right)^{(n-1)/n} - 1 \right] \tag{12-10}$$

where the terms are the same as those used in Eq. (12-9).

Example Determine the theoretical horsepower required to compress 100 cu ft of free air per minute, measured at standard conditions, from atmospheric pressure to 100 psi gauge pressure, under adiabatic conditions. The value of n will be 1.4 for air for adiabatic compression. Substituting in Eq. (12-10), we get

$$\text{hp} = \frac{1.4}{1.4 - 1} \times 0.0643 \times 100(7.8^{0.4/1.4} - 1)$$

$$= 22.5(7.8^{0.286} - 1)$$

$$= 22.5 \times 0.79$$

$$= 17.8$$

For air compressors used on construction projects the compression will be performed under conditions between isothermal and adiabatic. Thus, the theoretical horsepower will be between 13.2 and 17.8, the actual value depending on the extent to which the compressor is cooled during operation. The difference in the horsepowers required illustrates the importance of operating an air compressor at the lowest practical temperature.

EFFECT OF ALTITUDE ON THE POWER REQUIRED TO COMPRESS AIR

When a given volume of air, measured as free air prior to its entering a compressor, is compressed, the original pressure will average 14.7 psi absolute pressure at sea level. If the same volume of free air is compressed to the same gauge pressure at a higher altitude, the volume of the air after being compressed will be less than the volume compressed at sea level. The reason for this difference is that there is less air in a cubic foot of free air at 5,000 ft than at sea level. Thus, while a compressor may compress air to the same discharge pressure at a higher altitude, the volume supplied in a given time interval will be less at the higher altitude. The use of Eq. (12-2) and the information in Table 4-4 (page 97) will demonstrate the correctness of this statement.

Because a compressor of a specified capacity actually supplies a smaller volume of air at a given discharge pressure at a higher altitude, it requires less power to operate a compressor at a higher altitude, as illustrated in Table 12-1.

Table 12-1 Theoretical horsepower required to compress 100 cu ft of free air per min at different altitudes*

Altitude, ft	Isothermal compression Single- and two-stage gauge pressure				Adiabatic compression						
					Single-stage gauge pressure			Two-stage gauge pressure			
	60	80	100	125	60	80	100	60	80	100	125
0	10.4	11.9	13.2	14.4	13.4	15.9	18.1	11.8	13.7	15.4	17.1
1,000	10.2	11.7	12.9	14.1	13.2	15.6	17.8	11.6	13.5	15.1	16.8
2,000	10.0	11.4	12.6	13.8	13.0	15.4	17.5	11.4	13.2	14.8	16.4
3,000	9.8	11.2	12.3	13.5	12.8	15.2	17.2	11.2	13.0	14.5	16.1
4,000	9.6	11.0	12.1	13.2	12.6	14.9	16.9	11.0	12.7	14.2	15.7
5,000	9.4	10.7	11.8	12.8	12.4	14.7	16.5	10.8	12.5	13.9	15.4
6,000	9.2	10.5	11.5	12.5	12.2	14.4	16.2	10.6	12.2	13.6	15.1
7,000	9.0	10.3	11.2	12.2	12.0	14.2	16.0	10.4	12.0	13.4	14.8
8,000	8.9	10.0	11.0	11.9	11.8	14.0	15.7	10.2	11.8	13.1	14.5
9,000	8.7	9.8	10.7	11.6	11.6	13.7	15.4	10.0	11.6	12.8	14.1
10,000	8.5	9.6	10.4	11.4	11.5	13.5	15.1	9.8	11.3	12.6	13.8

* Compressed Air and Gas Institute.

AIR-COMPRESSOR DEFINITIONS AND TERMS

Many terms related to air compressors and compressed air have assumed uniform meanings. The essential terms are defined hereafter.

Air compressor   This is a machine which is used to increase the pressure of air by reducing its volume.

Reciprocating compressor   This is a machine which compresses air by means of a piston reciprocating in a cylinder.

Single-acting compressor   This compressor is a machine which compresses air in only one end of a cylinder.

Double-acting compressor   The double-acting compressor is a machine which compresses air in both ends of a cylinder.

Single-stage compressor   This is a machine which compresses air from atmospheric pressure to the desired discharge pressure in a single operation.

Two-stage compressor   This is a machine which compresses air in two separate operations. The first operation compresses the air to an intermediate pressure, while the second operation further compresses it to the desired final pressure.

Multistage compressor   This is a compressor which produces the desired final pressure through two or more stages.

Rotary compressor   The rotary compressor is a machine in which the compression is effected by the action of rotating elements.

Centrifugal compressor   This compressor is a machine in which the compression is effected by a rotating vane or impeller that imparts velocity to the flowing air to give it the desired pressure.

Intercooler   The intercooler is a heat exchanger which is placed between two compression stages to remove the heat of compression from the air.

Aftercooler   This is a heat exchanger which cools the air after it is discharged from a compressor.

Inlet pressure   This is the absolute pressure of the air at the inlet to a compressor.

Discharge pressure   Discharge pressure is the absolute pressure of the air at the outlet from a compressor.

Compression ratio   This is the ratio of the absolute discharge pressure to the absolute inlet pressure.

Free air   Free air is air as it exists under atmospheric conditions at any given location.

Cfm   Cfm is an abbreviation for cubic feet per minute.

Capacity   Capacity is the volume of air delivered by a compressor, expressed in cfm of free air.

Theoretical horsepower   This is the horsepower required to compress adiabatically the air delivered by a compressor through the specified pressure range, without any provision for lost energy.

Brake horsepower Brake horsepower is the actual horsepower input required by a compressor.

Compressor efficiency This is the ratio of the theoretical horsepower to the brake horsepower.

Volumetric efficiency This is the ratio of the capacity of a compressor to the piston displacement of the compressor.

Density of air This is the weight of a unit volume of air, usually expressed as pounds per cubic foot. Density varies with the pressure and temperature of the air. The weight of air at 60°F and 14.7 psi, absolute pressure, is 0.07658 lb per cu ft. The volume per pound is 13.059 cu ft.

Load factor The load factor is the ratio of the average load during a given period of time to the maximum rated load of a compressor.

Diversity factor This is the ratio of the actual quantity of air required for all uses to the sum of the individual quantities required for each use.

STATIONARY COMPRESSORS

Stationary compressors are generally used for installations where compressed air is required for a long period of time. The compressors may be reciprocating or rotary types, single-stage or multistage. The total quantity of air may be supplied by one or more compressors. The installed cost of a single compressor will usually be less than for several compressors having the same capacity. However, several compressors provide better flexibility for varying load demands, and, in

Figure 12-2 Two-stage stationary air compressor. *(Chicago Pneumatic Tool Company.)*

the event of a shutdown for repairs, the entire plant does not need to be stopped.

Stationary compressors may be driven by steam, electric motors, or internal-combustion engines.

PORTABLE COMPRESSORS

Portable compressors are used when it is necessary to move the equipment frequently to meet job demands. The compressors may be mounted on rubber tires, steel wheels, or skids. They may be driven by gasoline or diesel engines. They are available in single- or two-stage, reciprocating or rotary types.

Reciprocating compressors A reciprocating compressor depends on a piston, which moves back and forth in a cylinder, for the compressing action. The piston may compress air while moving in one or both directions. For the former it is defined as single-acting, while for the latter it is defined as double-acting. A compressor may have one or more cylinders.

Rotary compressors In recent years considerable effort has been directed toward the development of rotary compressors. These machines offer several advantages compared with reciprocating compressors, such as compactness, light weight, uniform flow, variable output, carefree operation, and long life.

Figure 12-4 illustrates a 600-cfm two-stage rotary compressor which has given excellent performance in the construction industry. Its operating weight is 9,500 lb, which is comparable with the weight of a 315-cfm portable reciprocating unit. The cost is approximately the same as for a 600-cfm reciprocating compressor.

Figure 12-3 Two stage diesel-engine-operated portable air compressor. *(Ingersoll-Rand Company.)*

Figure 12-4 Two-stage rotary air compressor. *(Ingersoll-Rand Company.)*

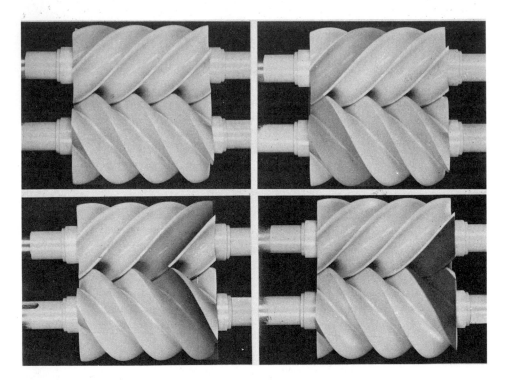

Figure 12-5 The operation of the helical rotors of a screw compressor. *(Atlas Copco, Inc.)*

344

Rotary Screw Compressors The working parts of a screw compressor are two helical rotors as illustrated in Fig. 12-5. The male rotor has four lobes and rotates 50 percent faster than the female rotor, which has six flutes, with which the male rotor meshes. As the air enters and flows through the compressor it is compressed in the space between the lobes and the flutes. The inlet and outlet ports are automatically covered and uncovered by the shaped ends of the rotors as they turn.

These compressors are available in a relatively wide range of capacities, with single- or multi-stage compression and with rotors which operate under oil-lubricated conditions or with no oil, the latter to produce oil-free air.

They offer several advantages when compared with other types of compressors, including but not limited to the following:

1. Quiet operation to satisfy a wide range of legal requirements limiting the permissible volume of noise, with little or no loss in output
2. Few moving parts, with minimum mechanical wear and little maintenance requirements
3. Automatic controls actuated by the output pressure, which regulate the speed of the driving unit and the compressor to limit the output to only the demand required
4. Little or no pulsation in the flow of air and hence reduced vibrations

Table 12-2 lists information applicable to representative screw compressors operated under standard conditions, namely absolute inlet air pressure equal to

Table 12-2 Representative specifications for rotary screw air compressors*

Capacity of free air		Normal operating pressure		Number of compression stages
cfm	cu m/min	psi	kp/cm²	
125	3.5	102	7	1
170	4.8	102	7	1
250	7.1	102	7	1
335	9.5	102	7	1
365	10.3	100	7	2
425	12.0	100	7	2
600	17.0	100	7	2
700	19.8	100	7	2
900	25.5	102	7	2
1,200	34.0	102	7	2
1,500	42.5	102	7	2

* Atlas Copco, Inc.

1 bar (1.02 kp/sq cm or 14.5 psi) and inlet air temperature and inlet coolant temperature equal to 15°C (60°F).

COMPRESSOR CAPACITY

Air compressors are rated by the piston displacement in cfm. However, the capacity of a compressor will be less than the piston displacement because of valve and piston leakage and the air left in the end-clearance spaces of the cylinders.

The capacity of a compressor is the actual volume of free air drawn into a compressor in a minute. It is expressed in cubic feet. For a reciprocating compressor in good mechanical condition the actual capacity should be 80 to 90 percent of the piston displacement. This is illustrated by an analysis of a 315-cfm two-stage portable compressor. The manufacturer's specifications give the following information:

No. low-pressure cylinders, 4
No. high-pressure cylinders, 2
Diameter of low-pressure cylinders, 7 in.
Diameter of high-pressure cylinders, $5\frac{3}{4}$ in.
Length of stroke, 5 in.
Rpm, 870

Consider the piston displacement of the low-pressure cylinders only as they determine the capacity of the unit.

Area of cylinder, $\dfrac{\pi \times 7^2}{4 \times 144}$ = 0.267 sq ft

Displacement per cylinder per stroke, $0.267 \times \frac{5}{12}$ = 0.111 cu ft
Displacement per minute, $4 \times 0.111 \times 870$ = 386 cu ft
Specified capacity, 315 cu ft
Volumetric efficiency, $315/386 \times 100$ = 81.6%

EFFECT OF ALTITUDE ON CAPACITY OF COMPRESSORS

The capacity of an air compressor is rated on the basis of its performance at sea level, where the normal absolute barometric pressure is about 14.7 psi. If a compressor is operated at a higher altitude, such as 5,000 ft above sea level, the absolute barometric pressure will be about 12.2 psi. Thus, at the higher altitude there is less air in a cubic foot of free volume than at sea level. If the air is discharged by the compressor at a given pressure, the compression ratio will be increased, and the capacity of the compressor will be reduced. This may be demonstrated by applying Eq. 12-2.

Assume that 100 cu ft of free air at sea level are compressed to 100 psi gauge with no change in temperature. Applying Eq. (12-2)

$$V_2 = \frac{P_1 V_1}{P_2}$$

where $V_1 = 100$ cu ft

$\quad\quad P_1 = 14.7$ psi absolute

$\quad\quad P_2 = 114.7$ psi absolute

$$V_2 = \frac{14.7 \times 100}{114.7} = 12.85 \text{ cu ft}$$

At 5,000 ft above sea level

$V_1 = 100$ cu ft

$P_1 = 12.2$ psi absolute

$P_2 = 112.2$ psi absolute

$$V_2 = \frac{12.2 \times 100}{112.2} = 10.87 \text{ cu ft}$$

Table 12-3 lists the factors that should be applied to single-stage compressors to correct for the loss in capacity at various altitudes. For example, a compressor having a sea-level capacity of 600 cfm operating at a pressure of 100 psi gauge will have a capacity at 5,000 ft equal to $600 \times 0.925 = 555.0$ cfm if the operating pressure is 100 psi gauge. At an altitude of 10,000 the capacity will be further reduced to $600 \times 0.840 = 504$ cfm.

INTERCOOLERS

Intercoolers frequently are installed between the stages of a compressor to reduce the temperature of the air and to remove moisture from the air. The reduction in temperature prior to additional compression can reduce the total power required by as much as 10 to 15 percent. Unless an intercooler is installed, the power required by a two-stage compressor will be the same as for a single-stage compressor.

An intercooler requires a continuous supply of circulating cool water to remove the heat from the air. It will require 1.0 to 1.5 gal of water per minute for each 100 cfm of air compressed, the actual amount depending on the temperature of the water.

AFTERCOOLERS

Aftercoolers are installed sometimes at the discharge side of a compressor to cool the air to the desired temperature and to remove moisture from the air. It is highly desirable to remove excess moisture from the air, as it tends to freeze during expansion in air tools, and it washes the lubricating oil out of tools, thereby reducing the lubricating efficiency.

Table 12-3 The effect of altitude on the capacity of single-stage air compressors*

Altitude above sea level, ft (m)	Operating pressure, psi gauge, [psi absolute], (Pa)							
	80 [94.7] (6.53 × 10⁵)		90 [104.7] (7.23 × 10⁵)		100 [114.7] (7.91 × 10⁵)		125 [139.7] (9.65 × 10⁵)	
	Compressor ratio†	Factor‡	Compressor ratio	Factor	Compressor ratio	Factor	Compressor ratio	Factor
0	6.44	1.000	7.12	1.000	7.81	1.000	9.51	1.000
1,000	6.64	0.992	7.34	0.988	8.05	0.987	9.81	0.982
(305)	6.64	0.992	7.34	0.988	8.05	0.987	9.81	0.982
2,000	6.88	0.977	7.62	0.972	8.35	0.972	10.20	0.962
(610)	6.88	0.977	7.62	0.972	8.35	0.972	10.20	0.962
3,000	7.12	0.967	7.87	0.959	8.63	0.957	10.55	0.942
(915)	7.12	0.967	7.87	0.959	8.63	0.957	10.55	0.942
4,000	7.36	0.953	8.15	0.944	8.94	0.942	10.92	0.923
(1,220)	7.36	0.953	8.15	0.944	8.94	0.942	10.92	0.923
5,000	7.62	0.940	8.44	0.931	9.27	0.925	11.32	0.903
(1,525)	7.62	0.940	8.44	0.931	9.27	0.925	11.32	0.903
6,000	7.84	0.928	8.69	0.917	9.55	0.908	11.69	0.883
(1,830)	7.84	0.928	8.69	0.917	9.55	0.908	11.69	0.883
7,000	8.14	0.915	9.03	0.902	9.93	0.890	12.17	0.863
(2,135)	8.14	0.915	9.03	0.902	9.93	0.890	12.17	0.863
8,000	8.42	0.900	9.33	0.886	10.26	0.873	12.58	0.844
(2,440)	8.42	0.900	9.33	0.886	10.26	0.873	12.58	0.844
9,000	8.70	0.887	9.65	0.868	10.62	0.857	13.02	0.824
(2,745)	8.70	0.887	9.65	0.868	10.62	0.857	13.02	0.824
10,000	9.00	0.872	10.00	0.853	11.00	0.840	13.50	0.804
(3,050)	9.00	0.872	10.00	0.853	11.00	0.840	13.50	0.804
11,000	9.34	0.858	10.38	0.837	11.42	0.823	14.03	
(3,355)	9.34	0.858	10.38	0.837	11.42	0.823	14.03	
12,000	9.70	0.839	10.79	0.818	11.88	0.807	14.60	
(3,660)	9.70	0.839	10.79	0.818	11.88	0.807	14.60	
14,000	10.42	0.805	11.60		12.78		15.71	
(4,270)	10.42	0.805	11.60		12.78		15.71	
15,000	10.88	0.784	12.12		13.36		16.43	
(4,575)	10.88	0.784	12.12		13.36		16.43	

* Compressed Air and Gas Institute.

† The compressor ratio is the ratio of the volume of free air divided by the volume of the same air at the indicated pressure.

‡ When this factor is multiplied by the specified capacity of the compressor, at sea level, it will give the capacity at the indicated altitude and operating pressure.

RECEIVERS

An air receiver should be installed on the discharge side of a compressor to equalize the compressor pulsations and to serve as a condensing chamber for the removal of water and oil vapors. A receiver should have a drain cock at its bottom to permit the removal of the condensate. Its volume should be one-tenth to one-sixth of the capacity of the compressor. A blowoff valve, to limit the maximum pressure, is desirable.

LOSS OF AIR PRESSURE IN PIPE DUE TO FRICTION

The loss in pressure due to friction as air flows through a pipe or a hose is a factor which must be considered in selecting the size of a pipe or hose. Failure to use a sufficiently large line may cause the air pressure to drop so low that it will not satisfactorily perform the service for which it is provided.

The selection of the size of line is a problem in economy. The efficiency of most equipment operated by compressed air drops off rapidly as the pressure of the air is reduced. When the cost of lost efficiency exceeds the cost of providing a larger line, it is good economy to install a larger line. The manufacturers of pneumatic equipment generally specify the minimum air pressure at which the equipment will operate satisfactorily. However, these values should be considered as minimum and not desirable operating pressures. The actual pressure should be higher than the specified minimum.

> **Example** The cost of lost efficiency on a project resulting from the operation of pneumatic equipment at reduced pressure is estimated to be $1,000. The lost efficiency can be eliminated by installing a larger pipe line at an additional cost of $600. In this instance the contractor will save $400 by installing the larger pipe. Thus, it is good economy to use a larger pipe. However, it is not good economy to spend $1,000 to eliminate an operating loss of $600.

Several formulas are used to determine the loss of pressure in a pipe due to friction. The following formula has been used extensively [1]:

$$f = \frac{CL}{r} \frac{Q^2}{d^5} \qquad (12\text{-}11)$$

where f = pressure drop, psi
L = length of pipe, ft
Q = cu ft of free air per sec
r = ratio of compression
d = actual ID of pipe, in.
C = experimental coefficient

For ordinary steel pipe the value of C has been found to equal $0.1025/d^{0.31}$. If this value is substituted in Eq. (12-11) we get

$$f = \frac{0.1025L}{r} \frac{Q^2}{d^{5.31}} \qquad (12\text{-}12)$$

A chart for determining the loss in pressure in a pipe is given in Fig. 12-6.

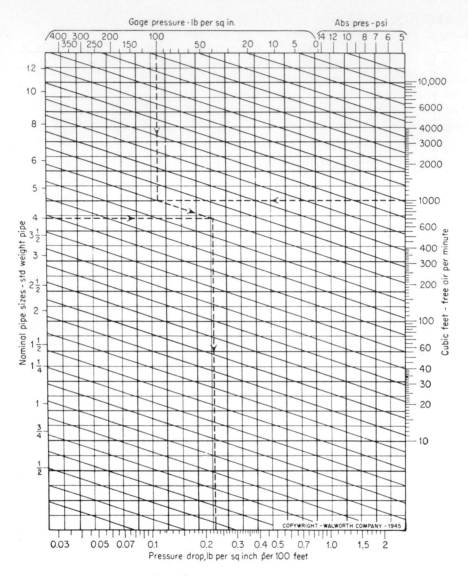

Figure 12-6 Compressed-air flow chart.

Example This example illustrates the use of the chart in Fig. 12-6. Determine the pressure loss per 100 ft of pipe resulting from transmitting 1,000 cfm of free air, at 100 psi gauge pressure, through a 4-in. standard-weight steel pipe. Enter the chart at the top at 100 psi; then proceed vertically downward to a point opposite 1,000 cfm; thence proceed parallel to the sloping guide lines to a point opposite the 4-in. pipe; thence proceed vertically downward to the bottom of the chart, where the pressure drop is indicated to be 0.225 psi.

Table 12-4 gives the loss of air pressure in 1,000 ft of standard-weight pipe due to friction. For longer or shorter lengths of pipe the friction loss will be in

Table 12-4 Loss of pressure in psi in 1,000 ft of standard-weight pipe due to friction for an inital gauge pressure of 100 psi

Free air per min., cu ft	Nominal diameter, in.												
	$\frac{1}{2}$	$\frac{3}{4}$	1	$1\frac{1}{4}$	$1\frac{1}{2}$	2	$2\frac{1}{2}$	3	$3\frac{1}{2}$	4	$4\frac{1}{2}$	5	6
10	6.50	0.99	0.28										
20	25.90	3.90	1.11	0.25	0.11								
30	68.50	9.01	2.51	0.57	0.26								
40	.....	16.00	4.45	1.03	0.46								
50	.....	25.10	6.96	1.61	0.71	0.19							
60	.....	36.20	10.00	2.32	1.02	0.28							
70	.....	49.30	13.70	3.16	1.40	0.37							
80	.....	64.50	17.80	4.14	1.83	0.49	0.19						
90	.....	82.80	22.60	5.23	2.32	0.62	0.24						
100	.....	.....	27.90	6.47	2.86	0.77	0.30						
125	.....	.....	48.60	10.20	4.49	1.19	0.46						
150	.....	.....	62.80	14.60	6.43	1.72	0.66	0.21					
175	.....	.....	.....	19.80	8.72	2.36	0.91	0.28					
200	.....	.....	.....	25.90	11.40	3.06	1.19	0.37	0.17				
250	.....	.....	.....	40.40	17.90	4.78	1.85	0.58	0.27				
300	.....	.....	.....	58.20	25.80	6.85	2.67	0.84	0.39	0.20			
350	.....	.....	.....	.....	35.10	9.36	3.64	1.14	0.53	0.27			
400	.....	.....	.....	.....	45.80	12.10	4.75	1.50	0.69	0.35	0.19		
450	.....	.....	.....	.....	58.00	15.40	5.98	1.89	0.88	0.46	0.25		
500	.....	.....	.....	.....	71.60	19.20	7.42	2.34	1.09	0.55	0.30		
600	.....	.....	.....	.....	.....	27.60	10.70	3.36	1.56	0.79	0.44		
700	.....	.....	.....	.....	.....	37.70	14.50	4.55	2.13	1.09	0.59		
800	.....	.....	.....	.....	.....	49.00	19.00	5.89	2.77	1.42	0.78		
900	.....	.....	.....	.....	.....	62.30	24.10	7.60	3.51	1.80	0.99		
1,000	.....	.....	.....	.....	.....	76.90	29.80	9.30	4.35	2.21	1.22		
1,500	.....	.....	.....	.....	.....	.....	67.00	21.00	9.80	4.90	2.73	1.51	0.57
2,000	.....	.....	.....	.....	.....	.....	.....	37.40	17.30	8.80	4.90	2.73	0.99
2,500	.....	.....	.....	.....	.....	.....	.....	58.40	27.20	13.80	8.30	4.20	1.57
3,000	.....	.....	.....	.....	.....	.....	.....	84.10	39.10	20.00	10.90	6.00	2.26
3,500	.....	.....	.....	.....	.....	.....	.....	.....	58.20	27.20	14.70	8.20	3.04
4,000	.....	.....	.....	.....	.....	.....	.....	.....	69.40	35.50	19.40	10.70	4.01
4,500	.....	.....	.....	.....	.....	.....	.....	.....	.....	45.00	24.50	13.50	5.10
5,000	.....	.....	.....	.....	.....	.....	.....	.....	.....	55.60	30.20	16.80	6.30
6,000	.....	.....	.....	.....	.....	.....	.....	.....	.....	80.00	43.70	24.10	9.10
7,000	.....	.....	.....	.....	.....	.....	.....	.....	.....	.....	59.50	32.80	12.20
8,000	.....	.....	.....	.....	.....	.....	.....	.....	.....	.....	77.50	42.90	16.10
9,000	.....	.....	.....	.....	.....	.....	.....	.....	.....	.....	.....	54.30	20.40
10,000	.....	.....	.....	.....	.....	.....	.....	.....	.....	.....	.....	.....	25.10
11,000	.....	.....	.....	.....	.....	.....	.....	.....	.....	.....	.....	.....	30.40
12,000	.....	.....	.....	.....	.....	.....	.....	.....	.....	.....	.....	.....	36.20
13,000	.....	.....	.....	.....	.....	.....	.....	.....	.....	.....	.....	.....	42.60
14,000	.....	.....	.....	.....	.....	.....	.....	.....	.....	.....	.....	.....	49.20
15,000	.....	.....	.....	.....	.....	.....	.....	.....	.....	.....	.....	.....	56.60

proportion to the length. The losses given in the table are for an initial gauge pressure of 100 psi. If the initial pressure is other than 100 psi, the corresponding losses may be obtained by multiplying the values in Table 12-4 by a suitable factor. Reference to Eq. (12-12) reveals that for a given rate of flow through a given size pipe the only variable is r, which is the ratio of compression, based on absolute pressures. For a gauge pressure of 100 psi, $r = 114.7/14.7 = 7.8$, while, for a gauge pressure of 80 psi, $r = 94.7/14.7 = 6.44$. The ratio of these values of $r = 7.8/6.44 = 1.21$. Thus, the loss for an initial pressure of 80 psi will be 1.21 times the loss for an initial pressure of 100 psi. For other initial pressures the factors are given below.

Gauge pressure, psi	Factor
80	1.210
90	1.095
100	1.000
110	0.912
120	0.853
125	0.822

LOSS OF AIR PRESSURE THROUGH SCREW-PIPE FITTINGS

In order to provide for the loss of pressure resulting from the flow of air through fittings, it is common practice to convert a fitting to its equivalent length of pipe

Table 12-5 Equivalent length in feet of standard-weight pipe having the same pressure losses as screwed fittings

Nominal pipe size, in.	Gate valve	Globe valve	Angle valve	Long-radius ell or on run of standard tee	Standard ell or on run of tee	Tee through side outlet
$\frac{1}{2}$	0.4	17.3	8.6	0.6	1.6	3.1
$\frac{3}{4}$	0.5	22.9	11.4	0.8	2.1	4.1
1	0.6	29.1	14.6	1.1	2.6	5.2
$1\frac{1}{4}$	0.8	38.3	19.1	1.4	3.5	6.9
$1\frac{1}{2}$	0.9	44.7	22.4	1.6	4.0	8.0
2	1.2	57.4	28.7	2.1	5.2	10.3
$2\frac{1}{2}$	1.4	68.5	34.3	2.5	6.2	12.3
3	1.8	85.2	42.6	3.1	6.2	15.3
4	2.4	112.0	56.0	4.0	7.7	20.2
5	2.9	140.0	70.0	5.0	10.1	25.2
6	3.5	168.0	84.1	6.1	15.2	30.4
8	4.7	222.0	111.0	8.0	20.0	40.0
10	5.9	278.0	139.0	10.0	25.0	50.0
12	7.0	332.0	166.0	11.0	29.8	59.6

having the same nominal diameter. This equivalent length should be added to the actual length of the pipe in determining losses in pressure. Table 12-5 gives the equivalent length of standard weight pipe for computing pressure losses.

LOSS OF AIR PRESSURE IN HOSE

The loss of pressure resulting from the flow of air through hose is given in Table 12-6.

RECOMMENDED SIZES OF PIPE FOR TRANSMITTING COMPRESSED AIR

In transmitting air from a compressor to pneumatic equipment, it is necessary to limit the pressure drop along the line. If this precaution is not taken, the pressure may drop below that for which the equipment was designed and production will suffer.

At least two factors should be considered in determining the minimum size pipe. One is the necessity of supplying air at the required pressure. The other is the desirability of supplying energy, through compressed air, at the lowest total cost, considering the cost of the pipe and the cost of production obtained from the equipment. Considering the first factor, a smaller pipe may be used for a short run than for a long run. While this is possible, it may not be economical. For the latter factor, economy may dictate the use of a pipe larger than the minimum possible size. The cost of installing large pipe will be more fully justified for an installation that will be used for a long period of time than for one that will be used for a short period of time.

No book, table, or fixed data can give the correct size pipe for all installations. The correct method of determining the size pipe for a given installation is to make a complete engineering analysis of the particular installation.

Table 12-7 gives recommended sizes of pipe for transmitting compressed air for various lengths of run. This information is useful as a guide in selecting pipe sizes.

RECOMMENDED SIZES OF HOSE FOR TRANSMITTING COMPRESSED AIR

Most pneumatic equipment and tools require a length of flexible hose between the source of air and the equipment. As the loss of pressure in the hose is relatively high, the length should be no greater than is required for satisfactory operation.

Table 12-8 gives the recommended sizes of hose for transmitting various quantities of compressed air and for various types of pneumatic equipment and tools frequently used on construction projects.

Table 12-6 Loss of pressure, in psi, in 50 ft of hose and end couplings

Size of hose, in.	Gauge pressure at line, psi	Volume of free air through hose, cfm													
		20	30	40	50	60	70	80	90	100	110	120	130	140	150
$\frac{1}{2}$	50	1.8	5.0	10.1	18.1										
	60	1.3	4.0	8.4	14.8	23.5									
	70	1.0	3.4	7.0	12.4	20.0	28.4								
	80	0.9	2.8	6.0	10.8	17.4	25.2	34.6							
	90	0.8	2.4	5.4	9.5	14.8	22.0	30.5	41.0						
	100	0.7	2.3	4.8	8.4	13.3	19.3	27.2	36.6						
	110	0.6	2.0	4.3	7.6	12.0	17.6	24.6	33.3	44.5					
$\frac{3}{4}$	50	0.4	0.8	1.5	2.4	3.5	4.4	6.5	8.5	11.4	14.2				
	60	0.3	0.6	1.2	1.9	2.8	3.8	5.2	6.8	8.6	11.2				
	70	0.2	0.5	0.9	1.5	2.3	3.2	4.2	5.5	7.0	8.8	11.0			
	80	0.2	0.5	0.8	1.3	1.9	2.8	3.6	4.7	5.8	7.2	8.8	10.6		
	90	0.2	0.4	0.7	1.1	1.6	2.3	3.1	4.0	5.0	6.2	7.5	9.0		
	100	0.2	0.4	0.6	1.0	1.4	2.0	2.7	3.5	4.4	5.4	6.6	7.9	9.4	11.1
	110	0.1	0.3	0.5	0.9	1.3	1.8	2.4	3.1	3.9	4.9	5.9	7.1	8.4	9.9
1	50	0.1	0.2	0.3	0.5	0.8	1.1	1.5	2.0	2.6	3.5	4.8	7.0		
	60	0.1	0.2	0.3	0.4	0.6	0.8	1.2	1.5	2.0	2.6	3.3	4.2	5.5	7.2
	70	...	0.1	0.2	0.4	0.5	0.7	1.0	1.3	1.6	2.0	2.5	3.1	3.8	4.7
	80	...	0.1	0.2	0.3	0.5	0.7	0.8	1.1	1.4	1.7	2.0	2.4	2.7	3.5
	90	...	0.1	0.2	0.3	0.4	0.6	0.7	0.9	1.2	1.4	1.7	2.0	2.4	2.8
	100	...	0.1	0.2	0.2	0.4	0.5	0.6	0.8	1.0	1.2	1.5	1.8	2.1	2.4
	110	...	0.1	0.2	0.2	0.3	0.4	0.6	0.7	0.9	1.1	1.3	1.5	1.8	2.1
$1\frac{1}{4}$	50	...	...	0.2	0.2	0.2	0.3	0.4	0.5	0.7	1.1				
	60	...	...	....	0.1	0.2	0.3	0.3	0.5	0.6	0.8	1.0	1.2	1.5	
	70	...	...	....	0.1	0.2	0.2	0.3	0.4	0.4	0.5	0.7	0.8	1.0	1.3
	80	...	...	....	....	0.1	0.2	0.2	0.3	0.4	0.5	0.6	0.7	0.8	1.0
	90	...	...	....	....	0.1	0.2	0.2	0.3	0.3	0.4	0.5	0.6	0.7	0.8
	100	...	....	....	....	....	0.1	0.2	0.2	0.3	0.4	0.4	0.5	0.6	0.7
	110	...	...	....	....	....	0.1	0.2	0.2	0.3	0.3	0.4	0.5	0.5	0.6
$1\frac{1}{2}$	50	...	...	....	....	....	0.1	0.2	0.2	0.2	0.3	0.3	0.4	0.5	0.6
	60	...	...	....	....	....	....	0.1	0.2	0.2	0.2	0.3	0.3	0.4	0.5
	70	...	...	....	....	....	....	....	0.1	0.2	0.2	0.2	0.3	0.3	0.4
	80	...	...	....	....	....	....	....	....	0.1	0.2	0.2	0.2	0.3	0.4
	90	...	...	....	....	....	....	....	....	....	0.1	0.2	0.2	0.2	0.2
	100	...	...	....	....	....	....	....	....	....	....	0.1	0.2	0.2	0.2
	110	...	...	....	....	....	....	....	....	....	....	0.1	0.2	0.2	0.2

Table 12-7 Recommended pipe sizes for transmitting compressed air at 80 to 125 psi gauge

Volume of air, cfm	Length of pipe, ft				
	50–200	200–500	500–1,000	1,000–2,500	2,500–5,000
	Nominal size pipe, in.				
30–60	1	1	$1\frac{1}{4}$	$1\frac{1}{2}$	$1\frac{1}{2}$
60–100	1	$1\frac{1}{4}$	$1\frac{1}{4}$	2	2
100–200	$1\frac{1}{4}$	$1\frac{1}{2}$	2	$2\frac{1}{2}$	$2\frac{1}{2}$
200–500	2	$2\frac{1}{2}$	3	$3\frac{1}{2}$	$3\frac{1}{2}$
500–1,000	$2\frac{1}{2}$	3	$3\frac{1}{2}$	4	$4\frac{1}{2}$
1,000–2,000	$2\frac{1}{7}$	4	$4\frac{1}{2}$	5	6
2,000–4,000	$3\frac{1}{7}$	5	6	8	8
4,000–8,000	6	8	8	10	10

DIVERSITY OR CAPACITY FACTOR

While it is necessary to provide as much compressed air as will be required to supply the needs of all operating equipment, it is unnecessarily extravagant to provide more air capacity than will be needed. It is probable that all equipment nominally used on a project will not be in operation at any given time. An analysis of the job should be made to determine the maximum actual need prior to designing the compressed-air system.

If 10 jackhammers are nominally drilling, it is probable that not more than 5 or 6 will be consuming air at a given time. The others will be out of use temporarily for changes in bits or drill steel or moving to new locations. Thus, the actual amount of air demand will be based on 5 or 6 drills instead of 10. The same condition will apply to other pneumatic tools.

Capacity factor is the ratio of the average load to the maximum mathematical load that would exist if all tools were operating at the same time. This ratio is also referred to as a diversity factor. For example, if a jackhammer required 90 cfm of air, 10 hammers would require a total of 900 cfm if they were all operated at the same time. However, with only 5 hammers operating at one time, the demand for air would be 450 cfm. Thus, the diversity factor would be 450 ÷ 900 = 0.5.

Table 12-9 illustrates a method of applying diversity factors to a project in which excavation is the primary operation.

Table 12-8 Recommended sizes of hose, in inches, for transmitting compressed air at 80- to 125-psi gauge

Volume of air, cfm	Types of air tools	Length of hose, ft		
		0–25	25–50	50–200
0–15	Spray guns $\frac{1}{4}$-in. drills Light chipping and scaling hammers $\frac{3}{8}$-in. impact wrenches	$\frac{5}{16}$	$\frac{3}{8}$	$\frac{1}{2}$
15–30	$\frac{5}{16}-\frac{1}{2}$-in. drills $\frac{5}{8}$-in. impact wrenches Chipping hammers 15-lb rock drills	$\frac{3}{8}$	$\frac{1}{2}$	$\frac{1}{2}$
30–60	$\frac{5}{8}$–1-in. drills $\frac{3}{4}$-in. impact wrenches Light grinders Rivet hammers Clay diggers Backfill tampers Small concrete vibrators Light and medium demolition tools 25-lb rock drills	$\frac{1}{2}$	$\frac{3}{4}$	$\frac{3}{4}$
60–100	1–2-in. drills $1\frac{1}{4}-1\frac{3}{4}$-in. impact wrenches Heavy grinders Large concrete vibrators Sump pumps 35–55-lb rock drills Heavy demolition tools	$\frac{3}{4}$	$\frac{3}{4}$	1
100–200	Winches and hoists Drifters Wagon drills 75-lb rock drills	1	1	$1\frac{1}{4}$

AIR REQUIRED BY PNEUMATIC EQUIPMENT AND TOOLS

The approximate quantities of compressed air required by pneumatic equipment and tools are given in Table 12-10. The quantities are based on continuous operation at a pressure of 90 psi gauge.

Table 12-9 Illustration of the application of diversity factors in designing a compressed-air system

Equipment	Air required per unit, cfm	Number of units on job	Number of units working	Maximum air demand, cfm	Diversity factor	Probable air demand, cfm
Wagon drills	200	6	4	1,200	0.67	800
Jackhammers	100	16	8	1,600	0.50	800
Drill sharpeners	160	2	1	320	0.50	160
Oil furnaces	80	2	2	160	1.00	160
Grinders	50	2	1	100	0.50	50
Sump pumps	160	3	2	480	0.67	320
Line loss	. . .	. . .	. . .	220	. . . .	220
Total	. . .	. . .	. . .	4,080	. . . .	2,510
Job diversity factor	. . .	. . .	. . .	. . . .	0.80	
Total actual demand, 0.80 × 2,510	. . .	. . .	. . .	. . . . .	. . . .	2,008

Table 12-10 Quantities of compressed air required by pneumatic equipment and tools*

Equipment or tools	Capacity or size	Air consumption, cfm
Chipping hammers	Light	15–25
	Heavy	25–30
Clay diggers	Light, 20 lb	20–25
	Medium, 25 lb	25–30
	Heavy, 35 lb	30–35
Concrete vibrators	$2\frac{1}{2}$-in. tube diameter	20–30
	3-in. tube diameter	40–50
	4-in. tube diameter	45–55
	5-in. tube diameter	75–85
Drills or borers	1-in. diameter	35–40
	2-in. diameter	50–75
	4-in. diameter	50–75
Hoist	Single-drum, 2,000 lb pull	200–220
	Double-drum, 2,400 lb pull	250–260
Impact wrenches	$\frac{5}{8}$-in. bolt	15–20
	$\frac{3}{4}$-in. bolt	30–40
	$1\frac{1}{4}$-in. bolt	60–70
	$1\frac{1}{2}$-in. bolt	70–80
	$1\frac{3}{4}$-in. bolt	80–90

* Air pressure 90 psi gauge.

Table 12-10 Quantities of compressed air required by pneumatic equipment and tools* (continued)

Equipment or tools	Capacity or size		Air consumption, cfm
	Weight, lb	Depth of hole, ft	
Jackhammers	10	0–2	15–25
	15	0–2	20–35
	25	2–8	30–50
	35	8–12	55–75
	45	12–16	80–100
	55	16–24	90–110
	75	8–24	150–175
Paving breakers	35	.....	30–35
	60	.....	40–45
	80	.....	50–50
Riveting hammers	$\frac{5}{8}$-in. rivet		25–30
	$\frac{3}{4}$-in. rivet		30–35
	$\frac{7}{8}$-in. rivet		35–40
	$1\frac{1}{8}$-in. rivet		40–45
	$1\frac{1}{4}$-in. rivet		40–45
Saws:			
Circular	12-in. blade		40–60
Chain	18-30-in. blade		85–95
	36-in. blade		135–150
	48-in. blade		150–160
Reciprocating	20-in.		45–50
Spray guns	Light-duty		2–3
	Medium-duty		8–15
	Heavy duty		14–30
Sump pump	Single-stage, 10–40 ft head		80–90
	Single-stage, 100–150 ft head		150–170
	Two-stage, 100–150 ft head		160–180
Trampers, earth	35 lb		30–35
	60 lb		40–45
	80 lb		50–60
Wagon drills—drifters	3-in. piston		150–175
	$3\frac{1}{2}$-in. piston		180–210
	4-in. piston		225–275

EFFECT OF ALTITUDE ON THE CONSUMPTION OF AIR BY ROCK DRILLS

As previously explained in this chapter, the capacity of an air compressor is the volume of free air that enters the compressor during a stated time, usually expressed in cfm. Because of the lower atmospheric pressure at higher altitudes, the quantity of air supplied by a compressor at a given gauge pressure will be less than at sea level. It is necessary to provide more compressor capacity at higher altitudes to assure an adequate supply of air at the specified pressure to rock drills.

Table 12-11 gives representative factors to be applied to specified compressor capacities to determine the required capacities at different altitudes. For example, if a single drill requires a capacity of 600 cfm of air at sea level, it will require a capacity of $600 \times 1.2 = 720$ cfm at an altitude of 5,000 ft, and $600 \times 1.3 = 780$ cfm at an altitude of 10,000 ft.

The values of the factors are adjusted to reflect representative diversity factors for the use of multidrills. Because these factors will not necessarily apply to all drills and projects, they should be used as a guide only.

THE COST OF COMPRESSED AIR

The cost of compressed air may be determined at the compressor or at the point of use. The former will include the cost of compressing, while the latter will include the cost of compressing plus transmitting, including line losses.

Table 12-11 Factors to be used in determining the capacities of compressed air required by rock drills at different altitudes*

Alti-tude, ft	Number of drills									
	1	2	3	4	5	6	7	8	9	10
	Factor									
0	1.0	1.8	2.7	3.4	4.1	4.8	5.4	6.0	6.5	7.1
1,000	1.0	1.9	2.8	3.5	4.2	4.9	5.6	6.2	6.7	7.3
2,000	1.1	1.9	2.9	3.6	4.4	5.1	5.8	6.4	7.0	7.6
3,000	1.1	2.0	3.0	3.7	4.5	5.3	5.9	6.6	7.2	7.8
5,000	1.1	2.1	3.1	3.9	4.7	5.5	6.1	6.8	7.4	8.1
5,000	1.2	2.1	3.2	4.0	4.8	5.6	6.3	7.0	7.6	8.3
6,000	1.2	2.2	3.2	4.1	4.9	5.8	6.5	7.2	7.8	8.5
7,000	1.2	2.2	3.3	4.2	5.0	5.9	6.6	7.4	8.0	8.7
8,000	1.3	2.3	3.4	4.3	5.2	6.1	6.8	7.6	8.2	9.0
9,000	1.3	2.3	3.5	4.4	5.3	6.2	7.0	7.7	8.4	9.2
10,000	1.3	2.4	3.6	4.5	5.4	6.3	7.1	7.9	8.6	9.4
12,000	1.4	2.5	3.7	4.6	5.6	6.6	7.4	8.2	8.9	9.7
15,000	1.4	2.6	3.9	4.7	5.9	6.9	7.7	8.6	9.3	1.02

* Compressed Air and Gas Institute.

The cost of compressing should include the cost of the compressor, insurance, taxes, interest, maintenance, repair, fuel, lubrication, and labor. The cost is usually based on 1,000 cu ft of free air.

Example Determine the cost of compressing 1,000 cu ft of free air to a gauge pressure of 100 psi by using a 600-cfm two-stage portable compressor driven by a 180-hp diesel engine. The following information will apply:

Cost f.o.b. factory	=	$26,805
Freight, 11,000 lb @ $2.00 per cwt	=	220
Sales tax	=	1,425
Total cost delivered to buyer	=	$28,450

Life, 5 yr at 2,000 hr per yr
Average investment, $0.6 \times \$28,450 = \$17,070$
Fuel consumed per hr, full load, $0.04 \times 180 = 7.2$ gal
Lubricating oil consumed per hr, 0.125 gal
The costs will be:
Annual costs:

Depreciation, $28,450 ÷ 5	=	$ 5,690
Repairs, 75% of $5,690	=	4,268
Investment, 15% × $17,070	=	2,560
Total annual fixed cost	=	$12,518

Hourly costs:

Fixed cost, $12,518 ÷ 2,000 hr	=	$ 6.26
Fuel, 7.2 gal @ $0.50	=	3.60
Lubricating oil, 0.125 gal @ $1.60	=	0.20
Operator, 1/2 time @ $8.00 per hr*	=	4.00
Total cost per hr,	=	$14.06

* This cost may vary with location and union requirements.

Volume of air compressed per hr, $60 \times 600 = 36,000$ cu ft
Cost per 1,000 cu ft, $14.06 ÷ 36 = $0.39
   The cost per 1,000 cu ft of air for a compressor operating under various load factors will be as follows:

	Load factor, %		
	100	75	50
Hourly costs:			
Fixed cost*	$6.26	$6.26	$6.26
Fuel	3.60	2.69	2.14
Lubricating oil	0.20	0.15	0.12
Operator, $\frac{1}{2}$ time†	4.00	4.00	4.00
Total cost per hr	$14.06	$13.10	$12.52
Volume of air per hr, cu ft	36,000	27,000	18,000
Cost per 1,000 cu ft	$0.39	$0.50	$0.70

   * This cost may vary slightly with the load factor.
   † This cost may vary with the location and with the requirements of the local union.

Table 12-12 Cost per month for air leakage

Size of opening in.	Cu ft of air lost per month at 100 psi	For indicated cost per 1,000 cu ft			
		$0.30	$0.45	$0.60	$0.75
$\frac{1}{32}$	45,500	$ 13.65	$ 19.14	$ 27.30	$ 34.14
$\frac{1}{16}$	182,300	54.75	82.20	109.50	136.95
$\frac{1}{8}$	740,200	222.00	333.00	444.00	555.00
$\frac{1}{4}$	2,920,800	876.00	1,314.00	1,782.00	2,190.00
$\frac{3}{8}$	6,671,900	2,013.00	3,018.00	4,126.00	5,031.00

THE COST OF AIR LEAKS

The loss of air through leakage in a transmission line can be surprisingly large and costly. It results from poor pipe connections, loose valve stems, deteriorated hose, and loose hose connections. If the cost of such leaks were more fully known, most of them would be eliminated. The rate of leakage through an opening of known size can be determined by applying a formula for the flow of air through an orifice.

Table 12-12 illustrates the cost of air leakage for various sizes of openings and costs per 1,000 cu ft of air.

THE COST OF USING LOW AIR PRESSURE

The effect on the cost of production of operating pneumatic equipment at less than the recommended air pressure can be demonstrated by analyzing the performance of a group of jackhammers under different pressures. The hammers receive the air from a common header-type pipe line. Similar results would be obtained when using other kinds of pneumatic equipment.

Example Determine the economy of using a 3-in. pipe instead of a $2\frac{1}{2}$-in. pipe to transmit compressed air to jackhammers. The air will be supplied to the entrance of each pipe at a pressure of 100 psi gauge. The stated conditions will apply.

Length of pipe, 1,000 ft
Installed cost of 3-in. pipe, $5,040
Installed cost of $2\frac{1}{2}$-in. pipe, $3,780
Extra cost of 3-in. pipe, $1,260
Extra cost chargeable to this project, considering the salvage value of the pipe, $900
Estimated length of project, 4 months
Hours worked per month, 180
No. jackhammers on the job, 16
No. jackhammers operating at one time, 8
Size of jackhammers, 55 lb
Air required per hammer at 90 psi, 100 cfm
    Total air required, 8 × 100 = 800 cfm

Loss of pressure in 3-in. pipe, from Table 12-4, 1.0 × 5.89 = 5.9 psi
Loss of pressure in 50 ft of 3/4-in. hose, from Table 12-6 = 4.7 psi, interpolated for 100 cfm at
    a pressure of 94 psi
Total loss in pressure through pipe and hose, 10.6 psi
Air pressure at the hammer, 100 − 10.6 = 89.4 psi
Loss of pressure in $2\frac{1}{2}$-in. pipe, from Table 12-4, 19.0 psi
Pressure entering 3/4-in. hose, 81 psi
Loss of pressure in 50 ft of 3/4-in. hose, 5.8 psi
Total loss in pressure through $2\frac{1}{2}$-in. pipe and hose, 24.8 psi
Pressure at the hammer, 100.0 − 24.8 = 75.2 psi

If the pressure of air at the hammer is reduced to 75.2 psi, the quantity of air required to operate each hammer will be 90 cfm instead of 100 cfm.
    Total quantity of air required, 8 × 90 = 720 cfm
    Hammer efficiency at 75.2 psi will be about 80% of that at 90 psi.
    Assume that the cost of air will be $0.45 per 1,000 cu ft. Consider the effect of using each size pipe for one hour, as it applies to the rates of drilling rock, and the indicated costs. The results will be:

Item	Size of pipe, in.	
	$2\frac{1}{2}$	3
Volume of air consumed, cu ft per hr		
by $2\frac{1}{2}$-in. pipe, 60 × 720	43,200	
by 3-in. pipe, 60 × 800		48,000
Cost of air @ $0.45 per 1,000 cu ft	$ 19.44	$ 21.60
Cost of labor, 20 men @ $6.00 per hr	120.00	120.00
Cost of jackhammers, steel, and bits*	24.00	28.80
Total cost per hr	$ 163.44	$ 170.40

* The cost per hour for jackhammer, steel, and bits is increased from $1.50 to $1.80 to compensate for the greater wear and reduced life of the units operated at the higher pressure provided by the 3-in. pipe.

Tests conducted on drilling equipment indicate that the drills operating at the lower pressure, namely 75.2 psi, will have an efficiency equal to about 80 percent of those operated at 89.4 psi. Thus, the increase in the depth of hole drilled at the higher pressures will be 100 − 80 = 20%.

Value of increased production as related
  to total cost per hr, 0.20 × $163.44   = $32.69
Increase in cost per hr with 3-in.
  pipe, $170.40 − $163.44   =   6.96
Net value of increased production per hr = $25.73

The total value of the increased rate of production during the project will be:

Length of project, 4 mo × 180 hr = 720 hr
Value of increased production, 720 hr @ $25.73 = $18,525.60

Thus, it is evident that spending an extra $900 to provide the larger pipe is an excellent investment. If the duration of the project is greater than 4 months, the increase in value resulting from use of the larger pipe will be proportionally greater.

PROBLEMS

12-1 An air compressor draws in 800 cu ft of free air at a gauge pressure of 0 psi and a temperature of 80°F. The air is compressed to a gauge pressure of 100 psi at a temperature of 140°F. The atmospheric pressure is 14.0 psi. Determine the volume of air after it is compressed.

12-2 An air compressor draws in 100 cu ft of free air at a gauge pressure of 0 psi and a temperature of 50°F. The air is compressed to a gauge pressure of 100 psi at a temperature of 130°F. The atmospheric pressure is 12.30 psi. Determine the volume of air after it is compressed.

12-3 Determine the theoretical horsepower required to compress 800 cfm of free air, measured at standard conditions, from atmospheric pressure to 100 psi gauge when the compression is performed under isothermal conditions.

12-4 Solve Prob. 12-3 if the air is compressed under adiabatic conditions.

12-5 Determine the difference in horsepower required to compress 800 cfm of free air under adiabatic conditions for altitudes of 2,000 and 9,000 ft. The air will be compressed to 100 psi gauge at each altitude.

12-6 A compressor has a capacity of 500 cfm of free air at 100 psi gauge at zero altitude. If the compressor is operating at an altitude of 6,000 ft, determine the capacity when the air is compressed to 100 psi gauge, with no change in temperature.

12-7 Compressors operating at zero altitude will supply enough air to operate eight drills. If the compressors and drills are operated at an altitude of 8,000 ft, how many drills can the compressors serve?

12-8 A 4-in. pipe with screwed fittings is used to transmit 1,200 cfm of free air at an initial pressure of 100 psi gauge. The pipeline includes the following items:

    800 ft of pipe
    3 gate valves
    8 on-run tees
    6 standard ells

Determine the total loss in pressure through the pipe.

12-9 If the air from the end of the pipeline of Prob. 12-8 is delivered through 50 ft of 1-in. hose to a rock drill that requires 160 cfm of air, determine the pressure at the drill.

REFERENCES

1. Harris, E. G.: *University of Missouri Bulletin*, vol. 1, no. 4, 1912.
2. Atlas Copco, Inc., 70 Demarest Drive, Wayne, NJ 07470.
3. Chicago Pneumatic Tool Company, 6 East 44th Street, New York, NY 10017.
4. Ingersoll-Rand Company, Phillipsburg, NJ 08865.

THIRTEEN

DRILLING ROCK AND EARTH

INTRODUCTION

This chapter will deal with the equipment and methods used by the construction and mining industries to drill holes in both rock and earth. Although the same or similar equipment may in some instances be used for drilling both materials, they will be treated separately in this chapter.

Because the purposes for which drilling is performed vary a great deal from general to highly specialized, it is highly desirable to select the equipment and methods best suited to the specific service. For example, a contractor engaged in highway construction which requires drilling rock under varying conditions should select equipment that is suitable for various services. However, if equipment is selected to drill rock in a quarry where the material and conditions will not vary, specialized equipment should be considered. In some instances custom-made equipment, designed for use on that project only, may be justified.

More complete information related to the performance characteristics of drilling equipment will be presented in this chapter.

DEFINITIONS OF TERMS

Terms which are commonly used in describing drilling equipment and procedures are given below as a guide for the reader.

Percussion drill This is a drill which breaks rock into small particles by the impact from repeated blows.

Abrasion drill This drill grinds rock into small particles through the abrasive effect of a bit that rotates in the hole.

Cuttings Cuttings are the disintegrated rock particles that are removed from a hole.

Jackhammer, or sinker This device is an air-operated percussion-type drill that is small enough to be handled by one worker.

Drifter A drifter is an air-operated percussion-type drill, similar to a jack-hammer, but so large that it requires mechanical mounting.

Wagon drill This is a drifter mounted on a mast supported by two or more wheels.

Stoper A stoper is an air-operated percussion-type drill, similar to a drifter, that is used for overhead drilling, as in a tunnel.

Churn drill The churn drill is a percussion-type drill consisting of a long steel bit that is mechanically lifted and dropped to disintegrate the rock. It is used to drill deep holes, usually 6 in. in diameter or larger.

Blast-hole drill This is a rotary drill consisting of a steel-pipe drill stem on the bottom of which is a roller bit that disintegrates the rock as it rotates over it. The cuttings are removed by a stream of compressed air.

Shot drill This is a rotary abrasive-type drill whose bit consists of a section of steel pipe with a roughened surface at the bottom. As the bit is rotated under pressure, chilled-steel shot are supplied under the bit to accomplish the disintegration of the rock. The cuttings are removed by water.

Diamond drill The diamond drill is a rotary abrasive-type drill whose bit consists of a metal matrix in which there are embedded a large number of diamonds. As the drill rotates, the diamonds disintegrate the rock. This drill is used extensively to obtain core samples.

Dry drill This is a drill which uses compressed air to remove the cuttings from a hole.

Wet drill A wet drill is one that uses water to remove the cuttings from a hole.

Core drilling Core drilling is the obtaining of core samples of rock from a hole, usually for exploratory purposes. The diamond and shot drills are used for core drilling.

Bit This is the portion of a drill which contacts the rock and disintegrates it. Many types are used.

Detachable bit This is a bit which may be attached to or removed from the drill steel or drill stem.

Forged bit This is a bit which is forged on drill steel.

Carbide-insert bit The carbide-insert bit is a detachable bit whose cutting edges consist of tungsten carbide embedded in a softer steel base.

Diamond bit The diamond bit is a detachable bit whose cutting elements consist of diamonds embedded in a metal matrix.

Depth per bit This is the depth of hole that can be drilled by a bit before it is replaced.

Drilling rate Drilling rate is the number of feet of hole drilled per hour per drill.

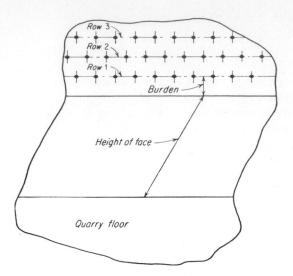

Figure 13-1 Dimensional terminology for drilling rock.

Face Face is the approximately vertical surface extending upward from the floor of a pit to the level at which drilling is being done.

Burden This is the horizontal distance from a face back to the first row of drill holes.

Drilling pattern Drilling pattern is the spacing of the drill holes.

Figure 13-1 illustrates the dimension terminology frequently used for drilling.

BITS

The bit is the essential part of a drill, as it is the part which must engage and disintegrate the rock. The success of a drilling operation depends on the ability of the bit to remain sharp under the impact of the drill. Many types and sizes are available.

Until recent years the bits for jackhammers and drifters were forged on one end of the drill steel. This practice has been pretty well discontinued in favor of detachable bits, which are screwed to the drill steel. Detachable bits have many advantages compared with forged bits. They are easily replaced and resharpened, are available in various sizes, shapes, and hardness, and are relatively inexpensive. They are usually resharpened on a grinder.

Steel bits for jackhammers and drifters are illustrated in Fig. 13-2. They are available in sizes from 1 to $4\frac{1}{2}$ in., the gauge size varying in steps of $\frac{1}{8}$ in. These bits may be resharpened two to six times.

The depth of hole that can be drilled with a steel bit will vary from a few inches to 30 or 40 ft or more, depending on the type of rock.

Figure 13-2 Removable shoulder-drive-type rock bits. *(The Timken Company.)*

Carbide-insert bits Some types of rock are so abrasive that steel bits must be replaced after they have drilled only a few inches of hole. The cost of the bits and the time lost in changing are so great that it will usually be economical to use carbide-insert bits. This bit is illustrated in Figs 13-2, 13-3, and 13-4. As noted in the figures, the actual drilling points consist of a very hard metal, tungsten carbide, which is embedded in steel. Although these bits are considerably more expensive than steel bits, the increased drilling rate and depth of hole obtained per bit will give an over-all economy in drilling hard rock.

A contractor on a highway project in Pennsylvania found that when drilling diabase rock the depth per steel bit was $\frac{1}{2}$ to 2 in. When he changed to carbide bits, he obtained an average depth per bit of 1,992 ft. The estimated saving by using carbide bits, in drilling 30,000 cu yd of rock, was in excess of $100,000. The cost analysis for this project is as follows:

Total quantity of rock, 300,000 cu yd
Depth of holes, 12 ft
Size of bits, $2\frac{1}{4}$ in.
Cu yd of rock per ft of hole, $2\frac{1}{2}$
Total depth of hole required, 300,000 ÷ 2.5 = 120,000 ft

Figure 13-3 Removable tapered-socket-type rock bits. *(The Timken Company.)*

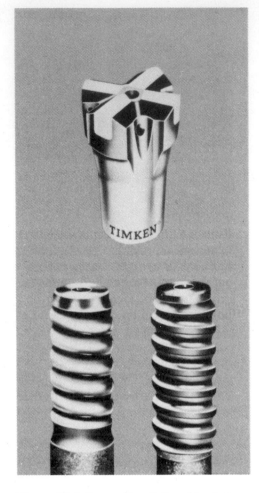

Figure 13-4 Removable bottom-drive-type carbide insert rock bit. *(The Timken Company.)*

Average depth of hole per steel bit, with resharpening, 0.48 ft
No. bits required, 120,000 ÷ 0.48 = 250,000
Cost of bits, 250,000 @ $0.45 each = $112,500
Average depth of hole per carbide bit, 1,992 ft
No. bits required, 120,000 ÷ 1,992 = 60
Cost of bits, 60 @ $15.90 each = $954.00
Saving through the use of carbide bits, $111,546

This figure does not include the value of time saved in changing bits. This is an exceptional case, as such savings are not possible on all projects.

Tapered socket bits Figure 13-3 illustrates removable tapered socket bits, which are available in gauge sizes varying in $\frac{1}{8}$-in. (3.2-mm) steps from about 1 in. (25 mm) to 4 in. (102 mm) or more.

Bottom-drive bits Figure 13-4 illustrates removable bottom-drive bits, which are available in gauge sizes varying from about $1\frac{1}{2}$ in. (38 mm) to 6 in. (152 mm) or more.

Button bits Figure 13-5 illustrates removable button bits, which are available in numerous sizes. These bits, which are available in different cutting face designs with a choice of insert grades, require no regrinding or sharpening. Their demonstrated performance has been superior to that of other types of bits when they are used to drill rocks that are more suitable for them, as indicated later in this chapter.

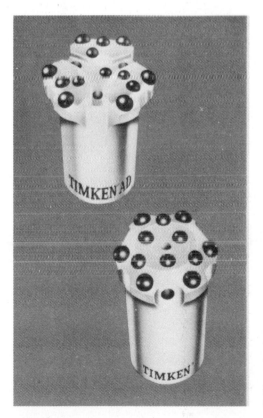

Figure 13-5 Removable button bits. *(The Timken Company.)*

JACKHAMMERS

Jackhammers are hand-held air-operated percussion-type drills which are used primarily for drilling down holes. For this reason, they are frequently called sinkers. They are classified according to their weight, such as 45 or 55 lb. A complete drilling unit consists of a hammer, drill steel, and bit. As the compressed air flows through a hammer, it causes a piston to reciprocate at a speed up to 2,200 blows per minute, which produces the hammer effect. The energy of this piston is transmitted to a bit through the drill steel. Some of the air flows through a hole in the drill steel and the bit to remove the cuttings from the hole and to cool the bit. For wet drilling, water is used instead of air to remove the cuttings. Figure 13-6 shows a sectionalized jackhammer with the essential parts indicated. The drill steel is rotated slightly following each blow so that the points of the bit will not strike at the same spot each time.

Although jackhammers may be used to drill holes in excess of 20 ft deep, they seldom are used for holes exceeding 10 ft deep. The heavier hammers will

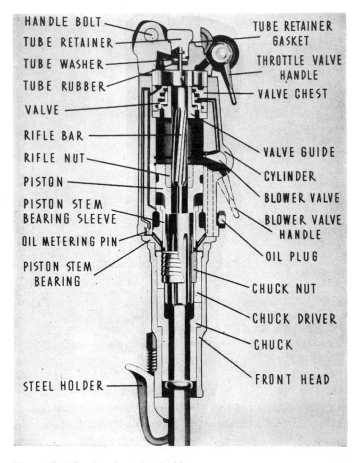

Figure 13-6 Section through a jackhammer.

Table 13-1 Representative specifications for jackhammers

Model	S33	S55	S73
Length overall, in.	$20\frac{1}{8}$	$23\frac{3}{8}$	25
Cylinder bore, in.	$2\frac{3}{8}$	$2\frac{5}{8}$	$2\frac{3}{4}$
Weight, lb	31	$56\frac{1}{2}$	67
Size steel recommended, in.	$\frac{7}{8}$	$\frac{7}{8}-1$	$\frac{7}{8}-1\frac{1}{4}$
Size air hose recommended, in.	$\frac{3}{4}$	$\frac{3}{4}-1$	$\frac{3}{4}-1$
Size water hose recommended, in.	$\frac{1}{2}$	$\frac{1}{2}$	$\frac{1}{2}$

drill holes up to $2\frac{1}{2}$ in. in diameter. Drill steel usually is supplied in 2-ft-length variations, but longer lengths are available.

DRIFTERS

Drifter drills are similar to jackhammers in operation, but they are larger and are used as mounted tools for drilling down, horizontal, or up holes. They vary in weight from 75 to 260 lb and are capable of drilling holes up to $4\frac{1}{2}$ in. in diameter. These tools are used extensively in mining and tunneling. Either air or water may be used to remove the cuttings.

When drifters are used for horizontal or up drilling, the feed pressure is supplied by a hand-operated screw or a pneumatic or hydraulic piston. The weight is usually sufficient to supply the necessary pressure for down drilling. Steel changes may be obtained in lengths of 24, 30, 36, 45, and 60 in.

WAGON DRILLS

Wagon drills consist of drifters mounted on masts which are mounted on wheels to provide portability. They are used extensively to drill holes up to $4\frac{1}{2}$ in. in diameter and up to 30 ft or more in depth. They give better performance than jackhammers when used on terrain where it is possible for them to operate. They

Table 13-2 Representative specifications for automatic-feed drifters

Model	79	89	93	99
Cylinder bore, in.	3	$3\frac{1}{2}$	$3\frac{1}{2}$	4
Size chuck available, in.	$\frac{7}{8}-1\frac{1}{4}$	$\frac{7}{8}-1\frac{1}{4}$	$\frac{7}{8}-1\frac{1}{4}$	$\frac{1}{4}-1\frac{1}{2}$
Size air hose recommended, in.	1	1	1	1
Size water hose recommended, in.	$\frac{1}{2}$	$\frac{1}{2}$	$\frac{1}{2}$	$\frac{1}{2}$
Weight of drill, less mounting, lb	111	134	140	181
Overall length, in.	$31\frac{3}{4}$	34	35	$35\frac{1}{8}$

Figure **13-7** Gasoline-engine-operated hand drill. *(Atlas Copco, Inc.)*

Figure 13-8 Drifters used to drill horizontal holes.

Figure 13-9 Wagon drill.

may be used to drill at any angle from down to slightly above horizontal. The length of drill steel may be 6, 10, or 15 ft, or more, depending on the length of feed of the particular wagon drill.

TRACK-MOUNTED DRILLS

The track-mounted drills illustrated in Figs. 13-10, 13-11 and 13-12 have substantially replaced the wagon drill on construction work. Because of its ability to move quickly to a new location, and, using the hydraulically operated boom, position the drill for resumption of drilling, its production rate may be three or more times that of a wagon drill. Holes can be drilled at any angle from under 15° back from vertical to above the horizontal, ahead, or on either side of the unit. All operations, including tramming, are powered by compressed air.

Depending on the size unit selected, these machines can drill holes up to about 6 in. in diameter, and to depths of 50 ft or more.

Figure 13-10 Track-mounted drill equipped with dust collector. *(Atlas Copco, Inc.)*

Figure 13-11 Track-mounted dual drills equipped with dust collector. *(Atlas Copco, Inc.)*

Figure 13-12 Track-mounted drill. *(Penn-Mar Mining Company.)*

ROTARY-PERCUSSION DRILLS

These drills combine the hard-hitting reciprocal action of the percussion drill with the turning-under-pressure action of the rotary drill. Whereas the percussion drill only has a rotary action to reposition the bit's cutting edges, the rotation of this combination drill, with the bit under constant pressure, has

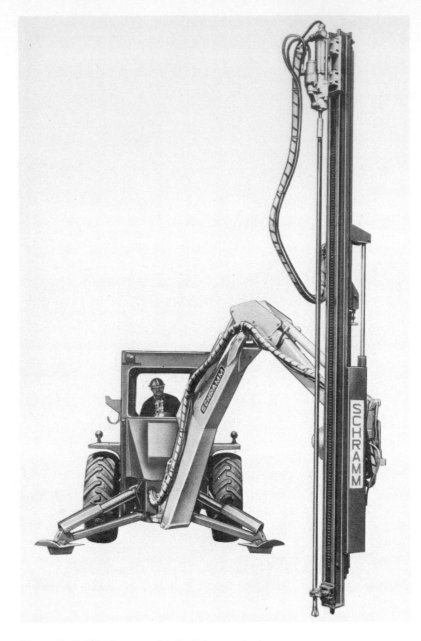

Figure 13-13 Wheel-mounted drill. *(Schramm, Inc.)*

Figure 13-14 Wheel-mounted drill. *(Joy Manufacturing Company.)*

demonstrated its ability to drill much faster than the regular percussion drill. On the Smith Power tunnel near Eugene, Oregon, rotary-percussion drills are reported to have drilled blast holes three times as fast as regular percussion drills [1]. These drills require special carbide bits with the carbide inserts set at a different angle than those used with standard carbide bits.

In the Smith Power tunnel, four of these drills operating on a two-deck rail-mounted jumbo are reported to have drilled $1\frac{3}{4}$-in.-diameter holes at rates

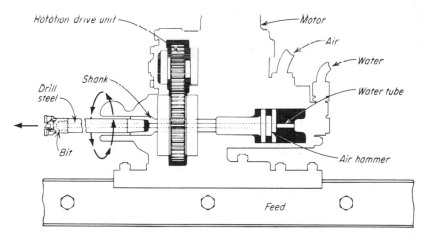

Figure 13-15 Rotary-percussion drill. *(Joy Manufacturing Company.)*

that varied from 5 to 10 fpm, depending on the hardness of the rock. A round of 40 to 48 holes, having an average depth of 8 ft, was drilled in as little as 15 min.

PISTON DRILLS

These are percussion-type drills with the hollow drill tube attached to the piston. The stroke and rotation of the piston are adjustable to give the best performance for the particular type of rock being drilled. It is available with carbide-insert bits which are up to 6 in. in diameter. The drill has a practical depth limit of approximately 70 ft. As indicated in Fig. 13-16 it is a self-propelled machine mounted on crawler tracks.

BLASTHOLE DRILLS

The blasthole drill is a self-propelled drill which is mounted on a truck or on crawler tracks. Drilling is accomplished with a tri-cone roller-type bit attached to the lower end of a drill pipe. As the bit is rotated in the hole, a continuous blast of compressed air is forced down through the pipe and the bit to remove the rock cuttings and cool the bit. Rigs are available to drill holes to different diameters and to depths up to approximately 300 ft. This drill is suitable for drilling soft to medium rock, such as hard dolomite and limestone, but is not suitable for drilling the harder igneous rocks.

Figure 13-16 Quarrymaster piston drill.

Figure 13-17 Blasthole drill. *(Schramm, Inc.)*

In drilling dolomite for the Ontario Hydro-canal, heavyweight drills were used to drill 25- and 50-ft-deep holes. The 25-ft holes were drilled on 10- by 10- and 12- by 12-ft patterns, using $6\frac{1}{4}$- and $6\frac{3}{4}$-in. bits. The average drilling speed was approximately 30 ft per hr, including moving. The average life of the bits was 958 ft for the $6\frac{1}{4}$-in. and 1,374 ft for the $6\frac{3}{4}$-in. bits.

Figure 13-18 Blasthole drill. *(Schramm, Inc.)*

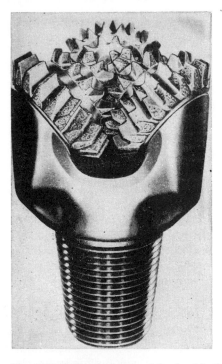

Figure 13-19 Representative bits for blastholes. *(a)* Tricone bit *(Joy Manufacturing Company).* *(b)* Button-type bit *(Reed Tool Company).*

On other projects, drilling speeds have varied from $1\frac{1}{2}$ ft per hr in dense, hard dolomite to 50 ft per hr in limestone. The speed of drilling is regulated by pressure delivered through a twin-cylinder hydraulic feed.

SHOT DRILLS

A shot drill is a tool which depends on the abrasive effect of chilled steel shot to penetrate the rock. The essential parts include a shot bit, core barrel, sludge barrel, drill rod, water pump, and power-driven rotation unit. The bit consists of a section of steel pipe, with a serrated lower end. As the bit is rotated, shot are fed to the lower end through the drill rod. Under the pressure of the bit these shot erode the rock to form a kerf around the core. Water, which is supplied through the drill rod, forces the rock cuttings up around the outside of the drill, where they settle in a sludge barrel, to be removed when the entire unit is pulled from the hole. Periodically it is necessary to break the core off and remove it from the hole in order that drilling may proceed.

Figure 13-20 illustrates a type of shot drill that has been used extensively. Figure 13-21 illustrates a drilling unit which is used to rotate the bit. The drive is through the spindle extending below the drill head.

Standard shot drills are capable of drilling holes up to 600 ft or more in depth, with diameters varying from $2\frac{1}{2}$ to 20 in. Special equipment has been used to drill up to 6 ft in diameter with depths in excess of 1,000 ft. Rock of any hardness may be drilled.

Although large holes are expensive, they permit a man to be lowered into them for a thorough examination of the formation in place. For this purpose holes 30 in. in diameter or larger are sometimes drilled. Smaller holes provide continuous cores for examination for structural information.

The rate of drilling with a shot drill is relatively slow, sometimes less than 1 ft per hr, depending on the size of the drill and the hardness of the rock.

Example On a project for an electric utility company near Oak Park, Ohio, the contractor used a shot drill to drill 100 large diameter footings for columns in hard limestone rock. The holes varied from 30 in. (76 cm) to 60 in. (152 cm) in diameter and averaged about 12 ft (3.7 m) in depth. Holes 42 in. (107 cm) in diameter were drilled at an average rate of 1 to $1\frac{1}{2}$ ft (0.3 to 0.5 m) per hr, while holes 60 in. (152 cm) in diameter were drilled at an average rate of about 1 ft (0.3 m) per hr [2].

DIAMOND DRILLS

Diamond drills are used primarily for exploration drilling, where cores are desired for the purpose of studying the rock structure. The Diamond Core Drill Manufacturers' Association lists four sizes as standard—$1\frac{1}{2}$, $1\frac{7}{8}$, $2\frac{3}{8}$, and 3 in. Larger sizes are available, but the investment in diamonds increases so rapidly with an increase in size that shot drills may be more economical for larger-diameter holes.

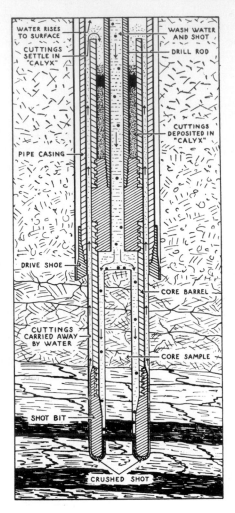

Figure 13-20 Shot or calyx core drill. *(Ingersoll-Rand Company.)*

A drilling rig consists of a diamond bit, a core barrel, a jointed driving tube, and a rotary head to supply the driving torque. Water is pumped through the driving tube to remove the cuttings. The pressure on the bit is regulated through a screw or hydraulic-feed swivel head. Core barrels are available in lengths varying from 5 to 15 ft. When the bit advances to a depth equal to the length of the core barrel, the core is broken off and the drill is removed from the hole. Diamond drills can drill in any desired direction from vertically downward to upward.

The selection of the size of diamonds depends on the nature of the formation to be drilled. Large stones are preferred for the softer formations and small stones for fine-grained solid formations.

Diamond drills are capable of drilling to depths in excess of 1,000 ft. Bit speeds may vary from approximately 200 to 1,200 rpm. The drilling rate will

Figure 13-21 Drilling unit for shot core drill. *(Acker Drill Company.)*

vary from less than a foot to several feet per hour, depending on the type of rock.

Table 13-3 gives information on the dimensions and diamond content of bits. The cost of diamonds varies with the quality and quantity used with the bit.

MANUFACTURERS' REPORT ON DRILLING EQUIPMENT AND TECHNIQUES [3]

In 1976 a magazine devoted primarily to construction methods and equipment published an article discussing and describing the contributions of drills to production profits. The article presented the views of representatives of drilling equipment manufacturers, with suggestions listed for selecting and using the equipment to achieve increased production at reduced costs. Their views are presented below.

The views of drilling equipment manufacturers The manufacturers' representatives who assessed the ingredients of drilling productivity included as important factors selection, maintainability, mobility, operator expertise, operability of

Table 13-3 Representative information for standard diamond coring bits

| Size of bit, in. | Nominal | | Net dimension | | Minimum carat content |
	Hole diameter, in.	Core diameter, in.	OD, in.	ID, in.	
EX	$1\frac{1}{2}$	$\frac{7}{8}$	1.460	0.845	6.75
AX	$1\frac{7}{8}$	$1\frac{1}{8}$	1.865	1.185	10.00
BX	$2\frac{3}{8}$	$1\frac{5}{8}$	2.330	1.655	14.00
NX	3	$2\frac{1}{8}$	2.945	2.155	18.00
$2\frac{3}{4} \times 3\frac{7}{8}$	$3\frac{7}{8}$	$2\frac{3}{4}$	3.840	2.690	36.00
$4 \times 5\frac{1}{2}$	$5\frac{1}{2}$	4	5.435	3.970	60.00
$6 \times 7\frac{3}{4}$	$7\frac{3}{4}$	6	7.655	5.970	90.00

Figure 13-22 Drilling unit for diamond core drill. *(Acker Drill Company.)*

Figure 13-23 Diamond-point bits. *(Sprague & Henwood, Inc.)*

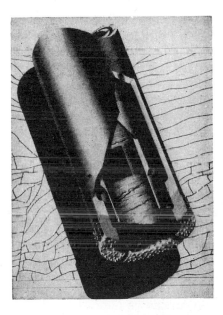

Figure 13-24 Diamond coring bit and double-tube core barrel. *(Sprague & Henwood, Inc.)*

equipment, and use of auxiliary attachments. The methods of drilling employed, the attitude of management toward this activity, and the interrelationship between the drill bit and the drilling rig also contribute to the ability to attain maximum production at minimum cost. Each user or prospective user of drilling equipment should examine these views and adopt the ones that seem to apply to his operations.

The views of the manufacturers are presented below.

The user of drills to be operated in a quarry should select equipment that will maximize productivity within the limits of his loading, hauling, and crushing equipment. The equipment which he selects must work under the most severe and gruelling conditions of the given project. Before any equipment is selected, it should be tested for performance and the results of the tests should be made available to the prospective purchaser.

One representative suggested that use of increased air pressure and larger hammers and internal improvements such as valveless construction of air compressors, where the piston is its own valve (resulting in the reduction of moving parts) should contribute to better performance. It was also suggested that when drilling holes deeper than about 50 ft, down-the-hole drilling, i.e., the process of moving the cylinder and its percussive impact into the hole, should be considered. This move can increase the effective energy by as much as 10 percent by eliminating the loss of energy in extended lengths of drill rods.

Another suggestion was that more tests be conducted to determine the best sizes of blast holes, ratios of burden to spacing, density of explosives, and delay patterns to increase the yield of blasted rock per foot of hole, to determine the effect which such actions would have on the cost of production.

Greater care could perhaps be exercised by the drill operators as they add sections of steel rods to produce deeper holes to be certain that the abutting ends of drill rods bear tightly against each other to transmit the drilling forces to the bits. If these forces are transmitted by the couplings, they may cause excessive splitting of the couplings, with possible loss of bits, drill rods, and holes.

The use of button bits as a means of more evenly distributing the forces of the drills on the rock may be desirable on some projects. The superior geometric pattern of the buttons can help increase the penetration by as much as 10 to 20 percent, smooth the drilling operation, and reduce the stress on the drilling equipment when compared with conventional blade bits. However, button bits are not recommended for drilling long, close, parallel holes, as in presplitting, where holes drilled with button bits may drift or even cross each other. Moreover, their small contact surface may cause greater wear in drilling of hard, abrasive rock.

In some drilling operations productivity has been increased by increasing the pressure and volume of air supplied to the drill by maintaining a cleaner blast hole. At the same time, increasing the down pressure on the bit has improved the cutting action of the bit.

Maintenance and repair services for equipment can be improved, with less down time for repairs and replacement of parts, if the equipment is standardized to the extent permitted by the operations for which it is used. With fewer models of equipment to be serviced, an inventory of spare parts that fail most frequently can be maintained on the job.

Manufacturers have made drilling equipment to provide more service-free time by enclosing many feed, swing, and other assemblies in oil to reduce the wear.

Track drills have been improved by offering hydraulic or mechanical oscillation. Improved horsepower-to-weight ratios permit drills to navigate terrain that was considered inaccessible without winch assistance at one time. And automatic brakes assist in holding the drills in difficult positions.

The availability of extendable booms on track drills has increased the service ranges and performance of drills.

Also, the availability of drills with dust control systems permits use of drills in locations where environmental restrictions would otherwise preclude them.

Because of the high cost, complexity, and sophistication of much drilling equipment, some manufacturers have developed training programs to assist the users and operators of their equipment in increasing its efficiency.

SELECTING THE DRILLING METHOD AND EQUIPMENT

Holes are drilled for various purposes, such as to receive charges of explosives, for exploration, for the injection of grout, etc. Within practical limits the equipment which will produce the greatest overall economy for the particular project is the most satisfactory. Many factors affect the selection of equipment. Among them are the following:

1. The nature of the terrain. Rough surfaces may dictate jackhammers, regardless of other factors.
2. The required depth of holes.
3. The hardness of the rock.
4. The extent to which the formation is broken or fractured.
5. The size of the project.
6. The extent to which the rock is to be broken for handling or crushing.
7. The availability of water for drilling purposes. Lack of water favors dry drilling.
8. The purpose of the holes, such as blasting, exploration, or grout injection.
9. The size cores required for exploration. Small cores permit the use of diamond drills, while large cores suggest shot drills.

For small-diameter shallow blastholes, especially on rough surfaces where larger drills cannot operate, it is usually necessary to use jackhammers, even though the production rates will be low and the costs high.

For blastholes up to about 6 in. in diameter and up to about 50 ft deep, where crawler-mounted machines can operate, the choice may be between track-mounted, rotary-percussion, or piston drills.

If it is necessary to drill holes from 6 to 12 in. in diameter, from 50 to 300 ft deep, the blasthole or rotary drill is usually the best choice.

If cores up to 3 in. are desired, the diamond coring drill is the most satisfactory.

If intermediate-size cores, 3 to 8 in. outside diameter, are desired, the choice will be between a diamond drill and a shot drill. A diamond drill will usually drill faster than a shot drill; also, a diamond drill can drill holes in any direction, while a shot drill is limited to holes that are vertical, or nearly so.

If larger-size cores are desired, a shot drill should be used, as diamond drills are not practical in sizes greater than approximately 8 in. outside diameter.

SELECTING THE DRILLING PATTERN

The pattern selected for drilling holes to be loaded with explosives will vary with the type and size drill used, the depth of the holes, the kind of rock, the maximum size rocks permissible, and other factors.

If the holes are drilled to produce rock aggregate, the drilling pattern should be planned to produce rock pieces small enough to permit most of them to be handled by the excavator, such as a power shovel, or to pass into the crusher opening without secondary blasting. While this condition is possible, the cost of excess drilling and explosives to produce it may be so high that the production of some oversize rocks is permissible, in the interest of economy.

If small-diameter holes are spaced close together, the better distribution of the explosives will result in a more uniform rock breakage. However, if the added cost of drilling exceeds the value of the benefits resulting from better breakage, the close spacing is not justified.

As large-diameter holes permit greater explosive loading per hole, it is possible to increase the spacing between large holes and thereby reduce the cost of drilling.

In analyzing a job for drilling and blasting operations, there are three factors which should be considered. They are:

1. The cubic yards of rock per linear foot of hole
2. The number of pounds of explosive per cubic yard of rock
3. The number of pounds of explosive per linear foot of hole

The value of each of the three factors may be estimated in advance of drilling and blasting operations, but after experimental drilling operations are conducted, it probably will be desirable to modify the values to give better results.

The relationships between the three factors are illustrated in Table 13-4. The volumes of rock per linear foot of hole are based on the net depth of holes and do not include subdrilling, which frequently is necessary. The pounds of explosive per linear foot of hole are based on filling the holes completely with 60 percent dynamite. The pounds of explosive per cubic yard of rock are based on filling each hole to 100, 75, and 50 percent of its total capacity with dynamite. When a hole is not filled completely with dynamite, the surplus volume is filled with stemming.

Table 13-4 Drilling and blasting data

| Size hole, in. | Hole pattern, ft | Area per hole, sq ft | Volume of rock per lin ft of hole, cu yd | Lb of explosive per lin ft of hole* | Lb of explosive per cu yd of rock* % of hole filled | | |
					100	75	50
$1\frac{1}{2}$	4 × 4	16	0.59	0.9	1.52	1.14	0.76
	5 × 5	25	0.93	0.9	0.97	0.73	0.48
	6 × 6	36	1.33	0.9	0.68	0.51	0.34
	7 × 7	49	1.81	0.9	0.50	0.38	0.25
2	5 × 5	25	0.93	1.7	1.83	1.37	0.92
	6 × 6	36	1.33	1.7	1.28	0.96	0.64
	7 × 7	49	1.81	1.7	0.94	0.71	0.47
	8 × 8	64	2.37	1.7	0.72	0.54	0.36
3	7 × 7	49	1.81	3.9	2.15	1.61	1.08
	8 × 8	64	2.37	3.9	1.65	1.24	0.83
	9 × 9	81	3.00	3.9	1.30	0.97	0.65
	10 × 10	100	3.70	3.9	1.05	0.79	0.53
	11 × 11	121	4.48	3.9	0.87	0.65	0.44
4	8 × 8	64	2.37	7.5	3.16	2.37	1.58
	10 × 10	100	3.70	7.5	2.03	1.52	1.02
	12 × 12	144	5.30	7.5	1.42	1.06	0.71
	14 × 14	196	7.25	7.5	1.03	0.77	0.52
	16 × 16	256	9.50	7.5	0.79	0.59	0.40
5	12 × 12	144	5.30	10.9	2.05	1.54	1.02
	14 × 14	196	7.25	10.9	1.50	1.13	0.75
	16 × 16	256	9.50	10.9	1.15	0.86	0.58
	18 × 18	324	12.00	10.9	0.91	0.68	0.46
	20 × 20	400	14.85	10.9	0.73	0.55	0.37
6	12 × 12	144	5.30	15.6	2.94	2.20	1.47
	14 × 14	196	7.25	15.6	2.05	1.54	1.02
	16 × 16	256	9.50	15.6	1.64	1.23	0.82
	18 × 18	324	12.00	15.6	1.30	0.97	0.65
	20 × 20	400	14.85	15.6	1.05	0.79	0.53
	24 × 24	576	21.35	15.6	0.73	0.55	0.37
9	20 × 20	400	14.85	35.0	2.36	1.77	1.18
	24 × 24	576	21.35	35.0	1.64	1.23	0.82
	28 × 28	784	29.00	35.0	1.21	0.91	0.61
	30 × 30	900	33.30	35.0	1.05	0.79	0.53
	32 × 32	1,024	37.90	35.0	0.92	0.69	0.46

* Based on using dynamite weighing 80 lb per cu ft.

RATES OF DRILLING ROCK

The rates of drilling rock will vary with a number of factors, such as the type and size drill used, hardness of the rock, depth of holes, drilling pattern, time lost waiting for other operations, etc. Also, if pneumatic drills are used, the rate of drilling will vary considerably with the pressure of the air, as demonstrated in the section starting on page 391.

Another item that influences the rate of drilling is the availability factor. Because of the nature of the work that they do, drills are subjected to severe usage, which may result in frequent failures of critical parts, or a deterioration of the whole unit, entailing delays in drilling. The portion of time that a drill is operative is defined as the availability factor, which is usually expressed as a percent of the total time the drill is expected to be working.

Examples of rates and costs of drilling rock During 1964 a mining company operating an open-pit mine in British Columbia, Canada, made an analysis of extensive records related to the production rates of several types and makes of drills [4]. The results of the analysis appear in Table 13-5.

The ore in the pit consisted of low-grade chalcopyrite, which is associated with hematite and magnetite.

As indicated in the table, four drills were used during the tests. The types were

A. Electric-powered rotary
B. Diesel-engine-powered rotary
C. Diesel-engine-powered rotary
D. Electric-powered percussion

Because drill bits account for about 50 percent of the operating cost of the drills, cost tests were conducted using several types and makes of bits. The results of the tests indicated that tri-cone bits were the most economical.

Table 13-5 Comparative production and cost of rock drills

Item	\multicolumn{4}{c}{Type drill}
	A	B	C	D
Diameter of hole, in.	9	9	$7\frac{7}{8}$	6
Availability, %	89	70	67	88
Tons drilled per shift	10,350	6,570	3,020	4,360
Operating cost per ton	$0.0085	$0.0154	$0.0210	$0.0126
Labor cost per ton	0.0034	0.0053	0.0113	0.0078
Total cost per ton	$0.0119	$0.0207	$0.0323	$0.0204

Table 13-6 Rates and costs of drilling and blasting rock

Item	Performance or cost
Drilling performance	
Tons drilled	368,250
Depth of holes drilled, ft	71,407
Tons per foot of hole	5.16
Depth of hole per bit, ft	174
Depth of hole per drill rod, ft	1,300
Depth of hole per coupling, ft	750
Depth of hole per drill shift, 8 hr, ft	238
Drilling costs per ton of rock	
Labor	$0.025
Supplies	0.059
Compressed air	0.017
Machine maintenance labor	0.002
Machine maintenance supplies	0.007
Miscellaneous	0.009
Total	$0.119
Blasting costs per ton of rock	
Average powder factor, lb/ton	0.429
Explosives	$0.084
Labor	0.009
Total cost	$0.093

Another example of the rates of drilling rock and the distribution of costs appears in Table 13-6. The project is an open-pit copper and zinc mine in Ontario, Canada [4]. The ores were greenstones and sulphides, the latter being hard and abrasive. The two units used were track-mounted rotary-percussion drills, which drilled 3-in.-diameter holes on patterns of 9 by 9 ft and 7 by 7 ft.

The effect of air pressure on the rate of drilling rock The cost of energy furnished by compressed air is high when compared with the cost of energy supplied by electricity or diesel fuel. The ratio of costs may be as high as 6 : 1. For this reason it is essential that every reasonable effort be made to increase the efficiency of the compressed air system and the equipment which uses compressed air as a source of energy. One method of increasing the efficiency of pneumatic drills is to be certain that the specified air pressure at the drill is available.

It has been shown that the energy of a rock drill can be represented by the following formula [5, 6]

$$E \propto \frac{P^{1.5}A^{1.5}S^{0.5}}{W^{0.5}}$$

(13-1)

where $E=$ energy per blow
$\quad\quad P=$ air pressure
$\quad\quad A=$ area of piston
$\quad\quad S=$ length of piston stroke
$\quad\quad W=$ weight of piston

With all the factors constant in a given drill except the pressure of the air, this formula indicates that the energy delivered per blow varies with the 1.5 power of the pressure.

Factors which during the past have discouraged the use of higher pressures to increase the rate of drilling have been the limitations imposed by the design of the drills and reduced life spans of the drill steel and bits. However, these limitations have been overcome to a large extent in recent years.

The potential increase in production of a drill when operating at a higher pressure should not be the sole factor in a decision to use higher pressure. The value of the increased production should be compared with the probable increase in the cost of air and maintenance and repairs for the drill, including drill steel and bits. Also, any increase in maintenance and repairs may reduce the availability factor for the drill. The optimum pressure is the pressure that will result in the minimum cost of drilling a unit of hole depth, considering all factors related to the drilling including, but not limited to, the following:

1. The value of the increased production
2. The increased cost of providing air at a higher pressure
3. The cost of increased line leakage
4. The increased cost of maintenance and repairs for the drill
5. The adverse effect, if any, of increased noise in some instances such as tunneling
6. The effect which a higher pressure may have on the availability factor for the drill or air compressor

On most construction projects it is not practical to conduct studies to evaluate each of these factors. However, a limited number of studies have been made under conditions that did permit evaluation of the effects of varying the pressure of the air. The results of one such test are given in the next article.

Determining the optimum air pressure for drilling rock This is a report on the results of tests that were conducted in a mine in Ontario, Canada, recently [3]. The walls of the test station were marked off in panels, so that, by drilling in each of the panels at every stage of testing, variations in the drillability of the rock were minimized. Stop watches, an air flowmeter, pressure-reducing valves, pressure gauges, micrometer gauges, and tools were used to assure adequate controls and information.

Prior to starting the tests seven new jackleg drills were obtained from five manufacturers and divided into two groups, as indicated in Table 13-7. Holes were drilled at pressures of 90, 100, 110, 120, 130, and 140 psi. For each pressure

Table 13-7 Variations in the rates of penetration by rock drills with varying air pressure

Drill group	Bore, in. (mm)	Stroke, in. (mm)	90 (7.2)†	100 (7.9)†	110 (8.6)†	120 (9.3)†	130 (10.0)†	140 (10.6)†
			Dynamic air pressure, psi gauge (Pa)* Rate of penetration, in. per min (mm/min)					
A_1	$2\frac{21}{32}$ (67.4)	$2\frac{7}{8}$ (73.0)	12.47 (317)	14.31 (364)	16.10 (409)	20.60 (524)	21.84 (555)	24.49 (623)
A_2	$2\frac{11}{16}$ (68.3)	$2\frac{9}{16}$ (65.2)	12.90 (329)	16.06 (408)	17.41 (443)	21.87 (556)	23.76 (603)	24.55 (625)
A_3	$2\frac{3}{4}$ (69.7)	$2\frac{3}{4}$ (75.0)	13.90 (355)	17.49 (444)	16.78 (426)	22.88 (582)	23.58 (600)	26.63 (678)
Average for group A			13.09 (322)	15.95 (405)	16.76 (427)	21.78 (554)	23.06 (587)	25.22 (641)
Percent increase				21.85	28.04	66.38	76.16	92.67
B_1	$3\frac{1}{8}$ (79.5)	$2\frac{3}{8}$ (60.5)	14.48 (367)	18.49 (469)	16.08 (408)	21.75 (553)	21.01 (535)	25.96 (659)
B_2	3 (76.0)	$2\frac{9}{16}$ (65.2)	14.15 (360)	19.04 (484)	19.72 (500)	22.94 (582)	21.32 (540)	22.89 (582)
B_3	3 (76.0)	$2\frac{5}{8}$ (66.6)	14.58 (370)	15.82 (402)	15.23 (387)	21.95 (558)	18.93 (481)	20.87 (531)
B_4	3 (76.0)	$1\frac{15}{16}$ (49.2)	10.32 (263)	12.59 (320)	17.77 (432)	20.28 (515)	21.97 (583)	24.01 (610)
Average for group B			13.39 (340)	16.49 (419)	17.20 (438)	21.73 (551)	20.81 (529)	23.43 (596)
Percent increase				23.15	28.45	62.28	55.41	74.97

* Psi pressures are gauge, while Pa pressures are absolute. Thus 14.7 must be added to the psi values before multiplying by the conversion to Pa units.

† Each of the listed values is multiplied by 10^5 to obtain the correct Pa units. Thus (7.2) is 7.2×10^5, (7.9) is 7.9×10^5, etc.

increment a new carbide-insert bit was used on both 6-ft and 12-ft steel. All bits were $1\frac{1}{4}$ in. in diameter.

Table 13-7 lists the rates of penetration for each drill for each of the air pressures, while Table 13-8 lists the volume of air consumed, in cubic feet of free air per minute, for each drill and pressure.

Figure 13-25 shows the relationship between the average rate of penetration and the operating pressure for each group of drills. Figure 13-26 is a nomogram based on the information appearing in Fig. 13-25 which indicates the percent increase in penetration resulting from an increase in air pressure. For example, if the pressure is increased from 90 to 100 psi, the increase in penetration will be 38 percent.

Table 13-8 Variations in the volume of air consumed with varying air pressures

Drill group	Dynamic air pressure, psi gauge (Pa),*					
	90 (7.2)[†]	100 (7.9)[†]	110 (8.6)[†]	120 (9.3)[†]	130 (10.0)[†]	140 (10.6)[†]
	Volume of air consumed, cfm (cu m/sec)					
I_1	132.2 (0.062)	154.2 (0.073)	160.5 (0.076)	178.5 (0.084)	185.0 (0.087)	210.0 (0.099)
A_2	133.5 (0.063)	150.6 (0.071)	162.5 (0.077)	182.5 (0.086)	193.0 (0.091)	221.0 (0.104)
A_3	159.2 (0.075)	171.0 (0.081)	193.2 (0.091)	214.0 (0.102)	228.5 (0.108)	255.7 (0.121)
Average for group A	141.6 (0.067)	158.6 (0.075)	172.1 (0.081)	191.7 (0.090)	202.2 (0.095)	228.9 (0.108)
Percent increase	.....	12.0	21.5	35.4	42.8	61.7
B_1	185.2 (0.087)	207.3 (0.098)	233.6 (0.111)	257.0 (0.121)	284.5 (0.134)	302.4 (0.143)
B_2	165.1 (0.078)	188.2 (0.089)	208.5 (0.098)	241.3 (0.114)	252.5 (0.119)	273.0 (0.129)
B_3	163.0 (0.077)	183.0 (0.086)	206.7 (0.097)	226.5 (0.107)	255.0 (0.121)	267.7 (0.126)
B_4	182.2 (0.086)	195.2 (0.092)	213.8 (0.102)	241.2 (0.114)	269.5 (0.127)	290.5 (0.137)
Average for group B	173.9 (0.082)	193.4 (0.091)	215.6 (0.103)	241.5 (0.114)	265.4 (0.125)	283.4 (0.133)
Percent increase	......	11.21	24.0	38.9	52.6	63.0

* Psi pressures are gauge, while Pa pressures are absolute. Thus 14.7 must be added to the psi values before multiplying by the conversion factor to obtain Pa units.

[†] Each of the listed values is multiplied by 10^5 to obtain the correct Pa units. Thus (7.2) is 7.2×10^5, (7.9) is 7.9×10^5, etc.

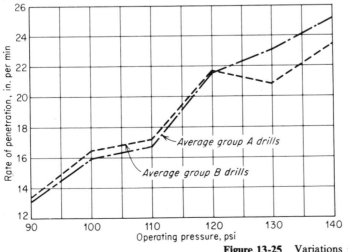

Figure 13-25 Variations in the rate of penetration with air pressure.

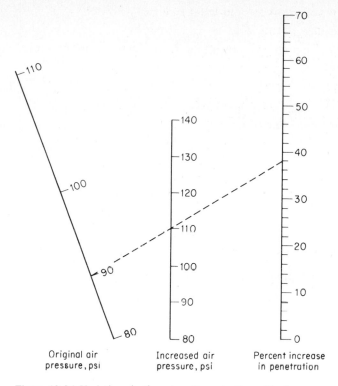

Figure 13-26 Variations in the rates of penetration with air pressure.

DETERMINING THE INCREASE IN PRODUCTION RESULTING FROM AN INCREASE IN AIR PRESSURE

If a drill is presently operating at a given air pressure, such as 90 psi, Fig. 13-26 indicates that if the pressure is increased to 110 psi, the rate of penetration of the drill will be increased 38 percent. This will not result in an increase of 38 percent in the production on the project. The increased rate of penetration is effective only during the time the drill is actually producing hole or drilling. Thus, the increase does not apply to the time that the drill is not actually drilling, which generally will remain the same, regardless of the rate of penetration.

Let us develop a formula which can be used to determine the increase in production resulting from an increase in the rate of penetration. The following symbols will be used:

T = elapsed time that the drill is on the job, hr

D = drilling factor, the portion of the elapsed time devoted to drilling = $\dfrac{T_1}{T}$

T_1 = time actually devoted to drilling, hr

Q_1 = total depth of hole drilled during T hr, ft

R_1 = average rate of drilling during T hr = $\dfrac{Q_1}{T}$, ft per hr

P = increase in rate of penetration resulting from increase in pressure, expressed as a fraction

R_2 = average rate of drilling resulting from increase in pressure = $R_1(1 + P)$

T_2 = time required to drill Q_1 ft of hole at increased rate R_2, hr = $\dfrac{T_1}{1 + P}$

T_s = time saved by increased rate of drilling

$$T_s = T_1 - T_2 = T_1 - \frac{T_1}{1 + P}$$
$$= \frac{T_1(1 + P) - T_1}{1 + P} = \frac{T_1 + T_1 P - T_1}{1 + P} = \frac{T_1 P}{1 + P} \tag{a}$$

But $T_1 = TD$. Thus,

$$T_s = \frac{TDP}{1 + P} \tag{b}$$

Let Q_2 = the increased depth of hole drilled at the increased rate of penetration during time T. Thus,

$$Q_2 = T_s R_2$$
$$= \frac{TDP}{1 + P} \times R_1(1 + P)$$
$$= TDPR_1 \tag{c}$$

But $Q_1 = TR_1$. Thus

$$Q_2 = Q_1 DP$$

and

$$\frac{Q_2}{Q_1} = DP \tag{13-2}$$

which is the ratio of the increased production divided by the original production, expressed as a fraction.

Example Consider a 1,000-hr elapsed time for a drill on a project. During this time the drill actually penetrates rock 300 hr for a drilling factor of 0.3, for a total depth of hole equal to 10,000 ft. The initial operating air pressure at the drill is 90 psi. If the pressure is increased to 110 psi, what is the probable total depth of hole drilled in 1,000 hr, based on the information appearing in Fig. 13-26? Reference to this figure indicates an increased rate of penetration equal to 38 percent. Thus $P = 0.38$.

Applying formula (13-2),

$$\frac{Q_2}{Q_1} = DP = 0.3 \times 0.38 = 0.114$$

$$Q_2 = 0.114Q_1 = 0.114 \times 10,000$$

$$= 1,140 \text{ ft additional depth of hole}$$

The total depth of hole will be 10,000 + 1,140 = 11,140 ft. This should result in an increase of 11.4 percent in production if the increased depth of hole is reflected in increased production.

It should be emphasized that the information appearing in Fig. 13-26 does not necessarily apply to all drilling conditions. For other projects the increase in the rate of penetration may be more or less than the values obtained from this figure.

THE EFFECT OF INCREASED AIR PRESSURE ON THE COSTS OF MAINTENANCE AND REPAIRS OF DRILLS

During the time that tests were conducted by the mining company in Ontario, Canada, to evaluate the effect of increasing air pressure on the rate of penetration the company also determined the effect of increased pressure on the cost of providing compressed air and the cost of drills, bits, and drill steel. This information appears in Table 13-9.

CONDUCTING A STUDY TO DETERMINE THE ECONOMY OF INCREASING AIR PRESSURE

The decision to increase or not increase the air pressure at the drills should not be determined solely on the basis of the anticipated increase in production and the increase in the cost of compressed air and drilling equipment. Drilling is only one item in a chain of operations, which may include drilling, blasting, loading, and hauling to a disposal area, or it may involve providing quarry rock for crushing into aggregate. The cost effect which operating at an increased pressure will have on the rate of production and also on cost of the related operations should be considered in reaching a decision. The objective is to provide rock at its disposal point, at a waste area, in a fill, or as crushed stone in stockpiles at the lowest practical cost per unit of material.

Figure 13-27 represents a curve that establishes the lowest total cost of producing the end product of a drilling operation. The curve is plotted to indicate this cost for varying air pressures. As noted, the optimum pressure is 102 psi.

Table 13-9 Increase in drilling expense resulting from using increased air pressure

Item	Percent increase in expense Operating air pressure, psi			
	90	100	110	120
Compressor operation and maintenance	0	13.0	26.0	39.5
Drills	0	27.0	55.0	83.0
Bits	0	21.5	43.0	64.5
Steel	0	21.5	43.5	66.0

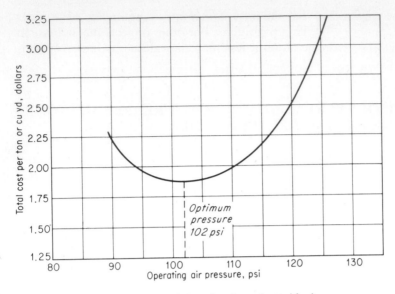

Figure 13-27 Variation in the total cost of rock product with air pressure.

TEST TO DETERMINE THE EFFECT OF AIR PRESSURE ON THE RATE OF PENETRATION OF A DRILL

During 1964 tests were conducted under the supervision of the author to determine the effect of air pressure on the rate of penetration of a track-mounted drill using 3-in.-diameter carbide-inset bits. The materials drilled were limestone in a commercial quarry and a large mass of homogeneous concrete, whose 28-day compressive strength averaged 6,790 psi, cast in a rectangular pit in the ground.

Adequate controls, such as valves, a pressure regulator, a recording pressure gauge, and an auxiliary 100-cu-ft air receiver in the line were used to assure the maintenance of the desired pressure. A constant down thrust was maintained on the drifter drill during all drilling operations.

The results of the tests are illustrated in Figs. 13-28 and 13-29. The maximum pressure of 105 psi was imposed by the inability of the 600-cfm compressor to supply air at a higher pressure.

It will be noted that, using values obtained from the curve in Fig. 13-28, the rate of penetration in concrete at 90 psi is 13.3 in. per min, while the rate at 100 psi is 14.4 in. per min. This is an increase of 8.3 percent in the rate of penetration. The corresponding increase for limestone is 6.7 percent. In each instance the percent increase in the rate of penetration was less than the percent increase in air pressure. Thus it appears that the use of an increased air pressure may not be economically justified.

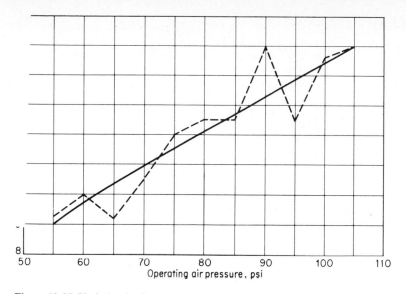

Figure 13-28 Variation in the rate of penetration of concrete with air pressure.

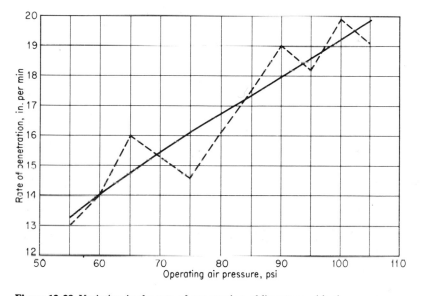

Figure 13-29 Variation in the rate of penetration of limestone with air pressure.

DRILLING EARTH

General information This section of the book will illustrate and discuss various types of equipment used to drill holes in earth, as distinguished from rock. Some equipment, such as that used for exploratory purposes in securing core samples and similar operations, may be used for drilling rock or earth.

Purposes for drilling holes in earth In the construction and mining industries holes are drilled into earth for many purposes, including, but not limited to, the following:

1. To obtain samples of soil for test purposes
2. To locate and evaluate deposits of aggregate suitable for construction purposes
3. To locate and evaluate deposits of minerals
4. To permit the installation of cast-in-place piles or shafts to support structures
5. To enable the driving of load-bearing piles into hard and tough formations
6. To provide wells for supplies of water or for deep drainage purposes

Figure 13-30 Tractor-mounted auger-type earth drill. *(Acker Drill Company.)*

7. To provide shafts for ventilating mines, tunnels, and other underground facilities
8. To provide horizontal holes through embankments, such as those for highways, for the installation of utility conduits

Sizes and depths of holes drilled into earth As illustrated by the accompanying figures, most holes are drilled by rotating bits or heads attached to the lower end of a shaft called a kelly bar. This bar, which is supported by a truck or a tractor or another suitable mount, is rotated by an external motor or engine.

The sizes of holes drilled may vary from a few inches to more than 12 ft (3.7 m). Drills may be equipped with a device attached to the lower end of the drill shaft, described as an underreamer, which will permit a gradual increase in the

Figure 13-31 Truck-mounted auger-type earth drill. *(Mobile Drilling Company.)*

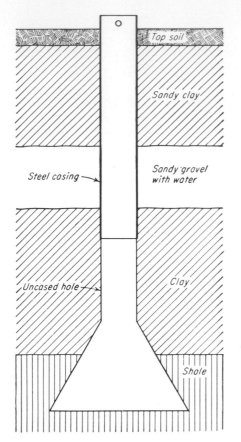

Figure 13-32 Steel casing used to permit footing to be drilled through unstable soil.

diameter of the hole, as illustrated in Fig. 13-32. This enlargement permits a substantial increase in the bearing area under a shaft-type concrete footing.

Holes may be drilled to almost any desired depth, several thousand feet in some instances, by adding more sections to the drill shaft.

Removal of cuttings Several methods are used to remove the cuttings from the holes.

One method of removing the cuttings is to attach the drill head, the actual cutting tool at the bottom of the drill shaft, to the lower end of an auger, as illustrated in Fig. 13-33, which extends from the drill head to above the surface of the ground. As the drill shaft and the auger rotate, the earth is forced to the top of the hole, where it is removed and wasted. However, the depth of a hole for which this method may be used is limited by the diameter of the hole, the class of soil, and the moisture content of the soil.

Another method of removing the cuttings is to attach the drill head to the lower end of a section of the auger. When the auger is filled with cuttings, it is raised above the surface of the ground and rotated rapidly to free it of the cuttings.

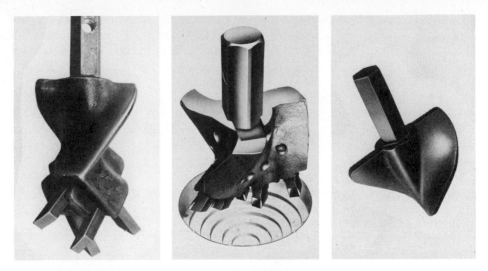

Figure 13-33 Drill heads or bits to be attached to the bottom of a drill kelly for drilling earth or soft rock. *(Mobile Drilling Company.)*

Figure 13-34 Gasoline-engine-powered auger-type boring machine. *(McLaughlin Manufacturing Company.)*

A third method of removing the cuttings is to use a combination of a drill head with a cylindrical bucket, whose diameter is the same as the diameter of the hole. As the bucket is rotated, steel cutting blades attached to the bottom of the bucket force the cuttings up and into the bucket. When the bucket is filled, it is raised to the surface of the ground and emptied.

A fourth method of removing the cuttings is to force air or water through the hollow kelly bar and drill shaft to the bottom of the hole and then upward around the drill shaft, so that the cuttings are carried to the surface of the ground.

Drilling holes through unstable soils When holes are drilled through unstable soils, such as mud, silt, sand, or gravel-containing water, it may be necessary to install a temporary or permanent steel casing, as illustrated in Fig. 13-32, to prevent the flow of soil into the hole.

Earth boring machines Figure 13-34 illustrates a self-contained gasoline-engine-powered open-auger-type boring machine, which is used to bore uncased holes through earth. The machine illustrated will bore holes varying from 3 to 12 in. (76 to 304 mm) in diameter to depths up to 80 ft (28 m), depending on the type and condition of the soil and the job conditions.

Figure 13-35 Gasoline-engine-powered auger-type boring machine with the auger enclosed in a steel casing. *(McLaughlin Manufacturing Company.)*

Figure 13-35 illustrates a self-contained gasoline-engine-powered auger-type boring machine with the auger enclosed in a steel pipe or casing, which is forced through the hole excavated by the auger. The machine illustrated is capable of boring holes for casing sizes varying from 4 to 30 in. (102 to 762 mm) or more to depths up to 200 ft (61 m), depending on the type and condition of the soil and the job conditions. As the boring advances, the machine automatically maintains a forward thrust on the casing and the auger.

These machines may also be powered hydraulically, by air, or by electric motors.

REFERENCES

1. Smith, Gordon R: Drilling, New Equipment, New Techniques, *Construction Methods and Equipment*, vol. 44, pp. 110–115, August 1962.
2. Shot-drill Cuts Hard Rock Sockets for Column Footings, *Construction Methods and Equipment*, vol. 53, pp 84–85, May 1971.
3. Higgins, Lindley R: Drills Play Dramatic Role in Profit Production, *Construction Methods and Equipment*, vol. 58, pp. 54–61, September 1976.
4. The Cost of Drilling and Blasting Today's Pits, *Engineering and Mining Journal*, vol. 166, pp. 110–113, September 1965.
5. Pasieka, A. R., and J. C. Wilson: The Importance of High-Pressure Compressed Air to Mining Operations, *The Canadian Mining and Metallurgical Bulletin*, vol. 59, pp. 1093–1102, September 1966.
6. Knox, John: Factors Influence the Design and Application of Downhole Drills, *The Canadian Mining and Metallurgical Bulletin*, vol. 58, pp. 547–550, May 1965.
7. Acker Drill Company, Inc., P.O. Box 830, Scranton, Pennsylvania 18501.
8. Atlas Copco, Inc., 70 Demarest Drive, Wayne, New Jersey 07470.
9. Ingersoll-Rand Company, Phillipsburg, New Jersey 08865.
10. Joy Manufacturing Company, Claremont, New Hampshire 03743.
11. McLaughlin Manufacturing Company, P.O. Box 303, Plainfield, Illinois 60544.
12. Mobile Drilling Company, Inc., 3807 Madison Avenue, Indianapolis, Indiana 46227.
13. Penn-Mar Mining Company, Route 5, Leitersburg Pike, Hagerstown, Maryland 21740.
14. Reed Tool Company, 12400 North Freeway, Houston, Texas 77090.
15. Schramm, Inc., 800 East Virginia Avenue, West Chester, Pennsylvania 19380.
16. Sprague & Henwood, Inc., Scranton, Pennsylvania 18501.
17. The Timken Company, Canton, Ohio 44706.

FOURTEEN

BLASTING ROCK

BLASTING

The operation referred to as blasting is performed to loosen rock in order that it may be excavated or removed from its existing position. Blasting is accomplished by discharging an explosive that has been placed in a hole specially provided for this purpose. The energy associated with an explosion is the result of the pressure produced in the gases that are formed by the explosive.

There are many types of explosives and methods of using them. A full treatment of each explosive and method is too comprehensive for inclusion in this book. For more complete discussions of this subject the reader is referred to handbooks on blasting, published by manufacturers of explosives.

DEFINITION OF TERMS

The more common terms which are used in describing blasting operations are given below as a guide for the reader.

ANFO This is an explosive that is produced by mixing prilled ammonium nitrate with fuel oil.

Blasthole This is a hole that is drilled into rock to permit the placing of an explosive in it.

Blasting This is the detonation of an explosive to fracture the rock.

Blasting agent This is an explosive compound that is placed in a blasthole and detonated.

Blasting cap This is a hollow metal cap which is filled with a high explosive and detonated within or adjacent to the blasting agent as a means of detonating the agent.

Blasting machine This is a machine that is used to generate the electric current that detonates an electric blasting cap.

Blasting powder This is a slow-burning low explosive made from saltpeter, sulfur, and charcoal. It is seldom used for blasting rock.

Block holing This is the drilling of holes in oversize boulders to permit secondary blasting.

Booster This is a high explosive that is placed in a hole at desired spacings to assure that the explosives will detonate throughout the hole.

Borehole This is a blasthole.

Brisance This is an indication of the shattering effect shown by an explosive.

Burden This is the horizontal distance from the face, as in quarrying, to the line of blastholes nearest the face.

Cap-sensitive explosive This is an explosive which can be detonated by a No. 6 cap when the cap is detonated within or adjacent to the explosive.

Coyote tunnel This is a tunnel, several feet in diameter, into which a large quantity of explosive is placed for detonating purposes.

Crimping This is an operation to reduce the diameter of a cap near the open end to hold the fuse securely in the cap.

Cutoff This is the breaking of a fuse or electric circuit to the cap in a primer, usually by explosions in adjacent holes, before the cap in this hole is detonated.

Deck stemming This is the operation of placing inert material in a blasthole at spacings to separate explosive charges in the hole.

Density This is a measure of the energy of an explosive in a stated volume.

Detonation rate This is a measure of the speed at which an explosion travels from one location in an explosive to another location.

Downline This is a cord containing an enclosed explosive which extends from a trunkline into a blasthole where it is used to detonate an attached blasting cap.

Dynamite This is a high explosive whose primary constituent is nitroglycerin.

Electric blasting cap This is a small metal tube loaded with a charge of sensitive explosive. The cap is detonated by the heat produced by an electric current flowing through a wire bridge inside the cap.

Explosive This is a chemical compound which, under favorable conditions, will detonate quickly to produce a very high pressure.

Fuse primer This is a quantity of high explosive which is detonated by a fuse as a means of initiating the explosion of a main charge of explosive.

Gelatin dynamite This is a jellylike explosive made by dissolving nitrocotton in nitroglycerin. This explosive is entirely waterproof.

High explosive This is an explosive that reacts to detonation at an extremely rapid rate.

Leading wires These are wires that are used to conduct the electric current from its source to the leg wires from electric blasting caps.

Leg wires These are wires that conduct the electric current from the lead wires to an electric cap.

Low explosive This is an explosive that produces pressure by progressive burning, thereby releasing energy relatively slowly.

LP delay cap This is a cap, electric or nonelectric, that delays the detonation for a long period of time as compared with MS caps.

MS delay cap This is a cap, electric or nonelectric, that delays the detonation of an explosive for a short period of time, measured in thousandths of a second.

Mud capping This is an operation in which an explosive is placed on an oversize boulder and covered with mud or earth, after which the explosive is detonated to fracture the boulder.

Nitroglycerin This is a colorless explosive liquid obtained by treating glycerol with a mixture of nitric and sulfuric acids.

Nonelectric delay blasting cap This is a blasting cap that is detonated by a fuse or a detonating cord.

Overbreak This is rock which is fractured outside of the desired space, as when tunneling.

Powder factor This is the quantity of explosive used to fracture a specified volume of rock, e.g., pounds of explosive per cubic yard of rock.

PETN This is the abbreviation for the chemical content of a high explosive with a very high rate of detonation.

Presplitting This operation involves drilling small holes at close intervals, loading them lightly with explosives, and detonating the explosives before the main charges to rupture the webs between the presplit holes.

Primacord This is a high-explosive detonating fuse or cord whose PETN core is contained in a waterproof covering of considerable strength. It is used to detonate high explosives and nonelectric blasting caps.

Primadet delay cap This nonelectric blasting cap is a small metal tube loaded with a charge of sensitive explosive, which is detonated by a detonating cord such as Primacord or Primaline.

Primaline This is a high-explosive detonating fuse or cord whose core is contained in a waterproof covering. It may be used as a downline with one end attached to a detonating cord trunkline and the other end inserted in a nonelectric blasting cap to detonate an explosive charge.

Primer This is the portion of a charge, consisting of a cap-sensitive explosive loaded with a firing device, which initiates the explosion.

Rounds This is a term which includes all the blastholes that are drilled, loaded, and exploded in one firing operation.

Safety fuse This is a fuse containing a low explosive enclosed in a suitable covering. When the fuse is ignited, it will burn at a predetermined speed. It is used to initiate explosions under certain conditions.

Secondary blasting This is an operation performed to reduce to desirable size the oversize boulders remaining after the primary explosion.

Slurry This is an explosive that is produced by mixing ammonium nitrate with TNT or with metals, such as aluminum, and water to form a gelatinlike mixture.

Stemming Stemming is the adding of inert material, such as rock dust or drill cuttings, in a blasthole on top of an explosive to confine the energy of the explosion.

Trunkline This is the main line of a detonating cord, extending from the ignition point to the blastholes containing explosives to be detonated. Secondary lines of detonating cords attached to the trunkline are used to detonate the blasting caps in the primers.

TNT This is a high explosive whose chemical content is trinitrotoluene.

DYNAMITE

Dynamite is available in many grades and sizes to meet the requirements of a particular job. The approximate strength is specified as a percentage, which is an indication of the ratio of the weight of nitroglycerin to the total weight of a cartridge. Individual cartridges vary in size from approximately 1 to 8 in. in diameter and 8 to 24 in. long.

Dynamite is used extensively for charging boreholes, especially for the smaller sizes. As it is placed in a hole, it is tamped sharply with a wooden pole to expand the cartridges so that they fill the hole. For this purpose it may be desirable to split the sides of a cartridge, or cartridges with perforated shells may be obtained. A charge may be fired by a blasting cap or a Primacord fuse. If a cap is used, it is placed in a hole made in one of the cartridges, which serves as a primer. Electric caps are supplied with two leg wires in lengths varying from 2 to 100 ft. These wires are connected with the wires from other holes to form a closed electric circuit for firing purposes.

AMMONIUM NITRATE EXPLOSIVES

This explosive is used extensively on construction projects for both above surface and underground blasting. The cost is only about one-fifth the cost of dynamite. Because this explosive must be detonated by special primers it is much safer than dynamite.

The explosive most commonly used is made by blending about 1 gal of diesel fuel with 100 lb of prilled ammonium nitrate fertilizer, which accounts for the common name used to identify it, ANFO. The mixture should be allowed to set for up to 24 hr to permit the oil to saturate the ammonium nitrate thoroughly.

Because the mixture is free flowing it can be poured directly into vertical holes, or it can be blown into horizontal holes using a suitable container, a hose, and compressed air at a pressure of approximately 10 psi.

Ammonium nitrate is not water resistant. If it is to be used in wet holes, it should be enclosed in sealed plastic bags, or the holes should be prelined with plastic tubing, closed at the bottom, to exclude the water. The tubes, whose diameters should be slightly larger than holes, are installed in the holes by placing rocks or other weights in the bottoms of the tubes.

If holes are wet up to a certain depth and dry above that depth, the wet portions may be loaded with dynamite gel, ammonium nitrate in plastic bags, or slurry, and the dry portions loaded with bulk ammonium nitrate.

Ammonium nitrate is detonated by primers consisting of charges of dynamite placed at the bottoms of the holes and sometimes at intermediate depths. Electric blasting caps or Primacord may be used to detonate the dynamite.

In driving a 2,850-ft tunnel for the Blue Ridge Parkway the contractor used dynamite for one-half of the length, then changed to ammonium nitrate for the balance of the length, using the same size holes ($1\frac{7}{8}$ in. in diameter, depth, 10 ft) and the same pattern [1]. The ammonium nitrate gave better fragmentation plus about 1 ft more advance per round than the dynamite.

SLURRIES

This is a plastic water-resistant explosive that is made by blending several materials, such as inert gel, ammonium nitrate, and aluminum particles, with water to produce the desired consistency. It may be poured directly into the holes, or it may be packaged in plastic bags for placement in the holes. Because it is denser than water, it will sink to the bottom of the holes containing water. Also, its free-flowing properties assure that it will fill the holes completely, which improves its fragmentation effects.

Slurries are detonated by special primers, such as dynamite, TNT, or PETN, using electric blasting caps or Primacord.

Slurry is less expensive than dynamite and more expensive than ammonium nitrate. However, any cost comparison should be based on the total cost in the holes and the magnitude and degree of fragmentation produced by the explosive.

In its Eagle Mountain Mine in Southern California, Kaiser Steel Corporation conducted numerous tests of different explosives to develop one that best suited its needs [2]. The tests resulted in the selection of three types of metallic slurries for use in the 9-in. and $9\frac{7}{8}$-in. blastholes. The slurries had densities varying from 84.5 to 91 lb per cu ft, and bulk strengths varying from 1.4 to 2.5 times that of ammonium nitrate and fuel oil.

STEMMING

After a hole is filled with an explosive to the required depth, the balance of the hole should be filled with stemming. Stemming, which may consist of rock cuttings or other suitable inert material, confines the energy and increases the effectiveness of an explosion. If a continuous charge of explosive is not required from the bottom to the top of the charge, stemming may be placed between

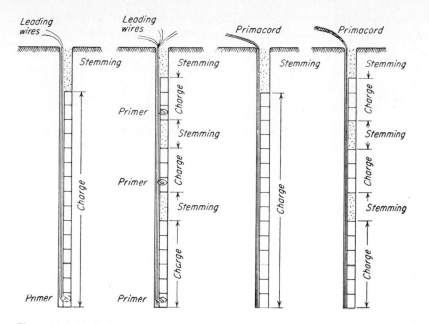

Figure 14-1 Methods of loading blastholes with explosives.

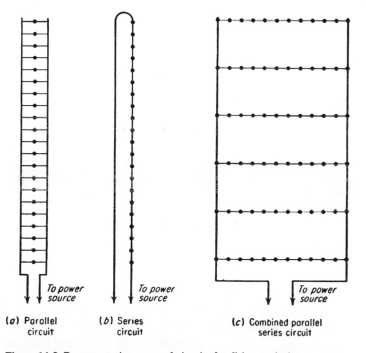

(*a*) Parallel circuit   (*b*) Series circuit   (*c*) Combined parallel series circuit

Figure 14-2 Representative types of circuits for firing explosives.

charges at predetermined intervals. When charges are separated with stemming, a separate primer should be provided for each charge. Figure 14-1 illustrates several methods of loading boreholes for firing with electric blasting caps.

FIRING CHARGES

It is common practice to fire several holes at one time, using either parallel or series circuits or a combination thereof. Prior to making the final connection to the source of electric current, a circuit should be tested with a galvanometer in the line. Each circuit must be tested as a precaution to eliminate open breaks and misfires. Figure 14-2 illustrates three types of circuits.

In order to secure good breakage, with the desired degree of fragmentation, it is frequently necessary to place a higher concentration of explosive near the bottom of a hole than near the top. This may be done by using a strong dynamite near the bottom and a less strong one near the top, or the same effect may be obtained by separating the charges near the top with stemming, provided the total charge in a hole is adequate.

SAFETY FUSE

This device is a continuous core of black powder enclosed in a covering of suitable material. When the core is ignited, it will convey a flame to an explosive attached to the opposite end. The flame will travel along the fuse at a predetermined uniform rate. Thus, the delay between lighting the fuse and the explosion is determined by selecting the proper length of fuse. Figure 14-3 illustrates the correct method of attaching the blasting cap to the end of the fuse.

ELECTRIC BLASTING CAPS

Electric blasting caps are used to detonate charges of dynamite or Primacord fuse. A cap is exploded by passing an electric current through a wire bridge inside the cap. The current, which should be approximately 1.5 amp, heats the bridge, which detonates the explosive in the cap with sufficient violence to fire a charge of dynamite.

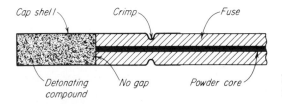

Figure 14-3 Method of seating square-cut fuse against detonating compound.

Table 14-1 Resistance of regular and delay blasting caps

Length of leg wires, ft (m)	Resistance, ohms per cap	
	Regular	Delay
4 (1.22)	0.94	1.45
6 (1.83)	1.00	1.51
8 (2.44)	1.07	1.58
10 (3.00)	1.13	1.64
12 (3.66)	1.20	1.71
16 (4.88)	1.32	1.84
20 (6.10)	1.45	1.97
24 (7.32)	1.58	2.10
30 (9.15)	1.41	1.93
40 (12.20)	1.62	2.13
50 (15.30)	1.82	2.33
60 (18.30)	2.02	2.53

Regular-type electric blasting caps are supplied with leg wires whose lengths are indicated in Table 14-1. Number 22 gauge copper wires are used for leg lengths up to 24 ft and No. 20 gauge copper wires for lengths of 30 ft and longer.

In order to analyze an electric circuit used to fire blasting caps, it is necessary to know the resistance of the caps and the leading wires, which conduct the current to the caps. Table 14-2 gives the resistance of single-strand copper wire in the sizes most commonly used for firing electric caps.

Example A total of 20 regular electric blasting caps, connected in a single series circuit, are to be fired. Determine the required voltage at the source of supply. The following information is available:

Current required to fire the caps, 1.5 amp
Length of leg wires per cap, 40 ft
Resistance per cap, 1.62 ohms
Distance from source of electricity to blast area, 400 ft
Length of leading wires, 2 × 400 = 800 ft
Size of leading wires, No. 20 gauge
Combined resistance of caps, 20 × 1.62 = 32.4 ohms
Resistance of leading wires, 0.8 × 10.15 = 8.1 ohms
    Total resistance of circuit   = 40.5 ohms

From Ohm's law the voltage required is obtained from the equation

$E = IR$

where E = volts
    I = current, amp
    R = resistance, ohms
Thus,

$E = 1.5 \times 40.5 = 60.7$ volts

Thus, any source of electricity that can supply at least 1.5 amp at 60.7 volts will be satisfactory. A 110-volt circuit is adequate.

Table 14-2 Resistance of copper wire

B. and S. gauge No.	Resistance, ohms per 1,000 ft (329 m)
8	0.628
10	0.999
12	1.588
14	2.525
16	4.015
18	6.385
20	10.150
22	16.140

Example If the blasting caps of the previous example are fired in a parallel circuit, with other conditions the same except as noted, the required voltage and current may be determined as follows:

Current required per cap, 0.5 amp
Total current required, $20 \times 0.5 = 10$ amp
Leading wires, No. 14 gauge
Resistance of leading wires, $0.8 \times 2.525 = 2.0$ ohms
Resistance of caps, $1.62 \div 20$ $= 0.08$ ohm
  Total resistance $= 2.08$ ohms
Required voltage $E = IR$
               $= 10 \times 2.08 = 20.8$ volts

Example Determine the voltage required to fire the blasting caps in the circuit of Fig. 14-2c for the stated conditions.

Current required per cap, 1.5 amp
Current required by the 6 circuits, $6 \times 1.5 = 9.0$ amp
Resistance per parallel circuit, $10 \times 1.62 = 16.2$ ohms
Resistance of 6 circuits, $16.2 \div 6 = 2.7$ ohms
Distance from blast area to source of electricity, 400 ft
Leading wires, No. 14 gauge
Resistance of leading wires, $0.8 \times 2.525 = 2.0$ ohms
Resistance of caps $= 2.7$ ohms
  Total resistance $= \overline{4.7}$ ohms
Required voltage $E = IR$
               $= 9 \times 4.7 = 42.3$ volts

DELAY BLASTING CAPS

When the explosive charges in two or more rows of holes parallel to a face are fired at the same time, it is desirable to fire the charges in the holes nearest the face a short time ahead of those in the second row. This procedure will reduce the burden on the holes in the second row and thereby permit the explosive in the second row to break the rock more effectively. If there are more than two rows of holes, the detonations may progress in the order 1, 2, 3, 4, etc., where the numbers indicate the rows, starting with the row nearest the face.

Delay blasting caps are used to obtain this firing sequence. Such caps are available for delay intervals varying from a small fraction of a second to 10 or more seconds. For the shortest delay intervals the caps are called millisecond delay caps and are designated as MS-25, MS-50, MS-200, etc. The number indicates the period of delay in thousandths of a second.

Primacord Primacord [3] is a high-explosive fuse that is used to detonate dynamite and other cap-sensitive explosives and sometimes the special primers that may be required to detonate ammonium nitrate explosives. The core of the fuse, which is the explosive PETN, is covered with a sheath for protection, tensile strength, waterproofing, and identification. The explosive has a detonation rate of about 22,000 ft per sec. When PETN is properly initiated, it explodes with great violence. When used as an explosive in Primacord, it is capable of initiating any cap-sensitive explosive with which it comes in contact.

The cord is manufactured in several types, grades, tensile strengths, and resistances to damage from external forces. Each type is specified as having the properties indicated below:

Reinforced Primacord

Core	Nominal grains per ft	Outside diameter, in.	Minimum tensile strength	Shipping weight per 2,000 ft
PETN	50	0.200 ± 0.008	200 lb	33 lb

When several blastholes are fired in a round, the cord is laid along the holes as a trunkline. At each hole, one end of a detonating cord serving as a downline is attached to the trunkline, while the other end extends into the blasthole. If it is necessary to use a blasting cap and/or a primer to initiate the blast in the hole, the bottom end of the downline may be cut square and securely inserted into a blasting cap as illustrated in Fig. 14-3.

Primadet delay blasting caps Primadet delays are nonelectric blasting caps of sufficient explosive strength to provide direct initiation of properly formulated ANFO mixtures when pneumatically loaded into blast holes up to $2\frac{1}{2}$ in. in diameter under normal conditions of density, confinement, and dryness. This eliminates the need for a primer cartridge of explosives. These caps provide the precise timing of delay electric caps in both millisecond and long-period ranges but are immune to static electricity that may be generated during pneumatic loading operations, as well as other types of extraneous electricity that may be encountered. They are available with various delay intervals, as indicated in Table 14-3 [3].

A blasthole is loaded with a Primadet by attaching the cap to the lower end of a detonating cord, whose opposite end is attached to a trunkline detonating cord, as illustrated in Fig. 14-4. Also, the downline may be detonated by firing a blasting cap properly attached to the outer end of the line.

Table 14-3 Standard delay timings for MS and LP series Primadet delay caps

	MS Primadet delays			LP Primadet delays	
Period	Average firing times, milliseconds	Average period interval, milliseconds	Period	Average firing times, seconds	Average period interval, second
0	Instant	Instant	1	0.2	0.2
1	25	25	2	0.4	0.2
2	50	25	3	0.6	0.2
3	75	25	4	1.0	0.4
4	100	25	5	1.4	0.4
5	125	25	6	1.8	0.4
6	150	25	7	2.4	0.6
7	175	25	8	3.0	0.6
8	200	25	9	3.8	0.8
9	250	50	10	4.6	0.8
10	300	50	11	5.5	0.9
11	350	50	12	6.4	0.9
12	400	50			
13	450	50			
14	500	50			
15	575	75			
16	650	75			

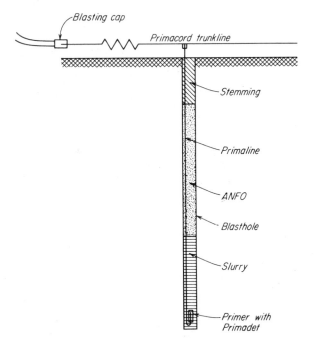

Figure 14-4 Loaded blasthole.

HANDLING MISFIRES

In shooting charges of explosives, it may be that one or more charges will fail to explode. This is referred to as a misfire. It is necessary to dispose of this explosive before excavating the loosened rock. The most satisfactory method is to shoot it if possible.

If electric blasting caps are used, the leading wires should be disconnected from the source of power prior to investigating the cause of the misfire. If the leg wires to the cap are available, test the cap circuit, and if the circuit is satisfactory, try again to set off the charge.

When it is necessary to remove the stemming to gain access to a charge in a hole, it should be removed with a wooden tool instead of a metal tool. If water or compressed air is available, either one may be used with a rubber hose to wash the stemming out of the hole. A new primer, set on top of or near the original charge, may be used to fire the charge.

PRESPLITTING ROCK

This is a technique of drilling and blasting which breaks rock along a relatively smooth surface, as illustrated in Fig. 14-5. Holes $2\frac{1}{2}$ to 3 in. in diameter are drilled along the desired surface at spacings varying from 18 to 36 in., or more in some instances, depending on the characteristics of the rock [4]. These holes are

Figure 14-5 An example of presplitting rock. *(E. I. du Pont de Nemours & Company.)*

loaded with one or two sticks of dynamite at the bottoms, with smaller charges, such as $1\frac{1}{4}$- by 4-in. sticks spaced at 12-in. intervals to the top of the portion of the holes to be loaded. The sticks may be attached to Primacord with tape, or hollow sticks may be used, which permits the Primacord to pass through the sticks with cardboard tube spacers between the charges. After a hole is loaded, it should be stemmed to full depth with a free-flowing material.

When the explosives in these holes are detonated ahead of the production blast, the webs between the holes will fracture, leaving a surface joint which serves as a barrier to the shock waves from the production blast, thereby essentially eliminating breakage beyond the fractured surface.

Because of the variations in the characteristics of rocks the spacings of the holes and the quantity of explosive per hole should be determined by tests conducted at a given project [5].

This technique has been used successfully with vertical holes and with slanted holes whose slopes are not less than about 1 to 1. It has been used with limited success in tunnels.

INCREASING EFFICIENCY OF EXPLOSIVES WITH HOLES DRILLED AT AN ANGLE

Figure 14-6 illustrates two methods of drilling blastholes—one vertical, the other slanted. Studies conducted on the effectiveness of explosives in the two types of holes have demonstrated that the slanted holes allow greater efficiency, as well as offering other advantages such as [6]:

1. More uniform burden for full depth permits a uniform loading of slanted holes, with a reduced need for a heavy charge at the bottom.

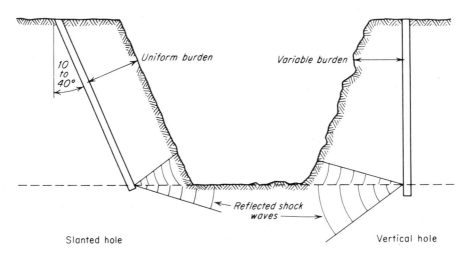

Figure 14-6 Slanted versus vertical blastholes.

2. An increased spacing of holes.
3. Less subdrilling.
4. Smoother faces and pit bottoms.
5. Generally better fragmentation of rock.

When an explosive is detonated in a blasthole, shock waves are propagated in all directions. Only those waves that move toward a free face are highly effective in breaking rock. When a hole is slanted, more of the shock waves are directed upward, and thus they are more effective.

PROPER SPACING OF BLASTHOLES

Formula (14-1), which was developed and tested by Monsanto Chemical Company [7], may be used as a guide in determining the proper spacing of blastholes when using ammonium nitrate and fuel oil as an explosive. The formula indicates the maximum distance from the center of the hole that the explosive will fracture rock of a known or estimated tensile strength.

$$R = \frac{K}{12} \sqrt{\frac{P}{S}} \qquad\qquad (14\text{-}1)$$

where R = critical radius to outer circle of fracture, ft
K = a coefficient whose average value is 0.8 for most rocks
P = maximum explosion pressure, psi
S = ultimate tensile strength of rock, psi

Table 14-4 gives the maximum spacings of blastholes per inch of diameter of hole.

Formula (14-1) and Table 14-4 assume that shock waves are propagated outward horizontally from the blastholes to form cylinders of fracture whose diameters are equal to $2R$. This assumption is more likely to be true with deep holes than with shallow ones. If cylinders of fracture are formed, as illustrated in Fig. 14-7, the staggering of holes in alternate rows should leave less unaffected volumes than unstaggered holes of equal center-to-center spacing. However, staggering holes will reduce the spacing between the rows, as illustrated.

Because the spacing of holes determined from formula (14-1) may not apply under all conditions, it may be necessary to make some adjustments in the spacing of holes after observing the results of test blasting.

The formula may not be valid for small-diameter holes because the size of a hole may change appreciably before the blast attains maximum pressure. If all holes are blasted simultaneously, it may be possible to increase the spacing of the holes by as much as 50 percent of the values obtained from the formula [3, 8].

Table 14-4 Representative spacing of blastholes

Type of rock	Tensile strength of rock, psi (Pa)	Spacing of blastholes, ft per in. (mm/mm) of hole diameter
Anhydrite, strong	1,200 (8.27 × 10⁶)	1.97 (23.6)
Anhydrite, weak	800 (5.52 × 10⁶)	2.45 (29.5)
Granite, strong	1,298 (8.96 × 10⁶)	1.92 (23.1)
Granite, average	888 (6.11 × 10⁶)	2.32 (27.9)
Granite, weak	422 (2.90 × 10⁶)	3.37 (40.5)
Graywacke	700 (4.82 × 10⁶)	2.62 (31.5)
Greenstone	380 (2.62 × 10⁶)	3.55 (42.7)
Limestone, strong	890 (6.13 × 10⁶)	2.30 (27.6)
Limestone, average	480 (3.31 × 10⁶)	3.15 (37.9)
Limestone, weak	280 (1.93 × 10⁶)	4.12 (49.5)
Marble	860 (5.92 × 10⁶)	2.37 (28.4)
Marlstone	480 (3.30 × 10⁶)	3.15 (37.9)
Sandstone, strong	583 (4.01 × 10⁶)	2.85 (34.3)
Sandstone, average	412 (2.83 × 10⁶)	3.40 (40.8)
Sandstone, weak	280 (1.93 × 10⁶)	4.12 (49.5)

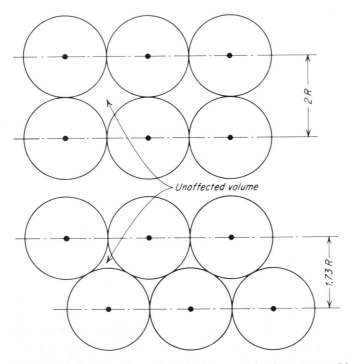

Figure 14-7 Reduction in unaffected volume resulting from staggered blastholes.

MONITORING THE SEISMIC EFFECT OF BLASTING

Because blasting operations may cause actual or alleged damages to buildings, structures, and other properties located in the vicinity of blasting operations, it may be desirable to examine, and possibly photograph, any structures for which charges of damage may be made later. Before beginning blasting operations, seismic recording instruments can be placed in the vicinity of the blasting to monitor the magnitudes of the effects of blasting. The monitoring may be conducted by the persons responsible for the blasting, or, if insurance covering this activity is carried by the company responsible for the blasting, a representative of the insurance carrier may provide this service [8, 9].

CARE IN THE USE OF DETONATING CORD

The following information is excerpted from the booklet "Do's and Dont's," Safety Library Publication No. 4, Institute of Makers of Explosives [10, 3]:

General Information

1. Obey all federal, state, and local laws and regulations applicable to obtaining, owning, transporting, storing, handling, and using explosives.
2. Do not abandon any explosives, in any location, for any reason. Never leave explosives lying around where children or unauthorized persons can get them.
3. Do not smoke, permit smoking, or have matches or any other source of fire or flame within 100 ft of a blast area or within 50 ft of a building in which explosives are being stored, handled, or used.
4. Do not place explosives where they may be exposed to flames, excessive heat, sparks, or impact.
5. Do not fight fires after they have come in contact with explosives. Remove all personnel to a safe location immediately and guard the area against intruders.
6. Do not shoot into explosives or allow the discharge of firearms in the vicinity of a magazine, explosives-loaded vehicle, or where explosives are being used.
7. Do not allow children or unauthorized or unnecessary persons to be present where explosives are handled or used.
8. Do see that other explosives, including detonating cord, are separated from all types of detonators where it is permitted to transport them in the same vehicle.
9. Do not store detonators in the same box, container, or magazine with other explosives. In a situation of practical necessity, detonators may be stored in the same magazine with detonating cord or detonating-cord millisecond-delay connectors, provided the magazine is bullet- and missile-resistant and

account is taken of the total explosive content in figuring compliance with separation distance requirements.

10. Do not attempt to reclaim or use safety fuse, detonating cord, igniter cord, detonators, or any explosives that have been water-soaked, even if they have apparently dried out. Consult the manufacturer for more specific information.

When Preparing the Primer

11. Make up primers in accordance with proven and established methods. Make sure that the detonator shell is completely encased in the dynamite cartridge or cast primer or booster and so secured that in loading no tension will be placed on the wires, safety fuse, or detonating cord at the point of entry into the detonator. The detonating cord should be firmly tied to the dynamite cartridge or passed through the appropriate hole or holes in the cast primer or booster and secured with an appropriate knot. When side priming a heavy wall or heavy-weight cartridge, wrap adhesive or other suitable tape around the hole punched in the cartridge so the detonator cannot come out.

12. Do not kink or injure the safety fuse, detonating cord, or electric blasting cap wires when tamping.

When Blasting with Detonating Cord

13. Select a detonating cord that has the physical and performance characteristics, including explosive core load, consistent with correct blasting methods and the type of explosives, primers, or boosters being used.

14. Handle the detonating cord with the same respect and care given other explosive products.

15. Handle and use the detonating cord with care to avoid damaging or severing the cord before firing.

16. Cut or remove from the spool the line of detonating cord extending into the borehole before loading the remainder of the charge.

17. Make positive and tight connections in accordance with proven and established methods. Knot-type or other cord-to-cord connections should be made only where the detonating cord is dry. Detonating cord which has a wet explosive core can be dependably detonated only by means of special boosters or end-priming techniques. Consult the manufacturer or explosive supplier.

18. Avoid loops or sharp kinks or angles that direct the cord back toward the oncoming line of detonation.

19. Do not attach blasting caps or electric blasting caps to the detonating cord until everything else is in readiness for the blast.

20. Connect the blasting caps or the electric blasting caps to the detonating cord by a positive method recommended by the manufacturer. The caps should always be pointed in the desired direction of detonating-cord detonation.

When Blasting with Non-Electric Delay Blasting Caps

21. Use explosives, blasting agents, or primers that are sensitive to reliable initiation from a No. 6 blasting cap, but are insensitive to initiation from miniaturized detonating cord.
22. Use a detonating cord trunkline of adequate strength to initiate reliably the miniaturized detonating cord leads of the nonelectric delay blasting caps.
23. Attach the nonelectric delay blasting-cap leads to detonating cord to trunklines, using positive and tight connections in accordance with the manufacturer's recommendations.
24. Do not attempt to join two lengths of miniaturized detonating cord, as it will not reliably initiate itself through knots or connections.
25. Do not allow the trunkline to come into contact with nonelectric delay blasting-cap leads, except at the knot or connection.
26. Dispose of or destroy explosives in accordance with approved methods. Consult the manufacturer or follow the instructions in the Institute of Makers of Explosives' Safety Library Publication No. 21, "How to Destroy Explosives" [11].
27. Do not leave explosives, empty cartridges, boxes, liners, or other materials used in the packing of explosives lying around where children, unauthorized persons, or livestock can get them.

TRANSPORTING AND HANDLING EXPLOSIVES

Most states and cities have laws regulating the transporting and handling of explosives. Persons responsible for handling explosives on a project should be familiar with such laws.

The Recommendations for Storing, Handling and Transporting Explosives, issued under the Federal Explosives Act of Dec. 26, 1941, revised as of June 1, 1944, suggests safe procedures for storing, handling, and transporting explosives. Among the recommendations for transporting explosives are the following:

1. Any vehicle transporting explosives should be marked or placarded on the front end, both sides, and rear with the word "Explosives" in letters not less than 4 in. in height in colors contrasting with the background; or the vehicle should carry in a conspicuous place a red flag not less than 24 in. square with the word "Explosives" in white letters at least 3 in. in height or the word "Danger" in letters 6 in. in height.
2. Vehicles should not carry blasting caps or detonators while carrying other explosives; and no metal, metal tools, oils, matches, firearms, acids, inflam-

mable substances, or similar material should be carried on vehicles transporting explosives.

3. Vehicles transporting explosives should not be overloaded, and in no case should the explosives containers be piled higher than the closed sides of the body. Any vehicle with an open body should have a tarpaulin to cover the explosives containers.

4. All vehicles, when transporting explosives, should be inspected to determine that: the brakes and steering mechanism are in effective working condition; the electric wiring is well insulated and firmly secured; the body and chassis are clean and free from accumulations of oil and greases; the fuel tank and feed line are secure and have no leaks; two suitable fire extinguishers in working order and located near the driver's seat are provided; and, in general, the vehicle is in proper condition for safe transportation of explosives.

5. The floors of all vehicles should be tight. Any exposed metal on the inside of the body that might come in contact with any package of explosives should be covered or protected with wood or other nonmetallic material.

6. No explosives should be transported in any form of pole-type trailer, nor should any trailer be attached to a vehicle hauling explosives.

7. Passengers or other unauthorized persons should not ride on a vehicle transporting explosives. Smoking or the carrying of matches and smoker's articles should not be permitted on or around a vehicle transporting explosives.

8. Packages or containers of explosives should not be thrown or dropped while being loaded or unloaded or otherwise handled, but they should be carefully deposited and stored or placed in such a manner as to prevent the packages or containers from sliding or falling or being otherwise displaced.

9. Motors of vehicles transporting explosives should be stopped before loading or unloading the explosives.

The recommendations for handling explosives are as follows:

1. Cases or kegs containing explosives should always be lifted and set down carefully and never slid over one another or dropped from one level to another or otherwise roughly handled.

2. Containers of explosives should not be opened inside a magazine nor within 50 ft of a magazine.

3. Tools made of wood or other nonmetallic material should be used in opening boxes or kegs or other containers of explosives. Metallic tools should not be used.

4. Explosives and detonators issued to individual workmen should be placed in separate insulated carriers or containers equipped with lids so constructed and fastened that they cannot come open during transportation.

5. No person except the attendant should be permitted to ride with explosives or detonators when they are being transported in a shaft, slope, or other underground working.

STORING EXPLOSIVES

Explosives and detonators should be stored separately in detached, dry, ventilated, bulletproof, and fire-resistant magazines, away from other buildings, railroads, and highways. The American Table of Distances [12] gives the safe distances between magazines and other buildings, railroads, and highways for varying quantities of detonators and explosives.

A magazine for the storage of dynamite should be constructed in such a manner that it will prevent the freezing of the dynamite during extended periods of cold weather. If the dynamite does freeze, it should be thawed before it is handled or used, as the danger of premature firing is much greater when it is frozen.

REFERENCES

1. ANFO Passes First Big Test as a Tunnel Explosive, *Construction Methods and Equipment*, vol. 44, pp. 90-93, September 1962.
2. Conger, H. M.: Metallized Slurry Blasting at Eagle Mountain, *Mining Engineering*, vol. 17, pp. 52-55, November 1965.
3. Ensign Bickford Company, P.O. Box 7, Simsbury, Connecticut 06070.
4. Presplitting, What It Can Do, How It Works, *Construction Methods and Equipment*, vol. 46, pp. 136-141, June 1964.
5. Presplitting Done Under Sand Blanket for Suburban Freeway, *Roads and Streets*, vol. 116, pp. 31-33, February 1973.
6. Smith, Gordon R.: Drilling, New Equipment, New Techniques, *Construction Methods and Equipment*, vol. 44, pp. 110-115, August 1962.
7. Spaeth, G. L.: Formula for Proper Blasthole Spacing, *Engineering News-Record*, vol. 164, p. 53, April 1960.
8. Flying Long-reaching Drills Override Rugged Cliff Obstacles, *Construction Methods and Equipment*, vol. 52, pp. 66-72, March 1970.
9. Precision Blasting for Highway Cut Protects Old Rail Tunnel Nearby, *Construction Methods and Equipment*, vol. 59, pp. 53-55, February 1977.
10. "Do's and Dont's," Safety Library Publication No. 4, Institute of Makers of Explosives, 420 Lexington Avenue, New York, New York 10017.
11. "How to Destroy Explosives," Safety Library Publication No. 21, Institute of Makers of Explosives, 420 Lexington Avenue, New York, New York 10017.
12. "The American Table of Distances," Safety Library Publication No. 2, Institute of Makers of Explosives, 420 Lexington Avenue, New York, New York 10017, November 1971.

FIFTEEN

TUNNELING

SCOPE OF THIS SUBJECT

The subject of tunneling is too broad to permit adequate coverage in this book. Therefore, only the fundamentals will be presented, with a limited number of examples to illustrate at least some of the construction methods used and current practices. Tunneling is an activity which is undergoing a great deal of study and development throughout a substantial portion of the world.

The references listed at the end of this chapter should assist readers who wish additional information on the subject in exploring it more fully. The list is representative of the types of information that are available. An examination of *Engineering Index*, available in many libraries, will assist readers in locating more sources of information.

Purposes of tunnels Tunnels are constructed for various purposes, including, but not limited to provision of:

1. Passageways for railroads and automotive vehicles
2. Conduits for water and other liquids
3. Accesses to mines and underground spaces
4. Conduits for utility services
5. Passageways for persons.

Types of earth excavated for tunnels Tunnels may be excavated in all types of soil, varying from loose earth, such as sand, gravel, clay, and shale, through the hardest rocks. This book will deal with tunnels driven through all these materials.

TYPES OF ROCK

The rocks which are encountered in tunneling operations can be divided into three major groups, igneous, sedimentary, and metamorphic. Each group can be subdivided according to origin, mineral content, physical condition, etc.

Igneous rocks Igneous rocks have cooled from molten masses which emerged through fissures from the interior of the earth. If a molten mass cooled prior to reaching the surface of the earth, the rock is defined as intrusive. Examples of intrusive rocks are granite and gabbro. If a molten mass cooled after reaching the surface of the earth, the rock is defined as extrusive. Examples of extrusive rocks are rhyolite and basalt.

Sedimentary rocks The sedimentary rocks with which the engineer is concerned include those which were deposited by flowing water, such as conglomerates, sandstones, shales, and clays, and those which were deposited by marine organisms, such as limestones and dolomites.

Metamorphic rocks If igneous or sedimentary rocks are subjected to high temperatures and pressures, they undergo changes in structure and texture. Rocks which have been subjected to such changes are described as metamorphic rocks.

Under the influence of moderate temperatures and pressures, clay and shales are transformed into slates and schists, which are low-grade metamorphic rocks. When subjected to high temperatures and pressures, slates and schists are metamorphosed into hard and dense gneiss. Limestone metamorphoses into marble and sandstone into quartzite.

PHYSICAL DEFECTS OF ROCKS

All rocks, regardless of the type, have physical or structural defects which have considerable effect on tunneling operations. These defects consist of fractures, whose magnitudes and spacings vary considerably. Simple fractures are defined as joints, whereas major fractures, associated with relatively large displacements, are defined as faults.

Joints Joints are surfaces of physical failure or separation with little or no displacement between the rock components on opposite sides of a joint. The joints may exist in two or three planes approximately at right angles with each other.

In driving a tunnel through a rock formation, the existence of joints will affect the extent to which the sides and roof must be supported during the tunneling operation. Also, joints provide passageways through which ground water may flow into a tunnel.

Faults A fault is a zone in a formation where a large displacement has occurred along the plane of failure. The displacement may be horizontal, vertical, or a combination thereof. A fault usually constitutes an undesirable hazard to tunnel driving. Because of the enormous forces that produce a fault the rock formation in the fault zone will be badly broken. The crushed material may vary in size from fine sand to large blocks, which tend to flow into a tunnel as it is driven through a fault zone. If ground water is present in the formation, the broken material within the fault zone will provide excellent passageways for the water to flow into the tunnel unless corrective steps are taken prior to excavating through the zone. It may be necessary to pressure-grout the formation ahead of the tunneling operation in order to eliminate the hazard of ground water.

PRELIMINARY EXPLORATIONS

While the approximate location of a tunnel is dictated by the service it is to provide, the final location should be based on the results of surface and subsurface explorations. Such explorations are made prior to selecting the exact location of a tunnel in order to determine the kinds of formation that exist and the extent to which ground water is present in the formations along the route of a proposed tunnel. The formations may include unconsolidated muck, sand, gravel, or clay, with or without ground water. There may be solid or badly broken rock, or there may be faults and folds to contend with. If a tunnel is driven through solid rock, little or no roof support may be required, whereas if it is driven through badly broken rock, it will be necessary to provide extensive wall and roof supports. If an exploration indicates the presence of significant quantities of ground water, it may be desirable to seek a more favorable location, or if this is not possible, it may be necessary to pressure-grout the formation ahead of excavation as a means of reducing the flow of water. Plans should be made to have adequate pumps available to remove the water.

Seismic exploratory methods have been used to obtain information on the characteristics of the formation along the proposed routes of tunnels. These studies are made by recording and analyzing the behavior of shock waves, generally propagated by explosives detonated in holes along the route, as the waves travel from the source to the recording instruments. Prior to driving the Musco Tunnel in Sweden intensive seismic studies were made. Where the studies indicated poor rock or fissures, borings were made with diamond core drills in order to obtain additional information.

Valuable information may be obtained from a surface exploration by a competent geologist who is reasonably familiar with the area. More definite information concerning a formation may be obtained by drilling holes along the proposed route and securing samples of the formation. The holes should be drilled at least to the bottom of the proposed tunnel and should be spaced sufficiently close to give representative samples of the formation. If the formation is free of severe structural irregularities and variations, the spacing of the holes may be greater than for a formation that contains faults, folds, or other structural irregularities.

If a formation is soft enough, the holes may be drilled with earth augers or split tubes, which will permit the recovery of undisturbed samples for examination. If the formation consists of unconsolidated material, such as sand or small gravel, holes may be jetted with water. For this purpose it will be necessary to supply a reasonably large quantity of water, under pressure, and enough pipe to permit holes to be jetted to the desired depth. However, the material recovered from jetted holes may not give true samples of the formation, and the information obtained from such samples may not be sufficiently dependable for selecting the final location of a tunnel.

If a formation is rock, the holes may be drilled with wagon, churn, rotary, or other types of drills that produce cuttings. Since these drills produce cuttings instead of undisturbed samples or cores, the material recovered from the holes will not indicate whether the formation is solid or broken rock. As water must be added to holes drilled with churn drills in order to remove the cuttings, the cuttings will not indicate the extent to which ground water exists in a formation.

When cores from the exploratory holes are desired, they may be obtained with core or shot drills. Cores obtained with diamond bits usually vary in diameter from $\frac{7}{8}$ to 4 in., while cores obtained with shot drills usually vary in diameter from about 4 to 8 in. However, larger sizes may be obtained with either bit. Large-diameter cores will permit a more intelligent analysis of the structure of the formation. Cores should be assembled in the same order as they come from the hole. In general, the length of the core recovered from a hole will be less than the depth of the hole, the length varying with the kind of rock and the degree of solidity. Typical core recoveries should be about 80 to 90 percent for igneous rocks, 60 to 70 percent for limestone, 70 to 80 percent for sandstone, and 40 to 50 percent for shale.

After the preliminary explorations have been completed and the results analyzed, the location that will permit the construction of a satisfactory tunnel at the lowest practical cost can be selected.

NUMBER OF ENTRANCES

If a tunnel is relatively short, not more than a few hundred feet long, it may be driven from one entrance only. However, as the length is increased, conducting all operations from one entrance may result in excessive haul distances and high haulage costs, together with a general congestion between the portal and the head of the tunnel. Such a condition may be eliminated or alleviated by driving a tunnel from both ends. For long tunnels it may be advantageous to provide intermediate openings, such as shafts, to facilitate the removal of muck and water and the delivery of materials, supplies, air, and utilities. Intermediate shafts or openings permit operations at a greater number of headings, thus making possible an increase in the rate of driving a tunnel. This may be especially important for a project when an early completion is desirable.

SEQUENCE OF OPERATIONS FOR DRILL AND BLAST CONSTRUCTION

As soon as the construction of a tunnel is under way, the various operations should be carried on in a well-planned sequence. The actual operations will vary with the type and size tunnel, the method of attacking the heading, and the kind of formation encountered. The construction may be on the basis of one, two, or three shifts per day.

For a tunnel driven through rock the following operations might apply:

1. Setting up and drilling
2. Loading holes and shooting the explosives
3. Ventilating and removing the dust following an explosion
4. Loading and hauling muck
5. Removing ground water if necessary
6. Erecting supports for the roof and sides if necessary
7. Placing reinforcing steel
8. Placing the concrete lining

The first four operations are related to the driving of the tunnel and frequently establish the rate of progress in constructing a tunnel. Progress on the other operations should be coordinated with the rate of driving insofar as it is practical to do so.

A representative sequence of operations and the time required for each are given hereinafter for a railroad tunnel at the Conemaugh Damsite [1]. The tunnel, whose bore was 36 ft wide and 32 ft high, was driven through sandstone. In driving the main bore, artificial ventilation was not necessary because a pilot tunnel had been driven the full distance prior to starting excavation for the main bore. Each round required 80 holes, 20 ft deep, which were drilled by nine drifters, mounted on a jumbo. The muck was loaded by $1\frac{1}{4}$-cu-yd electric power shovel into narrow-gauge cars, whose capacity was 5 cu yd each. The rate of progress was approximately 20 ft per day for two shifts.

The time required for several operations in a cycle was as follows:

Shift	Operation	Time, hr	
		Min	Max
1	Drill the holes	5	6
	Load the holes	1	1
	Explode the dynamite		
2	Load and haul muck	9	9
Total time		15	16

The contractor who drove the power tunnel for the Kemano hydro-electric project in British Columbia chose to complete a drilling cycle in each 8-hr shift [2]. The tunnel was a 25-ft horseshoe bore. Each round required 87 to 96 holes,

13 to 15 ft deep, which were drilled with 15 drifters, mounted on a jumbo. The average rate of advance was about 12 ft per shift.

A typical time for each operation and for a cycle was as follows:

Operation	Time, hr
Drill the holes	$1\frac{3}{4}$
Load the holes	$\frac{3}{4}$
Explode the dynamite	
Ventilate during lunch	$\frac{3}{4}$
Load and haul muck	$4\frac{3}{4}$
Total time	8

DRIVING TUNNELS IN ROCK

There are several methods of attacking the faces of tunnels driven through rock. The method selected will depend on the size of the bore, the equipment available, the condition of the formation, and the extent to which timbering is required. The more common methods of attack are:

1. Full face
2. Heading and bench
3. Drift
4. Pilot tunnel

Each of these methods is described in the articles which follow.

Full-face attack When a tunnel is driven by the full-face attack method, the entire bore or face is drilled, the holes are loaded, and the explosives are discharged. Small tunnels whose dimensions do not exceed about 10 ft are always driven by this method. Large-size tunnels in rock frequently are driven by the full-face method. With the development of the jumbo, or drill carriage, the use of this method has become increasingly more popular in driving large tunnels. A number of drills may be mounted on the front end of a jumbo and operated simultaneously with a high efficiency.

Heading and bench method The heading and bench method of driving a tunnel involves the driving of the top portion of the tunnel ahead of the bottom portion, as illustrated in Fig. 15-1. If the rock is firm enough to permit the roof to stand without supports, the top heading usually is advanced one round ahead of the bottom heading. If the rock is badly broken, the top heading may be driven well ahead of the bench and the bench used in installing the timbers to support the roof. The development of the jumbo has reduced the use of the heading and bench method of driving a tunnel.

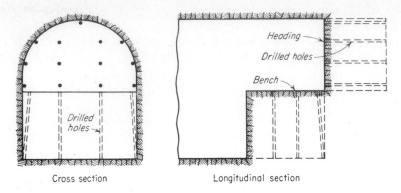

Cross section   Longitudinal section

Figure 15-1 Bench method of driving a tunnel.

Drift method In driving a large tunnel, it may be advantageous to drive a small tunnel, called a drift, through all or a portion of the length of the tunnel prior to excavating the full bore. A drift may be classified as center, bottom, side, or top, depending on its position relative to the main bore. Figure 15-2 illustrates the position of each type of drift.

The use of the drift method of driving a tunnel has several advantages and disadvantages.

Among the advantages are:

1. Any zone of bad rock or excessive water will be discovered prior to driving the full bore, thus permitting corrective steps to be taken early.

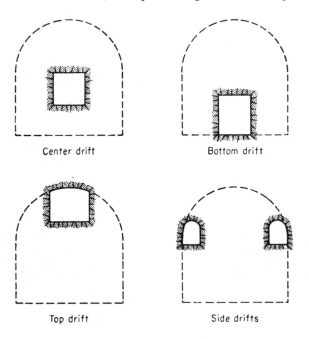

Center drift   Bottom drift

Top drift   Side drifts   **Figure 15-2** Types of drifts.

2. The drift will assist in ventilating the tunnel during later operations.
3. The quantity of explosives required may be reduced.
4. Side drifts may facilitate the installation of timbers to support the roof, especially for a tunnel driven through broken rock.

Among the disadvantages are:

1. Driving the main bore must be delayed until the drift is finished.
2. The cost of drilling and handling muck in a small drift will be high because much of the work must be performed by hand instead of by power-operated equipment.

DRILLING ROCK

In driving a tunnel through rock, it is necessary to drill holes for the explosives that loosen the rock. The most commonly used drill is a drifter, equipped with drill steel and detachable bits, either steel or carbide-insert. Drills and bits are of the types described in Chap. 13. Water frequently is used instead of compressed air to remove the cuttings from the holes, as a means of reducing the amount of dust in the air.

For any given project the best depth and spacing of holes over the face of the tunnel should be determined experimentally. The depth of holes will vary with the size and shape of the tunnel, the kind of rock, and the drilling equipment used. The depth advanced during one drilling and shooting operation is called a round. This distance frequently varies from 5 to 20 ft. It will be necessary to drill holes deeper than the advance per round because of loss in depth resulting in blasting. For example, it may be necessary to drill holes 14 ft deep in order to pull 12 ft, the latter value being the effective depth per round.

DRILL MOUNTINGS FOR SMALL TUNNELS

Drills used in small tunnels and drifts usually are mounted on bars or columns, which are made from sections of steel pipe, equipped with a screw jack at one or both ends. Bars are installed horizontally in a tunnel whose width is less than the height, while columns are installed vertically in a tunnel whose height is less than the width. Installation consists in placing the bar or column in position and extending the jack until the bar or column is securely wedged in position. Figure 15-3 illustrates the use of bars, while Fig. 15-4 illustrates the use of columns.

The drill may be mounted directly on the bar through an adjustable clamp, which permits movement along the length of the bar. When a column is used, the drill is mounted on an arm, which in turn is mounted on the column through an adjustable clamp. The drill may be moved along the arm or the column.

While bars and columns are satisfactory for use in small tunnels, the excess

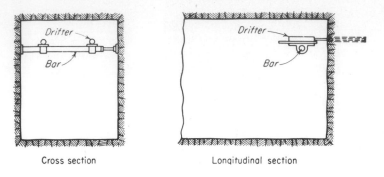

Figure 15-3 Drifter supported by a bar.

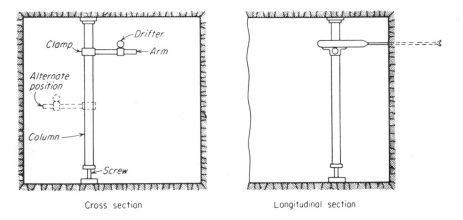

Figure 15-4 Drill mounted on a column.

lengths and weight required for use in large tunnels make them too difficult to handle. In drilling in large tunnels, it is more satisfactory to mount the drills on jumbos.

DRILL JUMBOS

A drill jumbo is a portable carriage with one or more working platforms, equipped with bars, columns, or booms to support the drills. The supports are designed to permit the drills to be spaced to any desired pattern. The main members of some jumbos have been constructed from welded steel pipe designed to transmit compressed air to the drills.

A recent improvement in drilling equipment is a hydraulic or airpowered boom to support rock drills. This boom, which is mounted on a jumbo, is equipped with controls that permit the operator to spot a drill in any desired position in a few seconds. Figure 15-6 illustrates a powered boom mounting in operation.

Figure 15-5 Drill mounted on a column. *(Chicago Pneumatic Tool Company.)*

Figure 15-6 Drill mounted on a power boom. *(Ingersoll-Rand Company.)*

Figure 15-7 Jumbo mounting 16 drifters, with hinged centers to permit passage of trucks. *(Joy Manufacturing Company.)*

A jumbo may be constructed with one or more working platforms, depending on the size of the tunnel in which it will be used. The platforms may be connected to the jumbo structure with hinges which permit them to be raised or lowered to allow other equipment, such as a mucker or cars, to pass under the jumbo. Several drills may be operated from each platform.

A jumbo may be mounted on skids, on wheels for traveling on rails, or on pneumatic tires. Tire mounting gives a jumbo considerable freedom of movement, which facilitates spotting it in position for drilling operations, since it is not restricted to movement on rails.

Self-propelled jumbos, with one or more working platforms, have been constructed on trucks and tractors. When an air compressor is mounted on or attached to the same vehicle, it provides a highly mobile and versatile drilling machine. If the machine is powered with an internal combustion engine, the engine should be diesel driven and equipped with an exhaust scrubber to eliminate the discharge of carbon monoxide gas in the tunnel.

DRILLING PATTERNS

A drilling pattern represents the positions of the holes drilled into the face of a tunnel in advancing one round. The pattern that will produce the most economical and satisfactory breakage of rock for a given tunnel should be determined by conducting tests, using different patterns and quantities of explosives.

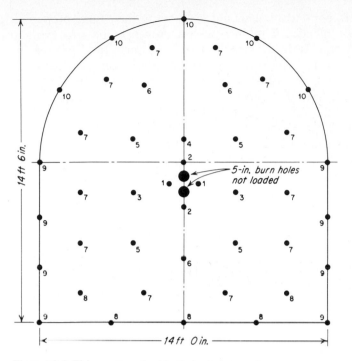

Figure 15-8 Firing pattern for blastholes in a tunnel.

Figure 15-8 illustrates a pattern of holes 12 ft deep and $1\frac{3}{4}$ in. in diameter used in driving a tunnel for water in California. The two 5-in.-diameter burn holes, located near the center of the face, were drilled to increase the effectiveness of the blasts in holes 1 and 2, which were detonated in the sequence indicated by the numbers. The numbers adjacent to the other holes indicate the sequence of firing the holes, using MS electric blasting caps. The explosives produced an average advance of 11 ft per round.

Contracts for driving tunnels usually provide that the contractor will be paid a given price per linear foot of tunnel, or per cubic yard of excavation lying within a specified payline. Also, if the tunnel is lined with concrete, it will be necessary to increase the quantity of concrete to replace the excess rock removed beyond the payline, perhaps at the contractor's expense. Therefore, it is desirable to keep overbreak to a minimum. It is good practice to use a template to locate the payline and all holes to be drilled. A daub of paint at each hole location will assist in spotting the drills more quickly.

LOADING AND SHOOTING HOLES

In general the information concerning explosives appearing in Chap. 14 will apply to the explosives used in driving tunnels. However, when selecting explosives for use in tunnels, consideration should be given to their fume properties.

Ammonium nitrate blended with fuel oil has proven to be effective and economical for use in tunnels. In driving the Canyon Tunnel in California the contractor used ANFO to load $1\frac{3}{4}$-in.-diameter holes 12 ft deep with considerable success [3, 4]. Among the advantages resulting from the use of ANFO compared with dynamite were the following:

1. Fragmentation was 40 percent better with the same hole pattern.
2. Loading and blasting time was reduced 15 to 20 percent.
3. Cost of ANFO was about 5 cents per lb versus 22 cents per lb for dynamite, and the overall cost of explosives for the job ran about one-half the cost of using dynamite only.
4. ANFO produced appreciably less toxic blast fumes than dynamite produced.
5. ANFO was simpler and safer to store and handle.

DRIVING TUNNELS WITH TUNNEL-BORING MACHINES

A recently developed technique in driving tunnels through both earth and rock is the use of tunnel-boring machines, frequently identified in the literature as TBM's or mechanical moles. Several types of moles are illustrated in Figures 15-9, 15-10, 15-11, and 15-12.

The function of a mole is to loosen the earth or break the rock to be removed from a tunnel into cuttings, which can be conveyed to the rear of the machine, where they can be loaded into muck cars or trucks or onto conveyor belts to be transported to the ultimate disposal site.

The essential parts of a mole Depending on the manufacturer and the type of service to be provided, the essential parts of a mole might include the following items, beginning at the front end and continuing to the rear:

1. A rotating cutterhead, mounting teeth for excavating earth or discs for excavating rock
2. Muck buckets mounted on a rotating muck ring to elevate the muck and to discharge it into or onto a primary conveyor, which transports it to the rear of the machine
3. A cylindrical metal shield, whose diameter is essentially the same as the diameter of the tunnel
4. Extendable and retractable clamp legs, with shoes to engage the inner surface of the tunnel bore to prevent the mole from rotating while in operation
5. Thrust cylinders or rams, usually hydraulically operated, to maintain a forward pressure on the cutting head
6. A control console
7. Rear support legs

Figure 15-9 Disc cutterhead for semihard rock formations. *(Caldwell Division of Smith Industries International.)*

Figure 15-10 Mechanical mole with oscillating arms. *(Caldwell Division of Smith Industries International.)*

8. Auxiliary sprag legs (may be optional)
9. Hydraulically operated extendable and retractable rams, which bear against the tunnel lining members or the tunnel surfaces, to provide the thrust needed to advance the mole
10. The motor or motors, usually electric, required to operate all energy-requiring components of the mole
11. Possibly a laser guidance system.

Figure 15-11 Mechanical mole with a rotating head. *(Reed Tool Company.)*

The operation of a mole When a mole is in position to operate, the cutterhead and discs are pressed against the face of the tunnel. As this thrust is maintained, the cutterhead is rotated and the muck is delivered to the rear of the mole. When the cutterhead reaches the end of the advance stroke, the rear legs are extended downward to support the machine. The clamp legs are retracted to free the main frame and the thrust rams move the frame forward. The clamp legs are then extended to anchor the mole in position for the beginning of the next cycle.

Methods of transporting muck Figure 15-13 illustrates a mechanical mole equipped with a self-contained belt conveyor, which transports the cuttings from the face of the tunnel to the rear of the machine, where it is discharged into hauling equipment for removal from the tunnel.

Other methods of removing the cuttings are illustrated and described in the following articles.

Sizes of moles There are no theoretical limits on the sizes of moles, either minimum or maximum. In actual practice they have been used to drive tunnels whose diameters vary from less than 5 to 40 ft or more. While many moles have been designed and manufactured to be used on a given project and have a

Figure 15-12 Mechanical mole equipped with disc-type cutter head. *(Robbins Company.)*

specified diameter, some machines have been equipped to permit increases or decreases in their diameters, so that they may be used to drive tunnels having different diameters.

Limits on the types of earth rock that can be excavated by moles Moles have been used to drive tunnels through all types of earth and solid rock with compressive strength as high as 40,000 psi [5]. However, when driving a tunnel through hard rock, the rate of advance may be slow, and the cost of replacing the cutter teeth or discs may be so high that alternate methods of driving the tunnel are more desirable.

Rates of driving tunnels with moles The rate of advance of a mole when driving a tunnel will depend on several factors, including but not limited to the following:

1. Type of earth or rock excavated
2. Amount of ground water present, if any
3. Power of the driving equipment
4. Skill of the operator

Figure 15-13 Mechanical mole equipped with belt conveyor to transport muck to hauling units. *(Robbins Company.)*

5. Method of removing the muck
6. Extent of ground support required
7. Type of ground support provided

The following examples indicate production rates attained by moles.

Example This example concerns the Azotea tunnel in New Mexico [6].

Diameter of bore, 13 ft 6 in., max
Type of rock, shale and sandstone
Hardness of shale, 2.5 Moh's scale
Compression strength of shale, 1,380 to 5,890 psi
Hardness of sandstone, 5.0 Moh's scale
Compression strength of sandstone, 3,015 to 8,500 psi
Maximum advance during a three-shift day, 241.5 ft
Average advance while mole was operating, 12.1 ft per hr

Example This following information applies to the Blanco tunnel in New Mexico [6].

Diameter of bore, 10 ft
Type of rock, shale and sandstone
Maximum advance per month, three shifts, 6,713 ft
Maximum advance per day, 375 ft
Advance during 12 months, 41,179 ft
Average advance per month, 3,432 ft

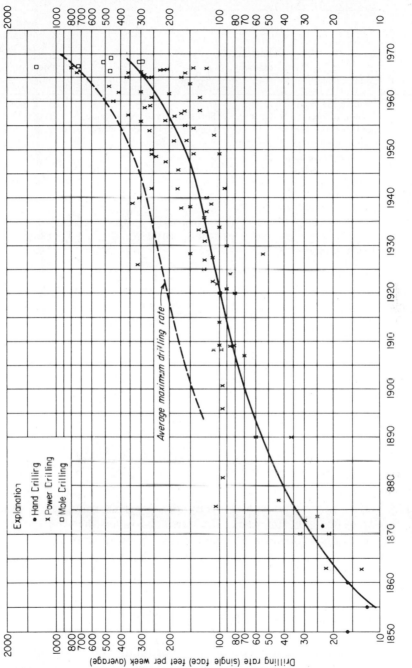

Figure 15-14 Progress in driving tunnels. (*Journal of the Construction Division, American Society of Civil Engineers.*)

443

Table 15-1   Rates of progress on tunnels driven by moles [4]

Date	Location	External diameter, ft-in.	Type of rock	Rate of advance, ft per 24 hr Maxi-mum	Aver-age
1954	Mittry mole, Oahe dam diversion tunnels	25-9	Soft shale, faulted squeezing	96	46
1955	Oahe miner Oahe dam	25-9	Clay and soft shale, faulted	120	38
1958	M-K miner Oahe dam	29-6	Soft shale, bentonite	135	32
1959	Prairie miner Oahe dam	29-6	Soft shale	153	63
1959	Humber River sewer at Toronto	10-9	Shale and limestone, hardness, 2.5	94	*
1961–63	Poatina tunnel, Australia	16-0	Sandstone—hardness 3.5 to 5.0, compressive strength 13,000 to 16,000 psi	150	84
1963–64	Vancouver interceptor sewer	7-6	Sandstone, shale, and coal	200	*
1965	Philadelphia sewer	13-8	Mica schist, hornblende, 6,000 to 25,000 psi	*	41
1965–66	St. Louis metropolitan sewer	8-0	Limestone, compressive strength 14,000 to 17,000 psi	*	48
1965–66	Navaho No. 1, New Mexico	20-10	Layered sandstone and shale, 5,000 to 6,000 psi	160	61
1964–66	Azotea, New Mexico	13-5	Sandstone and shale	241	55
1966–67	Oso, New Mexico	10-2	Shale	414	157
1965–67	Blanco, New Mexico	10-0	Shale	375	107

* Information not available.

While these examples report rates of advance that have been attained, they do not represent rates attained on other projects, some of which have been considerably less.

Figure 15-14 demonstrates graphically the progress in rates of drilling tunnels during more than 100 years [4]. It will be noted that the rates have increased significantly since introduction of the mechanical mole.

Table 15-1 gives information on the rates of advance for tunnels that have been driven with moles.

PRODUCTION EXPERIENCES WITH MOLES

The following examples furnish information illustrating and describing experiences and results of using moles to drive tunnels under various conditions. The references appearing at the end of this chapter list publications containing additional information on this subject.

Mangla Dam Tunnels [7] This project in West Pakistan involved driving five diversion and power tunnels, using what was then the world's largest full-face tunnel-boring machine. The diameter of the bore was 36 ft 8 in. The tunnels were driven through soft rock. An extensible rope belt conveyor was employed, which continuously increased in length as the machine advanced. An overhead monorail crane was used to carry steel ribs to the mole and place them on the machine's upper deck ring-beam conveyor. This was the second machine to employ a shield of flexible steel fingers to protect against caving rock at the point where the steel ribs, wire mesh, and lagging were placed. This shield provided continuous support without relaxation from a point close behind the cutters to the final emplacement of the primary lining. The machine established a record by excavating 4,160 cu yd of *in situ* rock in a 24-hr day while advancing 106 lin ft.

Mersey River Tunnels, Liverpool, England [7] When the mole used to drive the tunnels for the Mangla Dam finished that assignment, it was transported to Liverpool, England, where it was modified in size and used to drive two highway tunnels under the Mersey River. The mole was reduced in size from a diameter of 36 ft 8 in. to 33 ft 11 in. Also, the contractor redesigned the machine's propulsion and tunnel support erection system to permit installation of precast concrete segments for the final lining of the tunnel. Figure 15-15 illustrates longitudinal and cross-sectional views of this machine, showing the working

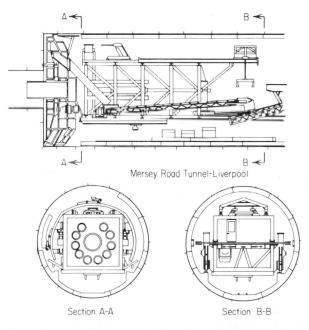

Figure 15-15 Mersey Road tunnel machine. *(Journal of the Construction Division, American Society of Civil Engineers.)*

platform and the precast concrete segments installed at a location immediately behind the cutter head.

New developments in tunneling [8] Tunnel-boring machines, or moles, exemplify the ingenuity of the manufacturing industry in developing new equipment for rapid excavation of tunnels. The machines have been used with considerable success to set new records in rapid excavation of several tunnels on Bureau of Reclamation projects. In excavating the two-mile long, 20-ft diameter tunnel No. 1 on the Navajo Indian irrigation project in northern New Mexico, the contractor completed the excavation in nine months, from June 23, 1965 to March 19, 1966, averaging 61 ft of advance each operating day. By comparison, the rate of excavation of a comparable tunnel using conventional methods would have averaged only 45 ft per day. Three tunnels of the San Juan-Chama project in New Mexico, the 8.6-mile Blanco, the 5-mile Oso, and the 12.7-mile Azotea Tunnel, were also excavated by boring machines. Excavation of the Blanco and Oso Tunnels set world records for progress. Using a mole, the crews for the 8-ft-7-in.-diameter Blanco Tunnel advanced 367 ft in one day and 375 ft in another day. During the month of March 1967 they advanced 6,713 ft. The crews for the 8-ft-7-in.-diameter Oso Tunnel excavated 403 ft in one day. During the month of March 1967 they advanced 6,851 ft.

The geological formations through which these boring machines were used were relatively soft sandstones and shales. However, the industry is continuing to develop boring machines for rapid excavation through much harder rock. For example, the 10-ft-diameter, 4-mile-long River Mountain Tunnel on the Southern Nevada Water Project is largely being driven through hard volcanic rock. Using tungsten carbide insert-type bits and hard steel kerf-type cutters on the mole's rotating head, the rate of advance was as great as 250 ft per day, with an average rate of 6.5 ft per shift hour.

San Francisco Bay Area Rapid Transit system [9] In driving the tunnels for this transit system, which was started in 1968, two types of soft-ground tunneling machines were used.

The Memco machine employed a cutting wheel working the entire face, scraping the ground and dropping the cuttings onto a conveyor belt, from which they were carried out by the muck trains. The wheel was turned clockwise or counterclockwise by planetary gears driven by hydraulic motors having 2,000,000 ft-lb of torque. Fifty jacks of 115 tons capacity each shoved the cutter wheel against the face during excavation. The advance for each shove was about 30 in. One machine excavated 19,056 ft of tunnel in clayey sand, 1,200 ft of which required compressed air with outside dewatering. Another machine excavated 7,600 ft in fairly graded sand and clay, also under compressed air.

Another type of mole with oscillating cutter arms was a Caldwell machine, similar to the one illustrated in Fig. 15-10, which employed four independently activated cutter blades, each operating in its own quadrant, sweeping back and forth to scrape the ground away at the face. When operated under 6,000 psi of

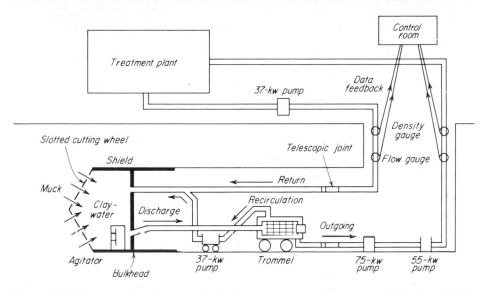

Figure 15-16 Automated mole's pressurized-mix support system. *(Construction Methods and Equipment.)*

hydraulic pressure, each arm could produce a torque of 972,000 ft-lb. A bulkhead mounted behind the cutting arm channeled the excavated material downward onto a 36-in. drag-chain conveyor belt and thence to the muck train. The machine was advanced by means of 20 hydraulic jacks, with a total capacity of 3,020 tons, in increments of 30 in.

The Memco machine was 17 ft 1 in. in outside diameter and 12 ft 5 in. long, with a 163-ft long trailing conveyor and power pack and a total of 1,350 hp.

The Caldwell machine was 18 ft 0 in. in outside diameter and 15 ft 0 in. long, with 24 hydraulic jacks, each having a capacity of 125 tons and an advance stroke of 36 in.

Three different mucking methods were used to move the excavated material out of the shield:

1. A backhoe mounted on the framing of the shield dumped the muck onto a conveyor belt.
2. An Eimco model 620 rail-mounted and pneumatically operated loader cast the material into muck cars behind the shield.
3. Diesel-engine-powered rubber-tired loaders carried the muck back through the tunnel to an outside stockpile.

Japan, tunnel mole [10] Figure 15-16 illustrates a full-face mole with a supporting system controlled almost entirely from above the ground, that was used to drive an 11-ft diameter water tunnel under a railroad yard in Osaka, Japan. As the highly automated mole bored through sandy gravel soil containing cobblestones, it supported the face of the tunnel with a pressurized clay-water slurry between its cutting head and a watertight steel bulkhead.

Excavated muck entering the mole shield through the cutting wheel joined the slurry in a mix, which was forced through a discharge pipe to a trommel, or rotary screen, for treatment. Some muck was extracted and delivered to the surface of the ground, while clay-water slurry was recirculated to the head of the mole, where it replaced the mix being pumped out. The controlled pressure of the slurry at the face counterbalanced the ground-water pressure, which permitted the space to the rear of the bulkhead to be maintained at atmospheric pressure.

The 15-ft long mole was driven forward by ten 80-ton jacks with 42-in. strokes, which pushed against the tunnel lining.

A data feedback system linked to a station on the surface of the ground monitored and controlled the tubehead pressure, the mucking conditions, and the pipeline flows. Information from this monitoring system was relayed to the mole operator to enable him to perform the operations that would produce the maximum production.

The slurry pressure in front of the bulkhead was continuously measured by a diaphragm gauge that activated the pressure-adjusting instrument. In turn, this instrument activated the incoming pipeline pump to vary its speed and to adjust the pressure in front of the bulkhead.

Readings from gauges on incoming and outgoing pipelines, plus the measured weights of stones removed by the trommel, were instantly and continuously processed by a computer. Thus, the exact volume of muck removed was determined. The results appeared on digital indicators and level gauges in the surface control room. From that room, the mole operator was directed to adjust the rotation of the cutting wheel and the thrust of the machine when necessary to maintain the desired production rate.

When the slurry-muck flowed to the trommel, all cobblestones were removed ahead of the screen and hauled out of the tunnel. A portion of the muck flowed through a pipeline to the treatment plant at the surface of the ground, where it was processed. That which was returned to the mole was mixed in the proportions of about 25 percent clay and 75 percent water, plus 0.04 percent of an additive to improve viscosity.

Tunnel in alluvial soil makes fast advance at low cost [11] A tunnel-boring machine with a bentonite-slurry shield was used to drive a 13-ft 6-in. diameter tunnel through wet sand and gravel for the Fleet Underground Railway Line in London, England. The methods used were similar to those used in the previous example.

As the machine moved forward a distance equal to one advance stroke, a complete ring of cast iron segments was installed under the tail of the mole; then the annular space between the outer surface of the lining and the surface of the tunnel was pressure grouted with a thick bentonite grout. This concluded the installation of the permanent lining for the tunnel.

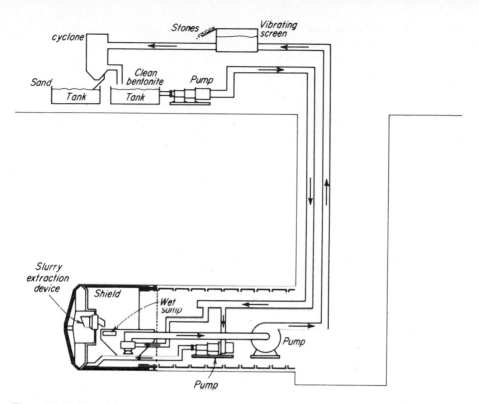

Figure 15-17 Use of slurry method to excavate tunnel in alluvial soil. *(Roads & Streets.)*

Use of this method permitted all operations to be carried out at atmospheric pressure and resulted in an estimated cost reduction of about one-third compared with conventional methods of driving the tunnel.

It was reported that no measurable subsidence resulted from driving the tunnel.

Figure 15-17 illustrates the assembly of equipment and the methods used to drive this tunnel.

MULTIHEAD TUNNELING MACHINE

Figure 15-18 illustrates a self-contained wheel-mounted multihead machine, which has demonstrated its ability to excavate tunnels having large cross sections in a single pass. As noted, this machine is mounted on a jumbo, which permits considerable flexibility in maneuvering within a tunnel. Also, the jumbo provides a floor for use in performing other operations that are necessary in driving a tunnel.

Figure 15-18 Multihead tunneling machine. *(Alpine Equipment Corporation.)*

USE OF LASER BEAMS TO GUIDE MOLES

A relatively new but effective method of guiding a mole, jumbo, or other tunnel-driving equipment is to use a laser beam for position control. These beams have been used on projects requiring accurate control of position and direction, where they have demonstrated their advantages compared with earlier or conventional methods [4, 8, 12].

The word LASER stands for "Light Amplification by Stimulated Emission of Radiation." The light from a laser tube differs from ordinary light from other sources such as the sun or an electric light bulb. Because ordinary light is a combination of many frequencies, a beam of such light will disperse in many directions. A laser produces light of only one frequency or wavelength. For this reason the rays of light travel essentially along a straight line, with little or no dispersion. If a laser generator emits a light beam of small diameter, the diameter remains small as the distances from the generator increase.

Figure 15-19 illustrates the basic method of producing a laser beam with a tube filled with helium and neon gas. A full mirror is located at one end of the tube, point A. A mirror with a small optical opening is located at the other end

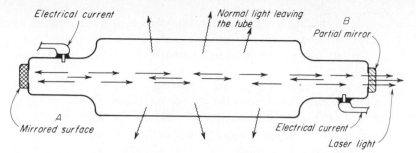

Figure 15-19 Section through a laser-beam generating tube. *(AGL Corporation.)*

of the tube, point B. When an electric current is sent through the tube, the atoms of the gas are excited, which causes the gas to produce light similar to the glow of a neon light. This light in turn produces stimulated-emission light from other atoms in the gas. As this second light is reflected back and forth between the mirrors, its intensity increases. When the correct level of intensity is reached, light passes out of the tube through the optical opening in mirror B as a continuous and narrow beam. It is this light that is used as a guiding beam.

Installing a laser beam system in a tunnel Figure 15-20 illustrates the basic method of installing and operating a laser beam system in a tunnel to guide a tunnel-boring machine. The same method may be used to guide a jumbo or

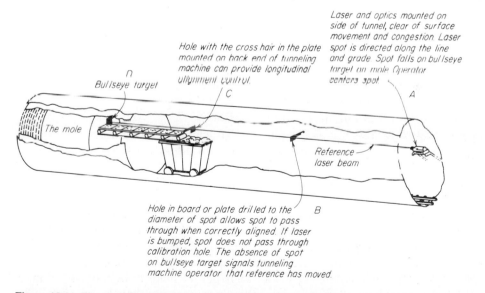

Figure 15-20 The use of a laser beam to control a mole. *(Journal of the Construction Division, American Society of Civil Engineers.)*

other equipment used in driving a tunnel. Literature furnished by the manufacturers of laser beam assemblies will explain the installation procedures more fully and will assist a purchaser of such an instrument in learning how to install and operate it [13, 14].

The installation illustrated in Fig. 15-20 is located inside a tunnel, with all items securely and accurately attached to the wall or ceiling of the tunnel lining. A surveyor's transit is used to assist in locating the items. The laser generator is located at position A. An adjustable target with a small opening is located at position B. A second target with a small opening is attached to the rear of the mole at point C, while a third target, which is illuminated by the laser beam, is attached to the forward end of the mole at position D, where it is in clear view of the operator. The position of the light beam on target D enables the operator to guide the mole.

Accuracy of a laser beam Laser beams currently used on construction projects are accurate to within $\frac{1}{8}$ in. at 100 ft and $\frac{1}{4}$ in. at 400 ft.

As the distance from the source of light to the target is increased, the vertical error in determining elevations increases in proportion to the square of the distance. This error is caused by the curvature of the earth.

ADVANTAGES OF USING MOLES

When driving tunnels through materials varying from unconsolidated earth to firm rock, moles have demonstrated that they have advantages including, but not limited to the following:

1. Moles can drive at faster rates of advance.
2. Moles produce round, smooth, and unshattered bores.
3. Moles reduce overbreak to an average of about 5 percent, compared with 20 percent or more with drill and blast methods.
4. Tunnels driven with moles require less concrete for lining.
5. Because the ground around and adjacent to a tunnel is not disturbed and/or fractured by moles as by blasting, the formation is not weakened, which permits the use of less expensive ground support. Thus, rock bolts are more effective, and thinner concrete linings are adequate.
6. Moles reduce the danger of injury from falling rocks and from toxic gases.
7. Moles permit more continuous operations, because excavation and muck removal can be performed at the same time. Because of the reduction in nonproductive time, both labor and equipment will operate more efficiently.
8. Because the smaller sizes of the cuttings permit them to be removed from a tunnel more easily by conveyor belts or as pumped slurries, congestion in the tunnel is reduced. This leaves more space for other operations, such as installation of ground supports, linings, and ventilation ducts.

9. Because moles eliminate the need for blasting to loosen rock, there is little or no weakening of or damage to the rock adjacent to the tunnel. Also, the danger of damaging property along the route of a tunnel by blasting is eliminated.
10. Analyses of the costs of driving tunnels with moles or by the drill, blast, and muck methods have demonstrated that reductions in costs amounting to 40 percent or more are possible.
11. Moles can be equipped with dust controls and with nozzles which permit water to be sprayed on the face of a tunnel and onto the muck as it is transported from the tunnel. The elimination of dust, in addition to the elimination of toxic gases produced by blasting, permits adequate ventilation within a tunnel at less cost.

DISADVANTAGES OF USING MOLES [4, 15]

There are several disadvantages in using moles to drive tunnels that may have limited their use. Such disadvantages include, but are not limited to, the following:

1. The high initial cost, varying with each project, but reportedly in the range of 4,000 to 6,000 times the square of the diameter in feet of a tunnel, expressed in dollars.
2. The very high cost of cutters and teeth when driving through hard rock. In driving portions of the tunnels for the Bay Area Rapid Transit system in California, the average cutter cost was $30.00 per lin ft of tunnel [5]. However, the compressive strength of the rock varied from 1,000 psi to 40,000 psi.

   In driving the 13-ft-5-in.-diameter Azotea tunnel in New Mexico through sandstone and shale during 1964-66, the contractor reported an initial cutter cost of $12.50 per lin ft. However, as a result of improvements that were made in the type, use, and makeup of the cutting head and cutters and in the pressures used to adapt them more nearly to the specific problems of the project, the cost was reduced to $0.66 per lin ft.
3. Because it is not possible or economically feasible to use moles in driving through hard rock, they are not now suitable for this condition. The development of cutters with longer lives may reduce this disadvantage.
4. Because most of the tunnels that have been driven by moles at this time have been completed under favorable geological conditions, there may not be enough experience to permit predetermination of the drillability of a given tunnel with a mole.
5. Because of the high initial cost of a mole, plus the relatively high cost of assembling and disassembling a unit at a project, it may not be economical to use a mole for driving a short tunnel.
6. Because moles are limited to driving circular tunnels, they cannot be used to drive tunnels having other cross sections, for example, horseshoe tunnels.

VENTILATING TUNNELS

It is necessary to ventilate a tunnel for various reasons, including the following:

1. To furnish fresh air for the workers
2. To remove obnoxious gases and the fumes produced by explosives
3. To remove the dust caused by drilling, blasting, mucking, and other operations

If a drift is driven through a tunnel from portal to portal, it may provide sufficient natural ventilation for the enlarging operations. When natural ventilation is not adequate, as is the case for most tunnels, a positive method of ventilation must be provided.

Mechanical ventilation usually is supplied by one or more electric-motor-driven fans, which may blow fresh air into a tunnel or exhaust the dust and foul air from the tunnel. If air is blown into a tunnel, it may be forced through a lightweight pipe or a fabric duct. If the air is exhausted, it is necessary to use a duct sufficiently rigid to prevent it from collapsing under partial vacuum. Many installations are designed to permit the ventilating system to operate by blowing or exhausting. The reversal of flow can be accomplished by a valve-and-duct arrangement, as illustrated in Fig. 15-21.

If fresh air is blown into a tunnel, it is released near the working face, and as it flows to the portal through the tunnel, it carries the dust and gases with it. If the exhaust method is used, the foul air and dust are drawn into the duct

Figure 15-21 Blower rated at 12,000 cfm at 2 psi, equipped with reversing valve. *(Ingersoll-Rand Company.)*

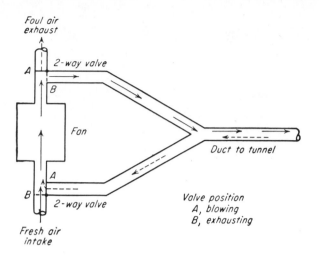

Figure 15-22 Valve and duct arrangement to reverse the direction of flow of air.

opening near the working face, thereby causing fresh air to flow into the tunnel from the portal. The latter method has the advantage of more quickly removing objectionable air from the spaces occupied by the workers.

Volume of air required for ventilation The volume of air required to ventilate a tunnel will vary with the number of workers, the frequency of blasting, the method of controlling dust, and the extent to which air-consuming equipment, if any, is used in the tunnel.

Each worker should be supplied with 200 to 500 cfm of fresh air. Compressed air, furnished to the drills, should not be included in computing the volume of air required for a project, as this air is contaminated with oil and dust before it is released by the drilling operations.

The firing of explosives to loosen rock fills the space near the face of the tunnel with gases and dust, which makes the air unfit for breathing. This foul air must be removed and replaced with fresh air before the workers can start mucking out the broken rock. The cycle of operations may be organized so that the workers retire a safe distance from the face prior to firing the explosives and eat lunch during the time required to remove the gases. If a 30-min lunch period is scheduled, the capacity of the ventilating equipment should be sufficient to clear the tunnel in that period of time.

In driving the 22- by 31-ft railroad tunnel near Aspen, Wyoming, the contractor supplied 18,000 cfm of air through a 26-in. vent pipe. The first 1,000 ft of each of the 36- by $26\frac{1}{2}$-ft twin bores of the Squirrel Hill Tunnel on the Penn-Lincoln Parkway was ventilated with a vane-axial fan capable of blowing 43,000 cfm of air through a 36-in. vent pipe, as illustrated in Fig. 15-23. After the tunnels were driven about 1,000 ft, the ventilation system was revised to permit air to flow from one tunnel into the other through passageways excavated between the two tunnels at 500-ft spacings. An air lock at the portal of one tunnel made it possible to control the direction of flow of air into or through

Figure 15-23 Twin radial fan used to ventilate the Squirrel Hill Tunnel. *(Joy Manufacturing Company.)*

either tunnel. The capacity of the ventilation system was increased to 240,000 cfm for both tunnels by installing additional fans.

Size and capacity of vent pipe After the quantity of air required to ventilate a tunnel is determined, the next step is to determine the size pipe and blower or blowers that will give the lowest total cost [16]. The total cost will include the installed costs of the blowers and pipe, with an allowance for salvage value upon completion of the project, plus the cost of electrical energy required to operate the blowers. If a fixed amount of air is to be supplied at the face of a tunnel, the use of a small pipe will require the installation of a larger blower, which will result in a high installation and operating cost. If a large pipe is used, the cost of the blower and the operating cost will be less but the cost of the pipe will be higher. For every project there is a combination of sizes which will give the lowest total cost. This is the most economical installation.

Consider a tunnel, with a 250- to 300-sq-ft bore, whose maximum length will be 16,000 ft. It is determined that 3,000 cfm of free air will be required for the tunnel. The effect which the size of pipe used has on the pressure lost in the pipe is shown in Fig. 15-25. As the tunnel progresses, the length of the pipe must be increased and the capacity of the blowers also must be increased to overcome the greater back pressure resulting from longer pipe. The cost of energy required to operate the blowers will increase as the length of the tunnel is increased. However, a reasonably accurate estimate of the total cost of energy can be obtained by computing the cost for each of several convenient equal lengths, such as at the quarter points.

Figure 15-24 Fan used for ventilating a tunnel. *(Bonanza Fans, Inc.)*

Table 15-2 illustrates a method of determining the most economical size pipe for the tunnel under consideration. For this project the 22-in. pipe is the most economical, considering all costs.

Dust control The operations such as drilling, blasting, loading, and hauling muck cause dust to accumulate in the air in a tunnel. Unless precautions are taken to limit the concentration, the dust will constitute a serious health hazard to the workers. This is especially true when a tunnel is driven through rock containing a high percent of silica, as extended exposure to silica dust may cause

Table 15-2 The combined cost of compressors, pipe, and energy for ventilating a tunnel

Size pipe, in.	Cost			
	Compressor	Pipe	Energy	Total
18	$50,560	$67,480	$30,640	$148,680
20	32,920	76,900	19,580	129,400
22	19,340	85,160	11,040	115,540
24	12,260	99,500	6,960	118,720
26	10,580	116,360	4,720	131,660

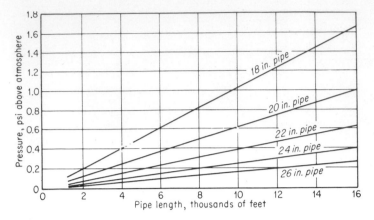

Figure 15-25 The effect of the size of the vent pipe on the loss in pressure.

silicosis, a lung disease for which there is no positive cure. Most states have laws governing mining and tunneling practices which are designed to protect workers against this disease by limiting the concentration of silica dust particles in the air.

Various methods are used to limit the amount of dust in the air in a tunnel, including the following:

1. The use of water instead of air to remove the cuttings from drilled holes
2. The use of a vacuum hood that fits around the drill steel at the rock face to remove the dust that comes from a hole during the drilling operation
3. Complete ventilation of the space near the face, preferably by the exhaust method, following each round of blasting
4. Keeping the muck pile wet during loading operations
5. Using a detergent dissolved in water, which is injected into the blasthole with the air when the hole is blown.

A system of dust control that was used successfully on the Delaware Aqueduct was to install on the drill jumbo several suction pipes with openings near the face of the heading. These pipes drew the dust-laden air from the face and passed it through filters, located at the rear of the jumbo, which removed most of the dust.

MUCKING

The operation of loading broken rock or earth for removal from a tunnel is referred to as mucking. This operation may be performed by hand, power shovels, mucking machines, slushers, or tractor loaders.

Hand mucking is limited to small tunnels and drifts which are not large enough to justify or permit the use of mechanical muckers.

Figure 15-26 A mucking machine. *(Goodman Manufacturing Company.)*

Special power shovels, with short booms and dipper sticks, have been used for mucking in large tunnels. If ventilation is not a serious problem, a diesel-engine-powered unit may be used. If the exhaust fumes are objectionable, a unit powered with an electric motor should be used.

Several types of mechanical muckers are available for use in tunnels. Figure 15-26 illustrates a popular mucking machine, while Fig. 15-27 illustrates the same machine loading muck in a tunnel. This machine, which operates on rails, moves forward to push the dipper into the pile of muck When the dipper is

Figure 15-27 Mucking machine loading muck in a tunnel. *(Goodman Manufacturing Company.)*

Figure 15-28 Rocker shovel loading muck in a tunnel. *(The Eimco Corporation.)*

filled, the machine backs up a short distance and tips the dipper up to discharge the load onto a belt, which conveys it back to a muck car, attached temporarily to the mucking machine. This machine is manufactured in several sizes, with a dipper capacity up to 1 cu yd and a loading capacity up to 162 cfm loose volume. The side swing of the dippers of the larger models gives them a cleanup range in excess of 10 ft on each side of the center line of the track. This machine is operated by an electric motor.

The mucking machine illustrated in Fig. 15-28 is designed to discharge onto a conveyor belt, attached to the rear of the machine, or it will discharge directly into a muck car, attached at the rear of the machine.

Several types of tractor-mounted loaders are available for use in tunnels. The bucket of the loader, illustrated in Fig. 15-29, is lowered to a position in front of the tractor, filled by the forward movement of the tractor, and then lifted over the tractor to discharge the load into a truck.

Tractors or other loading equipment powered with internal-combustion engines should not be used in a tunnel unless the ventilation system, natural or mechanical, is adequate to remove the exhaust fumes without injury to the workers. As carbon monoxide gas is the most dangerous fume, special care must

Figure 15-29 Overshot loader loading muck into a truck. *(Western Construction.)*

be exercised if gasoline-engine-powered equipment is used. Because diesel engines do not produce carbon monoxide, they are safer than gasoline engines for use in tunnels.

Removing muck Muck may be removed from a tunnel by narrow-gauge muck cars pulled by locomotives, by diesel-engine-powered trucks, by conveyor belts, or as slurry pumped through pipelines.

The use of pumps and pipelines to remove muck as a slurry has been satisfactory and economical on a number of projects where tunnels were driven through earth that could be converted into a slurry. A pipeline requires less space and should not interfere with the movement of materials and equipment through a tunnel.

Tracks When muck is hauled in cars, steel rails are required. For this use relatively lightweight rails are laid to a narrow gauge, most frequently 24 or 36 in. For a long tunnel it is necessary to provide a double track in order that loaded cars may be moved out while empty cars are moved into the tunnel. As the width of a muck car is usually twice the gauge of the rails, the maximum gauge is limited to slightly less than one-fourth the width of the tunnel. The weight of the rail, expressed in pounds per yard, should be heavy enough to prevent objectionable sag between the supporting ties when the locomotive and loaded cars travel over them. Also, if the same rails will be used for all haulage,

Figure 15-30 Automatic side-dump muck cars.

including timbering, reinforcing, and concrete for the lining, considerable expense in laying the rails on a good foundation will be justified. Low rolling resistance, plus freedom from excessive maintenance cost and reduced output due to car derailments, depend largely on the use of a good track.

Muck cars Various types and sizes of cars are used to haul muck from tunnels. The capacity may be expressed in cubic feet or cubic yards. In general, the largest size that can be used in a tunnel will be the most economical, as large cars reduce the time lost in switching at the loading operation.

The cars commonly used are constructed with sides hinged at the top and fastened with latches at the bottom to permit easy dumping.

LOCOMOTIVES

Three types of electric locomotives are available for tunnel hauling—the trolley, battery, and combination trolley and battery. All three are available in various weights and for operation on different track gauges, as indicated by the manufacturers.

The trolley-type locomotive is relatively easy to operate, but it requires a bare trolley wire, which may interfere with other operations in a tunnel and which represents a source of potential danger to workers. Also, it is necessary to ground the rails which serve as a return circuit for the electricity.

The battery-type locomotive is operated from a group of storage batteries mounted directly on the locomotive. These batteries should operate a locomotive

Figure 15-31 Battery-type locomotive pulling cars of muck out of a tunnel. *(Goodman Manufacturing Company.)*

for 8 hr, after which they must be recharged, which requires about 8 hr. If a locomotive is to operate more than one 8-hr shift per day, it is necessary to provide at least two sets of batteries so that one set may be charged while the other set is in use.

The combination trolley-and-battery-type locomotive is satisfactory for use on a project which requires haulage inside and outside of a tunnel. The batteries are used in the tunnel and the trolley outside the tunnel. If the operation from the trolley is long enough, the batteries may completely recharge each round trip.

The size of a locomotive is indicated by its weight, expressed in tons. If it has sufficient power to slip the driving wheels when standing on dry steel rails, the maximum tractive effort will be equal to the product of the weight times the coefficient of friction between the wheels and the rails. The coefficient of friction will usually be 0.2 to 0.25. Thus, an 8-ton locomotive should provide a tractive effort of at least

$$16,000 \times 0.2 = 3,200 \text{ lb}$$

A method of determining the maximum number of cars that can be hauled is illustrated in the following examples.

Example Determine the maximum number of cars that can be hauled on a level track by an 8-ton locomotive. The rolling resistance will be 30 lb per ton and the starting resistance 20 lb per ton of gross load, including the weight of the locomotive. The cars, which have a capacity of 80 cu ft each, weigh 2,800 lb empty and 10,800 lb loaded.

Available tractive effort, $16,000 \times 0.2 = 3,200$ lb
Total resistance, 30 lb + 20 lb = 50 lb per ton
Maximum gross load, 3,200 lb ÷ 50 lb per ton = 64 tons
Deduct weight of locomotive _____ = 8 tons
  Maximum net load _____ = 56 tons
No. of cars, $56 \times 2,000 \div 10,800 = 10.4$, or 10
Volume of muck per trip, $10 \times 80 \div 27 = 29.6$ cu yd

Example Determine the maximum number of loaded cars that can be hauled up a 1 percent grade with all other conditions the same as for the preceding example.

Grade resistance, 20 lb per ton
Total resistance, 70 lb per ton
Maximum gross load, 3,200 lb ÷ 70 lb per ton = 45.7 tons
Deduct weight of locomotive _____ = 8 tons
  Maximum net load _____ = 37.7 tons
No. of cars, $37.7 \times 2,000 \div 10,800 = 7$
Volume of muck per trip, $7 \times 80 \div 27 = 20.7$ cu yd

GROUND SUPPORT

When a tunnel is driven, it may be necessary to support the ground adjacent to the tunnel until a permanent concrete lining can be installed. The temporary supports must be strong enough to resist the pressures transmitted to them by the ground. These pressures are caused by faulted, folded, or fractured rock masses or the swelling of the surrounding earth following the removal of the material from a tunnel.

The operation of placing supports in a tunnel to resist the movement of ground is referred to as timbering. The type and extent of timbering are determined to a large degree by the kind and physical condition of ground to be supported. In the early years of tunnel driving heavy wooden timbers were commonly used for supports, but in recent years wood has been replaced by steel H beams. These beams can be fabricated from any desired section to produce ribs that fit the shape of any given tunnel bore. A rib may consist of two or more segments, which are carried into the tunnel, assembled, and bolted together as the driving progresses. Figure 15-32 illustrates the use of steel-H-beam timbering.

The advantages of steel sections instead of wood include the following:

1. Because smaller sizes are used it is possible to reduce the size of the bore of a tunnel. This reduces the cost of excavation and permits faster driving.
2. They can be installed more quickly and economically than wood.
3. They supplement the steel reinforcing in the concrete lining.
4. Their smaller dimensions may permit the use of thinner concrete linings.

The safe spacing of ribs may vary from 18 in. to as much as 6 to 8 ft, depending on the physical condition of the ground. Most grounds tend to bridge over at some height above the roof of a tunnel. As the rock above the natural

Figure 15-32 Steel H-beam supports for a tunnel.

bridge will be self-supporting, only that rock between the roof of a tunnel and the bridge surfaces must be supported by the timbering. Figure 15-33 illustrates how the physical condition of the rock affects the height of the natural bridge formed over the roof of a tunnel. As shown in the figure, rock having greater solidity or larger pieces will bridge more quickly than rock which is badly broken. The timbering must support the weight of the rock lying below the bridge surfaces. If the physical condition of the rock is known in advance of driving a tunnel, the spacing of the ribs may be determined with reasonable accuracy. However, because of the changes in the condition of rock encountered as a tunnel is driven, it is found in actual practice that the spacing of ribs should be modified to meet the conditions that exist at any given section in a tunnel.

Prior to awarding a contract for driving eight power and outlet tunnels at Garrison Dam, the United States Army Engineers drove a full-size test section 240 ft long in order to determine what forces the timbering and lining must withstand. These circular tunnels, whose excavated diameters varied from 27 to $36\frac{1}{2}$ ft, were driven through a formation of clay and shale. Figure 15-34 shows a section of a steel rib being hoisted to position for installation by a top-mounted jumbo, which rode on rails at the spring line, as shown in Fig. 15-35.

Before award of the contract for driving the twin-bore Straight Creek tunnel, which carries Interstate Highway 70 through the Rocky Mountains in

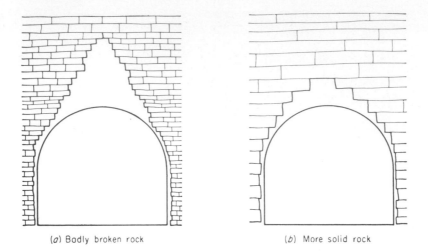

(*a*) Badly broken rock   (*b*) More solid rock

Figure 15-33 The effect of the physical condition of rock on bridging action.

Colorado, an 8,400-ft pilot tunnel was driven through the mountain at the site of the future tunnel. Pressure cells installed in the roof and sides of this tunnel provided valuable information, which was used in designing the ground supports for both tunnels.

The pilot tunnel, which connected the two portals, was also used to haul men and materials from one portal to the other during the driving of the main tunnels.

Figure 15-34 Hoisting sections of steel ribs into position for tunnel supports.

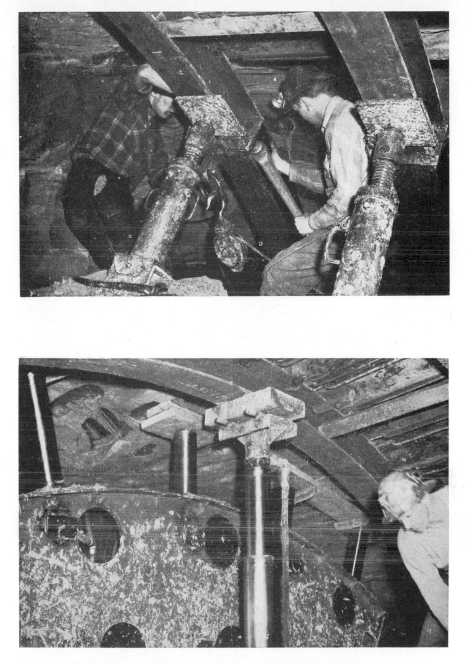

Figure 15-35 Forcing rib sections into place with jacks mounted on jumbos.

In order that the sets of ribs may resist the forces from the ground and prevent broken pieces of rock from falling into the bore of a tunnel, it is necessary to install some type of cover, called lagging, outside of the ribs. This lagging may consist of heavy pieces of lumber, extending from rib to rib, or it may consist of a series of steel plates. The space between the lagging and the undisturbed ground or rock should be filled with timbers, large pieces of rock, or gravel packing to prevent the ground from shifting toward the timbering. The use of lagging and rock packing is illustrated in Fig. 15-32.

USING ROCK MECHANICS STUDIES TO DESIGN TUNNEL SUPPORTS AND LININGS

While driving twin tunnels in 1964 and 1965 the Wyoming Highway Department used a rock mechanics instrumentation program to determine the actual tunnel support requirements [17]. The studies were conducted by Terrametrics, Inc., Golden, Colorado [18].

Before an opening is excavated, the forces on a normal rock mass are in equilibrium. The stress field in the rock depends on the thickness of the overburden, the geological continuity and physical character of the rock, and potential extraneous factors such as tectonic stress. As the opening is increased in size, equilibrium is disturbed, and the rock adjacent to the opening undergoes a dynamic strain readjustment. The support originally provided by the confined rock must be at least partially replaced by the timber, steel, or concrete.

If the opening is to be maintained, a major part of the induced load must ultimately be carried by the rock in the walls of the opening. The redistribution of the load to adjacent rock requires time. Peak support loads, which usually occur during the strain redistribution cycle, must be resisted by the initial steel support system. Usually these loads must be supported only for short periods of

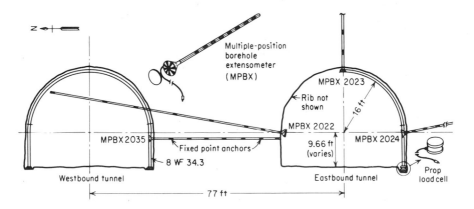

Figure 15-36 Cross section of a tunnel showing the locations of instruments for measuring rock strain and steel set loads. *(Civil Engineering.)*

Table 15-3 Projected rock loads on tunnel supports

| Station | | Rock loads, psf (Pa) | | |
From south tunnel	To south tunnel	Peak	Stable	Limiting
108 + 00	107 + 50	1,050 (50,200)	300 (14,360)	3,000 (143,600)
RMI − 1*	106 + 50	700 (33,500)	200 (9,575)	2,000 (95,750)
107 + 50	103 + 85	700 (33,500)	200 (9,575)	2,000 (95,750)
RMI + 2*	103 + 50	250 (11,950)	200 (9,575)	2,100 (100,500)
103 + 85	100 + 60	250 (11,950)	200 (9,575)	2,100 (100,500)
100 + 60	97 + 92	385 (18,400)	200 (9,575)	1,250 (59,800)
RMI − 4*	98 + 25	385 (18,400)	200 (9,575)	1,250 (59,800)
97 + 82	97 + 32	500 (23,950)	260 (12,450)	1,625 (77,750)
From north tunnel	**To north tunnel**			
108 + 06	107 + 56	1,050 (50,200)	300 (14,360)	3,000 (143,600)
107 + 56	105 + 50	700 (33,500)	200 (9,575)	2,000 (95,750)
RMI − 3*	105 + 15	690 (33,000)	260 (12,450)	1,700 (81,300)
105 + 50	103 + 80	690 (33,000)	260 (12,450)	1,700 (81,300)
103 + 80	100 + 75	250 (11,950)	200 (9,575)	1,250 (59,800)
100 + 75	97 + 82	385 (18,400)	200 (9,575)	1,250 (59,800)
97 + 82	97 + 32	500 (23,950)	260 (12,450)	1,625 (77,750)

* These results are based on actual tests.

time, ranging from a few hours to a few days. Under heavy loads a support system that is too rigid may tend to prevent the redistribution process, resulting in excessive loads and possible failure of the supports. After the peak loads have diminished the system must be strong enough to support permanently the stable rock loads.

The study conducted in the tunnels in Wyoming involved the measurements of displacement-load profiles at four representative locations, as indicated in Fig. 15-36. Each station tested consisted of four load-measuring devices, prop load cells, and three displacement measuring devices, multiposition borehole extensometers.

Table 15-3 gives the projected rock loads that act on or might act on the tunnel supports. It is recommended that the final support system should be designed to resist the limiting rock load, which is the load that might occur if the total weight of the rock in the tension arch were transferred to the support system.

It is reported that the information gained from the studies was used to reduce the cost of the initial support system by approximately 25 percent.

Considerable information related to the use of instruments in testing soils and rocks is available. The information obtained from such tests may be used in designing the ground supports for tunnels. Such information permits the design of adequate but not excessive supports. The references at the end of this chapter list publications containing relevant information.

ROCK BOLTING

Steel bolts are frequently set in holes drilled into the rock to assist in supporting the entire roof, or individual rock slabs that tend to fall into a tunnel. If the characteristics of the rock are such that the bolts will suffice in supporting the roof or parts thereof, the use of bolts is both safe and economical.

The effective use of bolts requires some understanding of the natural forces that exist underground. In an underground excavation all downward-acting forces are transmitted to the walls of the excavation. Most of the rock above the excavation is supported by natural arch action that bears on the walls. The remaining rock below the arch is suspended by the arch. If this suspended rock lacks sufficient strength, it sags and tension cracks develop. As the cracks work up into the roof, weakening the suspended strata, rock begins to fall—all at once or over an extended period of time. If the rock is strong enough and free of large slips and cracks, the rock that is subject to falling usually should not exceed one-third of the width of the roof. It is this rock that bolts can support. Figure 15-37 illustrates the natural forces that cause rock falls, as well as the remedy, which involves the use of rock bolts [19].

If bolts are to be effective, they must be long enough to be securely seated into the rock that is not subject to falling. Also, the rock into which they are seated must be strong enough to provide the necessary anchorage.

Table 15-4 gives the yield and breaking loads for frequently used rock bolts. Table 15-5 gives representative anchorage strengths of different types of rock.

Figure 15-38 illustrates one method used to anchor bolts into rock. As the bolt is tightened by applying a torque to the exposed head or nut, the tapered plug is drawn into the expansion shell, forcing it to bear against the rock adjacent to the hole. If the rock is sufficiently strong, the tensile strength of the bolt may be developed.

Another type of anchor bolt consists of a steel rod, with one end slotted and the other end threaded. Prior to inserting the slotted end of the rod into the hole

Table 15-4 Safe loads on rock bolts [4]

Bolt type and diameter	Load, lb (kg)	
	Yield	Breaking
1-in.(25.4-mm) slotted rod	23,000 (10,410)	40,000 (18,150)
$\frac{3}{4}$-in.(19.1-mm) steel	15,000 (6,800)	25,000 (11,350)
$\frac{3}{4}$-in.(19.1-mm) high-strength steel	22,000 (9,950)	38,000 (17,230)
$\frac{5}{8}$-in.(15.9-mm) high-strength steel	15,000 (6,800)	24,000 (10,890)

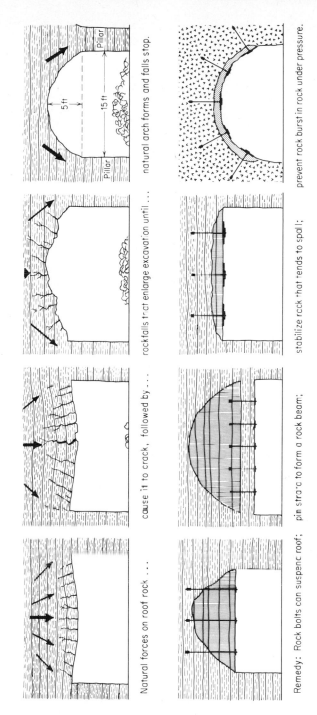

Natural forces on roof rock . . . cause it to crack, followed by . . . rockfalls that enlarge excavation until . . . natural arch forms and falls stop.

Remedy: Rock bolts can suspend roof; pin strata to form a rock beam; stabilize rock that tends to spall; prevent rock burst in rock under pressure.

Figure 15-37 Methods of supporting tunnel roofs with rock bolts. (*Engineering News-Record.*)

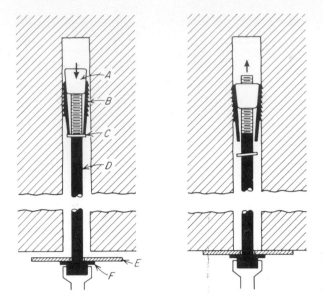

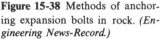

Figure 15-38 Methods of anchoring expansion bolts in rock. *(Engineering News-Record.)*

a steel wedge is driven into the slot a short distance. Then the rod is inserted into the hole until the wedge presses against the bottom of the hole. A driving force is applied to the projecting end of the rod to force the wedge deeper into the slot, thus expanding the rod against the rock adjacent to the hole. A roof plate, washer, and nut are attached to the projecting end of the rod, and the required torque is applied to the nut. The torque is usually limited to 175 ft-lb, which should be adequate to develop the tensile strength of the bolt.

When preparing the foundation for a building at the United States Military Academy at West Point, New York, the contractor used Williams [20] hollow core rock bolts inserted into drilled holes to strengthen the rock and hold it in position permanently. After the bolts were installed in the holes, a slurry of

Table 15-5 Representative anchor strength of rocks [4]

Type of rock	Approximate anchor strength, tons (kg)
Granite and basalt	20 to 30 (18,100 to 27,150)
Sandstone and quartzite	15 to 22 (13,600 to 19,950)
Limestone and marble	12 to 18 (10,850 to 16,300)
Firm sandy shale and gypsum	10 to 15 (9,072 to 13,600)
Shale	8 to 12 (7,250 to 10,850)
Wet or weak shale and coal	3 to 6 (2,720 to 5,440)
Unconsolidated weak, wet material	0 to 3 (0 to 2,720)

cement and drill cuttings was pumped through the bolt holes to fill all of the space around the bolts.

A bolt support system whose trade name is Fastloc has been developed by the Du Pont Company [21]. This system is composed of a specially designed steel bolt and a resin cartridge. When the bolt is installed in a hole, the resin covers the entire length of the bolt and anchors it to the surrounding stratum.

Celite, Inc. has developed a system of rock bolts which uses resin to anchor the entire lengths of bolts in the surrounding strata [22].

CONTROLLING GROUND WATER

In driving a tunnel, the control of water will consist of one or two operations, namely, preventing excess quantities of water from entering the tunnel and removing the water that does enter.

Most of the water in a tunnel comes from two sources, that used to wash the cuttings from the drill holes and that which flows in from the ground through which the tunnel is driven. The former may be estimated with reasonable accuracy, but the latter is subject to great variation. For example, shooting a charge of explosives may open fissures into a ground-water reservoir, thus

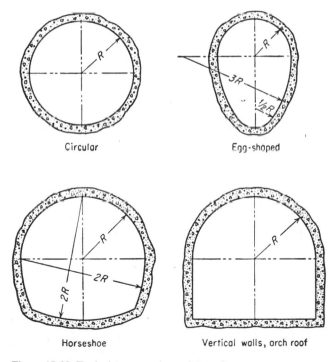

Circular   Egg-shaped

Horseshoe   Vertical walls, arch roof

Figure 15-39 Typical cross sections of tunnels.

permitting an unexpectedly large quantity of water to flow into a tunnel. It is good practice to drill exploratory holes ahead of and deeper than those drilled for explosives in order to determine whether there is badly broken rock or ground water ahead. If the exploratory holes indicate that such a condition exists, it is possible to grout off heavy flows of water and solidify the formation before the tunnel reaches the trouble zone.

Many types and sizes of pumps are available for removing water from a tunnel, as described in Chap. 18. The two types most commonly used are the air-driven centrifugal and the electric-motor-driven centrifugal. Both are compact units, with high capacities, which will operate satisfactorily under varying heads.

The water that accumulates near the face of a tunnel is collected in a sump. This water is picked up with air-driven centrifugal pumps and pumped back to another sump located nearer the portal, where most of the solid materials may settle out, after which it is pumped out of the tunnel with semipermanently installed electric-motor-driven centrifugal pumps.

An air-driven sump pump is satisfactory for use under the adverse conditions that usually exist near the face of a tunnel, but an electric-motor-driven pump usually is preferred for use in the main pumping operation. A switch control operated by a float set in the sump will make a pumping unit practically automatic.

Because of the possibility of encountering excessive flows of water into a tunnel it is good practice to provide stand-by pumps, which may be placed in operation very quickly.

See Chap. 18 for more complete information on various types of pumps.

THE CROSS SECTIONS OF TUNNELS

The shape of the cross section of a concrete-lined tunnel will depend on the pressure of the ground which the lining must resist and the purpose for which the tunnel is constructed. If the ground is solid rock, any desired shape may be selected. For an aqueduct the section may be circular, while for a vehicular tunnel the section may consist of a flat invert, vertical walls, and an arched roof. If the ground is broken rock, subject to horizontal pressure, the vertical wall section of a vehicular tunnel should be replaced with horseshoe curves to resist such pressure. If the ground is highly unstable, such as soft clay or sand, it may be necessary to use a circular section, because of its greater resistance to external pressures, regardless of the purpose for which the tunnel will be used.

The most common cross sections are illustrated in Fig. 15-39. They include the circular, elliptical, horseshoe, and vertical wall with arch-roof types. The circular and elliptical sections are popular for water and sewage conduits, while the horseshoe and vertical sections are popular for vehicular tunnels where the ground conditions permit such sections to be used.

THICKNESS OF CONCRETE LININGS

In the interest of economy it is desirable for a concrete tunnel wall to be as thin as practical. The thickness may be determined by the condition of the ground surrounding the tunnel, the size and shape of the cross section, the requirements of construction conditions, or the internal pressure in the event it is a water conduit.

The geological survey made prior to designing a tunnel lining should indicate whether the ground is solid or broken rock or unconsolidated soil, subject to horizontal and vertical pressures. If steel ribs and reinforcing are used in a concrete wall, the thickness may be reduced but the use of steel for the sole purpose of reducing the thickness of the lining is not economical. A rule which has been used to some extent as a guide only is to allow 1 in. of wall thickness for each foot of diameter.

As solid rock does not impose any load on a concrete lining, the thickness may be the minimum that can be placed behind the forms and cover any utility pipes, ducts, or appurtenances.

The designed thickness of a concrete lining which must resist the pressure from bad ground may include the concrete surrounding steel ribs and sections but should not include any concrete that is encroached on by wood timbers or any kind of lagging.

The 8-ft-diameter Carter Lake pressure tunnel of the Colorado-Big Thompson project, which was designed for a maximum dynamic head of 325 ft of water, has a minimum concrete thickness of $5\frac{1}{2}$ in. but is heavily reinforced with steel bars. The eight circular power and outlet tunnels at Garrison Dam, ranging from 27 to $36\frac{1}{2}$ ft in excavated diameter, have wall thicknesses varying from 30 to 42 in. The Gaviota Gorge Tunnel, a highway tunnel in California, whose inside dimensions are 35 ft 3 in. wide and 22 ft high, has three wall thicknesses, 18 in. in the cut and cover section, 24 in. in the section supported with steel ribs, and 36 in. in the section supported with timbers. All these are minimum thicknesses, which are subject to increases due to overbreak in the sizes of the bores during blasting operations.

SEQUENCE OF LINING A TUNNEL

If a tunnel is driven through solid rock, or if the supports will prevent objectionable movements of the rock until the entire bore is holed through, it is desirable to delay starting the lining until the excavation is finished. If this plan of construction is followed, the mucking and lining operations will not interfere with each other and a greater operating efficiency should be possible. However, if the ground is so unstable that it is difficult or impossible to restrain its movements, it will be necessary to install the lining as quickly as possible after blasting and mucking each round.

The sequence of installing the lining around the perimeter of a tunnel will

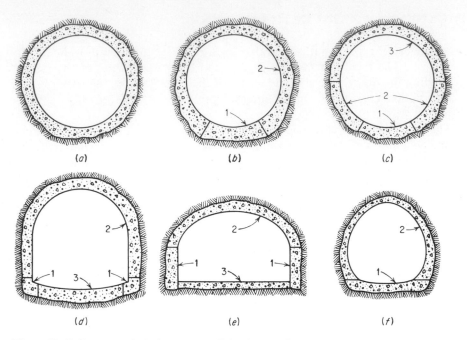

Figure 15-40 Sequence of placing concrete lining in tunnel.

depend on a number of factors. As illustrated in Fig. 15-40, any one of several sequences may be selected. The numbers 1, 2, and 3 indicate the sequence of placing the sections of the lining.

Plan *a* shows the entire wall placed in one operation. This method is limited to circular tunnels which are poured in relatively short sections. The top of the form must be rigidly blocked to prevent it from floating to the roof of the bore.

Plan *b* provides a rigid base on which the forms for the side walls and roof may be supported. If this plan is adopted, construction on the invert should be started at the most distant point and proceed toward the portal in order to eliminate the need of hauling materials over the concrete before it has set sufficiently.

Plan *c* is limited to large tunnels where it is desirable to separate the pours into the indicated sections.

Plan *d* offers several desirable advantages. The two curbs can be installed at the sides of a tunnel with little or no interference to the haulage tracks, located near the center of the tunnel. These tracks need not be removed or disturbed. After the curbs have cured sufficiently, they may be used to support wide-gauge rails on which the main form jumbos travel. Also, they may be used as guides, supports, and anchors for the bottoms of the wall forms. After the curbs, walls, and roof are completed, the original rails, which were used for hauling muck, supports, concrete, etc., can be removed just ahead of placing the invert. Thus, these rails need not be replaced, as would be necessary if the invert were placed first.

Plan *e* is used in placing the lining for large tunnels. Either the side walls or the invert may be placed first.

In plan *f* the invert is placed entirely across the tunnel floor; then the walls and roof are placed later in one operation. The chief objection to this method is that the haulage tracks must be removed prior to placing the invert, then relaid on top of the invert, if they are to be used to haul concrete or other materials for the walls and roof.

REINFORCING STEEL

If reinforcing steel is required in a concrete lining, it may consist of steel ribs, bars, or both. The design for a thick concrete lining may specify two layers of reinforcing bars, one near the inner and the other near the outer surface of the lining. The space between the two layers, especially near the top of the roof, must be great enough to permit the insertion of a pipe through which the concrete will be placed. Figure 15-41 shows the reinforcing steel in place for the Queen Creek Tunnel in Arizona. A jumbo was constructed for use by the ironworkers in placing the reinforcing.

FORMS FOR CONCRETE LININGS

Forms used for lining tunnels are, with few exceptions, of the traveling type, constructed of steel or a combination of steel and wood. While the initial cost of

Figure 15-41 Placing reinforcing steel for the lining of a tunnel.

Figure 15-42 Steel screed used to line invert of a tunnel. *(Chicago Bridge & Iron Co.)*

steel forms will exceed the cost of wood forms, the additional uses obtained from steel compared with wood, together with the savings in time and labor required to move and set up in using steel forms, usually will make steel forms cheaper than wood for any tunnels other than short ones.

The traveling-type form is constructed of steel members which are lined with steel plate or wood to give a surface which conforms with the shape of the inside surface of the portion of the tunnel for which it will be used. Thus, a form may be used for constructing the invert, the side walls, the roof, or any desired combination thereof. Each form is mounted on a traveler or a jumbo, which in turn is mounted on wheels that permit it to be moved along rails. A traveler is equipped with adjustable jacks or screw ratchets, which permit the form to be expanded into position for a concrete pour, then collapsed slightly to pull it away from the concrete in order that it may be moved into a new location.

Figure 15-42 shows a steel-screed form, mounted on wheels that roll on wide-gauge rails, used to line the invert of a tunnel.

Figure 15-43 shows a steel form 24 ft 6 in. in diameter by 32 ft long used to line the walls and roof of a circular tunnel. The form, which is hinged near the upper quarter points, is supported by a prefabricated steel jumbo mounted on eight wheels. Through a series of jacks, attached between the form and the jumbo, it is possible to expand the form to full size or to retract the side walls and lower the roof to permit movement to a new location. Forms of this type may be fabricated with hinged doors along the side walls or roof to permit inspection behind the form or the placing of concrete through the doors.

In lining a highway tunnel 42 ft wide by 22 ft 10 in. high in Arizona, the contractor used two sets of steel forms, each 30 ft long. The first form was set in

Figure 15-43 Steel form used to line tunnels. *(Chicago Bridge & Iron Co.)*

Figure 15-44 Two sets of steel forms used to place concrete lining in a tunnel.

Figure 15-45 Three sections of steel forms used to place concrete lining in a tunnel. *(Blaw-Knox Company.)*

position, and the concrete lining for the side walls and roof was installed. The form was left in place for 72 hr after the pour, then moved ahead far enough to leave a 30-ft-long gap of unlined tunnel. The second form was used later in lining this gap. This procedure was used throughout the tunnel. Figure 15-44 shows the first set of forms in place, supported by a jumbo. Note the pipeline used in pumping concrete for the lining.

Figure 15-45 shows the three 50-ft-long sections of steel forms used to line the twin-tube Squirrel Hill Tunnel. Each form was constructed with a continuous hinge along each side just above the spring line. A set of forms could be collapsed sufficiently to permit it to pass through a form set in position for a concrete pour. After the first section was anchored in position and the concrete was poured, the second section was moved ahead and anchored and the concrete was poured. This operation was repeated for the third section. By the time the concrete was poured for the third section, the first section was ready to be collapsed and moved through the other two sections into a new position. This procedure was repeated until the lining was completed. One 50-ft section of lining was poured each day.

TUNNEL LINING BY THE PUMPING METHOD

A common method of placing concrete lining for a tunnel is by a concrete pump. The machine includes an agitator, or remixer hopper, a single- or

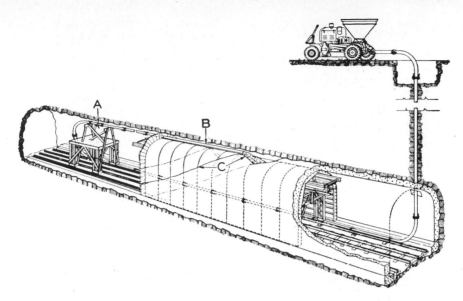

Figure 15-46 Placing concrete lining in a tunnel with a pump and a drop pipe.

double-cylinder piston pump, and a discharge pipe through which the concrete is pumped to the form.

Concrete that has been mixed by any convenient method is fed to the remixer hopper. This hopper, which serves as a storage reservoir ahead of the pump, is equipped with an agitator to ensure that a concrete of uniform quality will flow into the pump. The pump, which may consist of one or two horizontal cylinders, each with a single-acting piston, is located beneath the remixer hopper. When the piston is pulled back in a cylinder, concrete will flow by gravity from the remixing hopper through a valve-controlled opening into the cylinder. When the piston is pushed forward to eject the concrete from the cylinder, the inlet valve is closed and an outlet valve is opened by a system of mechanically operated levers and the concrete is forced the entire length of the discharge pipe and into the forms. Pumps are available with capacities varying from about 10 to 60 cu yd of concrete per hour.

A pump may be set up outside a tunnel, near a portal, or near a vertical shaft which provides passage into the tunnel. When such an installation is used, a pipe is laid and the concrete is pumped to the forms. As the maximum horizontal distance that concrete can be pumped is approximately 1,000 ft, it will be necessary, in installing lining more than 1,000 ft from a portal, either to take the pump into the tunnel or to use more than one machine, with the machine on the outside pumping concrete into the remixing hopper of a machine set up inside the tunnel.

Figure 15-46 illustrates a method of providing access to a tunnel by installing a drop pipe from a pump located at the surface of the ground above the tunnel. The drop pipe may be installed in a drilled hole or in a shaft.

PLACING THE CONCRETE LINING

The concrete walls may be placed by directing the flow of concrete from the discharge pipe through temporary openings in the form. As soon as the walls are poured to the desired height, the discharge pipe can be connected to an arch pipe, which is already installed over the top of the form. The arch pipe, frequently referred to as a slick pipe, usually extends to within a few feet of the opposite end of the form. As the concrete fills the space behind and above the form, the arch pipe is withdrawn until the entire space is filled. An alternate method is to place all the concrete from the arch pipe by letting the concrete for the side walls flow down the back sides of the form. Care should be exercised to keep the depth of concrete on each side wall nearly the same in order to eliminate unbalanced forces on the form.

The injection of a quantity of compressed air into the arch pipe through a quick-opening valve is referred to as air slugging. The slugger is operated at intervals by opening the air valve and permitting a large volume of compressed air to flow into the slick line. This has the effect of ejecting the concrete with sufficient velocity to push it away from the discharge end of the pipe into the most remote spaces. For the slugging action to be effective, at least 75 to 150 cu ft of free air at 100 psi should be injected through a $1\frac{1}{2}$- to 2-in. connection. The air usually is injected 20 to 60 ft behind the discharge end of the pipe.

As the space behind a set of forms is filled with concrete, the operation of the pump may be continued to build up considerable pressure between the form and the ground. Such a pressure is possible if the ends of the form are heavily bulkheaded to prevent the escape of concrete. This pressure forces concrete into all voids and spaces and produces a more solid lining.

The concrete should be vibrated as it is placed to eliminate voids and honeycombing. Internal vibrators may be used on the side walls if access to the concrete is possible, such as through doors in the walls of forms. If internal vibration is not practical, form vibrators may be used.

TUNNEL LINING WITH PNEUMATIC PLACERS

When a tunnel is so small that a pump cannot be set up in it and the length is so great that concrete cannot be pumped through a pipe, a pneumatic placer may be used to place the concrete lining.

Pneumatic placing concrete for a tunnel lining involves using compressed air to force the concrete out of an airtight hopper through a discharge pipe. Concrete is mixed outside the tunnel, loaded into cars, and hauled by a locomotive to the placing equipment. The concrete is transferred from the cars to the pneumatic placer or hopper, the charging door is closed tightly, and compressed air is injected into the placer to force the concrete through the discharge pipe into the forms. As the discharge pipe is generally placed above the roof of a form, it is necessary to provide a pipe support whose height can be

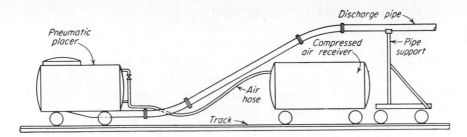

Figure 15-47 Equipment used to place concrete lining by pneumatic method.

adjusted. Air compressors, set up outside the tunnel, supply compressed air through a pipe to a portable receiver located near the placer. The purpose of the air receiver is to provide an adequate supply of compressed air during the placing operation. All the equipment used in the tunnel should be mounted on wheels to permit easy movement along the rails.

A modification of the pneumatic placer described in the previous paragraph is mounted on wheels and used as a car to haul the concrete from the mixer. The hopper of each car has a large door at the top, which can be sealed and made airtight. A number of these placer cars, loaded with concrete, are pushed by a small locomotive to the section of a tunnel to be lined. The front car is connected to the discharge pipe; then compressed air is injected to force the concrete into the discharge pipe. This operation is repeated until all the cars are emptied. Placers of this type were used in lining four aqueducts, 6 ft in diameter, for the city of San Diego. Each placer had a capacity of $1\frac{1}{4}$ cu yd of concrete.

When concrete is placed by the pneumatic method, care must be exercised to keep the velocity of the concrete low until the discharge end of the pipe is submerged in concrete. If this precaution is not observed, the concrete leaving the pipe will be segregated. Each pneumatic placer should be equipped with a throttling valve to regulate the flow of air into it.

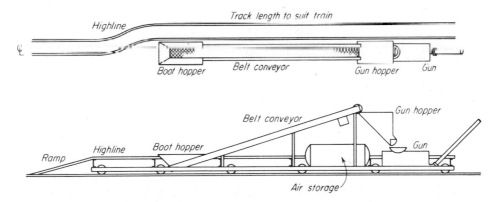

Figure 15-48 Typical concrete placing train. A train of side-dump cars is run onto the highline and dumped, one at a time, into the boot hopper, which feeds the belt conveyor. *(Elgood-Mayo Corp.)*

THE USE OF PRECAST CONCRETE SEGMENTS TO LINE TUNNELS

In recent years a number of tunnels driven through earth by using shields or moles in the United States and in foreign countries have been lined with precast concrete segments, which, in general, were placed immediately behind the excavating operation, for example within the tailpiece of the excavating machine. The number of segments used to produce a ring has varied from two to eight or more. The lengths of the rings have been in the range of 2 to 3 ft. This method of driving a tunnel and installing the lining has been very satisfactory

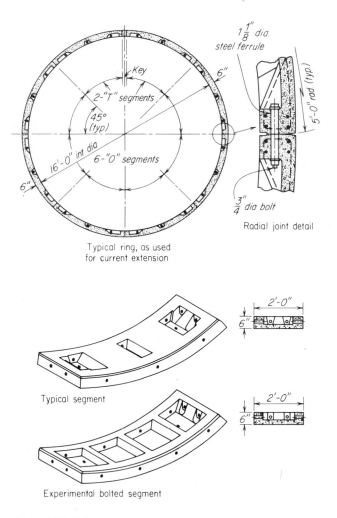

Figure 15-49 Details of prefabricated concrete linings for tunnel. *(Journal of the Construction Division, American Society of Civil Engineers.)*

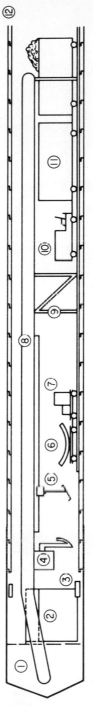

Figure 15-50 Schematic section (not to scale) of tunneling operation:

(1) Articulated head and flood doors
(2) Control section
(3) Thrust jacks
(4) Erector arm
(5) Monorail crane
(6) Segment carriage
(7) Grout hopper and pump
(8) Conveyor belt
(9) Trailing gear
(10) Locomotive
(11) Muck car
(12) Lining

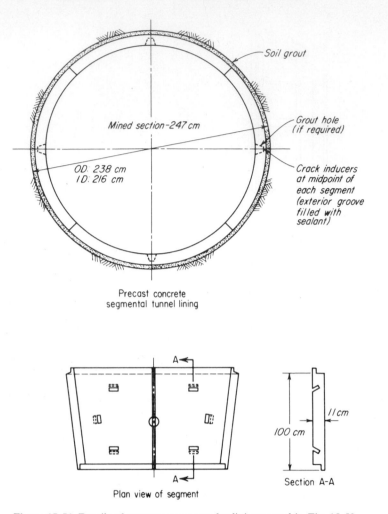

Figure 15-51 Details of concrete segments for lining tunnel in Fig. 15-50.

and economical when it was used under suitable conditions. The examples which follow describe projects where this method has been used.

Example The 3,735-ft long, 30-ft-diameter tunnel through sand, gravel, boulders, clay, and water in Mexico City was driven with a shield. This shield had a tailpiece extension, which enabled the crew to place the two-segment precast concrete rings immediately behind the excavation [23].

Example A method of driving and lining smaller tunnels through earth such as sand and clay, identified as the Mini Tunnel System, has proven effective and economical [24]. A tunnel is driven by using a cylindrical shield, usually with manual excavation. Precast concrete segments are installed immediately within the protection of the tailpiece of the shield. Cost savings varying from $50.00 to $200.00 per lin ft of tunnel have been reported, depending on ground conditions and the alternate methods of driving a tunnel.

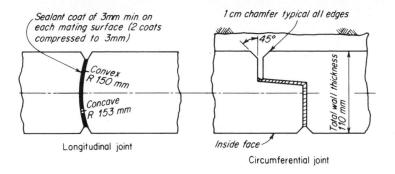

Longitudinal joint

Circumferential joint

Figure 15-52 Details of joints for concrete segments for tunnel in Fig. 15-50.

Example In driving a 16-ft-0-in.-inside-diameter extension for the Yonge subway tunnel in Toronto, Canada, precast reinforced concrete segments were installed to provide rings 2 ft 0 in. long. As indicated in Fig. 15-49, the segments were bolted together radially and longitudinally as they were assembled into rings under the steel tailpiece of the shield [25].

Example A procedure using a full-face tunnel-boring machine, together with a precast concrete tunnel lining, has been used successfully in Canada in constructing a sanitary trunk sewer for Thunder Bay, Ontario. The 2.16-m-diameter tunnel was driven through soft to firm clay [26].

Each ring of the lining consisted of four trapezoidal segments of unreinforced concrete 1 m long and 11 cm thick. The rings were installed within the protection of the tailpiece of the tunnel-boring machine to serve both as the preliminary support and the final lining of the tunnel. Figures 15-50, 15-51, and 15-52 illustrate the schematic section of the tunneling operation and the details of the lining segments and of the joints for the segments.

As noted in Fig. 15-51, the segments were cast in trapezoidal shapes to enable them to be installed in rings more effectively. When the four sections were installed to form a ring, the last segment installed was at the crown or top of the tunnel. By applying sufficient force parallel to the axis of the tunnel against this segment, it was driven into position, thereby expanding the ring to the desired diameter.

After each ring was installed, a pump mounted on the boring machine forced grout, consisting of clay and water, into the annular space between the lining and the outer surface of the tunnel.

The boring machine was designed to permit the use of compressed air at the face of the tunnel, if needed.

SUMMARY [7]

Tunneling technology has received a great deal of attention in recent years. Most of it has been directed at gaining a better knowledge of geologic conditions and at the mechanization of tunnel driving. However, maintaining reasonable and planned advance rates through unpredicted and varying geologic conditions should be identified as the major development frontier.

Contractors are seeking a universal tunnel support system which will provide both immediate ground support and a final lining, or a primary lining which eliminates cleanup problems before the final lining is placed. As noted earlier in this chapter, some contractors have turned to tunnel liner segments as the answer, and this has presented a challenge to the manufacturers of tunnel-boring machines to devise methods of handling and placing these segments quickly enough to maintain pace with the rates of advance of the machines.

The major share of technological progress should continue to come from the innovative daring of tunnel builders, teamed with tunnel designers and specialists devoted to the development of equipment and systems.

REFERENCES

1. Half-mile Tunnel Driven for P.R.R. Double-track Line, *Construction Methods*, vol. 29, pp. 104–105, 170–172, May 1947.
2. Methods Spur Underground Power House, Tunnels, *Construction Methods and Equipment*, vol. 34, pp. 72–85, December 1952.
3. Hardrock Tunneler Saves 50% on Explosives, *Engineering News-Record*, vol. 170, pp. 50–55, May 23, 1963.
4. Armstrong, Ellis L.: Development of Tunneling Methods and Controls, *Journal of the Construction Division, Proceedings ASCE*, vol. 96, pp. 99–118, October 1970.
5. Tunneling Rig Takes on Drill-and-Shoot Operation, *Construction Methods and Equipment*, vol. 52, pp. 76–79, March 1970.
6. Cannon, D. E.: Record Tunnel Excavation with Boring Machines, *Civil Engineering*, vol. 37, pp. 45–48, August 1967.
7. Robbins, Richard J.: Vehicular Tunnels in Rock—Direction for Development, *Journal of the Construction Division, Proceedings ASCE*, vol. 98, pp. 235–250, September 1972.
8. Bellport, Bernard P.: Construction Innovation in Reclamation Work, *Journal of the Construction Division, Proceedings ASCE*, vol. 97, pp. 79–93, March 1971.
9. Fox, George A. and Louis E. Nicolau: Half a Century Progress in Soft Ground Tunneling, *Journal of the Construction Division, Proceedings ASCE*, vol. 102, pp. 637–667, December 1976.
10. Wakabayashi, Jiro: Japan, Tunnel Mole, *Construction Methods and Equipment*, vol. 58, pp. 44–45, July 1976.
11. Tunnel in Alluvial Soil Makes Fast Advance at Low Cost, *Roads & Streets*, vol, 116, p. 120, June 1973.
12. Sacrison, Hans: Flathead Railroad Tunnel, *Journal of the Construction Division, Proceedings ASCE*, vol. 97, pp. 127–145, March 1971.
13. AGL Corporation, P.O. Box 189, Jacksonville, Arkansas 72076.
14. Micro-Grade Laser Systems, Inc., 2352 Charleston Road, Mountain View, California 94043.
15. Norman, N. E.: "The Inevitable Marriage of Underground Mining and Big Hole Drilling," Reed Tool Company, P.O. Box 998, Sherman, Texas 75090.
16. Mole Bores Tunnel No. 1, Miners No. 2, *Engineering News-Record*, vol. 175, pp. 26–33, November 11, 1965.
17. Dutro, Howard B.: Rock Mechanics Study Determines Design of Tunnel Supports and Lining, *Civil Engineering*, vol. 36, pp. 60–62, February 1966.
18. Hartman, Burt E.: "Rock Mechanics Instrumentation for Tunnel Construction," Terrametrics, Inc., Golden, Colorado 80401, 1967.
19. Allen, George W.: What You Should Know about Rock Bolts, *Engineering News-Record*, vol. 167, pp. 32–35, September 27, 1962.
20. Williams Form Engineering Corporation, P.O. Box 7343, Grand Rapids, Michigan 49510.
21. E. I. duPont deNemours & Company, Inc., 1007 Market Street, Wilmington, Delaware 19898.
22. Celite, Inc., 13670 York Road, Cleveland, Ohio 44133.
23. Custom Designed Shield Leaves No Space Behind As It Sets Tunnel Rings, *Construction Methods and Equipment*, vol. 52, pp. 64–72, August 1970.

24. Now Drive Tunnels Fast in Soft Ground without Liners, *Roads & Streets*, vol. 115, pp. 54–56, August 1972.
25. Bartlett, John V., Ted M. Noskiewicz, and James A. Ramsay: Precast Concrete Tunnel Linings for Toronto Subway, *Journal of the Construction Division, Proceedings ASCE*, vol. 97, pp. 241–256, November 1971.
26. Morton, J. D., D. D. Dunbar, and J. H. L. Palmer: Use of a Precast Segmented Concrete Lining for a Tunnel in Soft Clay, Paper prepared for submission to the International Symposium on Soft Clay, Bangkok, Thailand, July 1977. (J. D. Morton is a member of Morton, Dodds and Partners, Consulting Geotechnical and Geological Engineers, 50 Galaxy Boulevard, Rexdale, Ontario, Canada.)
27. Telescoping Forms Finish I-70 Tunnel, *Roads & Streets*, vol. 115, pp. 34–36, June 1972.
28. Automated Concrete Forms for Appalachian Tunnels, *Roads & Streets*, vol. 116, pp. 71–72, January 1973.
29. Dunbar, D. D.: Precast Concrete Liners in Tunneling, Paper presented at the 6th Annual Convention of the Ontario Sewer & Water Main Contractors' Association, February 10, 1977. R. V. Anderson Associates Limited, 194 Wilson Avenue, Toronto, Ontario, Canada.
30. Lane, K. S.: "Field Test Sections Save Cost in Tunnel Support," Underground Construction Research Council, American Society of Civil Engineers, 345 East 47th Street, New York, New York 10017, October, 1975.
31. Subsurface Exploration for Underground Excavation and Heavy Construction, Proceedings of a Specialty Conference held at New England College, Henniker, New Hampshire, August 11-16, 1974. Available from American Society of Civil Engineers, 345 East 47th Street, New York, New York 10017.
32. Hoskins, Earl R. Jr.: "Application of Rock Mechanics," Proceedings, Fifteenth Symposium on Rock Mechanics, held at The State Game Lodge, Custer State Park, South Dakota, September 17-19, 1973. Published by American Society of Civil Engineers, 345 East 47th Street, New York, New York 10017, 1975.
33. Day, David A. and Bradford P. Boisen: Fifty year Highlights of Tunneling Equipment, *Journal of the Construction Division, Proceedings ASCE*, vol. 101, pp. 265–280, June 1975.
34. Knight, Gail B.: Subway Tunnel Construction in New York City, *Journal of the Construction Division, Proceedings ASCE*, vol. 90, pp. 15–36, September 1964.
35. Underwood, Lloyd B.: Machine Tunneling on Missouri Dams, *Journal of the Construction Division, Proceedings ASCE*, vol. 91, pp. 1–27, May 1965.
36. Hill, George: What's Ahead for Tunneling Machines? *Journal of the Construction Division, Proceedings ASCE*, vol. 94, pp. 211–231, October 1968.
37. Pikarsky, Milton: Sixty Years of Rock Tunneling in Chicago, *Journal of the Construction Division, Proceedings ASCE*, vol. 97, pp. 189–210, November 1971.
38. Tunnel Under Alps Uses New Cost-Saving Lining Method, *Civil Engineering*, vol. 45, pp. 66–68, October 1975.
39. Rail Jumbos Handle Big Loads for Lining Tunnel, *Construction Methods and Equipment*, vol. 51, pp. 54–59, April 1969.
40. Smith, Lorraine: Auger Teams with Shield to Cut Mixed Tunnel Face, *Construction Methods and Equipment*, vol. 52, pp. 104–106, January 1970.
41. Small-bore Hydraulic Mining Machine Cuts Sewer Tunnel, *Roads & Streets*, vol. 115, pp. 66–69, August 1972.
42. Giles, J.: "Adventures Underground—The Story of the World's Great Tunnels," Doubleday & Company, Inc., New York, 1962.
43. AGL Corporation, P. O. Box 189, Jacksonville, Arkansas 72076.
44. Alpine Equipment Corporation, 140 North Gill Street, State College, Pennsylvania 16801.
45. Blaw-Knox Construction Equipment Division, Mattoon, Illinois 61938.
46. Caldwell Division of Smith Industries International, P. O. Box 2875, Santa Fe Springs, California 90670.
47. Chicago Pneumatic Tool Company, 6 East 44th Street, New York, NY 10017.
48. The Eimco Corporation, 634 South Fourth West Street, Salt Lake City, Utah 84110.

49. Ingersoll-Rand Company, Phillipsburg, New Jersey 08865.
50. Joy Manufacturing Company, River Road, Claremont, New Hampshire 03743.
51. Reed Tool Company Mining Equipment Division, 12400 North Freeway, Houston, Texas 77090.
52. Rex Chainbelt, Inc., 4710 W. Greenfield Avenue, Milwaukee, Wisconsin 53201.
53. The Robbins Company, 650 South Orcas Street, Seattle, Washington 98108.
54. Bonanza Fans, Inc., 1312 East Wakeham Street, Santa Ana, California 92705.
55. Elgood-Mayo Corp., 140 Varick Avenue, Brooklyn, New York 11237.

CHAPTER SIXTEEN

FOUNDATION GROUTING

NEED FOR GROUTING

Although large deposits of rock frequently are referred to as solid rock, in many instances they are not solid. These deposits may contain fissures, cavities, slips, faults, seams, or breaks, which make the deposits unsuitable for dams, reservoirs, buildings, bridge piers, locks, tunnels, etc. When subsurface investigations disclose the existence of such structural defects, it is necessary to adopt corrective steps if a foundation is to be made suitable for the intended use. If correction is impossible, or if it is unreasonably expensive, it may be necessary to abandon the site.

An operation to correct the foundation conditions is described as pressure grouting. The foundation under or adjacent to a structure is grouted for several reasons such as:

1. To solidify and strengthen the formation in order to increase its capacity to support a load
2. To reduce or eliminate the flow of water through a formation, such as under a dam or into a tunnel
3. To reduce the hydrostatic uplift under a dam

EXPLORING TO DETERMINE THE NEED FOR GROUTING

The most satisfactory method of determining whether a foundation should be grouted is to obtain core samples from representative locations within the foundation area. Cores may be obtained with diamond or shot drills, usually diamond for the smaller sizes and shot for the larger sizes. Several shot-drilled holes, 30 in. in diameter or larger, may be desirable in order that a man may be lowered into them for visual inspection of the formation. The size, number, depth, and spacing of the exploratory holes should be planned to provide the greatest amount of information for the lowest practical cost. Increasing the number of holes will provide more dependable information, but it will increase the cost of exploration. For each project there must be a weighted balance between the need for foundation information and the cost of obtaining this information. The decision should be made by a competent foundation engineer.

An accurate record should be kept for each exploratory hole. The record should show the location, size, and depth of the hole and, with the core recovered, should show the physical nature of the formation. If a core is recovered in long, continuous pieces, with little loss in length compared with the depth of the hole, this indicates a reasonably solid formation, which may require little or no grouting. However, if the core is badly broken, and if the recovered length is small in proportion to the depth of the hole, this indicates a bad foundation condition, which probably will require a large quantity of grout.

The approximate rate at which a hole will take grout may be determined by forcing water, under pressure, into the hole. For this purpose a section of pipe, $1\frac{1}{2}$ to 2 in. in diameter, and 2 to 4 ft long, is sealed into the top of a hole with a threaded end projecting from the hole. As water is forced into the hole, the rate of flow and pressure should be recorded. If the rate of flow drops quickly, with a corresponding increase in pressure, this indicates the presence of only a few thin seams or fissures, which can be closed easily with grout. If the rate of flow remains high, with little or no increase in pressure, this indicates a highly porous formation, with extensive fissures, for which a large amount of grout will be required.

MATERIAL USED FOR GROUT

The materials commonly used for grout include

1. Cement and water
2. Cement, rock flour, and water
3. Cement, clay, and water
4. Cement, clay, sand, and water
5. Asphalt
6. Clay and water
7. Chemicals

When a grout of cement and water only is to be injected into fine seams, it may be necessary to use as much as 10 parts of water to 1 part of cement, by volume, in order to obtain penetration. When the seams are large, the grout may be as dry as $\frac{3}{4}$ part water, or less, to 1 part cement. For most grouting

Table 16-1 Properties of admixtures used with cement grouts

Admixture	Property
Calcium chloride Sodium hydroxide Sodium silicate	Accelerates setting time
Gypsum Lime sugar Sodium tannate	Retards setting time
Finely ground bentonite	Increases plasticity Reduces grout shrinkage
Clay Ground shale Rock flour	Reduces cost of grout Reduces strength of grout

operations the ratio will vary from 1 to 2 parts water to 1 part cement. Usually, the most satisfactory grout is the stiffest mix that can be injected effectively. This should be determined by testing the rate of injection, using varying mix ratios.

Rock flour and clay may be added to cement grout in the interest of economy if the seams are small, while sand may be added if the seams are large enough to permit the sand to penetrate. Grout made of neat cement will give a higher strength than grout containing clay or sand. In grouting the foundation for the Norris Dam, the grout was mixed in the ratio of 1 part cement, 1 part rock flour, by volume, with 3 lb calcium chloride per 100 lb of cement added to speed setting. For the Chickamauga Dam the mixture was 2 parts cement, $\frac{1}{2}$ part bentonite, and 4 parts sand, by volume. As bentonite has the property of increasing up to several times its original volume when mixed with water, it is necessary to mix it thoroughly with water prior to adding cement and sand.

Table 16-1 gives the properties of certain admixtures when they are used with cement grout.

The use of asphalt and clay grouts will be discussed later in the chapter.

DRILLING PATTERNS

After a foundation has been explored and tested to determine the extent of grouting required, a drilling pattern should be adopted. The size, depth, and spacing of injection holes should give the best results at the lowest cost. It may be necessary to change the drilling pattern from time to time if the grouting operations encounter differences in foundation conditions.

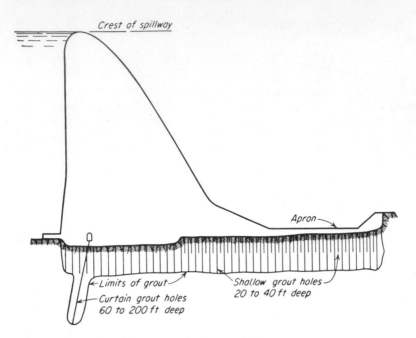

Figure 16-1 Method of grouting under the Norris Dam.

In general, the smallest holes which will permit the injection of grout are the most desirable, as the size of a hole seems to be secondary so long as grout can be injected through it. Because of their lower cost, small holes permit a greater number to be drilled for a limited expenditure and, thus, increase the probability of obtaining a successful grouting operation.

A simple pattern, such as a hole spacing of 20 by 20 ft, with all holes $2\frac{3}{4}$ in. in diameter and 40 ft deep, may be entirely satisfactory for one project but unsatisfactory for another. Figure 16-1 is a section through the Norris Dam showing shallow grout holes for consolidating the foundation under the dam and deeper holes for producing the impervious curtain to prevent the flow of water under the dam.

DRILLING INJECTION HOLES

Holes for the injection of grout may be drilled with jackhammers, wagon drills, diamond drills, or shot drills, depending on the terrain, class of foundation material, and size and depth of holes.

Diamond drills usually give holes that are uniform in shape and size, which are more satisfactory than holes drilled by other equipment when packers must be installed for washing or grouting individual seams. Wagon drills are satisfactory for holes whose depths do not exceed 30 to 40 ft.

PREPARATIONS FOR GROUTING

The preparations for washing or grouting seams by the full-length method consist in installing a section of pipe, usually $1\frac{1}{2}$ to 2 in. in diameter, 18 to 36 in. long, in the grout hole, with the top end projecting out a short distance for connection to an air line or a pump. The space around the bottom of the pipe is closed with oakum or other suitable material; then the balance of the space is filled with cement mortar, melted sulfur, or it may be calked with lead wool.

In order to reduce the danger of weakening the formation through fractures resulting from the application of excessive pressure, uplift gauges should be installed at several locations over the area to detect any lifting of the surface during the grouting operations.

WASHING THE SEAMS

When a formation is grouted with neat cement for consolidation purposes, it is desirable to deposit the cement in clean seams from which any clay or unconsolidated materials have been removed. The most effective method of removing such materials is to force a mixture of air and water through the seams. The removal of materials may be made more effective by alternately reversing the direction of flow of the air and water.

In washing a formation, a pattern of holes is selected. Some of the holes are capped for water, some for compressed air, and others are left open to permit the outflow of the washed materials. The direction of flow may be reversed by interchanging the pipe caps. When the water flowing from the uncapped holes clears up, indicating the removal of the unconsolidated materials, the caps are moved to another pattern of holes.

If the grout holes are deep and pass through several seams of unconsolidated materials, it may be desirable to isolate each seam in order that it may be washed individually. This is done by using an injection pipe, with the lower end closed, sufficiently long to extend below the lowest seam, with a perforated section long enough to extend completely through the seam. The pipe is equipped with an expandable packer above and below the perforated section, which is set opposite the seam to be washed. When the injection pipe is lowered into a hole and the packers are expanded, any air or water delivered to the pipe will be confined to a single seam.

It is possible to determine whether a seam is open from one hole to others by injecting into the seam water containing a coloring agent, such as fluorescein dye. If the colored water appears in other holes, this indicates open passages through the seam.

GROUTING PRESSURES

The most suitable pressure for grouting operations is difficult to determine in advance. Some engineers follow a general practice of using a pressure of 1 psi for each foot of depth of hole. There is no logical proof or demonstration that this is the most satisfactory pressure.

In the interest of economy and effectiveness it is desirable to use the highest pressure that is safe. However, when grout is forced into a seam under pressure, it is possible that the total upward force on the formation above the seam may exceed the combined weight and resisting strength of the formation. If this condition is permitted to occur, the entire formation may be lifted upward, with a resulting fracture that is more serious than the original condition that grouting is supposed to correct. Thus, it is possible for grouting to do more harm than good unless it is injected under careful supervision.

If the weight of a rock formation is 150 lb per cu ft, the unit pressure on a horizontal plane, 1 ft below the surface of the rock, will be 150 ÷ 144 sq in. = 1.04 psi. At a depth of 100 ft the pressure resulting from the weight only will be 104 psi. As most rocks weigh 150 lb or more per cubic foot, it is improbable that a grouting pressure equal to 1 psi for each foot of depth will endanger a foundation formation provided the pressure is confined to the intended depth.

When grout is injected by the full-length-hole method, care must be exercised to prevent the pressure of the grout near the surface of the ground from exceeding the maximum safe pressure. If the pressure at the bottom of a hole 40 ft deep is 40 psi, the pressure at a depth of 20 ft will be equal to 40 psi minus the hydrostatic pressure of 20 ft of grout. The hydrostatic pressure of cement grout may be determined from the curve in Fig. 16-2. If the grout is mixed in the ratio $1\frac{1}{2}$ parts of water to 1 part cement, the pressure change per foot of depth will be

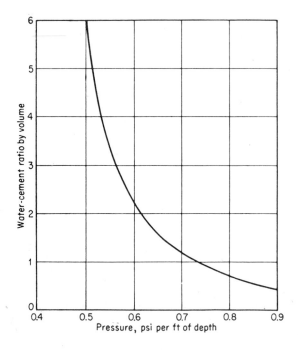

Figure 16-2 Hydrostatic pressure produced by cement grout.

0.66 psi. In 20 ft the reduction in pressure will be 20 × 0.66 = 13.2 psi. Thus, for the case cited above the pressure at a depth of 20 ft will be 40 − 13.2 = 26.8 psi. The pressure at the surface of the ground will be 40 − 40 × 0.66 = 13.6 psi. If the injection of grout by the full-length-hole method produces objectionably high pressures near the top of a hole, this objection may be overcome by injecting grout in limited depth zones.

The pressures at which grout is injected frequently are varied with the depth of injection and the stage at which the grout is injected. For example, when the foundation under a concrete dam is grouted for consolidation purposes, the grout may be injected in two or three stages. The first stage might consist in drilling holes 20 to 40 ft deep, with a spacing of 20 ft each way. The pressure at the bottom of these holes might be limited to a maximum of 40 to 50 psi. The second stage might consist in drilling holes 40 to 60 ft deep, with a spacing of 10 ft each way. If the grout is injected after the dam is partly constructed, the pressure at the bottom of the holes might safely be increased to 80 to 100 psi. The third and last stage might consist in drilling holes 60 to 100 ft or more deep for final high-pressure grouting under the dam. These holes might be spaced as close as 5 ft apart in a single row along the axis of the dam, to permit the grouting of a solid cutoff curtain, to prevent the flow of water under the dam. If these holes are not grouted until the dam is completed, the pressure may be as high as several hundred pounds per square inch. Figure 16-1 illustrates a method of grouting the foundation for a dam.

EQUIPMENT FOR CEMENT GROUTING

The most common method of injecting cement grout is to use one or more piston-type pumps to produce the necessary pressure. The pumps usually are air-driven duplex double-acting types so constructed that the number of strokes per minute and the pressure on the grout may be varied by regulating the quantity of compressed air supplied to the pump.

The equipment will include:

1. One or more air compressors
2. One or two grout mixers
3. One agitator-type reservoir tank
4. One or more grout pumps
5. Grout discharge pipe or hose, valves, pressure gauges, etc.

The grout mixer contains a shaft with paddles, operated by a motor. After the grout is mixed, it is discharged into a tank, with an agitator to prevent separation of the solids from the water. The pumps draw their charges directly from the agitator tank.

The essential parts of the Boulder-type grout unit are illustrated in Fig. 16-3. The location of the component parts may be modified to fit any particular injection conditions. The grout discharge line may be a pipe, a rubber hose, or a

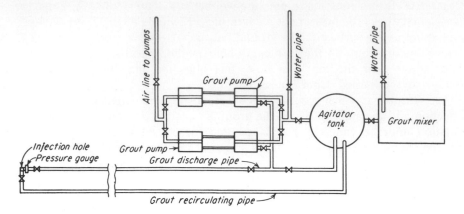

Figure 16-3 Boulder-type equipment used to inject cement grout.

combination thereof. The use of a hose will facilitate moving from one grout hole to another.

Figure 16-3 shows a grout recirculating pipe or line whose primary function is to permit grout to flow through the pumps and discharge pipe at a uniform rate even though the rate of injection into a hole is reduced as the cavities are filled.

It is good practice to install two grout pumps, even though one pump can supply all the grout that will be needed. In the event of a pump failure, the auxiliary pump can be placed in operation immediately, thereby reducing the danger of losing a partly filled hole or group of holes.

INJECTING CEMENT GROUT

The records that were kept at the time the grout holes were drilled, together with the records obtained from washing the holes, if such an operation was performed, should serve as a guide in estimating the grout mix to use. The best results are obtained by using the thickest grout that can be injected without plugging the hole. It may be necessary to start with a batch of thin grout, and then thicken each succeeding batch by reducing the water-cement ratio until the maximum practical thickness is determined.

The specifications covering the grouting of a project may require the injection of grout at a given pressure until the rate of injection for a given hole shall diminish to a specified amount or until a hole will not take any more grout at a specified pressure.

Grout may be injected into the full length of a hole at one time, or it may be injected into a portion of the length only. If the latter method is used, it is possible to apply a high pressure in injecting at the bottom of a hole. As the depth of injection is reduced, the pressure may be reduced accordingly. This is referred to as the zone method of grouting. In order to inject grout by the zone

Figure 16-4 Self-contained gasoline-engine-powered grout mixer and pump. *(Acker Drill Company.)*

method, it is necessary to use an injection pipe that is long enough to reach the lowest zone of injection. The zone to be grouted at a given time is isolated from the rest of the hole by means of a packer, which is set near the bottom of the injection pipe and just above the top of the zone. Most packers are of removable types, which permit them to be reused many times.

PRESSURE GROUTING WITH ASPHALT

If a formation contains fissures with water flowing through them, it will be difficult or even impossible to consolidate the formation with cement grout. The velocity of the water tends to sweep the grout through the openings without giving it an opportunity to solidify.

In numerous instances the injection of asphalt grout into fissures containing flowing water has sealed the fissures and stopped or reduced the flow of water. After the flow of water is stopped, it is possible to inject cement grout to complete the consolidation operation. Thus, the primary function of asphalt grout is to seal off the flow of water in order that cement grout may be retained in the fissures.

The heated asphalt is injected through a perforated pipe, which may have a steam line running through it, as a means of keeping the asphalt at the desired temperature until it flows into the formation. An alternate method of heating the asphalt in the injection pipe is to install an electric wire inside the pipe, with the pipe completing the electrical circuit. An electric current through the wire will heat the asphalt. When hot asphalt flows from an injection pipe into the openings in a formation, the outside surface of the asphalt tends to solidify, but, because of the low heat conductivity, the inside tends to remain a liquid for some time. The pressure from the injection pipe will keep the interior part of the asphalt flowing for a considerable distance, several hundred feet in some instances. As the grout solidifies under pressure, it conforms with the shape of the fissures and seals them against the flow of water.

The equipment required to inject asphalt grout consists of a heating kettle, a piston-type pump, an air compressor or an electric motor to operate the pump, a source of electrical current, plus a supply of pipe hose, valves, and pressure gauges.

An interesting example of the use of asphalt grout to stop the flow of water through a fissurized formation was developed in correcting the leakage from the reservoir at Great Falls Dam [1]. The limestone abutments to the dam had developed extensive fissures below the level of the water in the reservoir, through which a large quantity of water flowed from the reservoir into the river channel below the dam. Injection holes, which were drilled through the fissurized formations, were grouted first with asphalt to stop the flow of water, after which the consolidation was completed using cement grout. Asphalt grout, at temperatures varying from 300 to 350°F, was injected at rates varying from 40 to 60 cu ft per hr.

CLAY GROUTING

Grout mixtures of clay and water or cement, clay, and water have been used successfully to fill large seams and cavities subjected to low hydrostatic heads. While clay adds little, if any, strength to a foundation, its high resistance to the flow of water makes it an excellent barrier to water seepage. It can be mixed with water to any desired consistency and injected with equipment similar to that used for cement grouting. Pressures in excess of 100 psi have been used to inject clay grout into formations.

Clay is not a satisfactory grout for use in fissures which contain flowing water. The primary advantage of clay as a grouting material is its low cost compared with cement and asphalt, especially when a deposit of clay is available near the site to be grouted.

In sealing large seams and solution channels in the limestone along the ridges of the reservoir at Madden Dam in the Canal Zone, 70,000 cu yd of clay grout was used [2]. The water content of the mixture varied from 43 to 55 percent by weight, depending on the back pressure of the fissures.

Seams in the abutments of the Chickamauga Dam were sealed with a cement-clay grout [3]. For this project grout was mixed in the proportions $1\frac{1}{2}$ parts of cement, 7 parts of clay, and 6 parts of water, by volume. Prior to mixing, the clay was screened to remove any particles or objects that would not mix readily in the grout.

CHEMICAL GROUTING

During recent years considerable success has been experienced with chemical grouting. The chemical method has several advantages when compared with other methods, including the following:

1. Because it is a liquid it can be pumped into and through very small openings, which other grouts cannot penetrate.
2. The chemical forms a barrier to the flow of water through a formation by changing from a liquid to a gel at a predetermined time after it enters the formation. The gel time may be varied from 3 sec to several hours.
3. Fewer grout holes are required.
4. The time required to inject the chemical is usually less than for other grouting materials.

Figure 16-5 Two-tank grout plant with mixers and pump for slurries and chemicals. *(ChemGrout, Inc.)*

If a formation to be grouted is highly porous, with relatively large voids, preliminary grouting should be done using such materials as cement, a mixture of cement and clay, or a mixture of cement and bentonite, individually or in combination, to reduce the rate of flow of water to approximately 10 percent of the initial rate. Then the final grouting can be done with chemicals.

Chemicals that have been used with success include sodium silicate and calcium chloride and a chemical designated as AM-9, which is manufactured by the American Cyanamid Company. The latter is an aqueous solution of two acrylic monomers and a catalyst, dimethyl-aminopropionitrile (DMAPN), which is mixed with an aqueous solution of catalyst ammonium persulfate (AP) just before it is pumped into the ground [4].

During the construction of a tunnel for a storm sewer in Houston, Texas, the contractor injected a solution of 2 lb of calcium chloride dissolved in 1 gal of sodium silicate into the formation of wet sandy clay, jointed clay, and extended areas of water-bearing sand, ahead of excavation to stabilize and seal the formation [5].

Prior to constructing the Round Butte Dam in Oregon, the contractor injected cement grout into the curtain under the dam to stop 95 percent of the flow of water through the seamy rock foundation; then he used AM-9 chemicals to complete the grouting [6].

EXAMPLES DESCRIBING GROUTING OPERATIONS

The following examples describe and discuss projects where grouting has been used to correct or control soil conditions to permit construction of desirable structures.

Example: Logan Martin Dam [7] This is a multipurpose project on the Coosa River in Alabama. The foundation for the dam is a cavernous limestone, which required considerable pressure grouting to fill the cavities under the dam. Curtain grouting was used to consolidate and strengthen the foundation.

Tests which were conducted to assist in selecting the drilling equipment demonstrated that diamond core drills were most suitable for drilling the injection holes.

A maximum initial or primary hole spacing of 40 ft was chosen as one workable for exploratory purposes because it prescribed a recognizable area of influence confined to reasonable dimensions. Cores were required from this set of holes to give geologic information on bedrock structure and its influence on the occurrence of cavitation. The election of any practical drilling method capable of detecting cavities was permitted for all holes located between cored primary holes. The depths of the holes were varied as information gained from the drilling indicated such variations to be desirable and effective.

Figure 16-6 illustrates the layout for a grout mixing and pumping plant. After testing local clays, sand, rock dust, and fly ash, it was determined that a grout consisting of cement and fly ash was most suitable. When fly ash was in short supply, rock dust was used as a substitute.

Example: Paris rapid transit tunnels [8] During the driving of vehicular tunnels in Paris, France, chemical grout was applied under pressure to consolidate water-bearing sand ahead of the excavation with considerable success.

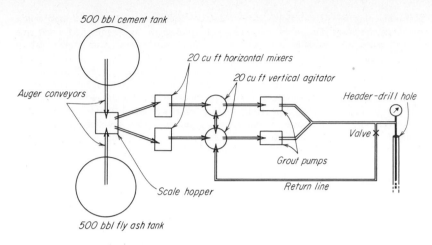

Figure 16-6 Layout of grout mixing plant for the Logan Martin Dam.

Two methods were used to accomplish the objectives. One method consisted of impregnating the sands with a diluted silica gel, giving a low strength, then partitioning the impregnated sand by cement grouting under high pressure. The other method consisted of grouting the sand through two closely drilled holes, using a pure silicate and a reagent such as calcium chloride. The main inconvenience with these methods is the required high pressure, which is not always permitted with the soil cover or structures.

For grouting medium to fine sands, viscous materials, generally colloidal, are used. These materials are designated as gels. They have a viscosity at the time of placing of about 25 centipoises. Their main characteristic, as far as grouting is concerned, is that their viscosity increases as a function of time. For equal strength, these silica gels are cheaper than other gels having the same viscosity-increase characteristics, such as lignosulfonates or derived products, vulcanizable oils, and alginates. In Europe, it has been determined that sodium silicate-based gels are the best.

When grouting clayey sands, gels are not suitable, and resins are used. A resin is a grouting material having a viscosity similar to that of water, which changes quickly at a given time by setting.

The essential difference between the two types of materials, gels and resins, is only a matter of viscosity characteristics, and it does not matter whether the materials are of organic or mineral origin. This variation in viscosity is considered the main criterion for selection of grout material. In each type, the materials are then classified according to the final strength they produce. In practice the two types of grout are generally used in combination on the same project. They must be compatible and have the same pH value. It is possible to use the more costly materials, resins, only when the more permeable areas have been treated with gels. However, gel grouting may follow, in some cases, an inexpensive clay cement pregrouting. This latter procedure was used on the project described here. This use was made possible by development of a new gel, sometimes referred to as Carongel. This reagent, of organic origin, is an ester, which has reactive properties on the silicate only after saponification. The reaction time and final strength are adjustable.

The use of these elaborate materials would not have been possible without the development of injection methods that permitted grouting to be competitive with other methods of stabilizing the soil. For this project, high-productivity drills and automatic grout mixing plants were used, ensuring regularity in the proportioning of component materials.

Because of variations in the characteristics and properties of the soil that was grouted, it was highly desirable to inject grouts that were most suitable for given conditions. In order to accomplish this objective, grout holes were drilled to their full depths and cased where necessary. Then there was introduced into each hole a polyvinylchloride pipe perforated with rings of small holes at intervals of 1 ft. Each ring of holes was covered with a short rubber sleeve, which fitted tightly around the tube and acted as a one-way valve, to permit grout to flow out from but nothing to flow into the tube. Injection of the grout into the formation was accomplished by lowering into this tube a grout pipe fitted with a double packer. The spacing between the two packers could be preset to limit the flow of grout to the desired part of the soil formation. The space in the grout pipe between the packers contained perforations to permit the grout to flow into the formation at controlled locations. Before injecting the grout, the casing, if used during the drilling of the hole, was removed from the hole.

The use of this technique provided several advantages, including:

1. It permitted the injection of grout in short stages and a better spread of the grout material.
2. It permitted the injection of grout that was best adapted to a given soil condition.
3. It permitted the injection of grout in several steps, using different mixes as desired, and it provided a method of repeating the procedure at a given level if desired.
4. It permitted separate drilling and grouting operations, thereby reducing possible interference between the two operations.

Because the polyvinylchloride tubes were easily broken, they did not impede the excavation that followed.

DETERMINING THE EFFECTIVENESS OF GROUTING

A question that usually arises in connection with a grouting operation is how to determine whether the operation has been successful. Several methods have been used with varying degrees of success.

To determine the extent of flow of grout from the injection holes through a formation, several holes are left open to see whether grout will appear in them. The appearance of grout in these holes serves as a guide to indicate the extent of flow.

Prior to concluding a grouting operation, additional exploratory holes may be drilled at various locations within the area that has been grouted in order to obtain cores from the formation. If these cores show the existence of sufficient grout to produce good consolidation where voids originally existed, this indicates that the grouting operation has been successful. The effectiveness of the grouting operation also may be tested by attempting to inject water or grout into the holes from which the cores were obtained. If these holes refuse to take grout, the test indicates that the formation has been consolidated adequately by previous injections.

REFERENCES

1. Weber, A. H.: Correction of Reservoir Leakage at Great Falls Dam, *Proceedings ASCE*, p. 101, January 1950.
2. Ackerman, Adolph J., and Charles H. Locher: "Construction Planning and Plant," 1st ed., pp. 215–216, McGraw-Hill Book Company, New York, 1940.

3. "Geology and Foundation Treatment," *Technical Report No.* 22, pp. 74, 267–269, Government Printing Office, Washington, D.C., 1949.
4. Chemical Grout Seals Shafts through Wet Sand, *Construction Methods and Equipment*, vol. 44, pp. 140–147, May 1962.
5. Murphy, W. D.: Machine Tunneling under Houston, *Civil Engineering*, vol. 34, pp. 44–45, September 1964.
6. Under Dams or over Subways Chemical Grout Plugs Leaks, *Engineering News-Record*, vol. 171, p. 62, August 8, 1963.
7. Grant, Leland F., and John S. Winefordner: Grouting a Dam Cutoff in Cavernous Limestone, *Journal of the Construction Division, Proceedings ASCE*, vol. 92, pp. 1–15, September 1966.
8. Janin, Jean J., and Guy F. LeSchiellour: Chemical Grouting for Paris Rapid Transit Tunnels, *Journal of the Construction Division, Proceedings ASCE*, vol. 96, pp. 61–74, June 1970.
9. Acker Drill Company, Inc., P.O. Box 830, Scranton, Pennsylvania 18501.
10. ChemGrout, Inc., P.O. Box 1140, La Grange Park, Illinois 60525.

SEVENTEEN

PILES AND PILE-DRIVING EQUIPMENT

INTRODUCTION

This chapter deals with the selection of load-bearing piles and the equipment required to drive the piles.

Load-bearing piles, as the name implies, are used primarily to transmit loads through soil formations with poor supporting properties into or onto formations that are capable of supporting the loads. If the load is transmitted to the soil through skin friction between the surface of the pile and the soil, the pile is called a *friction pile*. If the load is transmitted to the soil through the lower tip, the pile is called an *end-bearing pile*. Many piles depend on a combination of friction and end bearing for their supporting strengths.

TYPES OF PILES

Piles may be classified on the basis of their use or the materials from which they are made. On the basis of use there are two major classifications, *sheet* and *load-bearing*.

Sheet piling is used primarily to resist the flow of water and loose soil. Typical uses include cutoff walls under dams, cofferdams, bulkheads, trench sheeting, etc. On the basis of the materials from which they are made sheet piling may be classified as *steel*, *wood*, and *concrete*. The use of sheet piling will be discussed in Chap. 19.

On the basis of the material from which they are made and the method of constructing and driving them, load-bearing piles may be classified as follows:

1. Timber
   a. Untreated
   b. Treated with a preservative
2. Concrete
   a. Precast
   b. Cast-in-place
3. Steel
   a. H-section
   b. Steel-pipe
4. Composite

Each type of load-bearing pile has a place in the field of construction, and for some projects more than one type may seem satisfactory. It is the duty of the engineer to select that type of pile which is most satisfactory for a given project, considering all the factors that affect the selection. Among the factors that will influence his decision are the following:

1. Type, size, and weight of the structure to be supported
2. Physical properties of the soil at the site
3. Depth to a stratum capable of supporting the piles
4. Possibility of variations in the depth to a supporting stratum
5. Availability of materials for piles
6. Number of piles required
7. Facilities for driving piles
8. Comparative costs in place
9. Durability required
10. Types of structures adjacent to the project
11. Depth and kind of water, if any, above the ground into which the piles will be driven

To illustrate the effect which these factors have on the selection of types of piles, consider factor 4. If soil borings at the site of a project indicate that the depth to a stratum capable of supporting piles varies considerably, precast concrete piles should not be selected. Regardless of other desirable factors the difficulty and expense of increasing or decreasing the length of such piles should eliminate them from consideration. If concrete piles are desired, one of the cast-in-place types should be selected.

TIMBER PILES

Timber piles are made from the trunks of trees. While such piles are available in most sections of the nation and the world, it is becoming more difficult to obtain long, straight timber piles. Pine piles are reasonably available in lengths up to 60 ft, while Douglas fir piles are available in lengths in excess of 100 ft from the Pacific Northwest.

Among the advantages of timber piles are the following:

1. The more popular lengths and sizes are available on short notice.
2. They are economical in cost.
3. They are handled easily, with little danger of breakage.
4. They can be cut off to any desired length after they are driven.
5. They can be pulled easily in the event removal is necessary.

Among the disadvantages of timber piles are the following:

1. It may be difficult to obtain piles sufficiently long and straight for some projects.
2. It may be difficult or impossible to drive them into hard formations.
3. It is difficult to splice them to increase their lengths.
4. While they are satisfactory when used as friction piles, they are not suitable for use as end-bearing piles under heavy loads.
5. The length of life may be short unless the piles are treated with a preservative.

PRECAST CONCRETE PILES

Square and octagonal piles are cast in horizontal forms, while round piles are cast in vertical forms. After the piles are cast, they should be cured under damp sand, straw, or mats for the period required by the specifications, frequently 21 days.

With the exception of short lengths, precast concrete piles must be reinforced with sufficient steel to prevent damage or breakage while they are being handled from the casting beds to the driving positions. The Foundation Code of the City of New York, adopted in 1948, specifies that precast concrete piles shall contain longitudinal reinforcing steel in an amount not less than 2 percent of the volume of a pile. Lateral steel shall be at least $\frac{1}{4}$-in.-diameter round bars, spaced not more than 12 in. apart, except at the top and bottom 3 ft of a pile, where the spacing shall not exceed 3 in. The concrete cover over the reinforcing steel shall be at least 2 in. Figure 17-1 shows typical details of precast concrete piles.

Concrete piles should be cast as near the site of use as possible in order to reduce the cost of handling them from the casting beds to the pile driver. In the event it is necessary to transport them to a driver, this may be done by a truck. For handling concrete piles, care must be exercised to prevent breakage or damage due to flexural stresses. Long piles should be picked up at several points to reduce the unsupported lengths.

Concrete piles may be cast in any desired sizes and lengths. Those used in constructing the Morganza Floodway on the Mississippi River were square and

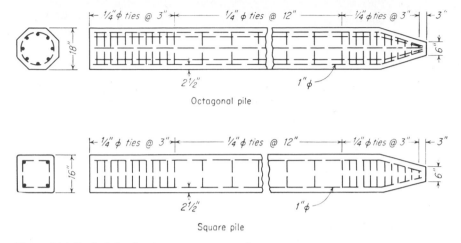

Figure 17-1 Typical details of precast concrete piles.

octagonal in cross section, 20 in. wide, and varied in length to more than 100 ft. Almost 360,000 lin ft of piles was driven on this project. The piles were cast in prefabricated steel forms, loaded on railroad cars by a gantry crane with a 135-ft span, and hauled to the driving site, where they were driven by special rigs. For a project as big as this the large investment in special equipment is justified, but for a small project the required investment in equipment probably would make

Figure 17-2 Preparing forms and reinforcing for precast concrete piles.

Figure 17-3 Crawler-mounted pile-driving rigs. *(Raymond International, Inc.)*

the cost prohibitive. Thus, the maximum-size concrete piles that can be used on a project may be determined by economy.

One of the disadvantages of using precast concrete piles, especially for a project where different lengths are required, is the difficulty of reducing or increasing the lengths of the piles.

If a pile proves to be too long, it is necessary to cut off the excess length. This is done, after a pile is driven to its maximum penetration, by chipping the concrete away from the reinforcing steel, cutting the reinforcing with a gas torch, then removing the surplus length of the concrete core. This operation represents a waste of material and time which can be very expensive.

When a precast concrete pile does not develop sufficient driving resistance to support the design load, it may be necessary to increase the length and drive the pile to a greater depth. Unless the reinforcing bars extend above the top of a pile, it will be necessary to chip the concrete back far enough to permit additional reinforcing to be welded to the original longitudinal bars. Then the concrete is placed for the added length.

Among the advantages of precast concrete piles are the following:

1. High resistance to chemical and biological attacks.
2. High strength.
3. A pipe may be installed along the center of a pile to facilitate jetting.

Among the disadvantages of precast concrete piles are the following:

1. It is difficult to reduce or increase the length.
2. Large sizes require heavy and expensive handling and driving equipment.
3. Inability to obtain piles by purchase may delay the starting of a project.
4. Possible breakage of piles during handling or driving produces a delay hazard.

CAST-IN-PLACE CONCRETE PILES

As the name implies, cast-in-place concrete piles are constructed by depositing the freshly mixed concrete in place in the ground and letting it cure there. The two principal methods of constructing such piles are:

1. Driving a metallic shell, leaving it in the ground, and filling it with concrete
2. Driving a metallic shell and filling it with concrete as the shell is pulled from the ground

There are several modifications for each of the two methods.

The more commonly used piles constructed by these two methods are described in the following sections.

RAYMOND STEP-TAPER CONCRETE PILES

The step-taper pile is installed by driving a spirally corrugated steel shell, made up of sections 4 or 8 ft long, with successive increases in diameter of 1 in. for each 8-ft section. A corrugated sleeve at the bottom of each section is screwed into the top of the section immediately below it. Piles of the necessary length, up to a maximum of 80 ft, are obtained by joining the proper number of sections at the job. The shells are available in various gauges of metal to fit different job conditions. The bottom of the shell, whose diameter can be varied from $8\frac{1}{2}$ to

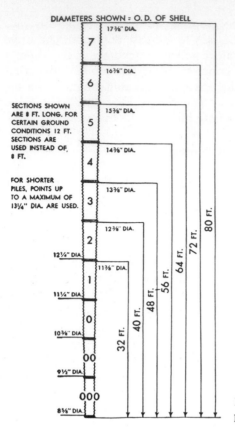
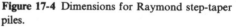

Figure 17-4 Dimensions for Raymond step-taper piles.

$13\frac{1}{8}$ in., is closed prior to driving by a flat steel plate or a hemispherical steel boot.

After a shell is assembled in the desired length, a step-tapered rigid-steel core is inserted and the shell is driven to the desired penetration. The core is removed, and the shell is filled with concrete. Figure 17-4 gives the dimensions of a step-taper pile shell. Figure 17-5 illustrates steps in driving these piles.

MONOTUBE PILES

The monotube pile is obtained by driving a fluted, tapered steel shell, closed at the tip with an 8-in.-diameter driving point, to the desired penetration. The shell is driven without a mandrel, inspected, and filled with concrete. Any desired length of shell, up to approximately 125 ft, may be obtained by welding extensions to a standard-length shell.

Table 17-1 gives dimensions and other information on one type of tube.

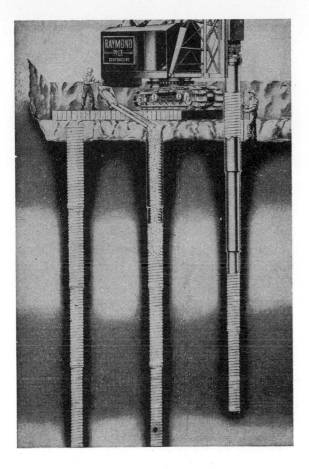

Figure 17-5 Driving Raymond step-taper piles.

ADVANTAGES AND DISADVANTAGES OF CAST-IN-PLACE CONCRETE PILES

Among the advantages of cast-in-place concrete piles are the following:

1. The lightweight shells may be handled and driven easily.
2. Variations in length do not present a serious problem. The length of a shell may be increased or decreased easily.
3. The shells may be shipped in short lengths and assembled at the job.
4. Excess reinforcing, to resist stresses caused by handling only, is eliminated.
5. The danger of breaking a pile while driving is eliminated.
6. Additional piles may be provided quickly if they are needed.

Figure 17-6 Driving No. 5 gauge 12 in. F taper Monotube piles up to 200 ft long with a 37,000 ft-lb steam hammer. *(The Union Metal Manufacturing Company.)*

Among the disadvantages of cast-in-place concrete piles are the following:

1. A slight movement of the earth around an unreinforced pile may break it.
2. An uplifting force, acting on the shaft of an uncased and unreinforced pile, may cause it to fail in tension.
3. The bottom of a pedestal pile may not be symmetrical.

Figure 17-7 Monotube piles. *(Union Metal Manufacturing Company.)*

STEEL-PIPE PILES

These piles are installed by driving pipes to the desired depth and filling them with concrete. A pipe may be driven with the lower end closed with a plate or a steel driving point, or the pipe may be driven with the lower end open. Pipes varying in diameter from 6 to 30 in. or more have been driven in lengths varying from a few feet to more than 200 ft.

A closed end pipe pile is driven in any conventional manner, usually with a pile hammer. If it is necessary to increase the length of a pile, two or more sections may be welded together or sections may be connected by using an inside sleeve for each joint. This type of pile is particularly advantageous for use on jobs when the headroom for driving is limited and short sections must be added to obtain the desired total length.

An open-end pipe pile is installed by driving the pipe to the required depth, removing the material from inside, and filling the space with concrete. Because open-end pipe piles offer less driving resistance than closed-end piles, a smaller pile hammer may be used. The use of a light hammer is desirable when piles are driven near a structure whose foundation might be damaged by the impact of the blows from a large hammer. Open-end piles may be driven to depths which could never be reached with closed-end piles.

Table 17-1 Data on Monotube piles

Type	Size, point diameter × butt diameter × length	Weight, lb per ft				Volume of concrete, cu yd
		9 ga	7 ga	5 ga	3 ga	
F	$8\frac{1}{2}''$ × 12″ × 25′	17	20	24	28	0.43
Taper	8″ × 12″ × 30′	16	20	23	27	0.55
0.14 in.	$8\frac{1}{2}''$ × 14″ × 40′	19	22	26	31	0.95
per ft	8″ × 16″ × 60′	20	24	28	33	1.68
	8″ × 18″ × 75′		26	31	35	2.59
J	8″ × 12″ × 17′	17	20	23	27	0.32
Taper	8″ × 14″ × 25′	18	22	26	30	0.58
0.25 in.	8″ × 16″ × 33′	20	24	28	32	0.95
per ft	8″ × 18″ × 40′		26	30	35	1.37
Y	8″ × 12″ × 10′	17	20	24	28	0.18
Taper	8″ × 14″ × 15′	19	22	26	30	0.34
0.40 in.	8″ × 16″ × 20′	20	24	28	33	0.56
per ft	8″ × 18″ × 25′		26	31	35	0.86

Extensions (Overall lengths 1 ft greater than indicated)

Type	Diameter × length	9 ga	7 ga	5 ga	3 ga	cu yd per ft
N 12	12″ × 12″ × 20′/40′	20	24	28	33	0.026
N 14	14″ × 14″ × 20′/40′	24	29	34	41	0.035
N 16	16″ × 16″ × 20′/40′	28	33	39	46	0.045
N 18	18″ × 18″ × 20′/40′		38	44	52	0.058

After a pile is driven to the desired depth, the material inside is removed by bursts of compressed air, a mixture of water and compressed air, an earth auger, or a small orange-peel bucket; then the pipe is filled with concrete. Figure 17-8 shows a barge-mounted driver driving 24-in. pipe piles up to 220 ft long for a dry dock in Portland, Oregon.

STEEL PILES

In constructing foundations that require piles driven to great depths, steel H piles probably are more suitable than any other type. Steel piles may be driven through hard materials to a specified depth to eliminate the danger of failure due to scouring, such as under a pier in a river. Also, steel piles may be driven to great depths through poor soils to bear on a solid rock stratum. The great strength of steel combined with the small displacement of soil permits a large portion of the energy from a pile hammer to be transmitted to the bottom of a

Figure 17-8 Barge-mounted rig driving 24-in. piles up to 220 ft long.

pile. As a result, it is possible to drive steel piles into soils which could not be penetrated by any other type of pile. However, in spite of the great strength of these piles the author has seen jobs where it was necessary to drill pilot holes into compacted sand ahead of steel H piles in order to obtain the specified penetration. By weld splicing sections together, lengths in excess of 200 ft have been driven.

THE RESISTANCE OF PILES TO PENETRATION

In general, the forces which enable a pile to support a load also cause the pile to resist the efforts made to drive it. The total resistance of a pile to penetration will equal the sum of the forces produced by skin friction and end bearing. The portion of the resistance supplied by either skin friction or end bearing may vary from almost 0 to 100 percent, depending on the soil more than on the type of pile. A steel H pile driven to refusal in stiff clay should be classified as a skin-friction pile, while the same pile driven through a mud deposit to rest on solid rock should be classified as an end-bearing pile.

Figure 17-9 Diesel hammer driving steel H-pile on 1 : 1 batter. *(Pileco, Inc.)*

Numerous tests have been conducted to determine values for skin friction for various types of piles and soils. A representative value for skin friction can be obtained by determining the total force required to pull a pile up slightly, using hydraulic jacks with calibrated pressure gauges.

The value of the skin friction is a function of the coefficient of friction between the pile and the soil and the pressure of the soil normal to the surface of the pile, or for a soil such as some types of clay the value of the skin friction may be limited to the shearing strength of the soil immediately adjacent to the pile. Consider a concrete pile driven into a soil that produces a normal pressure of 100 psi on the vertical surface of the pile. This is not an unusually high pressure for certain soils such as compacted sand. If the coefficient of friction is 0.25, the value of the skin friction will be $0.25 \times 100 \times 144 = 3,600$ psf. Table 17-2 gives representative values of skin friction on piles. The author of the table states that the information is intended as a qualitative guide, not as correct information to be used in any and all cases.

The magnitude of end-bearing pressure can be determined by driving a button-bottom-type pile and leaving the driving casing in place. A second steel pipe, slightly smaller than the driving casing, is lowered onto the concrete button. The force, applied through the second pipe, required to drive the button into the soil is a direct measure of the supporting strength of the soil. This is true because there is no skin friction on the inside pipe.

Table 17-2 Approximate allowable value of skin friction on piles*

Material	Skin friction, psf (kg/sq m)		
	Approximate depth		
	20 ft (6.1 m)	60 ft (18.3 m)	100 ft (30.5 m)
Soft silt and dense muck	50–100	50–120	60–150
	(244–488)	(244–586)	(273–738)
Silt (wet but confined)	100–200	125–250	150–300
	(488–976)	(610–1,220)	(738–1,476)
Soft clay	200–300	250–350	300–400
	(976–1,464)	(1,220–1,710)	(1,476–1,952)
Stiff clay	300–500	350–550	400–600
	(1,464–2,440)	(1,710–2,685)	(1,952–2,928)
Clay and sand mixed	300–500	400–600	500–700
	(1,464–2,440)	(1,952–2,928)	(2,440–3,416)
Fine sand (wet but confined)	300–400	350–500	400–600
	(1,464–1,952)	(1,710–2,440)	(1,952–2,928)
Medium sand and small gravel	500–700	600–800	600–800
	(2,440–3,416)	(2,928–3,904)	(2,928–3,904)

* Some allowance is made for the effect of using piles in small groups.

PILE HAMMERS

The function of a pile hammer is to furnish the energy required to drive a pile. Pile-driving hammers are designated by type and size.

The types commonly used include the following:

1. Drop
2. Single-acting steam
3. Double-acting steam
4. Differential-acting steam
5. Diesel
6. Vibratory
7. Hydraulic

The size of a drop hammer is designated by its weight, while the size of each of the other hammers is designated by the theoretical energy per blow, expressed in foot-pounds.

For each type of hammer listed the driving energy is supplied by a falling mass, which strikes the top of a pile. The various types are described in the following sections.

Drop hammers A drop hammer is a heavy metal weight that is lifted by a rope, then released and allowed to fall on top of the pile. The hammer may be

released by a trip and fall freely, or it may be released by loosening the friction
band on the hoisting drum and permitting the weight of the hammer to unwind
the rope from the drum. The latter type of release reduces the effective energy of
a hammer because of the friction loss in the drum and rope. Leads are used to
hold the pile in position and to guide the movement of the hammer so that it will
strike the pile with a solid blow.

Standard drop hammers are made in sizes which vary from about 500 to
3,000 lb. The height of drop or fall most frequently used varies from 5 to 20 ft.
When a large energy per blow is required to drive a pile, it is better to use a
heavy hammer with a small drop than a light hammer with a large drop.

Drop hammers are suitable for driving piles on remote projects which
require only a few piles and for which the time of completion is not an
important factor.

Among the advantages of drop hammers are the following:

1. Small investment in equipment
2. Simplicity of operation
3. Ability to vary the energy per blow by varying the height of fall

Among the disadvantages of drop hammers are the following:

1. Slow rate of driving piles
2. Danger of damaging piles by lifting a hammer too high
3. Danger of damaging adjacent buildings as a result of the heavy vibration
   caused by a hammer
4. Cannot be used directly for underwater driving

Single-acting steam hammers A single-acting steam hammer is a freely falling
weight, called a ram, which is lifted by steam or compressed air, whose pressure
is applied to the underside of a piston that is connected to the ram through a
piston rod. When the piston reaches the top of the stroke, the steam pressure is
released and the ram falls freely to strike the top of a pile. The energy supplied
by this type hammer is delivered by a heavy weight striking with a low velocity,
due to the relatively low fall. Whereas a drop hammer may strike 4 to 8 blows
per minute, a single-acting steam hammer will strike 50 or more blows per
minute when delivering the same energy per blow.

Single-acting steam hammers may be open or enclosed. Figure 17-10 shows
one of each type. This hammer is available in sizes varying from a few hundred
to more than 30,000 ft-lb of energy per blow. Table 17-3 gives data on several of
the more popular sizes of single-acting steam hammers. The length of the stroke
and the energy per blow for this type of hammer may be decreased slightly by
reducing the steam pressure below that recommended by the manufacturer. The
reduced pressure has the effect of decreasing the height to which the piston will
rise before it begins its free fall.

Among the advantages of single-acting steam compared with drop hammers are the following:

1. Greater number of blows per minute permits faster driving.
2. Greater frequency of blows reduces the increase in skin friction between blows.
3. Heavier ram falling at lower velocity transmits a greater portion of the energy to driving piles.
4. Reduction in the velocity of the ram decreases the danger of damage to piles during driving.
5. The enclosed types may be used for underwater driving.

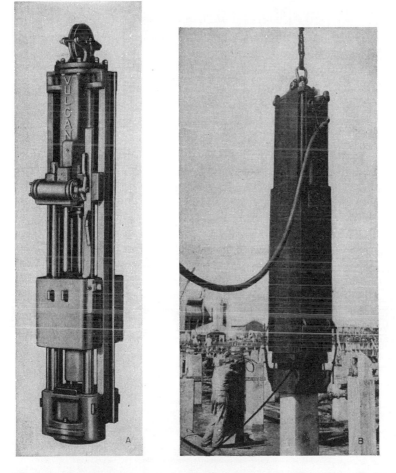

Figure 17-10 Single-acting steam hammers. (*a*) Open type *(Vulcan Iron Works)*. (*b*) Enclosed type *(MKT Geotechnical Systems).*

Table 17-3 Specifications for impact-type pile drivers

Make and model	Type[a]	Rated energy, ft·lb	Speed, blows per min	Weight of ram, lb	Maximum stroke, in	Boiler hp (ASME)	Air or steam, psi	Net weight, lb
BOLT CPD-15	Air-cushion Single action	30,000	55 85	14,200	36 23.5		250 120	30,000
BSP								
BSP B15	Dbl. Act. Diesel	26,200	80–100	3,300	100[d]			9,000
BSP B25	Dbl. Act. Diesel	45,700	800–100	5,500	100[d]			15,200
BSP B35	Dbl. Act. Diesel	63,900	80–100	7,700	100[d]			21,200
BSP B45	Dbl. Act. Diesel	80,000	80–100	10,000	100[d]			27,500
BSP 500N	Dbl. Act. Air	1,200	330	200	9		90	2,000
BSP 600N	Dbl. Act. Air	3,000	250	500	12		90	3,800
BSP 700N	Dbl. Act. Air	4,700	225	850	13		90	6,500
BSP 900	Dbl. Act. Air/Steam	8,750	145	1,600	17	85	90	7,100
BSP 1000	Dbl. Act. Air/Steam	13,100	105	3,000	19	104	90	10,850
BSP 1100	Dbl. Act. Air/Steam	19,150	95	5,000	19	126	90	14,000
CONMACO								
300	Sgl. Act. Air/Steam	90,000	55	30,000	36	247	150	55,390
200	Sgl. Act. Air/Steam	60,000	60	20,000	36	217	120	44,560
160	Sgl. Act. Air/Steam	48,750	60	16,250	36	198	120	33,200
140	Sgl. Act. Air/Steam	42,000	60	14,000	36	179	110	30,750
160D	Differ. Air/Steam	41,280	103	16,000	$15\frac{1}{2}$	237	160	35,400
125	Sgl. Act. Air/Steam	40,625	50	12,500	39	120	125	21,940
115	Sgl. Act. Air/Steam	37,375	50	11,500	39	99	120	20,780
140D	Differ. Air/Steam	36,000	103	14,000	$15\frac{1}{2}$	211	140	31,200
100	Sgl. Act. Air/Steam	32,500	50	10,000	39	85	100	19,280
80	Sgl. Act. Air/Steam	26,000	50	8,000	39	75	85	17,280
65	Sgl. Act. Air/Steam	19,500	60	6,500	36	67	100	11,200
50	Sgl. Act. Air/Steam	15,000	60	5,000	36	56	80	9,700
DELMAG[e,f]								
D-55		62,500 to 117.175	36–47	11,860	137			26,300
D-46-02[e,f]		48,400 to 105,000	37–53	10,100	128			19,900
D-44		43,500 to 87,000	37–56	9,460	137			22,440
D-36-02		38,000 to 83.100	37–53	7,940	128			17,700
D-30-05[e,f]		31,800 to 62,900	38–52	6,600	127			13,150
D-30		23,800 to 54,250	39–60	6,600	126			12,350
D-22-02[e,f]		24,600 to 48,400	38–52	4,850	127			11,400
D-22		39,700	40–60	4,850	127			11,100
D-15		27,100	40–60	3,300	132			6,600
D-12		22,500	40–60	2,750	130			6,050
D- 5		9,100	42–60	1,100	116			2,730
D- 4		3,630	50–60	836	52			1,360
D- 2		1,815	60–70	484	49			792
FOSTER/KOBE								
K150	Sgl. Act. Diesel	298,000	42–60	33,100	108			87,000
K60	Sgl. Act. Diesel	105,600	42–60	13,200	112			37,500
K45	Sgl. Act. Diesel	91,100	39–60	9,920	112			25,600
K42	Sgl. Act. Diesel	79,000	40–60	9,260	102			24,000
K35	Sgl. Act. Diesel	70,800	39–60	7,720	112			18,700
K32	Sgl. Act. Diesel	60,100	40–60	7,050	102			17,750
K25	Sgl. Act. Diesel	50,700	39–60	5,510	112			13,100
K22	Sgl. Act. Diesel	41,300	40–60	4,850	102			12,350
K13	Sgl. Act. Diesel	25,200	34–60	2,870	106			8,000
LINK-BELT								
660	Dbl. Act. Diesel	45,000	80–84	7,564	71[d]			23,500
520	Dbl. Act. Diesel	26,300	80–84	5,070	63[d]			12,545
440	Dbl. Act. Diesel	18,200	86–90	4,000	56[d]			9,839
180	Dbl. Act. Diesel	8,100	90–95	1,725	57[d]			4,546

NOTE: A diesel pile hammer has a variable stroke and hence a variable energy rating based upon the amount of resistance built up in the pile and the amount of compression in the cylinder.

[a] Type "U" indicates hammer is suitable for underwater driving. Type "E" indicates hammer can be converted to extractor.

[b] MKT air/steam hammers are listed with flat anvils. Vulcan hammers are listed with standard base, no drive cap. All diesels are listed without drive caps.

[c] MKT DA 35 diesel is convertible from single to double acting. Rated energy is 21,000 ft-lb double-acting, and 35,000 ft-lb single-acting.

[d] Equivalent ram stroke.

[e] Models showing two energy figures are equipped with adjustable fuel pumps—the numbers indicate the minimum and maximum settings. (Intermediate steps not shown.)

[f] Require revised "U" cylinder to operate in box leads.

Reproduced by permission of the editor, from *Construction Methods & Equipment*, pp. 68–69, March 1977. Copyright © 1977 by McGraw-Hill, Inc.

Table 17-3 Specifications for impact-type pile drivers (*Continued*)

	Type[a]	Rated energy, ft·lb	Speed, blows per min	Weight of ram, lb	Maximum stroke, in	Boiler hp (ASME)	Air steam, psi	Net weight, lb
MENCK								
MRBS 8000	Sgl. Act. Air Steam	867,960	32	176,365	59	1,500	156	330,695
MRBS 4600	Sgl. Act. Air Steam	499,070	36	101,410	59	850	156	176,371
MRBS 3000	Sgl. Act. Air Steam	325,480	40	66,135	59	520	156	108,025
MRBS 1800	Sgl. Act. Air Steam	189,850	40	38,580	59	320	156	64,596
MRBS 850	Sgl. Act. Air Steam	93,340	40	18,960	59	160	156	27,800
MITSUBISHI								
MB-70	Sgl. Act. Diesel	141,000	38–60	15,840	102			46,000
MH-45	Sgl. Act. Diesel	84,300	42–60	9,920	102			24,500
M-43	Sgl. Act. Diesel	84,000	40–60	9,460	102			22,660
MH-35	Sgl. Act. Diesel	65,900	42–60	7,720	102			18,500
M-33	Sgl. Act. Diesel	64,000	40–60	7,260	102			16,940
MH-25	Sgl. Act. Diesel	46,900	42–60	5,510	102			13,200
M-23	Sgl. Act. Diesel	45,000	42–60	5,060	102			11,220
MH-15	Sgl. Act. Diesel	28,100	42–60	3,310	102			8,400
M-14S	Sgl. Act. Diesel	26,000	42–60	2,970	102			7,260
MKT[b]								
DE70B	Sgl. Act. Diesel	63,000	40–50	7,000	126			15,400
S20	U Sgl. Act. Air Steam	60,000	60	20,000	36	190	150	38,650
MRBS-50	Sgl. Act. Air Steam	46,350	40	11,300			115	15,550
DE-50B	Sgl. Act. Diesel	45,000	40–50	5,000	126			12,250
DA55B	Sgl. Act. Diesel	45,000	40–50	5,000	126			17,000
DA55B	Dbl. Act. Diesel	38,200	78–82	5,000				17,000
S14-B	U Sgl. Act. Air Steam	37,500	60	14,000	32	155	100	31,700
S10	U Sgl. Act. Air Steam	32,500	55	10,000	39	130	80	22,380
DA35[c]	Sgl. Act. Diesel	25,200	40–50	2,800	150			10,000
DE30B	Sgl. Act. Diesel	25,200	45–50	2,800	129			7,500
DA35[c]	Dbl. Act. Diesel	21,000	78–82	2,800				10,000
11B3	U Dbl. Act. Air Steam	19,150	95	5,000	19	128	100	14,000
DE20	Sgl. Act. Diesel	16,000	40–50	2,000	111			5,375
10B3	U Sgl. Act. Air Steam	13,100	105	3,000	19	104	100	10,850
9B3	U Dbl. Act. Air Steam	8,750	145	1,600	17	85	100	7,000
7	E Dbl. Act. Air Steam	4,150	225	800	$9\frac{1}{2}$	65	100	5,000
6	E Dbl. Act. Air Steam	2,500	275	400	$8\frac{1}{4}$	45	100	2,900
5	E Dbl. Act. Air Steam	1,000	300	200	7	35	100	1,500
VULCAN[b]								
3100	Sgl. Act. Air/Steam	300,000	58	100,000	36	1,021	130	174,500
560	Sgl. Act. Air/Steam	300,000	45	62,500	60	875	150	134,060
060	Sgl. Act. Air/Steam	180,000	62	60,000	36	750	130	125,000
540	Sgl. Act. Air/Steam	200,000	48	40,900	60	635	130	102,980
040	Sgl. Act. Air/Steam	120,000	60	40,000	36	600	120	98,000
400C	Sgl. Act. Air/Steam	113,488	100	40,000	$16\frac{1}{2}$	700	150	91,180
030	Sgl. Act. Air/Steam	90,000	55	30,000	36	247	150	55,410
020	Sgl. Act. Air/Steam	60,000	60	20,000	36	217	120	43,785
200C	Dbl. Act. Air/Steam	50,200	98	20,000	$15\frac{1}{2}$	260	142	39,000
016	Sgl. Act. Air/Steam	48,750	60	16,250	36	210	120	33,340
014	Sgl. Act. Air/Steam	42,000	60	14,000	36	200	110	29,590
140C	Dbl. Act. Air/Steam	36,000	103	14,000	$15\frac{1}{2}$	211	140	27,984
010	Sgl. Act. Air/Steam	32,500	50	10,000	39	157	105	19,500
0R	Sgl. Act. Air/Steam	30,225	80	9,300	39	140	100	18,050
08	Sgl. Act. Air/Steam	26,000	50	8,000	39	127	83	16,750
80C	Dbl. Act. Air/Steam	24,450	111	8,000	$16\frac{1}{2}$	180	120	17,885
0	Sgl. Act. Air/Steam	24,375	50	7,500	39	120	80	16,250
06(106)	Sgl. Act. Air/Steam	19,500	60	6,500	36	94	100	11,200
65C	Dbl. Act. Air/Steam	19,200	117	6,500	$15\frac{1}{2}$	152	150	14,886
50C	Dbl. Act. Air/Steam	15,100	120	5,000	$15\frac{1}{2}$	125	120	11,782
1(106)	Sgl. Act. Air/Steam	15,000	60	5,000	36	81	80	9,700
30C	Dbl. Act. Air/Steam	7,260	133	3,000	$10\frac{1}{2}$	40	120	7,036
2	Sgl. Act. Air/Steam	7,260	70	3,000	29	49	80	6,700
DGH-900	Dbl. Act. Air/Steam	5,750	360	900	10	115	178	5,000
18C	Dbl. Act. Air/Steam	3,600	150	1,800	$10\frac{1}{2}$	45	120	4,139
DGH-100D	Dbl. Act. Air/Steam	643	505	100	6		100	786
5100	Sgl. Act. Air/Steam	500,000	48	100,000	60	1,400	150	197,000
4250	Sgl. Act. Air/Steam	1,000,000	54	250,000	48	3,000	150	400,000

Figure 17-11 Single-acting steam hammer driving steel pile shell. *(The Union Metal Manufacturing Company.)*

Among the disadvantages of single-acting steam compared with drop hammers are the following:

1. Require more investment in equipment such as a steam boiler or an air compressor
2. More complicated, with higher maintenance cost
3. Require more time to set up and take down
4. Require a larger operating crew

Double-acting steam hammers In the double-acting steam hammer steam pressure is applied to the underside of the piston to raise the ram; then during the downward stroke steam is applied to the top side of the piston to increase the energy per blow. Thus, with a given weight ram, it is possible to attain a desired amount of energy per blow with a shorter stroke than with a single-acting hammer. The number of blows per minute will be approximately twice as great as for a single-acting hammer with the same energy rating.

The lighter ram and higher striking velocity of the double-acting hammer may be advantageous when driving light- to medium-weight piles into soils having normal frictional resistance. It is claimed that the high frequency of blows will keep a pile moving downward continuously, thus preventing static skin friction from developing between blows. However, when heavy piles are driven, especially into soils having high frictional resistance, the heavier weight and slower velocity of a single-acting hammer will transmit a greater portion of the rated energy into driving the piles. Figure 17-12 shows the essential parts of a double-acting hammer. This hammer is fully enclosed by a steel case.

Table 17-3 gives dimensions and other data for several of the more popular sizes of double-acting hammers. As indicated in this table, the energy per blow

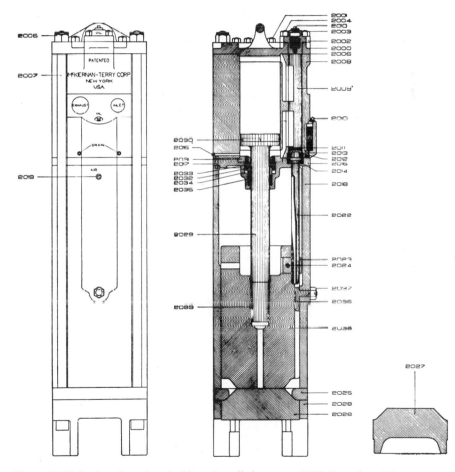

Figure 17-12 Section through a double-acting pile hammer. *(MKT Geotechnical Systems.)*

as well as the number of blows per minute can be modified by varying the steam pressure.

Among the advantages of double-acting compared with single-acting hammers are the following:

1. The greater number of blows per minute reduces the time required to drive piles.
2. The greater number of blows per minute reduces the development of static skin friction between blows.
3. Piles can be driven more easily without leads.

Among the disadvantages of double-acting compared with single-acting hammers are the following:

1. The relatively light weight and high velocity of the ram make this type of hammer less suitable for use in driving heavy piles into soils having high frictional resistance.
2. The hammer is more complicated.

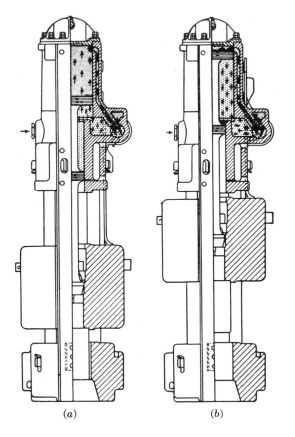

(a) (b)

Figure 17-13 Section through a differential-acting steam hammer. (*a*) Piston in lower position. (*b*) Piston in upper position. (*Vulcan Iron Works.*)

Differential-acting steam hammers A differential-acting steam hammer is a modified double-acting hammer in that steam pressure is used to lift the ram and to accelerate the ram on the downstroke. As shown in Fig. 17-13, the ram has a large piston which operates in an upper cylinder and a small piston which operates in a lower cylinder. The lifting of the ram is effected by the difference in the pressure forces acting on the two pistons. The number of blows per minute is comparable with that for a double-acting hammer, while the weight and the equivalent free fall of the ram are comparable with those of a single-acting hammer. Thus, it is claimed that this type of hammer has the advantages of the single- and double-acting hammers. It is reported that this hammer will drive a pile in one-half the time required by the same size single-acting hammer and in doing so will use 25 to 35 percent less steam. This hammer is available in open or closed types. Table 17-3 gives dimensions and data for these hammers. The values given in the table for rated energy per blow are correct provided the steam pressure is sufficient to produce the indicated normal blows per minute.

Hydraulic hammers These hammers operate on the differential principle of hydraulic fluid instead of steam or compressed air used by conventional hammers. Table 17-3 gives the specifications for the sizes manufactured by MKT Geotechnical Systems.

Dynamic pile-driving formulas in current use are applicable to these hammers.

Diesel hammers A diesel pile-driving hammer is a self-contained driving unit which does not require an external source of energy such as a steam boiler or an air compressor. In this respect it is simpler and more easily moved from one location to another than a steam hammer. A complete unit consists of a vertical cylinder, a piston or ram, an anvil, fuel- and lubricating-oil tanks, a fuel pump, injectors, and a mechanical lubricator.

After a hammer is placed on top of a pile, the combined piston and ram are lifted to the upper end of the stroke and released to start the unit operating. As the ram nears the end of the downstroke, it activates a fuel pump that injects the fuel into the combustion chamber between the ram and the anvil. The continued downstroke of the ram compresses the air and the fuel to ignition heat. The resulting explosion drives the pile downward and the ram upward to repeat its stroke. The energy per blow, which can be controlled by the operator, may be varied over a wide range. Table 17-3 lists the specifications for several makes and models of diesel hammers.

Advantages of the diesel hammer When compared with the steam hammer, the diesel hammer has several potential advantages, including the following:

1. The hammer needs no external source of energy. Thus, it is more mobile and it requires less time to set up and start operating.
2. The hammer is economical to operate. The rated fuel consumption for a

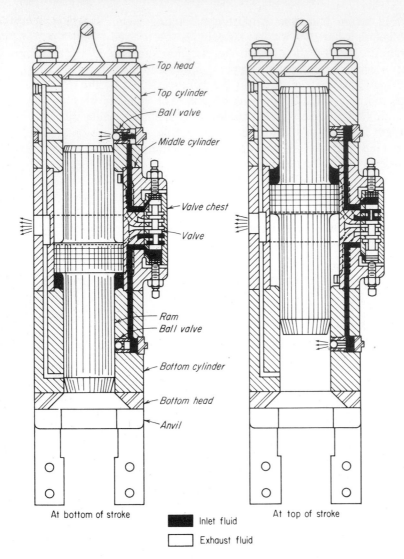

- Top head
- Top cylinder
- Ball valve
- Middle cylinder
- Valve chest
- Valve
- Ram
- Ball valve
- Bottom cylinder
- Bottom head
- Anvil

At bottom of stroke   At top of stroke

Inlet fluid

Exhaust fluid

Figure 17-14 Operation of a fluid-valve double-acting hammer. *(MKT Geotechnical Systems.)*

24,000 ft-lb hammer is 3 gal per hr when it is operating. Because a hammer does not operate continuously, the actual consumption is less.

3. It is convenient to operate in remote areas. Because it uses diesel oil as a source of energy, it is not necessary to provide a boiler, water for steam, and fuel oil.

4. It operates well in cold weather. Diesel hammers have been used at temperatures well below 0°F, where it would be difficult or impossible to provide steam.

Figure 17-15 Diesel hammer driving sheet piling. *(Pileco, Inc)*

5. The hammer is light in weight when compared with the weight of a steam hammer of equal rating.
6. Maintenance and servicing are simple and fast.
7. The energy per blow increases as the driving resistance of a pile increases.
8. Because the resistance of a pile to driving is necessary for continuing operation of a diesel hammer, this hammer will not operate if a pile breaks or falls out from under a hammer.
9. Because of the low velocity in easy driving, and also because the piston reacts to the impact needed for each blow by rebounding up its cylinder, a diesel hammer is less likely to batter the piles when driving them.
10. The energy per blow and the number of blows per minute can be varied easily to permit a diesel hammer to operate most effectively for an existing condition [1].

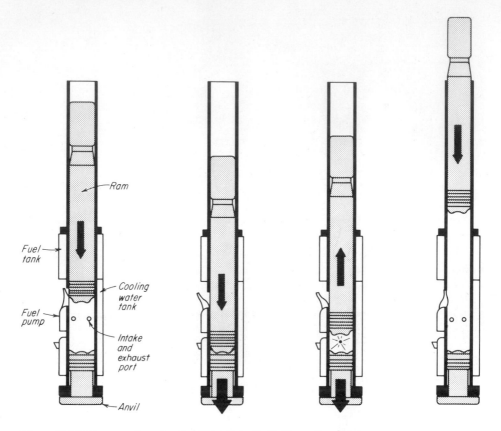

Figure 17-16 The operation of a diesel hammer. *(L. B. Foster Company.)*

Disadvantages of the diesel hammer Among the disadvantages of a diesel hammer are the following:

1. It is difficult to determine the energy per blow for this hammer. Because the height to which the piston ram will rise following the explosion of the fuel in the combustion chamber is a function of the driving resistance, the energy per blow will vary with the driving resistance. For this reason there is uncertainty about the accuracy of applying dynamic pile-driving formulas to diesel hammers.
2. The hammer may not operate well when driving piles into soft ground. Unless a pile offers sufficient driving resistance to activate the ram the hammer will not operate.
3. The number of strokes per minute is less than for a steam hammer. This is especially true for a diesel hammer with an open end or top.
4. The length of a diesel hammer is slightly greater than the length of a steam hammer of comparable energy rating.

VIBRATORY PILE DRIVERS

Vibratory pile drivers have demonstrated their effectiveness in speed and economy in driving piles into certain types of soils. These drivers are especially effective when the piles are driven into water-saturated noncohesive soils. The drivers may experience difficulty in driving piles into dry sand, or similar materials, or into tight cohesive soils that do not respond to the vibrations [2].

The drivers are equipped with horizontal shafts, to which eccentric weights are attached. As the shafts rotate in pairs, in opposing directions, at speeds that can be varied to in excess of 1,000 rpm, the forces produced by the rotating weights produce vibrations that are transmitted to a pile, and thence into the soil adjacent to the pile. The agitation of the soil, especially when it is saturated with water, reduces the skin friction between the soil and the pile materially. The combined weight of the pile and the driver resting on the pile will drive the pile quite rapidly.

Figure 17-17 illustrates the basic principle of the rotating weights, using six shafts. As noted in the figure, the two inner shafts, with lighter weights, rotate at twice the speeds of the two top and bottom shafts. During each revolution of the two top and bottom shafts the forces contributed by all weights will act downward at 0 and 360°, whereas at 180° the forces tend to counteract each other, as indicated in the exciting force curve [4].

Performance factors for vibratory drivers There are five performance factors that determine the effectiveness of a vibratory driver.

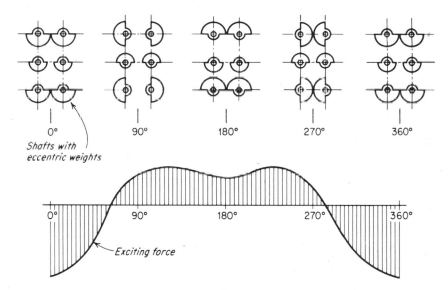

Figure 17-17 Operation of the eccentric weights for a vibratory pile driver. Diagram shows how exciting force of a six-shaft vibrator varies with the position of the eccentric weights attached to the shafts.

Figure 17-18 A vibratory driver driving sheet piling. *(L. B. Foster Company.)*

1. *Amplitude* This is the magnitude of the vertical movement of the pile produced by the vibratory unit. It may be expressed in inches or millimeters.
2. *Eccentric moment* The eccentric moment of a vibratory unit is a basic measure or indication of the size of a driver. It is the product of the weight of the eccentrics multiplied by the distance from the center of rotation of the shafts to the center of gravity of the eccentrics. The heavier the eccentric weights and the farther they are from the center of rotation of the shaft, the greater the eccentric moment of the unit.
3. *Frequency* This is expressed as the number of vertical movements of the vibrator per minute, which is also the number of revolutions of the rotating shafts per minute. Tests conducted on piles driven by vibratory drivers have indicated that the frictional forces between the piles being driven and the soil into which they are driven are at minimum values when frequencies are maintained in the range of 700 to 1,200 vibrations per minute. In general, the frequencies for piles driven into clay soils should be lower than for piles driven into sandy soils.
4. *Vibrating weight* The vibrating weight includes the vibrating case and the vibrating head of the vibrator unit, plus the pile being driven.
5. *Nonvibrating weight* This is the weight part of the system which does not vibrate, including the suspension mechanism and the motors. Nonvibrating weights push down on and aid in driving piles.

Figure 17-19 A vibratory hammer that is driving steel sheet piling. *(L. B. Foster Company.)*

The Foster vibro driver/extractor This driver uses two electric motors, powered by a portable generator or a commercial source of electrical energy, to drive eccentrically loaded shafts, whose speeds of rotation may be varied to produce the most effective frequency for a given soil. Table 17-4 lists the specifications for models of this driver.

JETTING PILES

The use of a water jet to assist in driving piles into sand or fine gravel frequently will speed the driving operation. The water, which is discharged through a nozzle at the lower end of a jet pipe, keeps the soil around a pile in agitation, thereby reducing the resistance due to skin friction. Successful jetting requires a plentiful supply of water at a pressure high enough to loosen the soil and remove

Table 17-4 Specifications for Foster pile driver/extractors

Model	2-3	2-17	10E-1	20SP-1	20E-3	40E-1	40E-3
Eccentric moment, in.-lb	174	650	870	1,740	1,740	3,470	3,470
Frequency, vibrations per min	1,800	1,090–1,290	955–1,100	890–1,500	955–1,100	700–1,300	700–1,120
Amplitude, in.	$\frac{1}{4}-\frac{1}{2}$	$\frac{1}{4}-\frac{3}{4}$	$\frac{3}{16}-\frac{3}{4}$	$\frac{5}{16}-1$	$\frac{5}{16}-1$	$\frac{5}{16}-1$	$\frac{5}{16}-1$
Horsepower	6	34	40	100	80	150	150
Maximum line pull for extraction, tons	$5\frac{1}{2}$	13	16	20	22	50	40
Pile clamping force, tons	$12\frac{1}{2}$	40	80	80/100	80/100	80/100	80/100
Suspended weight, lb*	1,500	5,500	7,400	9,100	13,500	16,500	20,300
Length, in.	36	57	88	85	105	110	128
Width, in.	19	27	29	34	36	42	54
Hammer height, in.	36	88	78	82	98	99	79
Head height, in.	6	24	26	26	26	26	26

* The suspended weight includes driver/extractor, typical driver/extractor head, and power cables or hydraulic hoses.

it from the hole ahead of the penetration of the pile. Jet pipes commonly used vary in size from 2 to 4 in. in diameter, with nozzles varying from $\frac{1}{2}$ to $1\frac{1}{2}$ in. in diameter. The water pressure at the nozzle may vary from approximately 100 to more than 300 psi, with the quantity commonly varying from 300 to 500 gpm, but as high as 1,000 gpm in some instances.

Although some piles have been jetted to final penetration, this is not considered good practice, primarily because it is impossible to determine the safe supporting capacity of a pile so driven. Most specifications require that piles shall be driven the last few feet without the benefit of jetting. The Foundation Code of the City of New York requires a contractor to obtain special permission prior to jetting piles and specifies that piles shall be driven the last 3 ft with a pile hammer.

DRIVING PILES BELOW WATER

If it is necessary to drive piles below water, either of two methods may be used. When the driving unit is a drop hammer, an open-type steam hammer, or a diesel hammer, the pile is driven until the top is just above the surface of the water. Then a follower is placed on top of the pile, and the driving is continued through the follower. The follower may be made of wood or steel and must be strong enough to transmit the energy from the hammer to the pile.

When the driving unit is an enclosed steam hammer, the driving may be continued below the surface of the water, without a follower. It is necessary to install an exhaust hose to the surface of the water for the steam. Also, it is necessary to supply about 60 cfm of compressed air to the lower part of the hammer housing to prevent water from flowing into the casing and around the ram. An air pressure of $\frac{1}{2}$ psi for each foot of depth below the surface of water will be satisfactory.

PILE-DRIVING FORMULAS

There are many pile-driving formulas, each of which is intended to give the supporting strength of a pile. The formulas are empirical, with coefficients that have been determined for certain existing or assumed conditions. While each formula may give dependable values for the conditions under which it was developed, there is no formula that will give dependable values for the supporting strength of piles for all the varying conditions that exist on foundation jobs.

It is not within the scope of this book to analyze the various pile-driving formulas or the theory related to them. For a more comprehensive study of this subject it is suggested that the reader consult the books listed at the end of this chapter [3, 4]. Perhaps the most popular formula in the United States is the *Engineering News* formula. Its popularity seems due primarily to its simplicity rather than its accuracy. For the three types of pile-driving hammers in current use it has the following forms:

For a drop hammer

$$R = \frac{2WH}{S + 1.0} \tag{17-1}$$

For a single-acting steam hammer

$$R = \frac{2WH}{S + 0.1} \tag{17-2}$$

For a double- and differential-acting steam hammer

$$R = \frac{2E}{S + 0.1} \tag{17-3}$$

where $R=$ safe load on a pile, lb

$W=$ weight of falling mass, lb

$H=$ height of free fall for mass W, ft

$E=$ total energy of ram at bottom of its downward stroke, ft-lb

$S=$ average penetration per blow for last 5 or 10 blows, in.

The *Engineering News* formula is based on a factor of safety of 6.

Another formula which is useful in analyzing the performance of a hammer in driving a pile is the *Hiley* formula. The author of the formula conducted numerous tests to verify it and to determine the values of coefficients used with it. The formula has two forms, based on the type of hammer with which it is used:

For drop, single-acting steam, and diesel hammers

$$U = \frac{eWH}{S + \frac{1}{2}(C_1 + C_2 + C_3)} \frac{W + k^2 P}{W + P} \tag{17-4}$$

For double-acting and differential-acting steam hammers

$$U = \frac{12eE}{S + \frac{1}{2}(C_1 + C_2 + C_3)} \frac{W + k^2 P}{W + P} \tag{17-5}$$

where $U=$ ultimate supporting capacity of a pile, lb

$W=$ weight of falling mass, lb

$P=$ weight of pile, including driving cap, head, anvil, or other driving accessories resting directly on pile, lb

$E=$ total theoretical energy of ram at bottom of its downward stroke, ft-lb

$h=$ height of free fall for mass W, in.

$S=$ average set or penetration per blow for last 5 or 10 blows, in.

$e=$ efficiency of hammer, equal to actual energy divided by rated energy per blow. The values of e for different hammers are as follows:

1.00 for drop hammers released by triggers

0.50 to 0.75 for drop hammers lifted by ropes and winches

0.75 to 0.90 for single-acting steam hammers

0.65 to 0.90 for double-acting steam hammers

0.75 to 0.85 for differential-acting steam hammers

0.90 to 1.00 for diesel hammers

$k=$ coefficient of restitution. The values of k for different conditions are as follows:

0.55 for steel hammer on steel pile, with no cushion

0.50 for well-compacted cushion in driving pipe piles

0.50 for double-acting steam hammer striking on steel anvil and driving steel piles or precast concrete piles

0.40 for ram of double-acting steam hammer striking steel anvil and driving wood piles

0.40 for medium-compacted wood cushion in driving steel or pipe piles

0.40 for ram of single-acting steam hammer or drop hammer striking directly on head of precast concrete pile

0.25 for ram of single-acting steam hammer or drop hammer striking on well-conditioned wood cap in driving precast concrete piles or directly on wood-pile heads

0.0 for badly broomed wood piles

C_1 = temporary compression of pile head and cap, in.

C_2 = temporary compression of pile, in.

C_3 = temporary compression, or quake of ground, for average cases where pile is driven into penetrable ground, in.

The unit stresses associated with a pile are as follows:

$$p_1 = \frac{U}{\text{area of pile head}} \qquad (17\text{-}6)$$

where p_1 = stress in driving cushion or on pile head if no cushion is used, psi and

$$p_2 = \frac{U}{\text{area of pile}} \qquad (17\text{-}7)$$

where p_2 = stress on average cross section area of a pile, including the mandrel if one is used, psi

$$p_3 = \frac{U}{\text{area of tip}} \qquad (17\text{-}8)$$

or

$$p_3 = \frac{U}{\text{gross area at ground surface}} \qquad (17\text{-}9)$$

where p_3 = stress under tip of constant cross section, and on gross area of a pile at ground surface for a tapered friction pile, psi

Representative values of C_1, C_2, C_3 are given in Tables 17-5, 17-6, and 17-7, respectively.

LOSS IN ENERGY DUE TO IMPACT

When a mass in motion striking a mass at rest transfers a portion of its kinetic energy to the mass at rest, there will always be some loss in energy due to impact. The proportion of energy dissipated through impact varies with the ratio of the weight of the moving mass to the weight of the stationary mass. The energy loss due to impact I is given by the following formulas:

For drop, single-acting steam, and diesel hammers

$$I = eWhP \frac{1 - k^2}{W + P} \qquad (17\text{-}10)$$

Table 17-5 Temporary compression allowance C_1 for pile and cap

Type of head and cap	Resistance to driving			
	Low, $p_1 = 500$ psi, in.	Medium, $p_1 = 1,000$ psi, in.	High, $p_1 = 1,500$ psi, in.	Very high, $p_1 = 2,000$ psi, in.
Head for timber pile	0.05	0.10	0.15	0.20
For precast concrete pile:				
Cap on head	0.05*	0.10*	0.15*	0.20*
3–4-in. packing inside cap	0.07*	0.15*	0.22*	0.30*
$\frac{1}{2}$–1-in. mat pad only on head				
of precast concrete pile	0.025	0.05	0.075	0.10
Steel-covered cap, containing				
wood packing for steel pile or				
pipe	0.04	0.08	0.12	0.16
Head of steel pile or pipe	0.0	0.0	0.0	0.0

* These values should be added if wood packing is used inside the head and cap.

Table 17-6 Temporary compression values of C_2 for piles

Resistance to driving	Low	Medium	High	Very high
p_2 for wood or concrete	500 psi	1,000 psi	1,500 psi	2,000 psi
p_2 for steel	7,500 psi	15,000 psi	22,500 psi	30,000 psi
	Values of C_2, in.			
Type of pile:				
Timber	$0.004L$*	$0.008L$*	$0.012L$*	$0.016L$*
Precast concrete	$0.002L$	$0.004L$	$0.006L$	$0.008L$
Sheet steel, pipe, and H pile	$0.003L$	$0.006L$	$0.009L$	$0.012L$

* L is the length from top of pile to center of driving resistance, ft.

Table 17-7 Temporary compression, or quake-of-ground, allowance C_3

Resistance to driving	Low	Medium	High	Very high
Value of p_3	500 psi	1,000 psi	1,500 psi	2,000 psi
	Values of C_3, in.			
For piles of constant cross section	0.0–0.10	0.10 – 0.20	0.10–0.30	0.05–0.20

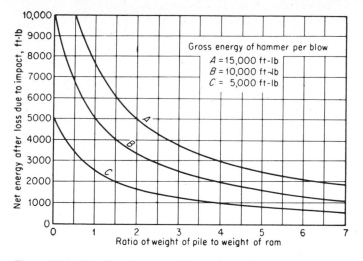

Figure 17-20 The effect of varying the weight of a ram on the net energy available for driving a pile.

For double-acting and differential-acting steam hammers

$$I = eEP \frac{1 - k^2}{W + P}$$ (17-11)

The kinetic energy of a hammer at the bottom of its stroke is $WV^2/2g$, where W is the weight of the moving mass in pounds, V is the velocity in feet per second, and g is the acceleration of gravity in feet per second per second. The energy is expressed in foot-pounds. Although the same amount of energy may be produced by a light weight and a high velocity or with a heavy weight and a low velocity, it is better to use a hammer with a heavy weight and a low velocity because more of the energy will be converted into driving a pile. The effect which varying the ratio of the weight of the ram to the weight of a pile has on the loss of energy due to impact is illustrated in Fig. 17-20. For a ratio of 1 the loss in energy is 50 percent, whereas for a ratio of $\frac{1}{2}$ the loss is about 33 percent. Instead of lifting a 1,000-lb drop hammer 10 ft to obtain 10,000 ft-lb of energy it is better to use a 2,000-lb hammer and lift it 5 ft. The same reasoning applies to steam and diesel hammers.

ENERGY LOSSES DUE TO CAUSES OTHER THAN IMPACT

A. Hiley, the author of formulas (17-4) and (17-5), conducted numerous tests to determine the energy losses due to causes other than impact. He found that the temporary compression of a pile head and cap, a pile, and the ground beneath and adjacent to a pile resulted in some energy losses. His analyses of these losses are primarily responsible for the values of C_1, C_2, and C_3, given in Tables 17-5, 17-6, and 17-7, respectively. Each of these losses may be expressed by a formula as follows: Energy loss due to temporary compression of a pile head and cap

$$\text{loss} = \frac{UC_1}{2} \tag{17-12}$$

Energy loss due to temporary compression of a pile

$$\text{Loss} = \frac{UC_2}{2} \quad \text{or} \quad \frac{U^2 l}{2AK} \tag{17-13}$$

where $l =$ length from top of a pile to center of driving resistance, in.
    $A =$ cross-sectional area of a pile, sq in.
    $K =$ modulus of elasticity of material in a pile, psi
Energy loss due to temporary compression of soil

$$\text{Loss} = \frac{UC_3}{2} \tag{17-14}$$

If the energy represented by formulas (17-10) to (17-14) is deducted from the net energy per blow supplied by a hammer, the remainder will be the energy that is available for driving a pile, which is given by one of the following formulas:

For drop, single-acting steam, and diesel hammers:

$$US = eWh - eWhP \frac{1 - k^2}{W + P} - \frac{UC_1}{2} - \frac{U^2 l}{2AK} - \frac{UC_3}{2} \tag{17-15}$$

For double-acting and differential-acting steam hammers

$$US = 12eE - 12eEP \frac{1 - k^2}{W + P} - \frac{UC_1}{2} - \frac{U^2 l}{2AK} - \frac{UC_3}{2} \tag{17-16}$$

Since the energy US is in inch-pounds, all weights in formulas (17-15) and (17-16) must be in pounds and all linear dimensions must be in inches.

The extent to which energy losses may vary in driving piles under different conditions is illustrated by Fig. 17-21. Pile (*a*), which was a 16-in.-square concrete pile, 51 ft long, weighing 6 tons, was driven with a 4-ton winch-operated drop hammer, with a fall of 3 ft 6 in. This pile was driven into soil having high frictional resistance. Pile (*b*), which was a composite 14- by 14-in. timber and concrete pile, 51 ft long, weighing 2.75 tons, was driven with a 2-ton freely falling drop hammer, with a fall of 4 ft 0 in. This pile was driven into soil having low frictional resistance.

The information given in Fig. 17-21 and below was obtained from calculations and tests made while the piles were being driven:

Item	Pile (a)	Pile (b)
Weight of pile, tons	6	2.75
Weight of hammer, tons	4	2
Drop of hammer, ft	3.5	4
Final set of pile, per blow, in.	$\frac{1}{13}$	3

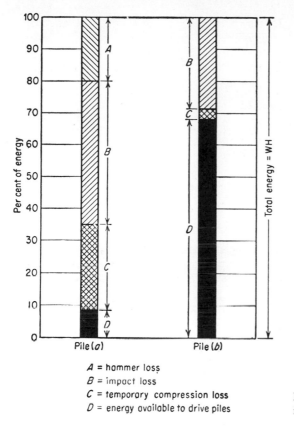

A = hammer loss
B = impact loss
C = temporary compression loss
D = energy available to drive piles

Figure 17-21 Representative energy loss in driving piles.

ANALYSIS OF PILE-DRIVING PROBLEMS

The examples which follow are intended to illustrate methods which may be used to determine whether a hammer is suitable for driving a given pile:

Example Concrete piles, 14 in. square and 50 ft long, are to be driven to full penetration into soil having normal frictional resistance. Tests indicate a pile will safely support a load of 40 tons, with a factor of safety of 3. It is planned to drive the piles with a Vulcan size 1 single-acting steam hammer. Determine the probable energy per blow available for driving a pile and the set per blow at full penetration.

For the specified hammer and piles the following information will apply:

$W = 5,000$ lb

$h = 36$ in.

$e = 0.75$

$k = 0.25$

Weight of pile $= \dfrac{14 \times 14}{144} \times 150 \times 50 = 10,220$ lb

Weight of pile cap and head $\quad=\quad$ 775 lb

$\quad$ Combined weight $P \quad\quad = \overline{10{,}995 \text{ lb}}$

$U = 3 \times 40 \times 2{,}000 = 240{,}000$ lb

$p_i = 240{,}000 \div 196 = 1{,}225$ psi

$C_1 = \dfrac{0.25 + 0.37}{2} = 0.31$ in. (from Table 17-5)

$p_2 = 240{,}000 \div 196 = 1{,}225$ psi

$C_2 = 0.0049 \times 33 = 0.162$ in. (from Table 17-6)

$p_3 = 240{,}000 \div 196 = 1{,}225$ psi

$C_3 = 0.15$ in. (from Table 17-7)

$\quad$ Assume that $L = \frac{2}{3} \times 50 = 33$ ft.
$\quad$ Apply formula (17-15).

Net energy delivered by hammer $= eWh = 0.75 \times 5{,}000 \times 36 = 135{,}000$ in.-lb

Impact loss $= eWhP \dfrac{1 - k^2}{W + P}$

$\quad\quad = 0.75 \times 5{,}000 \times 36 \times 10{,}995 \dfrac{1 - 0.0625}{5{,}000 + 10{,}995} = 87{,}000$ in.-lb

Cap loss $= \dfrac{UC_1}{2} = \dfrac{240{,}000 \times 0.31}{2} \quad\quad\quad\quad = 37{,}200$

Pile loss $= \dfrac{UC_2}{2} = \dfrac{U^2 l}{2AK} = \dfrac{240{,}000^2 \times 33 \times 12}{2 \times 196 \times 3{,}000{,}000} \quad = 19{,}400$

Soil loss $= \dfrac{UC_3}{2} = \dfrac{240{,}000 \times 0.15}{2} \quad\quad\quad\quad = 18{,}000$

$\quad$ Total energy loss $\quad\quad\quad\quad\quad\quad\quad\quad = \overline{161{,}600 \text{ in.-lb}}$

Since the net energy delivered by the hammer is less than the sum of the probable energy losses, it appears that this hammer will not be capable of driving a pile to full penetration. The set per blow will be zero prior to full penetration.

Example Consider all conditions the same as given in the preceding example, except that a Vulcan size 0 single-acting steam hammer will be used to drive the piles.
$\quad$ For the specified hammer and piles the following information will apply:

$W = 7{,}500$ lb

$h = 39$ in.

$\quad$ The other values will be the same as for preceding example.
$\quad$ Apply formula (17-15).

Net energy delivered by hammer $= eWh = 0.75 \times 7{,}500 \times 39 = 219{,}000$ in.-lb

Impact loss $= eWhP \dfrac{1 - k^2}{W + P}$

$\quad\quad = 0.75 \times 7{,}500 \times 39 \times 10{,}995 \dfrac{1 - 0.0625}{7{,}500 + 10{,}995} = 122{,}000$ in.-lb

Cap loss (see preceding example)	= 37,200
Pile loss (see preceding example)	= 19,400
Soil loss (see preceding example)	= 18,000
Total energy loss	= 196,600
Energy available to drive a pile	= 22,400
Net total energy delivered by hammer	= 219,000 in.-lb

The set of a pile per blow is obtained as follows:

$US = 22,400$ in.-lb

$U = 240,000$ lb

$S = \dfrac{22,400}{240,000} = 0.0933$ in.

MICHIGAN PILE-DRIVING TESTS

In 1961 the Michigan Highway Department and the United States Bureau of Public Roads began the most comprehensive tests ever conducted on pile driving [5, 6, 7]. The eight main objectives of the tests were

1. To develop a method for determining the driving energy output of various types of pile-driving hammers, including air, single- or double-acting steam, and diesel hammers.
2. To determine by load tests the load-bearing capacities of piles driven under test conditions.
3. To determine what factors, if any, relate the measured pile-driving energy to the load-bearing capacity of a pile.
4. To determine the proper wall thickness of pipe piles under certain driving conditions.
5. To determine the correlations between the tested load-bearing capacity and estimates of load-bearing capacity as obtained by nine of the best-known pile-driving formulas.*
6. To determine the best methods or procedures for jetting piles through intermediate soil layers when the driving resistance is large but the bearing capacity of the pile in these layers is not satisfactory.
7. To determine the effect of the pile cross section or the surface configuration on the energy required for driving piles.
8. To determine the effect of pile cross section or surface configuration on the load-bearing capacity of a pile.

A total of 88 piles were driven for test and analysis purposes. They included 12-in.-diameter pipe, open-end and closed-end, and 12-in. WF sections. The

* The formulas are: *Engineering-News*, Hiley, Pacific Coast Uniform Building Code, Redtenbocher, Eytelwein, Navy-McKay, Rankine, Canadian National Building Code, and the Rabe.

Table 17-8 Results of Michigan State Highway Department pile tests

Site	Hammer model	Maximum rated energy, ft-lb	Type pile	Accepted enthru determinations	Peak force, kips	Peak acceleration, G's	Average enthru, ft-lb	Ratio enthru/enthru Minimum	Maximum	Average
1	Vulcan No. 1	15,000	H	11	230	90	5,283	0.27	0.45	0.35
			Pipe	5	180	75	5,094	0.26	0.41	0.34
	Link-belt 312	18,000	H	27	380	170	7,726	0.28	0.56	0.43
			Pipe	12	440	210	8,226	0.32	0.62	0.46
	McKiernan-Terry DE-30	22,400	H	22	390	270	5,769	0.19	0.36	0.26
			Pipe	9	490	240	8,682	0.31	0.59	0.39
	Delmag D-12	22,500	H	30	800	360	9,123	0.19	0.53	0.41
			Pipe	13	690	350	11,870	0.39	0.64	0.53
2	Vulcan No. 1	15,000	H }Pipe	12	200	110	5,339	0.30	0.43	0.36
	Vulcan 50C	15,100	Pipe	3	490	270	9,822	0.55	0.76	0.65
	Link-belt 312	18,000	H }Pipe	3	200	100	7,554	0.37	0.50	0.42
	McKiernan-Terry DE-30	22,400	H }Pipe	14	370	190	8,417	0.31	0.46	0.38
	Delmag D-12	22,500	H }Pipe	9	600	320	10,033	0.24	0.60	0.45
3	Vulcan No. 1	15,000	Pipe	10	220	80	6,359	0.32	0.48	0.42
	Vulcan 80C	24,500	Pipe	6	650	310	13,872	0.52	0.64	0.57
	Link-belt 520	30,000	Pipe	8	560	150	16,637	0.44	0.66	0.55
	McKiernan-Terry DE-40	32,000	Pipe	4	700	310	18,088	0.52	0.65	0.57
	Delmag D-22	39,700	Pipe	9	1,050	470	24,660	0.53	0.78	0.62

results of the tests appear in Table 17-8. Enthru, as used in the table, is the actual energy delivered to a pile by a hammer, which was determined by instruments. As noted in the table, there was considerable variation in the net energy delivered to the piles by any given hammer. Also, the tests revealed that no dynamic formula currently in use can consistently provide an accurate estimate of the bearing capacity of a pile [7].

After observing the tests and analyzing the results, the highway department modified the *Engineering-News* formula as follows:

$$R = \frac{2.5E}{S + 0.1} \frac{W_r + e^2 W_p}{W_r + W_p} \tag{17-17}$$

where R = computed design pile load capacity, lb
   E = manufacturer's maximum rated energy per blow, ft-lb
   S = final average penetration of pile per blow, in.
   W_r = weight of ram, lb
   W_p = weight of pile, including driving appurtenances, lb
   e = coefficient of restitution

SELECTING A PILE-DRIVING HAMMER

Selecting the most suitable pile hammer for a given project involves a study of several factors, such as the size and type of piles, the number of piles, the character of the soil, the location of the project, the topography of the site, the type of rig available, whether driving will be done on land or in water, etc. A pile-driving contractor usually is concerned with selecting the hammer that will drive the piles for a project at the lowest practical cost. As most contractors must limit their ownership to a few representative sizes and types of hammers, a selection should be made from those hammers already owned unless conditions are such that it is economical or necessary to secure an additional size or type. Naturally, more consideration should be given to the selection of a hammer for a project that requires several hundred piles than for a project that requires only a few piles.

As previously stated, the function of a pile hammer is to furnish the energy required to drive a pile. This energy is supplied by a weight which is raised and permitted to drop on top of a pile, under the effect of gravity alone or with steam acting during the downward stroke. The theoretical energy per blow will equal the product of the weight times the equivalent free fall. Since some of this energy is lost in friction as the weight travels downward, the net energy per blow will be less than the theoretical energy, the actual amount depending on the efficiency of the particular hammer. As indicated on page 536, the efficiencies of pile hammers vary from 50 to 100 percent.

Table 17-9 gives recommended sizes of hammers for different types and sizes of piles and driving resistances. The sizes are indicated by the theoretical

Table 17-9 Recommended sizes of hammers for driving various types of piles
Size expressed in foot-pounds of energy per blow

Length of piles, ft	Depth of penetra- tion	Weight of various types of piles, lb per lin ft						
		Steel sheet*			Timber		Concrete	
		20	30	40	30	60	150	400
	Driving through ordinary earth, moist clay, and loose gravel, normal frictional resistance							
25	$\frac{1}{2}$	2,000	2,000	3,600	3,600	7,000	7,500	15,000
	Full	3,600	3,600	6,000	3,600	7,000	7,500	15,000
50	$\frac{1}{2}$	6,000	6,000	7,000	7,000	7,500	15,000	20,000
	Full	7,000	7,000	7,500	7,500	12,000	15,000	20,000
75	$\frac{1}{2}$	.....	7,000	7,500	......	15,000	......	30,000
	Full	.....	.....	12,000	......	15,000	......	30,000
	Driving through stiff clay, compacted sand, and gravel, high frictional resistance							
25	$\frac{1}{2}$	3,600	3,600	3,600	7,500	7,500	7,500	15,000
	Full	3,600	7,000	7,000	7,500	7,500	12,000	15,000
50	$\frac{1}{2}$	7,000	7,500	7,500	12,000	12,000	15,000	25,000
	Full	.....	7,500	7,500	......	15,000	......	30,000
75	$\frac{1}{2}$	.....	7,500	12,000	......	15,000	......	36,000
	Full	.....	.....	15,000	......	20,000	......	50,000

*The indicated energy is based on driving two steel-sheet piles simultaneously. In driving single piles, use approximately two-thirds of the indicated energy.

foot-pounds of energy delivered per blow. Table 17-3 gives the theoretical energy per blow for several types and sizes of hammer. For each hammer listed the specified theoretical energy per blow is correct provided the hammer is operated at the designated number of strokes per minute.

In general, it is good practice to select the largest hammer that can be used without overstressing or damaging a pile. As previously shown, when a large hammer is used, a greater portion of the energy is effective in driving a pile, which produces a higher operating efficiency. Therefore, the hammer sizes given in Table 17-9 should be considered as the minimum sizes. In some instances hammers as much as 50 per cent larger may be used advantageously.

DRILLED AND UNDERREAMED FOUNDATIONS

A method of foundation construction that has become popular in recent years is to drill holes deep enough to encounter or penetrate a stable formation that is capable of supporting heavy loads. These holes are filled with plain or reinforced concrete and thus serve the same purpose as piles in supporting structures. For many projects, this type of foundation is more satisfactory and less expensive than piles. It is an economical substitute for conventional spread footings.

As illustrated in Fig. 17-22, the holes may be drilled to a uniform diameter, or they may have an enlarged diameter at the bottom to give a greater bearing area. The footing illustrated in Fig. 17-22*a* is commonly referred to as a drilled footing, and the one illustrated in Fig. 17-22*b* is referred to as an underreamed footing. The upper portion of the latter is called the shaft, and the enlarged portion is called the underream. Shafts may be drilled to any desired diameter within reason, usually 12 to 96 in. Because of mechanical limitations on drilling equipment, the maximum diameter of the underream is related to the diameter of the shaft. Underream diameters as great as 144 in. or more have been drilled. Under favorable conditions it is possible to drill holes as deep as 200 ft for underreamed foundations.

The holes are drilled by a truck-mounted rig, whose essential parts include a power unit, cable drum, boom, rotary table, drill stem, and drill. The shaft is drilled first with a large earth auger or a bucket drill, equipped with cutting blades at the bottom; then the bottom portion of the hole is enlarged with a special drill known as an underreamer.

Figure 17-23 illustrates a method used to drill these holes through unstable soils, such as mud, sand, or gravel, containing water. If it is possible to do so, the

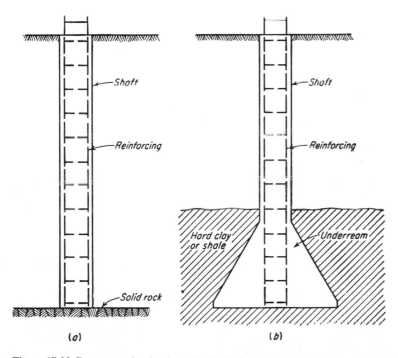

Figure 17-22 Representative footings. (*a*) Drilled footing. (*b*) Underreamed footing.

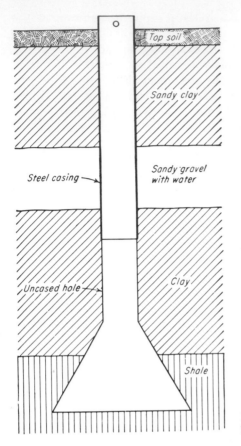

Figure 17-23 Steel casing used to permit footing to be drilled through unstable soil.

shaft is drilled entirely through the unstable soil; then a temporary steel casing is installed in the hole to eliminate ground water and caving. An alternate method is to add sections to the casing as drilling progresses until the full depth of bad soil is cased off. Then the hole is completed and filled with concrete, and the casing is pulled before the concrete sets.

This type of foundation has been used extensively in areas whose soils are subject to changes in moisture content to considerable depth. By placing the footings below the zone of moisture change the effect of soil movements due to changes in moisture is eliminated.

Among the advantages of drilled and underreamed foundations, compared with piles and conventional spread footings, are the following:

1. They are less expensive for some soils and projects.
2. They are easy to vary in length to adjust for soil conditions.
3. They permit inspection of soil prior to establishing depth or placing concrete.
4. They eliminate damage to adjacent structures due to vibration of the pile hammer.
5. They eliminate the use of forms for concrete.

REFERENCES

1. Rausche, Frank and George G. Goble. Performance of Pile-Driving Hammers, *Journal of the Construction Division, Proceedings ASCE*, vol. 98, pp. 201–218, September 1972.
2. Soil and Oil Troubles for Bridge Builders, *Engineering News-Record*, vol. 179, pp. 72–73, August 3, 1967.
3. Chellis, Robert D.: "Pile Foundations," 2d ed., McGraw-Hill Book Company, New York, 1961.
4. Dunham, Clarence W.: "Foundations of Structures," pp. 314–317, McGraw-Hill Book Company, New York, 1950.
5. Michigan Pile Test Program Results are Released, *Engineering News-Record*, vol. 164, pp. 26–34, May 20, 1965.
6. "A Performance Investigation of Pile-Driving Hammers and Piles, Final Report," Michigan State Highway Commission, Lansing, Michigan, March 1965.
7. Housel, W. S.: Michigan Study of Pile-Driving Hammers, *Journal of the Soil Mechanics and Foundation Division, Proceedings ASCE*, vol. 91, pp. 37–64, September 1965.
8. Sullivan, Richard A. and Clarence J. Ehlers: Planning for Driving Offshore Piles, *Journal of the Construction Division, Proceedings ASCE*, vol. 99, pp. 59–79, July 1973.
9. McClelland, B., J. A. Focht, Jr., and W. J. Emrich: Problems in Design and Installation of Offshore Piles, *Journal of the Soil Mechanics and Foundation Division, Proceedings ASCE*, vol. 95, pp. 1491–1514, November 1969.
10. Samson, C. H., T. J. Hirsch, and L. L. Lowery: Computer Study of Dynamic Behavior of Piling, *Journal of the Structural Division, Proceedings ASCE*, vol. 89, pp. 413–449, August 1963.
11. Bolt Associates, Inc., 205 Wilson Avenue, Norwalk, Connecticut 06954.
12. BSP: International Construction Equipment, P. O. Box 15291, Charlotte, North Carolina 28210.
13. Conmaco, Inc., 820 Kansas Avenue, Kansas City, Kansas 66119.
14. Delmag: Foundation Equipment Corporation, 100 Elizabeth Street, Newcomerstown, Ohio 43832.
15. L. B. Foster Company, Seven Parkway Center, Pittsburgh, Pennsylvania 15220.
16. Link-Belt: Crane & Excavator Division, FMC Corporation, 1201 Sixth Street, SW, Cedar Rapids, Iowa 52406.
17. Menck Division, Distributed by Conmaco, Inc. (See [13] above.)
18. Mitsubishi International Corporation, 4040 John Hancock Center, 875 N. Michigan Avenue, Chicago, Illinois 60611.
19. MKT Geotechnical Systems, P. O. Box 793, Dover, New Jersey 07801.
20. Pileco, Inc., P. O. Box 16099, Houston, Texas 77022.
21. Raymond International, Inc., 2801 South Post Oak Road, Houston, Texas 77027.
22. The Union Metal Manufacturing Company, P. O. Box 8530, Canton, Ohio 44711.
23. Vulcan Iron Works, Inc., 2725 N. Australian Avenue, West Palm Beach, Florida 33407.

EIGHTEEN

PUMPING EQUIPMENT

INTRODUCTION

Pumps are used extensively on construction projects for such operations as

1. Removing water from pits, tunnels, etc.
2. Unwatering cofferdams
3. Furnishing water for jetting and sluicing
4. Furnishing water for many types of utility services
5. Lowering the water table for excavations
6. Foundation grouting

Most projects require the use of one or more water pumps at various stages during the period of construction. Construction pumps frequently are required to perform under severe conditions, such as resulting from variations in the pumping head or from handling water that is muddy, sandy and trashy, or highly corrosive. The rate of pumping may vary several hundred per cent during the period of construction. The most satisfactory solution to the pumping problem may be a single all-purpose pump, or it may be to use several types and sizes of pumps, to permit flexibility in the operations. The proper solution is to select the equipment which will take care of the pumping needs adequately at the lowest total cost, considering the investment in pumping equipment, the cost of operating the pumps, and any losses that will result from possible failure of the pumps to operate satisfactorily.

For some projects a pump may be the most critical item of construction equipment. In constructing a multimillion-dollar concrete and earthfill dam, a contractor used a single centrifugal pump to supply water from a nearby stream.

The water was used to wash all concrete aggregate, for mixing and curing the concrete, and for moisture in the earth-fill dam. When the pump developed mechanical trouble and the rate of pumping dropped below the job requirements for several days, progress on the project suffered a loss of approximately 25 percent. With the fixed costs exceeding $4,000 per day, the loss due to the partial failure of the pump exceeded $1,000 per day.

Among the factors that should be considered in selecting construction pumps are the following:

1. Dependability
2. Availability of parts for making repairs
3. Simplicity to permit easy repairs
4. Economical installation and operation

CLASSIFICATION OF PUMPS

The pumps most commonly used on construction projects may be classified as:

1. Displacement
   a. Reciprocating
   b. Diaphragm
2. Centrifugal
   a. Conventional
   b. Self-priming
   c. Air-operated

Reciprocating pumps A reciprocating pump operates as the result of the movement of a piston inside a cylinder. When the piston is moved in one direction, the water ahead of the piston is forced out of the cylinder. At the same time additional water is drawn into the cylinder behind the piston. Regardless of the direction of movement of the piston, water is forced out of one end and drawn into the other end of the cylinder. This is classified as a double-acting pump. If water is pumped during a piston movement in one direction only, the pump is classified as single-acting. If a pump contains more than one cylinder, mounted side by side, it is classified as a duplex for two cylinders, triplex for three cylinders, etc. Thus a pump might be classified as duplex double-acting, duplex single-acting, etc.

The volume of water pumped in one stroke will equal the area of the cylinder times the length of the stroke, less a small deduction for slippage through the valves or past the piston, usually about 3 to 5 percent. If this volume is expressed in cubic inches, it may be converted to gallons by dividing by 231, the number of cubic inches in a gallon. The volume pumped in gpm by a simplex double-acting pump will be

$$Q = c\,\frac{\pi d^2 l n}{4 \times 231} \qquad\qquad (18\text{-}1)$$

where Q = capacity of a pump, gpm
    c = 1 − slip allowance; varies from 0.95 to 0.97
    d = diameter of cylinder, in.
    l = length of stroke, in.
    n = number of strokes per min (*Note*: The movement of the piston in either direction is a stroke)
    The volume pumped per minute by a multiplex double-acting pump will be

$$Q = Nc \frac{\pi d^2 l n}{4 \times 231} \tag{18-2}$$

where N = number of cylinders in pump.
    The energy required to operate a pump will be

$$W = \frac{wQh}{e}$$

where W = energy, ft-lb per min
    w = weight of 1 gal of water, lb
    h = total pumping head, ft, including friction loss in pipe
    e = efficiency of pump, expressed decimally
    The horsepower required by the pump will be

$$P = \frac{W}{33,000} = \frac{wQh}{33,000\,e} \tag{18-3}$$

where P = power, hp
  33,000 = ft-lb of energy per min for 1 hp

Example How many gallons of fresh water will be pumped per minute by a duplex double-acting pump, size 6 by 12 in., driven by a crankshaft making 90 rpm? If the total head is 160 ft and the efficiency of the pump is 60 percent, what is the minimum horsepower required to operate the pump? The weight of water is 8.34 lb per gal.

SOLUTION Assume a water slippage of 4 percent. Applying formula (18-2), the rate of pumping will be

$$Q = Nc \frac{\pi d^2 l n}{924}$$

$$= \frac{2 \times 0.96 \times \pi \times 36 \times 12 \times 180}{924} = 518 \text{ gpm}$$

Applying formula (18-3), the power required by the pump will be

$$P = \frac{wQh}{33,000e}$$

$$= \frac{8.34 \times 518 \times 160}{33,000 \times 0.60} = 34.9 \text{ hp}$$

The capacity of a reciprocating pump depends essentially on the speed at which the pump is operated and is independent of the head. The maximum head against which a pump will deliver water depends on the strength of the component parts of the pump and the power available to operate the pump. The capacity of this type of pump may be varied considerably by varying the speed of the pump.

Because the flow of water from each cylinder of a reciprocating pump stops and starts every time the direction of piston travel is reversed, a characteristic of this type of pump is to deliver water with pulsations. The amplitude of the pulsations may be reduced by using more cylinders and by installing an air chamber on the discharge side of a pump.

Among the advantages of reciprocating pumps are the following:

1. They are able to pump at a uniform rate against varying heads.
2. Their capacity can be increased by increasing the speed.
3. They have reasonably high efficiency regardless of the head and speed.
4. They are usually self-priming.

Among the disadvantages of reciprocating pumps are the following:

1. Heavy weight and large size for given capacity
2. Possibility of valve trouble, especially in pumping water containing trash
3. Pulsating flow of water
4. Danger of damaging a pump in operating against a high head

Diaphragm pumps The principle under which a diaphragm pump operates is illustrated in Fig. 18-1. The central portion of the flexible diaphragm is alternately raised and lowered by the pump rod, which is connected to a walking

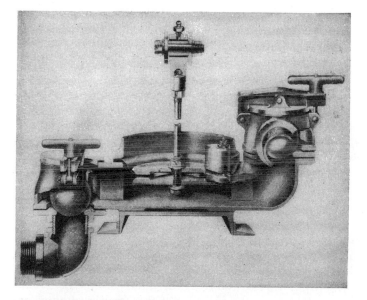

Figure 18-1 Section through a diaphragm pump.

Table 18-1 Minimum capacities for diaphragm pumps at 10-ft suction lifts*†

Size	Capacity, gal per hr
2-in. single	2,000
3-in. single	3,000
4-in. single	6,000
4-in. double	9,000

* Contractors Pump Bureau.
† Diaphragm pumps shall be tested with standard contractor's type suction hose 5 ft longer than the suction lift shown.

beam. This action draws water into and discharges it from the pump. Because this type of pump will handle clear water or water containing large quantities of mud, sand, sludge, and trash, it is popular as a construction pump. It is suitable for use on jobs where the quantity of water varies considerably, as the loss of prime during low flow does not prevent it from automatically repriming when the quantity of water increases. The accessible diaphragm may be replaced easily.

The Contractors Pump Bureau specifies that diaphragm pumps shall be manufactured in the size and capacity ratings given in Table 18-1.

Centrifugal pumps A centrifugal pump contains a rotating element, called an impeller, which imparts to water passing through the pump a velocity sufficiently great to cause it to flow from the pump even against considerable pressure. A mass of water may possess energy due to its height above a given datum or due to its velocity. The former is potential, while the latter is kinetic, energy. One type of energy can be converted into the other under favorable conditions. The kinetic energy imparted to a particle of water as it passes through the impeller is sufficient to cause the particles to rise to some determinable height.

The principle of the centrifugal pump may be illustrated by considering a drop of water at rest at a height h above a surface. If the drop of water is permitted to fall freely, it will strike the surface with a velocity given by the formula

$$V = \sqrt{2gh} \tag{18-4}$$

where V = velocity, fps
  g = acceleration of gravity, equal to 32.2 ft per sec per sec at sea level
  h = height of fall, ft

If the drop falls 100 ft, the velocity will be 80.4 fps. If the same drop is given an upward velocity of 80.4 fps, it will rise 100 ft. These values assume no loss in energy due to friction through air. It is the function of the centrifugal pump to give the water the necessary velocity as it leaves the impeller. If the speed of the pump is doubled, the velocity of the water will be increased from 80.4 to 160.8 fps, neglecting any increase in friction losses. With this velocity the water can be pumped to a height given by the formula

$$h = \frac{V^2}{2g} = \frac{160.8^2}{64.4} = 400 \text{ ft}$$

This indicates that if a centrifugal pump is pumping water against a total head of 100 ft, the same quantity of water can be pumped against a total head of 400 ft by doubling the speed of the impeller. In actual practice the maximum possible head for the increased speed will be less than 400 ft because of increases in losses in the pump due to friction. These results illustrate the effect which increasing the speed or the diameter of an impeller has on the performance of a centrifugal pump.

A centrifugal pump may be equipped with an open or an enclosed impeller. Although an enclosed impeller usually has higher efficiency, it will not handle water containing trash as well as an open impeller.

The power required to operate a centrifugal pump is given by formula (18-3). The efficiencies of these pumps may be as high as 75 percent.

Self-priming centrifugal pumps The centrifugal pumps most commonly installed in water and sewage plants are set below the level of water on the suction side because they are not self-priming. However, on construction projects, pumps frequently must be set up above the surface of the water to be pumped. Consequently, self-priming centrifugal pumps are more suitable than the conventional types for use on construction projects. The operation of a self-priming pump is illustrated in Fig. 18-2. A check valve on the suction side of the pump permits the chamber to be filled with water prior to starting the pump. When the pump is started, the water in the chamber produces a seal which enables the pump to draw air from the suction pipe. The air and water flow through channel *A* into the chamber, where the air escapes through the discharge, and the water flows down through channel *B* to the impeller. This action continues until all the air is exhausted from the suction line and water enters the pump. When a pump is stopped, it will retain its charge of priming water indefinitely. Such a pump is self-priming to heights in excess of 25 ft when in good mechanical condition.

Air-operated centrifugal-type sump pumps Air-operated centrifugal pumps are very useful in tunnels, foundation pits, trenches, and similar places, as they are designed to handle clear or dirty water, oil, sewage, or moderately heavy sludge. Figure 18-3 illustrates such a pump in operation on a typical job. This pump, which weighs about 56 lb, has a capacity of 185 gpm against a total head of 40 ft when supplied with compressed air at a pressure of 90 psi. Other types and models have capacities in excess of 200 gpm for total heads of 100 ft or more. Figure 18-4 shows typical performance curves for an air-operated centrifugal pump.

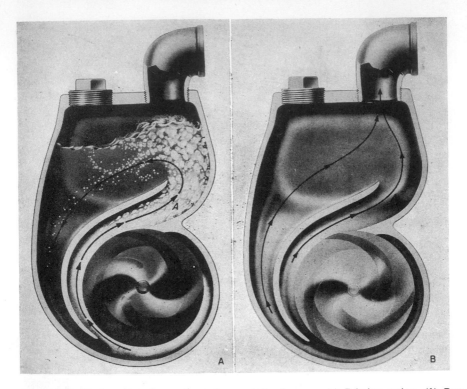

Figure 18-2 Section through a self-priming centrifugal pump. (*a*) Priming action. (*b*) Pumping action.

Figure 18-3 Single-stage air-operated centrifugal pump.

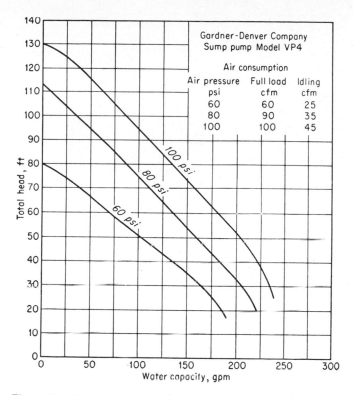

Figure 18-4 Performance curves for air-operated centrifugal pump.

Multistage centrifugal pumps If a centrifugal pump has a single impeller, it is described as single-stage, whereas if there are two or more impellers and the water discharged from one impeller flows into the suction of another, it is described as a multistage pump. Multistage pumps are especially suitable for pumping against high heads or pressures, as each stage imparts an additional pressure to the water. Pumps of this type are used frequently to supply water for jetting, where the pressure may run as high as several hundred psi.

Performance of centrifugal pumps The pump manufacturers will furnish sets of curves showing the performance of their pumps under different operating conditions. A set of curves for a given pump will show the variations in capacity, efficiency, and horsepower for different pumping heads. These curves can be very helpful in selecting the pump that is most suitable for a given pumping condition. Figure 18-5 illustrates a set of performance curves for a 10-in. centrifugal pump. For a total head of 60 ft the capacity will be 1,200 gpm, the efficiency 52 percent, and the required power 35 bhp. If the total head is reduced to 50 ft and the dynamic suction lift does not exceed 23 ft, the capacity will be 1,930 gpm, the efficiency 55 percent, and the required power 44 bhp. This

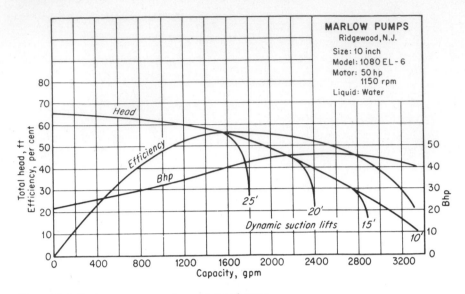

Figure 18-5 Performance curves for centrifugal pump.

pump will not deliver any water against a total head in excess of 66 ft, which is called the shutoff head.

Since a construction pump frequently is operated under varying heads, it is desirable to select a pump with relatively flat head-capacity and horsepower curves, even though efficiency must be sacrificed in order to obtain these conditions. A pump with a flat horsepower demand permits the use of an engine

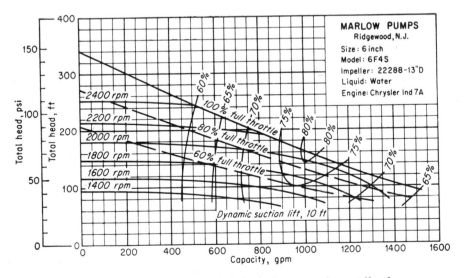

Figure 18-6 The effect of varying the speed on the performance of a centrifugal pump.

or an electric motor that will provide adequate power over a wide pumping range, without a substantial surplus or deficiency, regardless of the head.

The effect of varying the speed of a centrifugal pump is illustrated by the curves in Fig. 18-6

Capacity tables for self-priming centrifugal pumps The Contractors Pump Bureau of the AGC publishes pump standards for several types of pumps, including self-priming centrifugal. The standard capacities, which were approved in 1976, are given in Tables 18-2 and 18-3.

Table 18-2 Minimum capacities for M-rated self-priming centrifugal pumps manufactured in accordance with standards of the Contractors Pump Bureau

	Capacity, gpm (liters per min)			
Total head including friction, ft (meters)	Height of pump above water, ft (meters)			
	10 (3.0)	15 (4.6)	20 (6.1)	25 (7.6)
	Model 5-M($1\frac{1}{2}$ in.)			
15 (4.6)	85 (321.7)	—	—	—
20 (6.1)	84 (317.9)	68 (257.4)	—	—
25 (7.6)	82 (310.4)	67 (253.6)	—	—
30 (9.1)	79 (299.0)	66 (249.8)	49 (185.5)	35 (132.5)
40 (12.2)	71 (268.7)	60 (227.1)	46 (174.1)	33 (124.9)
50 (15.2)	59 (223.3)	52 (196.8)	41 (155.2)	28 (106.0)
60 (18.3)	42 (159.0)	40 (151.4)	32 (121.1)	22 (83.3)
70 (21.3)	22 (83.3)	22 (83.3)	20 (75.0)	12 (45.4)
	Model 7-M (2 in.)			
20 (6.1)	117 (442.8)	—	—	—
30 (9.1)	116 (439.1)	102 (386.1)	82 (310.4)	—
40 (12.2)	105 (397.4)	100 (378.5)	80 (302.8)	58 (219.5)
50 (15.2)	92 (348.2)	90 (340.7)	76 (287.7)	55 (208.2)
60 (18.3)	70 (265.0)	70 (265.0)	70 (265.0)	55 (208.2)
70 (21.3)	40 (151.4)	40 (151.4)	40 (151.4)	40 (151.4)
	Model 8-M (2 in.)			
20 (6.1)	135 (511.0)	—	—	—
25 (7.6)	134 (507.2)	117 (442.8)	—	—
30 (9.1)	132 (499.6)	115 (435.3)	93 (352.0)	65 (246.0)
40 (12.2)	123 (465.6)	109 (412.6)	88 (333.1)	63 (238.5)
50 (15.2)	109 (412.6)	99 (373.7)	81 (306.6)	59 (223.3)
60 (18.3)	90 (340.7)	84 (317.9)	70 (265.0)	51 (193.0)
70 (21.3)	66 (249.8)	65 (246.0)	57 (215.7)	41 (155.2)
80 (24.4)	40 (151.4)	40 (151.4)	40 (151.4)	28 (106.0)

Table 18-2

Model 10-M (2 in.)

Total head including friction, ft (meters)	Capacity, gpm (liters per min)			
	Height of pump above water, ft (meters)			
	10 (3.0)	15 (4.6)	20 (6.1)	25 (7.6)
25 (7.6)	166 (628.3)	—	—	—
30 (9.1)	165 (624.5)	140 (529.9)	110 (416.4)	—
40 (12.2)	158 (598.0)	140 (529.9)	110 (416.4)	75 (283.9)
50 (15.2)	145 (548.8)	130 (492.1)	106 (401.2)	70 (265.0)
60 (18.3)	126 (476.9)	117 (442.8)	97 (367.1)	68 (257.4)
70 (21.3)	102 (386.1)	100 (378.5)	85 (321.7)	60 (227.1)
80 (24.4)	74 (280.1)	74 (280.1)	68 (257.4)	48 (181.7)
90 (27.4)	40 (151.4)	40 (151.4)	40 (151.4)	32 (121.1)

Model 15-M (3 in.)

Total head including friction, ft (meters)	10 (3.0)	15 (4.6)	20 (6.1)	25 (7.6)
20 (6.1)	259 (980.3)	—	—	—
30 (9.1)	250 (946.3)	210 (794.9)	200 (757.0)	160 (605.6)
40 (12.2)	241 (912.2)	207 (783.5)	177 (669.9)	140 (529.9)
50 (15.2)	225 (851.6)	202 (764.6)	172 (651.0)	140 (529.9)
60 (18.3)	197 (745.6)	197 (745.6)	169 (639.7)	138 (522.3)
70 (21.3)	160 (605.6)	160 (605.6)	160 (605.6)	125 (473.1)
80 (24.4)	125 (473.1)	125 (473.1)	125 (473.1)	96 (363.4)
90 (27.4)	96 (363.4)	96 (363.4)	96 (363.4)	

Model 18-M (3 in.)

Total head including friction, ft (meters)	10 (3.0)	15 (4.6)	20 (6.1)	25 (7.6)
25 (7.6)	301 (1,139.3)	—	—	—
30 (9.1)	295 (1,116.6)	255 (965.2)	200 (757.0)	—
40 (12.2)	276 (1,044.7)	250 (946.3)	200 (757.0)	162 (613.2)
50 (15.2)	250 (946.3)	237 (897.0)	198 (749.4)	159 (601.8)
60 (18.3)	216 (817.6)	212 (8–2.4)	182 (688.9)	146 (552.6)
70 (21.3)	174 (658.6)	174 (658.6)	158 (598.0)	127 (480.7)
80 (24.4)	129 (488.3)	129 (488.3)	125 (473.1)	104 (393.6)
90 (27.4)	82 (310.4)	82 (310.4)	82 (310.4)	74 (280.1)
95 (29.0)	57 (215.7)	57 (215.7)	57 (215.7)	57 (215.7)

Model 20-M (3 in.)

Total head including friction, ft (meters)	10 (3.0)	15 (4.6)	20 (6.1)	25 (7.6)
30 (9.1)	333 (1,260.0)	280 (1,059.8)	235 (889.5)	165 (624.5)
40 (12.2)	315 (1,192.3)	270 (1,022.0)	230 (870.6)	162 (613.2)
50 (15.2)	290 (1,097.7)	255 (965.2)	220 (832.7)	154 (582.9)
60 (18.3)	255 (965.2)	235 (889.5)	205 (775.9)	143 (541.3)
70 (21.3)	212 (802.4)	209 (791.1)	184 (696.4)	130 (492.1)
80 (24.4)	165 (624.5)	165 (624.5)	157 (594.2)	114 (431.5)
90 (27.4)	116 (439.1)	116 (439.1)	116 (439.1)	94 (355.8)
100 (30.5)	60 (227.1)	60 (227.1)	60 (227.1)	60 (227.1)

Model 40-M (4 in.)

25 (7.6)	665 (2,517.0)	—	—	—
30 (9.1)	660 (2,498.1)	575 (2,176.4)	475 (1,797.9)	355 (1,343.7)
40 (12.2)	645 (2,441.3)	565 (2,138.5)	465 (1,760.0)	350 (1,324.8)
50 (15.2)	620 (2,346.7)	545 (2,062.8)	455 (1,722.2)	345 (1,305.8)
60 (18.3)	585 (2,214.2)	510 (1,930.3)	435 (1,646.5)	335 (1,268.0)
70 (21.3)	535 (2,025.0)	475 (1,797.9)	410 (1,551.9)	315 (1,192.3)
80 (24.4)	465 (1,760.0)	410 (1,551.9)	365 (1,381.5)	280 (975.8)
90 (27.4)	375 (1,419.4)	325 (1,230.1)	300 (1,135.5)	220 (832.7)
100 (30.5)	250 (946.3)	215 (813.8)	195 (738.1)	145 (548.8)
110 (33.5)	65 (246.0)	60 (227.1)	50 (189.2)	40 (151.4)

Model 90-M (6 in.)

25 (7.6)	1,500 (5,677.5)	—	—	—
30 (9.1)	1,480 (5,601.8)	1,280 (4,844.8)	1,050 (3,974.3)	790 (2,990.1)
40 (12.2)	1,430 (5,412.6)	1,230 (4,655.6)	1,020 (3,860.7)	780 (2,952.3)
50 (15.2)	1,350 (5,109.8)	1,160 (4,390.6)	970 (3,671.5)	735 (2,782.0)
60 (18.3)	1,225 (4,636.6)	1,050 (3,974.2)	900 (3,406.5)	690 (2,611.7)
70 (21.3)	1,050 (3,974.2)	900 (3,406.5)	775 (2,933.4)	610 (2,308.9)
80 (24.4)	800 (3,028.0)	680 (2,573.8)	600 (2,271.0)	490 (1,854.7)
90 (27.4)	450 (1,703.3)	400 (1,514.0)	365 (1,381.5)	300 (1,135.5)
100 (30.5)	100 (378.5)	100 (378.5)	100 (378.5)	100 (378.5)

Model 125-M (8 in.)

25 (7.6)	2,100 (7,948.5)	1,850 (7,002.3)	1,570 (5,942.5)	—
30 (9.1)	2,060 (7,797.1)	1,820 (6,888.7)	1,560 (5,904.6)	1,200 (4,542.0)
40 (12.2)	1,960 (7,418.6)	1,740 (6,585.9)	1,520 (5,753.2)	1,170 (4,428.5)
50 (15.2)	1,800 (6,813.0)	1,620 (6,131.7)	1,450 (5,488.3)	1,140 (4,314.9)
60 (18.3)	1,640 (6,207.4)	1,500 (5,677.5)	1,360 (5,147.6)	1,090 (4,125.7)
70 (21.3)	1,460 (5,526.1)	1,340 (5,071.9)	1,250 (4,731.3)	1,015 (3,840.8)
80 (24.4)	1,250 (4,731.1)	1,170 (4,428.5)	1,110 (4,201.4)	950 (3,595.8)
90 (27.4)	1,020 (3,860.7)	980 (3,709.3)	940 (3,557.9)	840 (3,179.4)
100 (30.5)	800 (3,028.0)	760 (2,876.6)	710 (2,687.4)	680 (2,573.8)
110 (33.5)	570 (2,157.5)	540 (2,043.9)	500 (1,892.5)	470 (1,779.0)
120 (36.6)	275 (1,040.9)	245 (927.3)	240 (908.4)	240 (908.4)

Model 200-M (10 in.)

20 (6.1)	3,350 (12,679.8)	3,000 (11,355.0)	—	—
30 (9.1)	3,000 (11,355.0)	2,800 (10,598.0)	2,500 (9,462.5)	1,550 (5,866.8)
40 (12.2)	2,500 (9,462.5)	2,500 (9,462.5)	2,250 (8,516.3)	1,500 (5,677.5)
50 (15.2)	2,000 (7,570.0)	2,000 (7,570.0)	2,000 (7,570.0)	1,350 (5,109.8)
60 (18.3)	1,300 (4,920.5)	1,300 (4,920.5)	1,300 (4,920.5)	1,150 (4,352.8)
70 (21.3)	500 (1,892.5)	500 (1,892.5)	500 (1,892.5)	500 (1,892.5)

Table 18-3 Minimum capacities for MT-rated, solids-handling, self-priming centrifugal pumps manufactured in accordance with the standards of the Contractors Pump Bureau

| | | Model 5MT (1 1/2 in.) | | | | | | | |

| Total head including friction, ft | (meters) | \multicolumn{8}{Capacity, gpm (liters per min) — Height of pump above water, ft (meters)} |

Model 5MT (1 1/2 in.)

Capacity, gpm (liters per min)

Height of pump above water, ft (meters)

Total head including friction, ft	(meters)	10	(3.0)	15	(4.6)	20	(6.1)	25	(7.6)
20	(6.1)	82	(310.4)	64	(242.2)				
30	(9.1)	70	(265.0)	64	(242.2)	50	(189.3)	33	(124.9)
40	(12.2)	50	(189.3)	50	(189.3)	50	(189.3)	33	(124.9)
50	(15.2)	25	(94.6)	22	(83.3)	22	(83.3)	22	(83.3)

Model 10MT (2 in.)

Total head including friction, ft	(meters)	10	(3.0)	15	(4.6)	20	(6.1)	25	(7.6)
20	(6.1)	164	(620.7)	132	(499.6)				
30	(9.1)	164	(620.7)	132	(499.6)	105	(397.4)	75	(283.9)
40	(12.2)	164	(620.7)	132	(499.6)	105	(397.4)	75	(283.9)
50	(15.2)	164	(620.7)	132	(499.6)	105	(397.4)	75	(283.9)
60	(18.3)	135	(511.0)	132	(499.6)	105	(397.4)	75	(283.9)
70	(21.3)	88	(333.1)	88	(333.1)	88	(333.1)	68	(257.4)
80	(24.4)	40	(151.4)	40	(151.4)	40	(151.4)	40	(151.4)

Model 18MT (3 in.)

Total head including friction, ft	(meters)	10	(3.0)	15	(4.6)	20	(6.1)	25	(7.6)
20	(6.1)	310	(1,173.4)	265	(1,003.0)				
30	(9.1)	305	(1,154.4)	265	(1,003.0)	200	(757.0)	115	(435.3)
40	(12.2)	300	(1,135.5)	265	(1,003.0)	200	(757.0)	110	(416.4)
50	(15.2)	275	(1,040.9)	260	(984.1)	200	(757.0)	105	(397.4)
60	(18.3)	215	(813.8)	215	(813.8)	200	(757.0)	100	(378.5)
70	(21.3)	170	(643.5)	170	(643.5)	170	(643.5)	100	(378.5)
80	(24.4)	87	(329.3)	87	(329.3)	87	(329.3)	87	(329.3)
90	(27.4)	25	(94.6)	25	(94.6)	25	(94.6)	25	(94.6)

Model 33MT (4 in.)

Total head including friction, ft	(meters)	10	(3.0)	15	(4.6)	20	(6.1)	25	(7.6)
30	(9.1)	550	(2,081.8)	460	(1,741.1)	350	(1,324.8)	240	(908.4)
40	(12.2)	540	(2,043.9)	455	(1,722.2)	350	(1,324.8)	240	(908.4)
50	(15.2)	500	(1,892.5)	430	(1,627.6)	340	(1,286.9)	230	(870.6)
60	(18.3)	450	(1,703.3)	395	(1,495.1)	320	(1,211.2)	220	(832.7)
70	(21.3)	370	(1,400.5)	360	(1,362.6)	300	(1,135.5)	210	(794.9)
80	(24.4)	275	(1,040.9)	275	(1,040.9)	260	(984.1)	180	(681.3)
90	(27.4)	190	(719.2)	190	(719.2)	190	(719.2)	150	(567.8)
100	(30.5)	100	(378.5)	100	(378.5)	100	(378.5)	100	(378.5)

Model 35MT (4 in.)

25	(7.6)	585	(2,214.2)	500	(1,892.5)	350	(1,324.8)		
30	(9.1)	585	(2,214.2)	500	(1,892.5)	350	(1,324.8)	240	(908.4)
40	(12.2)	585	(2,214.2)	500	(1,892.5)	350	(1,324.8)	240	(908.4)
50	(15.2)	585	(2,214.2)	500	(1,892.5)	350	(1,324.8)	240	(908.4)
60	(18.3)	545	(2,062.8)	500	(1,892.5)	350	(1,324.8)	240	(908.4)
70	(21.3)	495	(1,873.6)	480	(1,816.8)	350	(1,324.8)	240	(908.4)
80	(24.4)	430	(1,627.6)	420	(1,589.7)	340	(1,286.9)	240	(908.4)
90	(27.4)	320	(1,211.2)	320	(1,211.2)	260	(984.1)	220	(832.7)
100	(30.5)	100	(378.5)	100	(378.5)	100	(378.5)	100	(378.5)

Model 70MT (6 in.)

20	(6.1)	1,195	(4,523.1)	975	(3,690.4)				
30	(9.1)	1,180	(4,466.3)	975	(3,690.4)	715	(2,706.3)	350	(1,324.8)
40	(12.2)	1,175	(4,447.4)	950	(3,595.8)	715	(2,706.3)	350	(1,324.8)
50	(15.2)	1,160	(4,390.6)	935	(3,539.0)	715	(2,706.3)	350	(1,324.8)
60	(18.3)	1,150	(4,352.8)	925	(3,501.1)	715	(2,706.3)	350	(1,324.8)
70	(21.3)	1,120	(4,239.2)	900	(3,406.5)	715	(2,706.3)	350	(1,324.8)
80	(24.4)	950	(3,595.8)	875	(3,311.9)	700	(2,649.5)	350	(1,324.8)
90	(27.4)	700	(2,649.5)	700	(2,649.5)	600	(2,271.0)	350	(1,324.8)
100	(30.5)	450	(1,703.3)	450	(1,703.3)	450	(1,703.3)	300	(1,135.5)
110	(33.5)	200	(757.0)	200	(757.0)	200	(757.0)	200	(757.0)

LOSS OF HEAD DUE TO FRICTION IN PIPE

Table 18-4 gives the nominal loss of head due to water flowing through new steel pipe. The actual losses may differ from the values given in the table because of variations in the diameter of a pipe and in the condition of the inside surface.

The relationship between the head of fresh water in feet and pressure in psi is given by the formula

$$h = 2.31p$$

or

$$p = 0.434h$$

where $h=$ depth of water or head, ft

$p=$ pressure at depth h, psi

Table 18-5 gives the equivalent length of straight steel pipe having the same loss in head due to water friction as fittings and valves.

LOSS OF HEAD DUE TO FRICTION IN RUBBER HOSE

The flexibility of rubber hose makes it a desirable substitute for pipe for use with pumps on many jobs. Such hose may be used on the suction side of a pump if it

Table 18-4 Friction loss for water, in feet per 100 ft of clean wrought-iron or steel pipe*

Flow, gpm	Nominal diameter of pipe, in.											
	1	1¼	1½	2	2½	3	4	5	6	8	10	12
5	1.93	0.51										
10	6.86	1.77	0.83	0.25	0.11							
14	12.8	3.28	1.53	0.45	0.19							
20	25.1	6.34	2.94	0.87	0.36	0.13						
24	35.6	8.92	4.14	1.20	0.50	0.17						
30	54.6	13.6	6.26	1.82	0.75	0.26	0.07					
40	.....	23.5	10.79	3.10	1.28	0.44	0.12					
50	.....	36.0	16.4	4.67	1.94	0.66	0.18	0.06				
75	.....	.....	35.8	10.1	4.13	1.39	0.28	0.12				
100	.....	.....	62.2	17.4	8.51	2.39	0.62	0.20	0.08			
120	.....	.....	.....	24.7	10.0	3.37	0.88	0.29	0.12			
150	.....	.....	.....	38.0	15.4	5.14	1.32	0.33	0.17			
170	.....	.....	.....	48.4	19.6	6.53	1.67	0.54	0.22			
200	.....	.....	.....	66.3	26.7	8.90	2.27	0.74	0.30	0.08		
220	.....	.....	.....	.....	32.2	10.7	2.72	0.88	0.36	0.09		
260	.....	.....	.....	.....	44.5	14.7	3.24	1.20	0.49	0.13		
280	.....	.....	.....	.....	51.3	16.9	4.30	1.38	0.56	0.14		
300	.....	.....	.....	.....	.....	19.2	4.89	1.58	0.64	0.16		
340	.....	.....	.....	.....	.....	24.8	6.19	2.00	0.81	0.21		
400	.....	.....	.....	.....	.....	33.9	8.47	2.72	1.09	0.28	0.09	
500	.....	.....	.....	.....	.....	52.5	13.0	4.16	1.66	0.42	0.14	0.06
600	.....	.....	.....	.....	.....	.....	18.6	5.88	2.34	0.60	0.19	0.08
700	.....	.....	.....	.....	.....	.....	25.0	7.93	3.13	0.80	0.26	0.11
800	.....	.....	.....	.....	.....	.....	32.4	10.22	4.03	1.02	0.33	0.14
900	.....	.....	.....	.....	.....	.....	40.8	12.9	5.05	1.27	0.41	0.17
1,000	.....	.....	.....	.....	.....	.....	50.2	15.8	6.17	1.56	0.50	0.21
1,100	.....	.....	.....	.....	.....	.....	.....	19.0	7.41	1.87	0.59	0.25
1,200	.....	.....	.....	.....	.....	.....	.....	22.5	8.76	2.20	0.70	0.30
1,300	.....	.....	.....	.....	.....	.....	.....	.....	10.2	2.56	0.82	0.34
1,400	.....	.....	.....	.....	.....	.....	.....	.....	11.8	2.95	0.94	0.40
1,500	.....	.....	.....	.....	.....	.....	.....	.....	13.5	3.37	1.07	0.45
2,000	.....	.....	.....	.....	.....	.....	.....	.....	23.8	5.86	1.84	0.78
3,000	.....	.....	.....	.....	.....	.....	.....	.....	.....	12.8	4.00	1.68
4,000	.....	.....	.....	.....	.....	.....	.....	.....	.....	22.6	6.99	2.92
5,000	.....	.....	.....	.....	.....	.....	.....	.....	.....	.....	10.80	4.47

* Reprinted from "Tentative Standards of Hydraulic Institute, Pipe Friction," Copyright 1948 by the Hydraulic Institute, 122 E. 42d St., New York, New York, 10017.

is constructed with a wire insert to prevent collapse under partial vacuum. Rubber hose is available with end fittings corresponding with those for iron or steel pipe.

Table 18-6 gives the loss in head in feet per 100 ft due to friction caused by water flowing through the hose. The values in the table apply for rubber substitutes.

Table 18-5 Length of steel pipe, in feet, equivalent to fittings and valves*

Item	1	$1\frac{1}{4}$	$1\frac{1}{2}$	2	$2\frac{1}{2}$	3	4	5	6	8	10	12
						Nominal size, in.						
90° elbow	2.8	3.7	4.3	5.5	6.4	8.2	11.0	13.5	16.0	21.0	26.0	32.0
45° elbow	1.3	1.7	2.0	2.6	3.0	3.8	5.0	6.2	7.5	10.0	13.0	15.0
Tee, side outlet	5.6	7.5	9.1	12.0	13.5	17.0	22.0	27.5	33.0	43.5	55.0	66.0
Close return bend	6.3	8.4	10.2	13.0	15.0	18.5	24.0	31.0	37.0	49.0	62.0	73.0
Gate valve	0.6	0.8	0.9	1.2	1.4	1.7	2.5	3.0	3.5	4.5	5.7	6.8
Globe valve	27.0	37.0	43.0	55.0	66.0	82.0	115.0	135.0	165.0	215.0	280.0	335.0
Check valve	10.5	13.2	15.8	21.1	26.4	31.7	42.3	52.8	63.0	81.0	105.0	125.0
Foot valve	24.0	33.0	38.0	46.0	55.0	64.0	75.0	76.0	76.0	76.0	76.0	76.0

* Courtesy the Gormon-Rupp Company.

Table 18-6 Friction loss for water, in feet per 100 ft of rubber or rubber-substitute hose

Flow gpm	$\frac{3}{4}$	1	$1\frac{1}{4}$	$1\frac{1}{2}$	2	$2\frac{1}{2}$	3	4	5
				ID of hose, in.					
5	9.25	2.54	0.93	0.46					
10	32.3	9.25	2.78	1.15	0.46	0.23			
15	69.3	20.6	5.78	2.54	0.93	0.46			
20	125.0	32.3	9.93	4.16	1.62	0.69			
25	......	50.8	15.0	6.70	2.31	0.93			
30	......	71.7	21.2	9.25	3.23	1.15	0.23		
35	......	94.8	27.7	12.5	4.15	1.38	0.46		
40	......	125.0	34.6	15.5	5.55	1.85	0.69		
50	......	......	55.5	23.1	8.32	2.31	1.15		
60	......	......	80.9	32.3	11.8	3.23	1.38		
70	......	......	103.8	43.9	15.2	4.15	1.85		
80	......	......	134.0	55.5	19.9	5.31	2.54		
90	......	......	......	69.3	25.4	6.93	3.23	0.69	
100	......	......	......	85.5	28.8	8.1	3.93	1.15	0.23
125	......	......	......	......	46.2	12.2	5.78	1.38	0.46
150	......	......	......	......	62.4	17.3	8.1	1.62	0.69
175	......	......	......	......	85.5	23.1	10.6	2.54	0.93
200	......	......	......	......	106.1	30.0	13.6	3.23	1.15
250	......	......	......	......	......	37.0	16.1	4.16	1.38
300	......	......	......	......	......	43.8	21.0	4.85	1.62
350	......	......	......	......	......	62.3	27.7	6.70	2.31
400	......	......	......	......	......	106.0	48.5	9.25	3.93
450	......	......	......	......	......	......	60.0	14.5	4.85
500	......	......	......	......	......	......	74.0	17.1	6.00
1,000	......	......	......	......	......	......	......	62.3	22.2

SELECTING A PUMP

Prior to selecting a pump for a given job it is necessary to analyze all information and conditions that will affect the selection. The most satisfactory pumping equipment will be the combination of pump and pipe that will provide the required service for the least total cost. The total cost includes the installed and operating cost of the pump and pipe for the period that it will be used, with an appropriate allowance for salvage value at the completion of the project. In order to analyze the cost of pumping water, it is necessary to have certain information, such as the following:

1. Rate at which the water is to be pumped
2. Height of lift from the existing water surface to the point of discharge
3. Pressure head at discharge, if any
4. Variations in water level at suction or discharge
5. Altitude of the project
6. Height of the pump above the surface of water to be pumped
7. Size of pipe to be used, if already determined
8. Number, sizes, and types of fittings and valves in the pipeline

The examples which follow are intended to illustrate methods of selecting pumps and pumping systems:

Example Select a self-priming centrifugal pump, with a capacity of 600 gpm, for the project illustrated in Fig. 18-7. All pipe, fittings, and valves will be 6 in. with threaded connections.

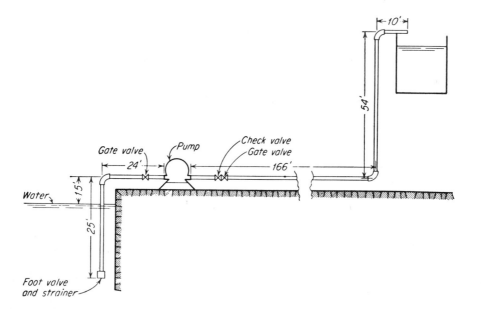

Figure 18-7 Pump and pipe installation.

Use the information given in Table 18-5 to convert the fittings and valves into equivalent lengths of pipe.

Item	Equivalent length of pipe, ft
1 foot valve and strainer	= 76
3 elbows @ 16 ft	= 48
2 gate valves @ 3.5 ft	= 7
1 check valve	= 63
Total	= 194
Add length of pipe	= 279
Total equivalent length of 6-in. pipe	= 473

From Table 18-4 the friction loss per 100 ft of 6-in. pipe will be 2.34 ft. The total head, including lift plus head lost in friction, will be

Lift, 15 + 54 = 69.0 ft
Head lost in friction, 473 ft @ 2.34 ft per 100 ft = 11.1 ft
Total head = 80.1 ft

Table 18-2 indicates that a model 90-M pump will deliver the required quantity of water.

Sometimes the problem is to select the pump and pipeline that will permit water to be pumped at the lowest total cost. The following example illustrates a method that may be used to select the most economical pumping system:

Example In operating a rock quarry it is necessary to pump 400 gpm of clear water. The pump and pipeline selected will be installed as illustrated in Fig. 18-8. It is estimated that the pump

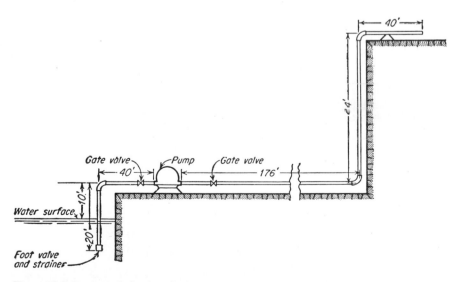

Figure 18-8 Pump and pipe installation.

will be operated a total of 1,200 hr per year. Compare the economy of using 4-in. and 6-in. steel pipe for the water line. Assume that the pump will have an economic life of 5 years and that the pipeline and fittings will have a life of 10 years. Also, assume that the cost of installing the pipeline will be the same regardless of the size, so that this cost may be disregarded.

Consider the use of 4-in. pipe. The total equivalent length of pipe will be:

Item	Equivalent length of pipe, ft
1 foot valve and strainer	= 75
3 elbows @ 11 ft	= 33
2 gate valves @ 2.5 ft	= 5
Pipe	= 320
Total equivalent length	= 433

The total head, including lift and head lost in friction, will be

Lift, 10 + 44 = 54.0 ft
Head lost in friction, 433 ft @ 8.47 ft per 100 ft = 36.7 ft
Total head = 90.7 ft

A model 90-M self-priming pump, with a capacity of approximately 450 gpm, will be required for this installation.

Consider the use of 6-in. pipe. The total equivalent length of pipe will be

Item	Equivalent length of pipe, ft
1 foot valve and strainer	= 76
3 elbows @ 16 ft	= 48
2 gate valves @ 3.5 ft	= 7
Pipe	= 320
Total equivalent length	= 451

The total head, including lift and head lost in friction, will be

Lift, 10 + 44 = 54.0 ft
Head lost in friction, 451 ft @ 1.09 ft per 100 ft = 4.9 ft
Total head = 58.9 ft

A model 30-M self-priming pump, with a capacity of approximately 450 gpm, will be satisfactory for this installation. The excess capacity of this pumping system is an advantage in favor of using 6-in. pipe.

The cost of each size pipeline, fittings, and valves will be

Item	Size pipe	
	4 in.	6 in.
320-ft pipeline	$776.00	$1,340.00
3 elbows	12.00	24.00
1 foot valve	24.00	36.00
2 gate valves	168.00	216.00
Total cost	$980.00	$1,616.00
Depreciation cost per year, based of 10-yr life	98.00	161.60
Depreciation cost per hr, based on 1,200 hr per yr	0.08	0.14

The cost per hour for owning and operating each size pump is given in Appendix A. The combined cost per hour for each size pump and pipeline system will be

Item	Cost per hr	
	4-in. pipe	6-in. pipe
Pump	$2.62	$1.74
Pipe, fittings, and valves	0.08	0.14
Total cost per hr	$2.70	$1.88

This analysis shows that the additional cost of the 6-in. pipe is more than offset by the reduction in the cost of the smaller pump.

WELLPOINT SYSTEMS

In excavating below the surface of the ground, it is not uncommon practice to encounter ground water before reaching the bottom of a pit. For pits excavated into sand and gravel, the flow of water will be large if some method is not adopted to remove the water before it enters the pit. While the water may be permitted to flow into sumps located in the pit, then removed by pumps, the presence of such water usually creates a nuisance and interferes with the construction operations. The installation of a wellpoint system along or around the pit may lower the water table below the bottom of the excavation, thus permitting the work to be done under relatively dry conditions.

A wellpoint is a perforated tube enclosed in a screen, which is installed below the surface of the ground to collect water in order that the water may be removed from the ground. The essential parts of a wellpoint are illustrated in Fig. 18-9. The top of a wellpoint is attached to a riser pipe, which extends a short distance above the surface of the ground, where it is connected to a large pipe called a header. The header pipe is connected to the suction of a centrifugal pump. A wellpoint system may include a few or several hundred wellpoints, all connected to one or more headers and pumps.

The principle by which a wellpoint system operates is illustrated in Fig. 18-10. Figure 18-10a shows how a single point will lower the surface of the water table in the soil adjacent to the point. Figure 18-10b shows how several points, installed reasonably close together, lower the water table over an extended area. A group of wellpoints properly installed along a trench or around a foundation pit will lower the water table below the depth of excavation.

Wellpoints will operate satisfactorily if they are installed in a permeable soil such as sand or gravel. If they are installed in a less permeable soil, such as silt, it may be necessary first to sink a large pipe, say 6 to 10 in. in diameter, for each point, remove the soil from inside the pipe, install a wellpoint, fill the space inside the pipe with sand or fine gravel, then withdraw the pipe. This leaves a volume of sand around each wellpoint to act as a water collector and a filter to increase the rate of flow for each point.

Wellpoints may be installed at any desired spacing, usually varying from 2 to 5 ft, along the header. The maximum height that water can be lifted is about

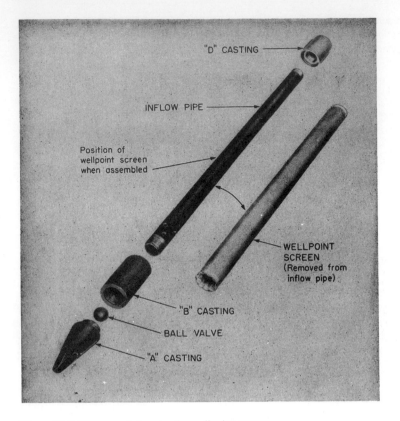

Figure 18-9 The essential parts of a wellpoint system.

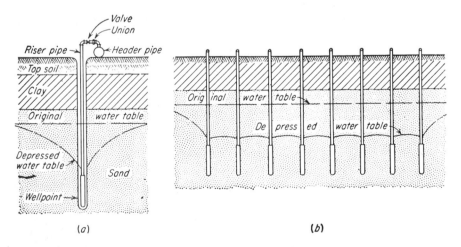

Figure 18-10 Lowering the water table adjacent to wellpoints.

Figure 18-11 Two-stage wellpoint installation. *(L. B. Foster Company.)*

18 to 20 ft. If it is necessary to lower the water table to a greater depth, one or more additional stages should be installed, each stage at a lower depth within the excavation. Figure 18-11 shows a project on which two stages were used. Figure 18-12 shows a typical wellpoint installation prior to starting excavation.

Installing a wellpoint system If the soil conditions are suitable, a wellpoint is jetted into position by forcing water through an opening at the bottom of the point. After each point is jetted into position, it is connected through a pipe or a rubber hose to a header pipe, usually 6, 8, or 10 in. in diameter. A valve is installed between each wellpoint and the header to regulate the flow of water. The header is connected to a self-priming centrifugal pump, which is equipped with an auxiliary air pump to remove any air from the water before it enters the pump proper.

Capacity of a wellpoint system The capacity of a wellpoint system depends on the number of points installed, the permeability of the soil, and the amount of

Figure 18-12 Typical wellpoint installation.

Figure 18-13 Three-stage wellpoint installation. *(Moretrench American Corp.)*

water present. An engineer who is experienced in this kind of work can make tests which will enable him to estimate with reasonable accuracy the capacity necessary to lower the water to the desired depth. The flow per wellpoint will vary from 3 or 4 gpm to as much as 30 or more on some installations.

When excavating 45 to 50 ft below the surface of the water in the Colorado River for the cutoff wall for the Morelos Dam, the contractor installed three main stages, with a supplemental fourth stage of wellpoints to enclose an area of 15 acres. A total of 2,750 wellpoints were serviced by 49 pumps. The maximum pumping rate was 17,400 gpm, with 2,150 wellpoints in operation. This gave an average yield of 8.1 gpm per point and 528 gpm per pump.

Prior to designing the wellpoint system for the Davis Dam on the Colorado River, a 45- by 58-ft test area was inclosed with 66 wellpoints, spaced $3\frac{1}{2}$ ft apart, each 21 ft long. The test, which was run for 172 hr, using two 8-in. pumps, gave an average yield of 13 gpm per wellpoint.

PROBLEMS

18-1 A two-cylinder duplex double-acting pump, size 6 by 12 in., is driven by a crankshaft which makes 125 rpm. If the water slippage is 7 percent, how many gallons of water will the pump deliver per minute? If the total head is 120 feet and the efficiency of the pump is 58 percent, what is the minimum horsepower required to operate the pump?

18-2 The centrifugal pump whose performance curves are given in Fig. 18-5 will be used to pump water against a total head of 60 ft. The dynamic suction lift will be 15 ft. Determine the capacity and efficiency of the pump and the horsepower required to operate the pump.

18-3 A centrifugal pump is to be used to pump all the water from a cofferdam whose dimensions are 70 ft long, 50 ft wide, and 12 ft deep. The water must be pumped against an average total head of 55 ft. The average height of the pump above the water will be 15 ft. If the cofferdam must be emptied in 18 hr, determine the minimum model self-priming pump Class M, to be used based on the ratings of the Contractors Pump Bureau.

18-4 Use Table 18-2 to select a centrifugal pump to handle 600 gpm of water. The water will be pumped from a pond through 460 ft of 6-in. pipe to a point 35 ft above the level of the pond, where it will be discharged into the air. The pump will be set 10 ft above the surface of the water in the pond. What is the designation of the pump selected?

18-5 Select a self-priming centrifugal pump to handle 500 gpm of water for the project illustrated in Fig. 18-7. Increase the height of the vertical pipe from 54 ft to 50 ft. All other conditions will be as shown in the figure.

18-6 Select a self-priming centrifugal pump to handle 1,000 gpm of water for the project illustrated in Fig. 18-7. Change the size of the pipe, fittings, and valves to 8 in.

REFERENCES

1. "Contractors Pump Manual," Contractors Pump Bureau, 13975 Connecticut Avenue, Silver Spring, Maryland 20906

NINETEEN

COFFERDAMS

INTRODUCTION

A cofferdam is a temporary structure which is built to exclude earth and water from an area in order that work may be performed there under reasonably dry conditions. Cofferdams are usually required for projects such as dams, locks, and piers that are constructed in rivers or in other bodies of water. Also, they may be installed to prevent the flow of earth and water into foundation pits excavated on land.

A cofferdam does not have to be entirely watertight in order to be successful. It usually is cheaper to permit some flow of water into the working area, which water can be removed with pumps, than to attempt to make the cofferdam watertight. The most satisfactory cofferdam is the one that has adequate strength to resist all destructive forces and that will permit the exclusion from or the control of water inside the dam at the lowest total cost. The total cost includes the cost of the cofferdam, the cost of damages due to water flowing into or over the dam, and the cost of pumping water from the area inside the dam, less any salvage value after the dam is removed. For many projects it is possible to determine these costs with reasonable accuracy prior to designing the cofferdam.

FORCES ACTING ON COFFERDAMS

The forces acting on a cofferdam may include the weight of the dam, the pressure of water, the scouring effect of moving water, the upward reaction of the earth, and the lateral pressure of earth in contact with the dam. A dam should be designed to resist the combined effect of all forces that will act on it.

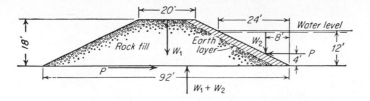

Figure 19-1 Forces acting on a rock-fill cofferdam.

Hydraulic pressure on cofferdams The unit pressure acting at any depth below the surface of water is given by the formula

$$p = wh \tag{19-1}$$

where p = pressure, psf
w = weight of a cubic foot of water, lb
h = depth below surface, ft

The total pressure acting on an area below the surface of water is given by the formula

$$P = pA = whA \tag{19-2}$$

where P = total pressure, lb
A = area, sq ft

If all the area A in formula (19-2) is not the same depth below the surface, h should be the depth to the center of gravity of A.

The forces acting on a section of a rock-fill cofferdam 1 ft long are shown in Fig. 19-1. For simplicity, the rock and the layer of impervious earth on the right side of the dam are assumed to weigh 120 lb per cu ft each.

The combined weight of rock and earth will be

$$W_1 = \frac{92 + 20}{2} \times 18 \times 120 = 121{,}000 \text{ lb}$$

The weight of water above the outer slope of the dam will be

$$W_2 = \frac{12 \times 24}{2} \times 62.5 = 9{,}000 \text{ lb}$$

The horizontal pressure of the water tending to push the dam to the left is

$$P = 62.5 \times 6 \times 12 = 4{,}500 \text{ lb}$$

The earth on which the dam rests must exert an upward force equal to $W_1 + W_2$, and a horizontal force to the right equal to P, in order to maintain the stability of the dam.

Seepage of water under cofferdams Since few cofferdams are watertight, the flow of water into a cofferdam must be considered in planning construction operations. The water may enter through openings in the dam, or it may enter through the soil underneath the dam. This discussion is devoted to the water that flows under a cofferdam and enters the construction area.

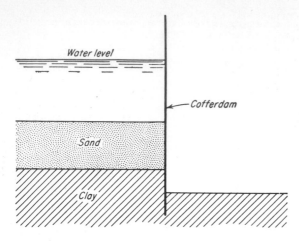

Figure 19-2 Sheet-piling cofferdam driven into impervious soil.

If a cofferdam is installed by driving a solid wall of sheeting, such as interlocking steel-sheet piling, through water or a pervious water-bearing soil, such as sand and gravel, into an impervious soil, such as clay or shale, the possibility of water flowing under the cofferdam is eliminated. This condition is illustrated in Fig. 19-2.

When it is not practical to drive sheeting into an impervious soil, water will flow under a cofferdam any time there is a difference in the hydrostatic levels on the two sides of the dam. The total quantity entering an area inside a cofferdam will depend on the velocity of flow and the area through which it flows. While many tests have been conducted to determine the rate of flow of ground water, variations in soil conditions prevent an accurate estimate of the flow. The results obtained by Hazen for sands varying from 0.1 to 3.0 mm in effective size are given by the formula

$$v = cd^2s \frac{t + 10}{60} \tag{19-3}$$

where $v =$ velocity of flow, m per day
$c =$ a constant, varying from 400 to 1,000
$d =$ effective size of sand, mm
$s =$ slope of hydraulic gradient
$t =$ temperature, °F

The velocity given in formula (19-3) is the velocity that would exist if no sand were present to reduce the area of passage. The presence of sand has the effect of increasing the true velocity to v/p. Hazen defined the effective size of soil as that size for which 10 percent is smaller and 90 percent is larger.

If the refinement of correcting for variations in temperature is omitted, as it probably should be on construction projects, and the velocity is expressed in feet per day, we get the formula

$$v = \frac{3.3cd^2}{p} s = ks \tag{19-4}$$

where v = true velocity of flow through the voids, ft per day

p = porosity ratio of soil

$k = 3.3cd^2/p$

The volume of flow through a given area, expressed in gpm, is given by the formula

$$Q = \frac{vAp}{192.5} \qquad (19\text{-}5)$$

Substituting the value of v from formula (19-4), we get

$$Q = \frac{3.3cd^2s}{p} \frac{Ap}{192.5} = \frac{cd^2As}{58.3} \qquad (19\text{-}6)$$

where Q = volume of flow, gpm

A = area of soil passage perpendicular to direction of flow, sq ft

Table 19-1 gives representative values of k or $3.3cd^2/p$ for use in formula (19-4). These values are based on experiments conducted by Hazen.

Example A steel-sheet-piling cofferdam encloses an area 20 ft wide by 40 ft long. The pit is excavated to a depth 20 ft below the level of water outside the dam. The average distance from the top of the sand outside the dam to the center of the bottom of the pit is 30 ft. The soil has an effective size of 0.5 mm and a porosity of 0.3. For this porosity the value of c will probably be 400.

In formula (19-4),

$c = 400 \qquad d = 0.5 \qquad p = 0.3 \qquad s = \frac{20}{30} = 0.667$

$k = \dfrac{3.3 \times 400 \times 0.5^2}{0.3} = 1{,}100 \qquad$ (see Table 19-1)

From formula (19-4),

$v = 1{,}100 \times 0.667 = 734$ ft per day

Substituting this value of v in formula (19-5), we get

$Q = \dfrac{734 \times 20 \times 40 \times 0.3}{192.5} = 915.1$ gpm

As indicated in Table 19-1, the effective size of the soil has considerable effect on the rate of flow of water through the soil. This is illustrated by the experience with the cofferdam for the Chain of Rocks Locks on the Mississippi River. Tests of the soil under the cofferdam and the area inside the dam

Table 19-1 Values of k in formula (19-4)

Porosity ratio	Fine		Medium	Coarse		Fine gravel			
	0.10	0.20	0.30	0.40	0.50	0.80	1.00	2.00	3.00
0.25	27	112	250	460	700	1,790	2,800	11,200	25,000
0.30	43	172	386	686	1,070	2,740	4,290	17,200	38,600
0.35	60	240	540	960	1,500	3,840	6,800	24,000	54,000
0.40	82	330	740	1,320	2,060	5,280	8,250	33,000	74,000

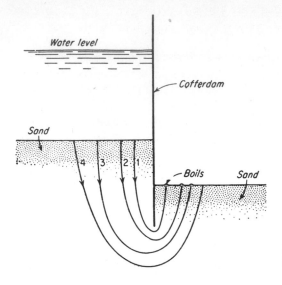
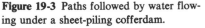

Figure 19-3 Paths followed by water flowing under a sheet-piling cofferdam.

indicated a probable flow of 100,000 gpm into the area. The actual flow proved to be only 5,000 to 8,000 gpm. Retests of the soil revealed that in conducting the original tests some of the fine material had washed out, which gave an apparent effective size that was too large.

The paths followed by particles of water flowing under a sheet-piling cofferdam are illustrated by lines 1, 2, 3, and 4 in Fig. 19-3. As line 1 offers the shortest path, the velocity of flow will be the greatest along this line. The velocity along lines 2, 3, and 4 will be correspondingly less. If the velocity of the water entering the cofferdam is sufficiently high, it may agitate the sand and cause boils at the bottom of the pit, as indicated.

If an impervious blanket is placed outside and a berm of earth is placed inside a sheet-piling cofferdam, as illustrated in Fig. 19-4, the increased flow distance will reduce the value of the hydraulic gradient s in formula (19-3),

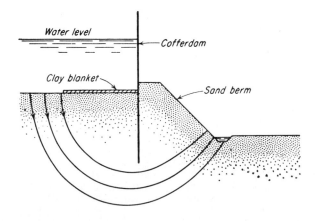

Figure 19-4 The use of a clay blanket and a berm to reduce the flow of water under a cofferdam.

which will reduce the velocity and quantity of water flowing under the cofferdam. In addition to reducing the flow of water, the berm adds horizontal stability to the cofferdam.

If the velocity of water flowing under a cofferdam is high enough, it may cause a channel to form through the sand which can result in a violent eruption of the sand and water into the cofferdam, producing what is referred to as a blow-in. This, of course, can be a major catastrophe.

When the wall of a cofferdam is installed to resist the horizontal pressure of earth and ground water, it may be desirable to leave enough openings in the wall to permit the water to flow through it as a means of reducing the pressure against the wall. This plan is reported to have been used with considerable success by White and Prentis in building cofferdams on the Mississippi River.

TYPES OF COFFERDAMS

Among the types of cofferdams frequently used are the following:

1. Water cofferdams
   a. Earth-fill
   b. Rock-fill
   c. Ohio type
   d. Rock-filled crib
   e. Sheet piling with bracing
   f. Steel-sheet piling, cells with diaphragms
   g. Steel-sheet piling with circular cells
2. Land cofferdams
   a. Wood-sheet piling
   b. Steel-sheet piling
   c. Horizontal sheeting

Earth-fill cofferdams When impervious earth is available near a project, a satisfactory and economical earth-fill cofferdam may be constructed in shallow water. As earth offers little resistance to erosion from moving water or wave action, this type of dam should be limited to use in water with little or no movement. An earth-fill dam is economical for low heights, but as the height is increased, it may prove to be more expensive than some other type. An earth dam should not be used where there is danger of overtopping by water. A typical earth-fill cofferdam is illustrated in Fig. 19-5.

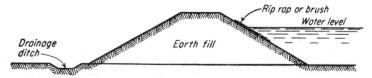

Figure 19-5 Earth-filled cofferdam.

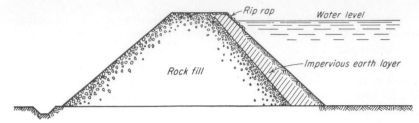

Figure 19-6 Rock-fill cofferdam.

Rock-fill cofferdams A rock-fill cofferdam is constructed by placing rock across a stream or around an area to be dewatered. Such a dam is quite satisfactory and economical if a large quantity of rock is available, such as from tunnels or excavations. A dam of this type is constructed by placing earth with the rock or by placing a layer of earth around the outside of the rock. The weight of the rock gives stability to the dam, while the earth supplies the watertight membrane. This type of dam may be overtopped by water without serious damage. Figure 19-6 shows a typical section through a rock-fill cofferdam.

Prior to constructing the Davis Dam on the Colorado River, the contractor excavated a diversion and forebay channel adjacent to the river. As soon as this channel was completed, the contractor began hauling rock onto a trestle which had been installed across the river below the entrance to the channel. Approximately 29,000 cu yd of rock was placed in 56 hr by 20 bottom-dump wagons. The river flow varied from 12,000 to 18,000 sec-ft during the diversion operation. It is estimated that approximately one-third of the rock was washed downstream by the river. After the rock fill was placed, the upstream face of the cofferdam was lined with impervious material to produce a watertight structure.

Ohio-River-type cofferdams This type of cofferdam derives its name from its use on the Ohio River. A dam is constructed by prefabricating a continuous row of timber frames with cross bracing and steel tie rods, as illustrated in Fig. 19-7. After the frames are in place, vertical sheeting is installed on each side of the frames and the space in between is filled with impervious earth. An earth or rock berm may be placed against a dam upstream and downstream to give greater stability and to reduce leakage through or under the dam. This type dam should not be used where the velocity of the water is high or where there is danger of serious overtopping.

Crib-type cofferdams A crib-type cofferdam is constructed by installing a series of connected cribs around or across an area to be dammed off. A crib is a framework of horizontal timbers installed in alternate courses to form pockets which are filled with rock and earth. The timber may be logs, or it may be heavy lumber, usually fastened together with driftpins, and sometimes with heavy vertical sheeting spiked to the timbers. A cross section through a typical crib-type cofferdam is shown in Fig. 19-8.

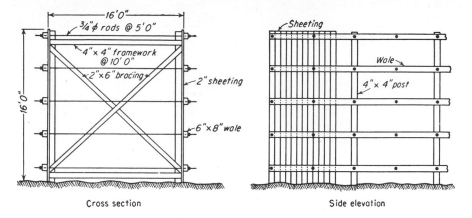

Cross section   Side elevation

Figure 19-7 Ohio-River-type cofferdam.

This type of cofferdam is used in a stream with a hard bottom, deep water, and swift current, where there is danger of overtopping, and where timber is relatively cheap. Unless these conditions exist, some other type cofferdam may be more economical. The Conwingo cofferdam had a maximum crib width of 30 ft and height of 35 ft, while the Bonneville cofferdam had a maximum crib width of 60 ft and height of 63 ft. The dimensions of a crib must be such that when it is filled with rock and earth it will be able to resist overturning and sliding with full water pressure on one side [see formulas (19-7) and (19-8)].

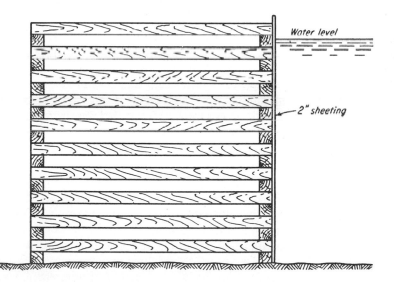

Figure 19-8 Crib-type cofferdam.

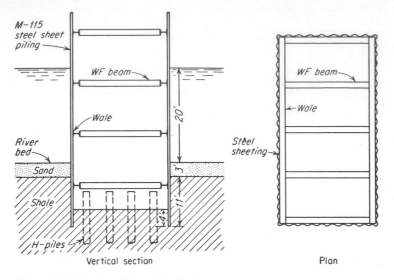

Figure 19-9 Single-wall braced cofferdam.

Single-wall steel-sheet-piling cofferdams A cofferdam of this type is satisfactory for use under certain conditions such as:

1. To enclose a small area for a bridge pier in water or on land, where the depth is not excessive
2. To enclose a land area for constructing the foundation for a building

As a single wall of steel-sheet piling has limited strength in resisting the horizontal pressure of water or earth, it is necessary to provide an internal system of bracing to resist the pressure. If the dimensions across a dam are not too great, rows of wales and cross braces will be satisfactory and economical. A single-wall braced cofferdam for a bridge pier is illustrated in Fig. 19-9.

If the dimensions inside a dam are great, such as for the basement of a building, it may not be practical to extend braces across from wall to wall. For this type of construction a system of bracing such as that illustrated in Fig. 19-10 may be used.

Diaphragm-type cellular cofferdams This structure is constructed of steel-sheet piling to give a self-sustaining cofferdam with two walls. The walls consist of a series of arc segments, which are connected at their intersections with diaphragms that extend through the cofferdam, to form a group of cells. A diaphragm is connected to the arcs with a Y pile at each connection. Figure 19-11 shows the details of a cellular cofferdam for the waterworks intake at St. Louis.

After a number of the cells are constructed, they are filled with earth, sand, gravel, or rock to increase the weight and stability of the dam and to reduce the

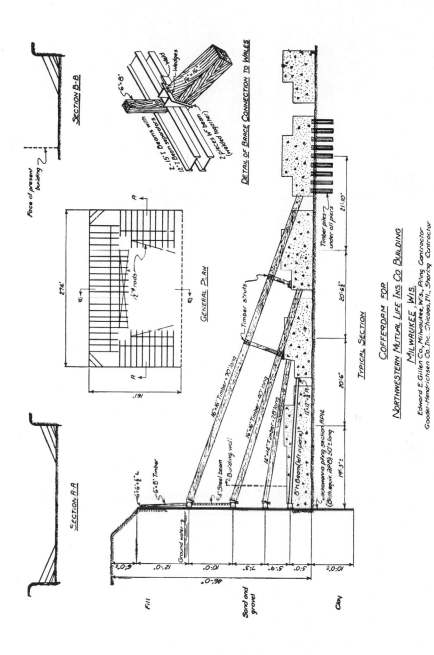

Figure 19-10 Representative bracing for a single-wall cofferdam. *(Bethlehem Steel Corporation.)*

583

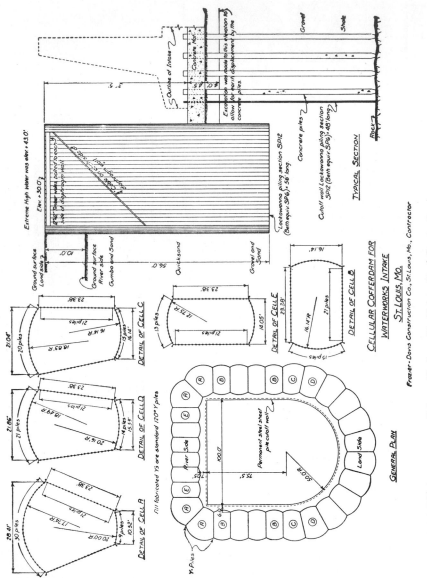

Figure 19-11 Diaphragm-type cellular cofferdam. (*Bethlehem Steel Corporation.*)

584

leakage of water through it. As the diaphragm which separates two cells is a straight wall, it is necessary to fill adjacent cells at approximately the same rate. If this is not done, the unbalanced pressure from the fill will distort the diaphragm, which may cause failure of the interlocks. This is one of the objections to the diaphragm-type cofferdam. The literature on steel-sheet piling published by the manufacturers gives recommended working strengths of interlocks expressed in pounds per linear inch.

The cellular-type cofferdam will withstand overtopping by water without serious damage to the dam. If overtopping is likely to occur, one or more gated openings should be installed through a dam in order that water may flow into the enclosure before it goes over the top of the dam. This precaution will reduce the damage caused by flooding the area inside a dam. The dam illustrated in Fig. 19-11 was overtopped by 13 ft of water.

Circular-type cellular cofferdams This structure is constructed of steel-sheet piling to give a self-sustaining cofferdam consisting of a group of circular cells joined with connecting arcs. The cells and arcs produce an enclosure to exclude water from the working area inside the dam. Figure 19-12 shows the details of a cellular cofferdam for the lock at Pickwick Landing Dam.

A cellular cofferdam is constructed by driving the piles which form the cells, then connecting the cells with two arcs, as shown in Fig. 19-14. Each cell should include four T piles, to which the arc piles are connected. In order to facilitate the spacing and driving of the piles, a circular steel template is located on steel supports where a cell is to be constructed. With the template as a guide, the piles, including the T piles, are driven in correct positions. After all the piles in a cell are driven, the template and supports are lifted out and relocated for another cell. Figure 19-13 shows several steps in constructing the cells for a circular-type cofferdam. The arcs are installed after the cells are completed.

As each cell is a stable unit, subjected to a tensile force only in the walls when filled with earth, it is possible to fill a cell immediately after it is constructed. In this respect the circular-type cofferdam is superior to the diaphragm type, which requires that adjacent cells be filled at the same time. After a cell is filled with earth, it is possible to locate on the earth a crane or other equipment needed to construct additional cells.

The piles in the cells and arcs on the water side of a cofferdam may be extended several feet above the tops of the inside piles to give a dam extra height at relatively low cost.

Representative dimensions and other information for circular-type cofferdams are given in Fig. 19-14 and Table 19-2.

In Fig. 19-14 and Table 19-2, E indicates the theoretical width of a rectangular wall having a resistance against overturning equal to that of the cellular wall. The value of E may be increased almost in proportion to the increase in the number of piles in and the diameter of a cell. The increase in the diameter of a cell will produce only a slight increase in the total number and weight of piles required for a given length cofferdam. For example, consider a

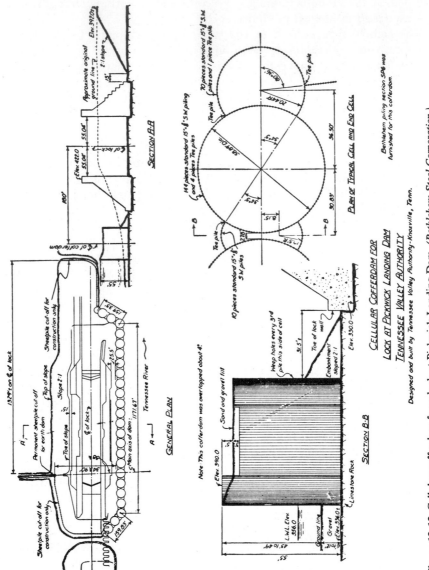

Figure 19-12 Cellular cofferdam for a lock at Pickwick Landing Dam. (*Bethlehem Steel Corporation.*)

(a)

(b)

Figure 19-13 Successive steps in constructing the cells for a circular-type cofferdam. (a) H piles are driven in square and braced with struts and supports, (b) prefabricated circular template is lowered over H piles, (c) sheet piles are driven around the template, (d) template is lifted out of finished cell to be used again, (e) stages in the construction of circular cells. (*Guy F. Atchison Company.*)

(c)

(d)

Figure 19-13 (*Continued*)

(*e*)

Figure 19-13 (*Continued*)

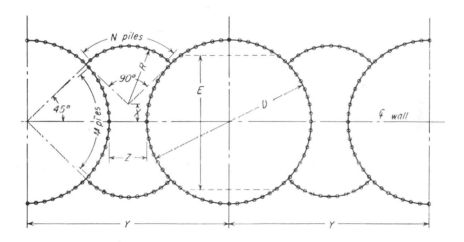

Figure 19-14 Dimension nomenclature for cellular structures of circular-type cofferdam. Use with Table 19-2. *(United States Steel Corporation.)*

Table 19-2 Representative dimensions and numbers of steel-sheet piling for circular-type cofferdams using 16-in.-wide piling*
(See Fig. 19-14)

No.† piles in cell	D, ft	Y, ft	R, ft	X, ft	Z, ft	E, ft	No. M piles	No. N piles	Area, sq ft Within circle	Between circles
48	20.36	26.47	8.54	1.16	6.11	17.40	11	9	325.6	156.3
52	22.06	27.67	8.54	1.76	5.61	18.73	12	9	382.2	160.5
56	23.76	30.08	9.39	1.76	6.32	20.11	13	10	443.4	192.8
60	25.46	31.28	9.39	2.36	5.82	21.50	14	10	509.1	196.8
64	27.16	32.48	9.39	2.97	5.32	22.91	15	10	579.4	200.0
68	28.85	34.88	10.24	2.96	6.03	24.32	16	11	653.7	236.3
72	30.55	36.15	10.24	3.60	5.60	25.70	17	11	733.1	239.5
76	32.25	37.28	10.24	4.16	5.03	27.12	18	11	816.9	241.5
80	33.95	38.48	10.24	4.77	4.53	28.53	19	11	905.3	242.8
84	35.65	40.88	11.08	4.77	5.23	29.95	20	12	998.2	283.9
88	37.34	42.08	11.08	5.36	4.74	31.24	21	12	1,095.1	285.0
92	39.04	43.28	11.08	5.97	4.24	32.52	22	12	1,197.0	285.4
96	40.74	44.48	11.08	6.57	3.74	33.94	23	12	1,303.6	284.8
100	42.43	46.88	11.93	6.56	4.45	35.36	24	13	1,414.0	330.7
104	44.14	48.09	11.93	7.17	3.95	36.70	25	13	1,530.2	330.0
108	45.83	49.28	11.93	7.77	3.45	38.10	26	13	1,649.6	328.4
112	47.52	51.68	12.78	7.76	4.16	39.51	27	14	1,773.6	378.3
116	49.22	52.88	12.78	8.36	3.66	40.91	28	14	1,902.7	376.6
120	50.92	54.08	12.78	8.97	3.16	42.34	29	14	2,036.4	374.1
124	52.62	56.48	13.63	8.97	3.86	43.77	30	15	2,174.7	428.1
128	54.31	57.68	13.63	9.56	3.37	45.10	31	15	2,316.6	425.4
132	56.01	60.08	14.48	9.57	4.07	46.55	32	16	2,463.9	482.9
136	57.71	61.28	14.48	10.17	3.57	48.00	33	16	2,615.7	480.0
140	59.41	62.48	14.48	10.77	3.07	49.42	34	16	2,772.1	476.1
144	61.11	64.88	15.33	10.76	3.77	50.83	35	17	2,933.0	537.8
148	62.80	66.08	15.33	11.37	3.28	52.21	36	17	3,097.5	533.8

* Courtesy United States Steel Corporation.
† Includes four T piles.

circular-type cofferdam having 60 piles per cell and another having 120 piles per cell. Reference to Table 19-2 indicates that for a length of 100 ft along the center line of the dam the following will apply:

For 60 piles per cell:
   No. cells, $100 \div 31.28 = 3.2$
   No. piles in cells, 3.2×60 $= 192$
   No. piles in arcs, $2 \times 3.2 \times 10$ $= 64$
      Total no. piles $= \overline{256}$
      Value of E $= 21.50$ ft

For 120 piles per cell:
  No. cells, $100 \div 54.08 = 1.85$
  No. piles in cells, 1.85×120 $= 222$
  No. piles in arcs, $2 \times 1.85 \times 14 = $ 52
    Total no. piles $= \overline{274}$
    Value of E $= 42.34$ ft

Thus, the value of E is almost doubled, whereas the number of piles required is increased by 7 percent. The larger-diameter cells will require more earth fill, which may add materially to the cost of a dam, and they produce higher stresses in the interlocks of the piles, which may endanger the safety of a dam.

Designing circular-type cellular cofferdams This type of cofferdam is filled with earth within the circles and between the circles. In order that such a dam may safely resist the pressure of water on the outside, it should be designed as a gravity dam. The forces acting on it are the weight of the earth and the piling, the pressure of the water on one side, the upward reaction of the soil under the dam and the resistance of the soil under the dam to sliding. All these forces are shown in Fig. 19-15. The relationship between all forces acting on a cofferdam should be such that the resultant of W and P will intersect the bottom of the dam not closer than $E/3$ from the inside toe at N.

Figure 19-15 shows a section through a cofferdam whose width is E, as given in Fig. 19-14 and Table 19-2. For calculation purposes, consider a section of a dam 1 ft long. Assume that all piling are the same length and that fresh water stands at the top of the dam. Assume that the earth fill inside the dam

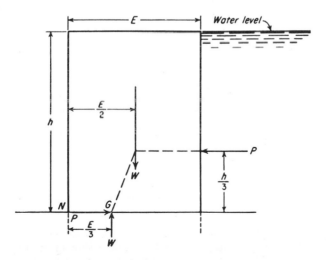

Figure 19-15 The forces acting on a cofferdam.

weighs 100 lb per cu ft and that the water weighs 62.5 lb per cu ft. Let

h = height of dam, ft
E = theoretical width, ft, of a rectangular dam having a resistance against overturning equal to that of the cellular dam
P = total pressure, lb, of water on a section of the dam 1 ft long
W = weight, lb, of the earth in a section of the dam 1 ft long
w = density of water, equal to 62.5 lb per cu ft
d = weight of 1 cu ft of earth, assumed to be 100 lb
A = area, sq ft, of section of dam on which P acts

Then

$$P = \frac{Awh}{2} = \frac{h \times 62.5h}{2} = \frac{62.5h^2}{2}$$
$$W = dEh = 100Eh$$

If we use the narrowest width of dam permissible, the resultant of W and P will intersect the base at point G. With this condition existing, if we equate the algebraic sum of all forces acting on the dam about N to zero, we get

$$\frac{WE}{2} - \frac{Ph}{3} - \frac{WE}{3} = 0$$

Substituting the values of W and P gives

$$\frac{100E^2h}{2} - \frac{62.5h^3}{6} - \frac{100E^2h}{3} = 0$$

Divide by h, and reduce to a common denominator.

$$300E^2 - 62.5h^2 - 200E^2 = 0$$
$$62.5h^2 = 100E^2$$
$$\frac{h^2}{E^2} = \frac{100}{62.5} = 1.6$$
$$\frac{h}{E} = \sqrt{1.6} = 1.265$$
$$h = 1.265E \tag{19-7}$$

This formula gives the theoretical maximum safe height for a dam. In deriving the formula the weight of the sheet piling and the effect of skin friction on the portion of the piling driven into the soil were neglected. These forces will increase the stability and safety of the dam. If a dam is constructed in salt water or in a flowing stream, the pressure of the water on the dam will be increased slightly, which will reduce the stability of the dam. In order to provide a factor of safety against variations that may occur, the height should be less than the value given by formula (19-7). A height not greater than the value given by formula (19-8) should be safe and satisfactory for most dams.

$$h = 1.2E \tag{19-8}$$

ECONOMY OF COFFERDAM HEIGHT

When a cofferdam is constructed in a river, it is necessary to determine the height that will be most satisfactory. The most satisfactory height is the one that will produce the lowest total cost considering the cost of the dam and the cost of risk that a flood may overtop the dam. In order to be satisfactory, a cofferdam in a river does not need to be high enough to exclude all floods that may occur in the river. The extra cost of constructing a dam to such a height might exceed the maximum damage that would be caused by a flood. Under this condition it is cheaper to assume the risk of loss due to flood damage than to build a dam high enough to eliminate the danger of overtopping.

For the rivers in the United States and throughout most of the world records are available which indicate with reasonable accuracy the frequency at which the stage of a river will rise to any desired height. For example, it is probable that the stage for a given river will reach or exceed 30 ft four times a year, 34 ft once a year, 38 ft once in 4 years, and 42 ft once in 10 years. It is impossible to predict the time at which any flood will occur, but the frequencies will apply over a reasonably long period of years. If a 34-ft-high cofferdam is in the river for 1 year, it is probable that it will be overtopped once. If the height is increased to 38 ft, the probability of it being overtopped is 1 in 4. Is it economical to increase the height from 34 to 38 ft at an extra cost of $42,800 if the probable loss from damage due to a flood will be $40,000? The cost of flood risk for a 34-ft-high dam is $40,000, resulting from 1 flood in 1 year. The cost of flood risk for a 38-ft-high dam is $40,000 ÷ 4 — $10,000, resulting from 1 flood

Figure 19-16 Final cofferdam for the McNary Dam.

Table 19-3 The most economical height for a cofferdam

Height of dam, ft	Frequency of floods overtopping the dam, floods per yr	Cost of dam	Cost of flood risk	Combined cost of dam and flood risk
30	4	$275,800	$160,000	$435,800
32	2	304,000	80,000	384,000
34	1	322,000	40,000	362,000
36	0.50	351,400	20,000	371,400
38	0.25	364,800	10,000	374,800
40	0.15	384,000	6,000	390,000
42	0.10	402,500	4,000	406,500

in 4 years. The increased cost of the dam is $42,800, while the reduction in flood risk is $40,000 − $10,000 = $30,000. As it is not economical to spend $42,800 to eliminate a $30,000 risk, the 38-ft height is not justified.

Table 19-3 illustrates a method of determining the most economical height for a cofferdam. The information in the table is based on the dam being in the river for 1 year and a probable loss due to flood damage equal to $40,000 each time the dam is overtopped. The results show that 34 ft is the most economical height listed. It is possible that the most economical height is between 34 and 36 ft.

Freezing a cofferdam A method of providing a substitute for a cofferdam which has been used in Europe and the United States is to freeze a wall of ice around a hole prior to excavating. This method of excluding earth and water from a hole is especially suitable in excavating a deep shaft through loose sand and gravel containing a large quantity of ground water.

When the Potash Company of America found it necessary to install a 15-ft inside-diameter shaft to a depth of 360 ft for its mines in New Mexico, it decided to freeze a cylinder of ice around the shaft opening as a means of excluding water and sand. It was decided to freeze the formation after an unsuccessful attempt had been made to consolidate it by pumping 1,000 sacks of cement into the sand.

Around the circumference of a 31-ft-diameter circle 28 holes were drilled to a depth of 360 ft, to penetrate below the deepest water-bearing formation. A 6-in.-diameter steel casing whose bottom was sealed with a welded steel plate was installed to the bottom of each hole. A 2-in.-diameter pipe, with its bottom end open, was installed inside of and to the bottom of the 6-in. pipe. The top of each 2-in. pipe was connected to an 8-in.-diameter brine pipe which encircled the shaft area. The top of each 6-in. pipe was closed with a hood and connected through a 2-in. pipe to a second 8-in. header pipe. Each injection pipe was equipped with a valve to regulate the flow of brine in order to produce an equal rate of freezing around the shaft. A single 6-in. pipe, with slots through the walls, was installed in a hole near the center of the shaft to provide a means of escape for water forced to the center by the freezing process.

Brine was pumped down through the 2-in. pipes and upward through the 6-in. pipes, and thence back through the refrigerating plant. After 48 days of operation the ice wall was sufficiently thick to permit the starting of excavation for the shaft.

A concrete lining was placed in 25-ft-long vertical sections as the excavation progressed. Where the excavation for the shaft encountered ice, the frozen wall was lined with corrugated-metal roofing prior to placing the concrete in order to provide an insulating membrane to prevent the concrete from freezing. Injection pipes were placed through the concrete wall to permit cement grout to be pumped behind the wall after its completion, to fill the air spaces. The grout was injected before the ice wall melted in order to prevent it from flowing outward through fissures and channels.

FREEZING SOIL FOR TEMPORARY GROUND SUPPORT

Introduction Controlled ground freezing for mining and construction applications has been practiced for over a century. Despite the technological developments that have occurred during this period, ground freezing is still used on projects today with considerable success when project and soil conditions warrant the use of this method of stabilization.

General advantages and disadvantages of freezing soil Ground freezing may be used in any soil or rock formation, regardless of structure, grain size, or permeability. However, it is best suited to soft ground, rather than rock conditions. Freezing may be used for any reasonable size, shape, or depth of excavation, and the same physical plant can be used from job to job despite wide variation in these factors.

Freezing is normally used to provide structural underpinning or temporary support for an excavation or to prevent ground water from flowing into an excavate area. Because the impervious frozen earth barrier is constructed prior to excavation, it generally eliminates the need for compressed air or dewatering and the concern for adjacent ground subsidence during dewatering or excavation. However, later ground-water flows may result in failure of the freezing program if not properly considered during the planning stage. Further, although subsidence may not be of concern, ground movements resulting from frost expansion of the soil during freezing may occur under certain conditions, and this condition must be considered in planning.

The freezing of soil may be accomplished rapidly if necessary or desirable. However, rapid freezing will usually be more expensive than slower freezing.

Frozen ground behaves as a viscoplastic material with strength properties which are primarily dependent on the ice content, duration of the applied load, and the temperature of the ground. The type and texture of the ground are relatively less important. Within limits, it is relatively insensitive to advance

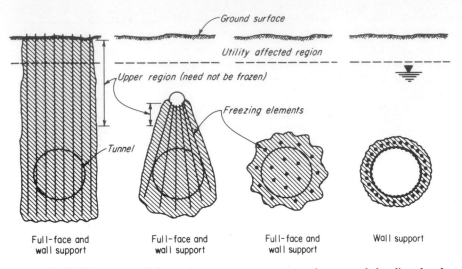

Figure 19-17 Alternate techniques for temporary support of a tunnel heading by freezing. *(Terrafreeze Corporation.)* [2]

geological prediction, and by changing the temperature or duration of loading, it will usually be possible to accommodate all types of ground conditions with one type of freezing method. As an example of the flexibility of support provided by freezing the ground, Fig. 19-17 illustrates some of the basic configurations that have been used in tunnel work.

Cost of freezing ground The direct costs of freezing for a specific project will depend largely on the ground conditions, the spacing of the freezing elements, the time available, and the type of refrigeration system used.

The relative economics of ground freezing are dependent on the specific conditions and requirements of a project. To evaluate the relative economics of various alternative methods of temporary ground support, it is necessary to consider their effect on the total project costs rather than on the direct costs of the specific alternative as a single item. In many instances, the direct costs of freezing alone may appear somewhat higher than the direct costs of an alternate method. However, when the added items of work required by the alternate method are considered, the total costs may favor the freezing method.

Alternate methods of freezing the ground As illustrated in Fig. 19-18, there are various methods or systems used for freezing ground. Each method has advantages and disadvantages compared with other methods, depending on job conditions, the location of the project, and other factors. For a more comprehensive treatment of this subject, several publications are available.

The effect of the properties of the ground on the shape of the frozen zone As illustrated in Fig. 19-19, when heterogeneous ground is frozen, the shape of the

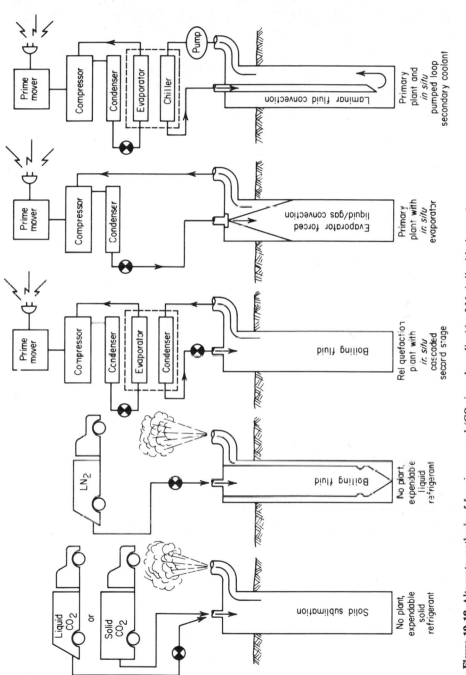

Figure 19-18 Alternate methods of freezing ground (CO_2 is carbon dioxide; LN_2 is liquid nitrogen). (*Terrafreeze Corporation.*) [2]

597

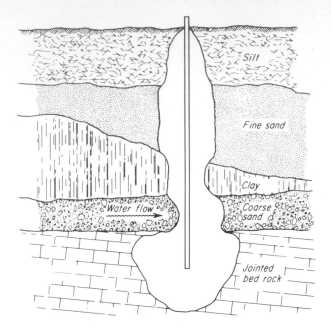

Figure 19-19 Irregular shape of frozen zone in heterogeneous ground. *(Terrafreeze Corporation.)* [2]

Figure 19-20 Excavation for 115- by 157- by 75-ft-deep pit for nuclear power plant stabilized by freezing. *(Terrafreeze Corporation.)* [2]

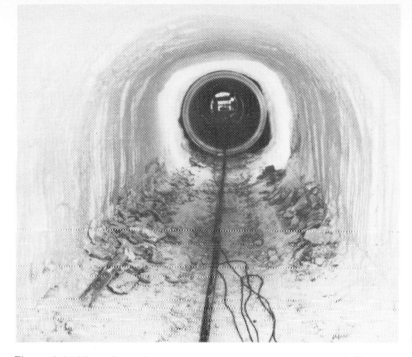

Figure 19-21 View of tunnel excavated through frozen ground. *(Terrafreeze Corporation.)*

frozen zone may be quite irregular. This possibility should be considered in selecting the spacings of the injection pipes.

ELECTROOSMOSIS

Electroosmosis is a means of stabilizing silts and soft clays by the introduction of direct electric current into the soil through electrodes placed in the ground around the area to be stabilized.

The stabilizing action is based on the phenomenon that, when a direct electric current is passed through a capillary, water moves through the capillary in the direction of the current. The water that is moved consists of the free water and of the inner part of the double layer of the boundary film of water that is adjacent to the wall of the capillary.

Considering the pores of a fine-grained soil as capillaries, the action of passing the direct current through the soil causes the positive ions adjacent to the soil particles to flow in the direction of the current. This action results in the free water being dragged along toward the negative electrodes, where the water accumulates and eventually flows out of the soil through pipes which are used for the negative electrodes. The constant removal of the free water from the soil causes a reduction in the water content, with a resultant increase in the shearing strength of the soil. By introducing anodes of a specific type of metal, a base exchange can be obtained in certain soils, which causes the soil to become permanently stabilized. This action results in a barrier of stable soil being created around the area, which serves as a wall to retain the unstable soil that exists beyond the area influenced by the electroosmosis system.

The equipment, layout, power, and time required to stabilize a soil are governed by the size of the project and the type of soil. In general, electroosmosis is applicable to soils having a grain size finer than that for which wellpoints normally are adaptable. The cost of this system is comparable with the cost of a wellpoint system if the latter were being used to unwater an area of similar size in a sand.

Several projects have been stabilized with electroosmosis in Europe and the United States. At the John C. Weadock power plant at Bay City, Mich., an area to be excavated was enclosed by steel-sheet piling. After the excavation had been carried down about 20 ft, the sheet piling started to move, which forced a work stoppage. An electroosmosis system was installed, and the project was completed without difficulty. The soil was a sandy silt and a clayey silt. Tests indicated that the shearing strength of the soil was increased 300 percent by the use of electroosmosis.

Laboratory or small-scale field tests are made to determine whether electroosmosis is applicable to a soil. From these tests, the practicability of using this method of stabilization, the overall cost of the project, and the time required for stabilization are determined.

Figure 19-22 shows excavation operation for the Weadock power plant after the electroosmosis system had been installed.

Figure 19-22 Soil stabilized by electroosmosis system.

REFERENCES

1. White, Lazarus, and Edmund Astley Prentis: "Cofferdams," Columbia University Press, New York, 1940.
2. Shuster, John A.: Controlled Freezing for Temporary Ground Support, reprint, *Proceedings of the 1st North American Rapid Excavation & Tunneling Conference, Chicago, Illinois, June 1972*, Terrafreeze Corporation.
3. Kersten, M. S.: "The Thermal Properties of Soils," *Bulletin* 28, Engineering Experiment Station, University of Minnesota, Minneapolis, Minnesota, 1949.
4. Highway Research Board, Bulletin 168, "Factors Influencing Ground Freezing" (a composite of papers presented at the 36th Annual Meeting, Washington, D.C., January 1957).
5. Mellor, M.: "Strength and Deformability of Rocks at Low Temperatures," *Research Report* 294, U.S. Army Cold Regions Research & Engineering Laboratory, Hanover, New Hampshire, May, 1971.
6. Brown, Bernal, and Allesandro Macchi: "Ground Freezing Techniques at Salerno," Terrafreeze Corporation, March 1974.
7. "Ground Freezing for Tunneling in Water-Bearing Soil at Dortmund, West Germany," Terrafreeze Corporation, no date.
8. Silinsh, J. J.: Freezing Keeps Shaft Dry and Holds Dirt in Place, *Construction Methods & Equipment*, vol. 42, January 1960.
9. "Deep Freeze" in New Mexico, *Western Construction*, vol. 27, pp. 78 79, May 1952.
10. Haworth, Russel C.: Apply Freezing Method in Potash Field, *Mining Congress Journal*, vol. 38, pp. 26-29, January 1952.
11. Casagrande, Leo: "Electro-osmotic Stabilization of Soils," *Harvard University Soil Mechanics Series, No.* 38.
12. Wakabayaski, Jiro: Peripheral Grouting Doubles Access Shaft Construction Speed, *Construction Methods & Equipment*, vol. 59, p. 46, February 1977.
13. Bethlehem Steel Corporation, Bethlehem, Pennsylvania 18016.
14. Terrafreeze Corporation, 8551 Backlick Road, Lorton, Virginia 22079.
15. United States Steel Corporation, 600 Grant Street, Pittsburgh, Pennsylvania 15230.

CHAPTER TWENTY

THE PRODUCTION OF
CRUSHED-STONE AGGREGATE

INTRODUCTION

The production of crushed-stone aggregate involves drilling, blasting, loading, transporting, crushing, screening, handling, and storing the aggregate. As the first four operations have already been discussed, this chapter will be devoted to studies of the last four operations.

In operating a quarry and a crushing plant, the drilling pattern, the amount of explosives, the size power shovel to load the stone, and the size of the primary crusher should be coordinated to assure that all stone from the quarry can pass through the opening to the crusher. It is desirable for the loading capacity of the shovel and the capacity of the crushing plant to be approximately equal. Table 20-1 gives the recommended minimum sizes of jaw and gyratory crushers required to handle the stone passing through power-shovel dippers of the specified capacities.

TYPES OF CRUSHERS

Crushers may be classified according to the stage of crushing which they accomplish, such as primary, secondary, tertiary, etc. A primary crusher receives the stone directly from a quarry and produces the first reduction in size. The output of the primary crusher is fed to a secondary crusher, which further reduces the size. Some of the stone may pass through four or more crushers before it is reduced to the necessary fineness.

Table 20-1 Recommended minimum sizes of primary crushers for use with shovel dippers of the indicated capacities

Capacity of dipper, cu yd (cu m)	Jaw crusher, in. (mm)*		Gyratory crusher, size of openings,† in. (mm)	
$\frac{3}{4}$	(0.575)	28 × 36	(712 × 913)	16	(406)
1	(0.765)	28 × 36	(712 × 913)	16	(406)
$1\frac{1}{2}$	(1.145)	36 × 42	(913 × 1,065)	20	(508)
$1\frac{3}{4}$	(1.340)	42 × 48	(1,065 × 1,200)	26	(660)
2	(1.530)	42 × 48	(1,065 × 1,200)	30	(760)
$2\frac{1}{2}$	(1.910)	48 × 60	(1,260 × 1,525)	36	(915)
3	(2.295)	48 × 60	(1,260 × 1,525)	42	(1,066)
$3\frac{1}{2}$	(2.668)	48 × 60	(1,260 × 1,525)	42	(1,066)
4	(3.060)	56 × 72	(1,420 × 1,830)	48	(1,220)
5	(3.820)	66 × 86	(1,675 × 2,182)	60	(1,520)

* The first two digits are the width of the opening at the top of the crusher, measured perpendicular to the jaw plates. The second two digits are the width of the opening, measured across the jaw plates.

† The recommended sizes are for gyratory crushers equipped with straight concaves.

While there is no rigid classification of crushers, the following is representative of common crusher uses.

1. Primary crushers
   a. Jaw
   b. Gyratory
   c. Hammer mill
2. Secondary crushers
   a. Cone
   b. Roll
   c. Hammer mill
3. Tertiary crushers
   a. Roll
   b. Rod mill
   c. Ball mill

As stone passes through a crusher, it undergoes a reduction in size, which may be expressed as a ratio of reduction. The ratio of reduction is the ratio of the distance between the fixed and moving faces at the top divided by the distance at the bottom of a crusher. Thus, if the distance between the two faces of a jaw crusher at the top is 16 in. and at the bottom is 4 in., the ratio of reduction is 4.

The ratio of reduction for a roll crusher is the ratio of the dimension of the largest stone that can be nipped by the rolls divided by the setting of the rolls, which is the smallest distance between the faces of the rolls.

Jaw crushers This machine is very popular as a primary crusher. It operates by allowing stone to flow into the space between two jaws, one of which is stationary, while the other is movable. The distance between the jaws diminishes as the stone travels downward under the effect of gravity and the movable jaw, until it ultimately passes through the lower opening. The movable jaw is capable of exerting a pressure sufficiently high to crush the hardest rock.

The Blake type, illustrated in Fig. 20-1, is a double-toggle crusher. The movable jaw is suspended from a shaft mounted on bearings on the crusher frame. The crushing operation is effected by rotating an eccentric shaft, which raises and lowers the pitman, which actuates the two toggles. As the two toggles are raised by the pitman, a high pressure is exerted near the bottom of the swing jaw, which partially closes the opening between the bottoms of the two jaws. This operation is repeated as the eccentric shaft is rotated.

The jaw plates, which are made of manganese steel, may be removed, replaced, or, in some cases, reversed. The jaws may be smooth, or, in the event the stone tends to break into slabs, corrugated jaws may be used to reduce the slabbing. The swing jaw may be straight, or it may be curved to reduce the danger of choking.

When the eccentric shaft of the single-toggle crusher, illustrated in Fig. 20-2, is rotated, it gives the movable jaw a vertical and horizontal motion. This type

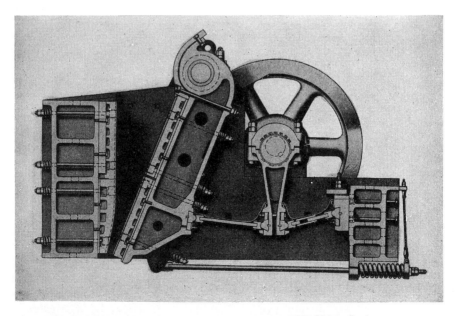

Figure 20-1 Blake-type jaw crusher. *(Fiat-Allis Construction Machinery, Inc.)*

Figure 20-2 Toggle-type jaw crusher. *(Portec, Inc., Pioneer Division.)*

crusher is used quite frequently in portable rock-crushing plants because of its compact size, light weight, and reasonably sturdy construction. The capacity of the single-toggle crusher is usually less than that of the Blake-type unit.

When a jaw crusher is used as a primary crusher, the size may be determined by the capacity of the shovel dipper, as indicated in Table 20-1, in which case the capacity of the crusher may be secondary. A jaw crusher should have a top opening at least 2 in. wider than the largest stones that will be fed to it.

Table 20-2 gives representative capacities for various sizes of jaw crushers. As the setting may be based on the open or closed position of the bottom of the swing jaw, a capacity table should specify which setting applies. The closed position is most commonly used and is the basis for the values given in Table 20-2. The capacity is given in tons per hour for stone weighing 100 lb per cu ft when crushed.

Table 20-2 Representative capacities of Blake-type jaw crushers, in tons per hour (metric tons per hour) of stone

Size crusher, in. (mm)*	Maximum rpm	Maximum hp (kW)	Closed setting of discharge opening, in. (mm)										
			1 (25.4)	1½ (38.1)	2 (50.8)	2½ (63.5)	3 (76.2)	4 (102)	5 (137)	6 (152)	7 (178)	8 (203)	9 (229)
10 × 6 (254 × 406)	300	15 (11.2)	11 (10)	16 (14)	20 (18)								
10 × 20 (254 × 508)	300	20 (14.9)	14 (13)	20 (18)	25 (23)	34 (31)							
15 × 24 (381 × 610)	275	30 (22.4)		27 (24)	34 (31)	42 (38)	50 (45)						
15 × 30 (381 × 762)	275	40 (29.8)		33 (30)	43 (39)	53 (48)	62 (56)						
18 × 36 (458 × 916)	250	60 (44.8)		46 (42)	61 (55)	77 (69)	93 (84)	125 (113)					
24 × 36 (610 × 916)	250	75 (56.0)			77 (69)	95 (86)	114 (103)	150 (136)					
30 × 42 (762 × 1,068)	200	100 (74.6)				125 (113)	150 (136)	200 (181)	250 (226)	300 (272)			
36 × 42 (916 × 1,068)	175	115 (85.5)				140 (127)	160 (145)	200 (181)	250 (226)	300 (272)			
36 × 48 (916 × 1,220)	160	125 (93.2)				150 (136)	175 (158)	225 (202)	275 (249)	325 (294)	375 (339)		
42 × 48 (1,068 × 1,220)	150	150 (111.9)				165 (149)	190 (172)	250 (226)	300 (272)	350 (318)	400 (364)	450 (408)	
48 × 60 (1,220 × 1,542)	120	180 (134.7)					220 (200)	280 (254)	340 (309)	400 (364)	450 (408)	500 (454)	550 (500)
56 × 72 (1,422 × 1,832)	95	250 (186.3)						315 (286)	380 (345)	450 (408)	515 (468)	580 (527)	640 (580)

* The first number indicates the width of the feed opening, while the second number indicates the width of the jaw plates.

Gyratory crushers A section through a gyratory crusher is illustrated in Fig. 20-3. The crusher unit consists of a heavy cast-iron or steel frame, with an eccentric shaft setting and driving gears in the lower part of the unit. In the upper part there is a cone-shaped crushing chamber, lined with hard-steel or manganese-steel plates called the concaves. The crushing member includes a hard-steel crushing head mounted on a vertical steel shaft. This shaft and head are suspended from the spider at the top of the frame, which is so constructed that some vertical adjustment of the shaft is possible. The eccentric support at the bottom causes the shaft and the crushing head to gyrate as the shaft rotates, thereby varying the width of the space between the concaves and the head. As the rock which is fed in at the top of the crushing chamber moves downward, it undergoes a reduction in size until it finally passes through the opening at the bottom of the chamber.

The size of a gyratory crusher is the width of the receiving opening, measured between the concaves and the crusher head. The setting is the width of the bottom opening and may be the open or closed dimension. When a setting is given, it should be specified if it is the open or closed dimension.

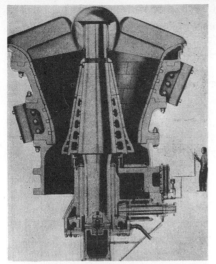

Figure 20-3 Hydroset gyratory crusher. *(Fiat-Allis Construction Machinery, Inc.)*

Figure 20-4 Gyrosphere crusher. *(Telsmith Division, Barber-Greene Company.)*

Table 20-3 Representative capacities of gyratory crushers, in tons per hour (metric tons per hour) of stone

Size of crusher, in. (mm)	Approximate power required, hp (kW)	Open-side setting of crusher, in. (mm)											
		$1\frac{1}{2}$ (38)	$1\frac{3}{4}$ (44)	2 (51)	$2\frac{1}{4}$ (57)	$2\frac{1}{2}$ (63)	3 (76)	$3\frac{1}{2}$ (89)	4 (102)	$4\frac{1}{2}$ (114)	5 (127)	$5\frac{1}{2}$ (140)	6 (152)
Straight concaves													
8 (20.0)	15–25 (11–19)	30 (27)	36 (33)	41 (37)	47 (42)								
10 (25.4)	25–40 (19–30)		40 (36)	50 (45)	60 (54)								
13 (33.1)	50–75 (37–56)				85 (77)	100 (90)	133 (120)						
16 (40.7)	60–100 (45–75)						160 (145)	185 (167)	210 (190)				
20 (50.8)	75–125 (56–93)							200 (180)	230 (208)	255 (271)			
30 (76.2)	125–175 (93–130)								310 (281)	350 (317)	390 (353)		
42 (106.7)	200–275 (150–205)										500 (452)	570 (515)	630 (569)
Modified straight concaves													
8 (20.0)	15–25 (11–19)	35 (32)	40 (36)	45 (41)									
10 (25.4)	25–40 (19–30)		54 (49)	60 (54)	65 (59)								
13 (33.1)	50–75 (37–56)					95 (86)	130 (117)						
16 (40.7)	60–100 (45–75)						150 (135)	172 (155)	195 (176)				
20 (50.8)	75–125 (56–93)							182 (165)	200 (180)	220 (199)			
30 (76.2)	125–175 (93–130)								340 (308)	370 (335)	400 (362)		
42 (106.7)	200–275 (150–205)										607 (550)	650 (589)	690 (625)
Nonchoking concaves													
8 (20.0)	15–25 (11–19)	42 (38)	46 (42)										
10 (25.4)	25–40 (19–30)	51 (46)	57 (52)	63 (57)	69 (62)								
13 (33.1)	50–75 (37–56)	79 (71)	87 (79)	95 (86)	103 (93)	111 (100)							
16 (40.7)	60–100 (45–75)			107 (96)	118 (106)	128 (115)	150 (135)						
20 (50.8)	75–125 (56–93)				155 (140)	169 (152)	198 (178)	220 (198)	258 (233)	285 (257)	310 (279)		

The ratio of reduction for gyratory crushers usually varies from about 5.5 to 7.5, with an average value around 6.5 for the sizes up to 42 in.

If a gyratory crusher is used as a primary crusher, the size selected may be dictated by the size of the rock from the quarry or it may be dictated by a desired capacity. When this machine is used as a secondary crusher, the capacity of a gyratory crusher may be increased by increasing the speed of the machine within reasonable limits.

Table 20-3 gives representative capacities of gyratory crushers, expressed in tons per hour, based on a continuous feed of stone weighing 100 lb per cu ft when crushed. The crushers with straight concaves are commonly used as primary crushers, while those with nonchoking concaves are commonly used as secondary crushers.

Cone crushers Cone, or reduction, crushers are used as secondary or tertiary crushers. They are capable of producing large quantities of uniformly fine crushed stone. A cone crusher differs from a gyratory crusher in the following respects:

1. It has a shorter cone.
2. It has a smaller receiving opening.
3. It rotates at a higher speed, from 430 to 580 rpm.
4. It produces a more uniformly sized stone with the maximum size equal to the width of the closed-side setting.

Figure 20-5 shows a section through a Symons standard cone crusher. The conical head, made usually of manganese steel and mounted on the vertical shaft, serves as one of the crushing surfaces. The other surface is the concave, which is attached to the upper part of the crusher frame. The bottom of the shaft

Figure 20-5 Symons standard cone crusher. *(Nordberg Manufacturing Company.)*

Table 20-4 Representative capacities of Symons/standard cone crushers, in tons per hour (metric tons per hour) of stone*

Size of crusher, ft (m)	Size of feed opening, in. (mm)	Minimum discharge settings, in. (mm)	Discharge setting, in. (mm)										
			$\frac{1}{4}$ (6.3)	$\frac{3}{8}$ (9.5)	$\frac{1}{2}$ (12.7)	$\frac{5}{8}$ (15.9)	$\frac{3}{4}$ (19.1)	$\frac{7}{8}$ (22.3)	1 (25.4)	$1\frac{1}{4}$ (31.8)	$1\frac{1}{2}$ (38.0)	2 (50.8)	$2\frac{1}{2}$ (63.5)
2 (0.61)	$2\frac{1}{4}$ (57)	$\frac{1}{4}$ (5.6)	15 (14)	20 (18)	25 (23)	30 (27)	35 (32)						
2 (0.61)	$3\frac{1}{4}$ (82)	$\frac{3}{8}$ (9.5)		20 (18)	25 (23)	30 (27)	35 (32)	40 (36)	45 (41)	50 (45)	60 (54)		
3 (0.91)	$3\frac{7}{8}$ (96)	$\frac{3}{8}$ (9.5)		35 (32)	40 (36)	55 (50)	70 (63)	75 (68)					
3 (0.91)	$5\frac{1}{8}$ (130)	$\frac{1}{2}$ (12.7)			40 (36)	55 (50)	70 (63)	75 (68)	80 (72)	85 (77)	90 (81)	95 (86)	
4 (1.22)	5 (127)	$\frac{3}{8}$ (9.5)		60 (54)	80 (72)	100 (90)	120 (109)	135 (122)	150 (136)				
4 (1.22)	$7\frac{3}{8}$ (187)	$\frac{3}{4}$ (19.0)					120 (109)	135 (122)	150 (136)	170 (154)	177 (160)	185 (167)	

			100	125	140	150	160	175	185	190	
			(90)	(113)	(126)	(136)	(145)	(158)	(167)	(172)	
$4\frac{1}{4}$ (1.29)	$4\frac{1}{2}$ (114)	$\frac{1}{2}$ (12.7)		125	140	150	160	175	185	190	
$4\frac{1}{4}$ (1.29)	$7\frac{3}{8}$ (187)	$\frac{5}{8}$ (15.8)		(113)	(126)	(136)	(145)	(158)	(167)	(172)	
$4\frac{1}{4}$ (1.29)	$9\frac{1}{2}$ (241)	$\frac{3}{4}$ (19.0)		160	200	235	275	300	340	375	450
$5\frac{1}{2}$ (1.67)	$7\frac{1}{8}$ (181)	$\frac{5}{8}$ (15.8)		(145)	(181)	(213)	(249)	(272)	(304)	(340)	(407)
$5\frac{1}{2}$ (1.67)	$8\frac{5}{8}$ (219)	$\frac{7}{8}$ (22.2)				235	275	300	340	375	450
$5\frac{1}{2}$ (1.67)	$9\frac{7}{8}$ (248)	1 (25.4)				(213)	(249)	(272)	(304)	(340)	(407)
7 (2.30)	10 (254)	$\frac{3}{4}$ (19.0)			330	390	450	560	600	800	900
7 (2.30)	$11\frac{1}{2}$ (292)	1 (25.4)			(300)	(353)	(407)	(507)	(543)	(725)	(815)
7 (2.30)	$13\frac{1}{2}$ (343)	$1\frac{1}{4}$ (31.7)					(407)	(507)	(543)	(725)	

* Courtesy Nordberg Manufacturing Company.

is set in an eccentric bushing to produce the gyratory effect as the shaft rotates.

While the maximum diameter of the crusher head may be used to designate the size of a cone crusher, the size of the feed opening, which limits the size of rocks that may be fed to the crusher, is the width of the opening at the entrance to the crushing chamber. The magnitude of the eccentric throw and the setting of the discharge opening may be varied within reasonable limits. Because of the high speed of rotation all particles passing through a crusher will be reduced to sizes no larger than the close-size setting, which should be used to designate the size of the discharge opening.

Table 20-4 gives representative capacities for the Symons standard cone crusher, expressed in tons of stone per hour for material weighing 100 lb per cu ft when crushed.

Hammer mills The hammer mill, which is the most widely used impact crusher, may be used for primary or secondary crushing. The basic parts of a unit include a housing frame, a horizontal shaft extending through the housing, a number of arms and hammers attached to a spool which is mounted on the shaft, one or more manganese-steel or other hard-steel breaker plates, and a series of grate bars whose spacings may be adjusted to regulate the width of openings through which the crushed stone flows. These parts are illustrated in the section through the crusher shown in Fig. 20-6.

As the stone to be crushed is fed to the mill, the hammers, which travel at a high speed, strike the particles, breaking them and driving them against the breaker plates, which further reduces their sizes.

The size of a hammer mill may be designated by the size of the feed opening. The capacity will vary with the size of the unit, the kind of stone crushed, the size of the material fed to the mill, and the speed of the shaft. Table 20-5 gives representative capacities of hammer mills expressed in tons of stone per hour for material weighing 100 lb per cu ft when crushed.

Roll crushers Roll crushers are used for producing additional reductions in the sizes of stone after the output of a quarry has been subjected to one or more stages of prior crushing. A roll crusher consists of a heavy cast-iron frame equipped with two hard-steel rolls, each mounted on a separate horizontal shaft. Most crushers are so constructed that each roll is driven independently by a flat-belt pulley or a V-belt sheave. One of the rolls is mounted on a slide frame, to permit an adjustment in the width of the discharge opening between the two rolls. The movable roll is spring-loaded to provide safety against damage to the rolls when trap iron or other noncrushable material passes through the machine. Figures 20-9, 20-10, and 20-11 illustrate roll crushers.

The maximum size of material that may be fed to a crusher is directly proportional to the diameter of the rolls. If the feed contains stones that are too large, the rolls will not grip them and pull them through the crusher. The angle of nip in Fig. 20-12, which is constant for smooth rolls, has been found to be 16°54'. The maximum-size particles that can be crushed is determined as

Figure 20-6 Cutaway of hammer mill rock crusher showing breaking action. *(Iowa Manufacturing Company.)*

follows. Let

  R = radius of rolls
  B = angle of nip
  $D = R \cos B = 0.9575R$
  A = maximum-size feed
  C − roll setting − size of finished product

Then

  $X = R - D$
   $= R - 0.9575R = 0.0425R$
  $A = 2X + C$
   $= 0.085R + C$ (20-1)

Example Determine the maximum-size stone that may be fed to a smooth-roll crusher whose rolls are 40 in. in diameter, when the roll setting is 1 in.

  $A = 0.085 \times 20 + 1$
   $= 2.7$ in.

Figure 20-7 Cutaway showing single-impeller impact breaker. *(Iowa Manufacturing Company.)*

The capacity of a roll crusher will vary with the kind of stone, size of feed, size of the finished product, width of rolls, speed at which the rolls rotate, and extent to which the stone is fed uniformly into the crusher. Referring to Fig. 20-12, the theoretical volume of a solid ribbon of material passing between the two rolls in 1 min would be the product of the width of the opening times the width of the rolls times the speed of the surface of the rolls. The volume may be expressed in cubic inches or cfm. In actual practice the ribbon of crushed stone will never be solid. A more realistic volume should approximate one-fourth to one-third of the theoretical volume. A formula which may be used as a guide in estimating the capacity is derived as follows. Let

C = distance between rolls, in.

W = width of rolls, in.

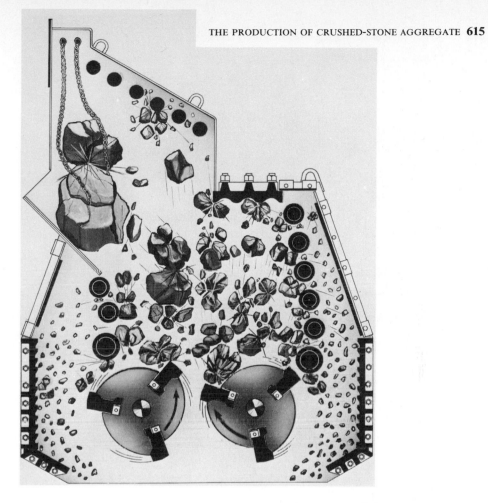

Figure 20-8 Cutaway showing double-impeller impact breaker. *(Iowa Manufacturing Company.)*

Table 20-5 Representative capacities for hammer mills, in tons per hour (metric tons per hour) of stone*

Size feed opening, in. (mm)	Size feed, in. (mm)	Power required, hp (kW)	Width of openings between grate bars, in. (mm)						
			$\frac{1}{8}$ (3.2)	$\frac{3}{16}$ (4.7)	$\frac{1}{4}$ (6.4)	$\frac{3}{8}$ (9.5)	$\frac{1}{2}$ (12.7)	1 (25.4)	$1\frac{1}{4}$ (31.8)
$6\frac{1}{4} \times 9$	3	15–20	2.5	3.5	5.0	8.0	10.0		
(159 × 229)	(76.2)	(11–15)	(2.3)	(3.2)	(4.5)	(7.2)	(9.1)		
12 × 15	3	50–60	9.0	13.0	17.0	23.0	29.0	36.0	39.0
(304 × 380)	(76.2)	(37–45)	(8.2)	(11.8)	(15.4)	(20.8)	(26.2)	(32.6)	(35.2)
15 × 25	6	100–125	18.0	25.0	31.0	40.0	47.0	65.0	70.0
(380 × 635)	(152.4)	(75–93)	(16.4)	(22.6)	(28.1)	(36.3)	(42.6)	(59.0)	(63.5)
15 × 37	6	150–200	27.0	37.0	47.0	60.0	71.0	97.0	105.0
(380 × 940)	(152.4)	(112–149)	(24.5)	(33.6)	(42.6)	(54.5)	(64.4)	(88.0)	(95.4)
15 × 49	6	200–250	36.0	50.0	63.0	80.0	95.0	130.0	140.0
(380 × 1,245)	(152.4)	(149–187)	(32.6)	(45.4)	(57.0)	(72.5)	(85.9)	(117.5)	(126.8)

* Courtesy Fiat-Allis Construction Machinery, Inc.

Figure 20-9 Cutaway showing triple-roll crusher. *(Portec, Inc., Pioneer Division.)*

$S =$ peripheral speed of rolls, in. per min

$N =$ speed of rolls, rpm

$R =$ radius of rolls, in.

$V_1 =$ theoretical volume, cu in. or cfm

$V_2 =$ actual volume, cu in. or cfm

$Q =$ probable capacity, tons per hr

Then

$$V_1 = CWS$$

Assume $V_2 = V_1/3$.

$$V_2 = \frac{CWS}{3} \qquad \text{cu in. per min}$$

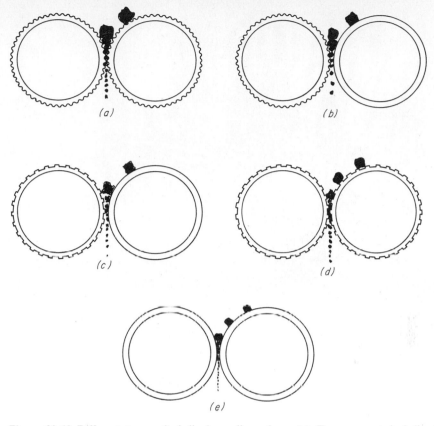

Figure 20-10 Different types of shells for roll crushers. (*a*) Two corrugated shells. (*b*) One corrugated and one smooth shell. (*c*) One step-tooth and one smooth shell. (*d*) Two step-tooth shells synchronized. (*e*) Two smooth shells. (*Grundler Crusher & Pulverizer Company.*)

Divide by 1,728 cu in. per cu ft.

$$V_2 = \frac{CWS}{5,184} \qquad \text{cfm}$$

Assume the crushed stone weighs 100 lb per cu ft.

$$Q = \frac{100 \times 60V_2}{2,000} = 3V_2$$

$$= \frac{CWS}{1,728} \qquad \text{tons per hr} \tag{20-2}$$

S may be expressed in terms of the diameter of the roll and the speed in rpm.

$$S = 2\pi RN$$

Substituting this value of S in formula (20-2) gives

$$Q = \frac{CW\pi RN}{864} \tag{20-3}$$

Figure 20-11 Cutaway of single-roll crusher showing deep-ribbed pittman and segment-type rotor. Breaker plate with ribs provides concentrated crushing action between teeth and ribs and acts as a sizing anvil for close control of product size. *(Grundler Crusher & Pulverizer Company.)*

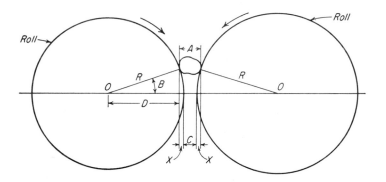

Figure 20-12 Crushing rock between two rolls.

Table 20-6 gives representative capacities for smooth-roll crushers, expressed in tons of stone per hour for material weighing 100 lb per cu ft when crushed. These capacities should be used as a guide only in estimating the probable output of a crusher. The actual capacity may be more or less than the given values.

If a roll crusher is producing a finished aggregate, the reduction ratio should not be greater than 4 : 1. However, if a roll crusher is used to prepare feed for a fine grinder, the reduction may be as high as 7 : 1.

Table 20-6 Representative capacities of smooth-roll crushers, in tons per hour (metric tons per hour) of stone*

Size of crusher,[†] in. (mm)	Speed, rpm	Power required, hp (kW)	Width of opening between rolls, in. (mm)						
			$\frac{1}{4}$ (6.3)	$\frac{1}{2}$ (12.7)	$\frac{3}{4}$ (19.1)	1 (25.4)	$1\frac{1}{2}$ (38.1)	2 (50.8)	$2\frac{1}{2}$ (63.5)
16 × 16	120	15–30	15.0	30.0	40.0	55.0	85.0	115.0	140.0
(414 × 416)		(11–22)	(13.6)	(27.2)	(36.2)	(49.7)	(77.0)	(104.0)	(127.0)
24 × 16	80	20–35	15.0	30.0	40.0	55.0	85.0	115.0	140.0
(610 × 416)		(15–26)	(13.6)	(27.2)	(36.2)	(49.7)	(77.0)	(104.0)	(127.0)
30 × 18	60	50–70	15.0	30.0	45.0	65.0	95.0	125.0	155.0
(763 × 456)		(37–52)	(13.6)	(27.2)	(40.7)	(59.0)	(86.0)	(113.1)	(140.0)
30 × 22	60	60–100	20.0	40.0	55.0	75.0	115.0	155.0	190.0
(763 × 558)		(45–75)	(18.1)	(36.2)	(49.7)	(67.9)	(104.0)	(140.0)	(172.0)
40 × 20	50	60–100	20.0	35.00	50.0	70.0	105.0	135.0	175.0
(1,016 × 508)		(45–75)	(18.1)	(31.7)	(45.2)	(63.4)	(95.0)	(122.0)	(158.5)
40 × 24	50	60–100	20.0	40.0	60.0	85.0	125.0	165.0	210.0
(1,016 × 610)		(45–75)	(18.1)	(36.2)	(54.3)	(77.0)	(113.1)	(149.5)	(190.0)
54 × 24	41	125–150	24.0	48.0	71.0	95.0	144.0	192.0	240.0
(1,374 × 610)		(93–112)	(21.7)	(43.5)	(64.3)	(86.0)	(130.0)	(173.8)	(217.5)

* Courtesy Iowa Manufacturing Company.

[†] The first number indicates the diameters of the rolls, and the second indicates the widths of the rolls.

Rod and ball mills These mills are used to produce fine aggregate, such as sand, from stone that has been crushed to suitable sizes by other crushing equipment. It is not uncommon for specifications for concrete to require the use of a homogeneous aggregate, regardless of size. If crushed stone is used for the coarse aggregate, sand manufactured from the same stone will satisfy the specifications.

A rod mill is a circular steel shell, lined on the inside with a hard mineral wearing surface, equipped with a suitable support or trunnion arrangement at each end, with a driving gear at one end. It is operated with its axis in a horizontal position. It is charged with steel rods, whose lengths are slightly less than the length of the mill. Crushed stone, which is fed through the trunnion at

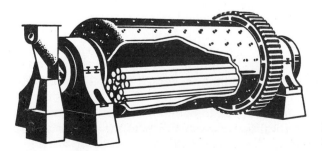

Figure 20-13 Section through a rod mill.

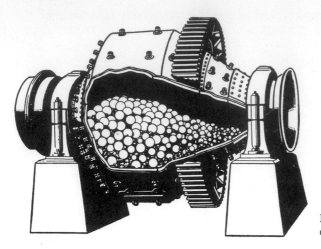

Figure 20-14   Section through a conical ball mill.

one end of the mill, flows to the discharge at the other end. As the mill rotates slowly, the stone is constantly subjected to the impact of the tumbling rods, which produce the desired grinding. A mill may be operated wet or dry, with or without water added. The size of a rod mill is specified by the diameter and the length of the shell, such as 8 by 12 ft, respectively. Figure 20-13 shows a section through a rod mill.

A ball mill, which uses steel balls instead of rods to supply the impact necessary to grind the stone, will produce fines with smaller grain sizes than those produced by a rod mill. Figure 20-14 shows a section through a ball mill.

Sizes of stone produced by jaw and roll crushers While the setting of the discharge opening of a crusher will determine the maximum-size stone produced, the aggregate sizes will range from slightly greater than the crusher setting to fine dust. Experience gained in the crushing industry indicates that for any given setting for a jaw or roll crusher approximately 15 percent of the total amount of stone passing through the crusher will be larger than the setting. If the openings of a screen which receives the output from such a crusher are the same size as the crusher setting, 15 percent of the output will not pass through the screen. Figure 20-15 gives representative values for the percent of crushed stone passing through or retained on screens having various sizes of openings for different crusher settings. The information in this figure will apply to jaw and roll crushers only.

In operating a crusher, it generally is desirable to know how the product varies in sizes from the maximum to the minimum sizes. The chart in Fig. 20-15 gives the percent of material passing or retained on screens having the size openings indicated. The chart can be applied to both jaw- and roll-type crushers. To read the chart, select the vertical line corresponding to the crusher setting. Then go down this line to the number which indicates the size of the screen

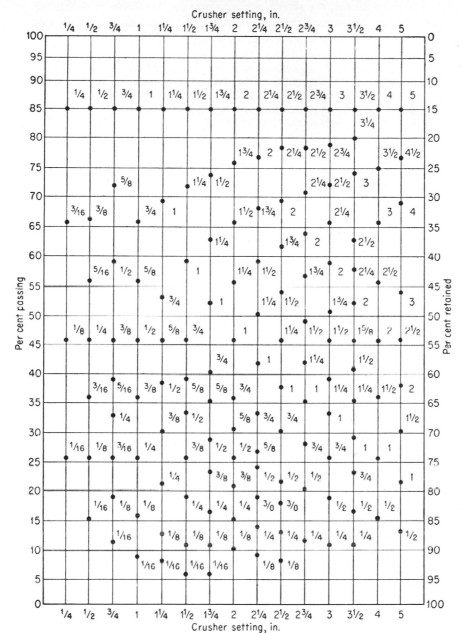

Figure 20-15 Analysis of the size of aggregate produced by jaw and roll crushers. (*Universal Engineering Company.*)

opening. From the size of the screen opening proceed horizontally to the left to determine the percent of material passing through the screen or to the right to determine the percent of material retained on the screen.

Example A jaw crusher, with a closed setting of 3 in., produces 50 tph of crushed stone. Determine the amount of stone produced in tons per hour within the following size ranges: in excess of 2 in.; between 2 and 1 in.; between 1 and $\frac{1}{4}$ in.; less than $\frac{1}{4}$ in.

From Fig. 20-15 the amount retained on a 2-in. screen is 42 percent of 50 = 21 tph. The amount in each of the size ranges is determined as follows:

Size range, in.	% passing screens	% in size range	Total output of crusher, tons per hr	Amount produced in size range, tons per hr
Over 2	100–58	42	50	21.0
2–1	58–33	25	50	12.5
1–$\frac{1}{4}$	33–11	22	50	11.0
$\frac{1}{4}$–0	11–0	11	50	5.5
Total		100		50.0

LOG WASHERS

When natural deposits of aggregate, such as sand and gravel, or individual pieces of crushed stone contain deleterious material as a part of the matrix or as deposits on the surface of the aggregate, it will be necessary to remove these materials before using the aggregate. One method of removing the material is to pass the aggregate through a machine called a log washer, which is illustrated in Fig. 20-16. This unit consists of a steel tank with two electric-motor-driven shafts, to which numerous replaceable paddles are attached. When the washer is placed in operation, the end of the tank on which the motor is mounted is raised above the opposite end. The aggregate to be processed is fed into the unit at the lower end, while a constant supply of water flows into the upper end. As the shafts are rotated in opposite directions, the paddles move the aggregate toward the upper end of the tank, while producing a continuing scrubbing action between the particles. The stream of water will remove the undesirable material and discharge it from the tank at the lower end, while the processed aggregate will be discharged at the upper end.

When a contractor submitted samples of a local aggregate which he proposed to use in producing concrete for an airport runway in New Mexico, he was advised that the particles were coated with a deposit that made the aggregate unfit for use. After the aggregate was processed with a log washer, it was found to be entirely acceptable.

Figure 20-16 Log washer for scrubbing coarse aggregate. *(Kolberg Manufacturing Corporation.)*

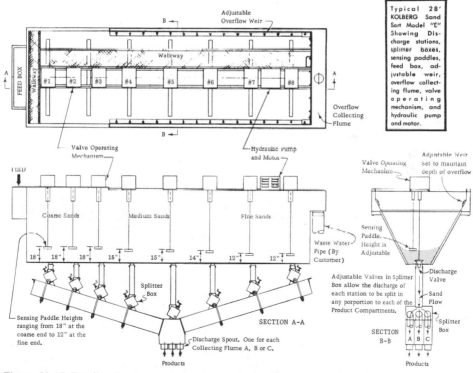

Typical 28' KOLBERG Sand Sort Model "E" Showing Discharge stations, splitter boxes, sensing paddles, feed box, adjustable weir, overflow collecting flume, valve operating mechanism, and hydraulic pump and motor.

Figure 20-17 Details of a sand preparation and classification machine. *(Kolberg Manufacturing Corporation.)*

Figure 20-18 Various sizes of sand produced by a preparation and classification machine. *(Kolberg Manufacturing Corporation.)*

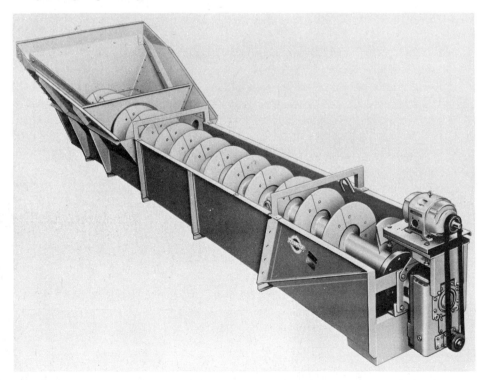

Figure 20-19 Screw classifier for producing specification sand. *(Telsmith Division, Barber-Greene Company.)*

SAND PREPARATION AND CLASSIFICATION MACHINES

When the specifications for sand and other fine aggregates require the materials to meet size gradations, it is frequently necessary to produce the gradations by mechanical equipment. Several types of equipment are available for this purpose. Figure 20-17 shows a plan and two sections of a machine that is used to classify sand into eight sizes. Sand and water are fed to the classifier as indicated at the left end of the unit. As the water flows to the outlet end of the tank, the sand particles settle to the bottom of the tank, the coarse ones first and the fine ones last. When the depth of a given size reaches a predetermined level, a sensing paddle will actuate a discharge valve at the bottom of the compartment to permit that material to flow into the splitter box, from which it can be removed and used.

Figure 20-18 illustrates the classification machine and four piles of sand from the machine, arranged by size of the grains.

Figure 20-19 illustrates a screw-type classifier which may be used to produce specification sand. When the machine is placed in operation, the discharge end, where the electric motor is mounted, is elevated above the opposite end. Sand and water are fed into the hopper. As the spiral screws rotate, the sand is moved up the tank to the discharge outlet under the motor. Undesirable material is flushed out of the tank by the overflowing water.

SELECTING CRUSHING EQUIPMENT

In selecting crushing and screening equipment it is essential that certain information be known prior to making the selection. The information needed should include, but will not necessarily be limited to, the following items:

1. The kind of stone to be crushed
2. The maximum size and perhaps the size ranges of the feed to the plant
3. The method of feeding the crushers
4. The required capacity of the plant
5. The percent of material falling within specified size ranges

The following example will illustrate a method which may be used to select crushing equipment:

Example Select a primary and a secondary crusher to produce 100 tph of crushed limestone. The maximum-size stones from the quarry will be 16 in. The quarry stone will be hauled by truck, dumped into a surge bin, and fed to the primary crusher by an apron feeder, which will maintain a reasonably uniform rate of feed. The aggregate will be used on a project whose specifications require the following size distributions:

Size screen opening, in.		
Passing	Retained on	Percent
$1\frac{1}{2}$		100
$1\frac{1}{2}$	$\frac{3}{4}$	42–48
$\frac{3}{4}$	$\frac{1}{4}$	30–36
$\frac{1}{4}$	0	20–26

Consider a jaw crusher for the primary and a roll crusher for the secondary crushing. The output of the jaw crusher will be screened to remove specification sizes before the oversize material is fed to the roll crusher.

Assume a setting of 3 in. for the jaw crusher. This will give a ratio of reduction of approximately 5 : 1, which is satisfactory. Table 20-2 indicates a size 24- by 36-in. crusher with a probable capacity of 114 tph. Figure 20-15 indicates that the product of the crusher will be distributed by sizes as follows:

Size range, in.	% passing screens	% in size range	Total output of crusher, tons per hr	Amount produced in size range, tons per hr
Over $1\frac{1}{2}$	100–46	54	100	54.0
$1\frac{1}{2}-\frac{3}{4}$	46–26	20	100	20.0
$\frac{3}{4}-\frac{1}{4}$	26–11	15	100	15.0
$\frac{1}{4}-0$	11–0	11	100	11.0
Total		100		100.0

As the roll crusher will receive the output from the jaw crusher, the rolls must be large enough to handle 3-in. stone. Assume a setting of $1\frac{1}{2}$ in. From formula (20-1) the minimum radius will be 17.7 in. Try a 40- by 20-in. crusher with a capacity of approximately 105 tph for a $1\frac{1}{2}$-in. setting.

For any given setting the crusher will produce about 15 percent stone having at least one dimension larger than the setting. Thus, for a given setting 15 percent of the stone that passes through the roll crusher will be returned for recrushing. The total amount of stone passing through the crusher, including the returned stone, is determined as follows. Let

Q = total amount of stone through the crusher

Then

$0.15Q$ = amount of returned stone

$0.85Q$ = amount of new stone

$$Q = \frac{\text{amount of new stone}}{0.85}$$

$$= \frac{54}{0.85} = 63.5 \text{ tph}$$

The 40- by 20-in. crusher will handle this amount of stone easily. The distribution of the output of this crusher by size range will be as follows:

Size range, in.	% passing screens	% in size range	Total amount through crusher, tph	Amount produced in size range, tph
$1\frac{1}{2}-\frac{3}{4}$	85–46	39	63.5	24.8
$\frac{3}{4}-\frac{1}{4}$	46–18	28	63.5	17.8
$\frac{1}{4}-0$	18–0	18	63.5	11.4
Total		85		54.0

Now combine the output of each crusher by specified sizes.

Size range, in.	From jaw crusher, tph	From roll crusher, tph	Total amount, tph	% in size range
$1\frac{1}{2}-\frac{3}{4}$	20.0	24.8	44.8	44.8
$\frac{3}{4}-\frac{1}{4}$	15.0	17.8	32.8	32.8
$\frac{1}{4}-0$	11.0	11.4	22.4	22.4
Total	46.0	54.0	100.0	100.0

SCALPING CRUSHED STONE

The term scalping, as used in this chapter, refers to a screening operation which is performed to remove from the main mass of stone to be processed that stone which is too large for the crusher opening or is small enough to be used without further crushing. Scalping may be performed ahead of a primary crusher, and it represents good crushing practice to scalp all crushed stone following each successive stage of reduction.

Scalping ahead of a primary crusher serves two purposes. The use of a grizzly, which consists of a number of widely spaced parallel bars, will prevent oversize stones from entering the crusher and blocking the opening. If the product of the quarry contains such stones, it is desirable to remove them ahead of the crusher.

The product of the quarry may contain dirt, mud, or other debris which is not acceptable in the finished product and therefore must be removed from the stone. Scalping should accomplish this removal. Also, the product of the quarry may contain an appreciable amount of stone which was reduced by the blasting operation to specification sizes. In this event it may be good economy to remove

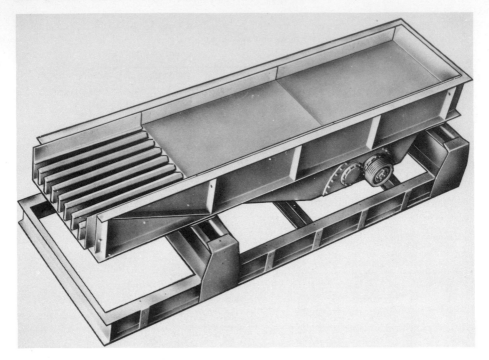

Figure 20-20 Vibrating grizzly feeder. *(Iowa Manufacturing Company.)*

such stone ahead of the primary crusher, thereby reducing the total load on the crusher and increasing the overall capacity of the plant. Figure 20-20 illustrates a commercial bar grizzly.

It usually is good practice and economical to install a scalper after each stage of reduction to remove specification sizes. This stone may be transported to grading screens, where it can be sized and placed in appropriate storage. Any stone removed ahead of a crusher will reduce the total load on the crusher, which will permit the use of a smaller crusher or an increase in the output of the plant.

FEEDERS

The capacity of a crusher will be increased if the stone is fed to it at a uniform rate. Surge feeding tends to overload a crusher, and then the surge is followed by an insufficient supply of stone. This type of feeding, which reduces the capacity of a crusher, may be eliminated by using a mechanical feeder ahead of a crusher. The installation of such a feeder may increase the capacity of a jaw crusher as much as 15 percent. An apron-type feeder, as illustrated in Fig. 20-21, is suitable for use ahead of a primary crusher.

Figure 20-21 Apron-type feeder. *(Universal Engineering Corp.)*

SURGE PILES

A stationary stone-crushing plant may include several types and sizes of crushers, each probably followed with a set of screens and a belt conveyor to transport the stone to the next crushing operation or to storage. A plant may be designed to provide temporary storage for stone between the successive stages of crushing. This plan has the advantage of eliminating or reducing the surge effect that frequently exists when the crushing, screening, and handling operations are conducted on a straight-line basis. The stone in temporary storage, which is referred to as a surge pile, ahead of a crusher may be used to keep at least a portion of a plant in operation. Within reasonable limits the use of a surge pile ahead of a crusher permits the crusher to be fed uniformly at the most satisfactory rate, regardless of variations in the output of other equipment ahead of the crusher. The use of surge piles has enabled some plants to increase the production by as much as 10 to 20 percent.

Among the arguments against the use of surge piles are the following:

1. They require additional area for storage.
2. They require the construction of storage bins or reclaiming tunnels.
3. They increase the amount of handling of stone.

The decision to use or not use surge piles should be based on the advantages and disadvantages for each plant.

SCREENING AGGREGATE

Screening of crushed stone is necessary in order that the aggregate may be separated by size ranges. Most specifications covering the use of aggregate stipulate that the different sizes shall be combined to produce a blend having a given size distribution. Persons who are responsible for preparing the specifications for the use of aggregate realize that crushing and screening cannot be done with complete precision, and, accordingly, they allow some tolerance in the size distribution. The extent of tolerance may be indicated by a statement such as that the quantity of aggregate passing a 1-in. screen and retained on a $\frac{1}{4}$-in. screen shall be not less than 30 or more than 40 percent of the total quantity of aggregate.

Revolving screens Revolving screens have several advantages over other types of screens, especially when they are used to wash and screen sand and gravel. The operating action is slow and simple, and the maintenance and repair costs are low. If the aggregate to be washed contains silt and clay, a scrubber can be installed near the entrance end of a screen in order that the material may be agitated in water. At the same time streams of water may be sprayed on the aggregate as it moves through the screen. Figure 20-22 shows a revolving screen with a scrubber in operation. The aggregate, which is separated by sizes, is stored temporarily in the bins below the screen.

Figure 20-22 Revolving screen with scrubber in operation.

Vibrating screens The vibrating screen is the most widely used screen for aggregate production. Figures 20-23 and 20-24 show multiple-deck screens units of this type. The steel frame may be designed to permit the installation of one or more screens, one above the other. Each screen is referred to as a deck. The vibration is obtained by means of an eccentric shaft, a counterweighted shaft, or electromagnets attached to the frame or to the screens.

A unit is installed with a slight slope from the receiving to the discharge end, which, combined with the vibrations, causes the aggregate to flow over the surface of the screen. Most of the particles that are smaller than the openings in a screen will drop through the screen, while the oversize particles will flow off the screen at the discharge end. For a multiple-deck unit the sizes of the openings will be progressively smaller for each lower deck.

A screen will not pass all material whose sizes are equal to or less than the dimensions of the openings in the screen. Some of this material may be retained on and carried over the discharge end of a screen. The efficiency of a screen may be defined as the ratio of the amount of material passing through a screen divided by the total amount that is small enough to pass through, with the ratio expressed as a percent. The highest efficiency is obtained with a single-deck screen, usually amounting to 90 to 95 percent. As additional decks are installed, the efficiencies of these decks will decrease, being about 85 percent for the second deck and 75 percent for the third deck.

Figure 20-23 Double-deck vibrating screen. *(Portec, Inc., Pioneer Division.)*

Figure 20-24 Triple-deck screen with spray bars for washing aggregate. *(Iowa Manufacturing Company.)*

The capacity of a screen is the number of tons of material that 1 sq ft will pass per hour. The capacity will vary with the size of the openings, kind of material screened, moisture content, and other factors. Because of the factors that affect the capacity of a screen it will seldom if ever be possible to calculate in advance the exact capacity of a screen. If a given number of tons of material must be passed per hour, it is good practice to select a screen whose total calculated capacity is 10 to 25 percent greater than the quantity to be screened.

The chart in Fig. 20-25 gives capacities for dry screening which may be used as a guide in selecting the correct size screen for a given flow of material. The capacities given in the chart should be modified by the application of appropriate correction factors. Representative values of these factors are given hereafter.

Efficiency factors If a low screening efficiency is permissible, the capacity of a screen may be higher than the values given in Fig. 20-25. Table 20-7 gives factors by which the chart values of capacities may be multiplied to obtain corrected capacities for given efficiencies.

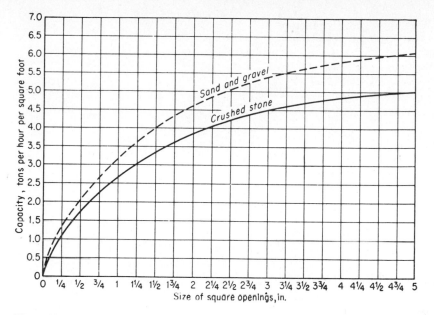

Figure 20-25 Screen-capacity chart.

Table 20-7 Efficiency factors

Permissible screen efficiency, %	Efficiency factor
95	1.00
90	1.25
85	1.50
80	1.75
75	2.00

Table 20-8 Deck factors

For deck no.	Deck factor
1	1.00
2	0.90
3	0.75
4	0.60

Table 20-9 Aggregate-size factors

% of aggregate less than $\frac{1}{2}$ the size of screen opening	Aggregate-size factor
10	0.55
20	0.70
30	0.80
40	1.00
50	1.20
60	1.40
70	1.80
80	2.20
90	3.00

Deck factors This is a factor whose value will vary with the particular deck position for multiple-deck screens. The values are given in Table 20-8.

Aggregate-size factors The capacities of screens given in Fig. 20-25 are based on screening dry material which contains particle sizes such as would be found in the output of a representative crusher. If the material to be screened contains a surplus of small sizes, the capacity of the screen will be increased, whereas if the material contains a surplus of large sizes, the capacity of the screen will be reduced. Table 20-9 gives representative factors which may be applied to the capacity of a screen to correct for the effect of fine or coarse particles.

Determining the size screen required Figure 20-25 gives the theoretical capacity of a screen in tons per hour per square foot based on material weighing 100 lb per cu ft when crushed. The corrected capacity of a screen is given by the formula

$$Q = ACEDG \tag{20-4}$$

where Q = capacity of screen, tph
A = area of screen, sq ft
C = theoretical capacity of screen, tph per sq ft
E = efficiency factor
D = deck factor
G = aggregate-size factor

The minimum area of a screen to provide a given capacity is determined from the formula

$$A = \frac{Q}{CEDG} \tag{20-5}$$

Example Determine the minimum-size single-deck screen, having $1\frac{1}{2}$-in.-square openings, for screening 120 tph of dry crushed stone, weighing 100 lb per cu ft when crushed. A screening efficiency of 90 percent is satisfactory. An analysis of the aggregate indicates that approximately 30 percent of it will be less than $\frac{3}{4}$ in. in size. The values of the factors to be used in formula (20-5) are

$Q = 120$ tph

$C = 3.32$ tph per sq ft   (Fig. 20-25)

$E = 1.25$ (Table 20-7)

$D = 1.0$ (Table 20-8)

$G = 0.8$ (Table 20-9)

Substituting these values in formula (20-5), we get

$$A = \frac{120}{3.32 \times 1.25 \times 1.0 \times 0.8} = 36.1 \text{ sq ft}$$

In view of the possibility of variations in the factors used, and to provide a margin of safety, it is recommended that a 4- by 10-ft screen be selected.

Portable crushing and screening plants Many types and sizes of portable crushing and screening plants are used in the construction industry. When there is a satisfactory deposit of stone near a project that requires stone aggregate, it frequently will be more economical to set up a portable plant and produce the crushed stone instead of purchasing it from a commercial source.

Typical portable crushing and screening plants are illustrated in Figs. 20-26 and 20-27. The stone from the quarry is fed to the plant by a belt conveyor at the right. This particular machine is designed to permit the quarry product to

Figure 20-26 Portable aggregate plant in operation. *(Iowa Manufacturing Company.)*

Figure 20-27 Cutaway of portable rock-crushing plant. *(Portec, Inc., Pioneer Division.)*

pass over a bottom-deck screen, which removes the material smaller than the screen, thereby reducing the load on the primary crusher. The oversize stone from this screen is fed to a jaw crusher, thence to a belt conveyor, which returns it to a top-deck screen, where the specification sizes are removed. The oversize stone is fed to a roll crusher. Portable plants commonly use a jaw crusher for primary crushing and a roll crusher for secondary crushing. Changes in the specification sizes may be met, over a reasonably wide range, by adjusting the crusher settings and changing the sizes of the screens.

FLOW DIAGRAMS OF AGGREGATE-PROCESSING PLANTS

Figures 20-28 and 20-29 illustrate flow diagrams for two portable aggregate-processing plants. By passing the stone from the quarry over a screen before it goes to the primary crusher, any stone within the specification sizes will be removed prior to crushing. This arrangement should increase the output of the plant.

Representative sizes of crushers and other equipment for this plant are as follows:

Jaw crusher, 10×36 in.
Roll crusher, 40×22 in.
Vibrator screen, 4×12 ft, $3\frac{1}{2}$ decks
Feeder, 4-ft hopper
Feeder conveyor, 30 in. wide, 50 ft long
Return conveyor, 24 in. wide

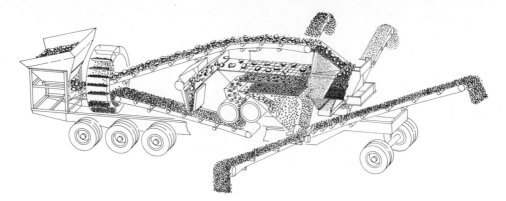

Figure 20-28 Flow diagram of a four-product portable aggregate plant. *(Iowa Manufacturing Company.)*

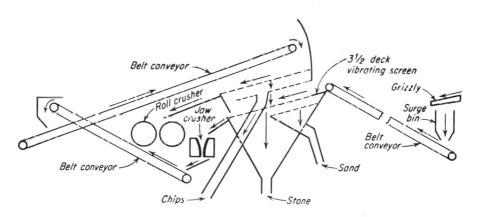

Figure 20-29 Flow diagram of a portable aggregate-processing plant.

Figure 20-30 illustrates the flow diagram of the aggregate processing plant for the Philpott Dam. This plant was located near the quarry, and trucks were used to haul the finished aggregate to the concrete mixing plant at the dam.

Example When constructing the Perris Dam in California, the contractor opened a rock quarry to drill, blast, crush, and deliver 50,000 tons per week of aggregate to the project [1].

He drilled 4-in. diameter holes to depths of 40 ft, loaded them with Dupont Pourvex slurry, then blasted 300 to 400 holes at a time to produce 40,000 to 50,000 tons of rock. All rock in excess of 48 in. in size was removed for riprap before sending the smaller-size material to a crusher plant.

Because the project required more than 2,500,000 cu yd of crushed rock, the crushing plant was designed to provide the quantities and sizes of material needed for the job. As illustrated in Fig. 20-31, the plant produced aggregate in three size ranges.

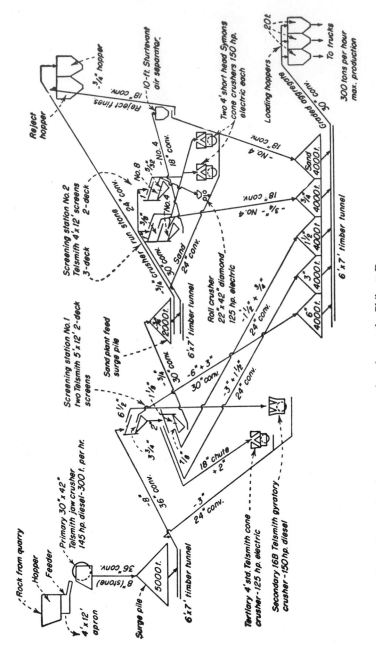

Figure 20-30 Flow diagram for the aggregate-processing plant at the Philpott Dam.

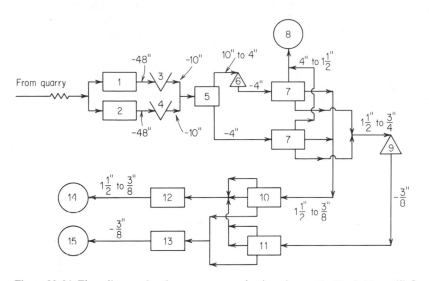

Figure 20-31 Flow diagram for the aggregate production plant at the Perris Dam: (1) 5 × 20′ grizzly feeder; (2) 5 × 16′ vibrating feeder; (3) 48 × 48″ jaw crusher; (4) 42 × 48″ jaw crusher; (5) 6 × 16′ scalping screen; (6) 7′ standard cone crusher; (7) 6 × 16′ doubledeck screens; (8) stock pile for 4 to $1\frac{1}{2}$″ aggregate; (9) $5\frac{1}{2}$′ shorthead cone crusher; (10) 8 × 20′ doubledeck screen; (11) 8 × 20′ doubledeck screen; (12) double screw classifier; (13) double screw classifier; (14) stock pile for $1\frac{1}{2}$ to 3/8″ aggregate; (15) stock pile for 3/8″ minus aggregate.

Figure 20-32 Belt-conveyor system for handling aggregate at production plant. *(Kolberg Manufacturing Corporation.)*

HANDLING CRUSHED-STONE AGGREGATE

After stone is crushed and screened to provide the desired size ranges, it is necessary to handle it carefully or the large and small particles may be separated, thereby destroying the blend in sizes, which frequently is essential to a satisfactory aggregate. If aggregate is permitted to flow freely off the end of a belt conveyor, especially at some height above the storage bin, the material will be segregated by sizes, as illustrated in Fig. 20-33. A strong cross wind tends to separate the smaller sizes from the larger sizes. Specifications covering the production of aggregate frequently stipulate that the aggregate transported by a belt conveyor shall not be permitted to fall freely from the discharge end of a belt. The end of the belt should be kept as low as possible, and the aggregate should be discharged through a rock ladder, containing baffles, to prevent segregation.

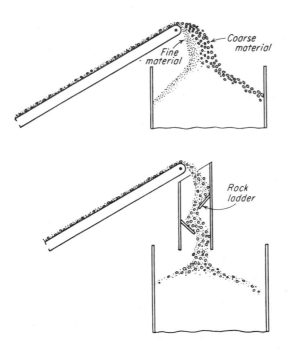

Figure 20-33 Method of preventing the segregation of aggregate discharged from a conveyor belt.

Figure 20-34 shows a pile of badly segregated aggregate, while Fig. 20-35 shows a rock ladder used to reduce segregation.

The references appearing at the end of this chapter list other publications containing information related to the production of aggregate.

Figure 20-34 Pile of aggregate showing segregation.

Figure 20-35 A rock ladder used to reduce the segregation of aggregate.

PROBLEMS

20-1 A jaw crusher, with a closed setting of $3\frac{1}{2}$ in., produces 250 tph of crushed stone. Determine the number of tons per hour produced in each of the following size ranges: in excess of 3 in.; between 3 in. and $1\frac{1}{2}$ in.; between $1\frac{1}{2}$ in. and $\frac{3}{4}$ in.; less than $\frac{3}{4}$ in.

20-2 A roll crusher, set at $1\frac{1}{2}$ in., produces 90 tph of crushed stone. Determine the number of tons per hour produced in each of the following size ranges: in excess of 1 in.; between 1 in. and $\frac{1}{2}$ in.; between $\frac{1}{2}$ in. and $\frac{1}{4}$ in.; and less than $\frac{1}{4}$ in.

20-3 Select a jaw crusher for primary crushing and a roll crusher for secondary crushing to produce 250 tph of limestone rock. The maximum size stone from the quarry will be 12 in. The stone is to be crushed to the following specifications:

Size screen opening, in.		
Passing	Retained on	Percent
$2\frac{1}{2}$		100
$2\frac{1}{2}$	$1\frac{1}{4}$	30–42
$1\frac{1}{4}$	$\frac{3}{4}$	20–30
$\frac{3}{4}$	$\frac{1}{4}$	20–30
$\frac{1}{4}$	0	15–25

Specify the size and setting for each crusher selected.

20-4 A jaw crusher and a roll crusher are used in an attempt to crush 160 tph of stone to the following specifications:

Size screen opening, in.		
Passing	Retained on	Percent
2		100
2	1	40–46
1	$\frac{1}{4}$	34–40
$\frac{1}{4}$	0	20–25

Select crushers to produce this aggregate. Is it possible to produce aggregate to meet these specifications with the indicated crushers without a surplus in any of the size ranges? If there is an accumulation of crushed stone in a specified size range, and a deficiency in another size range, is there any procedure by which the size ranges might be brought into better balance using only the two specified crushers?

20-5 A 30- by 42-in. jaw crusher is set to operate with a 3-in. opening. The output from the crusher is discharged onto a screen with $1\frac{1}{2}$-in. openings, whose efficiency is 90 percent. The aggregate that does not pass through the screen goes to a 40- by 20-in. roll crusher, set at $1\frac{1}{4}$ in. The output from the roll crusher is fed back over the screen.

Determine the maximum output of the plant in tons per hour.

Determine the output of the plant in tons per hour in each of the two sizes: $1\frac{1}{2}$ to $\frac{3}{4}$ in.; less than $\frac{3}{4}$ in.

20-6 A portable crushing plant is equipped with the following units:

1 jaw crusher, size 15 by 30 in.
1 roll crusher, size 30 by 22 in.
1 set of horizontal vibrating screens, 2 decks, with $1\frac{1}{2}$- and $\frac{1}{2}$-in. openings

The specifications require that 100 percent of the aggregate shall pass a $1\frac{1}{2}$ in. screen and 50 percent shall pass a $\frac{1}{2}$-in. screen.

Assume that 15 percent of the stone from the quarry will be smaller than $1\frac{1}{2}$ in. and that this aggregate will be removed by passing the quarry product over the screen before sending it to the jaw crusher. The aggregate will weigh 120 lb per cu ft.

Determine the maximum output of the plant, including the aggregate removed by the screens prior to crushing, expressed in tons per hour.

20-7 The output from a 36- by 42-in. jaw crusher, with a closed setting of 3 in., is passed over a single horizontal vibrating screen with $1\frac{1}{2}$ in. openings. If the permissible screen efficiency is 90 percent, use the information in this book to determine the minimum-size screen, expressed in square feet, required to handle the output of the crusher.

20-8 The output from a 36- by 42-in. jaw crusher, with a closed setting of 3 in., is to be screened into the three following sizes: $2\frac{1}{4}$ to $1\frac{1}{2}$ in.; $1\frac{1}{2}$ to $\frac{3}{4}$ in.; less than $\frac{3}{4}$ in. A three-deck horizontal vibrating screen will be used to separate the three sizes. The stone weighs 110 lb per cu ft. If the permissible screen efficiency is 90 percent, determine the minimum size screen for each deck, expressed in square feet, required to handle the output of the crusher.

REFERENCES

1. Contractor Planned Crushing Plant Keeps Dam on Schedule, *Roads & Streets*, vol. 115, pp. 46–48, August 1972.
2. Higgins, Lindley R.: Aggregates Today; Breakthrough in Methodology, Advances in Automation and Movement, *Construction Methods & Equipment*, vol. 54, pp. 72–75, January 1972.
3. Newman, Donald: Mathematical Method for Blending Aggregates, *Journal of the Construction Division, Proceedings ASCE*, vol. 90, pp. 1–13, September 1964.
4. Hancher, Donn E., and John A. Havers: "Mathematical Model of Aggregate Plant Production," American Society of Civil Engineers, 345 East 47th Street, New York, New York 10017, no date.
5. "Telsmith Mineral Processing Handbook," 1976, Telsmith Division, Barber-Greene Company, 532 East Capitol Drive, Milwaukee, Wisconsin 53212.
6. "Cedar Rapids Reference Book," 4th Pocket Edition, 1968, Iowa Manufacturing Company, 916 16th Street NE, Cedar Rapids, Iowa 52402.
7. "Facts and Figures Booklet," 16th ed., 1969, Portec Inc., Pioneer Division, 3200 Como Avenue SE, Minneapolis, Minnesota 55414.
8. Aggregate Reference Guide, 1976, Kolberg Manufacturing Corporation, 20 West 21st Street, Yankton, South Dakota 57078.
9. Fiat-Allis Construction Machinery, Inc., Box 1213, Milwaukee, Wisconsin 53201.
10. Grundler Crusher & Pulverizer Company, 2915 North Market Street, St. Louis, Missouri 63106.
11. Iowa Manufacturing Company, 916 16th Street NE, Cedar Rapids, Iowa 52402.
12. Kolberg Manufacturing Corporation, 20 West 21st Street, Yankton, South Dakota 57078.
13. Nordberg Division, Rex Chainbelt, Inc., 4710 West Greenfield Avenue, Milwaukee, Wisconsin 53201.
14. Portec, Inc., Pioneer Division, 3200 Como Avenue SE, Minneapolis, Minnesota 55414.
15. Telsmith Division, Barber-Greene Company, 532 East Capitol Drive, Milwaukee, Wisconsin 53212.
16. Universal Engineering Corporation, Subsidiary of Pettibone Corporation, 625 C Avenue NW, Cedar Rapids, Iowa.

TWENTY ONE

FORMS FOR CONCRETE STRUCTURES

INTRODUCTION

The cost of concrete for most structures includes the cost of the concrete in place plus the cost of the forms that are required to support the concrete while it gains sufficient strength and rigidity to support itself. The cost of the forms frequently will exceed the cost of the concrete alone. This is demonstrated by examples where ready-mixed concrete may be purchased delivered to a project at prices varying from $20.00 to $30.00 per cu yd, but the contract price for a finished structure may be as high as $50.00 to $80.00 per cu yd or more, excluding the cost of the reinforcing steel. Because of the large portion that forms contribute to the ultimate cost of concrete, it seems evident that efforts to effect economies in the costs of concrete structures should be devoted primarily to reducing the costs of forms.

The subject of forms for concrete structures is much too voluminous to develop sufficiently and completely in this book. For this reason, only limited fundamentals will be presented, information that may be helpful to persons who need this basic information. For a more comprehensive treatment of the subject it is recommended that publications which cover the subject more fully be consulted [1, 2].

FORM REQUIREMENTS

As concrete is in a plastic state when it is placed, it is necessary to use forms to confine and support it until it is rigid and self-supporting. Because of its initial plasticity, concrete can be cast in any desired shape, provided forms can be built to conform with that shape. However, complicated forms are expensive.

644

Forms for concrete structures should be:

1. Strong enough to resist the pressure or the weight of the fresh concrete plus any superimposed loads
2. Rigid enough to retain the shape without undue deformation
3. Economical in terms of the total cost of the forms, concrete, and surface finishing the concrete, when it is required

Forms should be designed by a person who has a knowledge of forces and the strength of materials. Guessing can result in forms which are underdesigned or overdesigned. The former is dangerous, because form failures are expensive, while the latter is unnecessarily expensive. A correct design should eliminate both of these possibilities.

Sometimes the specifications for a concrete structure impose rigid limitations on the variations in shape. Under such conditions form rigidity will be more important than strength.

When a concrete surface must be free from form marks and other blemishes, it may be economical to use expensive form materials in contact with the concrete surfaces in order to eliminate or reduce the cost of finishing the surfaces after the forms are removed. However, if the concrete surface will not be exposed or if surface defects are not objectionable, the form linings should be selected in the interest of economy. This may be illustrated by a concrete retaining wall which requires a smooth finish on the exposed surface. The sheathing for the exposed surface might be new plywood, while the sheathing for the back surface can be any material that is strong enough to resist the pressure of the concrete.

THE COST OF FORMS

The chief items which affect the cost of forms are materials and labor in making, erecting, and removing the forms.

Materials include lumber, steel, nails, bolts, and form connectors, such as wall ties, etc. If the shape of a concrete member is such that little or no salvage value can be realized from the materials after a single use, the cost of materials will be high, whereas if the materials can be used a great many times, the cost per use may be relatively low. A concrete wall may require 3 fbm of form lumber, costing $0.20 per fbm, for each square foot of exposed surface. If the lumber can be used only once, the cost will be $0.60 per square foot, whereas if it can be used 10 times, the cost will be $0.06 per square foot. Although the initial cost of steel forms usually will be considerably higher than for wood forms, the large number of uses under favorable conditions may reduce the cost per use to less than for wood.

The cost of labor includes the cost of making, erecting, and removing the forms. If forms can be fabricated into shapes that can be reused several times by simply reassembling the component parts, the labor cost of fabricating will occur only once. For successive uses the labor cost will involve erection and removal only.

> **Example** Compare the cost of lumber and labor for 100 sq ft of forms for concrete columns when the forms are used once and when they are used several times with no changes in dimensions. The forms will be made of lumber and assembled with adjustable steel clamps. If dressed and matched sheathing is used, it will require 1.8 fbm of lumber per sq ft of exposed surface.
>
> For a single use, assuming no salvage value for the lumber, the cost will be

Lumber, 100 sq ft × 1.8 fbm per sq ft = 180 fbm @ $0.20	= $ 36.00
Carpenter making, 100 sq ft × 3.0 hr per 100 sq ft = 3 hr @ $7.50	= 22.50
Helper making, 100 sq ft × 1.0 hr per 100 sq ft = 1 hr @ $5.00	= 5.00
Carpenter erecting, 100 sq ft × 6.0 hr per 100 sq ft = 6 hr @ $7.50	= 45.00
Helper erecting and removing, 100 sq ft × 5 hr per 100 sq ft = 5 hr @ $5.00	= 25.00
Total cost for first use	= $133.50
Cost per sq ft, $133.50 ÷ 100	= 1.34

For each additional use without remaking the cost will be	
Carpenter erecting, 6 hr @ $7.50	= $ 45.00
Helper erecting and removing, 5 hr @ $5.00	= 25.00
Total cost	= $ 70.00
Cost per sq ft, $70.00 ÷ 100	= 0.70

> *Note*: This analysis omits the cost of column clamps, which should be the same for each use of the forms. Also, the cost of nails should be less for each reuse of the forms.

The previous example illustrates the effect which the multiple use of forms has on the cost of forms per use. The reduction frequently is sufficient to justify designing a structure with members the same size even though loading conditions might permit the use of smaller members for a portion of the structure.

DESIGNING A PROJECT FOR FORM ECONOMY

Opportunities for form economy originate with the design of a structure. In order to permit the greatest economy consistent with the type of structure, the designer must have a reasonable knowledge of the cost of forms. Certain shape and finish requirements may be desirable, and in many instances they are justified, even though they increase the cost of a structure. At least the designer should consider their value to determine whether the increased cost is justified.

Among the steps which a designer can take to effect economy in concrete forms are the following:

1. Reduce the number of irregular shapes to a minimum.
2. Duplicate the sizes and shapes of structural members when practical to permit reuses of forms.
3. Design a structure to permit the use of cost-saving commercial forms, such as metal pans or corrugated steel sheets for decking for floor slabs.

4. Have a constructor review the preliminary plans to suggest methods of reducing the cost of forms without sacrificing the quality of the structure.
5. Consider the use of tilt-up, slip-form, or other cost-saving construction methods.
6. Allow the use of construction joints to permit the reuse of forms.
7. Specify a quality of workmanship no finer than is needed for the project.
8. Do not specify unreasonable limitations on the dimensions of structural members.
9. Design structural members to permit the use of commercial sizes of lumber without ripping, when practical.
10. Permit the constructor to use his own methods of building the forms by holding him responsible for adequacy only.
11. Permit the constructor to remove and reuse forms as soon as it is safe to do so.

THE CONSTRUCTOR AND FORM ECONOMY

Among the steps which a constructor can take to reduce the cost of forms for concrete structures are the following:

1. Design the forms to provide adequate but not excessive strength and rigidity.
2. Fabricate the forms into modular sizes to permit more reuses without refabricating, when practical.
3. Prepare working drawings for all except the simplest forms prior to fabricating the forms.
4. Prefabricate form sections on the ground, using power equipment, in order to reduce labor costs and unnecessary delays on the job. Labor is much more efficient when working on the ground than when working on a scaffold.
5. When possible adopt assembly-line methods in fabricating forms to increase the efficiency of the workers.
6. Use the most economical form material, considering initial cost and reuses.
7. Use labor-saving commercial connectors, such as wall ties, when their use is permitted.
8. Use commercial forms when they are cheaper than conventional forms.
9. Use no more nails than are needed to join the forms together safely.
10. When possible use scaffold or double-headed nails to facilitate their removal and to reduce the damage to lumber.
11. Remove forms as soon as it is permissible.
12. Clean and oil forms after each use.
13. If they are permissible, install construction joints to reduce the total quantity of form material required and to permit the carpenters to work more continuously.

MATERIALS FOR FORMS

The materials used for forms may be dictated by economy, necessity, or a combination of several factors. The materials most commonly used include, but are not limited to, lumber, plywood, plastics, fiber boards, steel, and aluminum, either separately or in combination. The material selected should be based on the requirements of the project and economy.

THE SIZE OF FORM SECTIONS

If forms are prefabricated into panels or sections, it is desirable to fabricate sizes as large as the concrete members or the methods of handling will permit, as such use should reduce the time and labor costs in erecting and removing the forms.

If the forms are handled by men, the weight of a panel should be limited to approximately 75 lb per man. If they are handled by power equipment, the size will be limited by the lengths of lumber available, the dimensions of the concrete structure, or the capacity of the hoisting equipment.

Figure 21-1 illustrates the use of large prefabricated form panels in constructing a flood wall along the Ohio River at Portsmouth, Ohio. The forms for this 7,290-ft-long structure were handled by a gantry crane.

Figure 21-1 Prefabricated forms used to construct a flood wall.

Table 21-1 Allowable unit stresses for lumber used for formwork at not more than 19 percent moisture content*

Species and commercial grade	Size classification	Allowable unit stress, lb per sq in.				
		Extreme fiber in bending	Horizontal shear	Compression perperdicular to grain	Compression parallel to grain	Modulus of elasticity, lb per sq in.
Douglas fir-larch, No. 2	2" to 4" wide and	1,800	230	480	1,250	1,700,000
		(1,450)	(185)	(385)	(1,000)	1,700,000
	2" to 4" thick	1,300	230	480	1,450	1,500,000
		(1,050)	(185)	(385)	(1,150)	1,500,000
Construction, No. 2	6" and wider	1,550	230	480	1,300	1,700,000
		(1,250)	(185)	(385)	(1,050)	1,700,000
Eastern spruce, No. 2	2" to 4" wide and	1,300	175	320	875	1,200,000
		(1,050)	(140)	(255)	(700)	1,200,000
	2" to 4" thick	975	175	320	1,000	1,100,000
		(775)	(140)	(255)	(800)	1,100,000
Construction, No. 2	6" and wider	1,125	175	320	940	1,200,000
		(900)	(140)	(255)	(750)	1,200,000
Southern pine, No. 2	2" to 4" thick	1,550	220	430	1,050	1,400,000
		(1,250)	(175)	(345)	(850)	1,400,000
	and 6" wide	1,300	220	430	1,375	1,400,000
		(1,050)	(175)	(345)	(1,100)	1,400,000
Construction, No. 2	6" and wider	1,300	220	430	1,125	1,400,000
		(1,050)	(175)	(345)	(900)	1,400,000
Hem-fir, No. 2	2" to 4" thick	1,450	187	305	1,000	1,400,000
		(1,150)	(150)	(245)	(800)	1,400,000
	and 2" to 4" wide	1,030	187	305	1,150	1,200,000
		(825)	(150)	(245)	(925)	1,200,000
Construction, No. 2	6" and wider	1,250	187	305	1,050	1,400,000
		(1,000)	(150)	(245)	(850)	1,400,000

* From R. L. Peurifoy, "Formwork for Concrete Structures," 2d ed., McGraw-Hill Book Company, New York, 1976.

The figures in parentheses indicate the allowable unit stresses for permanent loading. The figures immediately above the parentheses indicate the allowable unit stresses in form lumber.

Table 21-2 Properties of lumber $S4S$*

Nominal size, in.	Actual size, in.	Net area, sq. in.	X-X axis		Y-Y axis	
			I, in.^{4}	S, in.^{3}	I, in.^{4}	S, in.^{3}
1×4	$\frac{3}{4} \times 3\frac{1}{2}$	2.62	2.68	1.53	0.12	0.33
1×6	$\frac{3}{4} \times 5\frac{1}{2}$	4.12	10.40	3.78	0.19	0.52
1×8	$\frac{3}{4} \times 7\frac{1}{4}$	5.44	23.82	6.57	0.25	0.68
1×10	$\frac{3}{4} \times 9\frac{1}{4}$	6.94	49.47	10.70	0.32	0.87
1×12	$\frac{3}{4} \times 11\frac{1}{4}$	8.44	88.99	15.82	0.40	1.05
2×4	$1\frac{1}{2} \times 3\frac{1}{2}$	5.25	5.36	3.06	0.98	1.31
2×6	$1\frac{1}{2} \times 5\frac{1}{2}$	8.25	20.80	7.56	1.55	2.06
2×8	$1\frac{1}{2} \times 7\frac{1}{4}$	10.87	47.63	13.14	2.04	2.72
2×10	$1\frac{1}{2} \times 9\frac{1}{4}$	13.87	98.93	21 39	2.60	3.47
2×12	$1\frac{1}{2} \times 11\frac{1}{4}$	16.87	290.77	31.64	3.16	4.22
3×4	$2\frac{1}{2} \times 3\frac{1}{2}$	8.75	8.93	5.10	4.56	3.65
3×6	$2\frac{1}{2} \times 5\frac{1}{2}$	13.75	34.66	12.60	7.16	5.73
3×8	$2\frac{1}{2} \times 7\frac{1}{4}$	18.12	79.39	21.90	9.44	7.55
3×10	$2\frac{1}{2} \times 9\frac{1}{4}$	23.12	164.89	35.65	12.04	9.63
3×12	$2\frac{1}{2} \times 11\frac{1}{4}$	28.12	296.63	52.73	14.65	11.72
4×4	$3\frac{1}{2} \times 3\frac{1}{2}$	12.25	12.50	7.15	12.50	7.15
4×6	$3\frac{1}{2} \times 5\frac{1}{2}$	19.25	48.53	17.65	19.65	11.23
4×8	$3\frac{1}{2} \times 7\frac{1}{4}$	25.37	115.15	30.66	25.90	14.80
4×10	$3\frac{1}{2} \times 9\frac{1}{4}$	32.37	230.84	49.91	33.05	18.88
4×12	$3\frac{1}{2} \times 11\frac{1}{4}$	39.37	415.28	73.83	40.19	22.97
6×6	$5\frac{1}{2} \times 5\frac{1}{2}$	30.25	76.25	27.73	76.25	27.73
6×8	$5\frac{1}{2} \times 7\frac{1}{2}$	41.25	193.36	51.56	103.98	37.81
6×10	$5\frac{1}{2} \times 9\frac{1}{2}$	52.25	392.96	82.73	131.71	47.90
6×12	$5\frac{1}{2} \times 11\frac{1}{2}$	63.25	697.07	121.23	159.44	57.98
8×8	$7\frac{1}{2} \times 7\frac{1}{2}$	56.25	263.67	70.31	263.67	70.31
8×10	$7\frac{1}{2} \times 9\frac{1}{2}$	71.25	536.86	112.81	333.98	89.06
8×12	$7\frac{1}{2} \times 11\frac{1}{2}$	86.25	950.55	165.31	404.30	107.81
10×10	$9\frac{1}{2} \times 9\frac{1}{2}$	90.25	678.75	142.90	678.75	142.90
10×12	$9\frac{1}{2} \times 11\frac{1}{2}$	109.25	1204.03	209.40	821.65	172.98
12×12	$11\frac{1}{2} \times 11\frac{1}{2}$	132.25	1457.50	253.48	1457.50	253.48

* From R. L. Peurifoy, "Formwork for Concrete Structures," 2d ed., McGraw-Hill Book Company, New York, 1976.

PROPERTIES OF LUMBER

Table 21-1 gives the properties of various kinds of lumber used for forms. The given properties are based on using lumber of a quality not lower than the specified grade. If a lower-grade lumber is used, the working stresses should be reduced to values which are safe for the particular grade.

The dimensions and dimensional properties of various sizes of lumber commonly used for forms are given in Table 21-2. The values are based on using rough or $S4S$ lumber.

PRESSURE PRODUCED BY CONCRETE

When concrete is placed in forms, it produces a pressure perpendicular to the surface of the forms which is proportional to the density and the depth of the concrete in a liquid or semiliquid state. As the concrete sets, it changes from a liquid to a solid, with a reduction in the pressure exerted on the forms. The time required for the initial set of the concrete varies with the temperature, with a longer time required for a lower temperature. Thus the maximum pressure produced on the forms varies directly with the rate at which the forms are filled and inversely with the temperature of the concrete.

The American Concrete Institute, which has devoted considerable time and study to form construction practices, recommends the following formulas for determining the maximum pressure produced by internally vibrated concrete on forms:

For walls:

$$P_m = 150 + \frac{9,000R}{T} \qquad \text{for } R \text{ less than 7 ft per hr} \qquad (21\text{-}1)$$

$$P_m = 150 + \frac{43,400}{T} + \frac{2,800R}{T} \qquad \text{for } R \text{ greater than 7 ft per hr} \qquad (21\text{-}2)$$

For columns:

$$P_m = 150 + \frac{9,000R}{T} \qquad (21\text{-}3)$$

where $P_m =$ maximum pressure, lb per sq ft

$R =$ rate of filling forms, ft per hr

$T =$ temperature of concrete, °F

The maximum pressure for formula (21-2) is limited to 2,000 lb per sq ft, and for formula (21-3) it is limited to 3,000 lb per sq ft.

Table 21-3 Relations among the rate of filling wall forms, maximum pressure, and temperature (ACI)

Rate of filling forms, ft per hr (m/h)	Maximum concrete pressure, lb per sq ft (kg/m²)						
	40°F (4.4°C)	50°F (10.0°C)	60°F (15.5°C)	70°F (21.1°C)	80°F (26.7°C)	90°F (32.2°C)	100°F (37.7°C)
1	375	330	300	279	262	250	240
(0.31)	(1,830)	(1,510)	(1,465)	(1,360)	(1,275)	(1,220)	(1,175)
2	600	510	450	409	375	350	330
(0.61)	(2,940)	(2,490)	(2,200)	(2,000)	(1,830)	(1,710)	(1,616)
3	825	690	600	536	487	450	420
(0.92)	(4,035)	(3,380)	(2,940)	(2,620)	(2,480)	(2,200)	(2,055)
4	1,050	870	750	664	600	550	510
(1.22)	(5,135)	(4,250)	(3,665)	(3,250)	(2,940)	(2,690)	(2,495)
5	1,275	1,050	900	793	712	650	600
(1.52)	(6,250)	(5,135)	(4,400)	(3,880)	(3,480)	(3,175)	(2,940)
6	1,500	1,230	1,050	921	825	750	690
(1.83)	(7,325)	(6,025)	(5,135)	(4,525)	(4,035)	(3,660)	(3,370)
7	1,725	1,410	1,200	1,050	933	850	780
(2.14)	(8,430)	(6,900)	(5,870)	(5,135)	(4,550)	(3,675)	(3,810)
8	1,793	1,466	1,246	1,090	972	877	808
(2.44)	(8,760)	(7,175)	(6,100)	(5,330)	(4,750)	(4,290)	(3,950)
9	1,865	1,522	1,293	1,130	1,007	912	836
(2.74)	(9,120)	(7,445)	(6,385)	(5,525)	(4,925)	(4,465)	(4,085)
10	1,935	1,578	1,340	1,170	1,042	943	864
(3.05)	(9,470)	(7,736)	(6,555)	(5,725)	(5,100)	(4,615)	(4,220)
15	2,185*	1,858	1,573	1,370	1,217	1,099	1,004
(4.58)	(10,680)*	(9,100)	(7,700)	(6,700)	(5,950)	(5,385)	(4,910)
20	2,635*	2,138*	1,806	1,570	1,392	1,254	1,144
(6.12)	(12,850)*	(10,450)*	(8,860)	(7,685)	(6,815)	(6,130)	(5,590)

* These values are limited to 2,000 lb per sq ft (9,775 kg/m²).

Table 21-3 gives the relations among the rates of filling forms, temperatures, and the maximum pressures for wall forms.

Table 21-4 gives the relations among the rates of filling forms, temperatures, and the maximum pressures for column forms.

Figure 21-2 illustrates the relations among the rates of filling wall forms, temperatures, and the maximum pressures, and Fig. 21-3 illustrates the same information for column forms, based on using formulas (21-1) to (21-3).

The maximum pressures indicated in the tables and figures will not occur unless the forms are deep enough to permit the attainment of the pressures. Regardless of the values given in the tables and figures, the maximum pressure on a given area should not exceed $150H$, where H is the depth of the concrete above the area in feet.

Table 21-4 Relation among the rate of filling column forms, maximum pressure and temperature (ACI)

Rate of filling forms, ft per hr (m/h)	Maximum concrete pressure, lb per sq ft (kg/m²)						
	40°F (4.4°C)	50°F (10.0°C)	60°F (15.5°C)	70°F (21.1°C)	80°F (26.7°C)	90°F (32.2°C)	100°F (37.7°C)
1	375	330	300	279	262	250	240
(0.31)	(1,830)	(1,510)	(1,465)	(1,360)	(1,275)	(1,229)	(1,175)
2	600	510	450	409	375	350	330
(0.61)	(2,940)	(2,490)	(2,200)	(2,000)	(1,830)	(1,710)	(1,615)
3	825	690	600	536	487	450	420
(0.92)	(4,035)	(3,380)	(2,940)	(2,620)	(2,480)	(2,200)	(2,055)
4	1,050	870	750	664	600	550	510
(1.22)	(5,135)	(4,250)	(3,665)	(3,250)	(2,940)	(2,690)	(2,495)
5	1,275	1,050	900	793	712	650	600
(1.52)	(6,250)	(5,135)	(4,400)	(3,880)	(3,480)	(3,175)	(2,940)
6	1,500	1,230	1,050	921	825	750	690
(1.83)	(7,325)	(6,025)	(5,135)	(4,525)	(4,035)	(3,660)	(3,370)
7	1,725	1,410	1,200	1,050	937	850	780
(2.14)	(8,430)	(6,900)	(5,870)	(5,135)	(4,570)	(3,675)	(3,810)
8	1,950	1,590	1,350	1,179	1,050	950	870
(2.44)	(9,560)	(7,790)	(6,625)	(5,770)	(5,135)	(4,635)	(4,250)
9	2,175	1,770	1,500	1,307	1,162	1,050	960
(2.74)	(10,640)	(8,670)	(7,350)	(6,395)	(5,695)	(5,135)	(4,690)
10	2,400	1,950	1,650	1,436	1,275	1,150	1,050
(3.05)	(11,750)	(9,550)	(8,080)	(7,050)	(6,245)	(5,625)	(5,135)
12	2,850	2,310	1,950	1,693	1,500	1,350	1,230
(3.66)	(13,940)	(10,435)	(9,060)	(8,300)	(7,650)	(6,610)	(6,030)
15	3,525*	2,850	2,400	2,093	1,837	1,650	1,500
(4.58)	(17,220)*	(13,940)	(11,750)	(10,250)	(9,000)	(8,080)	(7,650)
20	4,650*	3,750*	3,150*	2,721	2,400	2,150	1,950
(6.12)	(22,550)*	(18,300)*	(15,400)*	(13,340)	(11,770)	(10,520)	(9,570)

* These values are limited to 3,000 lb per sq ft (14,663 kg/m²).

FUNDAMENTALS OF FORM DESIGN

As previously stated, forms should be strong enough to resist the stresses produced in them and rigid enough to limit the deformation to the values permitted. Table 21-1 gives maximum unit stresses which are considered safe for various kinds of lumber. These stresses, which are higher than are permitted in a permanent structure, have an adequate factor of safety for forms. If the lumber used is of a lower grade than that specified in the table, the stresses should be reduced accordingly.

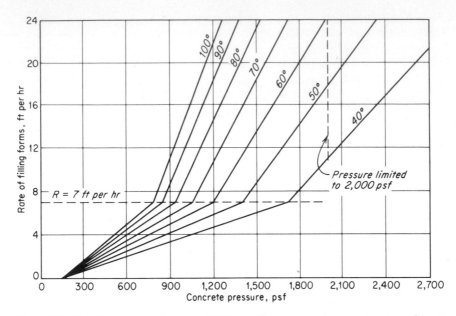

Figure 21-2 Relations among the rate of filling wall forms, maximum pressure, and temperature. (*ACI.*)

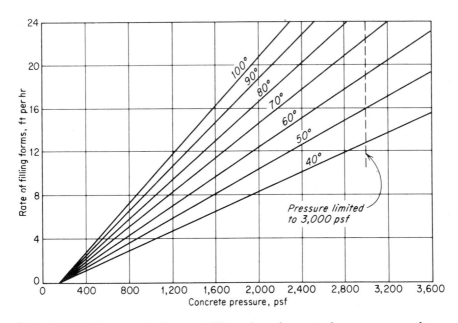

Figure 21-3 Relations among the rate of filling column forms, maximum pressure, and temperature. (*ACI.*)

Sometimes specifications limit the deflection of forms in order to eliminate objectionable bulges on the concrete surface. Representative deflection limits might be $\frac{1}{8}$ in. or $\frac{1}{270}$ of the span of the sheathing, studs, or wales. For most forms the size and spacing of studs and wales will be governed by the stresses in bending and shear, while deflection may limit the maximum span for sheathing.

In developing formulas for designing forms, the following symbols will be used:

$w=$ uniform load, lb per lin ft
$w'=$ uniform load, psf
$p=$ pressure, lb per lin ft
$p'=$ pressure, psf
$P=$ safe load on a shore, lb
$l=$ span from center to center of supports, in.
$L=$ span from center to center of supports, ft
$b=$ width of member, in.
$h=$ depth of member, in.
$g=$ height of shore, in.
$f=$ extreme fiber stress due to bending, psi
$v=$ horizontal shearing stress, psi
$V=$ external shear in a member, lb
$M=$ bending moment in a member, in.-lb
$M'=$ resisting moment of a member, in.-lb
$I=$ moment of inertia of a member $= bh^3/12$
$S=$ section modulus of a member $= bh^2/6$
$E=$ modulus of elasticity, psi
$D=$ deflection of a member, in.

In all instances the actual dimensions of a member should be used in designing forms (see Table 21-2).

STRESSES DUE TO BENDING

For most forms, sheathing, studs, and wales are continuous over several supports, and the maximum bending moment is given by the formula

$$M = \frac{12wL^2}{10} = 1.2wL^2 \tag{21-4}$$

The resisting moment of a member is given by the formula

$$M' = \frac{fbh^2}{6} \tag{21-5}$$

Equating formulas (21-4) and (21-5) and solving for L, we get

$$1.2wL^2 = \frac{fbh^2}{6}$$

$$L = 0.372h\sqrt{\frac{fb}{w}}$$

or

$$l = 4.464h\sqrt{\frac{fb}{w}} \tag{21-6}$$

The maximum safe load per linear foot is given by the formula

$$w = \frac{fbh^2}{7.2L^2} \tag{21-7}$$

SHEARING STRESSES

When a form member is subjected to transverse forces, shearing stresses in the member may govern the size of the member or the length of span. This is especially true for short spans and heavy loads. The external shear, which occurs at a support, is given by the formula

$$V = \frac{wL}{2} \tag{21-8}$$

The maximum unit shearing stress is

$$v = \frac{1.5V}{bh}$$

or

$$v = \frac{1.5wL}{2bh} \tag{21-9}$$

Solving for L, we get

$$L = \frac{2vbh}{1.5w}$$

or

$$l = \frac{16vbh}{w} \tag{21-10}$$

COMPRESSION STRESSES

When joists rest on sills or studs bear against wales, the areas of contact are subjected to compression stresses which act perpendicular to the wood fibers. As the safe stresses in compression perpendicular to the fibers are considerably less than those permitted in bending or parallel to the fibers, the stresses at these areas of contact should be checked to see that the safe values are not exceeded. Table 21-1 gives the maximum safe values of compression stresses perpendicular to the grain.

DEFLECTION OF FORMS

When a member, supported at each end, is subjected to a uniform load along its full length, the maximum deflection is given by the formula

$$D = \frac{5wl^4}{384 \times 12 \times EI} \tag{21-11}$$

Solving for l, we get

$$l = 5.51\sqrt[4]{\frac{EID}{w}} \tag{21-12}$$

If the lumber is grade 1 Douglas fir or southern pine, $E = 1,600,000$. $I = bh^3/12$. For sheathing assume D is limited to $1/8$ in. Substituting these values in formula (21-12), we get

$$l = 62.6\sqrt[4]{\frac{bh^3}{w}} \tag{21-13}$$

If a member extends continuously over several supports, such as sheathing over studs, the maximum deflection is given by the formula

$$D = \frac{wl^4}{384 \times 12 \times EI} \tag{21-14}$$

Solving for l, we get

$$l = 8.24\sqrt[4]{\frac{EID}{w}} \tag{21-15}$$

Substituting the values of E, I, and D, as given heretofore, we find the maximum value of l for sheathing to be

$$l = 93.5\sqrt[4]{\frac{bh^3}{w}} \tag{21-16}$$

The designer should use the value of l given by formula (21-13) instead of the value from formula (21-16) unless he is certain that the sheathing will be continuous over several supports. The length of a span adjacent to an end joint should be limited to the value given by formula (21-13).

WALL FORMS

The typical wall form shown in Fig. 21-4 includes sheathing, studs, wales, ties, and braces. If lumber is used for the sheathing, it may be 1, $1\frac{1}{4}$, $1\frac{1}{2}$, or 2 in. thick. Plywood usually is $\frac{5}{8}$ or $\frac{3}{4}$ in. thick.

As illustrated in Fig. 21-4, the opposite sides of the wall forms are held in the correct positions by steel-form ties, which resist the bursting pressure of the

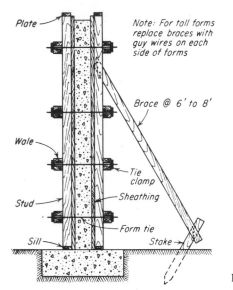

Figure 21-4 Wood forms for a concrete wall.

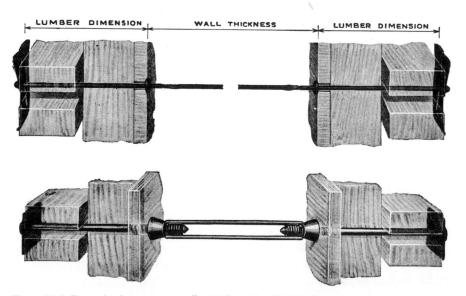

Figure 21-5 Form ties for concrete walls. (*a*) Snap tie. (*b*) Coil tie.

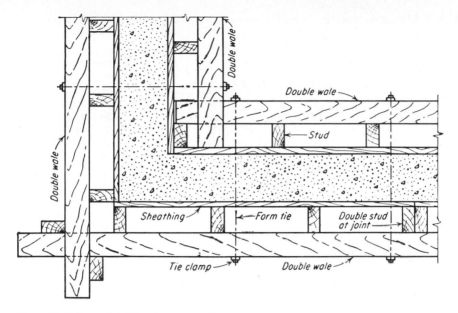

Figure 21-6 Form detail for the corner of a concrete wall.

concrete and serve as spreaders to govern the width of the space between the forms. Figure 21-5a illustrates a popular type of form tie for light wall construction. This tie has a safe working strength of 3,000 lb. It is designed to be snapped off 1 in. inside the concrete wall. Figure 21-5b illustrates a coil-type form tie which is suitable for use on heavy wall forms. It has safe working strengths of 6,000 and 9,000 lb. Many other types of form ties are available.

Figure 21-6 illustrates a representative method of constructing forms for the corner of a wall.

Table 21-5 gives safe spacings for studs, wales, and form ties for wall forms subjected to various pressures.

COLUMN FORMS

Forms for columns usually are made of vertical planks, with nominal thickness 1 in., or plywood. The component parts are prefabricated, then assembled in the location where they will be used. Adjustable steel clamps generally are used to resist the pressure from the concrete, as illustrated in Fig. 21-7.

Forms should be designed to resist the high pressure resulting from quick filling. If the forms are filled in 30 min or less, the concrete may exert the full hydrostatic pressure based on a weight of approximately 150 lb per cu ft.

Table 21-6 gives safe spacing for adjustable steel clamps based on the form material and limiting the deflection of the sheathing between clamps to not more than $\frac{1}{8}$ in.

Table 21-5 Maximum spacings, in in., for studs, wales, and form ties for wall forms*†

No.	Item	Maximum pressure, lb per sq ft								
		300	450	600	750	900	1,050	1,200	1,350	1,500
		Using 1-in. *S4S* sheathing and *S4S* lumber								
1	2″ × 4″ studs	25	21	18	16	14	1	12	12	11
	2″ × 4″ wales, 2 pc	29	26	24	23	22	21	21	20	19
	Form ties	38	33	30	27	25	24	22	21	21
	Load on tie, lb	2,375	2,680	3,000	3,235	3,440	3,675	3,850	4,330	4,375
	Tie spacing:									
	3,000-lb tie	38	33	30	25	22	19	17	14	14
	5,000-lb tie	38	33	30	27	25	24	22	21	21
	Fbm per sq ft	2.15	2.31	2.44	2.54	2.66	2.75	2.75	2.91	2.98
2	2″ × 4″ studs	25	21	18	16	14	13	12	12	11
	2″ × 6″ wales, 2 pc	29	26	24	23	22	21	21	20	19
	Form ties	60	52	48	43	40	38	35	34	32
	Load on tie, lb	3,620	4,225	4,800	5,150	5,500	5,820	6,120	6,375	6,330
	Tie spacing:									
	3,000-lb tie	50	37	30	25	22	19	17	16	15
	5,000-lb tie	60	52	48	41	36	32	28	26	25
	Fbm per sq ft	2.70	2.66	2.80	2.90	3.06	3.18	3.24	3.36	3.45
3	2″ × 6″ studs	25	21	18	16	14	13	12	12	11
	2″ × 6″ wales, 2 pc	46	40	38	36	35	34	33	31	31
	Form ties	49	42	37	34	31	30	29	27	26
	Load on tie, lb	4,700	5,250	5,860	6,375	6,780	7,440	7,975	7,850	8,400
	Tie spacing:									
	5,000-lb tie	47	40	31	26	22	20	18	17	15
	9,000-lb tie	49	42	37	34	31	30	29	27	26
	Fbm per sq ft	2.31	2.52	2.70	2.80	2.96	3.10	3.22	3.27	3.40
4	3″ × 4″ studs	25	21	18	16	14	13	12	12	11
	2″ × 4″ wales, 2 pc	38	33	31	30	29	28	27	25	25
	Form ties	33	29	25	23	22	21	20	19	18
	Load on tie, lb	2,610	2,990	3,230	3,530	4,000	4,290	4,500	4,450	4,690
	Tie spacing:									
	3,000-lb tie	33	29	23	19	16	14	13	13	11
	5,000-lb tie	33	29	25	23	22	21	20	19	18
	Fbm per sq ft	2.22	2.39	2.57	2.69	2.77	2.93	3.06	3.12	3.22
5	3″ × 4″ studs	25	21	18	16	14	13	12	12	11
	2″ × 6″ wales, 2 pc	38	33	31	30	29	28	27	25	25
	Form ties	52	46	41	38	33	32	31	30	29
	Load on tie, lb	4,120	4,740	5,300	5,340	5,980	6,530	6,975	7,030	7,550
	Tie spacing:									
	5,000-lb tie	52	46	38	35	27	24	22	21	19
	9,000-lb tie	52	46	41	38	33	32	31	30	29
	Fbm per sq ft	2.46	2.65	2.83	3.00	3.12	3.27	3.30	3.48	3.54

* Applicable conditions: (1) Allowable fiber stress in bending is 1,450 lb per sq in. (2) Allowable stress in horizontal shear is 200 lb per sq in. (3) Allowable stress in compression perpendicular to the grain is 500 lb per sq in. (4) Modulus of elasticity is 1,600,000 lb per sq in. (5) Permissible deflection is *l*/270. (6) Concrete will be vibrated as it is placed. (7) The load on a tie is the load that would occur if the maximum spacing of wales and ties were used.

† From R. L. Peurifoy, "Formwork for Concrete Structures," 2d ed., McGraw-Hill Book Company, New York, 1976.

FORMS FOR CONCRETE STRUCTURES **661**

Table 21-6 Safe spacing of adjustable steel-column clamps, in inches*

| Height of column, ft | Story height, ft | | | | | | | | | | | |
| | For 1-in. nominal-thickness sheathing with 1 × 4 cleats | | | | | | For ¾-in. plywood with vertical 2 × 4 cleats | | | | | |
	10	12	14	16	18	20	10	12	14	16	18	20
	32	32	32	32	32	32	33	33	33	33	33	33
	20	20	20	20	20	20	27	27	27	27	27	27
	16	16	16	16	16	16						
	13	13	13	13	13	13	24	24	24	24	24	24
	13	13	13	13	13	13						
	12	12	12	12	12	12	21	21	21	21	21	21
	8	12	12	12	12	12						
10	6						9	20	20	20	20	20
		12	12	12	12	12	6					
		8	11	11	11	11	13	19	19	19	19
12		6	11	11	11	11	6				
			10	10	10	10		18	18	18	18
14			6	10	10	10		6	15	17	17
				8	10	10			9		
				6	10	10				16	16
16				6	10	10			6		
					9	9				15	15
					9	9					
18					6	8				6	
						8					12
						8					12
20						6					6

* Basic information furnished by Symons Corporation.

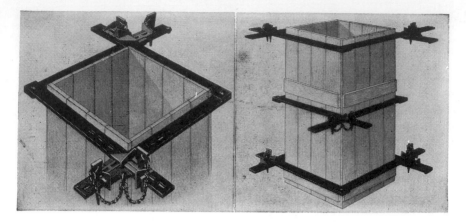

Figure 21-7 Wood forms and adjustable clamps for concrete columns.

ALLOWABLE LOADS ON WOOD SHORES

The following symbols are used in determining the allowable loads on wood shores installed in vertical positions, with the loads applied concentrically on the shores:

P = total load on a shore, lb
A = actual cross-sectional area of a shore, sq in.
b = actual dimension across the wide side of a shore, in.
d = actual dimension across the narrow side of a shore, in.
f_c = P/A = unit compressive stress parallel to the grain in a shore, lb per sq in.
E = modulus of elasticity of the wood in the shore, lb per sq in.
l = unsupported length of a shore, in.
l/d = slenderness ratio of a shore, which for wood should never exceed 50

The National Forest Products Association [3] recommends the use of Eq. (21-17) to determine the maximum allowable unit compressive stress in a wood column parallel to the grain. Equation (21-18) may be used to determine the maximum allowable total load on a wood shore or column.

$$f_c = \frac{P}{A} = \frac{0.3E}{(l/d)^2} \tag{21-17}$$

and

$$P = \frac{0.3AE}{(l/d)^2} \tag{21-18}$$

The two equations reveal that the supporting capacities of wood shores of constant cross-sectional area decrease with the square of the slenderness ratio.

Table 21-7 Allowable loads on $S4S$ wood shores, pounds*

$$P = \frac{0.3AE}{(l/d)^2}$$

Unsupported length of shore, ft	Nominal size of lumber, in.				
	2×4	3×4	4×4	4×6	6×6

f_c = 1,400 lb per sq in.; E = 1,700,000 lb per sq in.

4	2,631	12,105	17,150	26,950	42,350
5	1,673	7,747	17,150	26,950	42,350
6	1,162	5,380	14,870	23,361	42,350
7		3,952	10,846	17,044	42,350
8		3,027	8,322	13,076	42,350
9		2,402	6,585	10,343	40,153
10		1,937	5,341	9,394	32,462
12			3,700	5,812	22,135
14			2,711	4,261	16,584
16					14,167

f_c = 1,150 lb per sq in.; E = 1,400,000 lb per sq in.

4	2,177	9,963	14,000	22,000	34,750
5	1,380	6,375	14,000	22,000	34,750
6	965	4,431	12,180	19,150	34,750
7		3,260	8,910	13,450	34,750
8		2,425	6,840	10,475	34,750
9		1,970	5,410	8,500	33,000
10		1,585	4,340	6,910	26,650
12			3,030	4,800	18,250
14			2,225	3,475	13,620
16					10,350

f_c = 900 lb per sq in., E = 1,100,000 lb per sq in.

4	1,700	7,835	11,000	17,200	27,200
5	1,075	5,000	11,000	17,200	27,200
6	750	3,475	9,600	15,050	27,200
7		2,540	7,000	11,000	27,200
8		1,950	5,360	8,450	27,200
9		1,550	4,240	6,665	26,000
10		1,250	3,445	5,440	22,000
12			2,420	3,750	14,150
14			1,750	2,760	10,580
16					8,200

(Continued on next page)

Table 21-7 *(continued)*

$$P = \frac{0.3AE}{(l/d)^2}$$

Unsupported length of shore, ft	Nominal size of lumber, in.				
	2×4	3×4	4×4	4×6	6×6

$f_c = 700$ lb per sq in.; $E = 1,400,000$ lb per sq in.

Unsupported length of shore, ft	2×4	3×4	4×4	4×6	6×6
4	2,180	6,025	8,585	13,450	21,150
5	1,400	6,025	8,585	13,450	21,150
6	990	4,370	8,585	13,450	21,150
7		3,280	8,585	13,450	21,150
8		2,500	6,770	10,650	21,150
9		2,000	5,400	8,460	21,150
10		1,600	4,380	6,910	21,200
12			3,580	4,800	18,380
14			2,200	3,490	13,630
16					10,400

* From R. L. Peurifoy, "Formwork for Concrete Structures," 2d ed., McGraw-Hill Book Company, New York, 1976.

For this reason, the strength of shores in supporting vertical loads may be increased greatly by installing horizontal or equivalent braces to reduce the unsupported lengths of the shores.

Table 21-7 lists the maximum allowable loads on wood shores for different grades of lumber, as determined from Eq. (21-18).

FORMS FOR BEAM-AND-SLAB-TYPE FLOOR CONSTRUCTION

Figure 21-8 illustrates a method of constructing forms for the beams and slab for this type of floor system, using commercial lumber. Plywood, $\frac{5}{8}$- or $\frac{3}{4}$-in. thick, or 1-in. planks may be used for the decking. Plywood is installed more rapidly and has a higher salvage value, which may offset its higher cost compared to planks.

The maximum spacing of the joists will be limited by the strength or the permissible deflection of the decking. The maximum spacing of the stringers will be limited by the strength or the permissible deflection of the joists. The maximum spacing of shores under the stringers will be limited by the strength or the permissible deflection of the stringers or the capacity of the shores.

In designing forms for beams and slab, the design load should equal the weight of the concrete, plus an additional load of 40 to 50 psf, to provide for the weight of buggies and workers and for the storage of materials on the slab during construction.

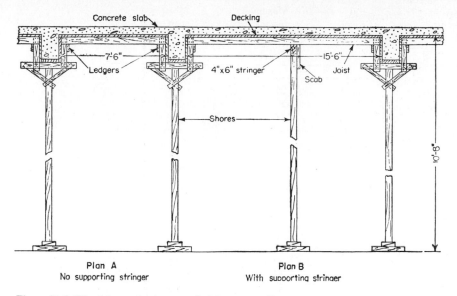

Figure 21-8 Wood forms for beam-and-slab concrete floor.

MAXIMUM SPANS FOR WOOD JOISTS AND WOOD STRINGERS

When wood joists and wood stringers are used to support the decking for a concrete slab, the total weight that must be supported will include the concrete plus any additional loads that may be applied during or after the placing of the concrete before the concrete is self-supporting. This should include an allowance for any vibrating loads that might occur.

Table 21-8 Maximum spans for *S4S* wood joists for floor slabs using grade No. 2 Douglas fir or equal
Live load 50 lb per sq ft

Thickness of slab, in.	Size of joist, in.	Maximum spacing of joist, in.	Maximum span of joist, in.
4	2 × 4	30	49
		24	54
	2 × 6	30	77
		24	86
5	2 × 6	30	68
		24	76
	2 × 8	30	90
		24	101

Table 21-8 *(continued)*

Thickness of slab, in.	Size of joist, in.	Maximum spacing of joist, in.	Maximum span of joist, in.
6	2 × 6	30	65
		24	72
	2 × 8	30	85
		24	95
8	2 × 6	30	59
		24	66
	2 × 8	30	78
		24	87
	2 × 10	30	99
		24	112
10	2 × 6	30	54
		24	61
	2 × 8	30	72
		24	80
	2 × 10	30	92
		24	103

Table 21-9 Maximum spans for $S4S$ wood stringers for floor slabs using grade No. 2 Douglas fir or equal
Live load 50 lb per sq ft

Thickness of slab, in.	Spacing of stringers, in.	Maximum span of stringer, in.			
		Nominal size of stringer, in.			
		2 × 8	3 × 8	4 × 6	4 × 8
4	60	66	84	78	102
	72	60	78	72	90
	84	54	72	66	84
	96	48	66	60	66
5	60	60	78	72	90
	72	54	72	66	84
	84	48	66	60	78
	96	48	60	54	72
6	60	60	78	66	90
	72	54	72	60	84
	84	48	66	60	78
	96	48	60	54	72
8	60		66	60	84
	72		60	54	78
	84		60	54	72
	96		54	48	66
10	60		66	54	72
	72		60	54	66
	84		54	48	66
	96		48	42	60

Table 21-8 gives the maximum spans for S4S wood joists, while Table 21-9 gives the maximum spans for wood stringers for the stated conditions. If it is anticipated that the live load on a concrete slab 6 in. thick will be 75 lb per sq ft, the spacing of the joists and stringers may be obtained from the values for a slab 8 in. thick.

FORMS FOR BEAMS

Figure 21-8 shows a common method of constructing forms for concrete beams for a beam-and-slab-type floor system.

Figure 21-9 shows a modified method of constructing and supporting beam forms which was developed by one contractor. The assembly was designed to be fastened together by wedges, with no erection nailing required. The primary objectives were to reduce the damage to the forms in order to obtain more uses and to reduce the amount of labor required to erect and remove the forms.

Bottom forms were $\frac{5}{8}$-in. plywood stiffened by a continuous 2- by 3-in. plank, fastened beneath and flush with each long edge. Nailed under the 2- by 3-in. stiffeners were 1- by 4-in. transverse cleats, which extended far enough out on each side to carry a continuous longitudinal 2- by 3-in. ribband nailed to their tops. Between the stiffened edge of the bottom sheathing and the inner beveled face of the ribband there was a space for a side-form panel to be rested

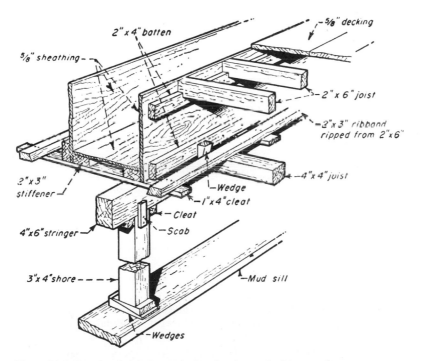

Figure 21-9 Beam-and-slab forms designed to be used without nails.

on the cleats and held tightly by wood wedges. The $\frac{5}{8}$-in. plywood sheathing of the beam side forms carried two continuous horizontal 2- by 4-in. battens. The lower batten coincided with the bottom edge of the sheathing, while the upper batten was located to serve as a ledger for notched joists that supported the $\frac{5}{8}$-in. plywood decking for the floor slab.

Beam forms rested on a framework of transverse 4- by 4-in. joists atop longitudinal 4- by 6-in. stringers, which were supported by 3- by 4-in. shores. To hold the members in place, yet make removal easy, cleats on the underside of the stringers fitted over the tops of the shores, whose opposite sides were fitted with scabs to keep them centered under the stringer.

PROBLEMS

21-1 Determine the maximum safe spacing of studs when using 1-in. nominal-thickness sheathing for each of the following conditions:

Rate of filling forms, ft per hr	Temperature of concrete, °F
3	80
4	90
6	70
8	60

Grade No. 2 southern pine will be used for the sheathing. The maximum deflection is limited to $\frac{1}{8}$ in. Limit the spacing of the studs to the values determined by the deflection of the sheathing or the allowable bending stresses.

21-2 A concrete wall 90 ft long, 11 ft high, and 12 in. thick will be placed in one pour. The forms will be filled at the rate of 3 ft per hr at a temperature of 70°F.

The sheathing will be 1 by 6 in., the studs 2 by 4 in., and the wales double 2 by 4 in., all $S4S$ yellow pine lumber. Form ties will be 3,000 lb working stress. Use the information in the tables in this book to design the forms.

Prepare a bill of materials for the lumber, including 2- by 4-in. braces spaced approximately 6 ft apart on one side of the forms only. Also, determine the number of form ties required. List each size of lumber as follows:

75 pc   2 × 4 in. × 16 ft   800 fbm

21-3 The forms selected to support a 6-in.-thick concrete slab will consist of the following materials:

Decking, 1-in. grade No. 2 southern pine
Joists, 2 × 8 in., grade No. 2 southern pine
Stringers, 3 × 8 in., $S4S$ grade No. 2 southern pine
Shores, 4,500 lb safe load

Determine the maximum safe spacings for the joists, stringers, and shores as limited by the allowable unit stresses in bending, shear, and compression between the joists and the stringers. The maximum deflection of each member is limited to $\frac{1}{8}$ in.

Assume a live load of 50 lb per sq ft on the concrete slab.

REFERENCES

1. Peurifoy, R. L.: "Formwork for Concrete Structures," 2d ed., McGraw-Hill Book Company, New York, 1976.
2. "Formwork for Concrete," *Publication SP*-4, 3d ed., American Concrete Institute, Detroit, Michigan, 1973.
3. "National Design Specifications for Stress-Grade Lumber and Its Fastenings," National Forest Products Association, Washington, D. C., 1973.

TWENTY TWO

CONCRETE

INTRODUCTION

Concrete is basically cement, aggregate, and water which have been mixed together, deposited, and permitted to solidify. Sometimes admixtures are used for various purposes, such as to produce a desired color, improve the workability, entrain air, reduce the segregation, or accelerate setting and hardening.

The operations in the production of concrete will vary with the type of project requiring the concrete and the type of concrete produced. In general, the operations, which are represented graphically in Fig. 22-1, include the following:

1. Batching the materials
2. Mixing
3. Handling and transporting
4. Placing
5. Finishing
6. Curing

DESIGN OF CONCRETE MIXTURES

The design of a concrete mixture involves determining the proper proportions of cement, aggregate, and water, plus any admixtures, to produce a concrete having the desired properties. Because of the many variables which affect the design of concrete for a given project it is impossible to include in this book specific information which can be used safely as a guide under all conditions. However, some general information will apply to all projects.

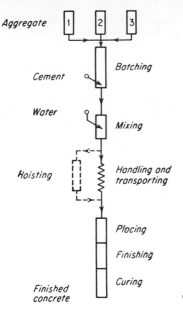

Aggregate

Cement

Water

Hoisting

Finished
concrete

Batching

Mixing

Handling and
transporting

Placing

Finishing

Curing

Figure 22-1 Flow diagram showing the operations perform‐
ed in constructing a concrete project.

The fine and coarse aggregate constitute about 75 to 80 percent of the ultimate mass of concrete. They are joined together into a solid body by the solidification of a paste made of cement and water. The water serves two purposes. It causes the cement to hydrate into a solid mass, and it gives the fresh concrete sufficient plasticity to permit it to be formed into the desired shape. If an excess quantity of water is used, it dilutes the paste and weakens the concrete. If an insufficient quantity of cement is used, there will not be enough paste to join all the particles of aggregate together solidly and the strength of the concrete will be affected. Thus, it seems apparent that the quantity of water used in making concrete should be the minimum amount needed to give the concrete the required plasticity.

Economical concrete, having the required properties, can be produced by using the largest practical sizes of coarse aggregate and the smallest practical quantity of water. Large pieces of aggregate are already joined together by nature, and they require no cement for this purpose. If the water content is kept low, the strength of the cement paste will be high and a strong concrete can be produced with less cement.

HANDLING AND BATCHING MATERIALS

In order to produce concrete having the required properties, it is necessary to control the quantity of each material that goes into a batch. This is referred to as batching the materials. Although batching may be done by volume or by weight, the former method is so unreliable that it should not be used on any job where the properties of concrete are of importance. Weight batching is much more dependable and more commonly used than volume batching.

Handling cement Cement may be shipped to a job in paper bags, containing 1 cu ft and weighing 94 lb, or as bulk cement in special railroad cars, in boxcars, or by trucks. Bulk cement is cheaper than bag cement but unless a job is large enough to justify the installation of facilities to handle bulk cement, it will be more satisfactory to use cement in bags.

Bag cement must be stored in a dry place and should be left in the original bags until used for concrete. If a batch of concrete requires one or more whole bags of cement, the use of bag cement simplifies the batching operation.

Bulk cement usually is unloaded from the cars or trucks and stored in a suitable silo or a fully enclosed overhead bin. Figure 22-2 shows an overhead cement bin suitable for storing one or more railroad cars of cement. An auxiliary silo may be added to increase the storage capacity. The cement flows from the bottom hopper of a railroad car into an under-track screw conveyor to a bucket-type elevating conveyor and thence into the overhead storage bin.

A weighing hopper, suspended beneath the storage bin, is used to measure the correct amount of cement. Weighing may be done by means of a beam scale or a springless dial scale, the latter being more expensive but more dependable.

Batching the aggregate The specifications for a project may require that concrete be made with aggregate having two to six different size ranges. The

Figure 22-2 Silo for the storage of bulk cement.

Figure 22-3 Four-compartment trolley-type aggregate batching plant.

quantity of material from each size range must be measured carefully. It is the function of the batching equipment to perform this measuring operation.

If a project is large enough to justify the additional investment in equipment for handling and batching aggregate, an elevated storage bin, equipped with a weighing batcher, should be used. It will be necessary to provide a clamshell, tractor-mounted scoop, or other suitable equipment to handle the aggregate from the stock pile to the bin. Figure 22-3 shows a trolley-type batching plant

Figure 22-4 Central batching plant for cement and aggregate.

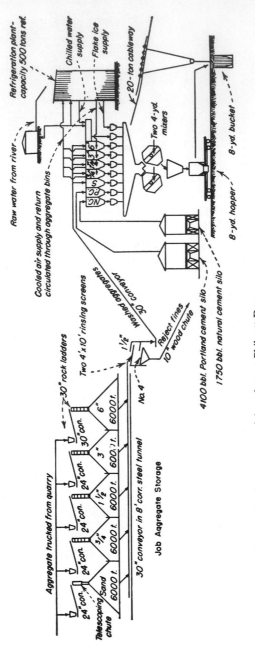

Figure 22-5 Flow diagram for the concrete-mixing plant at Philpott Dam.

which may be filled with a tractor-mounted scoop. When the specified quantities of aggregate have flowed from the bins into the weighing hopper, the hopper is moved along the trolley to permit the aggregate to be discharged into the skip of the concrete mixer. Bins of this type have capacities varying from about 3 to 40 tons. The batchers have capacities varying from 1,000 to 4,000 lb and are equipped with two, three, or four weighing beams, in addition to a tare beam.

For a large project it may be desirable to install one or more multiple-compartment overhead bins of the type illustrated in Fig. 22-4. This is a three-compartment storage bin equipped with a beam-type weighing batcher. Bins are available with two or more compartments, each compartment holding up to 50 tons of aggregate. The batched aggregate may be discharged into a truck, a transit mixer, or a chute and thence to a concrete mixer.

The capacity of a batching bin is the sum of the capacities of the several compartments, expressed in tons or in cubic yards.

The capacity of the hopper of a weighing batcher should be at least $1\frac{1}{3}$ times the rated capacity of the concrete mixer with which it is used.

Figure 22-5 shows the layout for storing, handling, and batching aggregates and for mixing and handling concrete for the Philpott Dam. Note that a batch required four different sizes of aggregate, plus sand, two types of cement, flaked ice, and water.

MEASURING WATER

In view of the significant effect which the quantity of water has on the properties of concrete it is necessary to provide a method of accurately measuring the quantity of water per batch. Concrete mixers usually are equipped with water-measuring tanks, which may be adjusted to supply any reasonable amount of water per batch. These tanks should be checked periodically to verify the amount of water supplied.

Other water-measuring devices include water meters and water-weighing tanks.

If the aggregate contains free surface water, such water should be included as part of the total quantity required for the concrete.

CONCRETE MIXERS

Concrete mixers may be classified as

1. Construction mixers
2. Paving mixers
3. Transit mixers

The old practice of specifying the size of a mixer as one-bag, two-bag, etc., has been pretty well abandoned in favor of specifying the size by the nominal volume of concrete that can be mixed in a batch, expressed in cubic feet for construction and paving mixers and in cubic yards for transit mixers.

The Mixer Manufacturers Bureau of the AGC lists the various sizes of construction and paving mixers that shall be considered standard. Other sizes are available and may be entirely satisfactory.

For construction mixers with a single-compartment drum the standard sizes are $3\frac{1}{2}$S, 6S, 11S, 16S, 28S, 56S, 84S, and 112S. The number indicates the nominal volume of mixed concrete in cubic feet, while the letter S designates that the equipment is a construction mixer. These mixers must be capable of mixing 10 percent more than the rated capacities when they are operating in a level position.

For paving mixers with single-compartment drums the standard sizes are 27E and 34E. For mixers with two-compartment drums the standard sizes are 16E and 34E. The number indicates the nominal volume of mixed concrete in cubic feet, while the letter E designates that the equipment is a paving mixer. These mixers are capable of mixing 20 percent more concrete than the rated capacities when they are operating on a level surface.

Outputs of construction mixers The output of a concrete mixer usually is expressed in cubic yards of concrete mixed per hour. Obviously, the output will vary with the size of a mixer and the conditions under which it is operated. For any given mixer and job conditions the output will be the product of the volume per batch times the number of batches per hour.

The actual volume of concrete mixed per batch usually will not equal the rated size of a mixer. Since it is desirable to avoid the use of fractional bags of cement, the size of a batch may be more or less than the size of the mixer. For example, if a 16S mixer is used to mix concrete requiring six bags per cubic yard, a batch should include three bags of cement. This will produce a batch having a volume of 13.5 cu ft instead of 16 cu ft.

The number of batches mixed per hour will depend on the average time per cycle, which varies with the mixing time and the method of discharging the concrete. The American Society for Testing Materials (ASTM) specifies that concrete shall be mixed 1 min for mixer sizes through 1 cu yd and that for larger sizes 15 sec shall be added to the mixing time for each additional cubic yard of size or fraction thereof.

The method of discharging a mixer has considerable influence on the time per cycle. If a 16S mixer can discharge the entire batch into a single container such as a bucket or a hopper, the mixer can be emptied in 15 sec or less. However, if the batch is discharged into five wheelbarrows, each requiring 10 sec, the total time required to discharge the mixer will be 50 sec. In the former case the mixer might produce 40 batches per hour without allowing for interruptions, whereas in the latter case the mixer might produce not more than 25 batches per hour.

In determining the output of a mixer over an extended period of time, any losses in output resulting from delays should be included by using an appropriate operating factor such as a 45- or 50-min hour.

Example Determine the quantities of materials required per batch and the probable output for a 16S construction mixer. The quantities of materials per cubic yard are

Cement, 5.6 bags
Sand, 1,438 lb
Gravel, 1,846 lb
Water, 39 gal

If the batch is 16 cu ft, the required volume of cement will be $(16 \times 5.6)/27 = 3.32$ bags. Instead of mixing 16 cu ft per batch, which would require a fractional bag of cement, reduce the quantity of cement to three bags, and the quantities of other materials in the same proportion. The volume per batch will be $(3 \times 27)/5.6 = 14.5$ cu ft. The quantities of materials per batch will be

Cement, 3 bags

Sand, $\dfrac{14.5}{27} \times 1,438 = 771$ lb

Gravel, $\dfrac{14.5}{27} \times 1,846 = 990$ lb

Water, $\dfrac{14.5}{27} \times 39 = 20.9$ gal

If the mixer discharges the entire batch of concrete into a single bucket, the time per cycle should be about as follows:

Charging mixer   = 0.25 min
Mixing concrete   = 1.00 min
Discharging mixer = 0.25 min
Lost time   = 0.10 min
Total time   = 1.60 min
No. batches per hr, $60 \div 1.60 = 37.5$
Output per hr, 37.5 batches $\times$ 14.5 cu ft per batch $\div$ 27 = 20.1 cu yd
The output in a 50-min hr will be $20.1 \times \frac{50}{60} = 16.7$ cu yd

Table 22-1 gives representative ranges in the output of standard sizes of construction mixers.

CENTRAL MIXING PLANTS

A central mixing plant may be installed to mix concrete for a large structure, such as a dam, or for sale to the public. Such a plant includes equipment for handling and storing aggregate and cement, batchers, and one to four construction-type concrete mixers in sizes from 28S to 112S. The mixers may be tilting or nontilting types. The mixed concrete may be discharged into buckets, agitator trucks, or dump trucks if air-entrained concrete is used.

Table 22-1 Representative ranges in the outputs for construction mixers

Size mixer	Time per cycle, min		Batches per hr		Output,* cu yd per hr	
	Min	Max	Min	Max	Min	Max
$3\frac{1}{2}$S	1.5	2.25	27	40	3.5	5.2
6S	1.5	2.25	27	40	6.0	8.9
11S	1.5	2.5	24	40	9.8	16.3
16S	1.5	2.5	24	40	14.2	20.1
28S	1.75	2.75	22	34	22.6	35.3
56S	2.00	2.75	22	30	45.6	62.3
84S	2.25	3.00	20	27	62.2	84.0
112S	2.50	3.25	18	24	74.5	99.5

* These values are based on a 60-min hour and should be adjusted to fit actual job conditions.

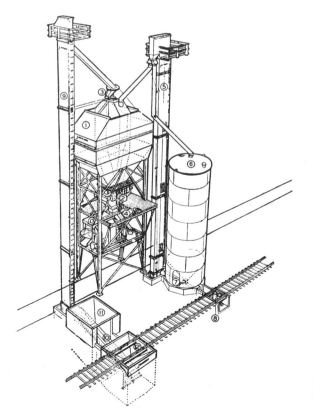

Figure 22-6 Layout for a central mixing plant.

Figure 22-7 Central mixing plant with tilt-type mixer.

Figure 22-6 illustrates one arrangement for a central mixing plant, using a single nontilting concrete mixer. The plant layout can be revised to permit the delivery of cement and aggregate by truck or by any other desired method of transportation.

PAVING MIXERS

Paving mixers are used primarily to mix and place concrete for highways, streets, and airport runways. They are mounted on crawler tracks in order that they may move along with the placing of the concrete. Figure 22-8 illustrates a paving mixer in operation.

As previously stated under Concrete Mixers, the Mixer Manufacturers Bureau of the AGC specifies as standard the 27E and 34E single-drum and the 16E and 34E double-drum units. As illustrated in Fig. 22-9, the double-drum mixer has two compartments. The aggregate is charged into the first compartment, where it is premixed, following which it is transferred to the second compartment as soon as this compartment is emptied. This operation permits a

Figure 22-8 Paving mixer in operation.

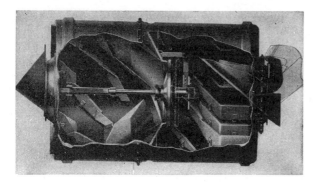

Figure 22-9 Section through a double-drum paving mixer.

substantial increase in the output of a double-drum mixer compared with a single-drum unit.

The aggregate is hauled to a paving mixer in dump trucks whose beds are divided into two or more compartments, each compartment being large enough to hold one batch of aggregate.

Table 22-2 gives recommended sizes of aggregate bins, clamshell buckets, and cranes for batching plants for paving mixers.

The output of a paving mixer will vary with the size of the mixer, the number of compartments, and the nature of the job. Under favorable conditions a paving mixer can mix a 20 percent overload of concrete. The batch cycle for a single-drum mixer should run about 1.5 to 2 min and for a double-drum mixer

Table 22-2 Recommended batching-plant equipment for paving mixers

Size mixer	Minimum size bin, tons	Size clamshell bucket, cu yd	Size crane, cu yd	Length of boom, ft
One 27E single-drum	75	$\frac{3}{4}$	$\frac{3}{4}$	45
One 34E single-drum	75	1	1	45
One 16E double-drum	50	$\frac{1}{2}$	$\frac{1}{2}$	40
One 34E double-drum	100	$1\frac{3}{4}$	$1\frac{1}{2}$	50
Two 34E double-drum	190	3	$2\frac{1}{2}$	60

about 0.8 to 1.25 min. While the lower cycle times are possible, it is not probable that they will be maintained over an extended period of time except under favorable conditions. For example, in paving city streets, requiring curbs and gutters, frequent driveway entrances, intersections, and other delay-producing operations, the actual operating factor may be as low as 0.5, corresponding to a 30-min hour.

Example Determine the probable output of a 34E double-drum paving mixer under various conditions.

If the highway is level and job conditions are favorable, it is possible to produce a batch of concrete in 50 sec.

Maximum size batch, $34 \times 1.20 = 40.8$ cu ft
Batches per hr, $60 \times 60 \div 50 = 72$
Maximum output per hr, $72 \times 40.8 \div 27 = 109$ cu yd
Output for a 45-min hr, $109 \times \frac{45}{60} = 81.6$ cu yd
Output for a 30-min hr, $109 \times \frac{30}{60} = 54.5$ cu yd

Table 22-3 gives representative outputs for paving mixers operating on level ground. If the slope of the ground is as great as 6 percent, the maximum

Table 22-3 Representative outputs for paving mixers

Size mixer	Time per cycle, min Min	Max	Batches per hr Min	Max	Output,* cu yd per hr Min	Max
27E single	1.5	2.0	30	40	36.0	48.0
34E single	1.5	2.0	30	40	45.4	60.5
16E double	0.8	1.25	48	75	34.2	53.3
34E double	0.8	1.25	48	75	72.6	113.5

* These values are based on a 60-min hour and should be adjusted to fit actual job conditions.

capacity per batch will be 10 percent greater than the rated size of the mixer. For such conditions the outputs given in the table should be reduced about 10 percent.

Transit-mixer and agitator trucks A transit-mixer or agitator truck is a truck on which there is mounted a concrete mixer. If the aggregate, including the cement, is charged into the mixer at a central batching plant, with mixing to be done en route to the job, the unit is called a transit mixer. If the unit is used to haul ready-mixed concrete, which requires agitation en route to the project only to prevent it from segregating, the unit is called an agitator.

Transit mixers are available in sizes varying from 1 to $7\frac{1}{2}$ cu yd. If a unit is used as an agitator, the capacity will be considerably greater than when it is used as a transit mixer, because the concrete is premixed, and thus it occupies a volume less than that of the aggregates measured separately.

When concrete is delivered by transit-mixer or agitator trucks, the effect of mixing concrete for long periods may be questioned. Tests that have been conducted over periods of several hours indicate that, when concrete is mixed for a long time, the slump will decrease and the compressive strength will increase for periods up to $2\frac{1}{2}$ hr or longer. The Standard Specifications for Ready-mixed Concrete (ASTM C94) requires that the concrete must be delivered and discharged from the truck mixer or agitator truck within $1\frac{1}{2}$ hr after the introduction of the water to the cement and aggregate or the cement to the aggregate. Table 22-4 illustrates the effect of mixing time on the slump and strength of concrete.

Figure 22-10 Discharging concrete from a transit-mixer truck.

Figure 22-11 Sectional view through the drum of a transit mixer.

Table 22-4 The effect of mixing time on the slump and strength of concrete*

Time of mixing, min	Slump, in.	Compressive strength, psi		
		3-day	7-day	28-day
1	9.0	1,370	2,150	3,410
15	8.4	1,710	2,530	3,720
30	6.4	1,800	2,590	3,640
60	2.6	2,230	3,100	4,160

* Courtesy Portland Cement Association.

HANDLING AND TRANSPORTING CONCRETE

The method used to handle and place concrete should be selected to accomplish several objectives, including:

1. Economy
2. The prevention of segregation
3. Final placing before concrete attains initial set

Concrete may be handled and transported by several methods, such as buggies, buckets handled by cranes, hoisting towers, or cables, chutes, belt conveyors, trucks, transit-mix or dump, pumps and pipelines. Each method, which has advantages and disadvantages, is suitable for use under certain conditions. The method selected should permit the use of a concrete having the required properties, such as consistency, maximum-size aggregate, etc.

In order to reduce segregation, concrete should flow vertically downward as it is discharged into the forms or from one unit of equipment to another.

Hand buggies Hand buggies or carts, equipped with pneumatic tires, which are available in sizes of 6 to 11 cu ft, are suitable for use on many projects. The smaller size will haul about 4.5 cu ft and the larger size about 9 cu ft per load. They are superior to wheelbarrows because the two wheels provide a better balance for the load.

Power-driven buggies Within recent years power buggies have been used at increasing rates to haul concrete. They have capacities of $\frac{1}{3}$ to $\frac{1}{2}$ cu yd and speeds up to about 15 mph, can make a 180° turn in about 4 ft, and can climb grades up to about 20 percent when loaded. On projects where they may be used advantageously, power buggies may pay for themselves in 1 to 6 months by economies which they can effect compared with the cost of transporting concrete with hand buggies.

Buckets Buckets may be divided into two groups—those used with material towers and those used with power cranes, cables, etc. The former, which are referred to as tower buckets, vary in size from about 8 to 36 cu ft, while the latter, which are referred to as concrete buckets, vary in size from about $\frac{1}{2}$ to 8 cu yd.

Concrete buckets have bottom gates which may be opened in such a manner that the concrete will flow vertically downward. The gates on the smaller buckets are operated manually, while the gates on the larger buckets are operated by compressed air or by some other mechanical method. Gates should be designed so that they may be opened or closed at will to regulate the flow of the concrete.

Figure 22-13 shows a bucket discharging concrete directly into the forms of a structure.

Figure 22-12 Power-driven concrete buggies.

Figure 22-13 Discharging concrete directly from bucket into forms.

Hoisting concrete with a crane versus a material tower On some projects, such as multistory buildings, it may be possible to use a crane or a material tower to hoist the buckets of concrete. Each has advantages which may make it more suitable than the other under certain conditions.

The advantages of a crane and bucket are as follows:

1. Greater mobility permits the crane to deposit the concrete at different locations around the structure, provided there is access to the building, thus reducing the haul distance with buggies.
2. The crane may be used for other operations.
3. The cost of getting a crane ready to operate will be less than for a tower.

The advantages of a tower and bucket are as follows:

1. The investment in the tower and hoisting equipment will be less than for a crane.
2. The method requires less space in a congested location.

Chutes The use of chutes to transport concrete has been restricted considerably in recent years, primarily because of the tendency to segregate the concrete. Unless care is exercised to prevent it, segregation may occur along a chute or as the concrete flows from the lower end of the chute.

Chutes should be made of metal with round bottoms. The slope should be such that the concrete will flow at a uniform speed, with all materials flowing at the same speed, to eliminate segregation. Unless a chute can transport concrete without producing segregation, it should not be used.

Belt conveyors Under certain conditions belt conveyors are satisfactory for transporting concrete. The uniform flow and high capacity represent advantages, while the tendency to segregate the concrete at the discharge end represents a disadvantage. A suitable type of ladder or down pipe should be installed at the discharge end to assure that the concrete will drop vertically. Usually it is necessary to install a belt cleaner at the discharge end to prevent a portion of the mortar from adhering to the belt.

Figures 22-14 and 22-15 illustrate the use of conveyor belts to place concrete for a floor slab and for other sections of concrete structures. This system provides considerable flexibility in placing concrete for different parts of structures. Also note that a relatively small crew of laborers is required to place the concrete.

Figure 22-16 illustrates the use of belt conveyors to place concrete in forms for columns. Because the conveyor units are mounted on wheels, they may be moved easily and quickly to other locations. Again, the concrete is being placed with a very small crew of workers.

Figure 22-17 illustrates the use of several flights of wheel-mounted conveyor belts to place concrete for a bridge structure. As the length of the structure

Figure 22-14 Use of conveyor belts to place concrete for floor slab. *(Morgen Manufacturing Company.)*

Figure 22-15 Use of conveyor belts to place concrete. *(Rotec Industries.)*

Figure 22-16 Use of conveyor belts to place concrete in column forms. *(Morgen Manufacturing Company.)*

Figure 22-17 Use of conveyor belts to place concrete for a bridge. *(Morgen Manufacturing Company.)*

Figure 22-18 Use of conveyor belts and crane to place concrete. *(Rotec Industries.)*

increases, additional flights of conveyors may be added to extend the total reach.

Figure 22-18 illustrates a wheel-mounted telescoping boom supporting a belt conveyor that is placing concrete through an elephant snout to prevent segregation. Note that the concrete is delivered from the mixing plant to the crane by using conveyor belts.

Placing concrete with pumps A wide variety of pumps are available for placing concrete. These pumps can handle all kinds of mixes and can pump up to 125 cu yd per hr. Recommended pumping distances vary from 250 to 2,000 ft horizontally, and from 75 to 400 ft vertically. The pumps may be mounted on trucks, trailers, or skids [1, 2].

The truck-mounted pump-and-boom combination is proving particularly effective in saving labor and eliminating pipeline handling and set up time and costs. Hydraulically operated and articulated, the booms come in various lengths up to nearly 100 ft.

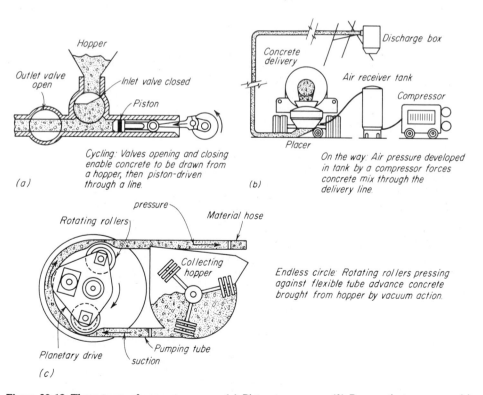

(a) Cycling: Valves opening and closing enable concrete to be drawn from a hopper, then piston-driven through a line.

(b) On the way: Air pressure developed in tank by a compressor forces concrete mix through the delivery line.

(c) Endless circle: Rotating rollers pressing against flexible tube advance concrete brought from hopper by vacuum action.

Figure 22-19 Three types of concrete pumps: (*a*) Piston-type pump. (*b*) Pneumatic-type pump. (*c*) Squeeze-pressure-type pump. (*Construction Methods and Equipment.*)

Three types of pumps are available, namely:

1. Piston
2. Pneumatic
3. Squeeze-type

Figure 22-19 illustrates the principal features of each of these types.

In the piston pump cycle, valves open and close, enabling concrete drawn from a hopper to be driven by the piston into and through the delivery line. These pumps may be mechanically or hydraulically operated.

Pneumatic pumps contain placers into which the concrete is deposited. With the lid of the placer closed, compressed air is introduced to force the concrete

Figure 22-20 Truck-mounted squeeze-type concrete pump with hydraulic-crane-supported delivery line. *(Challenge-Cook Bros. Inc.)*

Figure 22-21 Truck-mounted squeeze-type concrete pump with hydraulic-crane-supported delivery line. *(Challenge-Cook Bros. Inc.)*

through the delivery line. This type of pump has been used extensively to place concrete linings for tunnels.

As illustrated in Fig. 22-19, a squeeze-type pump consists of a mixing hopper, a suction tube, and a rotating planetary drive which presses against the tube containing the concrete and forces the concrete forward through the delivery line.

Improvements in materials used in the pumps and in the construction have produced pumps that can operate up to 10,000 to 15,000 hr before major maintenance or replacement is required.

Placing concrete using the shotcrete or gunite method Figure 22-22 illustrates the use of a shotcrete method of placing concrete for the lining of a canal. This method has been used successfully in placing concrete both above and below the surface of the ground, including canals, tunnels, mines, and other projects. Figure 22-23 illustrates the equipment which proportions and mixes the materials, consisting of cement, aggregate, accelerator if specified, and water and delivers it under pressure to the delivery line, which is equipped with a nozzle enabling the operator to direct the stream of material to the surface to be

Figure 22-22 Using the shotcrete method to place the concrete lining for a canal. *(Challenge-Cook Bros. Inc.)*

Figure 22-23 Equipment used to produce shotcrete concrete. *(Challenge-Cook Bros. Inc.)*

covered. The concrete is applied until the desired thickness is attained.

When the concrete is properly applied, the loss resulting from rebound may be held to 5 to 10 percent.

Because this method of placing concrete permits the reduction or elimination of formwork, the cost of concrete placed by the shotcrete method may be less than that of concrete placed against formwork. Also, when the shotcrete method is used under favorable conditions, the rate of placing may be faster than when the concrete is placed by conventional methods.

PLACING CONCRETE

If concrete is placed on earth, the earth should be moistened sufficiently to prevent it from robbing the concrete of its water. If fresh concrete is to be placed on or adjacent to concrete that has set, the surface of the old concrete should be cleaned thoroughly, preferably with a high-pressure air and water jet and steel-wire brushes. The surface should be wet, but there should be no standing water. A small quantity of cement grout should be brushed over the entire area, then followed immediately with the application of a $\frac{1}{2}$-in. layer of mortar. The fresh concrete should be placed on or against the mortar.

In order to reduce the segregation resulting from movement after it is placed, concrete should be placed as nearly as practicable in its final location. It should be placed in layers whose thickness will permit uniform compaction. The time lapse between the placing of layers should be limited to assure perfect bond between the fresh and previously placed concrete.

In placing concrete in deep forms, a tremie should be used to limit the free fall to not over 3 or 4 ft, in order to prevent segregation. A tremie is a pipe made of lightweight metal, having adjustable lengths and attached to the bottom of a hopper into which the concrete is deposited. As the forms are filled, sections of the pipe may be removed.

Immediately after concrete is placed, it should be compacted by hand puddling or a mechanical vibrator to eliminate voids. The vibrator should be left in one position only long enough to reduce the concrete around it to a plastic mass; then the vibrator should be moved, or segregation of the aggregate will occur. In general, the vibrator should not be permitted to penetrate concrete in the prior lift.

The primary advantage of vibrating is that it permits the use of a drier concrete, which has a higher strength because of the reduced water content. Among the advantages of vibrating concrete are the following:

1. The reduced water permits a reduction in the cement and fine aggregate because less cement paste is needed.
2. The lower water content reduces shrinkage and voids.
3. The drier concrete reduces the cost of finishing the surface.

4. Mechanical vibration can replace three to eight hand puddlers.
5. The lower water content increases the strength of the concrete.
6. The drier mix permits the removal of some forms more quickly, which may reduce the cost of forms.

CURING CONCRETE

If concrete is to attain its maximum strength and other desirable properties, it should be cured with adequate moisture and at a favorable temperature. Failure to provide these conditions may result in an inferior concrete.

The initial moisture in concrete is adequate to hydrate all the cement, provided it is not permitted to evaporate before it is used. Curing should prevent the loss of initial moisture, or it should replace the moisture that does evaporate. This may be accomplished by several methods, such as leaving the forms in place, keeping the surface wet, or covering the surface with a liquid curing compound, which forms a watertight membrane that prevents the escape of the initial water. Curing compounds may be applied by brushes or pressure sprayers. A gallon will cover 200 to 300 sq ft.

Concrete should be placed at a temperature not less than 40 or more than 80°F. A lower temperature will reduce the rate of setting, while a higher temperature will reduce the ultimate strength.

PLACING CONCRETE IN COLD WEATHER

When concrete is placed during cold weather, it usually is necessary to preheat the water, the aggregate, or both in order that the initial temperature will assure an early set and gain in strength. Preheating the water is the most effective method of providing the required temperature. For this purpose a water reservoir should be equipped with pipe coils through which steam can be passed, or steam may be discharged directly into the water, several outlets being used to give better distribution of the heat.

When the temperatures of the ingredients are known, the chart in Fig. 22-24 may be used to determine the temperature of concrete. A straight line across all three scales, passing through any two known temperatures, will permit the determination of the third temperature. If the sand is surface-dry, the solid lines of the scales giving the temperature of concrete should be used. However, if the sand contains about 3 percent moisture, the dotted lines should be used.

Specifications frequently require that freshly placed concrete shall be maintained at a temperature of not less than 70°F for 3 days or 50°F for 5 days after it is placed. Some suitable method must be provided to maintain the required temperature when cold weather is anticipated.

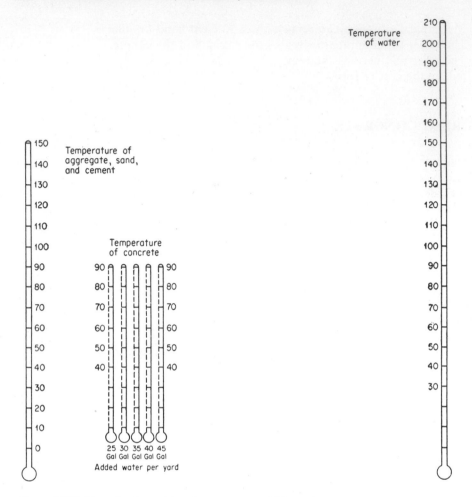

Figure 22-24 Chart for determining the temperature of concrete.

PLACING CONCRETE IN HOT WEATHER

When concrete is placed during hot weather, it may be necessary to precool the concrete in order to keep the temperature within the prescribed limits. For a massive concrete structure such as a dam, this may be accomplished by installing an ice-manufacturing plant near the concrete-mixing plant, as was done at the Philpott Dam, illustrated in Fig. 22-5. Flaked ice was added to the concrete as part of the water.

The specifications for the Pine Flat Dam required that the concrete be placed at a temperature not over 50°F. In order to cool the concrete, it was necessary to use as much as 350 lb of flaked ice in a 4-cu-yd batch. With a maximum output of 136 cu yd of concrete per hour the peak ice demand was 6 tph.

PLACING CONCRETE IN WATER

When it is necessary to place concrete in water, the concrete should be dropped through a pipe long enough to reach to the bottom of the water. As the concrete rises in the forms, the bottom of the pipe should be kept continuously below the surface of the concrete in order that the fresh concrete will not come in contact with the water. This method of placing will reduce the loss of mortar to a minimum.

PROBLEMS

22-1 A 16S construction mixer will be used to mix concrete for several culverts on a highway project. The specified quantities per cubic yard of concrete, based on surface dry sand and gravel, are:

Cement, 5.6 bags
Sand, 1,420 lb
Gravel, 1,840 lb
Water, 34 gal

The sand will contain 8 percent moisture and the gravel will contain 3 percent moisture.

Determine the weight each of cement, sand, and gravel, and the volume of added water required for each batch.

22-2 A concrete retaining wall whose total volume will be 236 cu yd is to be constructed by using job-mixed concrete containing the following quantities per cubic yard, based on surface dry sand and gravel:

Cement, 5.6 bags
Sand, 1,340 lb
Gravel, 1,864 lb
Water, 33 gal

The sand and gravel will be purchased by ton weight, including any moisture present at the time they are weighed. The gross weights, including the moisture present at the time of weighing are as follows:

Item	Gross weight, lb per cu yd	Percent moisture by gross weight
Sand	2,945	6
Gravel	2,968	3

It is estimated that 7 percent of the sand and 6 percent of the gravel will be lost or not recovered in the stockpile at the job.

Determine the total number of tons each of sand and gravel required for the project.

22-3 The aggregate, sand, and cement used in a concrete have an initial temperature of 76°F. The sand contains 4 percent moisture. If 35 gal of water, at a temperature of 46°F, is used per cubic yard of concrete, determine the temperature of the concrete.

22-4 The aggregate, sand, and cement used in a concrete have an initial temperature of 44°F. The sand contains 4 percent moisture. If 30 gal of water is used per cubic yard of concrete, what should be the temperature of the water to produce a concrete having a temperature of 72°F?

REFERENCES

1. Donnelly, C. William: Concrete Pumping, *Construction Methods & Equipment*, vol. 54, pp. 61–71, January 1972.
2. Donnelly, C. William: Concrete Pumping, *Construction Methods & Equipment*, vol. 54, pp. 88–96, February 1972.
3. Challenge-Cook Bros., Inc. 15421 East Gale Avenue, Industry, California 91745.
4. Morgen Manufacturing Company, P. O. Box 160-D2, Yankton, South Dakota 57078.
5. Rotec Industries, 333 West Lake Street, Elmhurst, Illinois 60126.

COST OF OWNING AND OPERATING
CONSTRUCTION EQUIPMENT

The costs listed in this appendix are intended to indicate the approximate costs per hour for ownership, fuel, and other expenses and the total ownership and operating costs per working hour for construction equipment. Costs of given equipment on any given project may vary considerably from the values given in the appendix, depending on job conditions, care of the equipment, location, and other conditions.

The costs per hour for ownership include depreciation, major repairs and overhauling, interest on the investment in the equipment, taxes, insurance, and storage.

The annual cost of depreciation is based on the estimated economic life of the equipment, using the straight-line method of determining the annual cost of depreciation. Thus, the annual cost of depreciation for equipment having an estimated life of 5 years is 20 percent of the original total cost of the equipment.

The annual cost of major repairs is based on experience obtained from the operation of the equipment under average conditions. The actual cost for any unit of equipment will not necessarily be the same as the value given in the appendix, as it will vary with the conditions under which the unit is used and the maintenance service that it receives. The cost of minor repairs, which are usually made in the field, is included under fuel and other expenses.

The annual cost of the investment in equipment includes interest on the investment, taxes, insurance, and storage equal to 15 percent of the average value of the equipment, divided as follows: interest 10 percent; taxes, insurance, and storage 5 percent.

The hours used per year are assumed for average conditions and will vary between jobs, with owners, and with locations. Estimators should modify the number of hours used per year, if necessary, to represent more nearly the actual conditions under which the equipment will be used. If the equipment is used more than the number of hours given in the table, the ownership cost per hour should be reduced, whereas if it is used fewer hours than given in the table, the ownership cost per hour should be increased. The ownership cost per working hour appearing in column 5 is obtained by multiplying the cost to the owner, column 1, by the annual expense, percent of cost, column 3, and then dividing by the number of hours used per year, column 4.

The cost per working hour for fuel and other expenses includes fuel, lubricating oil, greasing, filters, air cleaners, minor repairs, etc., for equipment powered by internal combustion engines. For equipment powered by electric motors, the cost appearing in column 6 includes the cost of electrical energy and minor repairs.

The costs appearing in column 6 for equipment powered by diesel engines are obtained as follows:

Cost of diesel fuel, $0.50 per gal, tax included
Fuel consumed per flywheel hp-hr at full load, 0.04 gal

Assume that the equipment operates at an average of $66\frac{2}{3}$ percent of rated horsepower.

Fuel consumed per rated hp-hr, $\frac{2}{3} \times 0.04 = 0.027$ gal
Fuel cost per rated hp-hr, 0.50×0.027 = $0.0135
Cost per rated hp-hr for oil, grease, filters,
  minor repairs, etc.   = 0.0090
   Total cost per rated hp-hr   = $0.0225

The costs given in column 6 for equipment powered by gasoline engines are obtained as follows:

Cost of gasoline, $0.60 per gal, tax included
Fuel consumed per flywheel hp-hr at full load, 0.06 gal

Assume that the equipment operates at an average of $66\frac{2}{3}$ percent of the rated horsepower.

Fuel consumed per rated hp-hr, $\frac{2}{3} \times 0.06 = 0.04$ gal
Fuel cost per rated hp-hr, 0.60×0.04 = $0.024
Cost per rated hp-hr for oil, grease, filters,
  minor repairs, etc.   = 0.012
   Total cost per rated hp-hr   = $0.036

The costs appearing in column 7 for equipment which has no direct power costs include greasing and minor repairs.

The total cost per working hour appearing in column 7 is the sum of the costs appearing in columns 5 and 6. The total costs do not include the wages for the operators. They do not include the costs of transporting the equipment to the job or setting it up for operation. These costs should be included as separate items in the total estimate for the job.

Example The following example illustrates the method used in estimating the cost per hour for owning and operating equipment: Equipment, power shovel, 160-hp diesel engine

Purchase price, fob factory, including taxes	= $164,520
Freight, factory to owner	= 4,840
Unloading and assembling at destination	= 720
Total cost to the owner	= $170,080
Estimated economical life, 6 yr	
Average investment, 0.5833 × $170,080	= $ 99,208
Annual cost:	
Depreciation, $170,080 ÷ 6 yr	= $ 28,347
Major repairs, 15% of $170,080	= 25,512
Investment, 15% of $99,208	= 14,881
Annual ownership cost	= $ 68,740
Hourly cost:	
Fixed cost, $68,740 ÷ 2,000 hr	= $ 34.37
Fuel and other costs, 160 hp @ $0.0225	= 3.60
Total estimated hourly cost	= $ 37.97

Estimated cost of owning and operating construction equipment

Equipment	Cost to owner	Life, years	Annual expense, % of cost	Hours used per year	Cost per working hour		
					Owner-ship	Fuel and other expense	Total
	(1)	(2)	(3)	(4)	(5)	(6)	(7)
Air compressors, portable, free air at 100 psi							
Reciprocating, gasoline engine							
75 cfm	$ 4,855	4	49	1,200	$ 1.98	$0.85	$ 2.83
105 cfm	7,125	4	49	1,200	2.91	1.12	4.08
125 cfm	7,385	4	49	1,200	3.01	1.26	4.27
160 cfm	7,590	4	49	1,200	3.10	1.87	4.97
250 cfm	12,110	5	44	1,200	4.43	3.10	7.53
Reciprocating, diesel engine							
105 cfm	9,985	4	49	1,200	4.07	0.53	4.60
125 cfm	11,200	4	49	1,200	4.57	0.68	5.25
160 cfm	12,875	4	49	1,200	5.25	0.95	6.20
250 cfm	17,180	5	44	1,200	6.54	1.13	7.67
300 cfm	22,245	5	44	1,200	8.16	1.38	9.54
600 cfm	28,450	5	44	1,200	10.45	2.48	12.93
Rotary, sliding-vane types, gasoline engine							
75 cfm	4,645	4	49	1,200	1.89	0.95	2.84
100 cfm	5,397	4	49	1,200	2.20	1.10	3.30
150 cfm	8,125	4	49	1,200	3.32	1.78	5.10
250 cfm	10,864	5	44	1,200	3.98	2.35	6.33

					Cost per working hour		
Equipment	Cost to owner	Life, years	Annual expense, % of cost	Hours used per year	Owner-ship	Fuel and other expense	Total
	(1)	(2)	(3)	(4)	(5)	(6)	(7)
Rotary, sliding-vane types, diesel engine							
125 cfm	$ 8,396	4	49	1,200	$ 3.44	$0.95	$ 4.39
150 cfm	10,185	4	49	1,200	4.17	1.05	5.22
250 cfm, 2 wheel	14,865	5	44	1,200	5.45	1.15	6.60
250 cfm, 4 wheel	19,380	5	44	1,200	7.10	1.15	8.25
365 cfm, 4 wheel	26,290	5	44	1,200	9.65	1.44	11.09
600 cfm, 4 wheel	35,855	5	44	1,200	13.10	2.45	15.55
Air compressors, screw types, diesel engine							
150 cfm, 2 wheel	8,245	4	49	1,200	2.36	1.05	3.41
175 cfm, 2 wheel	9,885	4	49	1,200	4.06	1.09	5.15
250 cfm, 4 wheel	17,840	5	44	1,200	6.55	1.25	7.80
365 cfm, 4 wheel	23,625	5	44	1,200	8.68	1.44	10.12
450 cfm, 4 wheel	26,720	5	44	1,200	9.80	1.85	11.65
600 cfm, 4 wheel	39,865	5	44	1,200	14.65	2.45	17.10
Air tools, no hose or steel							
Drifters							
Light, 3 in.	$ 1,850	4	49	1,200	$ 0.76		$ 0.76
Medium, $3\frac{1}{2}$ in.	3,815	4	49	1,200	1.55		1.55
Heavy, 4 in.	5,120	4	49	1,200	2.09		2.09
Jackhammers							
Light, 35 lb	1,075	3	58	1,200	0.52		0.52
Medium, 45 lb	1,100	3	58	1,200	0.53		0.53
Heavy, 57 lb	1,240	3	58	1,200	0.60		0.60
Paving breakers							
60 lb	790	3	58	1,200	0.38		0.38
80 lb	955	3	58	1,200	0.46		0.46
Track drills							
$4\frac{1}{2}$-in, piston, 12 ft	37,210	5	44	1,600	10.25	$1.52	11.77
5-in. piston, 20 ft	47,560	5	44	1,600	13.10	1.87	14.97
$5\frac{1}{2}$-in, piston, 20 ft	49,620	5	44	1,600	13.65	1.97	15.62
Bituminous equipment							
Distributors, with truck							
1,000 gal	$11,140	5	44	1,600	$ 3.06	$5.25	$ 8.31
1,500 gal	12,260	5	44	1,600	3.38	5.60	8.98
2,000 gal	12,875	5	44	1,600	3.54	6.05	9.59
2,500 gal	13,720	5	44	1,600	3.78	6.55	10.33
Pavers, complete							
Wheel, 8 ft, gasoline	29,875	4	49	1,600	9.14	2.10	11.24
Crawler, 10 ft, tamper screed, diesel	35,345	5	44	1,600	9.70	2.28	11.98
Crawler, 10 ft, vibratory screed, gasoline	45,395	5	44	1,600	12.45	2.84	15.29
Wheel, 10 ft, vibratory screed, gasoline	41,635	5	44	1,600	11.42	2.45	13.87

	Cost to owner	Life, years	Annual expense, % of cost	Hours used per year	Cost per working hour		
Equipment					Owner-ship	Fuel and other expense	Total
	(1)	(2)	(3)	(4)	(5)	(6)	(7)
Buggies, concrete, power-driven							
9 cu ft	$ 1,575	3	58	1,400	$ 0.66	$0.22	$0.88
11 cu ft	1,830	3	58	1,400	0.76	0.36	1.12
13 cu ft	2,440	3	58	1,400	1.03	0.40	1.43
Concrete buckets, bottom dump							
$\frac{3}{4}$ cu yd	$ 525	5	44	1,200	$ 0.19		$0.19
1 cu yd	595	5	44	1,200	0.22		0.22
$1\frac{1}{2}$ cu yd	755	5	44	1,200	0.28		0.28
2 cu yd	1,035	5	44	1,200	0.38		0.38
3 cu yd	1,460	5	44	1,200	0.54		0.54
4 cu yd	1,975	5	44	1,200	0.72		0.72
Concrete mixers, truck type, truck not included, gasoline engine							
Separate engine drive							
6 cu yd	$13,360	4	49	2,000	$ 3.27	$2.75	$6.02
7 cu yd	13,725	4	49	2,000	3.36	2.85	6.21
8 cu yd	14,140	4	49	2,000	3.46	3.15	6.61
Power take-off drive from truck, truck not included							
7 cu yd	11,645	4	49	2,000	2.85	2.85	5.70
8 cu yd	12,455	4	49	2,000	3.05	3.15	6.20
10 cu yd	13,625	4	49	2,000	3.35	3.45	6.80
Concrete vibrators, internal type							
Electric-motor-operated							
2 hp, 7-ft shaft	$ 630	4	49	1,600	$ 0.19	$0.11	$0.30
$2\frac{1}{7}$ hp, 7-ft shaft	785	4	49	1,600	0.24	0.13	0.37
$2\frac{1}{2}$ hp, 14-ft shaft	810	4	49	1,600	0.25	0.14	0.39
$2\frac{1}{3}$ hp, 21-ft shaft	885	4	49	1,600	0.27	0.15	0.42
$2\frac{1}{7}$ hp, 28-ft shaft	940	4	49	1,600	0.29	0.15	0.44
Gasoline-engine-operated							
2 hp, 7-ft shaft	515	3	58	1,600	0.19	0.09	0.28
2 hp, 14-ft shaft	580	3	58	1,600	0.21	0.09	0.30
4 hp, 14-ft shaft	670	3	58	1,600	0.24	0.16	0.40
4 hp, 21-ft shaft	845	3	58	1,600	0.31	0.16	0.47

Equipment	Cost to owner	Life, years	Annual expense, % of cost	Cost per working hour			
				Hours used per year	Owner-ship	Fuel and other expense	Total
	(1)	(2)	(3)	(4)	(5)	(6)	(7)

Cranes, basic unit, no attachments

Crawler-mounted, cable, gasoline engine

8 ton, PCSA 10-24	$ 61,290	5	44	1,600	$16.80	$1.60	$18.40
15 ton, PCSA 10-44	75,680	5	44	1,600	20.80	2.75	23.55
20 ton, PCSA 10-80	89,140	6	41	1,600	22.80	2.84	25.64
30 ton, PCSA 10-90	112,450	6	41	1,600	28.80	3.90	32.70
15 ton, PCSA 12-57	91,250	5	44	1,600	25.10	2.96	28.06
20 ton, PCSA 12-78	105,720	6	41	1,600	27.10	3.15	30.25

Crawler-mounted, cable, diesel engine

8 ton, PCSA 10-24	68,250	5	44	1,600	18.75	0.86	19.61
15 ton, PCSA 12-52	101,420	5	44	1,600	27.90	1.15	29.05
20 ton, PCSA 12-78	117,535	6	41	1,600	30.00	1.25	31.25
30 ton, PCSA 12-105	157,380	6	41	1,600	40.30	1.73	42.03

Truck-mounted, cable, gasoline engine

8 ton, PCSA 10-24	74,630	5	44	1,600	20.50	2.40	22.90
15 ton, PCSA 10-44	91,105	5	44	1,600	25.00	3.85	28.85
20 ton, PCSA 10-80	107,390	5	44	1,600	29.55	4.65	34.20

Truck-mounted, cable, diesel engine

8 ton, PCSA 10-24	82,390	5	44	1,600	22.60	1.13	23.73
12 ton, PCSA 12-36	104,675	6	41	1,600	26.80	1.57	28.37
30 ton, PCSA 12-92	154,925	6	41	1,600	39.85	2.50	42.35
45 ton, PCSA 15-267	173,185	6	41	1,600	44.50	2.95	47.45

Truck-mounted, hydraulic, diesel engine

25 ton, PCSA 12-104	113,530	6	41	1,600	29.10	1.70	30.80
45 ton, PCSA 10-170	148,185	6	41	1,600	38.00	2.35	40.35

Self-propelled, hydraulic, diesel engine

35 ton, PCSA 12-165	124,610	6	41	1,600	31.90	3.95	35.85

Draglines, complete with buckets, standard-length booms

Crawler-mounted, cable, diesel engine

$\frac{1}{2}$ cu yd	$ 46,750	4	49	2,000	$11.40	$1.05	$13.80
$\frac{3}{4}$ cu yd	63,435	5	44	2,000	13.90	1.23	15.13
1 cu yd	98,490	5	44	2,000	20.60	1.35	21.95
$1\frac{1}{2}$ cu yd	113,525	6	41	1,600	29.15	1.69	30.84
2 cu yd	159,640	6	41	1,600	40.90	2.47	43.37

Equipment	Cost to owner	Life, years	Annual expense, % of cost	Cost per working hour			
				Hours used per year	Owner- ship	Fuel and other expense	Total
	(1)	(2)	(3)	(4)	(5)	(6)	(7)
Crawler-mounted, hydraulic, diesel engine							
$\frac{1}{2}$ cu yd	$ 51,580	4	49	2,000	$12.65	$1.15	$13.80
$\frac{3}{4}$ cu yd	66,725	5	44	2,000	14.65	1.34	15.99
1 cu yd	101,630	5	44	2,000	22.35	1.46	23.81
$1\frac{1}{4}$ cu yd	113,890	5	44	1,600	31.35	1.65	33.00
Truck-mounted, hydraulic, diesel engine							
$\frac{1}{2}$ cu yd	53,510	4	49	2,000	13.10	1.20	14.30
$\frac{3}{4}$ cu yd	72,620	5	44	2,000	15.90	1.40	17.30
1 cu yd	113,775	5	44	2,000	25.00	1.55	26.55
$1\frac{1}{2}$ cu yd	130,895	5	44	1,600	36.10	1.85	37.95

Motors, electric, 3-phase, 60-cycle, 220/440 volt, 1,800 rpm, horizontal, portable

2 hp	$ 155	8	35	1,600	$ 0.03	$0.12	$ 0.17
3 hp	178	8	35	1,600	0.04	0.18	0.22
5 hp	258	8	35	1,600	0.06	0.30	0.36
10 hp	448	8	35	1,600	0.10	0.60	0.70
15 hp	596	8	35	1,600	0.13	0.90	1.03

Motor-generator sets, portable, 120 or 240 volt

Gasoline engine, air-cooled							
2,000 watts	$ 466	7	38	1,600	$ 0.11	$0.15	$ 0.26
3,000 watts	625	7	38	1,600	0.15	0.22	0.37
4,000 watts	1,530	7	38	1,600	0.36	0.30	0.66
7,000 watts	1,610	7	38	1,600	0.39	0.45	0.84
10,000 watts	2,145	7	38	1,600	0.51	0.66	1.12
Diesel engine, water-cooled							
30 kW, 120 volts	5,360	8	35	1,600	1 18	1.25	2.43
80 kW, 440 volts	8,660	8	35	1,600	1.90	2.60	4.50

Motor graders, diesel engine

12-ft blade, 100 hp	$ 24,360	5	44	2,000	$ 5.35	$1.20	$ 6.55
12-ft blade, 125 hp	32,485	5	44	2,000	7.15	1.45	8.60
13-ft blade, 157 hp	43,875	5	44	2,000	9.63	1.77	11.40
14-ft blade, 180 hp	58,360	5	44	2,000	12.80	2.10	14.90
16-ft blade, 250 hp	81,585	5	44	2,000	17.90	3.15	21.05

	Cost to owner	Life, years	Annual expense, % of cost	Hours used per year	Cost per working hour		
Equipment					Owner-ship	Fuel and other expense	Total
	(1)	(2)	(3)	(4)	(5)	(6)	(7)

Pile-driving hammers

Single-acting steam

Energy, ft-lb per blow	Blows per minute							
15,000	60	$ 16,785	6	41	1,400	$ 4.92		$ 4.92
19,500	60	18,885	6	41	1,400	5.55		5.55
26,000	50	22,245	6	41	1,400	6.52		6.52
32,500	50	23,935	6	41	1,400	7.00		7.00
42,000	60	32,945	6	41	1,200	11.25		11.25
60,000	60	45,875	6	41	1,200	15.70		15.70

Double-acting steam

Energy, ft-lb per blow	Blows per minute							
1,000	300	6,185	5	44	1,400	1.95		1.95
2,500	275	6,965	5	44	1,400	2.19		2.19
4,150	225	9,660	5	44	1,400	3.05		3.05
16,000	100	15,950	6	41	1,400	4.65		4.65
24,000	90	21,125	6	41	1,400	6.17		6.17

Diesel, open head

Energy, ft-lb per blow	Blows per minute							
3,600	60	11,780	4	49	1,400	4.12	$0.85	5.97
9,000	60	18,420	4	49	1,400	6.57	1.60	8.17
22,500	50	29,140	4	49	1,400	10.20	3.05	13.25
32,000	50	32,315	4	49	1,400	11.30	5.90	17.20
50,700	60	34,965	4	49	1,400	12.25	6.70	18.95
60,100	60	36,435	4	49	1,400	12.80	8.10	20.90
70,800	60	45,380	4	49	1,400	15.85	9.35	25.25

Power hoes and shovels, crawler-mounted, diesel engine, complete with bucket or dipper

Cable

	Cost to owner	Life, years	Annual expense, % of cost	Hours used per year	Ownership	Fuel and other expense	Total
$\frac{3}{4}$ cu yd	$ 73,425	4	49	2,000	$18.00	$2.20	$20.20
1 cu yd	76,920	5	44	2,000	16.95	2.35	19.30
$1\frac{1}{4}$ cu yd	82,335	5	44	2,000	18.15	2.80	20.95
$1\frac{1}{2}$ cu yd	106,535	5	44	2,000	23.50	3.05	26.55
2 cu yd	157,720	6	41	1,600	40.50	4.25	44.75
$2\frac{1}{2}$ cu yd	182,490	6	41	1,600	47.00	4.65	51.65
3 cu yd	198,270	6	41	1,600	51.00	5.35	56.35

Equipment	Cost to owner	Life, years	Annual expense, % of cost	Hours used per year	Cost per working hour		
					Owner-ship	Fuel and other expense	Total
	(1)	(2)	(3)	(4)	(5)	(6)	(7)

Hydraulic

Equipment	Cost to owner	Life, years	Annual expense, % of cost	Hours used per year	Owner-ship	Fuel and other expense	Total
$\frac{1}{2}$ cu yd	$ 78,685	4	49	2,000	$ 19.30	$1.80	$21.10
$\frac{3}{4}$ cu yd	102,750	4	49	2,000	25.20	2.20	27.40
1 cu yd	108,485	5	44	2,000	23.90	2.35	26.25
$1\frac{1}{4}$ cu yd	114,395	5	44	2,000	25.25	2.80	28.05

Pumps, self-priming centrifugal, base-mounted

Gasoline

Equipment	Cost to owner	Life, years	Annual expense, % of cost	Hours used per year	Owner-ship	Fuel and other expense	Total
$1\frac{1}{2}$ in., 5M	$ 415	5	44	1,200	$ 0.15	$0.12	$ 0.27
2 in., 5M	435	5	44	1,200	0.16	0.15	0.31
2 in., 10M	796	5	44	1,200	0.29	0.22	0.51
3 in., 20M	1,730	5	44	1,200	0.64	0.36	1.00
4 in., 30M	2,145	5	44	1,200	0.79	0.76	1.55
4 in., 40M	3,235	5	44	1,200	1.19	0.96	2.15
6 in., 90M	4,915	5	44	1,200	1.81	1.40	3.21

Electric

Equipment	Cost to owner	Life, years	Annual expense, % of cost	Hours used per year	Owner-ship	Fuel and other expense	Total
$1\frac{1}{2}$ in., 5M	745	6	41	1,200	0.25	0.08	0.33
2 in., 7M	915	6	41	1,200	0.31	0.15	0.46
3 in., 10M	1,050	6	41	1,200	0.36	0.24	0.60
3 in., 20M	1,425	6	41	1,200	0.49	0.45	0.94
4 in., 30M	2,120	6	41	1,200	0.73	0.95	1.68
4 in., 40M	2,725	6	41	1,200	0.93	1.45	2.38

Scrapers with diesel-engine wheel tractors

Struck capacity, cu yd	Tractor horsepower	Cost to owner	Life, years	Annual expense, % of cost	Hours used per year	Owner-ship	Fuel and other expense	Total
9	150	$ 72,580	5	44	2,000	$16.05	$2.25	$18.30
14	300	89,085	5	44	2,000	19.60	4.20	23.80
17	300	99,225	5	44	2,000	21.90	4.65	26.85
22	300	106,540	5	44	2,000	23.50	5.15	28.65
32	950 twin	226,380	5	44	2,000	49.95	11.25	61.20
40	950 twin	335,460	5	44	2,000	73.90	14.25	88.15

Tractors, crawler types, diesel, no attachments

Equipment	Cost to owner	Life, years	Annual expense, % of cost	Hours used per year	Owner-ship	Fuel and other expense	Total
75 hp, direct drive	$ 25,640	4	49	2,000	$ 6.28	$1.80	$ 8.08
75 hp, power shift	28,780	4	49	2,000	7.05	1.80	8.85
105 hp, direct drive	40,875	5	44	2,000	8.98	2.50	11.48
105 hp, power shift	44,260	5	44	2,000	9.75	2.50	12.25
140 hp, direct drive	54,690	5	44	2,000	12.05	3.35	15.40
180 hp, direct drive	64,380	5	44	2,000	14.15	4.32	18.47
270 hp, direct drive	85,980	5	44	2,000	18.90	6.47	25.37
300 hp, direct drive	110,670	5	44	2,000	24.35	7.18	31.53
410 hp, power shift	169,850	5	44	2,000	37.35	9.70	47.05

Estimated cost of owning and operating construction equipment

Equipment	Cost to owner	Life, years	Annual expense, % of cost	Hours used per year	Cost per working hour — Owner-ship	Cost per working hour — Fuel and other expense	Total
	(1)	(2)	(3)	(4)	(5)	(6)	(7)
Tractor attachments, bulldozers, hydraulic							
8-ft blade	$ 4,520	5	44	2,000	$ 1.00		$ 1.00
10-ft blade	4,835	5	44	2,000	1.06		1.06
12-ft blade	6,115	5	44	2,000	1.35		1.35
14-ft blade	8,725	5	44	2,000	1.92		1.92
Tractor loaders, including buckets							
Crawler-type, diesel							
1 cu yd	$ 26,750	4	49	2,000	$ 6.55	$1.24	$ 7.79
$1\frac{1}{2}$ cu yd	38,680	4	49	2,000	9.45	1.60	11.05
$1\frac{3}{4}$ cu yd	45,725	4	49	2,000	11.20	1.90	12.10
2 cu yd	56,620	5	44	2,000	12.45	2.60	15.05
$2\frac{3}{4}$ cu yd	85,385	5	44	2,000	18.85	3.10	21.95
$4\frac{1}{2}$ cu yd	90,265	5	44	2,000	20.40	5.35	25.75
Wheel-type, diesel							
3 cu yd	92,250	4	49	2,000	22.60	2.40	25.00
4 cu yd	98,175	4	49	2,000	24.10	3.05	27.15
5 cu yd	107,290	5	44	1,600	29.50	3.35	32.85
6 cu yd	116,545	5	44	1,600	32.00	3.75	35.75
Trenching machines, or ditchers							

Ladder type

Width of bucket, in.	Depth of trench, ft.	Cost to owner	Life, years	Annual expense, % of cost	Hours used per year	Owner-ship	Fuel and other expense	Total
8	3.5	$ 10,960	3	58	2,000	$ 3.18	$0.85	$ 4.03
12	3.0	14,285	3	58	2,000	4.15	1.50	5.65
16	11.0	57,485	5	44	1,600	15.80	1.85	17.65
24	15.0	76,325	5	44	1,600	21.05	2.32	23.37
24	25.0	137,935	5	44	1,600	38.00	3.78	41.78

Wheel type

Width of bucket, in.	Depth of trench, ft.	Cost to owner	Life, years	Annual expense, % of cost	Hours used per year	Owner-ship	Fuel and other expense	Total
12	7.0	42,325	4	49	1,600	13.00	1.76	14.76
16	7.0	69,240	4	49	1,600	21.30	2.32	23.62
28	8.0	99,635	4	49	1,600	30.60	3.63	34.23
26	8.0	87,495	4	49	1,600	26.85	3.81	30.66

Trucks, Dump

Equipment	Cost to owner	Life, years	Annual expense, % of cost	Hours used per year	Owner-ship	Fuel and other expense	Total
Gasoline							
4 cu yd	$12,100	4	49	2,000	$2.98	$2.48	$ 5.46
6 cu yd	15,000	5	44	2,000	3.30	3.10	6.40
8 cu yd	19,640	5	44	2,000	4.33		7.95
10 cu yd, heavy duty	28,850	5	44	1,600	7.93	5.40	13.33
Diesel							
5 tons	17,875	5	44	2,000	3.93	1.65	5.58
10 tons	25,750	5	44	1,800	6.30	2.25	8.55

DEFINITIONS OF CERTAIN SI UNITS

Name	Unit	Definition
Energy	joule	The joule is the work done when the point of application of a force of one newton is displaced a distance of one meter in the direction of the force.
Force	newton	The newton is that force which, when applied to a body having a mass of one kilogram, gives it an acceleration of one meter per second squared.
Frequency	hertz	The hertz is the frequency of a periodic phenomenon of which the period is one second.
Power	watt	The watt is the power which gives rise to the production of energy at the rate of one joule per second.
Pressure or stress	pascal	The pascal is the pressure or stress of one newton per square meter.
Temperature (thermodynamic)	kelvin	The kelvin is the unit of thermodynamic temperature measured from absolute zero; it is the same size as the degree Celsius.
Temperature (practical)	degree Celsius	The degree Celsius is the temperature in kelvins minus 273.15. The Celsius scale was formerly called centigrade.

Source: Standard for Metric Practice, ASTM E 380-76, IEEE 268-1976, American Society for Testing and Materials, 1916 Race Street, Philadelphia, PA 19103

ALPHABETICAL LIST OF UNITS WITH THEIR SI NAMES AND CONVERSION FACTORS

To convert from	to	Symbol	Multiply by
Acre (U.S. survey)	square meter	m^2	4.047×10^3
Acre-foot	cubic meter	m^3	1.233×10^3
Atmosphere (standard)	pascal	Pa	1.013×10^5
Board foot	cubic meter	m^3	$2.359 \div 10^3$
Degrees Celsius	kelvin	K	$t_K = t_{°C} + 273.15$
Degree Fahrenheit	Celsius degree	°C	$t_{°C} = (t_{°F} - 32)/1.8$
Degree Fahrenheit	kelvin	K	$t_K = (t_{°F} + 459.67)/1.8$
(Degree) Kelvin	Celsius degree	°C	$t_{°C} = t_K - 273.15$
Foot	meter	m	$3.048 \div 10$
Foot, square	square meter	m^2	$9.290 \div 10^2$
Foot, cubic	cubic meter	m^3	$2.831 \div 10^2$
Feet, cubic, per minute	cubic meters/per second	m^3/s	$4.917 \div 10^4$
Feet per second	meters/per second	m/s	$3.048 \div 10$
Foot-pound force	joule	J	1.355×1
Foot-pounds per minute	watt	W	$2.259 \div 10^2$
Foot-pounds per second	watt	W	1.355×1
Gallon (U.S. liquid)	cubic meter	m^3	$3.785 \div 10^3$
Gallons per minute	cubic meters per second	m^3/s	$6.309 \div 10^5$
Horsepower (550 ft-lb/sec)	watt	W	7.457×10^2
Horsepower	kilowatt	kW	$7.457 \div 10$
Inch	meter	m	$2.540 \div 10^2$
Inch, square	square meter	m^2	$6.452 \div 10^4$
Inch, cubic	cubic meter	m^3	$1.639 \div 10^5$
Inch	millimeter	mm	2.540×10
Kelvin	degree Celsius	°C	$t_{°C} = t_K - 273.15$
Mile	meter	m	1.609×10^3
Mile	kilometer	km	1.609×1
Miles per hour	kilometers per hour	km/h	1.609×1
Miles per minute	meters per second	m/s	2.682×10
Pound	kilogram	kg	$4.534 \div 10$
Pounds per cubic yard	kilograms per cubic meter	kg/m^3	$5.933 \div 10$
Pounds per cubic foot	kilograms per cubic meter	kg/m^3	1.602×10
Pounds per gallon (U.S.)	kilograms per cubic meter	kg/m^3	1.198×10^2
Pounds per square foot	kilograms per square meter	kg/m^2	4.882×1
Pounds per square inch (psi)	pascal	Pa	6.895×10^3
Ton (2,000 lb)	kilogram	kg	9.072×10^2
Ton (2,240 lb)	kilogram	kg	1.016×10^3
Ton (metric)	kilogram	kg	1.000×10^3
Tons (2,000 lb) per hour	kilograms per second	kg/s	$2.520 \div 10$
Yard, cubic	cubic meter	m^3	$7.646 \div 10$
Yards, cubic, per hour	cubic meter per hour	m^3/h	$7.646 \div 10$

Note: All SI symbols are expressed in lower-case letters except those that are used to designate a person, which are capitalized.

Sources: Standard for Metric Practice, ASTM E 380-76, IEEE 268-1976, American Society for Testing and Materials, 1916 Race Street, Philadelphia, PA 19103.

National Standard of Canada Metric Practice Guide, CAN-3-001-02-73/CSA Z 234.1-1973, Canadian Standards Association, 178 Rexdale Boulevard, Rexdale, Ontario, Canada M94 IRS.

FACTORS FOR CONVERTING CERTAIN U.S. CUSTOMARY (ENGLISH) UNITS TO METRIC UNITS

In general, the units appearing in this list do not appear in the list of SI units but they are used frequently, and it is probable that they will continue to be used by the construction industry. The units meter and liter may be spelled metre and litre. Both spellings are acceptable.

Multiply USC (English) unit	by	To obtain metric unit
Acre	0.4047	Hectare
Cubic foot	0.0283	Cubic meter
Foot-pound	0.1383	Kilogram-meter
Gallon (U.S.)	0.833	Imperial gallon
Gallon (U.S.)	3.785	Liters
Horsepower	1.014	Metric horsepower
Cubic inch	0.016	Liter
Square inch	6.452	Square centimeter
Miles per hour	1.610	Kilometers per hour
Ounce	28.350	Grams
Pounds per square inch	0.0689	Bars
Pounds per square inch	0.0703	kilograms per square centimeter

U.S. CUSTOMARY (ENGLISH) UNIT EQUIVALENTS

Unit	Equivalent
1 acre	43,560 square feet
1 atmosphere	14.7 lb per square inch
1 BTU	788 foot-pounds
1 BTU	0.000393 horsepower-hour
1 foot	12 inches
1 cubic foot	7.48 gallons liquid
1 square foot	144 square inches
1 gallon	231 cubic inches
1 gallon	4 quarts liquid
1 horsepower	550 foot-pounds per second
1 mile	5,280 feet
1 mile	1,760 yards
1 square mile	640 acres
1 pound	16 ounces avoirdupois
1 quart	32 fluid ounces
1 long ton	2,240 pounds
1 short ton	2,000 pounds

METRIC UNIT EQUIVALENTS

Unit	Equivalent
1 centimeter	10 millimeters
1 square centimeter	100 square millimeters
1 hectare	10,000 square meters
1 kilogram	1,000 grams
1 liter	1,000 cubic centimeters
1 meter	100 centimeters
1 kilometer	1,000 meters
1 cubic meter	1,000 liters
1 square meter	10,000 square centimeters
1 square kilometer	100 hectares
1 kilogram per square meter	0.97 atmosphere
1 metric ton	1,000 kilograms

INDEX

Acceleration, 100
Adiabatic compression, 335
Aggregate, 602
  crushed-stone, 602
    handling of, 640
  crushers (*sse* Crushers for aggregate)
  sand preparation and classification machines, 625
  screens (*see* Screens for aggregate)
  segregations of, 640
  surge piles for, 629
Air compressor(s):
  altitude, effect of, on power required to compress, 340
  capacity of, 346
    effect of altitude on, 346
  defined, 341
  definitions and terms: aftercooler, 341
    air density, 341
    compression ratio, 341
    compressor efficiency, 341
    discharge pressure, 341
    diversity factor, 342
    free air, 341
    horsepower required to compress, 341
    inlet pressure, 341
    intercooler, 347
    load factor, 341
    receivers, 349
    volumetric efficiency, 342
  double-acting, 341
  multistage, 341
  portable, 343
  reciprocating, 343
  rotary, 343
  rotary screw, 345
  single-stage, 341
  stationary, 342
  two-stage, 341
Air leaks, cost of, 361

Air pressure:
  loss of: through friction, 349
    in hose, 353
    in pipe, 349
    in screw-type fittings, 352
  low, cost of, 361
Altitude, effect of: on capacity of air compressors, 346
  on consumption of air by rock drills, 359
  on performance of engines, 94
  on power required to compress air, 340

Belt-conveyor systems, 309
  belt take-ups, 326
  conveyor belts, 312
    capacity of, 315
  design of, 328
  driving equipment, 324
  feeders for, 322
  holdbacks, 327
  idlers, 314
    friction in, 317
    spacing of, 315
    training, 316
  power required: to drive belt conveyor, 319
    to move empty belt, 319
    to move load horizontally, 321
      up an inclined conveyor, 323
    to turn pulleys, 326
  representative systems, 311
  transportation of materials with, economy of, 311
  trippers, 328
Bits, rock, 366
    carbide-insert, 367
    depth per bit, 367
    diamond, 381
Blasting caps, 412
  delay electric, 414

Blasting caps:
  electric, 412
  millisecond delay, 415
  Primadet, 415
  resistance of, 413
Blasting machine, 406
Blasting rock, 407
  definition of terms, 406–409
Boreholes, 407
Buckets, concrete, 684, 686
Buggies, concrete: hand, 684
    power, 684
Bulldozers, 155
  clearing land with, 161
  crawler versus wheel-mounted, 156
  moving earth with, 158
  output of, 158
Burden, 366

Clamshell buckets, 241
Clamshells, 240
  production rates for, 244
Clearing land, 160
Cofferdams, 574
  designing of, 591
  dimensions of, 590
  forces acting on, 574
  freezing of, 594
  height of, economy of, 593
  hydraulic pressure on, 575
  seepage of water into, 575
  types of, 579
    cellular: circular-type, 585
      diaphragm-type, 582
    crib, 580
    earth-fill, 579
    Ohio River, 580
    rock-fill, 580
    single-wall steel-sheet piling, 582
Compacting equipment, types of, 120
  manually operated rammer, 134
  pneumatic-tired rollers, 125
    with variable inflation pressure, 129
  smooth-wheel rollers, 124
  tamping rollers, 120
    grid, 123
    segmented, 121
    sheep's-foot, 121
  vibrating compactors, 130
    plates or shoes, 132, 134
    pneumatic-tired rollers, 129
    sheep's-foot rollers, 130
    steel-drum rollers, 131
Compressed air, 334
  altitude, effect on consumption of, by drills, 359
  Boyle's and Charles' laws, 336
  cost of, 359
  definition of terms, 334
  diversity factor, 355

Compressed air:
  energy required: to compress, 337
    by pneumatic tools, 356
  transmission of, recommended sizes for: of hose, 353
      of pipe, 353
Concrete, 670
  central mixing plants, 677
  chutes, use of, 686
  curing of, 695
  flow diagram for, 671
  handling and batching of materials, 671, 675
  hoisting of, with crane versus material tower, 686
  mixture design, 670
  placing of, 694
    in cold weather, 695
    in hot weather, 696
    by shotcrete or gunite method, 692
    in water, 697
  pressure produced by, 651
  pumps, 690
  strength and slump, effect of mixing time on, 683
  transit-mix and agitator trucks, 682
  transporting of: with conveyor belts, 687
      handling and, 684
  water, measuring of, 675
Concrete mixers, 675
  construction, 675
    outputs of, 676
  paving, 679
    outputs of, 681
Construction-cost control, 50
  records of, 52
Construction economy, 3–6
Construction equipment:
  cost of owning and operating, 65, 72
  depreciation of, 66
    declining-balance method, 66
    straight-line method, 66
    sum-of-the-years-digits method, 69
  economic life of, 76
    costs of: depreciation, 79
      downtime, 78
      investment, 68, 77
      maintenance and repairs, 68, 77
      obsolescence, 79
      summary of, 80
    equipment that serves other equipment, 82
  sources of, 82
    renting with option to purchase, 86
  special, 62
  standard, types of, 62
Construction industry, 2
Copper wire, resistance of, 414
Cores for exploration, 429
Coyote tunnel, 407
Cranes, 234
  classification of, 235
  rated loads, 235
    for hydraulic, 239
  specifications for, 236

Cranes:
  working ranges of, 237
Critical path method, 16
  arrow diagram, updating of, 24
  crash program, conducting of, 28
  definition of terms and symbols, 18
  float: determining free, 22
    determining total, 22
  manual versus computer analyses of, 31
  minimum total cost of a project, determining, 30
  overlapping activities, applying method to, 23
  schedule, developing a, 20
  scheduling, steps in, 18–19
  time-grid diagram method, 25
    advantages of, 27
    updating of, 27
Crushers for aggregate, 602
  ball mills, 619
  cone, 609
  feeders for, 628
  gyratory, 606
    representative capacity of, 608
  hammer mill, 612
    representative capacity of, 615
  jaw, 604
    Blake-type, 604
    representative capacity of, 606
    sizes of stone produced by, 620
    toggle-type, 604
  rod mills, 619
  roll, 612
    maximum-size feed into, 612
    representative capacities of, 619
  selection of crushing equipment, 625
  types of, 602
Crushing and screening plants:
  flow diagram, 636
  portable, 635

Depreciation of equipment, 66
  declining balance method, 66
  straight-line method, 66
  sum of-the-years-digits method, 67
Draglines, 221
  basic parts, 225
  excavation with, cost of, effect of class of material on, 232
  optimum depth of cut, 226
  output of, 227
    effect on: of angle of swing, 229
      of depth of cut, 229
      of job conditions, 229
      of length of boom, 229
      of management conditions, 229
      of size of bucket, 229
  size of, 224
  types of, 222
Drawbar pull, 98
Drilled and underreamed foundations, 546

Drilling and blasting data, 389
Drilling earth, 400
  earth boring machines, 404
  purposes for drilling, 400
  removal of cuttings, 402
  sizes and depths of holes drilled, 401
Drilling methods and equipment, selection of, 387
Drilling pattern, 366
  selection of, 388
Drilling rock, 365
  air pressure, effect of variations in: on cost of drilling, 390
    on rates of drilling, 391, 393, 395
  definition of terms, 364
  presplitting rock, 417
  rates for, 376
  (*See also* Drills, rock)
Drills, rock, 364
  abrasion, 365
  blast-hole, 378
  churn, 365
  diamond, 381
  drifter, 371
  dry, 365
  jackhammer, 370
  percussion, 375
  piston, 378
  shot, 381
  sinker, 365
  stoper, 365
  track-mounted, 373
  wagon, 371
  wet, 365
Dynamite, 409
  gelatin, 407

Electroosmosis, 599
Equipment costs, 65
  depreciation, 66
  fuel, 73
  investment, 68
  lubricating oil, 74
  maintenance and repairs, 68
  operating, 72
    examples of, 81
Equipment records, keeping of, 43
Equipment-use schedule, 34
Exploration:
  drilling, 428
  grouting, determining need for, 491
  preliminary, 427
  seismic, 428
  surface, 428
Explosives:
  ammonia nitrate, 409
  dynamite, 409
  high, 407
  low, 408
  slurries, 410

Explosives:
  storing of, 425
  transportation and handling of, 423

Faults, 428
Feeders for aggregate crushers, 628
Financing of project, 38
Firing charges, 412
Forms for concrete structures, 644
  beam-and-slab-type floor construction, 664
  beams, 667
  columns, 659
  constructor and form economy, 647
  cost of, 645
  deflection of, 657
  designing of project for economy, 646
  fundamentals of design, 653
  materials for, 648
  requirements of, 644
  sizes of sections, 648
  stresses in: due to bending, 655
    due to compression, 656
    due to shearing, 656
  wall, 658
  wood joists and stringers, maximum spans for, 665
  wood shores, allowable loads on, 662
Fuse:
  Primacord, 415
  safety, 412

Gas-law terms:
  absolute pressure, 335
  gauge pressure, 334
  standard conditions, 335
  temperature, 335
    absolute, 335
    Celsius, 335
    Fahrenheit, 335
    vacuum, 335
Gas laws, fundamental, 334
    Boyle's, 336
    Charles', 336
Gradability, 152
Grade, effect of, 91, 93
Grizzly, 627–628
Grouting of foundations, 491
  asphalt, 499
  cement: equipment for, 497
    injecting, 498
  chemical, 501
  clay, 500
  drilling for injection holes, 493
  drilling patterns, 493
  effectiveness of, determining, 504
  examples describing operations, 502
  materials used for, 492
  need for, 491
    exploring to determine, 491

Grouting of foundations:
  preparing for, 495
  pressure, 495
  washing of seams, 495

Hoes, 245
  basic parts of, 248
  output of, 249
  working ranges of, 248
Hose, loss of head in, due to water friction, 563

Isothermal compression, 335

Laborers, scheduling of, 38
Land clearing, 160
Lumber properties of, 651

Misfires, handling of, 417
Money, time value of, 9
    formulas: for single payments, 10
      for uniform end-of-period payments, 11
Motion and time studies, 287
  building houses, applied to, 299
  concrete paver for, 295
  constructing roof trusses, applied to, 298
  duration of, 289
  number of observations needed, 291
Moving pictures, time lapse, 294
    equipment needed for, 295

Nitroglycerin, 408

Operating efficiency and factor, 196

Parts, replacement of, 65
Pile-driving formulas, 535
Pile-driving hammers, 519
  data on, 519, 522
  diesel, 527
    advantages of, 527
    disadvantages of, 530
  drop, 519
  energy losses, 537
  hydraulic, 527
  recommended sizes, 522
  selection of, 545
  steam: differential-acting, 527
    double-acting, 524
    single-acting, 520
  vibratory, 531
    Foster driver/extractor, 533
    performance factors for, 531
Pile-driving problems, analyses of, 541

Pile-driving tests, Michigan, 543
Piles, 506
  composite, 507
  concrete, 507
    cast-in-place, 511
    Monotube, 512
    precast, 508
    Raymond step-taper, 511
  driving below water, 535
  jetting, 533
  resistance to penetration, 517
  steel, 515, 516
  timber, 507
  types, 506
Pipe:
  length equivalent to fittings, 565
  loss of head due to water friction, 563
Pneumatic equipment and tools, air required by, 357
Power shovels, 207
  basic parts of, 210
  dimensions and clearances, 212
  motion and time study applied to, 288
  optimum depth of cut, 214
  output of, effect on: of angle of swing, 216
    of depth of cut, 215
    of job conditions, 217
    of management conditions, 218
  selection of type and size, 211
  size of, 209
Presplitting rock, 417
Primacord, 415
Primer, blasting, 408
Project control, 41
Project supervision, 50
Pumps, water, 550
  centrifugal, 554
    air-operated, 555
    multistage, 557
    performance of, 557
    self-priming, 555
    capacity tables for, 559
  classification of, 551
  diaphragm, 553
  reciprocating, 551
  selection of, 566

Queues, applying theory of, to trucks, 300

Radio for supervising project, 49
Rocks, physical defects of, 427
  faults, 428
  joints, 427
Rocks:
  igneous, 427
  metamorphic, 427
  sedimentary, 427
Rolling resistance, 89

Sand preparation and classification machines, 625
Scalping of crushed stone, 627
Scrapers, tractor-pulled, 188
  cycle time for, 195
  increasing production rates of, 199
  load-growth curve, applying, 200
  number of scrapers per pushdozer, 197
  operation of, 193
  performance of, analyzing, 203
  performance charts for, 193
  size of, 192
  types of, 189
Screens for aggregate, 630
  aggregate-size factor, 634
  capacity of, 632
  deck factors, 634
  determining size required, 634
  efficiency factors, 632
  revolving, 630
  vibrating, 631
Shores, safe loads on, 662
Soil compaction, specifications for, 118
  end results only, 119
  method and end results, 119
  method only, 119
  suggested method and end results, 119
Soil stabilization, 115
  asphalt-soil, 119
  by blending and mixing, 116
  cement-soil, 118
  with hydrated lime, 117
Soils:
  glossary of terms used with, 105–106
  properties of, 107
  shrinkage of, 107
  swell of, 107
  tests of, 110
    field, 111
    laboratory, 111
    nuclear determination of moisture and density, 112
  types of, 110
Stemming, 409–410
Surge piles for aggregate, 629

Temperature, effect on performance of engines, 96
Traction, coefficient of, 93
Tractors:
  crawler, 145
  direct-drive, 145
  torque converter drive, 145
  wheel, 148
    performance data for, 149
Trap-loading materials, 258
Trenching machines, 251
  ladder-type, 254
  production rates of, 256
  wheel-type, 253
Trucks and wagons, 262
  altitude, effect of, on performance, 282

Trucks and wagons:
  balancing of, with size of excavator, 267
  bottom dump, 264
  capacities of, 266
  cost of hauling earth in, effect on: of grade,
     274
    of rolling resistance, 277
    of size of excavator, 272
    of size of truck, 271
  rear dump, 263
Tunnels:
  concrete linings: forms for, 477
    placing of: with pneumatic placers, 482
      by pumping method, 480
    precast segments, use of, 484
    reinforcing steel, 477
    sequence of, 475
    thickness of, 475
  control of groundwater, 473
  cross section of, 474
  drill mountings, 433
    bar, 411
    column, 434
    jumbo, 434
    powered boom, 435
  drilling patterns, 436
  drilling rock, 433
  entrances, number of, 429
  ground support, 469
    bolts, 470
    ribs, 469
    tests to determine need for, 468
  laser beams, use of, to guide moles, 450
    accuracy of, 452
    installing in a tunnel, 451
  mechanical boring machines (moles): essential parts
    of, 438
    muck, methods of transporting, 440
    operation of, 440

Tunnels:
  mechanical boring machines (moles): production
      experiences with, 444
    Japan, 447
    Mangla Dam, 445
    Mersey River, 445
    new developments in, 446
    San Francisco Bay Area Rapid Transit system, 446
  methods of driving: drift, 432
    full-face attack, 431
    heading and bench, 431
  mucking, 458
    cars, 462
    hauling, 461
    locomotives, 462
    tracks, 461
  purposes of, 426
  rocks, physical defects of, 427
    faults, 428
    joints, 427
  sequence of operations, 430
  timbering: steel, 464
    wood, 464
  ventilation, 454
    air required, volume of, 455
    dust control, 457
    vent pipe, size and capacities of, 456

Value engineering, 6
  examples of, 8
  making a study of, 7
  objections to, 7

Wagons (*see* Trucks and wagons)
Wellpoint systems, 569
  capacity of, 571
  installing of, 571